INTERNATIONAL FAMILY LAW:

Conventions, Statutes, and

Regulatory Materials

INTERNATIONAL FAMILY LAW:

Conventions, Statutes, and Regulatory Materials

Selected and Edited by

D. Marianne Blair
PROFESSOR OF LAW
UNIVERSITY OF TULSA COLLEGE OF LAW

Merle H. Weiner
ASSOCIATE PROFESSOR OF LAW
UNIVERSITY OF OREGON SCHOOL OF LAW

CAROLINA ACADEMIC PRESS
Durham, North Carolina

ISBN 0-89089-342-X
LCCN 2003109810

CAROLINA ACADEMIC PRESS
700 Kent Street
Durham, North Carolina 27701
Telephone (919) 489-7486
Fax (919) 493-5668
www.cap-press.com

Printed in the United States of America

Contents

CONTENTS

Preface

This book was created to assist American law students and attorneys who are studying or practicing international family law. It was designed to supplement materials in courses on private and/or public international family law, whether the courses utilize the authors' own casebook published by Carolina Academic Press, *Family Law in the World Community: Cases, Materials, and Problems in Comparative and International Family Law*, or other materials.

The dynamic field of international family law draws upon numerous sources of international and domestic law. While many volumes of documents could usefully be compiled, we have selected and edited those primary documents we feel are most critical to an introductory exploration of this exciting area. For reasons of space, we have excluded the numerous and often voluminous documents and reports issued by the United Nations, the Hague Conference on International Law, and the regional intergovernmental organizations relevant to matters falling within the field of international family law. Many of these excluded documents and reports are discussed in our casebook.

We have divided the book's contents into five parts. Part One primarily contains selected United Nations' instruments. We have included the multilateral conventions and human rights declarations of the General Assembly that are particularly pertinent to familial rights and obligations.

Part Two includes the selected conventions of the Hague Conference on Private International Law that address transnational family formation, dissolution, rights, and duties. We have included only the most current convention in those instances that the Hague Conference has promulgated successive conventions addressing the same topic, such as the recognition of maintenance obligations.

Part Three consists of selected conventions and regulations promulgated by regional intergovernmental organizations: the European Union, Council of Europe, Organization of American States, African Union, and League of Arab States. Many of these instruments are human rights conventions that shape the development of domestic family law within the member states. Other conventions in this section address courts' jurisdiction to adjudicate transnational family law disputes, and courts' obligation to recognize and enforce foreign judgments related to family disputes.

Part Four contains excerpts from U.S. federal statutes relevant to international family issues. These materials include the International Parental Kidnapping Crime Act, the

Trafficking Victims Protection Act, the International Child Abduction Remedies Act, the Intercountry Adoption Act of 2000, and statutes relevant to immigration and international child support enforcement. U.S. federal regulations governing international child abduction and international adoption are also included in this Part.

Part Five consists of two Uniform Acts promulgated by the National Conference of Commissioners on Uniform State Laws: the Uniform Child Custody Jurisdiction and Enforcement Act and the Uniform Interstate Family Support Act. These Acts, which address issues of jurisdiction and enforcement of foreign orders, are pertinent to disputes involving international child custody and international child support.

We hope this compilation of materials provides a convenient tool for exploring the field of international family law. We welcome your comments and suggestions.

Marianne Blair
Merle H. Weiner
May 2003

Acknowledgments

We gratefully acknowledge the following people and entities for their assistance:

The Council of Europe, for Council of Europe documents used with permission;

Mr. William Duncan, Deputy Secretary General of the Hague Conference on Private International Law, for his assistance in our republication of the Hague Conventions included in this volume;

The National Conference of Commissioners on Uniform State Laws, for its permission to reprint:

Uniform Child Custody Jurisdiction and Enforcement Act (1997), copyright © 1997 by the National Conference of Commissioners on Uniform State Laws, and

Uniform Interstate Family Support Act (1996), copyright © 1996 by the National Conference of Commissioners on Uniform State Laws;

Ms. Anne Cunningham, Secretary of the United Nations Publication Board, for her assistance in our republication of the United Nations documents included in this volume.

INTERNATIONAL FAMILY LAW:

Conventions, Statutes, and

Regulatory Materials

Part I

Selected United Nations and League of Nations Instruments

A. International Law and International Relations

Charter of the United Nations
June 26, 1945, 59 Stat. 1055, 2000 U.N.Y.B. 1451

[Ed. Note: The Charter of the United Nations entered into force on October 24, 1945. As of March 2003, 191 nations were members of the United Nations. The United States ratified the Charter on August 8, 1945. The text below reflects amendments made to the Charter in 1963, 1965, and 1971, all of which are currently in force, and can be found at 16 U.S.T. 1134, 557 U.N.T.S. 143, 19 U.S.T. 5450, 638 U.N.T.S. 308, and 24 U.S.T. 2225, 892 U.N.T.S. 119.]

PREAMBLE

WE THE PEOPLES OF THE UNITED NATIONS DETERMINED

to save succeeding generations from the scourge of war, which twice in our lifetime has brought untold sorrow to mankind, and

to reaffirm faith in fundamental human rights, in the dignity and worth of the human person, in the equal rights of men and women and of nations large and small, and

to establish conditions under which justice and respect for the obligations arising from treaties and other sources of international law can be maintained, and to promote social progress and better standards of life in larger freedom,

AND FOR THESE ENDS

to practice tolerance and live together in peace with one another as good neighbors, and to unite our strength to maintain international peace and security, and

to ensure, by the acceptance of principles and the institution of methods, that armed force shall not be used, save in the common interest, and

to employ international machinery for the promotion of the economic and social advancement of all peoples,

HAVE RESOLVED TO COMBINE OUR EFFORTS TO ACCOMPLISH THESE AIMS.

Accordingly, our respective Governments, through representatives assembled in the city of San Francisco, who have exhibited their full powers found to be in good and due form, have agreed to the present Charter of the United Nations and do hereby establish an international organization to be known as the United Nations.

Chapter I — Purposes and Principles

Article 1
The Purposes of the United Nations are:

1. To maintain international peace and security, and to that end: to take effective collective measures for the prevention and removal of threats to the peace, and for the suppression of acts of aggression or other breaches of the peace, and to bring about by peaceful means, and in conformity with the principles of justice and international law, adjustment or settlement of international disputes or situations which might lead to a breach of the peace;

2. To develop friendly relations among nations based on respect for the principle of equal rights and self-determination of peoples, and to take other appropriate measures to strengthen universal peace;

3. To achieve international cooperation in solving international problems of an economic, social, cultural, or humanitarian character, and in promoting and encouraging respect for human rights and for fundamental freedoms for all without distinction as to race, sex, language, or religion; and

4. To be a center for harmonizing the actions of nations in the attainment of these common ends.

Article 2
The Organization and its Members, in pursuit of the Purposes stated in Article 1, shall act in accordance with the following Principles.

1. The Organization is based on the principle of the sovereign equality of all its Members.

2. All Members, in order to ensure to all of them the rights and benefits resulting from membership, shall fulfil in good faith the obligations assumed by them in accordance with the present Charter.

3. All Members shall settle their international disputes by peaceful means in such a manner that international peace and security, and justice, are not endangered.

4. All Members shall refrain in their international relations from the threat or use of force against the territorial integrity or political independence of any state, or in any other manner inconsistent with the Purposes of the United Nations.

5. All Members shall give the United Nations every assistance in any action it takes in accordance with the present Charter, and shall refrain from giving assistance to any state against which the United Nations is taking preventive or enforcement action.

6. The Organization shall ensure that states which are not Members of the United Nations act in accordance with these Principles so far as may be necessary for the maintenance of international peace and security.

7. Nothing contained in the present Charter shall authorize the United Nations to intervene in matters which are essentially within the domestic jurisdiction of any state or shall require the Members to submit such matters to settlement under the present Charter; but this principle shall not prejudice the application of enforcement measures under Chapter VII.

Chapter II — Membership

Article 3
The original Members of the United Nations shall be the states which, having participated in the United Nations Conference on International Organization at San Francisco, or having previously signed the Declaration by United Nations of January 1, 1942, sign the present Charter and ratify it in accordance with Article 110.

Article 4
1. Membership in the United Nations is open to all other peace-loving states which accept the obligations contained in the present Charter and, in the judgment of the Organization, are able and willing to carry out these obligations.

2. The admission of any such state to membership in the United Nations will be effected by a decision of the General Assembly upon the recommendation of the Security Council.

Article 5
A member of the United Nations against which preventive or enforcement action has been taken by the Security Council may be suspended from the exercise of the rights and privileges of membership by the General Assembly upon the recommendation of the Security Council. The exercise of these rights and privileges may be restored by the Security Council.

Article 6
A Member of the United Nations which has persistently violated the Principles contained in the present Charter may be expelled from the Organization by the General Assembly upon the recommendation of the Security Council.

Chapter III — Organs

Article 7
1. There are established as the principal organs of the United Nations: a General Assembly, a Security Council, an Economic and Social Council, a Trusteeship Council, an International Court of Justice, and a Secretariat.

2. Such subsidiary organs as may be found necessary may be established in accordance with the present Charter.

Article 8

The United Nations shall place no restrictions on the eligibility of men and women to participate in any capacity and under conditions of equality in its principal and subsidiary organs.

Chapter IV — The General Assembly

Composition

Article 9

1. The General Assembly shall consist of all the Members of the United Nations.

2. Each Member shall have not more than five representatives in the General Assembly.

Functions and Powers

Article 10

The General Assembly may discuss any questions or any matters within the scope of the present Charter or relating to the powers and functions of any organs provided for in the present Charter, and, except as provided in Article 12, may make recommendations to the Members of the United Nations or to the Security Council or to both on any such questions or matters.

Article 11

1. The General Assembly may consider the general principles of cooperation in the maintenance of international peace and security, including the principles governing disarmament and the regulation of armaments, and may make recommendations with regard to such principles to the Members or to the Security Council or to both.

2. The General Assembly may discuss any questions relating to the maintenance of international peace and security brought before it by any Member of the United Nations, or by the Security Council, or by a state which is not a Member of the United Nations in accordance with Article 35, paragraph 2, and, except as provided in Article 12, may make recommendations with regard to any such questions to the state or states concerned or to the Security Council or to both. Any such question on which action is necessary shall be referred to the Security Council by the General Assembly either before or after discussion.

3. The General Assembly may call the attention of the Security Council to situations which are likely to endanger international peace and security.

4. The powers of the General Assembly set forth in this Article shall not limit the general scope of Article 10.

Article 12

1. While the Security Council is exercising in respect of any dispute or situation the functions assigned to it in the present Charter, the General Assembly shall not make any recommendation with regard to that dispute or situation unless the Security Council so requests.

2. The Secretary-General, with the consent of the Security Council, shall notify the General Assembly at each session of any matters relative to the maintenance of international peace and security which are being dealt with by the Security Council and shall similarly notify the General Assembly, or the Members of the United Nations if the General Assembly is not in session, immediately the Security Council ceases to deal with such matters.

Article 13

1. The General Assembly shall initiate studies and make recommendations for the purpose of:

a. promoting international cooperation in the political field and encouraging the progressive development of international law and its codification;

b. promoting international cooperation in the economic, social, cultural, educational, and health fields, and assisting in the realization of human rights and fundamental freedoms for all without distinction as to race, sex, language, or religion.

2. The further responsibilities, functions and powers of the General Assembly with respect to matters mentioned in paragraph 1(b) above are set forth in Chapters IX and X.

Article 14

Subject to the provisions of Article 12, the General Assembly may recommend measures for the peaceful adjustment of any situation, regardless of origin, which it deems likely to impair the general welfare or friendly relations among nations, including situations resulting from a violation of the provisions of the present Charter setting forth the Purposes and Principles of the United Nations.

Article 15

1. The General Assembly shall receive and consider annual and special reports from the Security Council; these reports shall include an account of the measures that the Security Council has decided upon or taken to maintain international peace and security.

2. The General Assembly shall receive and consider reports from the other organs of the United Nations.

Article 16

The General Assembly shall perform such functions with respect to the international trusteeship system as are assigned to it under Chapters XII and XIII, including the approval of the trusteeship agreements for areas not designated as strategic.

Article 17

1. The General Assembly shall consider and approve the budget of the Organization.

2. The expenses of the Organization shall be borne by the Members as apportioned by the General Assembly.

3. The General Assembly shall consider and approve any financial and budgetary arrangements with specialized agencies referred to in Article 57 and shall examine the administrative budgets of such specialized agencies with a view to making recommendations to the agencies concerned.

Voting

Article 18

1. Each member of the General Assembly shall have one vote.

2. Decisions of the General Assembly on important questions shall be made by a two-thirds majority of the members present and voting. These questions shall include: recommendations with respect to the maintenance of international peace and security, the election of the non-permanent members of the Security Council, the election of the members of the Economic and Social Council, the election of members of the Trusteeship Council in accordance with paragraph 1(c) of Article 86, the admission of new

Members to the United Nations, the suspension of the rights and privileges of membership, the expulsion of Members, questions relating to the operation of the trusteeship system, and budgetary questions.

3. Decisions on other questions, including the determination of additional categories of questions to be decided by a two-thirds majority, shall be made by a majority of the members present and voting.

Article 19

A Member of the United Nations which is in arrears in the payment of its financial contributions to the Organization shall have no vote in the General Assembly if the amount of its arrears equals or exceeds the amount of the contributions due from it for the preceding two full years. The General Assembly may, nevertheless, permit such a Member to vote if it is satisfied that the failure to pay is due to conditions beyond the control of the Member.

Procedure

Article 20

The General Assembly shall meet in regular annual sessions and in such special sessions as occasion may require. Special sessions shall be convoked by the Secretary-General at the request of the Security Council or of a majority of the Members of the United Nations.

Article 21

The General Assembly shall adopt its own rules of procedure. It shall elect its President for each session.

Article 22

The General Assembly may establish such subsidiary organs as it deems necessary for the performance of its functions.

Chapter V — The Security Council

Composition

Article 23

1. The Security Council shall consist of fifteen Members of the United Nations. The Republic of China, France, the Union of Soviet Socialist Republics, the United Kingdom of Great Britain and Northern Ireland, and the United States of America shall be permanent members of the Security Council. The General Assembly shall elect ten other Members of the United Nations to be non-permanent members of the Security Council, due regard being specially paid, in the first instance to the contribution of Members of the United Nations to the maintenance of international peace and security and to the other purposes of the Organization, and also to equitable geographical distribution.

2. The non-permanent members of the Security Council shall be elected for a term of two years. In the first election of the non-permanent members after the increase of the membership of the Security Council from eleven to fifteen, two of the four additional members shall be chosen for a term of one year. A retiring member shall not be eligible for immediate re-election.

3. Each member of the Security Council shall have one representative.

Functions and Powers

Article 24

1. In order to ensure prompt and effective action by the United Nations, its Members confer on the Security Council primary responsibility for the maintenance of international peace and security, and agree that in carrying out its duties under this responsibility the Security Council acts on their behalf.

2. In discharging these duties the Security Council shall act in accordance with the Purposes and Principles of the United Nations. The specific powers granted to the Security Council for the discharge of these duties are laid down in Chapters VI, VII, VIII, and XII.

3. The Security Council shall submit annual and, when necessary, special reports to the General Assembly for its consideration.

Article 25

The Members of the United Nations agree to accept and carry out the decisions of the Security Council in accordance with the present Charter.

Article 26

In order to promote the establishment and maintenance of international peace and security with the least diversion for armaments of the world's human and economic resources, the Security Council shall be responsible for formulating, with the assistance of the Military Staff Committee referred to in Article 47, plans to be submitted to the Members of the United Nations for the establishment of a system for the regulation of armaments.

Voting

Article 27

1. Each member of the Security Council shall have one vote.

2. Decisions of the Security Council on procedural matters shall be made by an affirmative vote of nine members.

3. Decisions of the Security Council on all other matters shall be made by an affirmative vote of nine members including the concurring votes of the permanent members; provided that, in decisions under Chapter VI, and under paragraph 3 of Article 52, a party to a dispute shall abstain from voting.

Procedure

Article 28

1. The Security Council shall be so organized as to be able to function continuously. Each member of the Security Council shall for this purpose be represented at all times at the seat of the Organization.

2. The Security Council shall hold periodic meetings at which each of its members may, if it so desires, be represented by a member of the government or by some other specially designated representative.

3. The Security Council may hold meetings at such places other than the seat of the Organization as in its judgment will best facilitate its work.

Article 29

The Security Council may establish such subsidiary organs as it deems necessary for the performance of its functions.

Article 30

The Security Council shall adopt its own rules of procedure, including the method of selecting its President.

Article 31

Any Member of the United Nations which is not a member of the Security Council may participate, without vote, in the discussion of any question brought before the Security Council whenever the latter considers that the interests of that Member are specially affected.

Article 32

Any Member of the United Nations which is not a member of the Security Council or any state which is not a Member of the United Nations, if it is a party to a dispute under consideration by the Security Council, shall be invited to participate, without vote, in the discussion relating to the dispute. The Security Council shall lay down such conditions as it deems just for the participation of a state which is not a Member of the United Nations.

[Ed. Note: Chapters VI to VIII, addressing peaceful settlement of disputes, responses to acts of aggression and breaches of the peace, and regional arrangements, are omitted]

Chapter IX — International Economic and Social Co-operation

Article 55

With a view to the creation of conditions of stability and well-being which are necessary for peaceful and friendly relations among nations based on respect for the principle of equal rights and self-determination of peoples, the United Nations shall promote:

a. higher standards of living, full employment, and conditions of economic and social progress and development;

b. solutions of international economic, social, health, and related problems; and international cultural and educational cooperation; and

c. universal respect for, and observance of, human rights and fundamental freedoms for all without distinction as to race, sex, language, or religion.

Article 56

All Members pledge themselves to take joint and separate action in cooperation with the Organization for the achievement of the purposes set forth in Article 55.

Article 57

1. The various specialized agencies, established by intergovernmental agreement and having wide international responsibilities, as defined in their basic instruments, in economic, social, cultural, educational, health, and related fields, shall be brought into relationship with the United Nations in accordance with the provisions of Article 63.

2. Such agencies thus brought into relationship with the United Nations are hereinafter referred to as specialized agencies.

Article 58

The Organization shall make recommendations for the coordination of the policies and activities of the specialized agencies.

Article 59

The Organization shall, where appropriate, initiate negotiations among the states concerned for the creation of any new specialized agencies required for the accomplishment of the purposes set forth in Article 55.

Article 60

Responsibility for the discharge of the functions of the Organization set forth in this Chapter shall be vested in the General Assembly and, under the authority of the General Assembly, in the Economic and Social Council, which shall have for this purpose the powers set forth in Chapter X.

Chapter X — The Economic and Social Council

Composition

Article 61

1. The Economic and Social Council shall consist of fifty-four Members of the United Nations elected by the General Assembly.

2. Subject to the provisions of paragraph 3, eighteen members of the Economic and Social Council shall be elected each year for a term of three years. A retiring member shall be eligible for immediate re-election.

3. At the first election after the increase in the membership of the Economic and Social Council from twenty-seven to fifty-four members, in addition to the members elected in place of the nine members whose term of office expires at the end of that year, twenty-seven additional members shall be elected. Of these twenty-seven additional members, the term of office of nine members so elected shall expire at the end of one year, and of nine other members at the end of two years, in accordance with arrangements made by the General Assembly.

4. Each member of the Economic and Social Council shall have one representative.

Functions and Powers

Article 62

1. The Economic and Social Council may make or initiate studies and reports with respect to international economic, social, cultural, educational, health, and related matters and may make recommendations with respect to any such matters to the General Assembly, to the Members of the United Nations, and to the specialized agencies concerned.

2. It may make recommendations for the purpose of promoting respect for, and observance of, human rights and fundamental freedoms for all.

3. It may prepare draft conventions for submission to the General Assembly, with respect to matters falling within its competence.

4. It may call, in accordance with the rules prescribed by the United Nations, international conferences on matters falling within its competence.

Article 63

1. The Economic and Social Council may enter into agreements with any of the agencies referred to in Article 57, defining the terms on which the agency concerned shall be brought into relationship with the United Nations. Such agreements shall be subject to approval by the General Assembly.

2. It may coordinate the activities of the specialized agencies through consultation with and recommendations to such agencies and through recommendations to the General Assembly and to the Members of the United Nations.

Article 64

1. The Economic and Social Council may take appropriate steps to obtain regular reports from the specialized agencies. It may make arrangements with the Members of the United Nations and with the specialized agencies to obtain reports on the steps taken to give effect to its own recommendations and to recommendations on matters falling within its competence made by the General Assembly.

2. It may communicate its observations on these reports to the General Assembly.

Article 65

The Economic and Social Council may furnish information to the Security Council and shall assist the Security Council upon its request.

Article 66

1. The Economic and Social Council shall perform such functions as fall within its competence in connection with the carrying out of the recommendations of the General Assembly.

2. It may, with the approval of the General Assembly, perform services at the request of Members of the United Nations and at the request of specialized agencies.

3. It shall perform such other functions as are specified elsewhere in the present Charter or as may be assigned to it by the General Assembly.

Voting

Article 67

1. Each member of the Economic and Social Council shall have one vote.

2. Decisions of the Economic and Social Council shall be made by a majority of the members present and voting.

Procedure

Article 68

The Economic and Social Council shall set up commissions in economic and social fields and for the promotion of human rights, and such other commissions as may be required for the performance of its functions.

Article 69

The Economic and Social Council shall invite any Member of the United Nations to participate, without vote, in its deliberations on any matter of particular concern to that Member.

Article 70

The Economic and Social Council may make arrangements for representatives of the specialized agencies to participate, without vote, in its deliberations and in those of the commissions established by it, and for its representatives to participate in the deliberations of the specialized agencies.

Article 71

The Economic and Social Council may make suitable arrangements for consultation with non-governmental organizations which are concerned with matters within its competence. Such arrangements may be made with international organizations and, where appropriate, with national organizations after consultation with the Member of the United Nations concerned.

Article 72

1. The Economic and Social Council shall adopt its own rules of procedure, including the method of selecting its President.

2. The Economic and Social Council shall meet as required in accordance with its rules, which shall include provision for the convening of meetings on the request of a majority of its members.

[Ed. Note: Chapters XI, XII, and XIII, addressing non-self-governing territories, the international trusteeship system, and the Trusteeship Council, are omitted.]

Chapter XIV — The International Court of Justice

Article 92

The International Court of Justice shall be the principal judicial organ of the United Nations. It shall function in accordance with the annexed Statute, which is based upon the Statute of the Permanent Court of International Justice and forms an integral part of the present Charter.

Article 93

1. All Members of the United Nations are *ipso facto* parties to the Statute of the International Court of Justice.

2. A state which is not a Member of the United Nations may become a party to the Statute of the International Court of Justice on conditions to be determined in each case by the General Assembly upon the recommendation of the Security Council.

Article 94

1. Each Member of the United Nations undertakes to comply with the decision of the International Court of Justice in any case to which it is a party.

2. If any party to a case fails to perform the obligations incumbent upon it under a judgment rendered by the Court, the other party may have recourse to the Security Council, which may, if it deems necessary, make recommendations or decide upon measures to be taken to give effect to the judgment.

Article 95

Nothing in the present Charter shall prevent Members of the United Nations from entrusting the solution of their differences to other tribunals by virtue of agreements already in existence or which may be concluded in the future.

Article 96

1. The General Assembly or the Security Council may request the International Court of Justice to give an advisory opinion on any legal question.

2. Other organs of the United Nations and specialized agencies, which may at any time be so authorized by the General Assembly, may also request advisory opinions of the Court on legal questions arising within the scope of their activities.

Chapter XV — The Secretariat

Article 97

The Secretariat shall comprise a Secretary-General and such staff as the Organization may require. The Secretary-General shall be appointed by the General Assembly upon the recommendation of the Security Council. He shall be the chief administrative officer of the Organization.

Article 98

The Secretary-General shall act in that capacity in all meetings of the General Assembly, of the Security Council, of the Economic and Social Council, and of the Trusteeship Council, and shall perform such other functions as are entrusted to him by these organs. The Secretary-General shall make an annual report to the General Assembly on the work of the Organization.

Article 99

The Secretary-General may bring to the attention of the Security Council any matter which in his opinion may threaten the maintenance of international peace and security.

Article 100

1. In the performance of their duties the Secretary-General and the staff shall not seek or receive instructions from any government or from any other authority external to the Organization. They shall refrain from any action which might reflect on their position as international officials responsible only to the Organization.

2. Each Member of the United Nations undertakes to respect the exclusively international character of the responsibilities of the Secretary-General and the staff and not to seek to influence them in the discharge of their responsibilities.

Article 101

1. The staff shall be appointed by the Secretary-General under regulations established by the General Assembly.

2. Appropriate staffs shall be permanently assigned to the Economic and Social Council, the Trusteeship Council, and, as required, to other organs of the United Nations. These staffs shall form a part of the Secretariat.

3. The paramount consideration in the employment of the staff and in the determination of the conditions of service shall be the necessity of securing the highest standards of efficiency, competence, and integrity. Due regard shall be paid to the importance of recruiting the staff on as wide a geographical basis as possible.

Chapter XVI — Miscellaneous Provisions

Article 102

1. Every treaty and every international agreement entered into by any Member of the United Nations after the present Charter comes into force shall as soon as possible be registered with the Secretariat and published by it.

2. No party to any such treaty or international agreement which has not been registered in accordance with the provisions of paragraph I of this Article may invoke that treaty or agreement before any organ of the United Nations.

Article 103

In the event of a conflict between the obligations of the Members of the United Nations under the present Charter and their obligations under any other international agreement, their obligations under the present Charter shall prevail.

Article 104

The Organization shall enjoy in the territory of each of its Members such legal capacity as may be necessary for the exercise of its functions and the fulfillment of its purposes.

Article 105

1. The Organization shall enjoy in the territory of each of its Members such privileges and immunities as are necessary for the fulfillment of its purposes.

2. Representatives of the Members of the United Nations and officials of the Organization shall similarly enjoy such privileges and immunities as are necessary for the independent exercise of their functions in connection with the Organization.

3. The General Assembly may make recommendations with a view to determining the details of the application of paragraphs 1 and 2 of this Article or may propose conventions to the Members of the United Nations for this purpose.

[Ed. Note: Chapter XVII, addressing transitional security arrangements, has been omitted.]

Chapter XVIII — Amendments

Article 108

Amendments to the present Charter shall come into force for all Members of the United Nations when they have been adopted by a vote of two thirds of the members of the General Assembly and ratified in accordance with their respective constitutional processes by two thirds of the Members of the United Nations, including all the permanent members of the Security Council.

Article 109

1. A General Conference of the Members of the United Nations for the purpose of reviewing the present Charter may be held at a date and place to be fixed by a two-thirds vote of the members of the General Assembly and by a vote of any nine members of the Security Council. Each Member of the United Nations shall have one vote in the conference.

2. Any alteration of the present Charter recommended by a two-thirds vote of the conference shall take effect when ratified in accordance with their respective constitutional processes by two thirds of the Members of the United Nations including all the permanent members of the Security Council.

3. If such a conference has not been held before the tenth annual session of the General Assembly following the coming into force of the present Charter, the proposal to call such a conference shall be placed on the agenda of that session of the General Assembly, and the conference shall be held if so decided by a majority vote of the members of the General Assembly and by a vote of any seven members of the Security Council.

Chapter XIX — Ratification and Signature

Article 110

1. The present Charter shall be ratified by the signatory states in accordance with their respective constitutional processes.

2. The ratifications shall be deposited with the Government of the United States of America, which shall notify all the signatory states of each deposit as well as the Secretary-General of the Organization when he has been appointed.

3. The present Charter shall come into force upon the deposit of ratifications by the Republic of China, France, the Union of Soviet Socialist Republics, the United Kingdom of Great Britain and Northern Ireland, and the United States of America, and by a majority of the other signatory states. A protocol of the ratifications deposited shall thereupon be drawn up by the Government of the United States of America which shall communicate copies thereof to all the signatory states.

4. The states signatory to the present Charter which ratify it after it has come into force will become original Members of the United Nations on the date of the deposit of their respective ratifications.

Article 111

The present Charter, of which the Chinese, French, Russian, English, and Spanish texts are equally authentic, shall remain deposited in the archives of the Government of the United States of America. Duly certified copies thereof shall be transmitted by that Government to the Governments of the other signatory states.

IN FAITH WHEREOF the representatives of the Governments of the United Nations have signed the present Charter.

DONE at the city of San Francisco the twenty-sixth day of June, one thousand nine hundred and forty-five.

Statute of the International Court of Justice
June 26, 1945, 59 Stat. 1031, 2000 U.N.Y.B. 1461

[Ed. Note: This statute was annexed to the United Nations Charter, and entered into force on October 24, 1945. All U.N. members become parties to the Statute. As of March 2003, two non-member nations, Switzerland and Nauru, were also parties to the Statute.]

Article 1

The International Court of Justice established by the Charter of the United Nations as the principal judicial organ of the United Nations shall be constituted and shall function in accordance with the provisions of the present Statute.

Chapter I — Organization of the Court

Article 2

The Court shall be composed of a body of independent judges, elected regardless of their nationality from among persons of high moral character, who possess the qualifications required in their respective countries for appointment to the highest judicial offices, or are jurisconsults of recognized competence in international law.

Article 3

1. The Court shall consist of fifteen members, no two of whom may be nationals of the same state.

2. A person who for the purposes of membership in the Court could be regarded as a national of more than one state shall be deemed to be a national of the one in which he ordinarily exercises civil and political rights.

Article 4

1. The members of the Court shall be elected by the General Assembly and by the Security Council from a list of persons nominated by the national groups in the Permanent Court of Arbitration, in accordance with the following provisions.

2. In the case of Members of the United Nations not represented in the Permanent Court of Arbitration, candidates shall be nominated by national groups appointed for this purpose by their governments under the same conditions as those prescribed for members of the Permanent Court of Arbitration by Article 44 of the Convention of The Hague of 1907 for the pacific settlement of international disputes.

3. The conditions under which a state which is a party to the present Statute but is not a Member of the United Nations may participate in electing the members of the Court shall, in the absence of a special agreement, be laid down by the General Assembly upon recommendation of the Security Council.

[Ed. Note: Articles 5 to 33 of Chapter I are omitted.]

Chapter II—Competence of the Court

Article 34

1. Only states may be parties in cases before the Court.

2. The Court, subject to and in conformity with its Rules, may request of public international organizations information relevant to cases before it, and shall receive such information presented by such organizations on their own initiative.

3. Whenever the construction of the constituent instrument of a public international organization or of an international convention adopted thereunder is in question in a case before the Court, the Registrar shall so notify the public international organization concerned and shall communicate to it copies of all the written proceedings.

Article 35

1. The Court shall be open to the states parties to the present Statute.

2. The conditions under which the Court shall be open to other states shall, subject to the special provisions contained in treaties in force, be laid down by the Security Council, but in no case shall such conditions place the parties in a position of inequality before the Court.

3. When a state which is not a Member of the United Nations is a party to a case, the Court shall fix the amount which that party is to contribute towards the expenses of the Court. This provision shall not apply if such state is bearing a share of the expenses of the Court

Article 36

1. The jurisdiction of the Court comprises all cases which the parties refer to it and all matters specially provided for in the Charter of the United Nations or in treaties and conventions in force.

2. The states parties to the present Statute may at any time declare that they recognize as compulsory *ipso facto* and without special agreement, in relation to any other state accepting the same obligation, the jurisdiction of the Court in all legal disputes concerning:

a. the interpretation of a treaty;

b. any question of international law;

c. the existence of any fact which, if established, would constitute a breach of an international obligation;

d. the nature or extent of the reparation to be made for the breach of an international obligation.

3. The declarations referred to above may be made unconditionally or on condition of reciprocity on the part of several or certain states, or for a certain time.

4. Such declarations shall be deposited with the Secretary-General of the United Nations, who shall transmit copies thereof to the parties to the Statute and to the Registrar of the Court.

5. Declarations made under Article 36 of the Statute of the Permanent Court of International Justice and which are still in force shall be deemed, as between the parties to the present Statute, to be acceptances of the compulsory jurisdiction of the International Court of Justice for the period which they still have to run and in accordance with their terms.

6. In the event of a dispute as to whether the Court has jurisdiction, the matter shall be settled by the decision of the Court.

[Ed Note: As of March 2003, 61 nations had declarations in effect accepting the compulsory jurisdiction of the Court under Article 36, paragraph 2.]

Article 37

Whenever a treaty or convention in force provides for reference of a matter to a tribunal to have been instituted by the League of Nations, or to the Permanent Court of International Justice, the matter shall, as between the parties to the present Statute, be referred to the International Court of Justice.

Article 38

1. The Court, whose function is to decide in accordance with international law such disputes as are submitted to it, shall apply:

a. international conventions, whether general or particular, establishing rules expressly recognized by the contesting states;

b. international custom, as evidence of a general practice accepted as law;

c. the general principles of law recognized by civilized nations;

d. subject to the provisions of Article 59, judicial decisions and the teachings of the most highly qualified publicists of the various nations, as subsidiary means for the determination of rules of law.

2. This provision shall not prejudice the power of the Court to decide a case *ex aequo et bono*, if the parties agree thereto.

[Ed. Note: Chapter III, addressing procedure of the Court, is omitted.]

Chapter IV — Advisory Opinons

Article 65

1. The Court may give an advisory opinion on any legal question at the request of whatever body may be authorized by or in accordance with the Charter of the United Nations to make such a request.

2. Questions upon which the advisory opinion of the Court is asked shall be laid before the Court by means of a written request containing an exact statement of the question upon which an opinion is required, and accompanied by all documents likely to throw light upon the question.

Article 66

1. The Registrar shall forthwith give notice of the request for an advisory opinion to all states entitled to appear before the Court.

2. The Registrar shall also, by means of a special and direct communication, notify any state entitled to appear before the Court or international organization considered by the Court, or, should it not be sitting, by the President, as likely to be able to furnish information on the question, that the Court will be prepared to receive, within a time limit to be fixed by the President, written statements, or to hear, at a public sitting to be held for the purpose, oral statements relating to the question.

3. Should any such state entitled to appear before the Court have failed to receive the special communication referred to in paragraph 2 of this Article, such state may express a desire to submit a written statement or to be heard; and the Court will decide.

4. States and organizations having presented written or oral statements or both shall be permitted to comment on the statements made by other states or organizations in the form, to the extent, and within the time limits which the Court, or, should it not be sitting, the President, shall decide in each particular case. Accordingly, the Registrar shall in due time communicate any such written statements to states and organizations having submitted similar statements.

Article 67

The Court shall deliver its advisory opinions in open court, notice having been given to the Secretary-General and to the representatives of Members of the United Nations, of other states and of international organizations immediately concerned.

Article 68

In the exercise of its advisory functions the Court shall further be guided by the provisions of the present Statute which apply in contentious cases to the extent to which it recognizes them to be applicable.

[Ed. Note: Chapter V, addressing amendments to the Statute, is omitted.]

Vienna Convention on the Law of Treaties
May 23, 1969, 1155 U.N.T.S. 331

[Ed. Note: On May 22, 1969, this Convention was adopted by the United Nations Conference on the Law of Treaties, which had been convened pursuant to a resolution of the

U.N. General Assembly. It entered into force on January 27, 1980. As of March 2003, 94 nations were parties to this convention. The United States has signed the Convention, but has never ratified it and is not a party.]

The States Parties to the present Convention,

Considering the fundamental role of treaties in the history of international relations,

Recognizing the ever-increasing importance of treaties as a source of international law and as a means of developing peaceful co-operation among nations, whatever their constitutional and social systems,

Noting that the principles of free consent and of good faith and the *pacta sunt servanda* rule are universally recognized,

Affirming that disputes concerning treaties, like other international disputes, should be settled by peaceful means and in conformity with the principles of justice and international law,

Recalling the determination of the peoples of the United Nations to establish conditions under which justice and respect for the obligations arising from treaties can be maintained,

Having in mind the principles of international law embodied in the Charter of the United Nations, such as the principles of the equal rights and self-determination of peoples, of the sovereign equality and independence of all States, of non-interference in the domestic affairs of States, of the prohibition of the threat or use of force and of universal respect for, and observance of, human rights and fundamental freedoms for all,

Believing that the codification and progressive development of the law of treaties achieved in the present Convention will promote the purposes of the United Nations set forth in the Charter, namely, the maintenance of international peace and security, the development of friendly relations and the achievement of co-operation among nations,

Affirming that the rules of customary international law will continue to govern questions not regulated by the provisions of the present Convention,

Have agreed as follows:

PART I — Introduction

Article 1. Scope of the present Convention

The present Convention applies to treaties between States.

Article 2. Use of terms

1. For the purposes of the present Convention:

(a) "Treaty" means an international agreement concluded between States in written form and governed by international law, whether embodied in a single instrument or in two or more related instruments and whatever its particular designation;

(b) "Ratification", "acceptance", "approval" and "accession" mean in each case the international act so named whereby a State establishes on the international plane its consent to be bound by a treaty;

(c) "Full powers" means a document emanating from the competent authority of a State designating a person or persons to represent the State for negotiating, adopting or authenticating the text of a treaty, for expressing the consent of the State to be bound by a treaty, or for accomplishing any other act with respect to a treaty;

(d) "Reservation" means a unilateral statement, however phrased or named, made by a State, when signing, ratifying, accepting, approving or acceding to a treaty, whereby it purports to exclude or to modify the legal effect of certain provisions of the treaty in their application to that State;

(e) "Negotiating State" means a State which took part in the drawing up and adoption of the text of the treaty;

(f) "Contracting State" means a State which has consented to be bound by the treaty, whether or not the treaty has entered into force;

(g) "Party" means a State which has consented to be bound by the treaty and for which the treaty is in force;

(h) "Third State" means a State not a party to the treaty;

(i) "International organization" means an intergovernmental organization.

2. The provisions of paragraph 1 regarding the use of terms in the present Convention are without prejudice to the use of those terms or to the meanings which may be given to them in the internal law of any State.

Article 3. International agreements not within the scope of the present Convention

The fact that the present Convention does not apply to international agreements concluded between States and other subjects of international law or between such other subjects of international law, or to international agreements not in written form, shall not affect:

(a) the legal force of such agreements;

(b) the application to them of any of the rules set forth in the present Convention to which they would be subject under international law independently of the Convention;

(c) the application of the Convention to the relations of States as between themselves under international agreements to which other subjects of international law are also parties.

Article 4. Non-retroactivity of the present Convention

Without prejudice to the application of any rules set forth in the present Convention to which treaties would be subject under international law independently of the Convention, the Convention applies only to treaties which are concluded by States after the entry into force of the present Convention with regard to such States.

Article 5. Treaties constituting international organizations and treaties adopted within an international organization

The present Convention applies to any treaty which is the constituent instrument of an international organization and to any treaty adopted within an international organization without prejudice to any relevant rules of the organization.

Part II — Conclusion and Entry Into Force of Treaties

Section 1. Conclusion of Treaties

Article 6. Capacity of States to conclude treaties

Every State possesses capacity to conclude treaties.

Article 7. Full powers

1. A person is considered as representing a State for the purpose of adopting or authenticating the text of a treaty or for the purpose of expressing the consent of the State to be bound by a treaty if:

(a) he produces appropriate full powers; or

(b) it appears from the practice of the States concerned or from other circumstances that their intention was to consider that person as representing the State for such purposes and to dispense with full powers.

2. In virtue of their functions and without having to produce full powers, the following are considered as representing their State:

(a) Heads of State, Heads of Government and Ministers for Foreign Affairs, for the purpose of performing all acts relating to the conclusion of a treaty;

(b) Heads of diplomatic missions, for the purpose of adopting the text of a treaty between the accrediting State and the State to which they are accredited;

(c) Representatives accredited by States to an international conference or to an international organization or one of its organs, for the purpose of adopting the text of a treaty in that conference, organization or organ.

Article 8. Subsequent confirmation of an act performed without authorization

An act relating to the conclusion of a treaty performed by a person who cannot be considered under article 7 as authorized to represent a State for that purpose is without legal effect unless afterwards confirmed by that State.

Article 9. Adoption of the text

1. The adoption of the text of a treaty takes place by the consent of all the States participating in its drawing up except as provided in paragraph 2.

2. The adoption of the text of a treaty at an international conference takes place by the vote of two-thirds of the States present and voting, unless by the same majority they shall decide to apply a different rule.

Article 10. Authentication of the text

The text of a treaty is established as authentic and definitive:

(a) by such procedure as may be provided for in the text or agreed upon by the States participating in its drawing up; or

(b) failing such procedure, by the signature, signature *ad referendum* or initialling by the representatives of those States of the text of the treaty or of the Final Act of a conference incorporating the text.

Article 11. Means of expressing consent to be bound by a treaty

The consent of a State to be bound by a treaty may be expressed by signature, exchange of instruments constituting a treaty, ratification, acceptance, approval or accession, or by any other means if so agreed.

Article 12. Consent to be bound by a treaty expressed by signature

1. The consent of a State to be bound by a treaty is expressed by the signature of its representative when:

(a) the treaty provides that signature shall have that effect;

(b) it is otherwise established that the negotiating States were agreed that signature should have that effect; or

(c) the intention of the State to give that effect to the signature appears from the full powers of its representative or was expressed during the negotiation.

2. For the purposes of paragraph 1:

(a) the initialling of a text constitutes a signature of the treaty when it is established that the negotiating States so agreed;

(b) the signature *ad referendum* of a treaty by a representative, if confirmed by his State, constitutes a full signature of the treaty.

Article 13. Consent to be bound by a treaty expressed by an exchange of instruments constituting a treaty

The consent of States to be bound by a treaty constituted by instruments exchanged between them is expressed by that exchange when:

(a) the instruments provide that their exchange shall have that effect; or

(b) it is otherwise established that those States were agreed that the exchange of instruments shall have that effect.

Article 14. Consent to be bound by a treaty expressed by ratification, acceptance or approval

1. The consent of a State to be bound by a treaty is expressed by ratification when:

(a) the treaty provides for such consent to be expressed by means of ratification;

(b) it is otherwise established that the negotiating States were agreed that ratification should be required;

(c) the representative of the State has signed the treaty subject to ratification; or

(d) the intention of the State to sign the treaty subject to ratification appears from the full powers of its representative or was expressed during the negotiation.

2. The consent of a State to be bound by a treaty is expressed by acceptance or approval under conditions similar to those which apply to ratification.

Article 15. Consent to be bound by a treaty expressed by accession

The consent of a State to be bound by a treaty is expressed by accession when:

(a) the treaty provides that such consent may be expressed by that State by means of accession;

(b) it is otherwise established that the negotiating States were agreed that such consent may be expressed by that State by means of accession; or

(c) all the parties have subsequently agreed that such consent may be expressed by that State by means of accession.

Article 16. Exchange or deposit of instruments of ratification, acceptance, approval or accession

Unless the treaty otherwise provides, instruments of ratification, acceptance, approval or accession establish the consent of a State to be bound by a treaty upon:

(a) their exchange between the contracting States;

(b) their deposit with the depositary; or

(c) their notification to the contracting States or to the depositary, if so agreed.

Article 17. Consent to be bound by part of a treaty and choice of differing provisions

1. Without prejudice to articles 19 to 23, the consent of a State to be bound by part of a treaty is effective only if the treaty so permits or the other contracting States so agree.

2. The consent of a State to be bound by a treaty which permits a choice between differing provisions is effective only if it is made clear to which of the provisions the consent relates.

Article 18. Obligation not to defeat the object and purpose of a treaty prior to its entry into force

A State is obliged to refrain from acts which would defeat the object and purpose of a treaty when:

(a) it has signed the treaty or has exchanged instruments constituting the treaty subject to ratification, acceptance or approval, until it shall have made its intention clear not to become a party to the treaty; or

(b) it has expressed its consent to be bound by the treaty, pending the entry into force of the treaty and provided that such entry into force is not unduly delayed.

Section 2. Reservations

Article 19. Formulation of reservations

A State may, when signing, ratifying, accepting, approving or acceding to a treaty, formulate a reservation unless:

(a) the reservation is prohibited by the treaty;

(b) the treaty provides that only specified reservations, which do not include the reservation in question, may be made; or

(c) in cases not falling under sub-paragraphs (a) and (b), the reservation is incompatible with the object and purpose of the treaty.

Article 20. Acceptance of and objection to reservations

1. A reservation expressly authorized by a treaty does not require any subsequent acceptance by the other contracting States unless the treaty so provides.

2. When it appears from the limited number of the negotiating States and the object and purpose of a treaty that the application of the treaty in its entirety between all the parties is an essential condition of the consent of each one to be bound by the treaty, a reservation requires acceptance by all the parties.

3. When a treaty is a constituent instrument of an international organization and unless it otherwise provides, a reservation requires the acceptance of the competent organ of that organization.

4. In cases not falling under the preceding paragraphs and unless the treaty otherwise provides:

(a) acceptance by another contracting State of a reservation constitutes the reserving State a party to the treaty in relation to that other State if or when the treaty is in force for those States;

(b) an objection by another contracting State to a reservation does not preclude the entry into force of the treaty as between the objecting and reserving States unless a contrary intention is definitely expressed by the objecting State;

(c) an act expressing a State's consent to be bound by the treaty and containing a reservation is effective as soon as at least one other contracting State has accepted the reservation.

5. For the purposes of paragraphs 2 and 4 and unless the treaty otherwise provides, a reservation is considered to have been accepted by a State if it shall have raised no objection to the reservation by the end of a period of twelve months after it was notified of the reservation or by the date on which it expressed its consent to be bound by the treaty, whichever is later.

Article 21. Legal effects of reservations and of objections to reservations

1. A reservation established with regard to another party in accordance with articles 19, 20 and 23:

(a) modifies for the reserving State in its relations with that other party the provisions of the treaty to which the reservation relates to the extent of the reservation; and

(b) modifies those provisions to the same extent for that other party in its relations with the reserving State.

2. The reservation does not modify the provisions of the treaty for the other parties to the treaty *inter se*.

3. When a State objecting to a reservation has not opposed the entry into force of the treaty between itself and the reserving State, the provisions to which the reservation relates do not apply as between the two States to the extent of the reservation.

Article 22. Withdrawal of reservations and of objections to reservations

1. Unless the treaty otherwise provides, a reservation may be withdrawn at any time and the consent of a State which has accepted the reservation is not required for its withdrawal.

2. Unless the treaty otherwise provides, an objection to a reservation may be withdrawn at any time.

3. Unless the treaty otherwise provides, or it is otherwise agreed:

(a) the withdrawal of a reservation becomes operative in relation to another contracting State only when notice of it has been received by that State;

(b) the withdrawal of an objection to a reservation becomes operative only when notice of it has been received by the State which formulated the reservation.

Article 23. Procedure regarding reservations

1. A reservation, an express acceptance of a reservation and an objection to a reservation must be formulated in writing and communicated to the contracting States and other States entitled to become parties to the treaty.

2. If formulated when signing the treaty subject to ratification, acceptance or approval, a reservation must be formally confirmed by the reserving State when expressing its consent to be bound by the treaty. In such a case the reservation shall be considered as having been made on the date of its confirmation.

3. An express acceptance of, or an objection to, a reservation made previously to confirmation of the reservation does not itself require confirmation.

4. The withdrawal of a reservation or of an objection to a reservation must be formulated in writing.

Section 3. Entry Into Force and Provisional Application of Treaties

Article 24. Entry into force

1. A treaty enters into force in such manner and upon such date as it may provide or as the negotiating States may agree.

2. Failing any such provision or agreement, a treaty enters into force as soon as consent to be bound by the treaty has been established for all the negotiating States.

3. When the consent of a State to be bound by a treaty is established on a date after the treaty has come into force, the treaty enters into force for that State on that date, unless the treaty otherwise provides.

4. The provisions of a treaty regulating the authentication of its text, the establishment of the consent of States to be bound by the treaty, the manner or date of its entry

into force, reservations, the functions of the depositary and other matters arising necessarily before the entry into force of the treaty apply from the time of the adoption of its text.

Article 25. Provisional application

1. A treaty or a part of a treaty is applied provisionally pending its entry into force if:
(a) the treaty itself so provides; or
(b) the negotiating States have in some other manner so agreed.

2. Unless the treaty otherwise provides or the negotiating States have otherwise agreed, the provisional application of a treaty or a part of a treaty with respect to a State shall be terminated if that State notifies the other States between which the treaty is being applied provisionally of its intention not to become a party to the treaty.

Part III — Observance, Application and Interpretation of Treaties

Section 1. Observance of Treaties

Article 26. "*Pacta sunt servanda*"

Every treaty in force is binding upon the parties to it and must be performed by them in good faith.

Article 27. Internal law and observance of treaties

A party may not invoke the provisions of its internal law as justification for its failure to perform a treaty. This rule is without prejudice to article 46.

Section 2. Application of Treaties

Article 28. Non-retroactivity of treaties

Unless a different intention appears from the treaty or is otherwise established, its provisions do not bind a party in relation to any act or fact which took place or any situation which ceased to exist before the date of the entry into force of the treaty with respect to that party.

Article 29. Territorial scope of treaties

Unless a different intention appears from the treaty or is otherwise established, a treaty is binding upon each party in respect of its entire territory.

Article 30. Application of successive treaties relating to the same subject-matter

1. Subject to Article 103 of the Charter of the United Nations, the rights and obligations of States parties to successive treaties relating to the same subject-matter shall be determined in accordance with the following paragraphs.

2. When a treaty specifies that it is subject to, or that it is not to be considered as incompatible with, an earlier or later treaty, the provisions of that other treaty prevail.

3. When all the parties to the earlier treaty are parties also to the later treaty but the earlier treaty is not terminated or suspended in operation under article 59, the earlier treaty applies only to the extent that its provisions are compatible with those of the later treaty.

4. When the parties to the later treaty do not include all the parties to the earlier one:
(a) as between States parties to both treaties the same rule applies as in paragraph 3;

(b) as between a State party to both treaties and a State party to only one of the treaties, the treaty to which both States are parties governs their mutual rights and obligations.

5. Paragraph 4 is without prejudice to article 41, or to any question of the termination or suspension of the operation of a treaty under article 60 or to any question of responsibility which may arise for a State from the conclusion or application of a treaty the provisions of which are incompatible with its obligations towards another State under another treaty.

Section 3. Interpretation of Treaties

Article 31. General rule of interpretation

1. A treaty shall be interpreted in good faith in accordance with the ordinary meaning to be given to the terms of the treaty in their context and in the light of its object and purpose.

2. The context for the purpose of the interpretation of a treaty shall comprise, in addition to the text, including its preamble and annexes:

(a) any agreement relating to the treaty which was made between all the parties in connection with the conclusion of the treaty;

(b) any instrument which was made by one or more parties in connection with the conclusion of the treaty and accepted by the other parties as an instrument related to the treaty.

3. There shall be taken into account, together with the context:

(a) any subsequent agreement between the parties regarding the interpretation of the treaty or the application of its provisions;

(b) any subsequent practice in the application of the treaty which establishes the agreement of the parties regarding its interpretation;

(c) any relevant rules of international law applicable in the relations between the parties.

4. A special meaning shall be given to a term if it is established that the parties so intended.

Article 32. Supplementary means of interpretation

Recourse may be had to supplementary means of interpretation, including the preparatory work of the treaty and the circumstances of its conclusion, in order to confirm the meaning resulting from the application of article 31, or to determine the meaning when the interpretation according to article 31:

(a) leaves the meaning ambiguous or obscure; or

(b) leads to a result which is manifestly absurd or unreasonable.

Article 33. Interpretation of treaties authenticated in two or more languages

1. When a treaty has been authenticated in two or more languages, the text is equally authoritative in each language, unless the treaty provides or the parties agree that, in case of divergence, a particular text shall prevail.

2. A version of the treaty in a language other than one of those in which the text was authenticated shall be considered an authentic text only if the treaty so provides or the parties so agree.

3. The terms of the treaty are presumed to have the same meaning in each authentic text.

4. Except where a particular text prevails in accordance with paragraph 1, when a comparison of the authentic texts discloses a difference of meaning which the applica-

tion of articles 31 and 32 does not remove, the meaning which best reconciles the texts, having regard to the object and purpose of the treaty, shall be adopted.

Section 4. Treaties and Third States

Article 34. General rule regarding third States

A treaty does not create either obligations or rights for a third State without its consent.

Article 35. Treaties providing for obligations for third States

An obligation arises for a third State from a provision of a treaty if the parties to the treaty intend the provision to be the means of establishing the obligation and the third State expressly accepts that obligation in writing.

Article 36. Treaties providing for rights for third States

1. A right arises for a third State from a provision of a treaty if the parties to the treaty intend the provision to accord that right either to the third State, or to a group of States to which it belongs, or to all States, and the third State assents thereto. Its assent shall be presumed so long as the contrary is not indicated, unless the treaty otherwise provides.

2. A State exercising a right in accordance with paragraph 1 shall comply with the conditions for its exercise provided for in the treaty or established in conformity with the treaty.

Article 37. Revocation or modification of obligations or rights of third States

1. When an obligation has arisen for a third State in conformity with article 35, the obligation may be revoked or modified only with the consent of the parties to the treaty and of the third State, unless it is established that they had otherwise agreed.

2. When a right has arisen for a third State in conformity with article 36, the right may not be revoked or modified by the parties if it is established that the right was intended not to be revocable or subject to modification without the consent of the third State.

Article 38. Rules in a treaty becoming binding on third States through international custom

Nothing in articles 34 to 37 precludes a rule set forth in a treaty from becoming binding upon a third State as a customary rule of international law, recognized as such.

Part IV — Amendment and Modification of Treaties

Article 39. General rule regarding the amendment of treaties

A treaty may be amended by agreement between the parties. The rules laid down in Part II apply to such an agreement except in so far as the treaty may otherwise provide.

Article 40. Amendment of multilateral treaties

1. Unless the treaty otherwise provides, the amendment of multilateral treaties shall be governed by the following paragraphs.

2. Any proposal to amend a multilateral treaty as between all the parties must be notified to all the contracting States, each one of which shall have the right to take part in:

(a) the decision as to the action to be taken in regard to such proposal;

(b) the negotiation and conclusion of any agreement for the amendment of the treaty.

3. Every State entitled to become a party to the treaty shall also be entitled to become a party to the treaty as amended.

4. The amending agreement does not bind any State already a party to the treaty which does not become a party to the amending agreement; article 30, paragraph 4(b), applies in relation to such State.

5. Any State which becomes a party to the treaty after the entry into force of the amending agreement shall, failing an expression of a different intention by that State:

(a) be considered as a party to the treaty as amended; and

(b) be considered as a party to the unamended treaty in relation to any party to the treaty not bound by the amending agreement.

Article 41. Agreements to modify multilateral treaties between certain of the parties only

1. Two or more of the parties to a multilateral treaty may conclude an agreement to modify the treaty as between themselves alone if:

(a) the possibility of such a modification is provided for by the treaty; or

(b) the modification in question is not prohibited by the treaty and:

(i) does not affect the enjoyment by the other parties of their rights under the treaty or the performance of their obligations;

(ii) does not relate to a provision, derogation from which is incompatible with the effective execution of the object and purpose of the treaty as a whole.

2. Unless in a case falling under paragraph 1(a) the treaty otherwise provides, the parties in question shall notify the other parties of their intention to conclude the agreement and of the modification to the treaty for which it provides.

Part V — Invalidity, Termination and Suspension of the Operation of Treaties

Section 1. General Provisions

Article 42. Validity and continuance in force of treaties

1. The validity of a treaty or of the consent of a State to be bound by a treaty may be impeached only through the application of the present Convention.

2. The termination of a treaty, its denunciation or the withdrawal of a party, may take place only as a result of the application of the provisions of the treaty or of the present Convention. The same rule applies to suspension of the operation of a treaty.

Article 43. Obligations imposed by international law independently of a treaty

The invalidity, termination or denunciation of a treaty, the withdrawal of a party from it, or the suspension of its operation, as a result of the application of the present Convention or of the provisions of the treaty, shall not in any way impair the duty of any State to fulfil any obligation embodied in the treaty to which it would be subject under international law independently of the treaty.

Article 44. Separability of treaty provisions

1. A right of a party, provided for in a treaty or arising under article 56, to denounce, withdraw from or suspend the operation of the treaty may be exercised only with respect to the whole treaty unless the treaty otherwise provides or the parties otherwise agree.

2. A ground for invalidating, terminating, withdrawing from or suspending the operation of a treaty recognized in the present Convention may be invoked only with respect to the whole treaty except as provided in the following paragraphs or in article 60.

3. If the ground relates solely to particular clauses, it may be invoked only with respect to those clauses where:

(a) the said clauses are separable from the remainder of the treaty with regard to their application;

(b) it appears from the treaty or is otherwise established that acceptance of those clauses was not an essential basis of the consent of the other party or parties to be bound by the treaty as a whole; and

(c) continued performance of the remainder of the treaty would not be unjust.

4. In cases falling under articles 49 and 50 the State entitled to invoke the fraud or corruption may do so with respect either to the whole treaty or, subject to paragraph 3, to the particular clauses alone.

5. In cases falling under articles 51, 52 and 53, no separation of the provisions of the treaty is permitted.

Article 45. Loss of a right to invoke a ground for invalidating, terminating, withdrawing from or suspending the operation of a treaty

A State may no longer invoke a ground for invalidating, terminating, withdrawing from or suspending the operation of a treaty under articles 46 to 50 or articles 60 and 62 if, after becoming aware of the facts:

(a) it shall have expressly agreed that the treaty is valid or remains in force or continues in operation, as the case may be; or

(b) it must by reason of its conduct be considered as having acquiesced in the validity of the treaty or in its maintenance in force or in operation, as the case may be.

Section 2. Invalidity of Treaties

Article 46. Provisions of internal law regarding competence to conclude treaties

1. A State may not invoke the fact that its consent to be bound by a treaty has been expressed in violation of a provision of its internal law regarding competence to conclude treaties as invalidating its consent unless that violation was manifest and concerned a rule of its internal law of fundamental importance.

2. A violation is manifest if it would be objectively evident to any State conducting itself in the matter in accordance with normal practice and in good faith.

Article 47. Specific restrictions on authority to express the consent of a State

If the authority of a representative to express the consent of a State to be bound by a particular treaty has been made subject to a specific restriction, his omission to observe that restriction may not be invoked as invalidating the consent expressed by him unless the restriction was notified to the other negotiating States prior to his expressing such consent.

Article 48. Error

1. A State may invoke an error in a treaty as invalidating its consent to be bound by the treaty if the error relates to a fact or situation which was assumed by that State to exist at the time when the treaty was concluded and formed an essential basis of its consent to be bound by the treaty.

2. Paragraph 1 shall not apply if the State in question contributed by its own conduct to the error or if the circumstances were such as to put that State on notice of a possible error.

3. An error relating only to the wording of the text of a treaty does not affect its validity; article 79 then applies.

Article 49. Fraud

If a State has been induced to conclude a treaty by the fraudulent conduct of another negotiating State, the State may invoke the fraud as invalidating its consent to be bound by the treaty.

Article 50. Corruption of a representative of a State

If the expression of a State's consent to be bound by a treaty has been procured through the corruption of its representative directly or indirectly by another negotiating State, the State may invoke such corruption as invalidating its consent to be bound by the treaty.

Article 51. Coercion of a representative of a State

The expression of a State's consent to be bound by a treaty which has been procured by the coercion of its representative through acts or threats directed against him shall be without any legal effect.

Article 52. Coercion of a State by the threat or use of force

A treaty is void if its conclusion has been procured by the threat or use of force in violation of the principles of international law embodied in the Charter of the United Nations.

Article 53. Treaties conflicting with a peremptory norm of general international law ("*jus cogens*")

A treaty is void if, at the time of its conclusion, it conflicts with a peremptory norm of general international law. For the purposes of the present Convention, a peremptory norm of general international law is a norm accepted and recognized by the international community of States as a whole as a norm from which no derogation is permitted and which can be modified only by a subsequent norm of general international law having the same character.

Section 3. Termination and Suspension of the Operation of Treaties

Article 54. Termination of or withdrawal from a treaty under its provisions or by consent of the parties

The termination of a treaty or the withdrawal of a party may take place:

(a) in conformity with the provisions of the treaty; or

(b) at any time by consent of all the parties after consultation with the other contracting States.

Article 55. Reduction of the parties to a multilateral treaty below the number necessary for its entry into force

Unless the treaty otherwise provides, a multilateral treaty does not terminate by reason only of the fact that the number of the parties falls below the number necessary for its entry into force.

Article 56. Denunciation of or withdrawal from a treaty containing no provision regarding termination, denunciation or withdrawal

1. A treaty which contains no provision regarding its termination and which does not provide for denunciation or withdrawal is not subject to denunciation or withdrawal unless:

(a) it is established that the parties intended to admit the possibility of denunciation or withdrawal; or

(b) a right of denunciation or withdrawal may be implied by the nature of the treaty.

2. A party shall give not less than twelve months' notice of its intention to denounce or withdraw from a treaty under paragraph 1.

Article 57. Suspension of the operation of a treaty under its provisions or by consent of the parties

The operation of a treaty in regard to all the parties or to a particular party may be suspended:

(a) in conformity with the provisions of the treaty; or

(b) at any time by consent of all the parties after consultation with the other contracting States.

Article 58. Suspension of the operation of a multilateral treaty by agreement between certain of the parties only

1. Two or more parties to a multilateral treaty may conclude an agreement to suspend the operation of provisions of the treaty, temporarily and as between themselves alone, if:

(a) the possibility of such a suspension is provided for by the treaty; or

(b) the suspension in question is not prohibited by the treaty and:

(i) does not affect the enjoyment by the other parties of their rights under the treaty or the performance of their obligations;

(ii) is not incompatible with the object and purpose of the treaty.

2. Unless in a case falling under paragraph 1(a) the treaty otherwise provides, the parties in question shall notify the other parties of their intention to conclude the agreement and of those provisions of the treaty the operation of which they intend to suspend.

Article 59. Termination or suspension of the operation of a treaty implied by conclusion of a later treaty

1. A treaty shall be considered as terminated if all the parties to it conclude a later treaty relating to the same subject-matter and:

(a) it appears from the later treaty or is otherwise established that the parties intended that the matter should be governed by that treaty; or

(b) the provisions of the later treaty are so far incompatible with those of the earlier one that the two treaties are not capable of being applied at the same time.

2. The earlier treaty shall be considered as only suspended in operation if it appears from the later treaty or is otherwise established that such was the intention of the parties.

Article 60. Termination or suspension of the operation of a treaty as a consequence of its breach

1. A material breach of a bilateral treaty by one of the parties entitles the other to invoke the breach as a ground for terminating the treaty or suspending its operation in whole or in part.

2. A material breach of a multilateral treaty by one of the parties entitles:

(a) the other parties by unanimous agreement to suspend the operation of the treaty in whole or in part or to terminate it either:

(i) in the relations between themselves and the defaulting State, or

(ii) as between all the parties;

(b) a party specially affected by the breach to invoke it as a ground for suspending the operation of the treaty in whole or in part in the relations between itself and the defaulting State;

(c) any party other than the defaulting State to invoke the breach as a ground for suspending the operation of the treaty in whole or in part with respect to itself if the treaty is of such a character that a material breach of its provisions by one party radically changes the position of every party with respect to the further performance of its obligations under the treaty.

3. A material breach of a treaty, for the purposes of this article, consists in:

(a) a repudiation of the treaty not sanctioned by the present Convention; or

(b) the violation of a provision essential to the accomplishment of the object or purpose of the treaty.

4. The foregoing paragraphs are without prejudice to any provision in the treaty applicable in the event of a breach.

5. Paragraphs 1 to 3 do not apply to provisions relating to the protection of the human person contained in treaties of a humanitarian character, in particular to provisions prohibiting any form of reprisals against persons protected by such treaties.

Article 61. Supervening impossibility of performance

1. A party may invoke the impossibility of performing a treaty as a ground for terminating or withdrawing from it if the impossibility results from the permanent disappearance or destruction of an object indispensable for the execution of the treaty. If the impossibility is temporary, it may be invoked only as a ground for suspending the operation of the treaty.

2. Impossibility of performance may not be invoked by a party as a ground for terminating, withdrawing from or suspending the operation of a treaty if the impossibility is the result of a breach by that party either of an obligation under the treaty or of any other international obligation owed to any other party to the treaty.

Article 62. Fundamental change of circumstances

1. A fundamental change of circumstances which has occurred with regard to those existing at the time of the conclusion of a treaty, and which was not foreseen by the parties, may not be invoked as a ground for terminating or withdrawing from the treaty unless:

(a) the existence of those circumstances constituted an essential basis of the consent of the parties to be bound by the treaty; and

(b) the effect of the change is radically to transform the extent of obligations still to be performed under the treaty.

2. A fundamental change of circumstances may not be invoked as a ground for terminating or withdrawing from a treaty:

(a) if the treaty establishes a boundary; or

(b) if the fundamental change is the result of a breach by the party invoking it either of an obligation under the treaty or of any other international obligation owed to any other party to the treaty.

3. If, under the foregoing paragraphs, a party may invoke a fundamental change of circumstances as a ground for terminating or withdrawing from a treaty it may also invoke the change as a ground for suspending the operation of the treaty.

Article 63. Severance of diplomatic or consular relations

The severance of diplomatic or consular relations between parties to a treaty does not affect the legal relations established between them by the treaty except in so far as the existence of diplomatic or consular relations is indispensable for the application of the treaty.

Article 64. Emergence of a new peremptory norm of general international law (*jus cogens*)

If a new peremptory norm of general international law emerges, any existing treaty which is in conflict with that norm becomes void and terminates.

Section 4. Procedure

Article 65. Procedure to be followed with respect to invalidity, termination, withdrawal from or suspension of the operation of a treaty

1. A party which, under the provisions of the present Convention, invokes either a defect in its consent to be bound by a treaty or a ground for impeaching the validity of a treaty, terminating it, withdrawing from it or suspending its operation, must notify the other parties of its claim. The notification shall indicate the measure proposed to be taken with respect to the treaty and the reasons therefor.

2. If, after the expiry of a period which, except in cases of special urgency, shall not be less than three months after the receipt of the notification, no party has raised any objection, the party making the notification may carry out in the manner provided in article 67 the measure which it has proposed.

3. If, however, objection has been raised by any other party, the parties shall seek a solution through the means indicated in article 33 of the Charter of the United Nations.

4. Nothing in the foregoing paragraphs shall affect the rights or obligations of the parties under any provisions in force binding the parties with regard to the settlement of disputes.

5. Without prejudice to article 45, the fact that a State has not previously made the notification prescribed in paragraph 1 shall not prevent it from making such notification in answer to another party claiming performance of the treaty or alleging its violation.

Article 66. Procedures for judicial settlement, arbitration and conciliation

If, under paragraph 3 of article 65, no solution has been reached within a period of twelve months following the date on which the objection was raised, the following procedures shall be followed:

(a) any one of the parties to a dispute concerning the application or the interpretation of articles 53 or 64 may, by a written application, submit it to the International Court of Justice for a decision unless the parties by common consent agree to submit the dispute to arbitration;

(b) any one of the parties to a dispute concerning the application or the interpretation of any of the other articles in Part V of the present Convention may set in motion the procedure specified in the Annex to the Convention by submitting a request to that effect to the Secretary-General of the United Nations.

Article 67. Instruments for declaring invalid, terminating, withdrawing from or suspending the operation of a treaty

1. The notification provided for under article 65, paragraph 1 must be made in writing.

2. Any act declaring invalid, terminating, withdrawing from or suspending the operation of a treaty pursuant to the provisions of the treaty or of paragraphs 2 or 3 of article 65 shall be carried out through an instrument communicated to the other parties. If the instrument is not signed by the Head of State, Head of Government or Minister for Foreign Affairs, the representative of the State communicating it may be called upon to produce full powers.

Article 68. Revocation of notifications and instruments provided for in articles 65 and 67

A notification or instrument provided for in articles 65 or 67 may be revoked at any time before it takes effect.

Section 5. Consequences of the Invalidity, Termination or Suspension of the Operation of a Treaty

Article 69. Consequences of the invalidity of a treaty

1. A treaty the invalidity of which is established under the present Convention is void. The provisions of a void treaty have no legal force.

2. If acts have nevertheless been performed in reliance on such a treaty:

(a) each party may require any other party to establish as far as possible in their mutual relations the position that would have existed if the acts had not been performed;

(b) acts performed in good faith before the invalidity was invoked are not rendered unlawful by reason only of the invalidity of the treaty.

3. In cases falling under articles 49, 50, 51 or 52, paragraph 2 does not apply with respect to the party to which the fraud, the act of corruption or the coercion is imputable.

4. In the case of the invalidity of a particular State's consent to be bound by a multilateral treaty, the foregoing rules apply in the relations between that State and the parties to the treaty.

Article 70. Consequences of the termination of a treaty

1. Unless the treaty otherwise provides or the parties otherwise agree, the termination of a treaty under its provisions or in accordance with the present Convention:

(a) releases the parties from any obligation further to perform the treaty;

(b) does not affect any right, obligation or legal situation of the parties created through the execution of the treaty prior to its termination.

2. If a State denounces or withdraws from a multilateral treaty, paragraph 1 applies in the relations between that State and each of the other parties to the treaty from the date when such denunciation or withdrawal takes effect.

Article 71. Consequences of the invalidity of a treaty which conflicts with a peremptory norm of general international law

1. In the case of a treaty which is void under article 53 the parties shall:

(a) eliminate as far as possible the consequences of any act performed in reliance on any provision which conflicts with the peremptory norm of general international law; and

(b) bring their mutual relations into conformity with the peremptory norm of general international law.

2. In the case of a treaty which becomes void and terminates under article 64, the termination of the treaty:

(a) releases the parties from any obligation further to perform the treaty;

(b) does not affect any right, obligation or legal situation of the parties created through the execution of the treaty prior to its termination, provided that those rights, obligations or situations may thereafter be maintained only to the extent that their maintenance is not in itself in conflict with the new peremptory norm of general international law.

Article 72. Consequences of the suspension of the operation of a treaty

1. Unless the treaty otherwise provides or the parties otherwise agree, the suspension of the operation of a treaty under its provisions or in accordance with the present Convention:

(a) releases the parties between which the operation of the treaty is suspended from the obligation to perform the treaty in their mutual relations during the period of the suspension;

(b) does not otherwise affect the legal relations between the parties established by the treaty.

2. During the period of the suspension the parties shall refrain from acts tending to obstruct the resumption of the operation of the treaty.

Part VI — Miscellaneous Provisions

Article 73. Cases of State succession, State responsibility and outbreak of hostilities

The provisions of the present Convention shall not prejudge any question that may arise in regard to a treaty from a succession of States or from the international responsibility of a State or from the outbreak of hostilities between States.

Article 74. Diplomatic and consular relations and the conclusion of treaties

The severance or absence of diplomatic or consular relations between two or more States does not prevent the conclusion of treaties between those States. The conclusion of a treaty does not in itself affect the situation in regard to diplomatic or consular relations.

Article 75. Case of an aggressor State

The provisions of the present Convention are without prejudice to any obligation in relation to a treaty which may arise for an aggressor State in consequence of measures taken in conformity with the Charter of the United Nations with reference to that State's aggression.

Part VII — Depositaries, Notifications, Corrections and Registration

Article 76. Depositaries of treaties

1. The designation of the depositary of a treaty may be made by the negotiating States, either in the treaty itself or in some other manner. The depositary may be one or more States, an international organization or the chief administrative officer of the organization.

2. The functions of the depositary of a treaty are international in character and the depositary is under an obligation to act impartially in their performance. In particular,

the fact that a treaty has not entered into force between certain of the parties or that a difference has appeared between a State and a depositary with regard to the performance of the latter's functions shall not affect that obligation.

Article 77. Functions of depositaries

1. The functions of a depositary, unless otherwise provided in the treaty or agreed by the contracting States, comprise in particular:

(a) keeping custody of the original text of the treaty and of any full powers delivered to the depositary;

(b) preparing certified copies of the original text and preparing any further text of the treaty in such additional languages as may be required by the treaty and transmitting them to the parties and to the States entitled to become parties to the treaty;

(c) receiving any signatures to the treaty and receiving and keeping custody of any instruments, notifications and communications relating to it;

(d) examining whether the signature or any instrument, notification or communication relating to the treaty is in due and proper form and, if need be, bringing the matter to the attention of the State in question;

(e) informing the parties and the States entitled to become parties to the treaty of acts, notifications and communications relating to the treaty;

(f) informing the States entitled to become parties to the treaty when the number of signatures or of instruments of ratification, acceptance, approval or accession required for the entry into force of the treaty has been received or deposited;

(g) registering the treaty with the Secretariat of the United Nations;

(h) performing the functions specified in other provisions of the present Convention.

2. In the event of any difference appearing between a State and the depositary as to the performance of the latter's functions, the depositary shall bring the question to the attention of the signatory States and the contracting States or, where appropriate, of the competent organ of the international organization concerned.

Article 78. Notifications and communications

Except as the treaty or the present Convention otherwise provide, any notification or communication to be made by any State under the present Convention shall:

(a) if there is no depositary, be transmitted direct to the States for which it is intended, or if there is a depositary, to the latter;

(b) be considered as having been made by the State in question only upon its receipt by the State to which it was transmitted or, as the case may be, upon its receipt by the depositary;

(c) if transmitted to a depositary, be considered as received by the State for which it was intended only when the latter State has been informed by the depositary in accordance with article 77, paragraph 1 (e).

Article 79. Correction of errors in texts or in certified copies of treaties

1. Where, after the authentication of the text of a treaty, the signatory States and the contracting States are agreed that it contains an error, the error shall, unless they decide upon some other means of correction, be corrected:

(a) by having the appropriate correction made in the text and causing the correction to be initialled by duly authorized representatives;

(b) by executing or exchanging an instrument or instruments setting out the correction which it has been agreed to make; or

(c) by executing a corrected text of the whole treaty by the same procedure as in the case of the original text.

2. Where the treaty is one for which there is a depositary, the latter shall notify the signatory States and the contracting States of the error and of the proposal to correct it and shall specify an appropriate time-limit within which objection to the proposed correction may be raised. If, on the expiry of the time-limit:

(a) no objection has been raised, the depositary shall make and initial the correction in the text and shall execute a *procés-verbal* of the rectification of the text and communicate a copy of it to the parties and to the States entitled to become parties to the treaty;

(b) an objection has been raised, the depositary shall communicate the objection to the signatory States and to the contracting States.

3. The rules in paragraphs 1 and 2 apply also where the text has been authenticated in two or more languages and it appears that there is a lack of concordance which the signatory States and the contracting States agree should be corrected.

4. The corrected text replaces the defective text *ab initio*, unless the signatory States and the contracting States otherwise decide.

5. The correction of the text of a treaty that has been registered shall be notified to the Secretariat of the United Nations.

6. Where an error is discovered in a certified copy of a treaty, the depositary shall execute a *procés-verbal* specifying the rectification and communicate a copy of it to the signatory States and to the contracting States.

Article 80. Registration and publication of treaties

1. Treaties shall, after their entry into force, be transmitted to the Secretariat of the United Nations for registration or filing and recording, as the case may be, and for publication.

2. The designation of a depositary shall constitute authorization for it to perform the acts specified in the preceding paragraph.

Part VIII — Final Provisions

Article 81. Signature

The present Convention shall be open for signature by all States Members of the United Nations or of any of the specialized agencies or of the International Atomic Energy Agency or parties to the Statute of the International Court of Justice, and by any other State invited by the General Assembly of the United Nations to become a party to the Convention, as follows: until 30 November 1969, at the Federal Ministry for Foreign Affairs of the Republic of Austria, and subsequently, until 30 April 1970, at United Nations Headquarters, New York.

Article 82. Ratification

The present Convention is subject to ratification. The instruments of ratification shall be deposited with the Secretary-General of the United Nations.

Article 83. Accession

The present Convention shall remain open for accession by any State belonging to any of the categories mentioned in article 81. The instruments of accession shall be deposited with the Secretary-General of the United Nations.

Article 84. Entry into force

1. The present Convention shall enter into force on the thirtieth day following the date of deposit of the thirty-fifth instrument of ratification or accession.

2. For each State ratifying or acceding to the Convention after the deposit of the thirty-fifth instrument of ratification or accession, the Convention shall enter into force on the thirtieth day after deposit by such State of its instrument of ratification or accession.

Article 85. Authentic texts

The original of the present Convention, of which the Chinese, English, French, Russian and Spanish texts are equally authentic, shall be deposited with the Secretary-General of the United Nations.

Annex

1. A list of conciliators consisting of qualified jurists shall be drawn up and maintained by the Secretary-General of the United Nations. To this end, every State which is a Member of the United Nations or a party to the present Convention shall be invited to nominate two conciliators, and the names of the persons so nominated shall constitute the list. The term of a conciliator, including that of any conciliator nominated to fill a casual vacancy, shall be five years and may be renewed. A conciliator whose term expires shall continue to fulfil any function for which he shall have been chosen under the following paragraph.

2. When a request has been made to the Secretary-General under article 66, the Secretary-General shall bring the dispute before a conciliation commission constituted as follows:

The State or States constituting one of the parties to the dispute shall appoint:

(a) one conciliator of the nationality of that State or of one of those States, who may or may not be chosen from the list referred to in paragraph 1; and

(b) one conciliator not of the nationality of that State or of any of those States, who shall be chosen from the list.

The State or States constituting the other party to the dispute shall appoint two conciliators in the same way. The four conciliators chosen by the parties shall be appointed within sixty days following the date on which the Secretary-General receives the request.

The four conciliators shall, within sixty days following the date of the last of their own appointments, appoint a fifth conciliator chosen from the list, who shall be chairman.

If the appointment of the chairman or of any of the other conciliators has not been made within the period prescribed above for such appointment, it shall be made by the Secretary-General within sixty days following the expiry of that period. The appointment of the chairman may be made by the Secretary-General either from the list or from the membership of the International Law Commission. Any of the periods within which appointments must be made may be extended by agreement between the parties to the dispute.

Any vacancy shall be filled in the manner prescribed for the initial appointment.

3. The Conciliation Commission shall decide its own procedure. The Commission, with the consent of the parties to the dispute, may invite any party to the treaty to submit to it its views orally or in writing. Decisions and recommendations of the Commission shall be made by a majority vote of the five members.

4. The Commission may draw the attention of the parties to the dispute to any measures which might facilitate an amicable settlement.

5. The Commission shall hear the parties, examine the claims and objections, and make proposals to the parties with a view to reaching an amicable settlement of the dispute.

6. The Commission shall report within twelve months of its constitution. Its report shall be deposited with the Secretary-General and transmitted to the parties to the dispute. The report of the Commission, including any conclusions stated therein regarding the facts or questions of law, shall not be binding upon the parties and it shall have no other character than that of recommendations submitted for the consideration of the parties in order to facilitate an amicable settlement of the dispute.

7. The Secretary-General shall provide the Commission with such assistance and facilities as it may require. The expenses of the Commission shall be borne by the United Nations.

Vienna Convention on Consular Relations and Optional Protocols
April 24, 1963, 21 U.S.T. 77, 596 U.N.T.S 261

[Ed. Note: This Convention entered into force on March 19, 1967. As of March 2003, 165 nations, including the United States, were parties to the Convention. Only the Preamble and Articles 35 to 38 are set forth below.]

The States Parties to the present Convention,

Recalling that consular relations have been established between peoples since ancient times,

Having in mind the Purposes and Principles of the Charter of the United Nation concerning the sovereign equality of States, the maintenance of international peace and security, and the promotion of friendly relations among nations,

Considering that the United Nations Conference on Diplomatic Intercourse and Immunities adopted the Vienna Convention on Diplomatic Relations which was opened for signature on 18 April 1961,

Believing that an international convention on consular relations, privileges and immunities would also contribute to the development of friendly relations among nations, irrespective of their differing constitutional and social systems,

Realizing that the purpose of such privileges and immunities is not to benefit individuals but to ensure the efficient performance of functions by consular posts on behalf of their respective States,

Affirming that the rules of customary international law continue to govern matters not expressly regulated by the provisions of the present Convention,

Have agreed as follows:

Article 35. Freedom of communication

1. The receiving State shall permit and protect freedom of communication on the part of the consular post for all official purposes. In communicating with the Government, the diplomatic missions and other consular posts, wherever situated, of the sending State, the consular post may employ all appropriate means, including diplomatic or consular couriers, diplomatic or consular bags and messages in code or cipher. However, the consular post may install and use a wireless transmitter only with the consent of the receiving State.

2. The official correspondence of the consular post shall be inviolable. Official correspondence means all correspondence relating to the consular post and its functions.

3. The consular bag shall be neither opened nor detained. Nevertheless, if the competent authorities of the receiving State have serious reason to believe that the bag contains something other than the correspondence, documents or articles referred to in paragraph 4 of this Article, they may request that the bag be opened in their presence by an authorized representative of the sending State. If this request is refused by the authorities of the sending State, the bag shall be returned to its place of origin.

4. The packages constituting the consular bag shall bear visible external marks of their character and may contain only official correspondence and documents or articles intended exclusively for official use.

5. The consular courier shall be provided with an official document indicating his status and the number of packages constituting the consular bag. Except with the consent of the receiving State he shall be neither a national of the receiving State, nor, unless he is a national of the sending State, a permanent resident of the receiving State. In the performance of his functions he shall be protected by the receiving State. He shall enjoy personal inviolability and shall not be liable to any form of arrest or detention.

6. The sending State, its diplomatic missions and its consular posts may designate consular couriers *ad hoc*. In such cases the provisions of paragraph 5 of this Article shall also apply except that the immunities therein mentioned shall cease to apply when such a courier has delivered to the consignee the consular bag in his charge.

7. A consular bag may be entrusted to the captain of a ship or of a commercial aircraft scheduled to land at an authorized port of entry. He shall be provided with an official document indicating the number of packages constituting the bag, but he shall not be considered to be a consular courier. By arrangement with the appropriate local authorities, the consular post may send one of its members to take possession of the bag directly and freely from the captain of the ship or of the aircraft.

Article 36. Communication and contact with nationals of the sending state

1. With a view to facilitating the exercise of consular functions relating to nationals of the sending State:

(a) consular officers shall be free to communicate with nationals of the sending State and to have access to them. Nationals of the sending State shall have the same freedom with respect to communication with and access to consular officers of the sending State;

(b) if he so requests, the competent authorities of the receiving State shall, without delay, inform the consular post of the sending State if, within its consular district, a national of that State is arrested or committed to prison or to custody pending trial or is detained in any other manner. Any communication addressed to the consular post by the person arrested, in prison, custody or detention shall also be forwarded by the said authorities without delay. The said authorities shall inform the person concerned without delay of his rights under this sub-paragraph;

(c) consular officers shall have the right to visit a national of the sending State who is in prison, custody or detention, to converse and correspond with him and to arrange for his legal representation. They shall also have the right to visit any national of the sending State who is in prison, custody or detention in their district in pursuance of a judgment. Nevertheless, consular officers shall refrain from taking action on behalf of a national who is in prison, custody or detention if he expressly opposes such action.

2. The rights referred to in paragraph 1 of this Article shall be exercised in conformity with the laws and regulations of the receiving State, subject to the proviso, however, that the said laws and regulations must enable full effect to be given to the purposes for which the rights accorded under this Article are intended.

Article 37. Information in cases of deaths, guardianship or trusteeship, wrecks and air accidents

If the relevant information is available to the competent authorities of the receiving State, such authorities shall have the duty:

(a) in the case of the death of a national of the sending State, to inform without delay the consular post in whose district the death occurred;

(b) to inform the competent consular post without delay of any case where the appointment of a guardian or trustee appears to be in the interests of a minor or other person lacking full capacity who is a national of the sending State. The giving of this information shall, however, be without prejudice to the operation of the laws and regulations of the receiving State concerning such appointments;

(c) if a vessel, having the nationality of the sending State, is wrecked or runs aground in the territorial sea or internal waters of the receiving State, or if an aircraft registered in the sending State suffers an accident on the territory of the receiving State, to inform without delay the consular post nearest to the scene of the occurrence.

Article 38. Communication with the authorities of the receiving state

In the exercise of their functions, consular officers may address:

(a) the competent local authorities of their consular district;

(b) the competent central authorities of the receiving State if and to the extent that this is allowed by the laws, regulations and usages of the receiving State or by the relevant international agreements.

B. Human Rights — General

Universal Declaration of Human Rights
G.A. res. 217A (III), U.N. GAOR, 3rd Sess., Pt.1, Resolutions at 71, U.N. Doc A/810 (1948)

PREAMBLE

Whereas recognition of the inherent dignity and of the equal and inalienable rights of all members of the human family is the foundation of freedom, justice and peace in the world,

Whereas disregard and contempt for human rights have resulted in barbarous acts which have outraged the conscience of mankind, and the advent of a world in which human beings shall enjoy freedom of speech and belief and freedom from fear and want has been proclaimed as the highest aspiration of the common people,

Whereas it is essential, if man is not to be compelled to have recourse, as a last resort, to rebellion against tyranny and oppression, that human rights should be protected by the rule of law,

Whereas it is essential to promote the development of friendly relations between nations,

Whereas the peoples of the United Nations have in the Charter reaffirmed their faith in fundamental human rights, in the dignity and worth of the human person and in the equal rights of men and women and have determined to promote social progress and better standards of life in larger freedom,

Whereas Member States have pledged themselves to achieve, in cooperation with the United Nations, the promotion of universal respect for and observance of human rights and fundamental freedoms,

Whereas a common understanding of these rights and freedoms is of the greatest importance for the full realization of this pledge,

Now, therefore, The General Assembly, proclaims this Universal Declaration of Human Rights as a common standard of achievement for all peoples and all nations, to the end that every individual and every organ of society, keeping this Declaration constantly in mind, shall strive by teaching and education to promote respect for these rights and freedoms and by progressive measures, national and international, to secure their universal and effective recognition and observance, both among the peoples of Member States themselves and among the peoples of territories under their jurisdiction.

Article 1

All human beings are born free and equal in dignity and rights. They are endowed with reason and conscience and should act towards one another in a spirit of brotherhood.

Article 2

Everyone is entitled to all the rights and freedoms set forth in this Declaration, without distinction of any kind, such as race, colour, sex, language, religion, political or other opinion, national or social origin, property, birth or other status.

Furthermore, no distinction shall be made on the basis of the political, jurisdictional or international status of the country or territory to which a person belongs, whether it be independent, trust, non-self-governing or under any other limitation of sovereignty.

Article 3

Everyone has the right to life, liberty and security of person.

Article 4

No one shall be held in slavery or servitude; slavery and the slave trade shall be prohibited in all their forms.

Article 5

No one shall be subjected to torture or to cruel, inhuman or degrading treatment or punishment.

Article 6

Everyone has the right to recognition everywhere as a person before the law.

Article 7

All are equal before the law and are entitled without any discrimination to equal protection of the law. All are entitled to equal protection against any discrimination in violation of this Declaration and against any incitement to such discrimination.

Article 8

Everyone has the right to an effective remedy by the competent national tribunals for acts violating the fundamental rights granted him by the constitution or by law.

Article 9

No one shall be subjected to arbitrary arrest, detention or exile.

Article 10

Everyone is entitled in full equality to a fair and public hearing by an independent and impartial tribunal, in the determination of his rights and obligations and of any criminal charge against him.

Article 11

1. Everyone charged with a penal offence has the right to be presumed innocent until proved guilty according to law in a public trial at which he has had all the guarantees necessary for his defence.

2. No one shall be held guilty of any penal offence on account of any act or omission which did not constitute a penal offence, under national or international law, at the time when it was committed. Nor shall a heavier penalty be imposed than the one that was applicable at the time the penal offence was committed.

Article 12

No one shall be subjected to arbitrary interference with his privacy, family, home or correspondence, nor to attacks upon his honour and reputation. Everyone has the right to the protection of the law against such interference or attacks.

Article 13

1. Everyone has the right to freedom of movement and residence within the borders of each State.

2. Everyone has the right to leave any country, including his own, and to return to his country.

Article 14

1. Everyone has the right to seek and to enjoy in other countries asylum from persecution.

2. This right may not be invoked in the case of prosecutions genuinely arising from non-political crimes or from acts contrary to the purposes and principles of the United Nations.

Article 15

1. Everyone has the right to a nationality.

2. No one shall be arbitrarily deprived of his nationality nor denied the right to change his nationality.

Article 16

1. Men and women of full age, without any limitation due to race, nationality or religion, have the right to marry and to found a family. They are entitled to equal rights as to marriage, during marriage and at its dissolution.

2. Marriage shall be entered into only with the free and full consent of the intending spouses.

3. The family is the natural and fundamental group unit of society and is entitled to protection by society and the State.

Article 17

1. Everyone has the right to own property alone as well as in association with others.
2. No one shall be arbitrarily deprived of his property.

Article 18

Everyone has the right to freedom of thought, conscience and religion; this right includes freedom to change his religion or belief, and freedom, either alone or in community with others and in public or private, to manifest his religion or belief in teaching, practice, worship and observance.

Article 19

Everyone has the right to freedom of opinion and expression; this right includes freedom to hold opinions without interference and to seek, receive and impart information and ideas through any media and regardless of frontiers.

Article 20

1. Everyone has the right to freedom of peaceful assembly and association.
2. No one may be compelled to belong to an association.

Article 21

1. Everyone has the right to take part in the government of his country, directly or through freely chosen representatives.
2. Everyone has the right to equal access to public service in his country.
3. The will of the people shall be the basis of the authority of government; this will shall be expressed in periodic and genuine elections which shall be by universal and equal suffrage and shall be held by secret vote or by equivalent free voting procedures.

Article 22

Everyone, as a member of society, has the right to social security and is entitled to realization, through national effort and international cooperation and in accordance with the organization and resources of each State, of the economic, social and cultural rights indispensable for his dignity and the free development of his personality.

Article 23

1. Everyone has the right to work, to free choice of employment, to just and favourable conditions of work and to protection against unemployment.
2. Everyone, without any discrimination, has the right to equal pay for equal work.
3. Everyone who works has the right to just and favourable remuneration ensuring for himself and his family an existence worthy of human dignity, and supplemented, if necessary, by other means of social protection.
4. Everyone has the right to form and to join trade unions for the protection of his interests.

Article 24

Everyone has the right to rest and leisure, including reasonable limitation of working hours and periodic holidays with pay.

Article 25

1. Everyone has the right to a standard of living adequate for the health and well-being of himself and of his family, including food, clothing, housing and medical care

and necessary social services, and the right to security in the event of unemployment, sickness, disability, widowhood, old age or other lack of livelihood in circumstances beyond his control.

2. Motherhood and childhood are entitled to special care and assistance. All children, whether born in or out of wedlock, shall enjoy the same social protection.

Article 26

1. Everyone has the right to education. Education shall be free, at least in the elementary and fundamental stages. Elementary education shall be compulsory. Technical and professional education shall be made generally available and higher education shall be equally accessible to all on the basis of merit.

2. Education shall be directed to the full development of the human personality and to the strengthening of respect for human rights and fundamental freedoms. It shall promote understanding, tolerance and friendship among all nations, racial or religious groups, and shall further the activities of the United Nations for the maintenance of peace.

3. Parents have a prior right to choose the kind of education that shall be given to their children.

Article 27

1. Everyone has the right freely to participate in the cultural life of the community, to enjoy the arts and to share in scientific advancement and its benefits.

2. Everyone has the right to the protection of the moral and material interests resulting from any scientific, literary or artistic production of which he is the author.

Article 28

Everyone is entitled to a social and international order in which the rights and freedoms set forth in this Declaration can be fully realized.

Article 29

1. Everyone has duties to the community in which alone the free and full development of his personality is possible.

2. In the exercise of his rights and freedoms, everyone shall be subject only to such limitations as are determined by law solely for the purpose of securing due recognition and respect for the rights and freedoms of others and of meeting the just requirements of morality, public order and the general welfare in a democratic society.

3. These rights and freedoms may in no case be exercised contrary to the purposes and principles of the United Nations.

Article 30

Nothing in this Declaration may be interpreted as implying for any State, group or person any right to engage in any activity or to perform any act aimed at the destruction of any of the rights and freedoms set forth herein.

International Covenant on Civil and Political Rights
Dec. 19, 1966, S. Exec. Doc. E, 95-2, 999 U.N.T.S. 171
With Selected Declarations, Reservations, and Objections

[Ed. Note: The ICCPR entered into force on March 23, 1976, for all provisions except Article 41, creating the Human Rights Committee. Article 41 entered into force on

March 28, 1979. As of March 2003, 149 nations were parties to the Covenant. The United States signed the Covenant on October 5, 1977, and ratified it on June 8, 1992. The text of the United States' reservations, understandings, and declarations and Finland's objections to the United States' reservations, understandings, and declarations are set forth below following the main text of the Convention.]

PREAMBLE

The States Parties to the present Covenant,

Considering that, in accordance with the principles proclaimed in the Charter of the United Nations, recognition of the inherent dignity and of the equal and inalienable rights of all members of the human family is the foundation of freedom, justice and peace in the world,

Recognizing that these rights derive from the inherent dignity of the human person,

Recognizing that, in accordance with the Universal Declaration of Human Rights, the ideal of free human beings enjoying civil and political freedom and freedom from fear and want can only be achieved if conditions are created whereby everyone may enjoy his civil and political rights, as well as his economic, social and cultural rights,

Considering the obligation of States under the Charter of the United Nations to promote universal respect for, and observance of, human rights and freedoms,

Realizing that the individual, having duties to other individuals and to the community to which he belongs, is under a responsibility to strive for the promotion and observance of the rights recognized in the present Covenant,

Agree upon the following articles:

PART I

Article 1

1. All peoples have the right of self-determination. By virtue of that right they freely determine their political status and freely pursue their economic, social and cultural development.

2. All peoples may, for their own ends, freely dispose of their natural wealth and resources without prejudice to any obligations arising out of international economic cooperation, based upon the principle of mutual benefit, and international law. In no case may a people be deprived of its own means of subsistence.

3. The States Parties to the present Covenant, including those having responsibility for the administration of Non-Self-Governing and Trust Territories, shall promote the realization of the right of self-determination, and shall respect that right, in conformity with the provisions of the Charter of the United Nations.

PART II

Article 2

1. Each State Party to the present Covenant undertakes to respect and to ensure to all individuals within its territory and subject to its jurisdiction the rights recognized in the present Covenant, without distinction of any kind, such as race, colour, sex, language, religion, political or other opinion, national or social origin, property, birth or other status.

2. Where not already provided for by existing legislative or other measures, each State Party to the present Covenant undertakes to take the necessary steps, in accor-

dance with its constitutional processes and with the provisions of the present Covenant, to adopt such legislative or other measures as may be necessary to give effect to the rights recognized in the present Covenant.

3. Each State Party to the present Covenant undertakes:

(a) to ensure that any person whose rights or freedoms as herein recognized are violated shall have an effective remedy, notwithstanding that the violation has been committed by persons acting in an official capacity;

(b) to ensure that any person claiming such a remedy shall have his right thereto determined by competent judicial, administrative or legislative authorities, or by any other competent authority provided for by the legal system of the State, and to develop the possibilities of judicial remedy;

(c) to ensure that the competent authorities shall enforce such remedies when granted.

Article 3

The States Parties to the present Covenant undertake to ensure the equal right of men and women to the enjoyment of all civil and political rights set forth in the present Covenant.

Article 4

1. In time of public emergency which threatens the life of the nation and the existence of which is officially proclaimed, the States Parties to the present Covenant may take measures derogating from their obligations under the present Covenant to the extent strictly required by the exigencies of the situation, provided that such measures are not inconsistent with their other obligations under international law and do not involve discrimination solely on the ground of race, colour, sex, language, religion or social origin.

2. No derogation from articles 6, 7, 8 (paragraphs 1 and 2), 11, 15, 16 and 18 may be made under this provision.

3. Any State Party to the present Covenant availing itself of the right of derogation shall immediately inform the other States Parties to the present Covenant, through the intermediary of the Secretary-General of the United Nations, of the provisions from which it has derogated and of the reasons by which it was actuated. A further communication shall be made, through the same intermediary, on the date on which it terminates such derogation.

Article 5

1. Nothing in the present Covenant may be interpreted as implying for any State, group or person any right to engage in any activity or perform any act aimed at the destruction of any of the rights and freedoms recognized herein or at their limitation to a greater extent than is provided for in the present Covenant.

2. There shall be no restriction upon or derogation from any of the fundamental human rights recognized or existing in any State Party to the present Covenant pursuant to law, conventions, regulations or custom on the pretext that the present Covenant does not recognize such rights or that it recognizes them to a lesser extent.

PART III

Article 6

1. Every human being has the inherent right to life. This right shall be protected by law. No one shall be arbitrarily deprived of his life.

2. In countries which have not abolished the death penalty, sentence of death may be imposed only for the most serious crimes in accordance with the law in force at the time of the commission of the crime and not contrary to the provisions of the present Covenant and to the Convention on the Prevention and Punishment of the Crime of Genocide. This penalty can only be carried out pursuant to a final judgement rendered by a competent court.

3. When deprivation of life constitutes the crime of genocide, it is understood that nothing in this article shall authorize any State Party to the present Covenant to derogate in any way from any obligation assumed under the provisions of the Convention on the Prevention and Punishment of the Crime of Genocide.

4. Anyone sentenced to death shall have the right to seek pardon or commutation of the sentence. Amnesty, pardon or commutation of the sentence of death may be granted in all cases.

5. Sentence of death shall not be imposed for crimes committed by persons below eighteen years of age and shall not be carried out on pregnant women.

6. Nothing in this article shall be invoked to delay or to prevent the abolition of capital punishment by any State Party to the present Covenant.

Article 7

No one shall be subjected to torture or to cruel, inhuman or degrading treatment or punishment. In particular, no one shall be subjected without his free consent to medical or scientific experimentation.

Article 8

1. No one shall be held in slavery; slavery and the slave-trade in all their forms shall be prohibited.

2. No one shall be held in servitude.

3. (a) No one shall be required to perform forced or compulsory labour.

(b) Paragraph 3 (a) shall not be held to preclude, in countries where imprisonment with hard labour may be imposed as a punishment for a crime, the performance of hard labour in pursuance of a sentence to such punishment by a competent court.

(c) For the purpose of this paragraph the term "forced or compulsory labour" shall not include:

(i) any work or service, not referred to in subparagraph (b), normally required of a person who is under detention in consequence of a lawful order of a court, or of a person during conditional release from such detention;

(ii) any service of a military character and, in countries where conscientious objection is recognized, any national service required by law of conscientious objectors;

(iii) any service exacted in cases of emergency or calamity threatening the life or well-being of the community;

(iv) any work or service which forms part of normal civil obligations.

Article 9

1. Everyone has the right to liberty and security of person. No one shall be subjected to arbitrary arrest or detention. No one shall be deprived of his liberty except on such grounds and in accordance with such procedure as are established by law.

2. Anyone who is arrested shall be informed, at the time of arrest, of the reasons for his arrest and shall be promptly informed of any charges against him.

3. Anyone arrested or detained on a criminal charge shall be brought promptly before a judge or other officer authorized by law to exercise judicial power and shall be entitled to trial within a reasonable time or to release. It shall not be the general rule that persons awaiting trial shall be detained in custody, but release may be subject to guarantees to appear for trial, at any other stage of the judicial proceedings, and, should occasion arise, for execution of the judgement.

4. Anyone who is deprived of his liberty by arrest or detention shall be entitled to take proceedings before a court, in order that court may decide without delay on the lawfulness of his detention and order his release if the detention is not lawful.

5. Anyone who has been the victim of unlawful arrest or detention shall have an enforceable right to compensation.

Article 10

1. All persons deprived of their liberty shall be treated with humanity and with respect for the inherent dignity of the human person.

2. (a) Accused persons shall, save in exceptional circumstances, be segregated from convicted persons and shall be subject to separate treatment appropriate to their status as unconvicted persons.

(b) Accused juvenile persons shall be separated from adults and brought as speedily as possible for adjudication.

3. The penitentiary system shall comprise treatment of prisoners the essential aim of which shall be their reformation and social rehabilitation. Juvenile offenders shall be segregated from adults and be accorded treatment appropriate to their age and legal status.

Article 11

No one shall be imprisoned merely on the ground of inability to fulfil a contractual obligation.

Article 12

1. Everyone lawfully within the territory of a State shall, within that territory, have the right to liberty of movement and freedom to choose his residence.

2. Everyone shall be free to leave any country, including his own.

3. The above-mentioned rights shall not be subject to any restrictions except those which are provided by law, are necessary to protect national security, public order (*ordre public*), public health or morals or the rights and freedoms of others, and are consistent with the other rights recognized in the present Covenant.

4. No one shall be arbitrarily deprived of the right to enter his own country.

Article 13

An alien lawfully in the territory of a State Party to the present Covenant may be expelled therefrom only in pursuance of a decision reached in accordance with law and shall, except where compelling reasons of national security otherwise require, be allowed to submit the reasons against his expulsion and to have his case reviewed by, and be represented for the purpose before, the competent authority or a person or persons especially designated by the competent authority.

Article 14

1. All persons shall be equal before the courts and tribunals. In the determination of any criminal charge against him, or of his rights and obligations in a suit at law, everyone

shall be entitled to a fair and public hearing by a competent, independent and impartial tribunal established by law. The press and the public may be excluded from all or part of a trial for reasons of morals, public order ("*ordre public*") or national security in a democratic society, or when the interest of the private lives of the parties so requires, or to the extent strictly necessary in the opinion of the court in special circumstances where publicity would prejudice the interests of justice; but any judgement rendered in a criminal case or in a suit at law shall be made public except where the interest of juvenile persons otherwise requires or the proceedings concern matrimonial disputes or the guardianship of children.

2. Everyone charged with a criminal offence shall have the right to be presumed innocent until proved guilty according to law.

3. In the determination of any criminal charge against him, everyone shall be entitled to the following minimum guarantees, in full equality:

(a) to be informed promptly and in detail in a language which he understands of the nature and cause of the charge against him;

(b) to have adequate time and facilities for the preparation of his defence and to communicate with counsel of his own choosing;

(c) to be tried without undue delay;

(d) to be tried in his presence, and to defend himself in person or through legal assistance of his own choosing; to be informed, if he does not have legal assistance, of this right; and to have legal assistance assigned to him, in any case where the interests of justice so require, and without payment by him in any such case if he does not have sufficient means to pay for it;

(e) to examine, or have examined, the witnesses against him and to obtain the attendance and examination of witnesses on his behalf under the same conditions as witnesses against him;

(f) to have the free assistance of an interpreter if he cannot understand or speak the language used in court;

(g) not to be compelled to testify against himself or to confess guilt.

4. In the case of juvenile persons, the procedure shall be such as will take account of their age and the desirability of promoting their rehabilitation.

5. Everyone convicted of a crime shall have the right to his conviction and sentence being reviewed by a higher tribunal according to law.

6. When a person has by a final decision been convicted of a criminal offence and when subsequently his conviction has been reversed or he has been pardoned on the ground that a new or newly discovered fact shows conclusively that there has been a miscarriage of justice, the person who has suffered punishment as a result of such conviction shall be compensated according to law, unless it is proved that the non-disclosure of the unknown fact in time is wholly or partly attributable to him.

7. No one shall be liable to be tried or punished again for an offence for which he has already been finally convicted or acquitted in accordance with the law and penal procedure of each country.

Article 15

1. No one shall be held guilty of any criminal offence on account of any act or omission which did not constitute a criminal offence, under national or international law, at the time when it was committed. Nor shall a heavier penalty be imposed than the one that was applicable at the time when the criminal offence was committed. If, subsequent to the commission of the offence, provision is made by law for the imposition of a lighter penalty, the offender shall benefit thereby.

2. Nothing in this article shall prejudice the trial and punishment of any person for any act or omission which, at the time when it was committed, was criminal according to the general principles of law recognized by the community of nations.

Article 16

Everyone shall have the right to recognition everywhere as a person before the law.

Article 17

1. No one shall be subjected to arbitrary or unlawful interference with his privacy, family, home or correspondence, nor to unlawful attacks on his honour and reputation.

2. Everyone has the right to the protection of the law against such interference or attacks.

Article 18

1. Everyone shall have the right to freedom of thought, conscience and religion. This right shall include freedom to have or to adopt a religion or belief of his choice, and freedom, either individually or in community with others and in public or private, to manifest his religion or belief in worship, observance, practice and teaching.

2. No one shall be subject to coercion which would impair his freedom to have or to adopt a religion or belief of his choice.

3. Freedom to manifest one's religion or beliefs may be subject only to such limitations as are prescribed by law and are necessary to protect public safety, order, health, or morals or the fundamental rights and freedoms of others.

4. The States Parties to the present Covenant undertake to have respect for the liberty of parents and, when applicable, legal guardians to ensure the religious and moral education of their children in conformity with their own convictions.

Article 19

1. Everyone shall have the right to hold opinions without interference.

2. Everyone shall have the right to freedom of expression; this right shall include freedom to seek, receive and impart information and ideas of all kinds, regardless of frontiers, either orally, in writing or in print, in the form of art, or through any other media of his choice.

3. The exercise of the rights provided for in paragraph 2 of this article carries with it special duties and responsibilities. It may therefore be subject to certain restrictions, but these shall only be such as are provided by law and are necessary:

(a) for respect of the rights or reputations of others;

(b) for the protection of national security or of public order ("*ordre public*"), or of public health or morals.

Article 20

1. Any propaganda for war shall be prohibited by law.

2. Any advocacy of national, racial or religious hatred that constitutes incitement to discrimination, hostility or violence shall be prohibited by law.

Article 21

The right of peaceful assembly shall be recognized. No restrictions may be placed on the exercise of this right other than those imposed in conformity with the law and which are necessary in a democratic society in the interests of national security or public safety, public order ("*ordre public*"), the protection of public health or morals or the protection of the rights and freedoms of others.

Article 22

1. Everyone shall have the right to freedom of association with others, including the right to form and join trade unions for the protection of his interests.

2. No restrictions may be placed on the exercise of this right other than those which are prescribed by law and which are necessary in a democratic society in the interests of national security or public safety, public order (*ordre public*), the protection of public health or morals or the protection of the rights and freedoms of others. This article shall not prevent the imposition of lawful restrictions on members of the armed forces and of the police in their exercise of this right.

3. Nothing in this article shall authorize States Parties to the International Labour Organisation Convention of 1948 concerning freedom of association and protection of the right to organize to take legislative measures which would prejudice, or to apply the law in such a manner as to prejudice, the guarantees provided for in that Convention.

Article 23

1. The family is the natural and fundamental group unit of society and is entitled to protection by society and the State.

2. The right of men and women of marriageable age to marry and to found a family shall be recognized.

3. No marriage shall be entered into without the free and full consent of the intending spouses.

4. States Parties to the present Covenant shall take appropriate steps to ensure equality of rights and responsibilities of spouses as to marriage, during marriage and at its dissolution. In the case of dissolution, provision shall be made for the necessary protection of any children.

Article 24

1. Every child shall have, without any discrimination as to race, colour, sex, language, religion, national or social origin, property or birth, the right to such measures of protection as are required by his status as a minor, on the part of his family, society and the State.

2. Every child shall be registered immediately after birth and shall have a name.

3. Every child has the right to acquire a nationality.

Article 25

Every citizen shall have the right and the opportunity, without any of the distinctions mentioned in article 2 and without unreasonable restrictions:

(a) to take part in the conduct of public affairs, directly or through freely chosen representatives;

(b) to vote and to be elected at genuine periodic elections which shall be by universal and equal suffrage and shall be held by secret ballot, guaranteeing the free expression of the will of the electors;

(c) to have access, on general terms of equality, to public service in his country.

Article 26

All persons are equal before the law and are entitled without any discrimination to the equal protection of the law. In this respect, the law shall prohibit any discrimination and guarantee to all persons equal and effective protection against discrimination on any ground such as race, colour, sex, language, religion, political or other opinion, national or social origin, property, birth or other status.

Article 27

In those States in which ethnic, religious or linguistic minorities exist, persons belonging to such minorities shall not be denied the right, in community with the other members of their group, to enjoy their own culture, to profess and practise their own religion, or to use their own language.

PART IV

Article 28

1. There shall be established a Human Rights Committee (hereafter referred to in the present Covenant as the Committee). It shall consist of eighteen members and shall carry out the functions hereinafter provided.

2. The Committee shall be composed of nationals of the States Parties to the present Covenant who shall be persons of high moral character and recognized competence in the field of human rights, consideration being given to the usefulness of the participation of some persons having legal experience.

3. The members of the Committee shall be elected and shall serve in their personal capacity.

Article 29

1. The members of the Committee shall be elected by secret ballot from a list of persons possessing the qualifications prescribed in article 28 and nominated for the purpose by the States Parties to the present Covenant.

2. Each State Party to the present Covenant may nominate not more than two persons. These persons shall be nationals of the nominating State.

3. A person shall be eligible for renomination.

Article 30

1. The initial election shall be held no later than six months after the date of the entry into force of the present Covenant.

2. At least four months before the date of each election to the Committee, other than an election to fill a vacancy declared in accordance with article 34, the Secretary-General of the United Nations shall address a written invitation to the States Parties to the present Covenant to submit their nominations for membership of the Committee within three months.

3. The Secretary-General of the United Nations shall prepare a list in alphabetical order of all the persons thus nominated, with an indication of the States Parties which have nominated them, and shall submit it to the States Parties to the present Covenant no later than one month before the date of each election.

4. Elections of the members of the Committee shall be held at a meeting of the States Parties to the present Covenant convened by the Secretary General of the United Nations at the Headquarters of the United Nations. At that meeting, for which two thirds of the States Parties to the present Covenant shall constitute a quorum, the persons elected to the Committee shall be those nominees who obtain the largest number of votes and an absolute majority of the votes of the representatives of States Parties present and voting.

Article 31

1. The Committee may not include more than one national of the same State.

2. In the election of the Committee, consideration shall be given to equitable geographical distribution of membership and to the representation of the different forms of civilization and of the principal legal systems.

Article 32

1. The members of the Committee shall be elected for a term of four years. They shall be eligible for re-election if renominated. However, the terms of nine of the members elected at the first election shall expire at the end of two years; immediately after the first election, the names of these nine members shall be chosen by lot by the Chairman of the meeting referred to in article 30, paragraph 4.

2. Elections at the expiry of office shall be held in accordance with the preceding articles of this part of the present Covenant.

Article 33

1. If, in the unanimous opinion of the other members, a member of the Committee has ceased to carry out his functions for any cause other than absence of a temporary character, the Chairman of the Committee shall notify the Secretary-General of the United Nations, who shall then declare the seat of that member to be vacant.

2. In the event of the death or the resignation of a member of the Committee, the Chairman shall immediately notify the Secretary-General of the United Nations, who shall declare the seat vacant from the date of death or the date on which the resignation takes effect.

Article 34

1. When a vacancy is declared in accordance with article 33 and if the term of office of the member to be replaced does not expire within six months of the declaration of the vacancy, the Secretary-General of the United Nations shall notify each of the States Parties to the present Covenant, which may within two months submit nominations in accordance with article 29 for the purpose of filling the vacancy.

2. The Secretary-General of the United Nations shall prepare a list in alphabetical order of the persons thus nominated and shall submit it to the States Parties to the present Covenant. The election to fill the vacancy shall then take place in accordance with the relevant provisions of this part of the present Covenant.

3. A member of the Committee elected to fill a vacancy declared in accordance with article 33 shall hold office for the remainder of the term of the member who vacated the seat on the Committee under the provisions of that article.

Article 35

The members of the Committee shall, with the approval of the General Assembly of the United Nations, receive emoluments from United Nations resources on such terms and conditions as the General Assembly may decide, having regard to the importance of the Committee's responsibilities.

Article 36

The Secretary-General of the United Nations shall provide the necessary staff and facilities for the effective performance of the functions of the Committee under the present Covenant.

Article 37

1. The Secretary-General of the United Nations shall convene the initial meeting of the Committee at the Headquarters of the United Nations.

2. After its initial meeting, the Committee shall meet at such times as shall be provided in its rules of procedure.

3. The Committee shall normally meet at the Headquarters of the United Nations or at the United Nations Office at Geneva.

Article 38

Every member of the Committee shall, before taking up his duties, make a solemn declaration in open committee that he will perform his functions impartially and conscientiously.

Article 39

1. The Committee shall elect its officers for a term of two years. They may be re-elected.

2. The Committee shall establish its own rules of procedure, but these rules shall provide, inter alia, that:

(a) twelve members shall constitute a quorum;

(b) decisions of the Committee shall be made by a majority vote of the members present.

Article 40

1. The States Parties to the present Covenant undertake to submit reports on the measures they have adopted which give effect to the rights recognized herein and on the progress made in the enjoyment of those rights:

(a) within one year of the entry into force of the present Covenant for the States Parties concerned;

(b) thereafter whenever the Committee so requests.

2. All reports shall be submitted to the Secretary-General of the United Nations, who shall transmit them to the Committee for consideration. Reports shall indicate the factors and difficulties, if any, affecting the implementation of the present Covenant.

3. The Secretary-General of the United Nations may, after consultation with the Committee, transmit to the specialized agencies concerned copies of such parts of the reports as may fall within their field of competence.

4. The Committee shall study the reports submitted by the States Parties to the present Covenant. It shall transmit its reports, and such general comments as it may consider appropriate, to the States Parties. The Committee may also transmit to the Economic and Social Council these comments along with the copies of the reports it has received from States Parties to the present Covenant.

5. The States Parties to the present Covenant may submit to the Committee observations on any comments that may be made in accordance with paragraph 4 of this article.

Article 41

1. A State Party to the present Covenant may at any time declare under this article that it recognizes the competence of the Committee to receive and consider communications to the effect that a State Party claims that another State Party is not fulfilling its obligations under the present Covenant. Communications under this article may be received and considered only if submitted by a State Party which has made a declaration

recognizing in regard to itself the competence of the Committee. No communication shall be received by the Committee if it concerns a State Party which has not made such a declaration. Communications received under this article shall be dealt with in accordance with the following procedure:

(a) If a State Party to the present Covenant considers that another State Party is not giving effect to the provisions of the present Covenant, it may, by written communication, bring the matter to the attention of that State Party. Within three months after the receipt of the communication, the receiving State shall afford the State which sent the communication an explanation or any other statement in writing clarifying the matter, which should include, to the extent possible and pertinent, reference to domestic procedures and remedies taken, pending, or available in the matter.

(b) If the matter is not adjusted to the satisfaction of both States Parties concerned within six months after the receipt by the receiving State of the initial communication, either State shall have the right to refer the matter to the Committee, by notice given to the Committee and to the other State.

(c) The Committee shall deal with a matter referred to it only after it has ascertained that all available domestic remedies have been invoked and exhausted in the matter, in conformity with the generally recognized principles of international law. This shall not be the rule where the application of the remedies is unreasonably prolonged.

(d) The Committee shall hold closed meetings when examining communications under this article.

(e) Subject to the provisions of sub-paragraph (c), the Committee shall make available its good offices to the States Parties concerned with a view to a friendly solution of the matter on the basis of respect for human rights and fundamental freedoms as recognized in the present Covenant.

(f) In any matter referred to it, the Committee may call upon the States Parties concerned, referred to in sub-paragraph (b), to supply any relevant information.

(g) The States Parties concerned, referred to in sub-paragraph (b), shall have the right to be represented when the matter is being considered in the Committee and to make submissions orally and/or in writing.

(h) The Committee shall, within twelve months after the date of receipt of notice under sub-paragraph (b), submit a report:

(i) if a solution within the terms of sub-paragraph (e) is reached, the Committee shall confine its report to a brief statement of the facts and of the solution reached;

(ii) if a solution within the terms of sub-paragraph (e) is not reached, the Committee shall confine its report to a brief statement of the facts; the written submissions and record of the oral submissions made by the States Parties concerned shall be attached to the report.

In every matter, the report shall be communicated to the States Parties concerned.

2. The provisions of this article shall come into force when ten States Parties to the present Covenant have made declarations under paragraph I of this article. Such declarations shall be deposited by the States Parties with the Secretary-General of the United Nations, who shall transmit copies thereof to the other States Parties. A declaration may be withdrawn at any time by notification to the Secretary-General. Such a withdrawal shall not prejudice the consideration of any matter which is the subject of a communication already transmitted under this article; no further communication by any State Party shall be received after the notification of withdrawal of the declaration has been received by the Secretary-General, unless the State Party concerned has made a new declaration.

Article 42

1. (a) If a matter referred to the Committee in accordance with article 41 is not resolved to the satisfaction of the States Parties concerned, the Committee may, with the prior consent of the States Parties concerned, appoint an *ad hoc* Conciliation Commission (hereinafter referred to as the Commission). The good offices of the Commission shall be made available to the States Parties concerned with a view to an amicable solution of the matter on the basis of respect for the present Covenant.

(b) The Commission shall consist of five persons acceptable to the States Parties concerned. If the States Parties concerned fail to reach agreement within three months on all or part of the composition of the Commission the members of the Commission concerning whom no agreement has been reached shall be elected by secret ballot by a two-thirds majority vote of the Committee from among its members.

2. The members of the Commission shall serve in their personal capacity. They shall not be nationals of the States Parties concerned, or of a State not Party to the present Covenant, or of a State Party which has not made a declaration under article 41.

3. The Commission shall elect its own Chairman and adopt its own rules of procedure.

4. The meetings of the Commission shall normally be held at the Headquarters of the United Nations or at the United Nations Office at Geneva. However, they may be held at such other convenient places as the Commission may determine in consultation with the Secretary-General of the United Nations and the States Parties concerned.

5. The secretariat provided in accordance with article 36 shall also service the Commissions appointed under this article.

6. The information received and collated by the Committee shall be made available to the Commission and the Commission may call upon the States Parties concerned to supply any other relevant information.

7. When the Commission has fully considered the matter, but in any event not later than twelve months after having been seized of the matter, it shall submit to the Chairman of the Committee a report for communication to the States Parties concerned.

(a) If the Commission is unable to complete its consideration of the matter within twelve months, it shall confine its report to a brief statement of the status of its consideration of the matter.

(b) If an amicable solution to the matter on the basis of respect for human rights as recognized in the present Covenant is reached, the Commission shall confine its report to a brief statement of the facts and of the solution reached.

(c) If a solution within the terms of sub-paragraph (b) is not reached, the Commission's report shall embody its findings on all questions of fact relevant to the issues between the States Parties concerned, and its views on the possibilities of an amicable solution of the matter. This report shall also contain the written submissions and a record of the oral submissions made by the States Parties concerned.

(d) If the Commission's report is submitted under sub-paragraph (c), the States Parties concerned shall, within three months of the receipt of the report, notify the Chairman of the Committee whether or not they accept the contents of the report of the Commission.

8. The provisions of this article are without prejudice to the responsibilities of the Committee under article 41.

9. The States Parties concerned shall share equally all the expenses of the members of the Commission in accordance with estimates to be provided by the Secretary-General of the United Nations.

10. The Secretary-General of the United Nations shall be empowered to pay the expenses of the members of the Commission, if necessary, before reimbursement by the States Parties concerned, in accordance with paragraph 9 of this article.

Article 43

The members of the Committee, and of the *ad hoc* conciliation commissions which may be appointed under article 42, shall be entitled to the facilities, privileges and immunities of experts on mission for the United Nations as laid down in the relevant sections of the Convention on the Privileges and Immunities of the United Nations.

Article 44

The provisions for the implementation of the present Covenant shall apply without prejudice to the procedures prescribed in the field of human rights by or under the constituent instruments and the conventions of the United Nations and of the specialized agencies and shall not prevent the States Parties to the present Covenant from having recourse to other procedures for settling a dispute in accordance with general or special international agreements in force between them.

Article 45

The Committee shall submit to the General Assembly of the United Nations through the Economic and Social Council, an annual report on its activities.

PART V

Article 46

Nothing in the present Covenant shall be interpreted as impairing the provisions of the Charter of the United Nations and of the constitutions of the specialized agencies which define the respective responsibilities of the various organs of the United Nations and of the specialized agencies in regard to the matters dealt with in the present Covenant.

Article 47

Nothing in the present Covenant shall be interpreted as impairing the inherent right of all peoples to enjoy and utilize fully and freely their natural wealth and resources.

PART VI

Article 48

1. The present Covenant is open for signature by any State Member of the United Nations or member of any of its specialized agencies, by any State Party to the Statute of the International Court of Justice, and by any other State which has been invited by the General Assembly of the United Nations to become a Party to the present Covenant.

2. The present Covenant is subject to ratification. Instruments of ratification shall be deposited with the Secretary-General of the United Nations.

3. The present Covenant shall be open to accession by any State referred to in paragraph 1 of this article.

4. Accession shall be effected by the deposit of an instrument of accession with the Secretary-General of the United Nations.

5. The Secretary-General of the United Nations shall inform all States which have signed this Covenant or acceded to it of the deposit of each instrument of ratification or accession.

Article 49

1. The present Covenant shall enter into force three months after the date of the deposit with the Secretary-General of the United Nations of the thirty-fifth instrument of ratification or instrument of accession.

2. For each State ratifying the present Covenant or acceding to it after the deposit of the thirty-fifth instrument of ratification or instrument of accession, the present Covenant shall enter into force three months after the date of the deposit of its own instrument of ratification or instrument of accession.

Article 50

The provisions of the present Covenant shall extend to all parts of federal States without any limitations or exceptions.

Article 51

1. Any State Party to the present Covenant may propose an amendment and file it with the Secretary-General of the United Nations. The Secretary-General of the United Nations shall thereupon communicate any proposed amendments to the States Parties to the present Covenant with a request that they notify him whether they favour a conference of States Parties for the purpose of considering and voting upon the proposals. In the event that at least one third of the States Parties favours such a conference, the Secretary-General shall convene the conference under the auspices of the United Nations. Any amendment adopted by a majority of the States Parties present and voting at the conference shall be submitted to the General Assembly of the United Nations for approval.

2. Amendments shall come into force when they have been approved by the General Assembly of the United Nations and accepted by a two-thirds majority of the States Parties to the present Covenant in accordance with their respective constitutional processes.

3. When amendments come into force, they shall be binding on those States Parties which have accepted them, other States Parties still being bound by the provisions of the present Covenant and any earlier amendment which they have accepted.

Article 52

Irrespective of the notifications made under article 48, paragraph 5, the Secretary-General of the United Nations shall inform all States referred to in paragraph 1 of the same article of the following particulars:

(a) Signatures, ratifications and accessions under article 48;

(b) The date of the entry into force of the present Covenant under article 49 and the date of the entry into force of any amendments under article 51.

Article 53

1. The present Covenant, of which the Chinese, English, French, Russian and Spanish texts are equally authentic, shall be deposited in the archives of the United Nations.

2. The Secretary-General of the United Nations shall transmit certified copies of the present Covenant to all States referred to in article 48.

In Faith Whereof the undersigned, being duly authorized thereto by their respective Governments, have signed the present Covenant, opened for signature at New York, on the nineteenth day of December, one thousand nine hundred and sixty-six.

Selected Declarations, Reservations, and Objections

[Ed. Note: The complete text of the declarations and reservations of those nations that ratified the convention can be found at the U.N. website, http://untreaty.un.org, listed alphabetically by nation. The following is the text of the reservations, declarations and understandings of the United States.]

United States of America
Reservations:
(1) That article 20 does not authorize or require legislation or other action by the United Sates that would restrict the right of free speech and association protected by the Constitution and laws of the United States.
(2) That the United States reserves the right, subject to its Constitutional constraints, to impose capital punishment on any person (other than a pregnant woman) duly convicted under existing or future laws permitting the imposition of capital punishment, including such punishment for crimes committed by persons below eighteen years of age.
(3) That the Unites States considers itself bound by article 7 to the extent that 'cruel, inhuman or degrading treatment or punishment' means the cruel and unusual treatment or punishment prohibited by the Fifth, Eighth, and/or Fourteenth Amendments to the Constitution of the United States.
(4) That because U.S. law generally applies to an offender the penalty in force at the time the offence was committed, the United States does not adhere to the third clause of paragraph 1 of article 15.
(5) That the policy and practice of the United States are generally in compliance with and supportive of the Covenant's provisions regarding treatment of juveniles in the criminal justice system. Nevertheless, the United States reserves the right, in exceptional circumstances, to treat juveniles as adults, notwithstanding paragraphs 2(b) and 3 of article 10 and paragraph 4 of article 14. The United States further reserves to these provisions with respect to States with respect to individuals who volunteer for military service prior to age 18.

Understandings
(1) That the Constitution and laws of the United States guarantee all persons equal protection of the law and provide extensive protections against discrimination. The United States understands distinctions based upon race, colour, sex, language, religion, political or other opinion, national or social origin, property, birth or any other status — as those terms are used in article 2, paragraph 1 and article 26 — to be permitted when such distinctions are, at minimum, rationally related to a legitimate governmental objective. The United States further understands the prohibition in paragraph 1 of article 4 upon discrimination, in time of public emergency, based 'solely' on the status of race, colour, sex, language, religion or social origin, not to bar distinctions that may have a disproportionate effect upon persons of a particular status.
(2) That the United States understands the right to compensation referred to in articles 9(5) and 14(6) to require the provision of effective and enforceable mechanisms by which a victim of an unlawful arrest or detention or a miscarriage of justice may seek and, where justified, obtain compensation from either the responsible individual or the appropriate governmental entity. Entitlement to compensation may be subject to the reasonable requirements of domestic law.

(3) That the United States understands the reference to 'exceptional circumstances' in paragraph 2(a) of article 10 to permit the imprisonment of an accused person with convicted persons where appropriate in light of an individual's overall dangerousness, and to permit accused persons to waive their right to segregation from convicted persons. The United States further understands that paragraph 3 of article 10 does not diminish the goals of punishment, deterrence, and incapacitation as additional legitimate purposes for a penitentiary system.

(4) That the United States understands that subparagraph 3(b) and (d) of article 14 do not require the provision of a criminal defendant's counsel of choice when the defendant is provided with court-appointed counsel on grounds of indigence, when the defendant is financially able to retain alternative counsel, or when imprisonment is not imposed. The United States further understands that paragraph 3(e) does not prohibit a requirement that the defendant make a showing that any witness whose attendance he seeks to compel is necessary for his defense. The United States understands the prohibition upon double jeopardy in paragraph 7 to apply only when the judgment of acquittal has ben rendered by a court of the same governmental unit, whether the Federal Government or a constituent unit, as is seeking a new trial for the same cause.

(5) That the United States understands that this Covenant shall be implemented by the Federal Government to the extent that it exercises legislative and judicial jurisdiction over the matters covered therein, and otherwise by the state and local governments; to the extent that state and local governments exercise jurisdiction over such matters, the Federal Government shall take measures appropriate to the Federal system to the end that the competent authorities of the state or local governments may take appropriate measures for the fulfillment of the Covenant.

Declarations:

(1) That the United States declares that the provisions of articles 1 through 27 of the Covenant are not self-executing.

(2) That it is the view of the United States that States Party to the Covenant should wherever possible refrain from imposing any restrictions or limitations on the exercise of the rights recognized and protected by the Covenant, even when such restrictions and limitations are permissible under the terms of the Covenant. For the United States, article 5, paragraph 2, which provides that fundamental human rights existing in any State Party may not be diminished on the pretext that the Covenant recognizes them to a lesser extent, has particular relevance to article 19, paragraph 3 which would permit certain restrictions on the freedom of expression. The United States declares that it will continue to adhere to the requirements and constraints of its Constitution in respect to all such restrictions and limitations.

(3) That the United States declares that the right referred to in article 47 may be exercised only in accordance with international law.

[Ed. Note: Following the reservations, understandings, and declarations of each country, the U.N. website lists the objections of each country to the reservations, understandings, and declarations of other countries. The declarations recognizing the competence of the Human Rights Committee under Article 41, which are omitted herein, are then listed separately following the general objections.

Many objections have been filed to the United States' reservations and declarations. The following objection submitted by Finland is one example.]

Finland
September 28, 1993

With regard to the reservations, understandings and declarations made by the United States of America:

...It is recalled that under international treaty law, the name assigned to a statement whereby the legal effect of certain provisions of a treaty is excluded or modified, does not determine its status as a reservation to the treaty. Understanding (1) pertaining to articles 2, 4, and 26 of the Covenant is therefore considered to constitute in substance a reservation to the Covenant, directed at some of its most essential provisions, namely those concerning the prohibition of discrimination. In the view of the Government of Finland, a reservation of this kind is contrary to the object and purpose of the Covenant, as specified in article 19 (c) of the Vienna Convention on the Law of Treaties.

As regards reservation (2) concerning article 6 of the Covenant, it is recalled that according to article 4(2), no restrictions of articles 6 and 7 of the Covenant are allowed for. In the view of the Government of Finland, the right to life is of fundamental importance in the Covenant and the said reservation therefore is incompatible with the object and purpose of the Covenant.

As regards reservation (3), it is in the view of the Government of Finland subject to the general principle of treaty interpretation according to which a party may not invoke the provisions of its internal law as justification for failure to perform a treaty.

For the above reasons the Government of Finland objects to reservations made by the United States to articles 2, 4 and 26 [cf. Understanding (1)], to article 6 [cf. Reservation (2)] and to article 7 [cf. Reservation (3)]. However, the Government of Finland does not consider that this objection constitutes an obstacle to the entry into force of the Covenant between Finland and the United States of America.

[Ed. Note: Finland's objections to the declarations and the reservation made by Kuwait are omitted.]

Optional Protocol to the International Covenant on Civil and Political Rights
Dec. 19, 1966, 999 U.N.T.S. 171, 302.

[Ed. Note: This Optional Protocol to the ICCPR entered into force on March 23, 1976. As of March 2003, 104 nations were parties to the Protocol. However, two nations, Jamaica and Trinidad and Tobago, denounced the Protocol after they became parties to it, and Guyana denounced and simultaneously re-acceded with a reservation, a procedure which has drawn objections from other nations that are party to the Protocol. The United States is not a party to this Protocol.]

The States Parties to the present Protocol,

Considering that in order further to achieve the purposes of the International Covenant on Civil and Political Rights (hereinafter referred to as the Covenant) and the implementation of its provisions it would be appropriate to enable the Human Rights Committee set up in part IV of the Covenant (hereinafter referred to as the Committee) to receive and consider, as provided in the present Protocol, communications from individuals claiming to be victims of violations of any of the rights set forth in the Covenant,

Have agreed as follows:

Article 1

A State Party to the Covenant that becomes a party to the present Protocol recognizes the competence of the Committee to receive and consider communications from individuals subject to its jurisdiction who claim to be victims of a violation by that State Party of any of the rights set forth in the Covenant. No communication shall be received by the Committee if it concerns a State Party to the Covenant which is not a Party to the present Protocol.

Article 2

Subject to the provisions of article 1, individuals who claim that any of their rights enumerated in the Covenant have been violated and who have exhausted all available domestic remedies may submit a written communication to the Committee for consideration.

Article 3

The Committee shall consider inadmissible any communciation under the present Protocol which is anonymous, or which it considers to be an abuse of the right of submission of such communications or to be incompatible with the provisions of the Covenant.

Article 4

1. Subject to the provisions of article 3, the Committee shall bring any communications submitted to it under the present Protocol to the attention of the State Party to the present Protocol alleged to be violating any provision of the Covenant.

2. Within six months, the receiving State shall submit to the Committee written explanations or statements clarifying the matter and the remedy, if any, that may have been taken by that State.

Article 5

1. The Committee shall consider communications received under the present Protocol in the light of all written information made available to it by the individual and by the State Party concerned.

2. The Committee shall not consider any communication from an individual unless it has ascertained that:

(a) The same matter is not being examined under another procedure of international investigation or settlement;

(b) The individual has exhausted all available domestic remedies. This shall not be the rule where the application of the remedies is unreasonably prolonged.

3. The Committee shall hold closed meetings when examining communications under the present Protocol.

4. The Committee shall forward its views to the State Party concerned and to the individual.

Article 6

The Committee shall include in its annual report under article 45 of the Covenant a summary of its activities under the present Protocol.

Article 7

Pending the achievement of the objectives of resolution 1514(XV) adopted by the General Assembly of the United Nations on 14 December 1960 concerning the Declaration on the Granting of Independence to Colonial Countries and Peoples, the provisions of the present Protocol shall in no way limit the right of petition granted to these peoples by the Charter of the United Nations and other international conventions and instruments under the United Nations and its specialized agencies.

Article 8

1. The present Protocol is open for signature by any State which has signed the Covenant.

2. The present Protocol is subject to ratification by any State which has ratified or acceded to the Covenant. Instruments of ratification shall be deposited with the Secretary-General of the United Nations.

3. The present Protocol shall be open to accession by any State which has ratified or acceded to the Covenant.

4. Accession shall be effected by the deposit of an instrument of accession with the Secretary-General of the United Nations.

5. The Secretary-General of the United Nations shall inform all States which have signed the present Protocol or acceded to it of the deposit of each instrument of ratification or accession.

Article 9

1. Subject to the entry into force of the Covenant, the present Protocol shall enter into force three months after the date of the deposit with the Secretary-General of the United Nations of the tenth instrument of ratification or instrument of accession.

2. For each State ratifying the present Protocol or acceding to it after the deposit of the tenth instrument of ratification or instrument of accession, the present Protocol shall enter into force three months after the date of the deposit of its own instrument of ratification or instrument of accession.

Article 10

The provisions of the present Protocol shall extend to all parts of federal States without any limitations or exceptions.

Article 11

1. Any State Party to the present Protocol may propose an amendment and file it with the Secretary-General of the United Nations. The Secretary-General shall thereupon communicate any proposed amendments to the States Parties to the present Protocol with a request that they notify him whether they favour a conference of States Parties for the purpose of considering and voting upon the proposal. In the event that at least one third of the States Parties favours such a conference, the Secretary-General shall convene the conference under the auspices of the United Nations. Any amendment adopted by a majority of the States Parties present and voting at the conference shall be submitted to the General Assembly of the United Nations for approval.

2. Amendments shall come into force when they have been approved by the General Assembly of the United Nations and accepted by a two-thirds majority of the States Parties to the present Protocol in accordance with their respective constitutional processes.

3. When amendments come into force, they shall be binding on those States Parties which have accepted them, other States Parties still being bound by the provisions of the present Protocol and any earlier amendment which they have accepted.

Article 12

1. Any State Party may denounce the present Protocol at any time by written notification addressed to the Secretary-General of the United Nations. Denunciation shall take effect three months after the date of receipt of the notification by the Secretary-General.

2. Denunciation shall be without prejudice to the continued application of the provisions of the present Protocol to any communication submitted under article 2 before the effective date of denunciation.

Article 13

Irrespective of the notifications made under article 8, paragraph 5, of the present Protocol, the Secretary-General of the United Nations shall inform all States referred to in article 48, paragraph 1, of the Covenant of the following particulars:

(a) Signatures, ratifications and accessions under article 8;

(b) The date of the entry into force of the present Protocol under article 9 and the date of the entry into force of any amendments under article 11;

(c) Denunciations under article 12.

Article 14

1. The present Protocol, of which the Chinese, English, French, Russian and Spanish texts are equally authentic, shall be deposited in the archives of the United Nations.

2. The Secretary-General of the United Nations shall transmit certified copies of the present Protocol to all States referred to in article 48 of the Covenant.

Second Optional Protocol to the International Covenant on Civil and Political Rights, Aiming at the Abolition of the Death Penalty
Dec. 15, 1989, 1642 U.N.T.S. 414

[Ed. Note: The Second Optional Protocol entered into force on July 11, 1991. As of March 2003, 49 nations were party to the Protocol. The United States is not a party to this Protocol.]

The States Parties to the present Protocol,

Believing that abolition of the death penalty contributes to enhancement of human dignity and progressive development of human rights,

Recalling article 3 of the Universal Declaration of Human Rights adopted on 10 December 1948 and article 6 of the International Covenant on Civil and Political Rights adopted on 16 December 1966,

Noting that article 6 of the International Covenant on Civil and Political Rights refers to abolition of the death penalty in terms that strongly suggest that abolition is desirable,

Convinced that all measures of abolition of the death penalty should be considered as progress in the enjoyment of the right to life,

Desirous to undertake hereby an international commitment to abolish the death penalty,

Have agreed as follows:

Article 1

1. No one within the jurisdiction of a State Party to the present Protocol shall be executed.

2. Each State Party shall take all necessary measures to abolish the death penalty within its jurisdiction.

Article 2

1. No reservation is admissible to the present Protocol, except for a reservation made at the time of ratification or accession that provides for the application of the death penalty in time of war pursuant to a conviction for a most serious crime of a military nature committed during wartime.

2. The State Party making such a reservation shall at the time of ratification or accession communicate to the Secretary-General of the United Nations the relevant provisions of its national legislation applicable during wartime.

3. The State Party having made such a reservation shall notify the Secretary-General of the United Nations of any beginning or ending of a state of war applicable to its territory.

Article 3

The States Parties to the present Protocol shall include in the reports they submit to the Human Rights Committee, in accordance with article 40 of the Covenant, information on the measures that they have adopted to give effect to the present Protocol.

Article 4

With respect to the States Parties to the Covenant that have made a declaration under article 41, the competence of the Human Rights Committee to receive and consider communications when a State Party claims that another State Party is not fulfilling its obligations shall extend to the provisions of the present Protocol, unless the State Party concerned has made a statement to the contrary at the moment of ratification or accession.

Article 5

With respect to the States Parties to the first Optional Protocol to the International Covenant on Civil and Political Rights adopted on 16 December 1966, the competence of the Human Rights Committee to receive and consider communications from individuals subject to its jurisdiction shall extend to the provisions of the present Protocol, unless the State Party concerned has made a statement to the contrary at the moment of ratification or accession.

Article 6

1. The provisions of the present Protocol shall apply as additional provisions to the Covenant.

2. Without prejudice to the possibility of a reservation under article 2 of the present Protocol, the right guaranteed in article 1, paragraph 1, of the present Protocol shall not be subject to any derogation under article 4 of the Covenant.

Article 7

1. The present Protocol is open for signature by any State that has signed the Covenant.

2. The present Protocol is subject to ratification by any State that has ratified the Covenant or acceded to it. Instruments of ratification shall be deposited with the Secretary-General of the United Nations.

3. The present Protocol shall be open to accession by any State that has ratified the Covenant or acceded to it.

4. Accession shall be effected by the deposit of an instrument of accession with the Secretary-General of the United Nations.

5. The Secretary-General of the United Nations shall inform all States that have signed the present Protocol or acceded to it of the deposit of each instrument of ratification or accession.

Article 8

1. The present Protocol shall enter into force three months after the date of the deposit with the Secretary-General of the United Nations of the tenth instrument of ratification or accession.

2. For each State ratifying the present Protocol or acceding to it after the deposit of the tenth instrument of ratification or accession, the present Protocol shall enter into force three months after the date of the deposit of its own instrument of ratification or accession.

Article 9

The provisions of the present Protocol shall extend to all parts of federal States without any limitations or exceptions.

Article 10

The Secretary-General of the United Nations shall inform all States referred to in article 48, paragraph 1, of the Covenant of the following particulars:

(a) Reservations, communications and notifications under article 2 of the present Protocol;

(b) Statements made under articles 4 or 5 of the present Protocol;

(c) Signatures, ratifications and accessions under article 7 of the present Protocol;

(d) The date of the entry into force of the present Protocol under article 8 thereof.

Article 11

1. The present Protocol, of which the Arabic, Chinese, English, French, Russian and Spanish texts are equally authentic, shall be deposited in the archives of the United Nations.

2. The Secretary-General of the United Nations shall transmit certified copies of the present Protocol to all States referred to in article 48 of the Covenant.

International Covenant on Economic, Social and Cultural Rights
Dec. 19, 1966, 993 U.N.T.S. 3

[Ed. Note: The ICESCR entered into force on January 3, 1976. As of March 2003, 146 nations were party to the Convention. The United States signed the Convention on October 5, 1977, but has never ratified it, and is therefore not a party to this Convention.]

PREAMBLE

The States Parties to the present Covenant,

Considering that, in accordance with the principles proclaimed in the Charter of the United Nations, recognition of the inherent dignity and of the equal and inalienable rights of all members of the human family is the foundation of freedom, justice and peace in the world,

Recognizing that these rights derive from the inherent dignity of the human person,

Recognizing that, in accordance with the Universal Declaration of Human Rights, the ideal of free human beings enjoying freedom from fear and want can only be achieved if conditions are created whereby everyone may enjoy his economic, social and cultural rights, as well as his civil and political rights,

Considering the obligation of States under the Charter of the United Nations to promote universal respect for, and observance of, human rights and freedoms,

Realizing that the individual, having duties to other individuals and to the community to which he belongs, is under a responsibility to strive for the promotion and observance of the rights recognized in the present Covenant,

Agree upon the following articles:

PART I

Article 1

1. All peoples have the right of self-determination. By virtue of that right they freely determine their political status and freely pursue their economic, social and cultural development.

2. All peoples may, for their own ends, freely dispose of their natural wealth and resources without prejudice to any obligations arising out of international economic co-operation, based upon the principle of mutual benefit, and international law. In no case may a people be deprived of its own means of subsistence.

3. The States Parties to the present Covenant, including those having responsibility for the administration of Non-Self-Governing and Trust Territories, shall promote the realization of the right of self-determination, and shall respect that right, in conformity with the provisions of the Charter of the United Nations.

PART II

Article 2

1. Each State Party to the present Covenant undertakes to take steps, individually and through international assistance and co-operation, especially economic and technical, to the maximum of its available resources, with a view to achieving progressively the full realization of the rights recognized in the present Covenant by all appropriate means, including particularly the adoption of legislative measures.

2. The States Parties to the present Covenant undertake to guarantee that the rights enunciated in the present Covenant will be exercised without discrimination of any kind as to race, colour, sex, language, religion, political or other opinion, national or social origin, property, birth or other status.

3. Developing countries, with due regard to human rights and their national economy, may determine to what extent they would guarantee the economic rights recognized in the present Covenant to non-nationals.

Article 3

The States Parties to the present Covenant undertake to ensure the equal right of men and women to the enjoyment of all economic, social and cultural rights set forth in the present Covenant.

Article 4

The States Parties to the present Covenant recognize that, in the enjoyment of those rights provided by the State in conformity with the present Covenant, the State may subject such rights only to such limitations as are determined by law only in so far as this may be compatible with the nature of these rights and solely for the purpose of promoting the general welfare in a democratic society.

Article 5

1. Nothing in the present Covenant may be interpreted as implying for any State, group or person any right to engage in any activity or to perform any act aimed at the destruction of any of the rights or freedoms recognized herein, or at their limitation to a greater extent than is provided for in the present Covenant.

2. No restriction upon or derogation from any of the fundamental human rights recognized or existing in any country in virtue of law, conventions, regulations or custom shall be admitted on the pretext that the present Covenant does not recognize such rights or that it recognizes them to a lesser extent.

PART III

Article 6

1. The States Parties to the present Covenant recognize the right to work, which includes the right of everyone to the opportunity to gain his living by work which he freely chooses or accepts, and will take appropriate steps to safeguard this right.

2. The steps to be taken by a State Party to the present Covenant to achieve the full realization of this right shall include technical and vocational guidance and training programmes, policies and techniques to achieve steady economic, social and cultural development and full and productive employment under conditions safeguarding fundamental political and economic freedoms to the individual.

Article 7

The States Parties to the present Covenant recognize the right of everyone to the enjoyment of just and favourable conditions of work which ensure, in particular:

(a) remuneration which provides all workers, as a minimum, with:

(i) fair wages and equal remuneration for work of equal value without distinction of any kind, in particular women being guaranteed conditions of work not inferior to those enjoyed by men, with equal pay for equal work;

(ii) a decent living for themselves and their families in accordance with the provisions of the present Covenant;

(b) safe and healthy working conditions;

(c) equal opportunity for everyone to be promoted in his employment to an appropriate higher level, subject to no considerations other than those of seniority and competence;

(d) rest, leisure and reasonable limitation of working hours and periodic holidays with pay, as well as remuneration for public holidays

Article 8

1. The States Parties to the present Covenant undertake to ensure:

(a) the right of everyone to form trade unions and join the trade union of his choice, subject only to the rules of the organization concerned, for the promotion and protection of his economic and social interests. No restrictions may be placed on the exercise of this right other than those prescribed by law and which are necessary in a democratic society in the interests of national security or public order or for the protection of the rights and freedoms of others;

(b) the right of trade unions to establish national federations or confederations and the right of the latter to form or join international trade-union organizations;

(c) the right of trade unions to function freely subject to no limitations other than those prescribed by law and which are necessary in a democratic society in the interests of national security or public order or for the protection of the rights and freedoms of others;

(d) the right to strike, provided that it is exercised in conformity with the laws of the particular country.

2. This article shall not prevent the imposition of lawful restrictions on the exercise of these rights by members of the armed forces or of the police or of the administration of the State.

3. Nothing in this article shall authorize States Parties to the International Labour Organization Convention of 1948 concerning Freedom of Association and Protection of the Right to Organize to take legislative measures which would prejudice, or apply the law in such a manner as would prejudice, the guarantees provided for in that Convention.

Article 9

The States Parties to the present Covenant recognize the right of everyone to social security, including social insurance.

Article 10

The States Parties to the present Covenant recognize that:

1. The widest possible protection and assistance should be accorded to the family, which is the natural and fundamental group unit of society, particularly for its establishment and while it is responsible for the care and education of dependent children. Marriage must be entered into with the free consent of the intending spouses.

2. Special protection should be accorded to mothers during a reasonable period before and after childbirth. During such period working mothers should be accorded paid leave or leave with adequate social security benefits.

3. Special measures of protection and assistance should be taken on behalf of all children and young persons without any discrimination for reasons of parentage or other conditions. Children and young persons should be protected from economic and social exploitation. Their employment in work harmful to their morals or health or dangerous to life or likely to hamper their normal development should be punishable by law. States should also set age limits below which the paid employment of child labour should be prohibited and punishable by law.

Article 11

1. The States Parties to the present Covenant recognize the right of everyone to an adequate standard of living for himself and his family, including adequate food, clothing and housing, and to the continuous improvement of living conditions. The States Parties will take appropriate steps to ensure the realization of this right, recog-

nizing to this effect the essential importance of international co-operation based on free consent.

2. The States Parties to the present Covenant, recognizing the fundamental right of everyone to be free from hunger, shall take, individually and through international co-operation, the measures, including specific programmes, which are needed:

(a) to improve methods of production, conservation and distribution of food by making full use of technical and scientific knowledge, by disseminating knowledge of the principles of nutrition and by developing or reforming agrarian systems in such a way as to achieve the most efficient development and utilization of natural resources;

(b) taking into account the problems of both food-importing and food-exporting countries, to ensure an equitable distribution of world food supplies in relation to need.

Article 12

1. The States Parties to the present Covenant recognize the right of everyone to the enjoyment of the highest attainable standard of physical and mental health.

2. The steps to be taken by the States Parties to the present Covenant to achieve the full realization of this right shall include those necessary for:

(a) the provision for the reduction of the stillbirth-rate and of infant mortality and for the healthy development of the child;

(b) the improvement of all aspects of environmental and industrial hygiene;

(c) the prevention, treatment and control of epidemic, endemic, occupational and other diseases;

(d) the creation of conditions which would assure to all medical service and medical attention in the event of sickness.

Article 13

1. The States Parties to the present Covenant recognize the right of everyone to education. They agree that education shall be directed to the full development of the human personality and the sense of its dignity, and shall strengthen the respect for human rights and fundamental freedoms. They further agree that education shall enable all persons to participate effectively in a free society, promote understanding, tolerance and friendship among all nations and all racial, ethnic or religious groups, and further the activities of the United Nations for the maintenance of peace.

2. The States Parties to the present Covenant recognize that, with a view to achieving the full realization of this right:

(a) primary education shall be compulsory and available free to all;

(b) secondary education in its different forms, including technical and vocational secondary education, shall be made generally available and accessible to all by every appropriate means, and in particular by the progressive introduction of free education;

(c) higher education shall be made equally accessible to all, on the basis of capacity, by every appropriate means, and in particular by the progressive introduction of free education;

(d) fundamental education shall be encouraged or intensified as far as possible for those persons who have not received or completed the whole period of their primary education;

(e) the development of a system of schools at all levels shall be actively pursued, an adequate fellowship system shall be established, and the material conditions of teaching staff shall be continuously improved.

3. The States Parties to the present Covenant undertake to have respect for the liberty of parents and, when applicable, legal guardians, to choose for their children schools,

other than those established by the public authorities, which conform to such minimum educational standards as may be laid down or approved by the State and to ensure the religious and moral education of their children in conformity with their own convictions.

4. No part of this article shall be construed so as to interfere with the liberty of individuals and bodies to establish and direct educational institutions, subject always to the observance of the principles set forth in paragraph 1 of this article and to the requirement that the education given in such institutions shall conform to such minimum standards as may be laid down by the State.

Article 14

Each State Party to the present Covenant which, at the time of becoming a Party, has not been able to secure in its metropolitan territory or other territories under its jurisdiction compulsory primary education, free of charge, undertakes, within two years, to work out and adopt a detailed plan of action for the progressive implementation, within a reasonable number of years, to be fixed in the plan, of the principle of compulsory education free of charge for all.

Article 15

1. The States Parties to the present Covenant recognize the right of everyone:
(a) to take part in cultural life;
(b) to enjoy the benefits of scientific progress and its applications;
(c) to benefit from the protection of the moral and material interests resulting from any scientific, literary or artistic production of which he is the author.

2. The steps to be taken by the States Parties to the present Covenant to achieve the full realization of this right shall include those necessary for the conservation, the development and the diffusion of science and culture.

3. The States Parties to the present Covenant undertake to respect the freedom indispensable for scientific research and creative activity.

4. The States Parties to the present Covenant recognize the benefits to be derived from the encouragement and development of international contacts and co-operation in the scientific and cultural fields.

PART IV
Article 16

1. The States Parties to the present Covenant undertake to submit in conformity with this part of the Covenant reports on the measures which they have adopted and the progress made in achieving the observance of the rights recognized herein.

2. (a) All reports shall be submitted to the Secretary-General of the United Nations, who shall transmit copies to the Economic and Social Council for consideration in accordance with the provisions of the present Covenant;

(b) The Secretary-General of the United Nations shall also transmit to the specialized agencies copies of the reports, or any relevant parts therefrom, from States Parties to the present Covenant which are also members of these specialized agencies in so far as these reports, or parts therefrom, relate to any matters which fall within the responsibilities of the said agencies in accordance with their constitutional instruments.

Article 17

1. The States Parties to the present Covenant shall furnish their reports in stages, in accordance with a programme to be established by the Economic and Social Council

within one year of the entry into force of the present Covenant after consultation with the States Parties and the specialized agencies concerned.

2. Reports may indicate factors and difficulties affecting the degree of fulfilment of obligations under the present Covenant.

3. Where relevant information has previously been furnished to the United Nations or to any specialized agency by any State Party to the present Covenant, it will not be necessary to reproduce that information, but a precise reference to the information so furnished will suffice.

Article 18

Pursuant to its responsibilities under the Charter of the United Nations in the field of human rights and fundamental freedoms, the Economic and Social Council may make arrangements with the specialized agencies in respect of their reporting to it on the progress made in achieving the observance of the provisions of the present Covenant falling within the scope of their activities. These reports may include particulars of decisions and recommendations on such implementation adopted by their competent organs.

Article 19

The Economic and Social Council may transmit to the Commission on Human Rights for study and general recommendation or as appropriate for information the reports concerning human rights submitted by States in accordance with articles 16 and 17, and those concerning human rights submitted by the specialized agencies in accordance with article 18.

Article 20

The States Parties to the present Covenant and the specialized agencies concerned may submit comments to the Economic and Social Council on any general recommendation under article 19 or reference to such general recommendation in any report of the Commission on Human Rights or any documentation referred to therein.

Article 21

The Economic and Social Council may submit from time to time to the General Assembly reports with recommendations of a general nature and a summary of the information received from the States Parties to the present Covenant and the specialized agencies on the measures taken and the progress made in achieving general observance of the rights recognized in the present Covenant.

Article 22

The Economic and Social Council may bring to the attention of other organs of the United Nations, their subsidiary organs and specialized agencies concerned with furnishing technical assistance any matters arising out of the reports referred to in this part of the present Covenant which may assist such bodies in deciding, each within its field of competence, on the advisability of international measures likely to contribute to the effective progressive implementation of the present Covenant.

Article 23

The States Parties to the present Covenant agree that international action for the achievement of the rights recognized in the present Covenant includes such methods as the conclusion of conventions, the adoption of recommendations, the furnishing of technical assistance and the holding of regional meetings and technical meetings for the purpose of consultation and study organized in conjunction with the Governments concerned.

Article 24

Nothing in the present Covenant shall be interpreted as impairing the provisions of the Charter of the United Nations and of the constitutions of the specialized agencies which define the respective responsibilities of the various organs of the United Nations and of the specialized agencies in regard to the matters dealt with in the present Covenant.

Article 25

Nothing in the present Covenant shall be interpreted as impairing the inherent right of all peoples to enjoy and utilize fully and freely their natural wealth and resources.

[Ed. Note: Part V of the ICESCR, containing Articles 26 to 31, which address the terms for signature, ratification, accession, entry into force, application to federal states, amendment, notification, and deposit, has been omitted.]

Slavery Convention, as amended by the Protocol signed on December 7, 1953
Dec. 7, 1953, 7 U.S.T. 479, 182 U.N.T.S. 51, 212 U.N.T.S. 17

[Ed. Note: The Slavery Convention, Sept. 25, 1926, T.S. 778, at 9, 60 L.N.T.S. 253, was drafted under the auspices of the League of Nations. It entered into force on March 9, 1927. It was amended by the Protocol of December 7, 1953, which entered into force on July 7, 1955, through which the United Nations assumed the duties and functions under the treaty formerly invested in the League of Nations. As of March 2003, 59 nations were parties to the Protocol itself and 95 nations were parties to the Slavery Convention as amended by the Protocol. The United States became a party to the Convention on March 21, 1929, and to the Protocol on March 7, 1956. The text set forth below contains the preamble to the original convention, and the body of the convention, as amended by the 1953 protocol.]

Whereas the signatories of the General Act of the Brussels Conference of 1889–90 declared that they were equally animated by the firm intention of putting an end to the traffic in African slaves,

Whereas the signatories of the Convention of Saint-Germain-en-Laye of 1919, to revise the General Act of Berlin of 1885 and the General Act and Declaration of Brussels of 1890, affirmed their intention of securing the complete suppression of slavery in all its forms and of the slave trade by land and sea,

Taking into consideration the report of the Temporary Slavery Commission appointed by the Council of the League of Nations on June 12th, 1924,

Desiring to complete and extend the work accomplished under the Brussels Act and to find a means of giving practical effect throughout the world to such intentions as were expressed in regard to slave trade and slavery by the signatories of the Convention of Saint-Germain-en-Laye, and recognizing that it is necessary to conclude to that end more detailed arrangements than are contained in that Convention,

Considering, moreover, that it is necessary to prevent forced labour from developing into conditions analogous to slavery, have decided to conclude a Convention and have accordingly appointed as their Plenipotentiaries [names omitted]...have agreed as follows:

Article 1

For the purpose of the present Convention, the following definitions are agreed upon:

(I) Slavery is the status or condition of a person over whom any or all of the powers attaching to the right of ownership are exercised.

(2) The slave trade includes all acts involved in the capture, acquisition or disposal of a person with intent to reduce him to slavery; all acts involved in the acquisition of a slave with a view to selling or exchanging him; all acts of disposal by sale or exchange of a slave acquired with a view to being sold or exchanged, and, in general, every act of trade or transport in slaves.

Article 2

The High Contracting Parties undertake, each in respect of the territories placed under its sovereignty, jurisdiction, protection, suzerainty or tutelage, so far as they have not already taken the necessary steps:

(a) To prevent and suppress the slave trade;

(b) To bring about, progressively and as soon as possible, the complete abolition of slavery in all its forms.

Article 3

The High Contracting Parties undertake to adopt all appropriate measures with a view to preventing and suppressing the embarkation, disembarkation and transport of slaves in their territorial waters and upon all vessels flying their respective flags.

The High Contracting Parties undertake to negotiate as soon as possible a general Convention with regard to the slave trade which will give them rights and impose upon them duties of the same nature as those provided for in the Convention of June 17th, 1925, relative to the International Trade in Arms (Articles 12, 20, 21, 22, 23, 24 and paragraphs 3, 4 and 5 of Section II of Annex II), with the necessary adaptations, it being understood that this general Convention will not place the ships (even of small tonnage) of any High Contracting Parties in a position different from that of the other High Contracting Parties.

It is also understood that, before or after the coming into force of this general Convention, the High Contracting Parties are entirely free to conclude between themselves, without, however, derogating from the principles laid down in the preceding paragraph, such special agreements as, by reason of their peculiar situation, might appear to be suitable in order to bring about as soon as possible the complete disappearance of the slave trade.

Article 4

The High Contracting Parties shall give to one another every assistance with the object of securing the abolition of slavery and the slave trade.

Article 5

The High Contracting Parties recognise that recourse to compulsory or forced labour may have grave consequences and undertake, each in respect of the territories placed under its sovereignty, jurisdiction, protection, suzerainty or tutelage, to take all necessary measures to prevent compulsory or forced labour from developing into conditions analogous to slavery.

It is agreed that:

(1) Subject to the transitional provisions laid down in paragraph (2) below, compulsory or forced labour may only be exacted for public purposes.

(2) In territories in which compulsory or forced labour for other than public purposes still survives, the High Contracting Parties shall endeavour progressively and as soon as possible to put an end to the practice. So long as such forced or compulsory labour exists, this labour shall invariably be of an exceptional character, shall always receive adequate remuneration, and shall not involve the removal of the labourers from their usual place of residence.

(3) In all cases, the responsibility for any recourse to compulsory or forced labour shall rest with the competent central authorities of the territory concerned.

Article 6

Those of the High Contracting Parties whose laws do not at present make adequate provision for the punishment of infractions of laws and regulations enacted with a view to giving effect to the purposes of the present Convention undertake to adopt the necessary measures in order that severe penalties may be imposed in respect of such infractions.

Article 7

The High Contracting Parties undertake to communicate to each other and to the Secretary-General of the United Nations any laws and regulations which they may enact with a view to the application of the provisions of the present Convention.

Article 8

The High Contracting Parties agree that disputes arising between them relating to the interpretation or application of this Convention shall, if they cannot be settled by direct negotiation, be referred for decision to the International Court of Justice. In case either or both of the States Parties to such a dispute should not be Parties to the Statute of the International Court of Justice, the dispute shall be referred, at the choice of the Parties and in accordance with the constitutional procedure of each State, either to the International Court of Justice or to a court of arbitration constituted in accordance with the Convention of October 18th, 1907, for the Pacific Settlement of International Disputes, or to some other court of arbitration.

Article 9

At the time of signature or of ratification or of accession, any High Contracting Party may declare that its acceptance of the present Convention does not bind some or all of the territories placed under its sovereignty, jurisdiction, protection, suzerainty or tutelage in respect of all or any provisions of the Convention; it may subsequently accede separately on behalf of any one of them or in respect of any provision to which any one of them is not a Party.

Article 10

In the event of a High Contracting Party wishing to denounce the present Convention, the denunciation shall be notified in writing to the Secretary-General of the United

Nations who will at once communicate a certified true copy of the notification to all the other High Contracting Parties, informing them of the date on which it was received.

The denunciation shall only have effect in regard to the notifying State, and one year after the notification has reached the Secretary-General of the United Nations.

Denunciation may also be made separately in respect of any territory placed under its sovereignty, jurisdiction, protection, suzerainty or tutelage.

Article 11

The present Convention, which will bear this day's date and of which the French and English texts are both authentic, will remain open for signature by the States Members of the League of Nations until April 1st, 1927.

The present Convention shall be open to accession by all States, including States which are not Members of the United Nations, to which the Secretary-General of the United Nations shall have communicated a certified copy of the Convention.

Accession shall be effected by the deposit of a formal instrument with the Secretary-General of the United Nations, who shall give notice thereof to all States Parties to the Convention and to all other States contemplated in the present article, informing them of the date on which each such instrument of accession was received in deposit.

Article 12

The present Convention will be ratified and the instruments of ratification shall be deposited in the office of the Secretary-General of the United Nations. The Secretary-General will inform all the High Contracting Parties of such deposit.

The Convention will come into operation for each State on the date of the deposit of its ratification or of its accession.

Supplementary Convention on the Abolition of Slavery, the Slave Trade, and Institutions and Practices Similar to Slavery
Sept. 7, 1956, 18 U.S.T. 3201, 266 U.N.T.S. 3

[Ed. Note: The Supplementary Convention on the Abolition of Slavery, the Slave Trade, and Institutions and Practices Similar to Slavery was adopted by the United Nations Conference of Plenipotentiaries convened pursuant to resolution of the Economic and Social Council of the United Nations. It entered into force on April 30, 1957. As of March 2003, 119 nations were parties to this supplementary convention. The United States became a party by accession on December 6, 1967.]

PREAMBLE

The States Parties to the present Convention;

Considering that freedom is the birthright of every human being;

Mindful that the peoples of the United Nations reaffirmed in the Charter their faith in the dignity and worth of the human person;

Considering that the Universal Declaration of Human Rights, proclaimed by the General Assembly of the United Nations as a common standard of achievement for all peoples and all nations, states that no one shall be held in slavery or servitude and that slavery and the slave trade shall be prohibited in all their forms;

Recognizing that, since the conclusion of the Slavery Convention signed at Geneva on 25 September 1926, which was designed to secure the abolition of slavery and of the slave trade, further progress has been made towards this end;

Having regard to the Forced Labour Convention of 1930 and to subsequent action by the International Labour Organisation in regard to forced or compulsory labour;

Being aware, however, that slavery, the slave trade and institutions and practices similar to slavery have not yet been eliminated in all parts of the world;

Having decided, therefore, that the Convention of 1926, which remains operative, should now be augmented by the conclusion of a supplementary convention designed to intensify national as well as international efforts towards the abolition of slavery, the slave trade and institutions and practices similar to slavery;

Have agreed as follows:

Section I — Institutions and Practices Similar to Slavery

Article 1

Each of the States Parties to this Convention shall take all practicable and necessary legislative and other measures to bring about progressively and as soon as possible the complete abolition or abandonment of the following institutions and practices, where they still exist and whether or not they are covered by the definition of slavery contained in article 1 of the Slavery Convention signed at Geneva on 25 September 1926:

(a) Debt bondage, that is to say, the status or condition arising from a pledge by a debtor of his personal services or of those of a person under his control as security for a debt, if the value of those services as reasonably assessed is not applied towards the liquidation of the debt or the length and nature of those services are not respectively limited and defined;

(b) Serfdom, that is to say, the condition or status of a tenant who is by law, custom or agreement bound to live and labour on land belonging to another person and to render some determinate service to such other person, whether for reward or not, and is not free to change his status;

(c) Any institution or practice whereby:

(i) A woman, without the right to refuse, is promised or given in marriage on payment of a consideration in money or in kind to her parents, guardian, family or any other person or group; or

(ii) The husband of a woman, his family, or his clan, has the right to transfer her to another person for value received or otherwise; or

(iii) A woman on the death of her husband is liable to be inherited by another person;

(d) Any institution or practice whereby a child or young person under the age of 18 years, is delivered by either or both of his natural parents or by his guardian to another person, whether for reward or not, with a view to the exploitation of the child or young person or of his labour.

Article 2

With a view to bringing to an end the institutions and practices mentioned in article 1(c) of this Convention, the States Parties undertake to prescribe, where appropriate, suitable minimum ages of marriage, to encourage the use of facilities whereby the consent of both parties to a marriage may be freely expressed in the presence of a competent civil or religious authority, and to encourage the registration of marriages.

Section II — The Slave Trade

Article 3

1. The act of conveying or attempting to convey slaves from one country to another by whatever means of transport, or of being accessory thereto, shall be a criminal offence under the laws of the States Parties to this Convention and persons convicted thereof shall be liable to very severe penalties.

2. (a) The States Parties shall take all effective measures to prevent ships and aircraft authorized to fly their flags from conveying slaves and to punish persons guilty of such acts or of using national flags for that purpose.

(b) The States Parties shall take all effective measures to ensure that their ports, airfields and coasts are not used for the conveyance of slaves.

3. The States Parties to this Convention shall exchange information in order to ensure the practical co-ordination of the measures taken by them in combating the slave trade and shall inform each other of every case of the slave trade, and of every attempt to commit this criminal offence, which comes to their notice.

Article 4

Any slave who takes refuge on board any vessel of a State Party to this Convention shall *ipso facto* be free.

Section III — Slavery and Institutions and Practices Similar to Slavery

Article 5

In a country where the abolition or abandonment of slavery, or of the institutions or practices mentioned in article 1 of this Convention, is not yet complete, the act of mutilating, branding or otherwise marking a slave or a person of servile status in order to indicate his status, or as a punishment, or for any other reason, or of being accessory thereto, shall be a criminal offence under the laws of the States Parties to this Convention and persons convicted thereof shall be liable to punishment.

Article 6

1. The act of enslaving another person or of inducing another person to give himself or a person dependent upon him into slavery, or of attempting these acts, or being accessory thereto, or being a party to a conspiracy to accomplish any such acts, shall be a criminal offence under the laws of the States Parties to this Convention and persons convicted thereof shall be liable to punishment.

2. Subject to the provisions of the introductory paragraph of article 1 of this Convention, the provisions of paragraph 1 of the present article shall also apply to the act of inducing another person to place himself or a person dependent upon him into the servile status resulting from any of the institutions or practices mentioned in article 1, to any attempt to perform such acts, to being accessory thereto, and to being a party to a conspiracy to accomplish any such acts.

Section IV — Definitions

Article 7

For the purposes of the present Convention:

(a) "Slavery" means, as defined in the Slavery Convention of 1926, the status or condition of a person over whom any or all of the powers attaching to the right of ownership are exercised, and "slave" means a person in such condition or status;

(b) "A person of servile status" means a person in the condition or status resulting from any of the institutions or practices mentioned in article 1 of this Convention;

(c) "Slave trade" means and includes all acts involved in the capture, acquisition or disposal of a person with intent to reduce him to slavery; all acts involved in the acquisition of a slave with a view to selling or exchanging him; all acts of disposal by sale or exchange of a person acquired with a view to being sold or exchanged; and, in general, every act of trade or transport in slaves by whatever means of conveyance.

Section V — Co-operation Between States Parties and Communication of Information

Article 8

1. The States Parties to this Convention undertake to co-operate with each other and with the United Nations to give effect to the foregoing provisions.

2. The Parties undertake to communicate to the Secretary-General of the United Nations copies of any laws, regulations and administrative measures enacted or put into effect to implement the provisions of this Convention.

3. The Secretary-General shall communicate the information received under paragraph 2 of this article to the other Parties and to the Economic and Social Council as part of the documentation for any discussion which the Council might undertake with a view to making further recommendations for the abolition of slavery, the slave trade or the institutions and practices which are the subject of this Convention.

Section VI — Final Clauses

Article 9

No reservations may be made to this Convention.

Article 10

Any dispute between States Parties to this Convention relating to its interpretation or application, which is not settled by negotiation, shall be referred to the International Court of Justice at the request of any one of the parties to the dispute, unless the parties concerned agree on another mode of settlement.

Article 11

1. This Convention shall be open until 1 July 1957 for signature by any State Member of the United Nations or of a specialized agency. It shall be subject to ratification by the signatory States, and the instruments of ratification shall be deposited with the Secretary-General of the United Nations, who shall inform each signatory and acceding State.

2. After 1 July 1957 this Convention shall be open for accession by any State Member of the United Nations or of a specialized agency, or by any other State to which an invitation to accede has been addressed by the General Assembly of the United Nations. Accession shall be effected by the deposit of a formal instrument with the Secretary-General of the United Nations, who shall inform each signatory and acceding State.

Article 12

1. This Convention shall apply to all non-self-governing, trust, colonial and other non-metropolitan territories for the international relations of which any State Party is responsible; the Party concerned shall, subject to the provisions of paragraph 2 of this article, at the time of signature, ratification or accession declare the non-metropolitan territory or territories to which the Convention shall apply *ipso facto* as a result of such signature, ratification or accession.

2. In any case in which the previous consent of a non-metropolitan territory is required by the constitutional laws or practices of the Party or of the non-metropolitan territory, the Party concerned shall endeavour to secure the needed consent of the non-metropolitan territory within the period of twelve months from the date of signature of the Convention by the metropolitan State, and when such consent has been obtained the Party shall notify the Secretary-General. This Convention shall apply to the territory or territories named in such notification from the date of its receipt by the Secretary General.

3. After the expiry of the twelve-month period mentioned in the preceding paragraph, the States Parties concerned shall inform the Secretary General of the results of the consultations with those non-metropolitan territories for whose international relations they are responsible and whose consent to the application of this Convention may have been withheld.

Article 13

1. This Convention shall enter into force on the date on which two States have become Parties thereto.

2. It shall thereafter enter into force with respect to each State and territory on the date of deposit of the instrument of ratification or accession of that State or notification of application to that territory.

Article 14

1. The application of this Convention shall be divided into successive periods of three years, of which the first shall begin on the date of entry into force of the Convention in accordance with paragraph 1 of article 13.

2. Any State Party may denounce this Convention by a notice addressed by that State to the Secretary-General not less than six months before the expiration of the current three-year period. The Secretary-General shall notify all other Parties of each such notice and the date of the receipt thereof.

3. Denunciations shall take effect at the expiration of the current three-year period.

4. In cases where, in accordance with the provisions of article 12, this Convention has become applicable to a non-metropolitan territory of a Party, that Party may at any time thereafter, with the consent of the territory concerned, give notice to the Secretary-General of the United Nations denouncing this Convention separately in respect of that territory. The denunciation shall take effect one year after the date of the receipt of such notice by the Secretary-General, who shall notify all other Parties of such notice and the date of the receipt thereof.

Article 15

This Convention, of which the Chinese, English, French, Russian and Spanish texts are equally authentic, shall be deposited in the archives of the United Nations Secretariat. The Secretary-General shall prepare a certified copy thereof for communication to States Parties to this Convention, as well as to all other States Members of the United Nations and of the specialized agencies.

International Convention on the Elimination of All Forms of Racial Discrimination
March 7, 1966, S. Exec. Doc. C, 95-2 (1978), 660 U.N.T.S. 195

[Ed. Note: The Convention entered into force on January 4, 1969. As of March 2003, 167 nations were party to the Convention. The United States is a party to this Convention, which it signed on September 28, 1966 and ratified on October 21, 1994. Only the Preamble and Articles 1 to 7 of the Convention are reproduced below.]

The States Parties to this Convention,

Considering that the Charter of the United Nations is based on the principles of the dignity and equality inherent in all human beings, and that all Member States have pledged themselves to take joint and separate action, in co-operation with the Organization, for the achievement of one of the purposes of the United Nations which is to promote and encourage universal respect for and observance of human rights and fundamental freedoms for all, without distinction as to race, sex, language or religion,

Considering that the Universal Declaration of Human Rights proclaims that all human beings are born free and equal in dignity and rights and that everyone is entitled to all the rights and freedoms set out therein, without distinction of any kind, in particular as to race, colour or national origin,

Considering that all human beings are equal before the law and are entitled to equal protection of the law against any discrimination and against any incitement to discrimination,

Considering that the United Nations has condemned colonialism and all practices of segregation and discrimination associated therewith, in whatever form and wherever they exist, and that the Declaration on the Granting of Independence to Colonial Countries and Peoples of 14 December 1960 (General Assembly resolution 1514 (XV)) has affirmed and solemnly proclaimed the necessity of bringing them to a speedy and unconditional end,

Considering that the United Nations Declaration on the Elimination of All Forms of Racial Discrimination of 20 November 1963 (General Assembly Resolution 1904 (XVIII)) solemnly affirms the necessity of speedily eliminating racial discrimination throughout the world in all its forms and manifestations and of securing understanding of and respect for the dignity of the human person,

Convinced that any doctrine of superiority based on racial differentiation is scientifically false, morally condemnable, socially unjust and dangerous, and that there is no justification for racial discrimination, in theory or in practice, anywhere,

Reaffirming that discrimination between human beings on the grounds of race, colour or ethnic origin is an obstacle to friendly and peaceful relations among nations and is capable of disturbing peace and security among peoples and the harmony of persons living side by side even within one and the same State,

Convinced that the existence of racial barriers is repugnant to the ideals of any human society,

Alarmed by manifestations of racial discrimination still in evidence in some areas of the world and by governmental policies based on racial superiority or hatred, such as policies of apartheid, segregation or separation,

Resolved to adopt all necessary measures for speedily eliminating racial discrimination in all its forms and manifestations, and to prevent and combat racist doctrines and practices in order to promote understanding between races and to build an international community free from all forms of racial segregation and racial discrimination,

Bearing in mind the Convention concerning Discrimination in respect of Employment and Occupation adopted by the International Labour Organisation in 1958, and the Convention against Discrimination in Education adopted by the United Nations Educational, Scientific and Cultural Organization in 1960,

Desiring to implement the principles embodied in the United Nations Declaration on the Elimination of All Forms of Racial Discrimination and to secure the earliest adoption of practical measures to that end,

Have agreed as follows:

PART I

Article 1

1. In this Convention, the term "racial discrimination" shall mean any distinction, exclusion, restriction or preference based on race, colour, descent, or national or ethnic origin which has the purpose or effect of nullifying or impairing the recognition, enjoyment or exercise, on an equal footing, of human rights and fundamental freedoms in the political, economic, social, cultural or any other field of public life.

2. This Convention shall not apply to distinctions, exclusions, restrictions or preferences made by a State Party to this Convention between citizens and non-citizens.

3. Nothing in this Convention may be interpreted as affecting in any way the legal provisions of States Parties concerning nationality, citizenship or naturalization, provided that such provisions do not discriminate against any particular nationality.

4. Special measures taken for the sole purpose of securing adequate advancement of certain racial or ethnic groups or individuals requiring such protection as may be necessary in order to ensure such groups or individuals equal enjoyment or exercise of human rights and fundamental freedoms shall not be deemed racial discrimination, provided, however, that such measures do not, as a consequence, lead to the maintenance of separate rights for different racial groups and that they shall not be continued after the objectives for which they were taken have been achieved.

Article 2

1. States Parties condemn racial discrimination and undertake to pursue by all appropriate means and without delay a policy of eliminating racial discrimination in all its forms and promoting understanding among all races, and, to this end:

(a) Each State Party undertakes to engage in no act or practice of racial discrimination against persons, groups of persons or institutions and to ensure that all public authorities and public institutions, national and local, shall act in conformity with this obligation;

(b) Each State Party undertakes not to sponsor, defend or support racial discrimination by any persons or organizations;

(c) Each State Party shall take effective measures to review governmental, national and local policies, and to amend, rescind or nullify any laws and regulations which have the effect of creating or perpetuating racial discrimination wherever it exists;

(d) Each State Party shall prohibit and bring to an end, by all appropriate means, including legislation as required by circumstances, racial discrimination by any persons, group or organization;

(e) Each State Party undertakes to encourage, where appropriate, integrationist multi-racial organizations and movements and other means of eliminating barriers between races, and to discourage anything which tends to strengthen racial division.

2. States Parties shall, when the circumstances so warrant, take, in the social, economic, cultural and other fields, special and concrete measures to ensure the adequate development and protection of certain racial groups or individuals belonging to them, for the purpose of guaranteeing them the full and equal enjoyment of human rights and fundamental freedoms. These measures shall in no case entail as a consequence the maintenance of unequal or separate rights for different racial groups after the objectives for which they were taken have been achieved.

Article 3

States Parties particularly condemn racial segregation and apartheid and undertake to prevent, prohibit and eradicate all practices of this nature in territories under their jurisdiction.

Article 4

States Parties condemn all propaganda and all organizations which are based on ideas or theories of superiority of one race or group of persons of one colour or ethnic origin, or which attempt to justify or promote racial hatred and discrimination in any form, and undertake to adopt immediate and positive measures designed to eradicate all incitement to, or acts of, such discrimination and, to this end, with due regard to the principles embodied in the Universal Declaration of Human Rights and the rights expressly set forth in article 5 of this Convention, *inter alia*:

(a) Shall declare an offence punishable by law all dissemination of ideas based on racial superiority or hatred, incitement to racial discrimination, as well as all acts of violence or incitement to such acts against any race or group of persons of another colour or ethnic origin, and also the provision of any assistance to racist activities, including the financing thereof;

(b) Shall declare illegal and prohibit organizations, and also organized and all other propaganda activities, which promote and incite racial discrimination, and shall recognize participation in such organizations or activities as an offence punishable by law;

(c) Shall not permit public authorities or public institutions, national or local, to promote or incite racial discrimination.

Article 5

In compliance with the fundamental obligations laid down in article 2 of this Convention, States Parties undertake to prohibit and to eliminate racial discrimination in all its forms and to guarantee the right of everyone, without distinction as to race, colour, or national or ethnic origin, to equality before the law, notably in the enjoyment of the following rights:

(a) The right to equal treatment before the tribunals and all other organs administering justice;

(b) The right to security of person and protection by the State against violence or bodily harm, whether inflicted by government officials or by any individual group or institution;

(c) Political rights, in particular the right to participate in elections—to vote and to stand for election—on the basis of universal and equal suffrage, to take part in the Government as well as in the conduct of public affairs at any level and to have equal access to public service;

(d) Other civil rights, in particular:

(i) The right to freedom of movement and residence within the border of the State;

(ii) The right to leave any country, including one's own, and to return to one's country;

(iii) The right to nationality;

(iv) The right to marriage and choice of spouse;

(v) The right to own property alone as well as in association with others;

(vi) The right to inherit;

(vii) The right to freedom of thought, conscience and religion;

(viii) The right to freedom of opinion and expression;

(ix) The right to freedom of peaceful assembly and association;

(e) Economic, social and cultural rights, in particular:

(i) The rights to work, to free choice of employment, to just and favourable conditions of work, to protection against unemployment, to equal pay for equal work, to just and favourable remuneration;

(ii) The right to form and join trade unions;

(iii) The right to housing;

(iv) The right to public health, medical care, social security and social services;

(v) The right to education and training;

(vi) The right to equal participation in cultural activities;

(f) The right of access to any place or service intended for use by the general public, such as transport, hotels, restaurants, cafés, theatres and parks.

Article 6

States Parties shall assure to everyone within their jurisdiction effective protection and remedies, through the competent national tribunals and other State institutions, against any acts of racial discrimination which violate his human rights and fundamental freedoms contrary to this Convention, as well as the right to seek from such tribunals just and adequate reparation or satisfaction for any damage suffered as a result of such discrimination.

Article 7

States Parties undertake to adopt immediate and effective measures, particularly in the fields of teaching, education, culture and information, with a view to combating prejudices which lead to racial discrimination and to promoting understanding, tolerance and friendship among nations and racial or ethnical groups, as well as to propagating the purposes and principles of the Charter of the United Nations, the Universal Declaration of Human Rights, the United Nations Declaration on the Elimination of All Forms of Racial Discrimination, and this Convention.

[Ed. Note: Part II, including Articles 8 to 16, which address the creation, procedures, and functions of the Committee on the Elimination of Racial Discrimination that oversees implementation of the Convention, and Part III, including Articles 17 to 25, which address procedures for signature, ratification, accession, reservations, denunciation, dispute resolution, notification, and deposit of the Convention, are omitted.]

Declaration on Race and Racial Prejudice
UNESCO, Gen. Conf. Res. 3/1.1/2, 20th Sess. (1978),
U.N. Doc. E/CN. 4/Sub. 2/1982/2/Add. 1, Annex V (1982)

PREAMBLE

The General Conference of the United Nations Educational, Scientific and Cultural Organization, meeting at Paris at its twentieth session, from 24 October to 28 November 1978,

Whereas it is stated in the Preamble to the Constitution of UNESCO, adopted on 16 November 1945, that "the great and terrible war which has now ended was a war made possible by the denial of the democratic principles of the dignity, equality and mutual respect of men, and by the propagation, in their place, through ignorance and prejudice, of the doctrine of the inequality of men and races", and whereas, according to Article I of the said Constitution, the purpose of UNESCO "is to contribute to peace and security by promoting collaboration among the nations through education, science and culture in order to further universal respect for justice, for the rule of law and for the human rights and fundamental freedoms which are affirmed for the peoples of the world, without distinction of race, sex, language or religion, by the Charter of the United Nations",

Recognizing that, more than three decades after the founding of UNESCO, these principles are just as significant as they were when they were embodied in its Constitution,

Mindful of the process of decolonization and other historical changes which have led most of the peoples formerly under foreign rule to recover their sovereignty, making the international community a universal and diversified whole and creating new opportunities of eradicating the scourge of racism and of putting an end to its odious manifestations in all aspects of social and political life, both nationally and internationally,

Convinced that the essential unity of the human race and consequently the fundamental equality of all human beings and all peoples, recognized in the loftiest expressions of philosophy, morality and religion, reflect an ideal towards which ethics and science are converging today,

Convinced that all peoples and all human groups, whatever their composition or ethnic origin, contribute according to their own genius to the progress of the civilizations and cultures which, in their plurality and as a result of their interpenetration, constitute the common heritage of mankind,

Confirming its attachment to the principles proclaimed in the United Nations Charter and the Universal Declaration of Human Rights and its determination to promote the implementation of the International Covenants on Human Rights as well as the Declaration on the Establishment of a New International Economic Order,

Determined also to promote the implementation of the United Nations Declaration and the International Convention on the Elimination of All Forms of Racial Discrimination,

Noting the Convention on the Prevention and Punishment of the Crime of Genocide, the International Convention on the Suppression and Punishment of the Crime of Apartheid and the Convention on the Non-Applicability of Statutory Limitations to War Crimes and Crimes against Humanity,

Recalling also the international instruments already adopted by UNESCO, including in particular the Convention and Recommendation against Discrimination in Education, the Recommendation concerning the Status of Teachers, the Declaration of the Principles of International Cultural Co-operation, the Recommendation concerning

Education for International Understanding, Co-operation and Peace and Education relating to Human Rights and Fundamental Freedoms, the Recommendations on the Status of Scientific Researchers, and the Recommendation on participation by the people at large in cultural life and their contribution to it,

Bearing in mind the four statements on the race question adopted by experts convened by UNESCO,

Reaffirming its desire to play a vigorous and constructive part in the implementation of the programme of the Decade for Action to Combat Racism and Racial Discrimination, as defined by the General Assembly of the United Nations at its twenty-eighth session,

Noting with the gravest concern that racism, racial discrimination, colonialism and apartheid continue to afflict the world in ever-changing forms, as a result both of the continuation of legislative provisions and government and administrative practices contrary to the principles of human rights and also of the continued existence of political and social structures, and of relationships and attitudes, characterized by injustice and contempt for human beings and leading to the exclusion, humiliation and exploitation, or to the forced assimilation, of the members of disadvantaged groups,

Expressing its indignation at these offences against human dignity, deploring the obstacles they place in the way of mutual understanding between peoples and alarmed at the danger of their seriously disturbing international peace and security,

Adopts and solemnly proclaims this Declaration on Race and Racial Prejudice:

Article 1

1. All human beings belong to a single species and are descended from a common stock. They are born equal in dignity and rights and all form an integral part of humanity.

2. All individuals and groups have the right to be different, to consider themselves as different and to be regarded as such. However, the diversity of life styles and the right to be different may not, in any circumstances, serve as a pretext for racial prejudice; they may not justify either in law or in fact any discriminatory practice whatsoever, nor provide a ground for the policy of apartheid, which is the extreme form of racism.

3. Identity of origin in no way affects the fact that human beings can and may live differently, nor does it preclude the existence of differences based on cultural, environmental and historical diversity nor the right to maintain cultural identity.

4. All peoples of the world possess equal faculties for attaining the highest level in intellectual, technical, social, economic, cultural and political development.

5. The differences between the achievements of the different peoples are entirely attributable to geographical, historical, political, economic, social and cultural factors. Such differences can in no case serve as a pretext for any rank-ordered classification of nations or peoples.

Article 2

1. Any theory which involves the claim that racial or ethnic groups are inherently superior or inferior, thus implying that some would be entitled to dominate or eliminate others, presumed to be inferior, or which bases value judgements on racial differentiation, has no scientific foundation and is contrary to the moral and ethical principles of humanity.

2. Racism includes racist ideologies, prejudiced attitudes, discriminatory behaviour, structural arrangements and institutionalized practices resulting in racial inequality as well as the fallacious notion that discriminatory relations between groups are morally

and scientifically justifiable; it is reflected in discriminatory provisions in legislation or regulations and discriminatory practices as well as in anti-social beliefs and acts; it hinders the development of its victims, perverts those who practise it, divides nations internally, impedes international co-operation and gives rise to political tensions between peoples; it is contrary to the fundamental principles of international law and, consequently, seriously disturbs international peace and security.

3. Racial prejudice, historically linked with inequalities in power, reinforced by economic and social differences between individuals and groups, and still seeking today to justify such inequalities, is totally without justification.

Article 3

Any distinction, exclusion, restriction or preference based on race, colour, ethnic or national origin or religious intolerance motivated by racist considerations, which destroys or compromises the sovereign equality of States and the right of peoples to self-determination, or which limits in an arbitrary or discriminatory manner the right of every human being and group to full development is incompatible with the requirements of an international order which is just and guarantees respect for human rights; the right to full development implies equal access to the means of personal and collective advancement and fulfilment in a climate of respect for the values of civilizations and cultures, both national and world-wide.

Article 4

1. Any restriction on the complete self-fulfilment of human beings and free communication between them which is based on racial or ethnic considerations is contrary to the principle of equality in dignity and rights; it cannot be admitted.

2. One of the most serious violations of this principle is represented by apartheid, which, like genocide, is a crime against humanity, and gravely disturbs international peace and security.

3. Other policies and practices of racial segregation and discrimination constitute crimes against the conscience and dignity of mankind and may lead to political tensions and gravely endanger international peace and security.

Article 5

1. Culture, as a product of all human beings and a common heritage of mankind, and education in its broadest sense, offer men and women increasingly effective means of adaptation, enabling them not only to affirm that they are born equal in dignity and rights, but also to recognize that they should respect the right of all groups to their own cultural identity and the development of their distinctive cultural life within the national and international contexts, it being understood that it rests with each group to decide in complete freedom on the maintenance, and, if appropriate, the adaptation or enrichment of the values which it regards as essential to its identity.

2. States, in accordance with their constitutional principles and procedures, as well as all other competent authorities and the entire teaching profession, have a responsibility to see that the educational resources of all countries are used to combat racism, more especially by ensuring that curricula and textbooks include scientific and ethical considerations concerning human unity and diversity and that no invidious distinctions are made with regard to any people; by training teachers to achieve these ends; by making the resources of the educational system available to all groups of the population without

racial restriction or discrimination; and by taking appropriate steps to remedy the handicaps from which certain racial or ethnic groups suffer with regard to their level of education and standard of living and in particular to prevent such handicaps from being passed on to children.

3. The mass media and those who control or serve them, as well as all organized groups within national communities, are urged—with due regard to the principles embodied in the Universal Declaration of Human Rights, particularly the principle of freedom of expression—to promote understanding, tolerance and friendship among individuals and groups and to contribute to the eradication of racism, racial discrimination and racial prejudice, in particular by refraining from presenting a stereotyped, partial, unilateral or tendentious picture of individuals and of various human groups. Communication between racial and ethnic groups must be a reciprocal process, enabling them to express themselves and to be fully heard without let or hindrance. The mass media should therefore be freely receptive to ideas of individuals and groups which facilitate such communication.

Article 6

1. The State has prime responsibility for ensuring human rights and fundamental freedoms on an entirely equal footing in dignity and rights for all individuals and all groups.

2. So far as its competence extends and in accordance with its constitutional principles and procedures, the State should take all appropriate steps, inter alia by legislation, particularly in the spheres of education, culture and communication, to prevent, prohibit and eradicate racism, racist propaganda, racial segregation and apartheid and to encourage the dissemination of knowledge and the findings of appropriate research in natural and social sciences on the causes and prevention of racial prejudice and racist attitudes with due regard to the principles embodied in the Universal Declaration of Human Rights and in the International Covenant on Civil and Political Rights.

3. Since laws proscribing racial discrimination are not in themselves sufficient, it is also incumbent on States to supplement them by administrative machinery for the systematic investigation of instances of racial discrimination, by a comprehensive framework of legal remedies against acts of racial discrimination, by broadly based education and research programmes designed to combat racial prejudice and racial discrimination and by programmes of positive political, social, educational and cultural measures calculated to promote genuine mutual respect among groups. Where circumstances warrant, special programmes should be undertaken to promote the advancement of disadvantaged groups and, in the case of nationals, to ensure their effective participation in the decision-making processes of the community.

Article 7

In addition to political, economic and social measures, law is one of the principal means of ensuring equality in dignity and rights among individuals, and of curbing any propaganda, any form of organization or any practice which is based on ideas or theories referring to the alleged superiority of racial or ethnic groups or which seeks to justify or encourage racial hatred and discrimination in any form. States should adopt such legislation as is appropriate to this end and see that it is given effect and applied by all their services, with due regard to the principles embodied in the Universal Declaration of Human Rights. Such legislation should form part of a political, economic and social framework conducive to its implementation. Individuals and other legal entities, both public and private, must conform with such legislation and use all appropriate means to help the population as a whole to understand and apply it.

Article 8

1. Individuals, being entitled to an economic, social, cultural and legal order, on the national and international planes, such as to allow them to exercise all their capabilities on a basis of entire equality of rights and opportunities, have corresponding duties towards their fellows, towards the society in which they live and towards the international community. They are accordingly under an obligation to promote harmony among the peoples, to combat racism and racial prejudice and to assist by every means available to them in eradicating racial discrimination in all its forms.

2. In the field of racial prejudice and racist attitudes and practices, specialists in natural and social sciences and cultural studies, as well as scientific organizations and associations, are called upon to undertake objective research on a wide interdisciplinary basis; all States should encourage them to this end.

3. It is, in particular, incumbent upon such specialists to ensure, by all means available to them, that their research findings are not misinterpreted, and also that they assist the public in understanding such findings.

Article 9

1. The principle of the equality in dignity and rights of all human beings and all peoples, irrespective of race, colour and origin, is a generally accepted and recognized principle of international law. Consequently any form of racial discrimination practised by a State constitutes a violation of international law giving rise to its international responsibility.

2. Special measures must be taken to ensure equality in dignity and rights for individuals and groups wherever necessary, while ensuring that they are not such as to appear racially discriminatory. In this respect, particular attention should be paid to racial or ethnic groups which are socially or economically disadvantaged, so as to afford them, on a completely equal footing and without discrimination or restriction, the protection of the laws and regulations and the advantages of the social measures in force, in particular in regard to housing, employment and health; to respect the authenticity of their culture and values; and to facilitate their social and occupational advancement, especially through education.

3. Population groups of foreign origin, particularly migrant workers and their families who contribute to the development of the host country, should benefit from appropriate measures designed to afford them security and respect for their dignity and cultural values and to facilitate their adaptation to the host environment and their professional advancement with a view to their subsequent reintegration in their country of origin and their contribution to its development; steps should be taken to make it possible for their children to be taught their mother tongue.

4. Existing disequilibria in international economic relations contribute to the exacerbation of racism and racial prejudice; all States should consequently endeavour to contribute to the restructuring of the international economy on a more equitable basis.

Article 10

International organizations, whether universal or regional, governmental or non-governmental, are called upon to co-operate and assist, so far as their respective fields of competence and means allow, in the full and complete implementation of the principles set out in this Declaration, thus contributing to the legitimate struggle of all men, born equal in dignity and rights, against the tyranny and oppression of racism, racial segregation, apartheid and genocide, so that all the peoples of the world may be forever delivered from these scourges.

Declaration on the Elimination of All Forms of Intolerance and of Discrimination Based on Religion or Belief

G.A. Res. 36/55, U.N. GAOR, 36th Sess., Supp. No 51
at 171, U.N. Doc. A/36/684 (1981)

The General Assembly,

Considering that one of the basic principles of the Charter of the United Nations is that of the dignity and equality inherent in all human beings, and that all Member States have pledged themselves to take joint and separate action in co-operation with the Organization to promote and encourage universal respect for and observance of human rights and fundamental freedoms for all, without distinction as to race, sex, language or religion,

Considering that the Universal Declaration of Human Rights and the International Covenants on Human Rights proclaim the principles of non-discrimination and equality before the law and the right to freedom of thought, conscience, religion and belief,

Considering that the disregard and infringement of human rights and fundamental freedoms, in particular of the right to freedom of thought, conscience, religion or whatever belief, have brought, directly or indirectly, wars and great suffering to mankind, especially where they serve as a means of foreign interference in the internal affairs of other States and amount to kindling hatred between peoples and nations,

Considering that religion or belief, for anyone who professes either, is one of the fundamental elements in his conception of life and that freedom of religion or belief should be fully respected and guaranteed,

Considering that it is essential to promote understanding, tolerance and respect in matters relating to freedom of religion and belief and to ensure that the use of religion or belief for ends inconsistent with the Charter of the United Nations, other relevant instruments of the United Nations and the purposes and principles of the present Declaration is inadmissible,

Convinced that freedom of religion and belief should also contribute to the attainment of the goals of world peace, social justice and friendship among peoples and to the elimination of ideologies or practices of colonialism and racial discrimination,

Noting with satisfaction the adoption of several, and the coming into force of some, conventions, under the aegis of the United Nations and of the specialized agencies, for the elimination of various forms of discrimination,

Concerned by manifestations of intolerance and by the existence of discrimination in matters of religion or belief still in evidence in some areas of the world,

Resolved to adopt all necessary measures for the speedy elimination of such intolerance in all its forms and manifestations and to prevent and combat discrimination on the ground of religion or belief,

Proclaims this Declaration on the Elimination of All Forms of Intolerance and of Discrimination Based on Religion or Belief:

Article 1

1. Everyone shall have the right to freedom of thought, conscience and religion. This right shall include freedom to have a religion or whatever belief of his choice, and freedom, either individually or in community with others and in public or private, to manifest his religion or belief in worship, observance, practice and teaching.

2. No one shall be subject to coercion which would impair his freedom to have a religion or belief of his choice.

3. Freedom to manifest one's religion or beliefs may be subject only to such limitations as are prescribed by law and are necessary to protect public safety, order, health or morals or the fundamental rights and freedoms of others.

Article 2

1. No one shall be subject to discrimination by any State, institution, group of persons, or person on the grounds of religion or other belief.

2. For the purposes of the present Declaration, the expression "intolerance and discrimination based on religion or belief" means any distinction, exclusion, restriction or preference based on religion or belief and having as its purpose or as its effect nullification or impairment of the recognition, enjoyment or exercise of human rights and fundamental freedoms on an equal basis.

Article 3

Discrimination between human beings on the grounds of religion or belief constitutes an affront to human dignity and a disavowal of the principles of the Charter of the United Nations, and shall be condemned as a violation of the human rights and fundamental freedoms proclaimed in the Universal Declaration of Human Rights and enunciated in detail in the International Covenants on Human Rights, and as an obstacle to friendly and peaceful relations between nations.

Article 4

1. All States shall take effective measures to prevent and eliminate discrimination on the grounds of religion or belief in the recognition, exercise and enjoyment of human rights and fundamental freedoms in all fields of civil, economic, political, social and cultural life.

2. All States shall make all efforts to enact or rescind legislation where necessary to prohibit any such discrimination, and to take all appropriate measures to combat intolerance on the grounds of religion or other beliefs in this matter.

Article 5

1. The parents or, as the case may be, the legal guardians of the child have the right to organize the life within the family in accordance with their religion or belief and bearing in mind the moral education in which they believe the child should be brought up.

2. Every child shall enjoy the right to have access to education in the matter of religion or belief in accordance with the wishes of his parents or, as the case may be, legal guardians, and shall not be compelled to receive teaching on religion or belief against the wishes of his parents or legal guardians, the best interests of the child being the guiding principle.

3. The child shall be protected from any form of discrimination on the grounds of religion or belief. He shall be brought up in a spirit of understanding, tolerance, friendship among peoples, peace and universal brotherhood, respect for freedom of religion or belief of others, and in full consciousness that his energy and talents should be devoted to the service of his fellow men.

4. In the case of a child who is not under the care either of his parents or of legal guardians, due account shall be taken of their expressed wishes or of any other proof of their wishes in the matter of religion or belief, the best interests of the child being the guiding principle.

5. Practices of a religion or belief in which a child is brought up must not be injurious to his physical or mental health or to his full development, taking into account article 1, paragraph 3, of the present Declaration.

Article 6

In accordance with article 1 of the present Declaration, and subject to the provisions of article 1, paragraph 3, the right to freedom of thought, conscience, religion or belief shall include, inter alia, the following freedoms:

(a) To worship or assemble in connection with a religion or belief, and to establish and maintain places for these purposes;

(b) To establish and maintain appropriate charitable or humanitarian institutions;

(c) To make, acquire and use to an adequate extent the necessary articles and materials related to the rites or customs of a religion or belief;

(d) To write, issue and disseminate relevant publications in these areas;

(e) To teach a religion or belief in places suitable for these purposes;

(f) To solicit and receive voluntary financial and other contributions from individuals and institutions;

(g) To train, appoint, elect or designate by succession appropriate leaders called for by the requirements and standards of any religion or belief;

(h) To observe days of rest and to celebrate holidays and ceremonies in accordance with the precepts of one's religion or belief;

(i) To establish and maintain communications with individuals and communities in matters of religion and belief at the national and international levels.

Article 7

The rights and freedoms set forth in the present Declaration shall be accorded in national legislation in such a manner that everyone shall be able to avail himself of such rights and freedoms in practice.

Article 8

Nothing in the present Declaration shall be construed as restricting or derogating from any right defined in the Universal Declaration of Human Rights and the International Covenants on Human Rights.

Declaration on the Rights of Persons Belonging to National or Ethnic, Religious and Linguistic Minorities

G.A. Res. 47/135, Annex, U.N. GAOR, 47th Sess., Supp. No. 49,
at 210, 211, U.N. Doc. A/47/49 (1992)

The General Assembly,

Reaffirming that one of the basic aims of the United Nations, as proclaimed in the Charter, is to promote and encourage respect for human rights and for fundamental freedoms for all, without distinction as to race, sex, language or religion,

Reaffirming faith in fundamental human rights, in the dignity and worth of the human person, in the equal rights of men and women and of nations large and small,

Desiring to promote the realization of the principles contained in the Charter, the Universal Declaration of Human Rights, the Convention on the Prevention and Punishment of the Crime of Genocide, the International Convention on the Elimination of All Forms of Racial Discrimination, the International Covenant on Civil and Political Rights, the International Covenant on Economic, Social and Cultural Rights, the Declaration on the Elimination of All Forms of Intolerance and of Discrimination Based on Religion or Belief, and the Convention on the Rights of the Child, as well as other relevant international instruments that have been adopted at the universal or regional level and those concluded between individual States Members of the United Nations,

Inspired by the provisions of article 27 of the International Covenant on Civil and Political Rights concerning the rights of persons belonging to ethnic, religious or linguistic minorities,

Considering that the promotion and protection of the rights of persons belonging to national or ethnic, religious and linguistic minorities contribute to the political and social stability of States in which they live,

Emphasizing that the constant promotion and realization of the rights of persons belonging to national or ethnic, religious and linguistic minorities, as an integral part of the development of society as a whole and within a democratic framework based on the rule of law, would contribute to the strengthening of friendship and cooperation among peoples and States,

Considering that the United Nations has an important role to play regarding the protection of minorities,

Bearing in mind the work done so far within the United Nations system, in particular by the Commission on Human Rights, the Subcommission on Prevention of Discrimination and Protection of Minorities and the bodies established pursuant to the International Covenants on Human Rights and other relevant international human rights instruments in promoting and protecting the rights of persons belonging to national or ethnic, religious and linguistic minorities,

Taking into account the important work which is done by intergovernmental and non-governmental organizations in protecting minorities and in promoting and protecting the rights of persons belonging to national or ethnic, religious and linguistic minorities,

Recognizing the need to ensure even more effective implementation of international human rights instruments with regard to the rights of persons belonging to national or ethnic, religious and linguistic minorities,

Proclaims this Declaration on the Rights of Persons Belonging to National or Ethnic, Religious and Linguistic Minorities:

Article 1

1. States shall protect the existence and the national or ethnic, cultural, religious and linguistic identity of minorities within their respective territories and shall encourage conditions for the promotion of that identity.

2. States shall adopt appropriate legislative and other measures to achieve those ends.

Article 2

1. Persons belonging to national or ethnic, religious and linguistic minorities (hereinafter referred to as persons belonging to minorities) have the right to enjoy their own culture, to profess and practise their own religion, and to use their own language, in private and in public, freely and without interference or any form of discrimination.

2. Persons belonging to minorities have the right to participate effectively in cultural, religious, social, economic and public life.

3. Persons belonging to minorities have the right to participate effectively in decisions on the national and, where appropriate, regional level concerning the minority to which they belong or the regions in which they live, in a manner not incompatible with national legislation.

4. Persons belonging to minorities have the right to establish and maintain their own associations.

5. Persons belonging to minorities have the right to establish and maintain, without any discrimination, free and peaceful contacts with other members of their group and with persons belonging to other minorities, as well as contacts across frontiers with citizens of other States to whom they are related by national or ethnic, religious or linguistic ties.

Article 3

1. Persons belonging to minorities may exercise their rights, including those set forth in the present Declaration, individually as well as in community with other members of their group, without any discrimination.

2. No disadvantage shall result for any person belonging to a minority as the consequence of the exercise or non-exercise of the rights set forth in the present Declaration.

Article 4

1. States shall take measures where required to ensure that persons belonging to minorities may exercise fully and effectively all their human rights and fundamental freedoms without any discrimination and in full equality before the law.

2. States shall take measures to create favourable conditions to enable persons belonging to minorities to express their characteristics and to develop their culture, language, religion, traditions and customs, except where specific practices are in violation of national law and contrary to international standards.

3. States should take appropriate measures so that, wherever possible, persons belonging to minorities may have adequate opportunities to learn their mother tongue or to have instruction in their mother tongue.

4. States should, where appropriate, take measures in the field of education, in order to encourage knowledge of the history, traditions, language and culture of the minorities existing within their territory. Persons belonging to minorities should have adequate opportunities to gain knowledge of the society as a whole.

5. States should consider appropriate measures so that persons belonging to minorities may participate fully in the economic progress and development in their country.

Article 5

1. National policies and programmes shall be planned and implemented with due regard for the legitimate interests of persons belonging to minorities.

2. Programmes of cooperation and assistance among States should be planned and implemented with due regard for the legitimate interests of persons belonging to minorities.

Article 6

States should cooperate on questions relating to persons belonging to minorities, inter alia, exchanging information and experiences, in order to promote mutual understanding and confidence.

Article 7

States should cooperate in order to promote respect for the rights set forth in the present Declaration.

Article 8

1. Nothing in the present Declaration shall prevent the fulfilment of international obligations of States in relation to persons belonging to minorities. In particular, States shall fulfil in good faith the obligations and commitments they have assumed under international treaties and agreements to which they are parties.

2. The exercise of the rights set forth in the present Declaration shall not prejudice the enjoyment by all persons of universally recognized human rights and fundamental freedoms.

3. Measures taken by States to ensure the effective enjoyment of the rights set forth in the present Declaration shall not prima facie be considered contrary to the principle of equality contained in the Universal Declaration of Human Rights.

4. Nothing in the present Declaration may be construed as permitting any activity contrary to the purposes and principles of the United Nations, including sovereign equality, territorial integrity and political independence of States.

Article 9

The specialized agencies and other organizations of the United Nations system shall contribute to the full realization of the rights and principles set forth in the present Declaration, within their respective fields of competence.

C. Women, Marriage, Dissolution, and Domestic Violence

Convention on the Political Rights of Women
Mar. 31, 1953, 27 U.S.T. 1909, 193 U.N.T.S. 135

[Ed. Note: The Convention entered into force on July 7, 1954. As of March 2003, 115 nations were party to the Convention. The United States became a party by accession on April 8, 1976.]

The Contracting Parties,

Desiring to implement the principle of equality of rights for men and women contained in the Charter of the United Nations,

Recognizing that everyone has the right to take part in the government of his country directly or indirectly through freely chosen representatives, and has the right to equal access to public service in his country, and desiring to equalize the status of men and women in the enjoyment and exercise of political rights, in accordance with the provisions of the Charter of the United Nations and of the Universal Declaration of Human Rights,

Having resolved to conclude a Convention for this purpose,

Hereby agree as hereinafter provided:

Article 1

Women shall be entitled to vote in all elections on equal terms with men, without any discrimination.

Article 2

Women shall be eligible for election to all publicly elected bodies, established by national law, on equal terms with men, without any discrimination.

Article 3

Women shall be entitled to hold public office and to exercise all public functions, established by national law, on equal terms with men, without any discrimination.

[Ed. Note: Articles 4 to 11, addressing signature, ratification, accession, reservations, denunciation, resolution of disputes, and deposit of the Convention, are omitted.]

Declaration on the Elimination of Discrimination against Women
G.A. Res. 2263, U.N. GAOR, 22nd Sess.,
Supp. No. 16, 35, U.N. Doc. A/6716 (1967)

The General Assembly,

Considering that the peoples of the United Nations have, in the Charter, reaffirmed their faith in fundamental human rights, in the dignity and worth of the human person and in the equal rights of men and women,

Considering that the Universal Declaration on Human Rights asserts the principle of non-discrimination and proclaims that all human beings are born free and equal in dignity and rights and that everyone is entitled to all the rights and freedoms set forth therein without distinction of any kind, including any distinction as to sex,

Taking into account the resolutions, declarations, conventions and recommendations of the United Nations and the specialized agencies designed to eliminate all forms of discrimination and to promote equal rights for men and women,

Concerned that, despite the Charter of the United Nations, the Universal Declaration of Human Rights, the International Covenants on Human Rights and other instruments of the United Nations and the specialized agencies and despite the progress made in the matter of equality of rights, there continues to exist considerable discrimination against women,

Considering that discrimination against women is incompatible with human dignity and with the welfare of the family and of society, prevents their participation, on equal terms with men, in the political, social, economic and cultural life of their countries and is an obstacle to the full development of the potentialities of women in the service of their countries and of humanity,

Bearing in mind the great contribution made by women to social, political, economic and cultural life and the part they play in the family and particularly in the rearing of children,

Convinced that the full and complete development of a country, the welfare of the world and the cause of peace require the maximum participation of women as well as men in all fields,

Considering that it is necessary to ensure the universal recognition in law and in fact of the principle of equality of men and women,

Solemnly proclaims this Declaration:

Article 1

Discrimination against women, denying or limiting as it does their equality of rights with men, is fundamentally unjust and constitutes an offence against human dignity.

Article 2

All appropriate measures shall be taken to abolish existing laws, customs, regulations and practices which are discriminatory against women, and to establish adequate legal protection for equal rights of men and women, in particular:

(a) The principle of equality of rights shall be embodied in the constitution or otherwise guaranteed by law;

(b) The international instruments of the United Nations and the specialized agencies relating to the elimination of discrimination against women shall be ratified or acceded to and fully implemented as soon as practicable.

Article 3

All appropriate measures shall be taken to educate public opinion and to direct national aspirations towards the eradication of prejudice and the abolition of customary and all other practices which are based on the idea of the inferiority of women.

Article 4

All appropriate measures shall be taken to ensure to women on equal terms with men, without any discrimination:

(a) The right to vote in all elections and be eligible for election to all publicly elected bodies;

(b) The right to vote in all public referenda;

(c) The right to hold public office and to exercise all public functions.

Such rights shall be guaranteed by legislation.

Article 5

Women shall have the same rights as men to acquire, change or retain their nationality. Marriage to an alien shall not automatically affect the nationality of the wife either by rendering her stateless or by forcing upon her the nationality of her husband.

Article 6

1. Without prejudice to the safeguarding of the unity and the harmony of the family, which remains the basic unit of any society, all appropriate measures, particularly legislative measures, shall be taken to ensure to women, married or unmarried, equal rights with men in the field of civil law, and in particular:

(a) The right to acquire, administer, enjoy, dispose of and inherit property, including property acquired during marriage;

(b) The right to equality in legal capacity and the exercise thereof;

(c) The same rights as men with regard to the law on the movement of persons.

2. All appropriate measures shall be taken to ensure the principle of equality of status of the husband and wife, and in particular:

(a) Women shall have the same right as men to free choice of a spouse and to enter into marriage only with their free and full consent;

(b) Women shall have equal rights with men during marriage and at its dissolution. In all cases the interest of the children shall be paramount;

(c) Parents shall have equal rights and duties in matters relating to their children. In all cases the interest of the children shall be paramount.

3. Child marriage and the betrothal of young girls before puberty shall be prohibited, and effective action, including legislation, shall be taken to specify a minimum age for marriage and to make the registration of marriages in an official registry compulsory.

Article 7

All provisions of penal codes which constitute discrimination against women shall be repealed.

Article 8

All appropriate measures, including legislation, shall be taken to combat all forms of traffic in women and exploitation of prostitution of women.

Article 9

All appropriate measures shall be taken to ensure to girls and women, married or unmarried, equal rights with men in education at all levels, and in particular:

(a) Equal conditions of access to, and study in, educational institutions of all types, including universities and vocational, technical and professional schools;

(b) The same choice of curricula, the same examinations, teaching staff with qualifications of the same standard, and school premises and equipment of the same quality, whether the institutions are co-educational or not;

(c) Equal opportunities to benefit from scholarships and other study grants;

(d) Equal opportunities for access to programmes of continuing education, including adult literacy programmes;

(e) Access to educational information to help in ensuring the health and well-being of families.

Article 10

1. All appropriate measures shall be taken to ensure to women, married or unmarried, equal rights with men in the field of economic and social life, and in particular:

(a) The right, without discrimination on grounds of marital status or any other grounds, to receive vocational training, to work, to free choice of profession and employment, and to professional and vocational advancement;

(b) The right to equal remuneration with men and to equality of treatment in respect of work of equal value;

(c) The right to leave with pay, retirement privileges and provision for security in respect of unemployment, sickness, old age or other incapacity to work;

(d) The right to receive family allowances on equal terms with men.

2. In order to prevent discrimination against women on account of marriage or maternity and to ensure their effective right to work, measures shall be taken to prevent their dismissal in the event of marriage or maternity and to provide paid maternity leave, with the guarantee of returning to former employment, and to provide the necessary social services, including child-care facilities.

3. Measures taken to protect women in certain types of work, for reasons inherent in their physical nature, shall not be regarded as discriminatory.

Article 11

1. The principle of equality of rights of men and women demands implementation in all States in accordance with the principles of the Charter of the United Nations and of the Universal Declaration of Human Rights.

2. Governments, non-governmental organizations and individuals are urged, therefore, to do all in their power to promote the implementation of the principles contained in this Declaration.

Declaration on Social Progress and Development
G.A. Res. 2542, U.N. GAOR, 24th Sess., Supp. No. 30, at 49,
U.N. Doc. A/7630 (1969)

The General Assembly,

Mindful of the pledge of Members of the United Nations under the Charter to take joint and separate action in co-operation with the Organization to promote higher standards of living, full employment and conditions of economic and social progress and development,

Reaffirming faith in human rights and fundamental freedoms and in the principles of peace, of the dignity and worth of the human person, and of social justice proclaimed in the Charter,

Recalling the principles of the Universal Declaration of Human Rights, the International Covenants on Human Rights, the Declaration of the Rights of the Child, the Declaration on the Granting of Independence to Colonial Countries and Peoples, the International Convention on the Elimination of All Forms of Racial Discrimination, the United Nations Declaration on the Elimination of All Forms of Racial Discrimination, the Declaration on the Promotion among Youth of the Ideals of Peace, Mutual Respect and Understanding between Peoples, the Declaration on the Elimination of Discrimination against Women and of resolutions of the United Nations,

Bearing in mind the standards already set for social progress in the constitutions, conventions, recommendations and resolutions of the International Labour Organisation, the Food and Agriculture Organization of the United Nations, the United Nations Educational, Scientific and Cultural Organization, the World Health Organization, the United Nations Children's Fund and of other organizations concerned,

Convinced that man can achieve complete fulfilment of his aspirations only within a just social order and that it is consequently of cardinal importance to accelerate social and economic progress everywhere, thus contributing to international peace and solidarity,

Convinced that international peace and security on the one hand, and social progress and economic development on the other, are closely interdependent and influence each other,

Persuaded that social development can be promoted by peaceful coexistence, friendly relations and co-operation among States with different social, economic or political systems,

Emphasizing the interdependence of economic and social development in the wider process of growth and change, as well as the importance of a strategy of integrated development which takes full account at all stages of its social aspects,

Regretting the inadequate progress achieved in the world social situation despite the efforts of States and the international community,

Recognizing that the primary responsibility for the development of the developing countries rests on those countries themselves and acknowledging the pressing need to narrow and eventually close the gap in the standards of living between economically more advanced and developing countries and, to that end, that Member States shall have the responsibility to pursue internal and external policies designed to promote social development throughout the world, and in particular to assist developing countries to accelerate their economic growth,

Recognizing the urgency of devoting to works of peace and social progress resources being expended on armaments and wasted on conflict and destruction,

Conscious of the contribution that science and technology can render towards meeting the needs common to all humanity,

Believing that the primary task of all States and international organizations is to eliminate from the life of society all evils and obstacles to social progress, particularly such evils as inequality, exploitation, war, colonialism and racism,

Desirous of promoting the progress of all mankind towards these goals and of overcoming all obstacles to their realization,

Solemnly proclaims this Declaration on Social Progress and Development and calls for national and international action for its use as a common basis for social development policies:

Part I — Principles

Article 1
All peoples and all human beings, without distinction as to race, colour, sex, language, religion, nationality, ethnic origin, family or social status, or political or other conviction, shall have the right to live in dignity and freedom and to enjoy the fruits of social progress and should, on their part, contribute to it.

Article 2
Social progress and development shall be founded on respect for the dignity and value of the human person and shall ensure the promotion of human rights and social justice, which requires:

(a) The immediate and final elimination of all forms of inequality, exploitation of peoples and individuals, colonialism and racism, including nazism and apartheid, and all other policies and ideologies opposed to the purposes and principles of the United Nations;

(b) The recognition and effective implementation of civil and political rights as well as of economic, social and cultural rights without any discrimination.

Article 3

The following are considered primary conditions of social progress and development:

(a) National independence based on the right of peoples to self-determination;

(b) The principle of non-interference in the internal affairs of States;

(c) Respect for the sovereignty and territorial integrity of States;

(d) Permanent sovereignty of each nation over its natural wealth and resources;

(e) The right and responsibility of each State and, as far as they are concerned, each nation and people to determine freely its own objectives of social development, to set its own priorities and to decide in conformity with the principles of the Charter of the United Nations the means and methods of their achievement without any external interference;

(f) Peaceful coexistence, peace, friendly relations and co-operation among States irrespective of differences in their social, economic or political systems.

Article 4

The family as a basic unit of society and the natural environment for the growth and well-being of all its members, particularly children and youth, should be assisted and protected so that it may fully assume its responsibilities within the community. Parents have the exclusive right to determine freely and responsibly the number and spacing of their children.

Article 5

Social progress and development require the full utilization of human resources, including, in particular:

(a) The encouragement of creative initiative under conditions of enlightened public opinion;

(b) The dissemination of national and international information for the purpose of making individuals aware of changes occurring in society as a whole;

(c) The active participation of all elements of society, individually or through associations, in defining and in achieving the common goals of development with full respect for the fundamental freedoms embodied in the Universal Declaration of Human Rights;

(d) The assurance to disadvantaged or marginal sectors of the population of equal opportunities for social and economic advancement in order to achieve an effectively integrated society.

Article 6

Social development requires the assurance to everyone of the right to work and the free choice of employment.

Social progress and development require the participation of all members of society in productive and socially useful labour and the establishment, in conformity with human rights and fundamental freedoms and with the principles of justice and the social function of property, of forms of ownership of land and of the means of production which preclude any kind of exploitation of man, ensure equal rights to property for all and create conditions leading to genuine equality among people.

Article 7

The rapid expansion of national income and wealth and their equitable distribution among all members of society are fundamental to all social progress, and they should therefore be in the forefront of the preoccupations of every State and Government.

The improvement in the position of the developing countries in international trade resulting among other things from the achievement of favourable terms of trade and of equitable and remunerative prices at which developing countries market their products is necessary in order to make it possible to increase national income and in order to advance social development.

Article 8

Each Government has the primary role and ultimate responsibility of ensuring the social progress and well-being of its people, of planning social development measures as part of comprehensive development plans, of encouraging and co-ordinating or integrating all national efforts towards this end and of introducing necessary changes in the social structure. In planning social development measures, the diversity of the needs of developing and developed areas, and of urban and rural areas, within each country, shall be taken into due account.

Article 9

Social progress and development are the common concerns of the international community, which shall supplement, by concerted international action, national efforts to raise the living standards of peoples.

Social progress and economic growth require recognition of the common interest of all nations in the exploration, conservation, use and exploitation, exclusively for peaceful purposes and in the interests of all mankind, of those areas of the environment such as outer space and the sea-bed and ocean floor and the subsoil thereof, beyond the limits of national jurisdiction, in accordance with the purposes and principles of the Charter of the United Nations.

Part II—Objectives

Social progress and development shall aim at the continuous raising of the material and spiritual standards of living of all members of society, with respect for and in compliance with human rights and fundamental freedoms, through the attainment of the following main goals:

Article 10

(a) The assurance at all levels of the right to work and the right of everyone to form trade unions and workers' associations and to bargain collectively; promotion of full productive employment and elimination of unemployment and under-employment; establishment of equitable and favourable conditions of work for all, including the improvement of health and safety conditions; assurance of just remuneration for labour without any discrimination as well as a sufficiently high minimum wage to ensure a decent standard of living; the protection of the consumer;

(b) The elimination of hunger and malnutrition and the guarantee of the right to proper nutrition;

(c) The elimination of poverty; the assurance of a steady improvement in levels of living and of a just and equitable distribution of income;

(d) The achievement of the highest standards of health and the provision of health protection for the entire population, if possible free of charge;

(e) The eradication of illiteracy and the assurance of the right to universal access to culture, to free compulsory education at the elementary level and to free education at all levels; the raising of the general level of life-long education;

(f) The provision for all, particularly persons in low income groups and large families, of adequate housing and community services.

Social progress and development shall aim equally at the progressive attainment of the following main goals:

Article 11

(a) The provision of comprehensive social security schemes and social welfare services; the establishment and improvement of social security and insurance schemes for all persons who, because of illness, disability or old age, are temporarily or permanently unable to earn a living, with a view to ensuring a proper standard of living for such persons and for their families and dependants;

(b) The protection of the rights of the mother and child; concern for the upbringing and health of children; the provision of measures to safeguard the health and welfare of women and particularly of working mothers during pregnancy and the infancy of their children, as well as of mothers whose earnings are the sole source of livelihood for the family; the granting to women of pregnancy and maternity leave and allowances without loss of employment or wages;

(c) The protection of the rights and the assuring of the welfare of children, the aged and the disabled; the provision of protection for the physically or mentally disadvantaged;

(d) The education of youth in, and promotion among them of, the ideals of justice and peace, mutual respect and understanding among peoples; the promotion of full participation of youth in the process of national development;

(e) The provision of social defence measures and the elimination of conditions leading to crime and delinquency especially juvenile delinquency;

(f) The guarantee that all individuals, without discrimination of any kind, are made aware of their rights and obligations and receive the necessary aid in the exercise and safeguarding of their rights.

Social progress and development shall further aim at achieving the following main objectives:

Article 12

(a) The creation of conditions for rapid and sustained social and economic development, particularly in the developing countries; change in international economic relations; new and effective methods of international co-operation in which equality of opportunity should be as much a prerogative of nations as of individuals within a nation;

(b) The elimination of all forms of discrimination and exploitation and all other practices and ideologies contrary to the purposes and principles of the Charter of the United Nations;

(c) The elimination of all forms of foreign economic exploitation, particularly that practised by international monopolies, in order to enable the people of every country to enjoy in full the benefits of their national resources.

Social progress and development shall finally aim at the attainment of the following main goals:

Article 13

(a) Equitable sharing of scientific and technological advances by developed and developing countries, and a steady increase in the use of science and technology for the benefit of the social development of society;

(b) The establishment of a harmonious balance between scientific, technological and material progress and the intellectual, spiritual, cultural and moral advancement of humanity;

(c) The protection and improvement of the human environment.

Part III—Means and Methods

On the basis of the principles set forth in this Declaration, the achievement of the objectives of social progress and development requires the mobilization of the necessary resources by national and international action, with particular attention to such means and methods as:

Article 14

(a) Planning for social progress and development as an integrated part of balanced overall development planning;

(b) The establishment, where necessary, of national systems for framing and carrying out social policies and programmes, and the promotion by the countries concerned of planned regional development, taking into account differing regional conditions and needs, particularly the development of regions which are less favoured or under-developed by comparison with the rest of the country;

(c) The promotion of basic and applied social research, particularly comparative international research applied to the planning and execution of social development programmes.

Article 15

(a) The adoption of measures, to ensure the effective participation, as appropriate, of all the elements of society in the preparation and execution of national plans and programmes of economic and social development;

(b) The adoption of measures for an increasing rate of popular participation in the economic, social, cultural and political life of countries through national governmental bodies, non-governmental organizations, co-operatives, rural associations, workers' and employers' organizations and women's and youth organizations, by such methods as national and regional plans for social and economic progress and community development, with a view to achieving a fully integrated national society, accelerating the process of social mobility and consolidating the democratic system;

(c) Mobilization of public opinion, at both national and international levels, in support of the principles and objectives of social progress and development;

(d) The dissemination of social information, at the national and the international level, to make people aware of changing circumstances in society as a whole, and to educate the consumer.

Article 16

(a) Maximum mobilization of all national resources and their rational and efficient utilization; promotion of increased and accelerated productive investment in social and economic fields and of employment; orientation of society towards the development process;

(b) Progressively increasing provision of the necessary budgetary and other resources required for financing the social aspects of development;

(c) Achievement of equitable distribution of national income, utilizing, inter alia, the fiscal system and government spending as an instrument for the equitable distribution and redistribution of income in order to promote social progress;

(d) The adoption of measures aimed at prevention of such an outflow of capital from developing countries as would be detrimental to their economic and social development.

Article 17

(a) The adoption of measures to accelerate the process of industrialization, especially in developing countries, with due regard for its social aspects, in the interests of the entire population; development of an adequate organization and legal framework conducive to an uninterrupted and diversified growth of the industrial sector; measures to overcome the adverse social effects which may result from urban development and industrialization, including automation; maintenance of a proper balance between rural and urban development, and in particular, measures designed to ensure healthier living conditions, especially in large industrial centres;

(b) Integrated planning to meet the problems of urbanization and urban development;

(c) Comprehensive rural development schemes to raise the levels of living of the rural populations and to facilitate such urban-rural relationships and population distribution as will promote balanced national development and social progress;

(d) Measures for appropriate supervision of the utilization of land in the interests of society.

The achievement of the objectives of social progress and development equally requires the implementation of the following means and methods:

Article 18

(a) The adoption of appropriate legislative, administrative and other measures ensuring to everyone not only political and civil rights, but also the full realization of economic, social and cultural rights without any discrimination;

(b) The promotion of democratically based social and institutional reforms and motivation for change basic to the elimination of all forms of discrimination and exploitation and conducive to high rates of economic and social progress, to include land reform, in which the ownership and use of land will be made to serve best the objectives of social justice and economic development;

(c) The adoption of measures to boost and diversify agricultural production through, inter alia, the implementation of democratic agrarian reforms, to ensure an adequate and well-balanced supply of food, its equitable distribution among the whole population and the improvement of nutritional standards;

(d) The adoption of measures to introduce, with the participation of the Government, low-cost housing programmes in both rural and urban areas;

(e) Development and expansion of the system of transportation and communications, particularly in developing countries.

Article 19

(a) The provision of free health services to the whole population and of adequate preventive and curative facilities and welfare medical services accessible to all;

(b) The enactment and establishment of legislative measures and administrative regulations with a view to the implementation of comprehensive programmes of social security schemes and social welfare services and to the improvement and co-ordination of existing services;

(c) The adoption of measures and the provision of social welfare services to migrant workers and their families, in conformity with the provisions of Convention No. 97 of the International Labour Organisation and other international instruments relating to migrant workers;

(d) The institution of appropriate measures for the rehabilitation of mentally or physically disabled persons, especially children and youth, so as to enable them to the fullest possible extent to be useful members of society—these measures shall include the provision of treatment and technical appliances, education, vocational and social guidance, training and selective placement, and other assistance required—and the creation of social conditions in which the handicapped are not discriminated against because of their disabilities.

Article 20

(a) The provision of full democratic freedoms to trade unions; freedom of association for all workers, including the right to bargain collectively and to strike; recognition of the right to form other organizations of working people; the provision for the growing participation of trade unions in economic and social development; effective participation of all members in trade unions in the deciding of economic and social issues which affect their interests;

(b) The improvement of health and safety conditions for workers, by means of appropriate technological and legislative measures and the provision of the material prerequisites for the implementation of those measures, including the limitation of working hours;

(c) The adoption of appropriate measures for the development of harmonious industrial relations.

Article 21

(a) The training of national personnel and cadres, including administrative, executive, professional and technical personnel needed for social development and for overall development plans and policies;

(b) The adoption of measures to accelerate the extension and improvement of general, vocational and technical education and of training and retraining, which should be provided free at all levels;

(c) Raising the general level of education; development and expansion of national information media, and their rational and full use towards continuing education of the whole population and towards encouraging its participation in social development activities; the constructive use of leisure, particularly that of children and adolescents;

(d) The formulation of national and international policies and measures to avoid the "brain drain" and obviate its adverse effects.

Article 22

(a) The development and co-ordination of policies and measures designed to strengthen the essential functions of the family as a basic unit of society;

(b) The formulation and establishment, as needed, of programmes in the field of population, within the framework of national demographic policies and as part of the welfare medical services, including education, training of personnel and the provision to families of the knowledge and means necessary to enable them to exercise their right to determine freely and responsibly the number and spacing of their children;

(c) The establishment of appropriate child-care facilities in the interest of children and working parents. The achievement of the objectives of social progress and development finally requires the implementation of the following means and methods:

Article 23

(a) The laying down of economic growth rate targets for the developing countries within the United Nations policy for development, high enough to lead to a substantial acceleration of their rates of growth;

(b) The provision of greater assistance on better terms; the implementation of the aid volume target of a minimum of 1 per cent of the gross national product at market prices of economically advanced countries; the general easing of the terms of lending to the developing countries through low interest rates on loans and long grace periods for the repayment of loans, and the assurance that the allocation of such loans will be based strictly on socioeconomic criteria free of any political considerations;

(c) The provision of technical, financial and material assistance, both bilateral and multilateral, to the fullest possible extent and on favourable terms, and improved co-ordination of international assistance for the achievement of the social objectives of national development plans;

(d) The provision to the developing countries of technical, financial and material assistance and of favourable conditions to facilitate the direct exploitation of their national resources and natural wealth by those countries with a view to enabling the peoples of those countries to benefit fully from their national resources;

(e) The expansion of international trade based on principles of equality and non-discrimination, the rectification of the position of developing countries in international trade by equitable terms of trade, a general nonreciprocal and non-discriminatory system of preferences for the exports of developing countries to the developed countries, the establishment and implementation of general and comprehensive commodity agreements, and the financing of reasonable buffer stocks by international institutions.

Article 24

(a) Intensification of international co-operation with a view to ensuring the international exchange of information, knowledge and experience concerning social progress and development;

(b) The broadest possible international technical, scientific and cultural co-operation and reciprocal utilization of the experience of countries with different economic and social systems and different levels of development, on the basis of mutual advantage and strict observance of and respect for national sovereignty;

(c) Increased utilization of science and technology for social and economic development; arrangements for the transfer and exchange of technology, including know-how and patents, to the developing countries.

Article 25

(a) The establishment of legal and administrative measures for the protection and improvement of the human environment, at both national and international level;

(b) The use and exploitation, in accordance with the appropriate international regimes, of the resources of areas of the environment such as outer space and the sea-bed and ocean floor and the subsoil thereof, beyond the limits of national jurisdiction, in order to supplement national resources available for the achievement of economic and social progress and development in every country, irrespective of its geographical location, special consideration being given to the interests and needs of the developing countries.

Article 26
Compensation for damages, be they social or economic in nature—including restitution and reparations—caused as a result of aggression and of illegal occupation of territory by the aggressor.

Article 27
(a) The achievement of general and complete disarmament and the channelling of the progressively released resources to be used for economic and social progress for the welfare of people everywhere and, in particular, for the benefit of developing countries;

(b) The adoption of measures contributing to disarmament, including, inter alia, the complete prohibition of tests of nuclear weapons, the prohibition of the development, production and stockpiling of chemical and bacteriological (biological) weapons and the prevention of the pollution of oceans and inland waters by nuclear wastes.

Convention on the Elimination of All Forms of Discrimination against Women
Dec. 18, 1979, 1249 U.N.T.S. 13

[Ed. Note: The Convention entered into force on September 3, 1981. As of March 2003, 172 nations were parties to the Convention. The United States is not a party to this Convention. Although the United States signed the Convention on July 17, 1980, it has not ratified or acceded to it.]

The States Parties to the present Convention,

Noting that the Charter of the United Nations reaffirms faith in fundamental human rights, in the dignity and worth of the human person and in the equal rights of men and women,

Noting that the Universal Declaration of Human Rights affirms the principle of the inadmissibility of discrimination and proclaims that all human beings are born free and equal in dignity and rights and that everyone is entitled to all the rights and freedoms set forth therein, without distinction of any kind, including distinction based on sex,

Noting that the States Parties to the International Covenants on Human Rights have the obligation to ensure the equal rights of men and women to enjoy all economic, social, cultural, civil and political rights,

Considering the international conventions concluded under the auspices of the United Nations and the specialized agencies promoting equality of rights of men and women,

Noting also the resolutions, declarations and recommendations adopted by the United Nations and the specialized agencies promoting equality of rights of men and women,

Concerned, however, that despite these various instruments extensive discrimination against women continues to exist,

Recalling that discrimination against women violates the principles of equality of rights and respect for human dignity, is an obstacle to the participation of women, on equal terms with men, in the political, social, economic and cultural life of their countries, hampers the growth of the prosperity of society and the family and makes more difficult the full development of the potentialities of women in the service of their countries and of humanity,

Concerned that in situations of poverty women have the least access to food, health, education, training and opportunities for employment and other needs,

Convinced that the establishment of the new international economic order based on equity and justice will contribute significantly towards the promotion of equality between men and women,

Emphasizing that the eradication of apartheid, all forms of racism, racial discrimination, colonialism, neo-colonialism, aggression, foreign occupation and domination and interference in the internal affairs of States is essential to the full enjoyment of the rights of men and women,

Affirming that the strengthening of international peace and security, relaxation of international tension, mutual co-operation among all States irrespective of their social and economic systems, general and complete disarmament, and in particular nuclear disarmament under strict and effective international control, the affirmation of the principles of justice, equality and mutual benefit in relations among countries and the realization of the right of peoples under alien and colonial domination and foreign occupation to self-determination and independence, as well as respect for national sovereignty and territorial integrity, will promote social progress and development and as a consequence will contribute to the attainment of full equality between men and women,

Convinced that the full and complete development of a country, the welfare of the world and the cause of peace require the maximum participation of women on equal terms with men in all fields,

Bearing in mind the great contribution of women to the welfare of the family and to the development of society, so far not fully recognized, the social significance of maternity and the role of both parents in the family and in the upbringing of children, and aware that the role of women in procreation should not be a basis for discrimination but that the upbringing of children requires a sharing of responsibility between men and women and society as a whole,

Aware that a change in the traditional role of men as well as the role of women in society and in the family is needed to achieve full equality between men and women,

Determined to implement the principles set forth in the Declaration on the Elimination of Discrimination against Women and, for that purpose, to adopt the measures required for the elimination of such discrimination in all its forms and manifestations,

Have agreed on the following:

PART I

Article I

For the purposes of the present Convention, the term "discrimination against women" shall mean any distinction, exclusion or restriction made on the basis of sex which has the effect or purpose of impairing or nullifying the recognition, enjoyment or exercise by women, irrespective of their marital status, on a basis of equality of men and women, of human rights and fundamental freedoms in the political, economic, social, cultural, civil or any other field.

Article 2

States Parties condemn discrimination against women in all its forms, agree to pursue by all appropriate means and without delay a policy of eliminating discrimination against women and, to this end, undertake:

(a) To embody the principle of the equality of men and women in their national constitutions or other appropriate legislation if not yet incorporated therein and to ensure, through law and other appropriate means, the practical realization of this principle;

(b) To adopt appropriate legislative and other measures, including sanctions where appropriate, prohibiting all discrimination against women;

(c) To establish legal protection of the rights of women on an equal basis with men and to ensure through competent national tribunals and other public institutions the effective protection of women against any act of discrimination;

(d) To refrain from engaging in any act or practice of discrimination against women and to ensure that public authorities and institutions shall act in conformity with this obligation;

(e) To take all appropriate measures to eliminate discrimination against women by any person, organization or enterprise;

(f) To take all appropriate measures, including legislation, to modify or abolish existing laws, regulations, customs and practices which constitute discrimination against women;

(g) To repeal all national penal provisions which constitute discrimination against women.

Article 3

States Parties shall take in all fields, in particular in the political, social, economic and cultural fields, all appropriate measures, including legislation, to ensure the full development and advancement of women, for the purpose of guaranteeing them the exercise and enjoyment of human rights and fundamental freedoms on a basis of equality with men.

Article 4

1. Adoption by States Parties of temporary special measures aimed at accelerating de facto equality between men and women shall not be considered discrimination as defined in the present Convention, but shall in no way entail as a consequence the maintenance of unequal or separate standards; these measures shall be discontinued when the objectives of equality of opportunity and treatment have been achieved.

2. Adoption by States Parties of special measures, including those measures contained in the present Convention, aimed at protecting maternity shall not be considered discriminatory.

Article 5

States Parties shall take all appropriate measures:

(a) To modify the social and cultural patterns of conduct of men and women, with a view to achieving the elimination of prejudices and customary and all other practices which are based on the idea of the inferiority or the superiority of either of the sexes or on stereotyped roles for men and women;

(b) To ensure that family education includes a proper understanding of maternity as a social function and the recognition of the common responsibility of men and women in the upbringing and development of their children, it being understood that the interest of the children is the primordial consideration in all cases.

Article 6

States Parties shall take all appropriate measures, including legislation, to suppress all forms of traffic in women and exploitation of prostitution of women.

PART II

Article 7

States Parties shall take all appropriate measures to eliminate discrimination against women in the political and public life of the country and, in particular, shall ensure to women, on equal terms with men, the right:

(a) To vote in all elections and public referenda and to be eligible for election to all publicly elected bodies;

(b) To participate in the formulation of government policy and the implementation thereof and to hold public office and perform all public functions at all levels of government;

(c) To participate in non-governmental organizations and associations concerned with the public and political life of the country.

Article 8

States Parties shall take all appropriate measures to ensure to women, on equal terms with men and without any discrimination, the opportunity to represent their Governments at the international level and to participate in the work of international organizations.

Article 9

1. States Parties shall grant women equal rights with men to acquire, change or retain their nationality. They shall ensure in particular that neither marriage to an alien nor change of nationality by the husband during marriage shall automatically change the nationality of the wife, render her stateless or force upon her the nationality of the husband.

2. States Parties shall grant women equal rights with men with respect to the nationality of their children.

PART III

Article 10

States Parties shall take all appropriate measures to eliminate discrimination against women in order to ensure to them equal rights with men in the field of education and in particular to ensure, on a basis of equality of men and women:

(a) The same conditions for career and vocational guidance, for access to studies and for the achievement of diplomas in educational establishments of all categories in rural as well as in urban areas; this equality shall be ensured in pre-school, general, technical, professional and higher technical education, as well as in all types of vocational training;

(b) Access to the same curricula, the same examinations, teaching staff with qualifications of the same standard and school premises and equipment of the same quality;

(c) The elimination of any stereotyped concept of the roles of men and women at all levels and in all forms of education by encouraging coeducation and other types of education which will help to achieve this aim and, in particular, by the revision of textbooks and school programmes and the adaptation of teaching methods;

(d) The same opportunities to benefit from scholarships and other study grants;

(e) The same opportunities for access to programmes of continuing education, including adult and functional literacy programmes, particularly those aimed at reducing, at the earliest possible time, any gap in education existing between men and women;

(f) The reduction of female student drop-out rates and the organization of programmes for girls and women who have left school prematurely;

(g) The same opportunities to participate actively in sports and physical education;

(h) Access to specific educational information to help to ensure the health and well-being of families, including information and advice on family planning.

Article 11

1. States Parties shall take all appropriate measures to eliminate discrimination against women in the field of employment in order to ensure, on a basis of equality of men and women, the same rights, in particular:

(a) The right to work as an inalienable right of all human beings;

(b) The right to the same employment opportunities, including the application of the same criteria for selection in matters of employment;

(c) The right to free choice of profession and employment, the right to promotion, job security and all benefits and conditions of service and the right to receive vocational training and retraining, including apprenticeships, advanced vocational training and recurrent training;

(d) The right to equal remuneration, including benefits, and to equal treatment in respect of work of equal value, as well as equality of treatment in the evaluation of the quality of work;

(e) The right to social security, particularly in cases of retirement, unemployment, sickness, invalidity and old age and other incapacity to work, as well as the right to paid leave;

(f) The right to protection of health and to safety in working conditions, including the safeguarding of the function of reproduction.

2. In order to prevent discrimination against women on the grounds of marriage or maternity and to ensure their effective right to work, States Parties shall take appropriate measures:

(a) To prohibit, subject to the imposition of sanctions, dismissal on the grounds of pregnancy or of maternity leave and discrimination in dismissals on the basis of marital status;

(b) To introduce maternity leave with pay or with comparable social benefits without loss of former employment, seniority or social allowances;

(c) To encourage the provision of the necessary supporting social services to enable parents to combine family obligations with work responsibilities and participation in public life, in particular through promoting the establishment and development of a network of child-care facilities;

(d) To provide special protection to women during pregnancy in types of work proved to be harmful to them.

3. Protective legislation relating to matters covered in this article shall be reviewed periodically in the light of scientific and technological knowledge and shall be revised, repealed or extended as necessary.

Article 12

1. States Parties shall take all appropriate measures to eliminate discrimination against women in the field of health care in order to ensure, on a basis of equality of men and women, access to health care services, including those related to family planning.

2. Notwithstanding the provisions of paragraph 1 of this article, States Parties shall ensure to women appropriate services in connection with pregnancy, confinement and the post-natal period, granting free services where necessary, as well as adequate nutrition during pregnancy and lactation.

Article 13

States Parties shall take all appropriate measures to eliminate discrimination against women in other areas of economic and social life in order to ensure, on a basis of equality of men and women, the same rights, in particular:

(a) The right to family benefits;

(b) The right to bank loans, mortgages and other forms of financial credit;

(c) The right to participate in recreational activities, sports and all aspects of cultural life.

Article 14

1. States Parties shall take into account the particular problems faced by rural women and the significant roles which rural women play in the economic survival of their families, including their work in the non-monetized sectors of the economy, and shall take all appropriate measures to ensure the application of the provisions of this Convention to women in rural areas.

2. States Parties shall take all appropriate measures to eliminate discrimination against women in rural areas in order to ensure, on a basis of equality of men and women, that they participate in and benefit from rural development and, in particular, shall ensure to such women the right:

(a) To participate in the elaboration and implementation of development planning at all levels;

(b) To have access to adequate health care facilities, including information, counselling and services in family planning;

(c) To benefit directly from social security programmes;

(d) To obtain all types of training and education, formal and non-formal, including that relating to functional literacy, as well as, inter alia, the benefit of all community and extension services, in order to increase their technical proficiency;

(e) To organize self-help groups and co-operatives in order to obtain equal access to economic opportunities through employment or self employment;

(f) To participate in all community activities;

(g) To have access to agricultural credit and loans, marketing facilities, appropriate technology and equal treatment in land and agrarian reform as well as in land resettlement schemes;

(h) To enjoy adequate living conditions, particularly in relation to housing, sanitation, electricity and water supply, transport and communications.

PART IV

Article 15

1. States Parties shall accord to women equality with men before the law.

2. States Parties shall accord to women, in civil matters, a legal capacity identical to that of men and the same opportunities to exercise that capacity. In particular, they shall give women equal rights to conclude contracts and to administer property and shall treat them equally in all stages of procedure in courts and tribunals.

3. States Parties agree that all contracts and all other private instruments of any kind with a legal effect which is directed at restricting the legal capacity of women shall be deemed null and void.

4. States Parties shall accord to men and women the same rights with regard to the law relating to the movement of persons and the freedom to choose their residence and domicile.

Article 16

1. States Parties shall take all appropriate measures to eliminate discrimination against women in all matters relating to marriage and family relations and in particular shall ensure, on a basis of equality of men and women:

(a) The same right to enter into marriage;

(b) The same right freely to choose a spouse and to enter into marriage only with their free and full consent;

(c) The same rights and responsibilities during marriage and at its dissolution;

(d) The same rights and responsibilities as parents, irrespective of their marital status, in matters relating to their children; in all cases the interests of the children shall be paramount;

(e) The same rights to decide freely and responsibly on the number and spacing of their children and to have access to the information, education and means to enable them to exercise these rights;

(f) The same rights and responsibilities with regard to guardianship, wardship, trusteeship and adoption of children, or similar institutions where these concepts exist in national legislation; in all cases the interests of the children shall be paramount;

(g) The same personal rights as husband and wife, including the right to choose a family name, a profession and an occupation;

(h) The same rights for both spouses in respect of the ownership, acquisition, management, administration, enjoyment and disposition of property, whether free of charge or for a valuable consideration.

2. The betrothal and the marriage of a child shall have no legal effect, and all necessary action, including legislation, shall be taken to specify a minimum age for marriage and to make the registration of marriages in an official registry compulsory.

PART V

Article 17

1. For the purpose of considering the progress made in the implementation of the present Convention, there shall be established a Committee on the Elimination of Discrimination against Women (hereinafter referred to as the Committee) consisting, at the time of entry into force of the Convention, of eighteen and, after ratification of or accession to the Convention by the thirty-fifth State Party, of twenty-three experts of high moral standing and competence in the field covered by the Convention. The experts shall be elected by States Parties from among their nationals and shall serve in their personal capacity, consideration being given to equitable geographical distribution and to the representation of the different forms of civilization as well as the principal legal systems.

2. The members of the Committee shall be elected by secret ballot from a list of persons nominated by States Parties. Each State Party may nominate one person from among its own nationals.

3. The initial election shall be held six months after the date of the entry into force of the present Convention. At least three months before the date of each election the Secretary-General of the United Nations shall address a letter to the States Parties inviting them to submit their nominations within two months. The Secretary-General shall prepare a list in alphabetical order of all persons thus nominated, indicating the States Parties which have nominated them, and shall submit it to the States Parties.

4. Elections of the members of the Committee shall be held at a meeting of States Parties convened by the Secretary-General at United Nations Headquarters. At that meeting, for which two thirds of the States Parties shall constitute a quorum, the persons elected to the Committee shall be those nominees who obtain the largest number of votes and an absolute majority of the votes of the representatives of States Parties present and voting.

5. The members of the Committee shall be elected for a term of four years. However, the terms of nine of the members elected at the first election shall expire at the end of two years; immediately after the first election the names of these nine members shall be chosen by lot by the Chairman of the Committee.

6. The election of the five additional members of the Committee shall be held in accordance with the provisions of paragraphs 2, 3 and 4 of this article, following the thirty-fifth ratification or accession. The terms of two of the additional members elected on this occasion shall expire at the end of two years, the names of these two members having been chosen by lot by the Chairman of the Committee.

7. For the filling of casual vacancies, the State Party whose expert has ceased to function as a member of the Committee shall appoint another expert from among its nationals, subject to the approval of the Committee.

8. The members of the Committee shall, with the approval of the General Assembly, receive emoluments from United Nations resources on such terms and conditions as the Assembly may decide, having regard to the importance of the Committee's responsibilities.

9. The Secretary-General of the United Nations shall provide the necessary staff and facilities for the effective performance of the functions of the Committee under the present Convention.

Article 18

1. States Parties undertake to submit to the Secretary-General of the United Nations, for consideration by the Committee, a report on the legislative, judicial, administrative or other measures which they have adopted to give effect to the provisions of the present Convention and on the progress made in this respect:

(a) Within one year after the entry into force for the State concerned; and

(b) Thereafter at least every four years and further whenever the Committee so requests.

2. Reports may indicate factors and difficulties affecting the degree of fulfilment of obligations under the present Convention.

Article 19

1. The Committee shall adopt its own rules of procedure.

2. The Committee shall elect its officers for a term of two years.

Article 20

1. The Committee shall normally meet for a period of not more than two weeks annually in order to consider the reports submitted in accordance with article 18 of the present Convention.

2. The meetings of the Committee shall normally be held at United Nations Headquarters or at any other convenient place as determined by the Committee.

Article 21

1. The Committee shall, through the Economic and Social Council, report annually to the General Assembly of the United Nations on its activities and may make suggestions and general recommendations based on the examination of reports and information received from the States Parties. Such suggestions and general recommendations shall be included in the report of the Committee together with comments, if any, from States Parties.

2. The Secretary-General shall transmit the reports of the Committee to the Commission on the Status of Women for its information.

Article 22

The specialized agencies shall be entitled to be represented at the consideration of the implementation of such provisions of the present Convention as fall within the scope of their activities. The Committee may invite the specialized agencies to submit reports on the implementation of the Convention in areas falling within the scope of their activities.

PART VI

Article 23

Nothing in this Convention shall affect any provisions that are more conducive to the achievement of equality between men and women which may be contained:
(a) In the legislation of a State Party; or
(b) In any other international convention, treaty or agreement in force for that State.

Article 24

States Parties undertake to adopt all necessary measures at the national level aimed at achieving the full realization of the rights recognized in the present Convention.

[Ed. Note: Articles 25 to 30, addressing signature, ratification, revision, entry into force, reservations, dispute resolution, and deposit of the Convention, are omitted.]

Optional Protocol to the Convention on the Elimination of Discrimination against Women

adopted October 6, 1999, G.A. Res. 54/4, Annex, U.N. GAOR, 54th Sess., Supp. No. 49, at 5, U.N. Doc. A/Res/54/4 (1999)

[Ed. Note: This Protocol was adopted by resolution of the United Nations General Assembly on October 6, 1999, and entered into force on December 22, 2000. As of March 2003, 49 nations were parties to the Protocol. The United States is neither a signatory nor a party to this Protocol.]

The States Parties to the present Protocol,

Noting that the Charter of the United Nations reaffirms faith in fundamental human rights, in the dignity and worth of the human person and in the equal rights of men and women,

Also noting that the Universal Declaration of Human Rights Resolution 217 A (III), proclaims that all human beings are born free and equal in dignity and rights and that everyone is entitled to all the rights and freedoms set forth therein, without distinction of any kind, including distinction based on sex,

Recalling that the International Covenants on Human Rights Resolution 2200 A (XXI), annex, and other international human rights instruments prohibit discrimination on the basis of sex,

Also recalling the Convention on the Elimination of All Forms of Discrimination against Women (the Convention), in which the States Parties thereto condemn discrimination against women in all its forms and agree to pursue by all appropriate means and without delay a policy of eliminating discrimination against women,

Reaffirming their determination to ensure the full and equal enjoyment by women of all human rights and fundamental freedoms and to take effective action to prevent violations of these rights and freedoms,

Have agreed as follows:

Article 1

A State Party to the present Protocol ("State Party") recognizes the competence of the Committee on the Elimination of Discrimination against Women ("the Committee") to receive and consider communications submitted in accordance with article 2.

Article 2

Communications may be submitted by or on behalf of individuals or groups of individuals, under the jurisdiction of a State Party, claiming to be victims of a violation of any of the rights set forth in the Convention by that State Party. Where a communication is submitted on behalf of individuals or groups of individuals, this shall be with their consent unless the author can justify acting on their behalf without such consent.

Article 3

Communications shall be in writing and shall not be anonymous. No communication shall be received by the Committee if it concerns a State Party to the Convention that is not a party to the present Protocol.

Article 4

1. The Committee shall not consider a communication unless it has ascertained that all available domestic remedies have been exhausted unless the application of such remedies is unreasonably prolonged or unlikely to bring effective relief.

2. The Committee shall declare a communication inadmissible where:

(a) The same matter has already been examined by the Committee or has been or is being examined under another procedure of international investigation or settlement;

(b) It is incompatible with the provisions of the Convention;

(c) It is manifestly ill-founded or not sufficiently substantiated;

(d) It is an abuse of the right to submit a communication;

(e) The facts that are the subject of the communication occurred prior to the entry into force of the present Protocol for the State Party concerned unless those facts continued after that date.

Article 5

1. At any time after the receipt of a communication and before a determination on the merits has been reached, the Committee may transmit to the State Party concerned for its urgent consideration a request that the State Party take such interim measures as may be necessary to avoid possible irreparable damage to the victim or victims of the alleged violation.

2. Where the Committee exercises its discretion under paragraph 1 of the present article, this does not imply a determination on admissibility or on the merits of the communication.

Article 6

1. Unless the Committee considers a communication inadmissible without reference to the State Party concerned, and provided that the individual or individuals consent to the disclosure of their identity to that State Party, the Committee shall bring any communication submitted to it under the present Protocol confidentially to the attention of the State Party concerned.

2. Within six months, the receiving State Party shall submit to the Committee written explanations or statements clarifying the matter and the remedy, if any, that may have been provided by that State Party.

Article 7

1. The Committee shall consider communications received under the present Protocol in the light of all information made available to it by or on behalf of individuals or groups of individuals and by the State Party concerned, provided that this information is transmitted to the parties concerned.

2. The Committee shall hold closed meetings when examining communications under the present Protocol.

3. After examining a communication, the Committee shall transmit its views on the communication, together with its recommendations, if any, to the parties concerned.

4. The State Party shall give due consideration to the views of the Committee, together with its recommendations, if any, and shall submit to the Committee, within six months, a written response, including information on any action taken in the light of the views and recommendations of the Committee.

5. The Committee may invite the State Party to submit further information about any measures the State Party has taken in response to its views or recommendations, if any, including as deemed appropriate by the Committee, in the State Party's subsequent reports under article 18 of the Convention.

Article 8

1. If the Committee receives reliable information indicating grave or systematic violations by a State Party of rights set forth in the Convention, the Committee shall invite that State Party to cooperate in the examination of the information and to this end to submit observations with regard to the information concerned.

2. Taking into account any observations that may have been submitted by the State Party concerned as well as any other reliable information available to it, the Committee

may designate one or more of its members to conduct an inquiry and to report urgently to the Committee. Where warranted and with the consent of the State Party, the inquiry may include a visit to its territory.

3. After examining the findings of such an inquiry, the Committee shall transmit these findings to the State Party concerned together with any comments and recommendations.

4. The State Party concerned shall, within six months of receiving the findings, comments and recommendations transmitted by the Committee, submit its observations to the Committee.

5. Such an inquiry shall be conducted confidentially and the cooperation of the State Party shall be sought at all stages of the proceedings.

Article 9

1. The Committee may invite the State Party concerned to include in its report under article 18 of the Convention details of any measures taken in response to an inquiry conducted under article 8 of the present Protocol.

2. The Committee may, if necessary, after the end of the period of six months referred to in article 8.4, invite the State Party concerned to inform it of the measures taken in response to such an inquiry.

Article 10

1. Each State Party may, at the time of signature or ratification of the present Protocol or accession thereto, declare that it does not recognize the competence of the Committee provided for in articles 8 and 9.

2. Any State Party having made a declaration in accordance with paragraph 1 of the present article may, at any time, withdraw this declaration by notification to the Secretary-General.

Article 11

A State Party shall take all appropriate steps to ensure that individuals under its jurisdiction are not subjected to ill treatment or intimidation as a consequence of communicating with the Committee pursuant to the present Protocol.

Article 12

The Committee shall include in its annual report under article 21 of the Convention a summary of its activities under the present Protocol.

Article 13

Each State Party undertakes to make widely known and to give publicity to the Convention and the present Protocol and to facilitate access to information about the views and recommendations of the Committee, in particular, on matters involving that State Party.

Article 14

The Committee shall develop its own rules of procedure to be followed when exercising the functions conferred on it by the present Protocol.

[Ed. Note: Articles 15 to 21, addressing the signature, ratification, entry into force, prohibition of reservations, amendment, denunciation, notifications, and deposit of the Convention, are omitted.]

Convention on the Recovery Abroad of Maintenance

June 20, 1956, 268 U.N.T.S. 3

[Ed. Note: This Convention entered into force on May 25, 1957. As of March 2003, 58 nations were party to the Convention. The United States is neither a signatory nor a party to this Convention.]

Preamble

Considering the urgency of solving the humanitarian problem resulting from the situation of persons in need dependent for their maintenance on persons abroad,

Considering that the prosecution or enforcement abroad of claims for maintenance gives rise to serious legal and practical difficulties, and

Determined to provide a means to solve such problems and to overcome such difficulties,

The Contracting Parties have agreed as follows:

Article 1 — Scope of the Convention

1. The purpose of this Convention is to facilitate the recovery of maintenance to which a person, hereinafter referred to as claimant, who is in the territory of one of the Contracting Parties, claims to be entitled from another person, hereinafter referred to as respondent, who is subject to the jurisdiction of another Contracting Party. This purpose shall be effected through the office of agencies which will hereinafter be referred to as Transmitting and Receiving Agencies.

2. The remedies provided for in this Convention are in addition to, and not in substitution for, any remedies available under municipal or international law.

Article 2 — Designation of agencies

1. Each Contracting Party shall, at the time when the instrument of ratification or accession is deposited, designate one or more judicial or administrative authorities which shall act in its territory as Transmitting Agencies.

2. Each Contracting Party shall, at the time when the instrument of ratification or accession is deposited, designate a public or private body which shall act in its territory as Receiving Agency.

3. Each Contracting Party shall promptly communicate to the Secretary-General of the United Nations the designations made under paragraphs 1 and 2 and any changes made in respect thereof.

4. Transmitting and Receiving Agencies may communicate directly with Transmitting and Receiving Agencies of other Contracting Parties.

Article 3 — Application to Transmitting Agency

1. Where a claimant is in the territory of one Contracting Party, hereinafter referred to as the State of the claimant, and the respondent is subject to the jurisdiction of another Contracting Party, hereinafter referred to as the State of the respondent, the claimant may make application to a Transmitting Agency in the State of the claimant for the recovery of maintenance from the respondent.

2. Each Contracting Party shall inform the Secretary-General as to the evidence normally required under the law of the State of the Receiving Agency for the proof of main-

tenance claims, of the manner in which such evidence should be submitted, and of other requirements to be complied with under such law.

3. The application shall be accompanied by all relevant documents, including, where necessary, a power of attorney authorizing the Receiving Agency to act, or to appoint some other person to act, on behalf of the claimant. It shall also be accompanied by a photograph of the claimant and, where available, a photograph of the respondent.

4. The Transmitting Agency shall take all reasonable steps to ensure that the requirements of the law of the State of the Receiving Agency are complied with; and, subject to the requirements of such law, the application shall include:

(a) the full name, address, date of birth, nationality, and occupation of the claimant, and the name and address of any legal representative of the claimant;

(b) the full name of the respondent, and, so far as known to the claimant, his addresses during the preceding five years, date of birth, nationality, and occupation;

(c) particulars of the grounds upon which the claim is based and of the relief sought, and any other relevant information such as the financial and family circumstances of the claimant and the respondent.

Article 4 — Transmission of documents

1. The Transmitting Agency shall transmit the documents to the Receiving Agency of the State of the respondent, unless satisfied that the application is not made in good faith.

2. Before transmitting such documents, the Transmitting Agency shall satisfy itself that they are regular as to form, in accordance with the law of the State of the claimant.

3. The Transmitting Agency may express to the Receiving Agency an opinion as to the merits of the case and may recommend that free legal aid and exemption from costs be given to the claimant.

Article 5 — Transmission of judgements and other judicial acts

1. The Transmitting Agency shall, at the request of the claimant, transmit, under the provisions of article 4, any order, final or provisional, and any other judicial act, obtained by the claimant for the payment of maintenance in a competent tribunal of any of the Contracting Parties, and, where necessary and possible, the record of the proceedings in which such order was made.

2. The orders and judicial acts referred to in the preceding paragraph may be transmitted in substitution for or in addition to the documents mentioned in article 3.

3. Proceedings under article 6 may include, in accordance with the law of the State of the respondent, exequatur or registration proceedings or an action based upon the act transmitted under paragraph 1.

Article 6 — Functions of the Receiving Agency

1. The Receiving Agency shall, subject always to the authority given by the claimant, take, on behalf of the claimant, all appropriate steps for the recovery of maintenance, including the settlement of the claim and, where necessary, the institution and prosecution of an action for maintenance and the execution of any order or other judicial act for the payment of maintenance.

2. The Receiving Agency shall keep the Transmitting Agency currently informed. If it is unable to act, it shall inform the Transmitting Agency of its reasons and return the documents.

3. Notwithstanding anything in this Convention, the law applicable in the determination of all questions arising in any such action or proceedings shall be the law of the State of the respondent, including its private international law.

Article 7 — Letters of request

If provision is made for letters of request in the laws of the two Contracting Parties concerned, the following rules shall apply:

(a) A tribunal hearing an action for maintenance may address letters of request for further evidence, documentary or otherwise, either to the competent tribunal of the other Contracting Party or to any other authority or institution designated by the other Contracting Party in whose territory the request is to be executed.

(b) In order that the parties may attend or be represented, the requested authority shall give notice of the date on which and the place at which the proceedings requested are to take place to the Receiving Agency and the Transmitting Agency concerned, and to the respondent.

(c) Letters of request shall be executed with all convenient speed; in the event of such letters of request not being executed within four months from the receipt of the letters by the requested authority, the reasons for such non-execution or for such delay shall be communicated to the requesting authority.

(d) The execution of letters of request shall not give rise to reimbursement of fees or costs of any kind whatsoever.

(e) Execution of letters of request may only be refused:

(1) If the authenticity of the letters is not established;

(2) If the Contracting Party in whose territory the letters are to be executed deems that its sovereignty or safety would be compromised thereby.

Article 8 — Variation of orders

The provisions of this Convention apply also to applications for the variation of maintenance orders.

Article 9 — Exemptions and facilities

1. In proceedings under this Convention, claimants shall be accorded equal treatment and the same exemptions in the payment of costs and charges as are given to residents or nationals of the State where the proceedings are pending.

2. Claimants shall not be required, because of their status as aliens or non-residents, to furnish any bond or make any payment or deposit as security for costs or otherwise.

3. Transmitting and Receiving Agencies shall not charge any fees in respect of services rendered under this Convention.

Article 10 — Transfer of funds

A Contracting Party, under whose law the transfer of funds abroad is restricted, shall accord the highest priority to the transfer of funds payable as maintenance or to cover expenses in respect of proceedings under this Convention.

Article 11 — Federal State clause

In the case of a Federal or non-unitary State, the following provisions shall apply:

(a) With respect to those articles of this Convention that come within the legislative jurisdiction of the federal legislative authority, the obligations of the Federal Government shall to this extent be the same as those of Parties which are not Federal States;

(b) With respect to those articles of this Convention that come within the legislative jurisdiction of constituent States, provinces or cantons which are not, under the constitutional system of the Federation, bound to take legislative action, the Federal Government shall bring such articles with a favourable recommendation to the notice of the appropriate authorities of States, provinces or cantons at the earliest possible moment;

(c) A Federal State Party to this Convention shall, at the request of any other Contracting Party transmitted through the Secretary-General, supply a statement of the law and practice of the Federation and its constituent units in regard to any particular provision of the Convention, showing the extent to which effect has been given to that provision by legislative or other action.

[Ed. Note: Articles 12 through 17, addressing territorial application, entry into force, denunciation, settlement of disputes, and reservations, are omitted.]

Article 18 — Reciprocity

A Contracting Party shall not be entitled to avail itself of this Convention against other Contracting Parties except to the extent that it is itself bound by the Convention.

[Ed. Note: Articles 19 to 21, addressing notification, revision, languages, and deposit of the Convention, are omitted.]

Convention on the Nationality of Married Women
Feb. 20, 1957, 309 U.N.T.S. 65

[Ed. Note: This Convention entered into force on August 11, 1958. As of March 2003, 71 nations were party to the Convention. The United States is neither a signatory nor a party to this Convention.]

The Contracting States,

Recognizing that conflicts in law and in practice with reference to nationality arise as a result of provisions concerning the loss or acquisition of nationality by women as a result of marriage, of its dissolution or of the change of nationality by the husband during marriage,

Recognizing that, in article 15 of the Universal Declaration of Human Rights, the General Assembly of the United Nations has proclaimed that "everyone has the right to a nationality" and that "no one shall be arbitrarily deprived of his nationality nor denied the right to change his nationality",

Desiring to co-operate with the United Nations in promoting universal respect for, and observance of, human rights and fundamental freedoms for all without distinction as to sex,

Hereby agree as hereinafter provided:

Article 1

Each Contracting State agrees that neither the celebration nor the dissolution of a marriage between one of its nationals and an alien, nor the change of nationality by the husband during marriage, shall automatically affect the nationality of the wife.

Article 2

Each Contracting State agrees that neither the voluntary acquisition of the nationality of another State nor the renunciation of its nationality by one of its nationals shall prevent the retention of its nationality by the wife of such national.

Article 3

1. Each Contracting State agrees that the alien wife of one of its nationals may, at her request, acquire the nationality of her husband through specially privileged naturalization procedures; the grant of such nationality may be subject to such limitations as may be imposed in the interests of national security or public policy.

2. Each Contracting State agrees that the present Convention shall not be construed as affecting any legislation or judicial practice by which the alien wife of one of its nationals may, at her request, acquire her husband's nationality as a matter of right.

[Ed. Note: Articles 4 to 12, addressing signature, ratification and accession, entry into force, application to territories, reservations, denunciation, dispute resolution, notification, and deposit, are omitted.]

Convention on Consent to Marriage, Minimum Age for Marriage and Registration of Marriages
Dec. 10, 1962, 521 U.N.T.S. 231

[Ed. Note: This Convention entered into force on December 9, 1964. As of March 2003, 50 nations were party to the Convention. Although the United States signed the Convention on December 10, 1962, it has never become a party to it by ratification or accession.]

The Contracting States,

Desiring, in conformity with the Charter of the United Nations, to promote universal respect for, and observance of, human rights and fundamental freedoms for all, without distinction as to race, sex, language or religion,

Recalling that article 16 of the Universal Declaration of Human Rights states that:

(1) "Men and women of full age, without any limitation due to race, nationality or religion, have the right to marry and to found a family. They are entitled to equal rights as to marriage, during marriage and at its dissolution."

(2) "Marriage shall be entered into only with the free and full consent of the intending spouses,"

Recalling further that the General Assembly of the United Nations declared, by resolution 843 (IX) of 17 December 1954, that certain customs, ancient laws and practices relating to marriage and the family were inconsistent with the principles set forth in the Charter of the United Nations and in the Universal Declaration of Human Rights,

Reaffirming that all States, including those which have or assume responsibility for the administration of Non-Self-Governing and Trust Territories until their achievement of independence, should take all appropriate measures with a view to abolishing such customs, ancient laws and practices by ensuring, inter alia, complete freedom in the choice of a spouse, eliminating completely child marriages and the betrothal of young girls before the age of puberty, establishing appropriate penalties where necessary and establishing a civil or other register in which all marriages will be recorded,

Hereby agree as hereinafter provided:

Article 1

1. No marriage shall be legally entered into without the full and free consent of both parties, such consent to be expressed by them in person after due publicity and in the presence of the authority competent to solemnize the marriage and of witnesses, as prescribed by law.

2. Notwithstanding anything in paragraph 1 above, it shall not be necessary for one of the parties to be present when the competent authority is satisfied that the circumstances are exceptional and that the party has, before a competent authority and in such manner as may be prescribed by law, expressed and not withdrawn consent.

Article 2

States Parties to the present Convention shall take legislative action to specify a minimum age for marriage. No marriage shall be legally entered into by any person under this age, except where a competent authority has granted a dispensation as to age, for serious reasons, in the interest of the intending spouses.

Article 3

All marriages shall be registered in an appropriate official register by the competent authority.

[Ed. Note: Articles 4 to 10, addressing signature, ratification, accession, entry into force, denunciation, dispute resolution, notification, and deposit of the Convention, are omitted.]

Recommendation on Consent to Marriage, Minimum Age for Marriage and Registration of Marriages
G.A. Res. 2018, U.N. GAOR, 20th Sess.,
Supp. No. 14, at 36, U.N. Doc. A/6014 (1965)

The General Assembly,

Recognizing that the family group should be strengthened because it is the basic unit of every society, and that men and women of full age have the right to marry and to found a family, that they are entitled to equal rights as to marriage and that marriage shall be entered into only with the free and full consent of the intending spouses, in accordance with the provisions of article 16 of the Universal Declaration of Human Rights,

Recalling its resolution 843 (IX) of 17 December 1954,

Recalling further article 2 of the Supplementary Convention on the Abolition of Slavery, the Slave Trade, and Institutions and Practices Similar to Slavery of 1956, which makes certain provisions concerning the age of marriage, consent to marriage and registration of marriages,

Recalling also that Article 13, paragraph 1 b, of the Charter of the United Nations provides that the General Assembly shall make recommendations for the purpose of assisting in the realization of human rights and fundamental freedoms for all without distinction as to race, sex, language or religion,

Recalling likewise that, under Article 64 of the Charter, the Economic and Social Council may make arrangements with the Members of the United Nations to obtain reports on the steps taken to give effect to its own recommendations and to recommendations on matters falling within its competence made by the General Assembly,

1. Recommends that, where not already provided by existing legislative or other measures, each Member State should take the necessary steps, in accordance with its constitutional processes and its traditional and religious practices, to adopt such legislative or other measures as may be appropriate to give effect to the following principles:

Principle I

(a) No marriage shall be legally entered into without the full and free consent of both parties, such consent to be expressed by them in person, after due publicity and in the presence of the authority competent to solemnize the marriage and of witnesses, as prescribed by law.

(b) Marriage by proxy shall be permitted only when the competent authorities are satisfied that each party has, before a competent authority and in such manner as may be prescribed by law, fully and freely expressed consent before witnesses and not withdrawn such consent.

Principle II

Member States shall take legislative action to specify a minimum age for marriage, which in any case shall not be less than fifteen years of age; no marriage shall be legally entered into by any person under this age, except where a competent authority has granted a dispensation as to age, for serious reasons, in the interest of the intending spouses.

Principle III

All marriages shall be registered in an appropriate official register by the competent authority.

2. Recommends that each Member State should bring the Recommendation on Consent to Marriage, Minimum Age for Marriage and Registration of Marriages contained in the present resolution before the authorities competent to enact legislation or to take other action at the earliest practicable moment and, if possible, no later than eighteen months after the adoption of the Recommendation;

3. Recommends that Member States should inform the Secretary-General, as soon as possible after the action referred to in paragraph 2 above, of the measures taken under the present Recommendation to bring it before the competent authority or authorities, with particulars regarding the authority or authorities considered as competent;

4. Recommends further that Member States should report to the Secretary-General at the end of three years, and thereafter at intervals of five years, on their law and practice with regard to the matters dealt with in the present Recommendation, showing the extent to which effect has been given or is proposed to be given to the provisions of the Recommendation and such modifications as have been found or may be found necessary in adapting or applying it;

5. Requests the Secretary-General to prepare for the Commission on the Status of Women a document containing the reports received from Governments concerning methods of implementing the three basic principles of the present Recommendation;

6. Invites the Commission on the Status of Women to examine the reports received from Member Status pursuant to the present Recommendation and to report thereon to the Economic and Social Council with such recommendations as it may deem fitting.

Convention for the Suppression of the Traffic in Persons and of the Exploitation of the Prostitution of Others and Final Protocol

March 21, 1950, 96 U.N.T.S. 271, 96 U.N.T.S. 316

[Ed. Note: The Convention entered into force on July 25, 1951. As of March 2003, 75 nations were party to this Convention and 34 nations were party to the Final Protocol. The United States is neither a signatory nor a party to either the Convention or the Final Protocol.

As the Introductory Section of the Convention indicates, the Convention for the Suppression of the Traffic in Persons and of the Exploitation of the Prostitution of Others ("Suppression Convention") was created to consolidate and update four instruments that were already in force at the time of its creation. Article 28 of the Suppression Convention provides that it will supersede these earlier agreements and conventions regarding relations between nations that are party to the Suppression Convention. It further provides that the earlier Agreement and Conventions will be terminated when all of the parties thereto have become parties to the Suppression Convention. As of March 2003, this had not yet occurred, and the Agreement and three Conventions listed in the Introductory Section of the Suppression Convention were all still in force. The United States is a party to only one of these, the International Agreement for the Suppression of White Slave Traffic, as amended by a Protocol of May 4, 1949. The United States is a party to the original agreement by accession, and became party to the Protocol of May 4, 1949 on August 14, 1950.]

Preamble

Whereas prostitution and the accompanying evil of the traffic in persons for the purpose of prostitution are incompatible with the dignity and worth of the human person and endanger the welfare of the individual, the family and the community,

Whereas, with respect to the suppression of the traffic in women and children, the following international instruments are in force:

(1) International Agreement of 18 May 1904 for the Suppression of the White Slave Traffic, as amended by the Protocol approved by the General Assembly of the United Nations on 3 December 1948,

(2) International Convention of 4 May 1910 for the Suppression of the White Slave Traffic, as amended by the above-mentioned Protocol,

(3) International Convention of 30 September 1921 for the Suppression of the Traffic in Women and Children, as amended by the Protocol approved by the General Assembly of the United Nations on 20 October 1947,

(4) International Convention of 11 October 1933 for the Suppression of the Traffic in Women of Full Age, as amended by the aforesaid Protocol,

Whereas the League of Nations in 1937 prepared a draft Convention extending the scope of the above-mentioned instruments, and

Whereas developments since 1937 make feasible the conclusion of a convention consolidating the above-mentioned instruments and embodying the substance of the 1937 draft Convention as well as desirable alterations therein:

Now therefore

The Contracting parties

Hereby agree as hereinafter provided:

Article 1

The Parties to the present Convention agree to punish any person who, to gratify the passions of another:

(1) Procures, entices or leads away, for purposes of prostitution, another person, even with the consent of that person;

(2) Exploits the prostitution of another person, even with the consent of that person.

Article 2

The Parties to the present Convention further agree to punish any person who:

(1) Keeps or manages, or knowingly finances or takes part in the financing of a brothel;

(2) Knowingly lets or rents a building or other place or any part thereof for the purpose of the prostitution of others.

Article 3

To the extent permitted by domestic law, attempts to commit any of the offences referred to in articles 1 and 2, and acts preparatory to the commission thereof, shall also be punished.

Article 4

To the extent permitted by domestic law, intentional participation in the acts referred to in articles 1 and 2 above shall also be punishable.

To the extent permitted by domestic law, acts of participation shall be treated as separate offences whenever this is necessary to prevent impunity.

Article 5

In cases where injured persons are entitled under domestic law to be parties to proceedings in respect of any of the offences referred to in the present Convention, aliens shall be so entitled upon the same terms as nationals.

Article 6

Each Party to the present Convention agrees to take all the necessary measures to repeal or abolish any existing law, regulation or administrative provision by virtue of which persons who engage in or are suspected of engaging in prostitution are subject either to special registration or to the possession of a special document or to any exceptional requirements for supervision or notification.

Article 7

Previous convictions pronounced in foreign States for offences referred to in the present Convention shall, to the extent permitted by domestic law, be taken into account for the purposes of:

(1) Establishing recidivism;

(2) Disqualifying the offender from the exercise of civil rights.

Article 8

The offences referred to in articles 1 and 2 of the present Convention shall be regarded as extraditable offences in any extradition treaty which has been or may hereafter be concluded between any of the Parties to this Convention.

The Parties to the present Convention which do not make extradition conditional on the existence of a treaty shall henceforward recognize the offences referred to in articles 1 and 2 of the present Convention as cases for extradition between themselves.

Extradition shall be granted in accordance with the law of the State to which the request is made.

Article 9

In States where the extradition of nationals is not permitted by law, nationals who have returned to their own State after the commission abroad of any of the offences referred to in articles 1 and 2 of the present Convention shall be prosecuted in and punished by the courts of their own State.

This provision shall not apply if, in a similar case between the Parties to the present Convention, the extradition of an alien cannot be granted.

Article 10

The provisions of article 9 shall not apply when the person charged with the offence has been tried in a foreign State and, if convicted, has served his sentence or had it remitted or reduced in conformity with the laws of that foreign State.

Article 11

Nothing in the present Convention shall be interpreted as determining the attitude of a Party towards the general question of the limits of criminal jurisdiction under international law.

Article 12

The present Convention does not affect the principle that the offences to which it refers shall in each State be defined, prosecuted and punished in conformity with its domestic law.

Article 13

The Parties to the present Convention shall be bound to execute letters of request relating to offences referred to in the Convention in accordance with their domestic law and practice.

The transmission of letters of request shall be effected:

(1) By direct communication between the judicial authorities; or

(2) By direct communication between the Ministers of Justice of the two States, or by direct communication from another competent authority of the State making the request to the Minister of Justice of the State to which the request is made; or

(3) Through the diplomatic or consular representative of the State making the request in the State to which the request is made; this representative shall send the letters of request direct to the competent judicial authority or to the authority indicated by the Government of the State to which the request is made, and shall receive direct from such authority the papers constituting the execution of the letters of request.

In cases 1 and 3 a copy of the letters of request shall always be sent to the superior authority of the State to which application is made.

Unless otherwise agreed, the letters of request shall be drawn up in the language of the authority making the request, provided always that the State to which the request is made may require a translation in its own language, certified correct by the authority making the request.

Each Party to the present Convention shall notify to each of the other Parties to the Convention the method or methods of transmission mentioned above which it will recognize for the letters of request of the latter State.

Until such notification is made by a State, its existing procedure in regard to letters of request shall remain in force.

Execution of letters of request shall not give rise to a claim for reimbursement of charges or expenses of any nature whatever other than expenses of experts.

Nothing in the present article shall be construed as an undertaking on the part of the Parties to the present Convention to adopt in criminal matters any form or methods of proof contrary to their own domestic laws.

Article 14

Each Party to the present Convention shall establish or maintain a service charged with the co-ordination and centralization of the results of the investigation of offences referred to in the present Convention.

Such services should compile all information calculated to facilitate the prevention and punishment of the offences referred to in the present Convention and should be in close contact with the corresponding services in other States.

Article 15

To the extent permitted by domestic law and to the extent to which the authorities responsible for the services referred to in article 14 may judge desirable, they shall furnish to the authorities responsible for the corresponding services in other States the following information:

(1) Particulars of any offence referred to in the present Convention or any attempt to commit such offence;

(2) Particulars of any search for and any prosecution, arrest, conviction, refusal of admission or expulsion of persons guilty of any of the offences referred to in the present Convention, the movements of such persons and any other useful information with regard to them. The information so furnished shall include descriptions of the offenders, their fingerprints, photographs, methods of operation, police records and records of conviction.

Article 16

The Parties to the present Convention agree to take or to encourage, through their public and private educational, health, social, economic and other related services, measures for the prevention of prostitution and for the rehabilitation and social adjustment of the victims of prostitution and of the offences referred to in the present Convention.

Article 17

The Parties to the present Convention undertake, in connection with immigration and emigration, to adopt or maintain such measures as are required, in terms of their obligations under the present Convention, to check the traffic in persons of either sex for the purpose of prostitution.

In particular they undertake:

(1) To make such regulations as are necessary for the protection of immigrants or emigrants, and in particular, women and children, both at the place of arrival and departure and while en route;

(2) To arrange for appropriate publicity warning the public of the dangers of the aforesaid traffic;

(3) To take appropriate measures to ensure supervision of railway stations, airports, seaports and en route, and of other public places, in order to prevent international traffic in persons for the purpose of prostitution;

(4) To take appropriate measures in order that the appropriate authorities be informed of the arrival of persons who appear, prima facie, to be the principals and accomplices in or victims of such traffic.

Article 18

The Parties to the present Convention undertake, in accordance with the conditions laid down by domestic law, to have declarations taken from aliens who are prostitutes, in order to establish their identity and civil status and to discover who has caused them to leave their State. The information obtained shall be communicated to the authorities of the State of origin of the said persons with a view to their eventual repatriation.

Article 19

The Parties to the present Convention undertake, in accordance with the conditions laid down by domestic law and without prejudice to prosecution or other action for violations thereunder and so far as possible:

(1) Pending the completion of arrangements for the repatriation of destitute victims of international traffic in persons for the purpose of prostitution, to make suitable provisions for their temporary care and maintenance;

(2) To repatriate persons referred to in article 18 who desire to be repatriated or who may be claimed by persons exercising authority over them or whose expulsion is ordered in conformity with the law. Repatriation shall take place only after agreement is reached with the State of destination as to identity and nationality as well as to the place and date of arrival at frontiers. Each Party to the present Convention shall facilitate the passage of such persons through its territory.

Where the persons referred to in the preceding paragraph cannot themselves repay the cost of repatriation and have neither spouse, relatives nor guardian to pay for them, the cost of repatriation as far as the nearest frontier or port of embarkation or airport in the direction of the State of origin shall be borne by the State where they are in residence, and the cost of the remainder of the journey shall be borne by the State of origin.

Article 20

The Parties to the present Convention shall, if they have not already done so, take the necessary measures for the supervision of employment agencies in order to prevent persons seeking employment, in particular women and children, from being exposed to the danger of prostitution.

Article 21

The Parties to the present Convention shall communicate to the Secretary-General of the United Nations such laws and regulations as have already been promulgated in their States, and thereafter annually such laws and regulations as may be promulgated, relating to the subjects of the present Convention, as well as all measures taken by them concerning the application of the Convention. The information received shall be published periodically by the Secretary-General and sent to all Members of the United Nations and to non-member States to which the present Convention is officially communicated in accordance with article 23.

[Ed. Note: Articles 22 to 26, addressing dispute resolution, signature, ratification, and accession, entry into force, denunciation, and notification regarding the Convention, are omitted.]

Article 27

Each Party to the present Convention undertakes to adopt, in accordance with its Constitution, the legislative or other measures necessary to ensure the application of the Convention.

Article 28

The provisions of the present Convention shall supersede in the relations between the Parties thereto the provisions of the international instruments referred to in sub-paragraphs 1, 2, 3 and 4 of the second paragraph of the Preamble, each of which shall be deemed to be terminated when all the Parties thereto shall have become Parties to the present Convention.

FINAL PROTOCOL

Nothing in the present Convention shall be deemed to prejudice any legislation which ensures, for the enforcement of the provisions for securing the suppression of the traffic in persons and of the exploitation of others for purposes of prostitution, stricter conditions than those provided by the present Convention.

The provisions of articles 23 to 26 inclusive of the Convention shall apply to the present Protocol.

Convention against Torture and Other Cruel, Inhuman or Degrading Treatment or Punishment

Dec. 10, 1984, S. Treaty Doc. No. 100-20, 1465 U.N.T.S. 85

[Ed. Note: The Convention entered into force on June 26, 1987. As of March 2003, 132 nations were party to the Convention. The United States became a party by ratification on October 21, 1994.

An Optional Protocol to this Convention was adopted by the U.N. General Assembly on December 18, 2002, by resolution A/RES/57/199, and opened for signature on February 4, 2003. If and when it enters into force, the Protocol will create a Sub-committee on Prevention of Torture of the Committee against Torture, which will establish a system of regular visits undertaken by independent and national bodies to locations where individuals are being held in detention, in order to prevent torture or other cruel or inhuman treatment or punishment. This Optional Protocol is not included in these materials.]

The States Parties to this Convention,

Considering that, in accordance with the principles proclaimed in the Charter of the United Nations, recognition of the equal and inalienable rights of all members of the human family is the foundation of freedom, justice and peace in the world,

Recognizing that those rights derive from the inherent dignity of the human person,

Considering the obligation of States under the Charter, in particular Article 55, to promote universal respect for, and observance of, human rights and fundamental freedoms,

Having regard to article 5 of the Universal Declaration of Human Rights and article 7 of the International Covenant on Civil and Political Rights, both of which provide that no one shall be subjected to torture or to cruel, inhuman or degrading treatment or punishment,

Having regard also to the Declaration on the Protection of All Persons from Being Subjected to Torture and Other Cruel, Inhuman or Degrading Treatment or Punishment, adopted by the General Assembly on 9 December 1975,

Desiring to make more effective the struggle against torture and other cruel, inhuman or degrading treatment or punishment throughout the world,

Have agreed as follows:

PART I

Article 1

1. For the purposes of this Convention, the term "torture" means any act by which severe pain or suffering, whether physical or mental, is intentionally inflicted on a person for such purposes as obtaining from him or a third person information or a confession, punishing him for an act he or a third person has committed or is suspected of having committed, or intimidating or coercing him or a third person, or for any reason based on discrimination of any kind, when such pain or suffering is inflicted by or at the instigation of or with the consent or acquiescence of a public official or other person acting in an official capacity. It does not include pain or suffering arising only from, inherent in or incidental to lawful sanctions.

2. This article is without prejudice to any international instrument or national legislation which does or may contain provisions of wider application.

Article 2

1. Each State Party shall take effective legislative, administrative, judicial or other measures to prevent acts of torture in any territory under its jurisdiction.

2. No exceptional circumstances whatsoever, whether a state of war or a threat of war, internal political instability or any other public emergency, may be invoked as a justification of torture.

3. An order from a superior officer or a public authority may not be invoked as a justification of torture.

Article 3 — General comment on its implementation

1. No State Party shall expel, return ("refouler") or extradite a person to another State where there are substantial grounds for believing that he would be in danger of being subjected to torture.

2. For the purpose of determining whether there are such grounds, the competent authorities shall take into account all relevant considerations including, where applicable, the existence in the State concerned of a consistent pattern of gross, flagrant or mass violations of human rights.

Article 4

1. Each State Party shall ensure that all acts of torture are offences under its criminal law. The same shall apply to an attempt to commit torture and to an act by any person which constitutes complicity or participation in torture.

2. Each State Party shall make these offences punishable by appropriate penalties which take into account their grave nature.

Article 5

1. Each State Party shall take such measures as may be necessary to establish its jurisdiction over the offences referred to in article 4 in the following cases:

(a) When the offences are committed in any territory under its jurisdiction or on board a ship or aircraft registered in that State;

(b) When the alleged offender is a national of that State;

(c) When the victim is a national of that State if that State considers it appropriate.

2. Each State Party shall likewise take such measures as may be necessary to establish its jurisdiction over such offences in cases where the alleged offender is present in any territory under its jurisdiction and it does not extradite him pursuant to article 8 to any of the States mentioned in paragraph 1 of this article.

3. This Convention does not exclude any criminal jurisdiction exercised in accordance with internal law.

Article 6

1. Upon being satisfied, after an examination of information available to it, that the circumstances so warrant, any State Party in whose territory a person alleged to have committed any offence referred to in article 4 is present shall take him into custody or take other legal measures to ensure his presence. The custody and other legal measures shall be as provided in the law of that State but may be continued only for such time as is necessary to enable any criminal or extradition proceedings to be instituted.

2. Such State shall immediately make a preliminary inquiry into the facts.

3. Any person in custody pursuant to paragraph 1 of this article shall be assisted in communicating immediately with the nearest appropriate representative of the State of which he is a national, or, if he is a stateless person, with the representative of the State where he usually resides.

4. When a State, pursuant to this article, has taken a person into custody, it shall immediately notify the States referred to in article 5, paragraph 1, of the fact that such person is in custody and of the circumstances which warrant his detention. The State which makes the preliminary inquiry contemplated in paragraph 2 of this article shall promptly report its findings to the said States and shall indicate whether it intends to exercise jurisdiction.

Article 7

1. The State Party in the territory under whose jurisdiction a person alleged to have committed any offence referred to in article 4 is found shall in the cases contemplated in article 5, if it does not extradite him, submit the case to its competent authorities for the purpose of prosecution.

2. These authorities shall take their decision in the same manner as in the case of any ordinary offence of a serious nature under the law of that State. In the cases referred to in article 5, paragraph 2, the standards of evidence required for prosecution and conviction shall in no way be less stringent than those which apply in the cases referred to in article 5, paragraph 1.

3. Any person regarding whom proceedings are brought in connection with any of the offences referred to in article 4 shall be guaranteed fair treatment at all stages of the proceedings.

Article 8

1. The offences referred to in article 4 shall be deemed to be included as extraditable offences in any extradition treaty existing between States Parties. States Parties undertake to include such offences as extraditable offences in every extradition treaty to be concluded between them.

2. If a State Party which makes extradition conditional on the existence of a treaty receives a request for extradition from another State Party with which it has no extradition treaty, it may consider this Convention as the legal basis for extradition in respect of such offences. Extradition shall be subject to the other conditions provided by the law of the requested State.

3. States Parties which do not make extradition conditional on the existence of a treaty shall recognize such offences as extraditable offences between themselves subject to the conditions provided by the law of the requested State.

4. Such offences shall be treated, for the purpose of extradition between States Parties, as if they had been committed not only in the place in which they occurred but also in the territories of the States required to establish their jurisdiction in accordance with article 5, paragraph 1.

Article 9

1. States Parties shall afford one another the greatest measure of assistance in connection with criminal proceedings brought in respect of any of the offences referred to in article 4, including the supply of all evidence at their disposal necessary for the proceedings.

2. States Parties shall carry out their obligations under paragraph 1 of this article in conformity with any treaties on mutual judicial assistance that may exist between them.

Article 10

1. Each State Party shall ensure that education and information regarding the prohibition against torture are fully included in the training of law enforcement personnel, civil or military, medical personnel, public officials and other persons who may be involved in the custody, interrogation or treatment of any individual subjected to any form of arrest, detention or imprisonment.

2. Each State Party shall include this prohibition in the rules or instructions issued in regard to the duties and functions of any such person.

Article 11

Each State Party shall keep under systematic review interrogation rules, instructions, methods and practices as well as arrangements for the custody and treatment of persons subjected to any form of arrest, detention or imprisonment in any territory under its jurisdiction, with a view to preventing any cases of torture.

Article 12

Each State Party shall ensure that its competent authorities proceed to a prompt and impartial investigation, wherever there is reasonable ground to believe that an act of torture has been committed in any territory under its jurisdiction.

Article 13

Each State Party shall ensure that any individual who alleges he has been subjected to torture in any territory under its jurisdiction has the right to complain to, and to have his case promptly and impartially examined by, its competent authorities. Steps shall be taken to ensure that the complainant and witnesses are protected against all ill-treatment or intimidation as a consequence of his complaint or any evidence given.

Article 14

1. Each State Party shall ensure in its legal system that the victim of an act of torture obtains redress and has an enforceable right to fair and adequate compensation, including the means for as full rehabilitation as possible. In the event of the death of the victim as a result of an act of torture, his dependants shall be entitled to compensation.

2. Nothing in this article shall affect any right of the victim or other persons to compensation which may exist under national law.

Article 15

Each State Party shall ensure that any statement which is established to have been made as a result of torture shall not be invoked as evidence in any proceedings, except against a person accused of torture as evidence that the statement was made.

Article 16

1. Each State Party shall undertake to prevent in any territory under its jurisdiction other acts of cruel, inhuman or degrading treatment or punishment which do not amount to torture as defined in article I, when such acts are committed by or at the instigation of or with the consent or acquiescence of a public official or other person acting in an official capacity. In particular, the obligations contained in articles 10, 11, 12 and 13 shall apply with the substitution for references to torture of references to other forms of cruel, inhuman or degrading treatment or punishment.

2. The provisions of this Convention are without prejudice to the provisions of any other international instrument or national law which prohibits cruel, inhuman or degrading treatment or punishment or which relates to extradition or expulsion.

PART II

Article 17

1. There shall be established a Committee against Torture (hereinafter referred to as the Committee) which shall carry out the functions hereinafter provided. The Committee shall consist of ten experts of high moral standing and recognized competence in the field of human rights, who shall serve in their personal capacity. The experts shall be elected by the States Parties, consideration being given to equitable geographical distribution and to the usefulness of the participation of some persons having legal experience.

2. The members of the Committee shall be elected by secret ballot from a list of persons nominated by States Parties. Each State Party may nominate one person from among its own nationals. States Parties shall bear in mind the usefulness of nominating persons who are also members of the Human Rights Committee established under the International Covenant on Civil and Political Rights and who are willing to serve on the Committee against Torture.

3. Elections of the members of the Committee shall be held at biennial meetings of States Parties convened by the Secretary-General of the United Nations. At those meetings, for which two thirds of the States Parties shall constitute a quorum, the persons elected to the Committee shall be those who obtain the largest number of votes and an absolute majority of the votes of the representatives of States Parties present and voting.

4. The initial election shall be held no later than six months after the date of the entry into force of this Convention. At least four months before the date of each election, the Secretary-General of the United Nations shall address a letter to the States Parties inviting them to submit their nominations within three months. The Secretary-

General shall prepare a list in alphabetical order of all persons thus nominated, indicating the States Parties which have nominated them, and shall submit it to the States Parties.

5. The members of the Committee shall be elected for a term of four years. They shall be eligible for re-election if renominated. However, the term of five of the members elected at the first election shall expire at the end of two years; immediately after the first election the names of these five members shall be chosen by lot by the chairman of the meeting referred to in paragraph 3 of this article.

6. If a member of the Committee dies or resigns or for any other cause can no longer perform his Committee duties, the State Party which nominated him shall appoint another expert from among its nationals to serve for the remainder of his term, subject to the approval of the majority of the States Parties. The approval shall be considered given unless half or more of the States Parties respond negatively within six weeks after having been informed by the Secretary-General of the United Nations of the proposed appointment.

7. States Parties shall be responsible for the expenses of the members of the Committee while they are in performance of Committee duties. [Ed. Note: This paragraph was added by amendment, endorsed by the General Assembly in Resolution 47/111 of 16 December 1992, which has been accepted by 23 nations, as of March 2003.]

Article 18

1. The Committee shall elect its officers for a term of two years. They may be re-elected.

2. The Committee shall establish its own rules of procedure, but these rules shall provide, inter alia, that:

(a) Six members shall constitute a quorum;

(b) Decisions of the Committee shall be made by a majority vote of the members present.

3. The Secretary-General of the United Nations shall provide the necessary staff and facilities for the effective performance of the functions of the Committee under this Convention.

4. The Secretary-General of the United Nations shall convene the initial meeting of the Committee. After its initial meeting, the Committee shall meet at such times as shall be provided in its rules of procedure.

5. The States Parties shall be responsible for expenses incurred in connection with the holding of meetings of the States Parties and of the Committee, including reimbursement to the United Nations for any expenses, such as the cost of staff and facilities, incurred by the United Nations pursuant to paragraph 3 of this article. [Ed. Note: This paragraph is an amendment endorsed by the General Assembly in Resolution 47/111 of 16 December 1992, which has been accepted by 23 nations as of March 2003.]

Article 19

1. The States Parties shall submit to the Committee, through the Secretary-General of the United Nations, reports on the measures they have taken to give effect to their undertakings under this Convention, within one year after the entry into force of the Convention for the State Party concerned. Thereafter the States Parties shall submit supplementary reports every four years on any new measures taken and such other reports as the Committee may request.

2. The Secretary-General of the United Nations shall transmit the reports to all States Parties.

3. Each report shall be considered by the Committee which may make such general comments on the report as it may consider appropriate and shall forward these to the State Party concerned. That State Party may respond with any observations it chooses to the Committee.

4. The Committee may, at its discretion, decide to include any comments made by it in accordance with paragraph 3 of this article, together with the observations thereon received from the State Party concerned, in its annual report made in accordance with article 24. If so requested by the State Party concerned, the Committee may also include a copy of the report submitted under paragraph 1 of this article.

Article 20

1. If the Committee receives reliable information which appears to it to contain well-founded indications that torture is being systematically practised in the territory of a State Party, the Committee shall invite that State Party to co-operate in the examination of the information and to this end to submit observations with regard to the information concerned.

2. Taking into account any observations which may have been submitted by the State Party concerned, as well as any other relevant information available to it, the Committee may, if it decides that this is warranted, designate one or more of its members to make a confidential inquiry and to report to the Committee urgently.

3. If an inquiry is made in accordance with paragraph 2 of this article, the Committee shall seek the co-operation of the State Party concerned. In agreement with that State Party, such an inquiry may include a visit to its territory.

4. After examining the findings of its member or members submitted in accordance with paragraph 2 of this article, the Commission shall transmit these findings to the State Party concerned together with any comments or suggestions which seem appropriate in view of the situation.

5. All the proceedings of the Committee referred to in paragraphs 1 to 4 of this article shall be confidential, and at all stages of the proceedings the co-operation of the State Party shall be sought. After such proceedings have been completed with regard to an inquiry made in accordance with paragraph 2, the Committee may, after consultations with the State Party concerned, decide to include a summary account of the results of the proceedings in its annual report made in accordance with article 24.

Article 21

1. A State Party to this Convention may at any time declare under this article that it recognizes the competence of the Committee to receive and consider communications to the effect that a State Party claims that another State Party is not fulfilling its obligations under this Convention. Such communications may be received and considered according to the procedures laid down in this article only if submitted by a State Party which has made a declaration recognizing in regard to itself the competence of the Committee. No communication shall be dealt with by the Committee under this article if it concerns a State Party which has not made such a declaration. Communications received under this article shall be dealt with in accordance with the following procedure;

(a) If a State Party considers that another State Party is not giving effect to the provisions of this Convention, it may, by written communication, bring the matter to the attention of that State Party. Within three months after the receipt of the communication the receiving State shall afford the State which sent the communication an explanation or any other statement in writing clarifying the matter, which should include, to the extent possible and pertinent, reference to domestic procedures and remedies taken, pending or available in the matter;

(b) If the matter is not adjusted to the satisfaction of both States Parties concerned within six months after the receipt by the receiving State of the initial communication, either State shall have the right to refer the matter to the Committee, by notice given to the Committee and to the other State;

(c) The Committee shall deal with a matter referred to it under this article only after it has ascertained that all domestic remedies have been invoked and exhausted in the matter, in conformity with the generally recognized principles of international law. This shall not be the rule where the application of the remedies is unreasonably prolonged or is unlikely to bring effective relief to the person who is the victim of the violation of this Convention;

(d) The Committee shall hold closed meetings when examining communications under this article;

(e) Subject to the provisions of subparagraph (c), the Committee shall make available its good offices to the States Parties concerned with a view to a friendly solution of the matter on the basis of respect for the obligations provided for in this Convention. For this purpose, the Committee may, when appropriate, set up an ad hoc conciliation commission;

(f) In any matter referred to it under this article, the Committee may call upon the States Parties concerned, referred to in subparagraph (b), to supply any relevant information;

(g) The States Parties concerned, referred to in subparagraph (b), shall have the right to be represented when the matter is being considered by the Committee and to make submissions orally and/or in writing;

(h) The Committee shall, within twelve months after the date of receipt of notice under subparagraph (b), submit a report:

(i) If a solution within the terms of subparagraph (e) is reached, the Committee shall confine its report to a brief statement of the facts and of the solution reached;

(ii) If a solution within the terms of subparagraph (e) is not reached, the Committee shall confine its report to a brief statement of the facts; the written submissions and record of the oral submissions made by the States Parties concerned shall be attached to the report.

In every matter, the report shall be communicated to the States Parties concerned.

2. The provisions of this article shall come into force when five States Parties to this Convention have made declarations under paragraph 1 of this article. Such declarations shall be deposited by the States Parties with the Secretary-General of the United Nations, who shall transmit copies thereof to the other States Parties. A declaration may be withdrawn at any time by notification to the Secretary-General. Such a withdrawal shall not prejudice the consideration of any matter which is the subject of a communication already transmitted under this article; no further communication by any State Party shall be received under this article after the notification of withdrawal of the declaration has been received by the Secretary-General, unless the State Party concerned has made a new declaration.

Article 22

1. A State Party to this Convention may at any time declare under this article that it recognizes the competence of the Committee to receive and consider communications from or on behalf of individuals subject to its jurisdiction who claim to be victims of a

violation by a State Party of the provisions of the Convention. No communication shall be received by the Committee if it concerns a State Party which has not made such a declaration.

2. The Committee shall consider inadmissible any communication under this article which is anonymous or which it considers to be an abuse of the right of submission of such communications or to be incompatible with the provisions of this Convention.

3. Subject to the provisions of paragraph 2, the Committee shall bring any communications submitted to it under this article to the attention of the State Party to this Convention which has made a declaration under paragraph 1 and is alleged to be violating any provisions of the Convention. Within six months, the receiving State shall submit to the Committee written explanations or statements clarifying the matter and the remedy, if any, that may have been taken by that State.

4. The Committee shall consider communications received under this article in the light of all information made available to it by or on behalf of the individual and by the State Party concerned.

5. The Committee shall not consider any communications from an individual under this article unless it has ascertained that:

(a) The same matter has not been, and is not being, examined under another procedure of international investigation or settlement;

(b) The individual has exhausted all available domestic remedies; this shall not be the rule where the application of the remedies is unreasonably prolonged or is unlikely to bring effective relief to the person who is the victim of the violation of this Convention.

6. The Committee shall hold closed meetings when examining communications under this article.

7. The Committee shall forward its views to the State Party concerned and to the individual.

8. The provisions of this article shall come into force when five States Parties to this Convention have made declarations under paragraph 1 of this article. Such declarations shall be deposited by the States Parties with the Secretary-General of the United Nations, who shall transmit copies thereof to the other States Parties. A declaration may be withdrawn at any time by notification to the Secretary-General. Such a withdrawal shall not prejudice the consideration of any matter which is the subject of a communication already transmitted under this article; no further communication by or on behalf of an individual shall be received under this article after the notification of withdrawal of the declaration has been received by the Secretary-General, unless the State Party has made a new declaration.

Article 23

The members of the Committee and of the ad hoc conciliation commissions which may be appointed under article 21, paragraph 1(e), shall be entitled to the facilities, privileges and immunities of experts on mission for the United Nations as laid down in the relevant sections of the Convention on the Privileges and Immunities of the United Nations.

Article 24

The Committee shall submit an annual report on its activities under this Convention to the States Parties and to the General Assembly of the United Nations.

Part III
[Ed. Note: Articles 25 to 27, addressing signature, ratification and accession, and entry into force, have been omitted.]

Article 28
1. Each State may, at the time of signature or ratification of this Convention or accession thereto, declare that it does not recognize the competence of the Committee provided for in article 20.

2. Any State Party having made a reservation in accordance with paragraph 1 of this article may, at any time, withdraw this reservation by notification to the Secretary-General of the United Nations.

[Ed. Note: Articles 29 to 33, addressing amendments, dispute resolution, denunciation, reservations, notification, and languages, are omitted.]

Declaration on the Elimination of Violence against Women
G.A. Res. 48/104, U.N. GAOR, 48th Sess., Supp. No. 49, at 217, U.N. Doc. A/RES/48/104 (1993)

The General Assembly,

Recognizing the urgent need for the universal application to women of the rights and principles with regard to equality, security, liberty, integrity and dignity of all human beings,

Noting that those rights and principles are enshrined in international instruments, including the Universal Declaration of Human Rights, the International Covenant on Civil and Political Rights, the International Covenant on Economic, Social and Cultural Rights, the Convention on the Elimination of All Forms of Discrimination against Women and the Convention against Torture and Other Cruel, Inhuman or Degrading Treatment or Punishment,

Recognizing that effective implementation of the Convention on the Elimination of All Forms of Discrimination against Women would contribute to the elimination of violence against women and that the Declaration on the Elimination of Violence against Women, set forth in the present resolution, will strengthen and complement that process,

Concerned that violence against women is an obstacle to the achievement of equality, development and peace, as recognized in the Nairobi Forward-looking Strategies for the Advancement of Women, in which a set of measures to combat violence against women was recommended, and to the full implementation of the Convention on the Elimination of All Forms of Discrimination against Women,

Affirming that violence against women constitutes a violation of the rights and fundamental freedoms of women and impairs or nullifies their enjoyment of those rights and freedoms, and concerned about the long-standing failure to protect and promote those rights and freedoms in the case of violence against women,

Recognizing that violence against women is a manifestation of historically unequal power relations between men and women, which have led to domination over and discrimination against women by men and to the prevention of the full advancement of women, and that violence against women is one of the crucial social mechanisms by which women are forced into a subordinate position compared with men,

Concerned that some groups of women, such as women belonging to minority groups, indigenous women, refugee women, migrant women, women living in rural or remote communities, destitute women, women in institutions or in detention, female children, women with disabilities, elderly women and women in situations of armed conflict, are especially vulnerable to violence,

Recalling the conclusion in paragraph 23 of the annex to Economic and Social Council resolution 1990/15 of 24 May 1990 that the recognition that violence against women in the family and society was pervasive and cut across lines of income, class and culture had to be matched by urgent and effective steps to eliminate its incidence,

Recalling also Economic and Social Council resolution 1991/18 of 30 May 1991, in which the Council recommended the development of a framework for an international instrument that would address explicitly the issue of violence against women,

Welcoming the role that women's movements are playing in drawing increasing attention to the nature, severity and magnitude of the problem of violence against women,

Alarmed that opportunities for women to achieve legal, social, political and economic equality in society are limited, inter alia, by continuing and endemic violence,

Convinced that in the light of the above there is a need for a clear and comprehensive definition of violence against women, a clear statement of the rights to be applied to ensure the elimination of violence against women in all its forms, a commitment by States in respect of their responsibilities, and a commitment by the international community at large to the elimination of violence against women,

Solemnly proclaims the following Declaration on the Elimination of Violence against Women and urges that every effort be made so that it becomes generally known and respected:

Article 1

For the purposes of this Declaration, the term "violence against women" means any act of gender-based violence that results in, or is likely to result in, physical, sexual or psychological harm or suffering to women, including threats of such acts, coercion or arbitrary deprivation of liberty, whether occurring in public or in private life.

Article 2

Violence against women shall be understood to encompass, but not be limited to, the following:

(a) Physical, sexual and psychological violence occurring in the family, including battering, sexual abuse of female children in the household, dowry-related violence, marital rape, female genital mutilation and other traditional practices harmful to women, non-spousal violence and violence related to exploitation;

(b) Physical, sexual and psychological violence occurring within the general community, including rape, sexual abuse, sexual harassment and intimidation at work, in educational institutions and elsewhere, trafficking in women and forced prostitution;

(c) Physical, sexual and psychological violence perpetrated or condoned by the State, wherever it occurs.

Article 3

Women are entitled to the equal enjoyment and protection of all human rights and fundamental freedoms in the political, economic, social, cultural, civil or any other field. These rights include, inter alia:

(a) The right to life;

(b) The right to equality;

(c) The right to liberty and security of person;

(d) The right to equal protection under the law;

(e) The right to be free from all forms of discrimination;

(f) The right to the highest standard attainable of physical and mental health;

(g) The right to just and favourable conditions of work;

(h) The right not to be subjected to torture, or other cruel, inhuman or degrading treatment or punishment.

Article 4

States should condemn violence against women and should not invoke any custom, tradition or religious consideration to avoid their obligations with respect to its elimination. States should pursue by all appropriate means and without delay a policy of eliminating violence against women and, to this end, should:

(a) Consider, where they have not yet done so, ratifying or acceding to the Convention on the Elimination of All Forms of Discrimination against Women or withdrawing reservations to that Convention;

(b) Refrain from engaging in violence against women;

(c) Exercise due diligence to prevent, investigate and, in accordance with national legislation, punish acts of violence against women, whether those acts are perpetrated by the State or by private persons;

(d) Develop penal, civil, labour and administrative sanctions in domestic legislation to punish and redress the wrongs caused to women who are subjected to violence; women who are subjected to violence should be provided with access to the mechanisms of justice and, as provided for by national legislation, to just and effective remedies for the harm that they have suffered; States should also inform women of their rights in seeking redress through such mechanisms;

(e) Consider the possibility of developing national plans of action to promote the protection of women against any form of violence, or to include provisions for that purpose in plans already existing, taking into account, as appropriate, such cooperation as can be provided by non-governmental organizations, particularly those concerned with the issue of violence against women;

(f) Develop, in a comprehensive way, preventive approaches and all those measures of a legal, political, administrative and cultural nature that promote the protection of women against any form of violence, and ensure that the re-victimization of women does not occur because of laws insensitive to gender considerations, enforcement practices or other interventions;

(g) Work to ensure, to the maximum extent feasible in the light of their available resources and, where needed, within the framework of international cooperation, that women subjected to violence and, where appropriate, their children have specialized assistance, such as rehabilitation, assistance in child care and maintenance, treatment, counselling, and health and social services, facilities and programmes, as well as support structures, and should take all other appropriate measures to promote their safety and physical and psychological rehabilitation;

(h) Include in government budgets adequate resources for their activities related to the elimination of violence against women;

(i) Take measures to ensure that law enforcement officers and public officials responsible for implementing policies to prevent, investigate and punish violence against women receive training to sensitize them to the needs of women;

(j) Adopt all appropriate measures, especially in the field of education, to modify the social and cultural patterns of conduct of men and women and to eliminate prejudices, customary practices and all other practices based on the idea of the inferiority or superiority of either of the sexes and on stereotyped roles for men and women;

(k) Promote research, collect data and compile statistics, especially concerning domestic violence, relating to the prevalence of different forms of violence against women and encourage research on the causes, nature, seriousness and consequences of violence against women and on the effectiveness of measures implemented to prevent and redress violence against women; those statistics and findings of the research will be made public;

(l) Adopt measures directed towards the elimination of violence against women who are especially vulnerable to violence;

(m) Include, in submitting reports as required under relevant human rights instruments of the United Nations, information pertaining to violence against women and measures taken to implement the present Declaration;

(n) Encourage the development of appropriate guidelines to assist in the implementation of the principles set forth in the present Declaration;

(o) Recognize the important role of the women's movement and non-governmental organizations world wide in raising awareness and alleviating the problem of violence against women;

(p) Facilitate and enhance the work of the women's movement and non-governmental organizations and cooperate with them at local, national and regional levels;

(q) Encourage intergovernmental regional organizations of which they are members to include the elimination of violence against women in their programmes, as appropriate.

Article 5

The organs and specialized agencies of the United Nations system should, within their respective fields of competence, contribute to the recognition and realization of the rights and the principles set forth in the present Declaration and, to this end, should, inter alia:

(a) Foster international and regional cooperation with a view to defining regional strategies for combating violence, exchanging experiences and financing programmes relating to the elimination of violence against women;

(b) Promote meetings and seminars with the aim of creating and raising awareness among all persons of the issue of the elimination of violence against women;

(c) Foster coordination and exchange within the United Nations system between human rights treaty bodies to address the issue of violence against women effectively;

(d) Include in analyses prepared by organizations and bodies of the United Nations system of social trends and problems, such as the periodic reports on the world social situation, examination of trends in violence against women;

(e) Encourage coordination between organizations and bodies of the United Nations system to incorporate the issue of violence against women into ongoing programmes, especially with reference to groups of women particularly vulnerable to violence;

(f) Promote the formulation of guidelines or manuals relating to violence against women, taking into account the measures referred to in the present Declaration;

(g) Consider the issue of the elimination of violence against women, as appropriate, in fulfilling their mandates with respect to the implementation of human rights instruments;

(h) Cooperate with non-governmental organizations in addressing the issue of violence against women.

Article 6

Nothing in the present Declaration shall affect any provision that is more conducive to the elimination of violence against women that may be contained in the legislation of a State or in any international convention, treaty or other instrument in force in a State.

Protocol to Prevent, Suppress and Punish Trafficking in Persons, Especially Women and Children, Supplementing the United Nations Convention against Transnational Organized Crime

Nov. 15, 2000, G.A. Res. 55/25, Annex II, U.N. GAOR, 55th Sess., Supp. No. 49 (Vol. 1), at 60, U.N. Doc. A/55/383; 40 I.L.M. 377 (2001)

[Ed. Note: This Protocol and the Convention against Transnational Organized Crime (which is not included in these materials) were adopted by the General Assembly of the United Nations on November 15, 2000 and opened for signature from December 12, 2000 to December 12, 2002. As of March 2003, 117 nations had signed and 25 nations were party to the Protocol, and it had not yet entered into force. The United States signed the Protocol on December 13, 2000, and is not yet a party.]

Preamble

The States Parties to this Protocol,

Declaring that effective action to prevent and combat trafficking in persons, especially women and children, requires a comprehensive international approach in the countries of origin, transit and destination that includes measures to prevent such trafficking, to punish the traffickers and to protect the victims of such trafficking, including by protecting their internationally recognized human rights,

Taking into account the fact that, despite the existence of a variety of international instruments containing rules and practical measures to combat the exploitation of persons, especially women and children, there is no universal instrument that addresses all aspects of trafficking in persons,

Concerned that, in the absence of such an instrument, persons who are vulnerable to trafficking will not be sufficiently protected,

Recalling General Assembly resolution 53/111 of 9 December 1998, in which the Assembly decided to establish an open-ended intergovernmental ad hoc committee for the purpose of elaborating a comprehensive international convention against transnational organized crime and of discussing the elaboration of, inter alia, an international instrument addressing trafficking in women and children,

Convinced that supplementing the United Nations Convention against Transnational Organized Crime with an international instrument for the prevention, suppression and punishment of trafficking in persons, especially women and children, will be useful in preventing and combating that crime,

Have agreed as follows:

I. General provisions

Article 1 — Relation with the United Nations Convention against Transnational Organized Crime

1. This Protocol supplements the United Nations Convention against Transnational Organized Crime. It shall be interpreted together with the Convention.

2. The provisions of the Convention shall apply, mutatis mutandis, to this Protocol unless otherwise provided herein.

3. The offences established in accordance with article 5 of this Protocol shall be regarded as offences established in accordance with the Convention.

Article 2 — Statement of purpose

The purposes of this Protocol are:

(a) To prevent and combat trafficking in persons, paying particular attention to women and children;

(b) To protect and assist the victims of such trafficking, with full respect for their human rights; and

(c) To promote cooperation among States Parties in order to meet those objectives.

Article 3 — Use of terms

For the purposes of this Protocol:

(a) "Trafficking in persons" shall mean the recruitment, transportation, transfer, harbouring or receipt of persons, by means of the threat or use of force or other forms of coercion, of abduction, of fraud, of deception, of the abuse of power or of a position of vulnerability or of the giving or receiving of payments or benefits to achieve the consent of a person having control over another person, for the purpose of exploitation. Exploitation shall include, at a minimum, the exploitation of the prostitution of others or other forms of sexual exploitation, forced labour or services, slavery or practices similar to slavery, servitude or the removal of organs;

(b) The consent of a victim of trafficking in persons to the intended exploitation set forth in subparagraph (a) of this article shall be irrelevant where any of the means set forth in subparagraph (a) have been used;

(c) The recruitment, transportation, transfer, harbouring or receipt of a child for the purpose of exploitation shall be considered "trafficking in persons" even if this does not involve any of the means set forth in subparagraph (a) of this article;

(d) "Child" shall mean any person under eighteen years of age.

Article 4 — Scope of application

This Protocol shall apply, except as otherwise stated herein, to the prevention, investigation and prosecution of the offences established in accordance with article 5 of this Protocol, where those offences are transnational in nature and involve an organized criminal group, as well as to the protection of victims of such offences.

Article 5 — Criminalization

1. Each State Party shall adopt such legislative and other measures as may be necessary to establish as criminal offences the conduct set forth in article 3 of this Protocol, when committed intentionally.

2. Each State Party shall also adopt such legislative and other measures as may be necessary to establish as criminal offences:

(a)Subject to the basic concepts of its legal system, attempting to commit an offence established in accordance with paragraph 1 of this article;

(b)Participating as an accomplice in an offence established in accordance with paragraph 1 of this article; and

(c)Organizing or directing other persons to commit an offence established in accordance with paragraph 1 of this article.

II. Protection of victims of trafficking in persons

Article 6 — Assistance to and protection of victims of trafficking in persons

1. In appropriate cases and to the extent possible under its domestic law, each State Party shall protect the privacy and identity of victims of trafficking in persons, including, inter alia, by making legal proceedings relating to such trafficking confidential.

2. Each State Party shall ensure that its domestic legal or administrative system contains measures that provide to victims of trafficking in persons, in appropriate cases:

(a)Information on relevant court and administrative proceedings;

(b)Assistance to enable their views and concerns to be presented and considered at appropriate stages of criminal proceedings against offenders, in a manner not prejudicial to the rights of the defense.

3.Each State Party shall consider implementing measures to provide for the physical, psychological and social recovery of victims of trafficking in persons, including, in appropriate cases, in cooperation with non-governmental organizations, other relevant organizations and other elements of civil society, and, in particular, the provision of:

(a)Appropriate housing;

(b)Counseling and information, in particular as regards their legal rights, in a language that the victims of trafficking in persons can understand;

(c)Medical, psychological and material assistance; and

(d)Employment, educational and training opportunities.

4. Each State Party shall take into account, in applying the provisions of this article, the age, gender and special needs of victims of trafficking in persons, in particular the special needs of children, including appropriate housing, education and care.

5. Each State Party shall endeavour to provide for the physical safety of victims of trafficking in persons while they are within its territory.

6. Each State Party shall ensure that its domestic legal system contains measures that offer victims of trafficking in persons the possibility of obtaining compensation for damage suffered.

Article 7 — Status of victims of trafficking in persons in receiving States

1. In addition to taking measures pursuant to article 6 of this Protocol, each State Party shall consider adopting legislative or other appropriate measures that permit victims of trafficking in persons to remain in its territory, temporarily or permanently, in appropriate cases.

2. In implementing the provision contained in paragraph 1 of this article, each State Party shall give appropriate consideration to humanitarian and compassionate factors.

Article 8 — Repatriation of victims of trafficking in persons

1. The State Party of which a victim of trafficking in persons is a national or in which the person had the right of permanent residence at the time of entry into the

territory of the receiving State Party shall facilitate and accept, with due regard for the safety of that person, the return of that person without undue or unreasonable delay.

2. When a State Party returns a victim of trafficking in persons to a State Party of which that person is a national or in which he or she had, at the time of entry into the territory of the receiving State Party, the right of permanent residence, such return shall be with due regard for the safety of that person and for the status of any legal proceedings related to the fact that the person is a victim of trafficking and shall preferably be voluntary.

3. At the request of a receiving State Party, a requested State Party shall, without undue or unreasonable delay, verify whether a person who is a victim of trafficking in persons is its national or had the right of permanent residence in its territory at the time of entry into the territory of the receiving State Party.

4. In order to facilitate the return of a victim of trafficking in persons who is without proper documentation, the State Party of which that person is a national or in which he or she had the right of permanent residence at the time of entry into the territory of the receiving State Party shall agree to issue, at the request of the receiving State Party, such travel documents or other authorization as may be necessary to enable the person to travel to and re-enter its territory.

5. This article shall be without prejudice to any right afforded to victims of trafficking in persons by any domestic law of the receiving State Party.

6. This article shall be without prejudice to any applicable bilateral or multilateral agreement or arrangement that governs, in whole or in part, the return of victims of trafficking in persons.

III. Prevention, cooperation and other measures

Article 9 — Prevention of trafficking in persons
1. States Parties shall establish comprehensive policies, programmes and other measures:

(a) To prevent and combat trafficking in persons; and

(b) To protect victims of trafficking in persons, especially women and children, from revictimization.

2. States Parties shall endeavour to undertake measures such as research, information and mass media campaigns and social and economic initiatives to prevent and combat trafficking in persons.

3. Policies, programmes and other measures established in accordance with this article shall, as appropriate, include cooperation with non-governmental organizations, other relevant organizations and other elements of civil society.

4. States Parties shall take or strengthen measures, including through bilateral or multilateral cooperation, to alleviate the factors that make persons, especially women and children, vulnerable to trafficking, such as poverty, underdevelopment and lack of equal opportunity.

5. States Parties shall adopt or strengthen legislative or other measures, such as educational, social or cultural measures, including through bilateral and multilateral cooperation, to discourage the demand that fosters all forms of exploitation of persons, especially women and children, that leads to trafficking.

Article 10 — Information exchange and training

1. Law enforcement, immigration or other relevant authorities of States Parties shall, as appropriate, cooperate with one another by exchanging information, in accordance with their domestic law, to enable them to determine:

(a) Whether individuals crossing or attempting to cross an international border with travel documents belonging to other persons or without travel documents are perpetrators or victims of trafficking in persons;

(b) The types of travel document that individuals have used or attempted to use to cross an international border for the purpose of trafficking in persons; and

(c) The means and methods used by organized criminal groups for the purpose of trafficking in persons, including the recruitment and transportation of victims, routes and links between and among individuals and groups engaged in such trafficking, and possible measures for detecting them.

2. States Parties shall provide or strengthen training for law enforcement, immigration and other relevant officials in the prevention of trafficking in persons. The training should focus on methods used in preventing such trafficking, prosecuting the traffickers and protecting the rights of the victims, including protecting the victims from the traffickers. The training should also take into account the need to consider human rights and child- and gender-sensitive issues and it should encourage cooperation with non-governmental organizations, other relevant organizations and other elements of civil society.

3. A State Party that receives information shall comply with any request by the State Party that transmitted the information that places restrictions on its use.

Article 11 — Border measures

1. Without prejudice to international commitments in relation to the free movement of people, States Parties shall strengthen, to the extent possible, such border controls as may be necessary to prevent and detect trafficking in persons.

2. Each State Party shall adopt legislative or other appropriate measures to prevent, to the extent possible, means of transport operated by commercial carriers from being used in the commission of offences established in accordance with article 5 of this Protocol.

3. Where appropriate, and without prejudice to applicable international conventions, such measures shall include establishing the obligation of commercial carriers, including any transportation company or the owner or operator of any means of transport, to ascertain that all passengers are in possession of the travel documents required for entry into the receiving State.

4. Each State Party shall take the necessary measures, in accordance with its domestic law, to provide for sanctions in cases of violation of the obligation set forth in paragraph 3 of this article.

5. Each State Party shall consider taking measures that permit, in accordance with its domestic law, the denial of entry or revocation of visas of persons implicated in the commission of offences established in accordance with this Protocol.

6. Without prejudice to article 27 of the Convention, States Parties shall consider strengthening cooperation among border control agencies by, inter alia, establishing and maintaining direct channels of communication.

Article 12 — Security and control of documents

Each State Party shall take such measures as may be necessary, within available means:

(a)To ensure that travel or identity documents issued by it are of such quality that they cannot easily be misused and cannot readily be falsified or unlawfully altered, replicated or issued; and

(b)To ensure the integrity and security of travel or identity documents issued by or on behalf of the State Party and to prevent their unlawful creation, issuance and use.

Article 13—Legitimacy and validity of documents

At the request of another State Party, a State Party shall, in accordance with its domestic law, verify within a reasonable time the legitimacy and validity of travel or identity documents issued or purported to have been issued in its name and suspected of being used for trafficking in persons.

IV. Final provisions

Article 14—Saving clause

1. Nothing in this Protocol shall affect the rights, obligations and responsibilities of States and individuals under international law, including international humanitarian law and international human rights law and, in particular, where applicable, the 1951 Convention and the 1967 Protocol relating to the Status of Refugees and the principle of non-refoulement as contained therein.

2. The measures set forth in this Protocol shall be interpreted and applied in a way that is not discriminatory to persons on the ground that they are victims of trafficking in persons. The interpretation and application of those measures shall be consistent with internationally recognized principles of non-discrimination.

[Ed. Note: Articles 15 to 20, addressing dispute resolution, signature, ratification and accession, entry into force, amendment, denunciation, depositary and languages, are omitted.]

General Recommendation No. 19, Violence against Women

U.N. CEDAW Comm., 11th Sess., U.N. Doc. A/47/38 (1992)
available at http://www.un.org/womenwatch/daw/cedaw/recomm.htm

Background

1. Gender-based violence is a form of discrimination that seriously inhibits women's ability to enjoy rights and freedoms on a basis of equality with men.

2. In 1989, the Committee recommended that States should include in their reports information on violence and on measures introduced to deal with it (General recommendation 12, eighth session).

3. At its tenth session in 1991, it was decided to allocate part of the eleventh session to a discussion and study on article 6 and other articles of the Convention relating to violence towards women and the sexual harassment and exploitation of women. That subject was chosen in anticipation of the 1993 World Conference on Human Rights, convened by the General Assembly by its resolution 45/155 of 18 December 1990.

4. The Committee concluded that not all the reports of States parties adequately reflected the close connection between discrimination against women, gender-based vio-

lence, and violations of human rights and fundamental freedoms. The full implementation of the Convention required States to take positive measures to eliminate all forms of violence against women.

5. The Committee suggested to States parties that in reviewing their laws and policies, and in reporting under the Convention, they should have regard to the following comments of the Committee concerning gender-based violence.

General comments

6. The Convention in article 1 defines discrimination against women. The definition of discrimination includes gender-based violence, that is, violence that is directed against a woman because she is a woman or that affects women disproportionately. It includes acts that inflict physical, mental or sexual harm or suffering, threats of such acts, coercion and other deprivations of liberty. Gender-based violence may breach specific provisions of the Convention, regardless of whether those provisions expressly mention violence.

7. Gender-based violence, which impairs or nullifies the enjoyment by women of human rights and fundamental freedoms under general international law or under human rights conventions, is discrimination within the meaning of article 1 of the Convention. These rights and freedoms include:

(a) The right to life;

(b) The right not to be subject to torture or to cruel, inhuman or degrading treatment or punishment;

(c) The right to equal protection according to humanitarian norms in time of international or internal armed conflict;

(d) The right to liberty and security of person;

(e) The right to equal protection under the law;

(f) The right to equality in the family;

(g) The right to the highest standard attainable of physical and mental health;

(h) The right to just and favourable conditions of work.

8. The Convention applies to violence perpetrated by public authorities. Such acts of violence may breach that State's obligations under general international human rights law and under other conventions, in addition to breaching this Convention.

9. It is emphasized, however, that discrimination under the Convention is not restricted to action by or on behalf of Governments (see articles 2(e), 2(f) and 5). For example, under article 2(e) the Convention calls on States parties to take all appropriate measures to eliminate discrimination against women by any person, organization or enterprise. Under general international law and specific human rights covenants, States may also be responsible for private acts if they fail to act with due diligence to prevent violations of rights or to investigate and punish acts of violence, and for providing compensation.

Comments on specific articles of the Convention

Articles 2 and 3

10. Articles 2 and 3 establish a comprehensive obligation to eliminate discrimination in all its forms in addition to the specific obligations under articles 5–16.

Articles 2(f), 5 and 10(c)

11. Traditional attitudes by which women are regarded as subordinate to men or as having stereotyped roles perpetuate widespread practices involving violence or coer-

cion, such as family violence and abuse, forced marriage, dowry deaths, acid attacks and female circumcision. Such prejudices and practices may justify gender-based violence as a form of protection or control of women. The effect of such violence on the physical and mental integrity of women is to deprive them of the equal enjoyment, exercise and knowledge of human rights and fundamental freedoms. While this comment addresses mainly actual or threatened violence the underlying consequences of these forms of gender-based violence help to maintain women in subordinate roles and contribute to their low level of political participation and to their lower level of education, skills and work opportunities.

12. These attitudes also contribute to the propagation of pornography and the depiction and other commercial exploitation of women as sexual objects, rather than as individuals. This in turn contributes to gender-based violence.

Article 6

13. States parties are required by article 6 to take measures to suppress all forms of traffic in women and exploitation of the prostitution of women.

14. Poverty and unemployment increase opportunities for trafficking in women. In addition to established forms of trafficking there are new forms of sexual exploitation, such as sex tourism, the recruitment of domestic labour from developing countries to work in developed countries and organized marriages between women from developing countries and foreign nationals. These practices are incompatible with the equal enjoyment of rights by women and with respect for their rights and dignity. They put women at special risk of violence and abuse.

15. Poverty and unemployment force many women, including young girls, into prostitution. Prostitutes are especially vulnerable to violence because their status, which may be unlawful, tends to marginalize them. They need the equal protection of laws against rape and other forms of violence.

16. Wars, armed conflicts and the occupation of territories often lead to increased prostitution, trafficking in women and sexual assault of women, which require specific protective and punitive measures.

Article 11

17. Equality in employment can be seriously impaired when women are subjected to gender-specific violence, such as sexual harassment in the workplace.

18. Sexual harassment includes such unwelcome sexually determined behaviour as physical contact and advances, sexually coloured remarks, showing pornography and sexual demand, whether by words or actions. Such conduct can be humiliating and may constitute a health and safety problem; it is discriminatory when the woman has reasonable grounds to believe that her objection would disadvantage her in connection with her employment, including recruitment or promotion, or when it creates a hostile working environment.

Article 12

19. States parties are required by article 12 to take measures to ensure equal access to health care. Violence against women puts their health and lives at risk.

20. In some States there are traditional practices perpetuated by culture and tradition that are harmful to the health of women and children. These practices include dietary restrictions for pregnant women, preference for male children and female circumcision or genital mutilation.

Article 14

21. Rural women are at risk of gender-based violence because [sic] traditional attitudes regarding the subordinate role of women that persist in many rural communities. Girls from rural communities are at special risk of violence and sexual exploitation when they leave the rural community to seek employment in towns.

Article 16 (and Article 5)

22. Compulsory sterilization or abortion adversely affects women's physical and mental health, and infringes the right of women to decide on the number and spacing of their children.

23. Family violence is one of the most insidious forms of violence against women. It is prevalent in all societies. Within family relationships women of all ages are subjected to violence of all kinds, including battering, rape, other forms of sexual assault, mental and other forms of violence, which are perpetuated by traditional attitudes. Lack of economic independence forces many women to stay in violent relationships. The abrogation of their family responsibilities by men can be a form of violence, and coercion. These forms of violence put women's health at risk and impair their ability to participate in family life and public life on a basis of equality.

Specific recommendation

24. In light of these comments, the Committee on the Elimination of Discrimination against Women recommends:

(a) States parties should take appropriate and effective measures to overcome all forms of gender-based violence, whether by public or private act;

(b) States parties should ensure that laws against family violence and abuse, rape, sexual assault and other gender-based violence give adequate protection to all women, and respect their integrity and dignity. Appropriate protective and support services should be provided for victims. Gender-sensitive training of judicial and law enforcement officers and other public officials is essential for the effective implementation of the Convention;

(c) States parties should encourage the compilation of statistics and research on the extent, causes and effects of violence, and on the effectiveness of measures to prevent and deal with violence;

(d) Effective measures should be taken to ensure that the media respect and promote respect for women;

(e) States parties in their reports should identify the nature and extent of attitudes, customs and practices that perpetuate violence against women and the kinds of violence that result. They should report on the measures that they have undertaken to overcome violence and the effect of those measures;

(f) Effective measures should be taken to overcome these attitudes and practices. States should introduce education and public information programmes to help eliminate prejudices that hinder women's equality (recommendation No. 3, 1987);

(g) Specific preventive and punitive measures are necessary to overcome trafficking and sexual exploitation;

(h) States parties in their reports should describe the extent of all these problems and the measures, including penal provisions, preventive and rehabilitation measures that have been taken to protect women engaged in prostitution or subject to trafficking and other forms of sexual exploitation. The effectiveness of these measures should also be described;

(i) Effective complaints procedures and remedies, including compensation, should be provided;

(j) States parties should include in their reports information on sexual harassment, and on measures to protect women from sexual harassment and other forms of violence of [sic] coercion in the workplace;

(k) States parties should establish or support services for victims of family violence, rape, sexual assault and other forms of gender-based violence, including refuges, specially trained health workers, rehabilitation and counselling;

(l) States parties should take measures to overcome such practices and should take account of the Committee's recommendation on female circumcision (recommendation No. 14) in reporting on health issues;

(m) States parties should ensure that measures are taken to prevent coercion in regard to fertility and reproduction, and to ensure that women are not forced to seek unsafe medical procedures such as illegal abortion because of lack of appropriate services in regard to fertility control;

(n) States parties in their reports should state the extent of these problems and should indicate the measures that have been taken and their effect;

(o) States parties should ensure that services for victims of violence are accessible to rural women and that where necessary special services are provided to isolated communities;

(p) Measures to protect them from violence should include training and employment opportunities and the monitoring of the employment conditions of domestic workers;

(q) States parties should report on the risks to rural women, the extent and nature of violence and abuse to which they are subject, their need for and access to support and other services and the effectiveness of measures to overcome violence;

(r) Measures that are necessary to overcome family violence should include:

(i) Criminal penalties where necessary and civil remedies in cases of domestic violence;

(ii) Legislation to remove the defence of honour in regard to the assault or murder of a female family member;

(iii) Services to ensure the safety and security of victims of family violence, including refuges, counselling and rehabilitation programmes;

(iv) Rehabilitation programmes for perpetrators of domestic violence;

(v) Support services for families where incest or sexual abuse has occurred;

(s) States parties should report on the extent of domestic violence and sexual abuse, and on the preventive, punitive and remedial measures that have been taken;

(t) States parties should take all legal and other measures that are necessary to provide effective protection of women against gender-based violence, including, inter alia:

(i) Effective legal measures, including penal sanctions, civil remedies and compensatory provisions to protect women against all kinds of violence, including inter alia violence and abuse in the family, sexual assault and sexual harassment in the workplace;

(ii) Preventive measures, including public information and education programmes to change attitudes concerning the roles and status of men and women;

(iii) Protective measures, including refuges, counselling, rehabilitation and support services for women who are the victims of violence or who are at risk of violence;

(u) States parties should report on all forms of gender-based violence, and such reports should include all available data on the incidence of each form of violence and on the effects of such violence on the women who are victims;

(v) That the reports of States parties should include information on the legal, preventive and protective measures that have been taken to overcome violence against women, and on the effectiveness of such measures.

D. Children

Declaration of the Rights of the Child, "Declaration of Geneva"

League of Nations O.J. Spec Supp. 28, at 66 (1924)

By the present Declaration of the Rights of the Child, commonly known as the Declaration of Geneva, men and women of all nations, recognising that mankind owes to the child the best that it has to give, declare and accept it as their duty that, beyond and above all considerations of race, nationality, or creed:

I. The child must be given the means requisite for its normal development, both materially and spiritually;

II. The child that is hungry must be fed, the child that is sick must be helped: the child that is backward must be helped; the delinquent child must be reclaimed; and the orphan and the waif must be sheltered and succoured;

III. The child must be the first to receive relief in times of distress;

IV. The child must be put in a position to earn a livelihood and must be protected against every form of exploitation;

V. The child must be brought up in the consciousness that its talents must be devoted to the service of its fellow men.

Declaration of the Rights of the Child

G.A. Res. 1386, U.N. GAOR, 14th Sess., Supp. No. 16, at 19, U.N. Doc. A/4354 (1959)

Preamble

Whereas the peoples of the United Nations have, in the Charter, reaffirmed their faith in fundamental human rights and in the dignity and worth of the human person, and have determined to promote social progress and better standards of life in larger freedom,

Whereas the United Nations has, in the Universal Declaration of Human Rights, proclaimed that everyone is entitled to all the rights and freedoms set forth therein, without distinction of any kind, such as race, colour, sex, language, religion, political or other opinion, national or social origin, property, birth or other status,

Whereas the child, by reason of his physical and mental immaturity, needs special safeguards and care, including appropriate legal protection, before as well as after birth,

Whereas the need for such special safeguards has been stated in the Geneva Declaration of the Rights of the Child of 1924, and recognized in the Universal Declaration of Human Rights and in the statutes of specialized agencies and international organizations concerned with the welfare of children,

Whereas mankind owes to the child the best it has to give,

Now therefore,

The General Assembly

Proclaims this Declaration of the Rights of the Child to the end that he may have a happy childhood and enjoy for his own good and for the good of society the rights and freedoms herein set forth, and calls upon parents, upon men and women as individuals, and upon voluntary organizations, local authorities and national Governments to recognize these rights and strive for their observance by legislative and other measures progressively taken in accordance with the following principles:

Principle I

The child shall enjoy all the rights set forth in this Declaration. Every child, without any exception whatsoever, shall be entitled to these rights, without distinction or discrimination on account of race, colour, sex, language, religion, political or other opinion, national or social origin, property, birth or other status, whether of himself or of his family.

Principle 2

The child shall enjoy special protection, and shall be given opportunities and facilities, by law and by other means, to enable him to develop physically, mentally, morally, spiritually and socially in a healthy and normal manner and in conditions of freedom and dignity. In the enactment of laws for this purpose, the best interests of the child shall be the paramount consideration.

Principle 3

The child shall be entitled from his birth to a name and a nationality.

Principle 4

The child shall enjoy the benefits of social security. He shall be entitled to grow and develop in health; to this end, special care and protection shall be provided both to him and to his mother, including adequate pre-natal and post-natal care. The child shall have the right to adequate nutrition, housing, recreation and medical services.

Principle 5

The child who is physically, mentally or socially handicapped shall be given the special treatment, education and care required by his particular condition.

Principle 6

The child, for the full and harmonious development of his personality, needs love and understanding. He shall, wherever possible, grow up in the care and under the responsibility of his parents, and, in any case, in an atmosphere of affection and of moral and material security; a child of tender years shall not, save in exceptional circumstances, be separated from his mother. Society and the public authorities shall have the duty to extend particular care to children without a family and to those without adequate means of support. Payment of State and other assistance towards the maintenance of children of large families is desirable.

Principle 7

The child is entitled to receive education, which shall be free and compulsory, at least in the elementary stages. He shall be given an education which will promote his general culture and enable him, on a basis of equal opportunity, to develop his abilities, his individual judgement, and his sense of moral and social responsibility, and to become a useful member of society.

The best interests of the child shall be the guiding principle of those responsible for his education and guidance; that responsibility lies in the first place with his parents.

The child shall have full opportunity for play and recreation, which should be directed to the same purposes as education; society and the public authorities shall endeavour to promote the enjoyment of this right.

Principle 8
The child shall in all circumstances be among the first to receive protection and relief.

Principle 9
The child shall be protected against all forms of neglect, cruelty and exploitation. He shall not be the subject of traffic, in any form. The child shall not be admitted to employment before an appropriate minimum age; he shall in no case be caused or permitted to engage in any occupation or employment which would prejudice his health or education, or interfere with his physical, mental or moral development.

Principle 10
The child shall be protected from practices which may foster racial, religious and any other form of discrimination. He shall be brought up in a spirit of understanding, tolerance, friendship among peoples, peace and universal brotherhood, and in full consciousness that his energy and talents should be devoted to the service of his fellow men.

Declaration on Social and Legal Principles relating to the Protection and Welfare of Children, with special reference to Foster Placement and Adoption Nationally and Internationally

G.A. Res. 41/85, U.N. GAOR, 41st Sess., Supp. No. 53, at 265, U.N. Doc. A/Res/41/85 (1986)

The General Assembly,

Recalling the Universal Declaration of Human Rights, the International Covenant on Economic, Social and Cultural Rights, the International Covenant on Civil and Political Rights, the International Convention on the Elimination of All Forms of Racial Discrimination and the Convention on the Elimination of All Forms of Discrimination against Women,

Recalling also the Declaration of the Rights of the Child, which it proclaimed by its resolution 1386 (XIV) of 20 November 1959,

Reaffirming principle 6 of that Declaration, which states that the child shall, wherever possible, grow up in the care and under the responsibility of his parents and, in any case, in an atmosphere of affection and of moral and material security,

Concerned at the large number of children who are abandoned or become orphans owing to violence, internal disturbance, armed conflicts, natural disasters, economic crises or social problems,

Bearing in mind that in all foster placement and adoption procedures the best interests of the child should be the paramount consideration,

Recognizing that under the principal legal systems of the world, various valuable alternative institutions exist, such as the Kafalah of Islamic Law, which provide substitute care to children who cannot be cared for by their own parents,

Recognizing further that only where a particular institution is recognized and regulated by the domestic law of a State would the provisions of this Declaration relating to that institution be relevant and that such provisions would in no way affect the existing alternative institutions in other legal systems,

Conscious of the need to proclaim universal principles to be taken into account in cases where procedures are instituted relating to foster placement or adoption of a child, either nationally or internationally,

Bearing in mind, however, that the principles set forth hereunder do not impose on States such legal institutions as foster placement or adoption,

Proclaims the following principles:

A. General, Family and Child Welfare

Article 1
Every State should give a high priority to family and child welfare.

Article 2
Child welfare depends upon good family welfare.

Article 3
The first priority for a child is to be cared for by his or her own parents.

Article 4
When care by the child's own parents is unavailable or inappropriate, care by relatives of the child's parents, by another substitute—foster or adoptive— family or, if necessary, by an appropriate institution should be considered.

Article 5
In all matters relating to the placement of a child outside the care of the child's own parents, the best interests of the child, particularly his or her need for affection and right to security and continuing care, should be the paramount consideration.

Article 6
Persons responsible for foster placement or adoption procedures should have professional or other appropriate training.

Article 7
Governments should determine the adequacy of their national child welfare services and consider appropriate actions.

Article 8
The child should at all times have a name, a nationality and a legal representative. The child should not, as a result of foster placement, adoption or any alternative regime, be deprived or his or her name, nationality or legal representative unless the child thereby acquires a new name, nationality or legal representative.

Article 9

The need of a foster or an adopted child to know about his or her background should be recognized by persons responsible for the child's care, unless this is contrary to the child's best interests.

B. Foster Placement

Article 10

Foster placement of children should be regulated by law.

Article 11

Foster family care, though temporary in nature, may continue, if necessary, until adulthood but should not preclude either prior return to the child's own parents or adoption.

Article 12

In all matters of foster family care, the prospective foster parents and, as appropriate, the child and his or her own parents should be properly involved. A competent authority or agency should be responsible for supervision to ensure the welfare of the child.

C. Adoption

Article 13

The primary aim of adoption is to provide the child who cannot be cared for by his or her own parents with a permanent family.

Article 14

In considering possible adoption placements, persons responsible for them should select the most appropriate environment for the child.

Article 15

Sufficient time and adequate counselling should be given to the child's own parents, the prospective adoptive parents and, as appropriate, the child in order to reach a decision on the child's future as early as possible.

Article 16

The relationship between the child to be adopted and the prospective adoptive parents should be observed by child welfare agencies or services prior to the adoption. Legislation should ensure that the child is recognized in law as a member of the adoptive family and enjoys all the rights pertinent thereto.

Article 17

If a child cannot be placed in a foster or an adoptive family or cannot in any suitable manner be cared for in the country of origin, intercountry adoption may be considered as an alternative means of providing the child with a family.

Article 18

Governments should establish policy, legislation and effective supervision for the protection of children involved in intercountry adoption. Intercountry adoption should, wherever possible, only be undertaken when such measures have been established in the States concerned.

Article 19

Policies should be established and laws enacted, where necessary, for the prohibition of abduction and of any other act for illicit placement of children.

Article 20

In intercountry adoption, placements should, as a rule, be made through competent authorities or agencies with application of safeguards and standards equivalent to those existing in respect of national adoption. In no case should the placement result in improper financial gain for those involved in it.

Article 21

In intercountry adoption through persons acting as agents for prospective adoptive parents, special precautions should be taken in order to protect the child's legal and social interests.

Article 22

No intercountry adoption should be considered before it has been established that the child is legally free for adoption and that any pertinent documents necessary to complete the adoption, such as the consent of competent authorities, will become available. It must also be established that the child will be able to migrate and to join the prospective adoptive parents and may obtain their nationality.

Article 23

In intercountry adoption, as a rule, the legal validity of the adoption should be assured in each of the countries involved.

Article 24

Where the nationality of the child differs from that of the prospective adoptive parents, all due weight shall be given to both the law of the State of which the child is a national and the law of the State of which the prospective adoptive parents are nationals. In this connection due regard shall be given to the child's cultural and religious background and interests.

Convention on the Rights of the Child
Nov. 20, 1989, 1577 U.N.T.S. 3

[Ed. Note: The Convention entered into force on September 2, 1990. As of March 2003, 191 nations were party to the Convention. The United States signed this Convention on Feb. 16, 1995, but remains one of only a few nations in the world that have not become a party to it.

In 1995, Costa Rica proposed an amendment to Article 43(2) of the Convention that raised the number of members of the Committee on the Rights of the Child, which is charged with overseeing implementation of the Convention, from ten to eighteen. At a Conference of the States Parties convened by the Secretary-General in accordance with Article 50(1), the Amendment was adopted on December 12, 1995 and subsequently approved by the General Assembly in Resolution No. 155 of December 21, 1995. The amendment, Doc. CRC/SP/1995/L.1/Rev. 1, entered into force on November 18, 2002.]

PREAMBLE

The States Parties to the present Convention,

Considering that, in accordance with the principles proclaimed in the Charter of the United Nations, recognition of the inherent dignity and of the equal and inalienable rights of all members of the human family is the foundation of freedom, justice and peace in the world,

Bearing in mind that the peoples of the United Nations have, in the Charter, reaffirmed their faith in fundamental human rights and in the dignity and worth of the human person, and have determined to promote social progress and better standards of life in larger freedom,

Recognizing that the United Nations has, in the Universal Declaration of Human Rights and in the International Covenants on Human Rights, proclaimed and agreed that everyone is entitled to all the rights and freedoms set forth therein, without distinction of any kind, such as race, colour, sex, language, religion, political or other opinion, national or social origin, property, birth or other status,

Recalling that, in the Universal Declaration of Human Rights, the United Nations has proclaimed that childhood is entitled to special care and assistance,

Convinced that the family, as the fundamental group of society and the natural environment for the growth and well-being of all its members and particularly children, should be afforded the necessary protection and assistance so that it can fully assume its responsibilities within the community,

Recognizing that the child, for the full and harmonious development of his or her personality, should grow up in a family environment, in an atmosphere of happiness, love and understanding,

Considering that the child should be fully prepared to live an individual life in society, and brought up in the spirit of the ideals proclaimed in the Charter of the United Nations, and in particular in the spirit of peace, dignity, tolerance, freedom, equality and solidarity,

Bearing in mind that the need to extend particular care to the child has been stated in the Geneva Declaration of the Rights of the Child of 1924 and in the Declaration of the Rights of the Child adopted by the General Assembly on 20 November 1959 and recognized in the Universal Declaration of Human Rights, in the International Covenant on Civil and Political Rights (in particular in articles 23 and 24), in the International Covenant on Economic, Social and Cultural Rights (in particular in article 10) and in the statutes and relevant instruments of specialized agencies and international organizations concerned with the welfare of children,

Bearing in mind that, as indicated in the Declaration of the Rights of the Child, "the child, by reason of his physical and mental immaturity, needs special safeguards and care, including appropriate legal protection, before as well as after birth",

Recalling the provisions of the Declaration on Social and Legal Principles relating to the Protection and Welfare of Children, with Special Reference to Foster Placement and Adoption Nationally and Internationally; the United Nations Standard Minimum Rules for the Administration of Juvenile Justice (The Beijing Rules); and the Declaration on the Protection of Women and Children in Emergency and Armed Conflict,

Recognizing that, in all countries in the world, there are children living in exceptionally difficult conditions, and that such children need special consideration,

Taking due account of the importance of the traditions and cultural values of each people for the protection and harmonious development of the child,

Recognizing the importance of international co-operation for improving the living conditions of children in every country, in particular in the developing countries,

Have agreed as follows:

PART I

Article 1
For the purposes of the present Convention, a child means every human being below the age of eighteen years unless, under the law applicable to the child, majority is attained earlier.

Article 2
1. States Parties shall respect and ensure the rights set forth in the present Convention to each child within their jurisdiction without discrimination of any kind, irrespective of the child's or his or her parent's or legal guardian's race, colour, sex, language, religion, political or other opinion, national, ethnic or social origin, property, disability, birth or other status.

2. States Parties shall take all appropriate measures to ensure that the child is protected against all forms of discrimination or punishment on the basis of the status, activities, expressed opinions, or beliefs of the child's parents, legal guardians, or family members.

Article 3
1. In all actions concerning children, whether undertaken by public or private social welfare institutions, courts of law, administrative authorities or legislative bodies, the best interests of the child shall be a primary consideration.

2. States Parties undertake to ensure the child such protection and care as is necessary for his or her well-being, taking into account the rights and duties of his or her parents, legal guardians, or other individuals legally responsible for him or her, and, to this end, shall take all appropriate legislative and administrative measures.

3. States Parties shall ensure that the institutions, services and facilities responsible for the care or protection of children shall conform with the standards established by competent authorities, particularly in the areas of safety, health, in the number and suitability of their staff, as well as competent supervision.

Article 4
States Parties shall undertake all appropriate legislative, administrative, and other measures for the implementation of the rights recognized in the present Convention. With regard to economic, social and cultural rights, States Parties shall undertake such measures to the maximum extent of their available resources and, where needed, within the framework of international co-operation.

Article 5
States Parties shall respect the responsibilities, rights and duties of parents or, where applicable, the members of the extended family or community as provided for by local custom, legal guardians or other persons legally responsible for the child, to provide, in a manner consistent with the evolving capacities of the child, appropriate direction and guidance in the exercise by the child of the rights recognized in the present Convention.

Article 6
1. States Parties recognize that every child has the inherent right to life.

2. States Parties shall ensure to the maximum extent possible the survival and development of the child.

Article 7

1. The child shall be registered immediately after birth and shall have the right from birth to a name, the right to acquire a nationality and, as far as possible, the right to know and be cared for by his or her parents.

2. States Parties shall ensure the implementation of these rights in accordance with their national law and their obligations under the relevant international instruments in this field, in particular where the child would otherwise be stateless.

Article 8

1. States Parties undertake to respect the right of the child to preserve his or her identity, including nationality, name and family relations as recognized by law without unlawful interference.

2. Where a child is illegally deprived of some or all of the elements of his or her identity, States Parties shall provide appropriate assistance and protection, with a view to speedily re-establishing his or her identity.

Article 9

1. States Parties shall ensure that a child shall not be separated from his or her parents against their will, except when competent authorities subject to judicial review determine, in accordance with applicable law and procedures, that such separation is necessary for the best interests of the child. Such determination may be necessary in a particular case such as one involving abuse or neglect of the child by the parents, or one where the parents are living separately and a decision must be made as to the child's place of residence.

2. In any proceedings pursuant to paragraph 1 of the present article, all interested parties shall be given an opportunity to participate in the proceedings and make their views known.

3. States Parties shall respect the right of the child who is separated from one or both parents to maintain personal relations and direct contact with both parents on a regular basis, except if it is contrary to the child's best interests.

4. Where such separation results from any action initiated by a State Party, such as the detention, imprisonment, exile, deportation or death (including death arising from any cause while the person is in the custody of the State) of one or both parents or of the child, that State Party shall, upon request, provide the parents, the child or, if appropriate, another member of the family with the essential information concerning the whereabouts of the absent member(s) of the family unless the provision of the information would be detrimental to the well-being of the child. States Parties shall further ensure that the submission of such a request shall of itself entail no adverse consequences for the person(s) concerned.

Article 10

1. In accordance with the obligation of States Parties under article 9, paragraph 1, applications by a child or his or her parents to enter or leave a State Party for the purpose of family reunification shall be dealt with by States Parties in a positive, humane and expeditious manner. States Parties shall further ensure that the submission of such a request shall entail no adverse consequences for the applicants and for the members of their family.

2. A child whose parents reside in different States shall have the right to maintain on a regular basis, save in exceptional circumstances personal relations and direct contacts with both parents. Towards that end and in accordance with the obligation of States Parties under article 9, paragraph 1, States Parties shall respect the right of the child and

his or her parents to leave any country, including their own, and to enter their own country. The right to leave any country shall be subject only to such restrictions as are prescribed by law and which are necessary to protect the national security, public order (ordre public), public health or morals or the rights and freedoms of others and are consistent with the other rights recognized in the present Convention.

Article 11

1. States Parties shall take measures to combat the illicit transfer and non-return of children abroad.

2. To this end, States Parties shall promote the conclusion of bilateral or multilateral agreements or accession to existing agreements.

Article 12

1. States Parties shall assure to the child who is capable of forming his or her own views the right to express those views freely in all matters affecting the child, the views of the child being given due weight in accordance with the age and maturity of the child.

2. For this purpose, the child shall in particular be provided the opportunity to be heard in any judicial and administrative proceedings affecting the child, either directly, or through a representative or an appropriate body, in a manner consistent with the procedural rules of national law.

Article 13

1. The child shall have the right to freedom of expression; this right shall include freedom to seek, receive and impart information and ideas of all kinds, regardless of frontiers, either orally, in writing or in print, in the form of art, or through any other media of the child's choice.

2. The exercise of this right may be subject to certain restrictions, but these shall only be such as are provided by law and are necessary:

(a) For respect of the rights or reputations of others; or

(b) For the protection of national security or of public order (ordre public), or of public health or morals.

Article 14

1. States Parties shall respect the right of the child to freedom of thought, conscience and religion.

2. States Parties shall respect the rights and duties of the parents and, when applicable, legal guardians, to provide direction to the child in the exercise of his or her right in a manner consistent with the evolving capacities of the child.

3. Freedom to manifest one's religion or beliefs may be subject only to such limitations as are prescribed by law and are necessary to protect public safety, order, health or morals, or the fundamental rights and freedoms of others.

Article 15

1. States Parties recognize the rights of the child to freedom of association and to freedom of peaceful assembly.

2. No restrictions may be placed on the exercise of these rights other than those imposed in conformity with the law and which are necessary in a democratic society in the interests of national security or public safety, public order (ordre public), the protection of public health or morals or the protection of the rights and freedoms of others.

Article 16

1. No child shall be subjected to arbitrary or unlawful interference with his or her privacy, family, home or correspondence, nor to unlawful attacks on his or her honour and reputation.

2. The child has the right to the protection of the law against such interference or attacks.

Article 17

States Parties recognize the important function performed by the mass media and shall ensure that the child has access to information and material from a diversity of national and international sources, especially those aimed at the promotion of his or her social, spiritual and moral well-being and physical and mental health. To this end, States Parties shall:

(a) Encourage the mass media to disseminate information and material of social and cultural benefit to the child and in accordance with the spirit of article 29;

(b) Encourage international co-operation in the production, exchange and dissemination of such information and material from a diversity of cultural, national and international sources;

(c) Encourage the production and dissemination of children's books;

(d) Encourage the mass media to have particular regard to the linguistic needs of the child who belongs to a minority group or who is indigenous;

(e) Encourage the development of appropriate guidelines for the protection of the child from information and material injurious to his or her well-being, bearing in mind the provisions of articles 13 and 18.

Article 18

1. States Parties shall use their best efforts to ensure recognition of the principle that both parents have common responsibilities for the upbringing and development of the child. Parents or, as the case may be, legal guardians, have the primary responsibility for the upbringing and development of the child. The best interests of the child will be their basic concern.

2. For the purpose of guaranteeing and promoting the rights set forth in the present Convention, States Parties shall render appropriate assistance to parents and legal guardians in the performance of their child-rearing responsibilities and shall ensure the development of institutions, facilities and services for the care of children.

3. States Parties shall take all appropriate measures to ensure that children of working parents have the right to benefit from child-care services and facilities for which they are eligible.

Article 19

1. States Parties shall take all appropriate legislative, administrative, social and educational measures to protect the child from all forms of physical or mental violence, injury or abuse, neglect or negligent treatment, maltreatment or exploitation, including sexual abuse, while in the care of parent(s), legal guardian(s) or any other person who has the care of the child.

2. Such protective measures should, as appropriate, include effective procedures for the establishment of social programmes to provide necessary support for the child and for those who have the care of the child, as well as for other forms of prevention and for identification, reporting, referral, investigation, treatment and follow-up of in-

stances of child maltreatment described heretofore, and, as appropriate, for judicial involvement.

Article 20

1. A child temporarily or permanently deprived of his or her family environment, or in whose own best interests cannot be allowed to remain in that environment, shall be entitled to special protection and assistance provided by the State.

2. States Parties shall in accordance with their national laws ensure alternative care for such a child.

3. Such care could include, inter alia, foster placement, kafalah of Islamic law, adoption or if necessary placement in suitable institutions for the care of children. When considering solutions, due regard shall be paid to the desirability of continuity in a child's upbringing and to the child's ethnic, religious, cultural and linguistic background.

Article 21

States Parties that recognize and/or permit the system of adoption shall ensure that the best interests of the child shall be the paramount consideration and they shall:

(a) Ensure that the adoption of a child is authorized only by competent authorities who determine, in accordance with applicable law and procedures and on the basis of all pertinent and reliable information, that the adoption is permissible in view of the child's status concerning parents, relatives and legal guardians and that, if required, the persons concerned have given their informed consent to the adoption on the basis of such counselling as may be necessary;

(b) Recognize that inter-country adoption may be considered as an alternative means of child's care, if the child cannot be placed in a foster or an adoptive family or cannot in any suitable manner be cared for in the child's country of origin;

(c) Ensure that the child concerned by inter-country adoption enjoys safeguards and standards equivalent to those existing in the case of national adoption;

(d) Take all appropriate measures to ensure that, in inter-country adoption, the placement does not result in improper financial gain for those involved in it;

(e) Promote, where appropriate, the objectives of the present article by concluding bilateral or multilateral arrangements or agreements, and endeavour, within this framework, to ensure that the placement of the child in another country is carried out by competent authorities or organs.

Article 22

1. States Parties shall take appropriate measures to ensure that a child who is seeking refugee status or who is considered a refugee in accordance with applicable international or domestic law and procedures shall, whether unaccompanied or accompanied by his or her parents or by any other person, receive appropriate protection and humanitarian assistance in the enjoyment of applicable rights set forth in the present Convention and in other international human rights or humanitarian instruments to which the said States are Parties.

2. For this purpose, States Parties shall provide, as they consider appropriate, co-operation in any efforts by the United Nations and other competent intergovernmental organizations or non-governmental organizations co-operating with the United Nations to protect and assist such a child and to trace the parents or other members of the family of any refugee child in order to obtain information necessary for reunification with

his or her family. In cases where no parents or other members of the family can be found, the child shall be accorded the same protection as any other child permanently or temporarily deprived of his or her family environment for any reason, as set forth in the present Convention.

Article 23

1. States Parties recognize that a mentally or physically disabled child should enjoy a full and decent life, in conditions which ensure dignity, promote self-reliance and facilitate the child's active participation in the community.

2. States Parties recognize the right of the disabled child to special care and shall encourage and ensure the extension, subject to available resources, to the eligible child and those responsible for his or her care, of assistance for which application is made and which is appropriate to the child's condition and to the circumstances of the parents or others caring for the child.

3. Recognizing the special needs of a disabled child, assistance extended in accordance with paragraph 2 of the present article shall be provided free of charge, whenever possible, taking into account the financial resources of the parents or others caring for the child, and shall be designed to ensure that the disabled child has effective access to and receives education, training, health care services, rehabilitation services, preparation for employment and recreation opportunities in a manner conducive to the child's achieving the fullest possible social integration and individual development, including his or her cultural and spiritual development.

4. States Parties shall promote, in the spirit of international cooperation, the exchange of appropriate information in the field of preventive health care and of medical, psychological and functional treatment of disabled children, including dissemination of and access to information concerning methods of rehabilitation, education and vocational services, with the aim of enabling States Parties to improve their capabilities and skills and to widen their experience in these areas. In this regard, particular account shall be taken of the needs of developing countries.

Article 24

1. States Parties recognize the right of the child to the enjoyment of the highest attainable standard of health and to facilities for the treatment of illness and rehabilitation of health. States Parties shall strive to ensure that no child is deprived of his or her right of access to such health care services.

2. States Parties shall pursue full implementation of this right and, in particular, shall take appropriate measures:

(a) To diminish infant and child mortality;

(b) To ensure the provision of necessary medical assistance and health care to all children with emphasis on the development of primary health care;

(c) To combat disease and malnutrition, including within the framework of primary health care, through, inter alia, the application of readily available technology and through the provision of adequate nutritious foods and clean drinking-water, taking into consideration the dangers and risks of environmental pollution;

(d) To ensure appropriate pre-natal and post-natal health care for mothers;

(e) To ensure that all segments of society, in particular parents and children, are informed, have access to education and are supported in the use of basic knowledge of child health and nutrition, the advantages of breast-feeding, hygiene and environmental sanitation and the prevention of accidents;

(f) To develop preventive health care, guidance for parents and family planning education and services.

3. States Parties shall take all effective and appropriate measures with a view to abolishing traditional practices prejudicial to the health of children.

4. States Parties undertake to promote and encourage international co-operation with a view to achieving progressively the full realization of the right recognized in the present article. In this regard, particular account shall be taken of the needs of developing countries.

Article 25

States Parties recognize the right of a child who has been placed by the competent authorities for the purposes of care, protection or treatment of his or her physical or mental health, to a periodic review of the treatment provided to the child and all other circumstances relevant to his or her placement.

Article 26

1. States Parties shall recognize for every child the right to benefit from social security, including social insurance, and shall take the necessary measures to achieve the full realization of this right in accordance with their national law.

2. The benefits should, where appropriate, be granted, taking into account the resources and the circumstances of the child and persons having responsibility for the maintenance of the child, as well as any other consideration relevant to an application for benefits made by or on behalf of the child.

Article 27

1. States Parties recognize the right of every child to a standard of living adequate for the child's physical, mental, spiritual, moral and social development.

2. The parent(s) or others responsible for the child have the primary responsibility to secure, within their abilities and financial capacities, the conditions of living necessary for the child's development.

3. States Parties, in accordance with national conditions and within their means, shall take appropriate measures to assist parents and others responsible for the child to implement this right and shall in case of need provide material assistance and support programmes, particularly with regard to nutrition, clothing and housing.

4. States Parties shall take all appropriate measures to secure the recovery of maintenance for the child from the parents or other persons having financial responsibility for the child, both within the State Party and from abroad. In particular, where the person having financial responsibility for the child lives in a State different from that of the child, States Parties shall promote the accession to international agreements or the conclusion of such agreements, as well as the making of other appropriate arrangements.

Article 28

1. States Parties recognize the right of the child to education, and with a view to achieving this right progressively and on the basis of equal opportunity, they shall, in particular:

(a) Make primary education compulsory and available free to all;

(b) Encourage the development of different forms of secondary education, including general and vocational education, make them available and accessible to every child, and take appropriate measures such as the introduction of free education and offering financial assistance in case of need;

(c) Make higher education accessible to all on the basis of capacity by every appropriate means;

(d) Make educational and vocational information and guidance available and accessible to all children;

(e) Take measures to encourage regular attendance at schools and the reduction of drop-out rates.

2. States Parties shall take all appropriate measures to ensure that school discipline is administered in a manner consistent with the child's human dignity and in conformity with the present Convention.

3. States Parties shall promote and encourage international cooperation in matters relating to education, in particular with a view to contributing to the elimination of ignorance and illiteracy throughout the world and facilitating access to scientific and technical knowledge and modern teaching methods. In this regard, particular account shall be taken of the needs of developing countries.

Article 29

1. States Parties agree that the education of the child shall be directed to:

(a) The development of the child's personality, talents and mental and physical abilities to their fullest potential;

(b) The development of respect for human rights and fundamental freedoms, and for the principles enshrined in the Charter of the United Nations;

(c) The development of respect for the child's parents, his or her own cultural identity, language and values, for the national values of the country in which the child is living, the country from which he or she may originate, and for civilizations different from his or her own;

(d) The preparation of the child for responsible life in a free society, in the spirit of understanding, peace, tolerance, equality of sexes, and friendship among all peoples, ethnic, national and religious groups and persons of indigenous origin;

(e) The development of respect for the natural environment.

2. No part of the present article or article 28 shall be construed so as to interfere with the liberty of individuals and bodies to establish and direct educational institutions, subject always to the observance of the principle set forth in paragraph 1 of the present article and to the requirements that the education given in such institutions shall conform to such minimum standards as may be laid down by the State.

Article 30

In those States in which ethnic, religious or linguistic minorities or persons of indigenous origin exist, a child belonging to such a minority or who is indigenous shall not be denied the right, in community with other members of his or her group, to enjoy his or her own culture, to profess and practise his or her own religion, or to use his or her own language.

Article 31

1. States Parties recognize the right of the child to rest and leisure, to engage in play and recreational activities appropriate to the age of the child and to participate freely in cultural life and the arts.

2. States Parties shall respect and promote the right of the child to participate fully in cultural and artistic life and shall encourage the provision of appropriate and equal opportunities for cultural, artistic, recreational and leisure activity.

Article 32

1. States Parties recognize the right of the child to be protected from economic exploitation and from performing any work that is likely to be hazardous or to interfere with the child's education, or to be harmful to the child's health or physical, mental, spiritual, moral or social development.

2. States Parties shall take legislative, administrative, social and educational measures to ensure the implementation of the present article. To this end, and having regard to the relevant provisions of other international instruments, States Parties shall in particular:

(a) Provide for a minimum age or minimum ages for admission to employment;

(b) Provide for appropriate regulation of the hours and conditions of employment;

(c) Provide for appropriate penalties or other sanctions to ensure the effective enforcement of the present article.

Article 33

States Parties shall take all appropriate measures, including legislative, administrative, social and educational measures, to protect children from the illicit use of narcotic drugs and psychotropic substances as defined in the relevant international treaties, and to prevent the use of children in the illicit production and trafficking of such substances.

Article 34

States Parties undertake to protect the child from all forms of sexual exploitation and sexual abuse. For these purposes, States Parties shall in particular take all appropriate national, bilateral and multilateral measures to prevent:

(a) The inducement or coercion of a child to engage in any unlawful sexual activity;

(b) The exploitative use of children in prostitution or other unlawful sexual practices;

(c) The exploitative use of children in pornographic performances and materials.

Article 35

States Parties shall take all appropriate national, bilateral and multilateral measures to prevent the abduction of, the sale of or traffic in children for any purpose or in any form.

Article 36

States Parties shall protect the child against all other forms of exploitation prejudicial to any aspects of the child's welfare.

Article 37

States Parties shall ensure that:

(a) No child shall be subjected to torture or other cruel, inhuman or degrading treatment or punishment. Neither capital punishment nor life imprisonment without possibility of release shall be imposed for offences committed by persons below eighteen years of age;

(b) No child shall be deprived of his or her liberty unlawfully or arbitrarily. The arrest, detention or imprisonment of a child shall be in conformity with the law and shall be used only as a measure of last resort and for the shortest appropriate period of time;

(c) Every child deprived of liberty shall be treated with humanity and respect for the inherent dignity of the human person, and in a manner which takes into account the needs of persons of his or her age. In particular, every child deprived of liberty shall be separated from adults unless it is considered in the child's best interest not to do so and shall have the right to maintain contact with his or her family through correspondence and visits, save in exceptional circumstances;

(d) Every child deprived of his or her liberty shall have the right to prompt access to legal and other appropriate assistance, as well as the right to challenge the legality of the deprivation of his or her liberty before a court or other competent, independent and impartial authority, and to a prompt decision on any such action.

Article 38

1. States Parties undertake to respect and to ensure respect for rules of international humanitarian law applicable to them in armed conflicts which are relevant to the child.

2. States Parties shall take all feasible measures to ensure that persons who have not attained the age of fifteen years do not take a direct part in hostilities.

3. States Parties shall refrain from recruiting any person who has not attained the age of fifteen years into their armed forces. In recruiting among those persons who have attained the age of fifteen years but who have not attained the age of eighteen years, States Parties shall endeavour to give priority to those who are oldest.

4. In accordance with their obligations under international humanitarian law to protect the civilian population in armed conflicts, States Parties shall take all feasible measures to ensure protection and care of children who are affected by an armed conflict.

Article 39

States Parties shall take all appropriate measures to promote physical and psychological recovery and social reintegration of a child victim of: any form of neglect, exploitation, or abuse; torture or any other form of cruel, inhuman or degrading treatment or punishment; or armed conflicts. Such recovery and reintegration shall take place in an environment which fosters the health, self-respect and dignity of the child.

Article 40

1. States Parties recognize the right of every child alleged as, accused of, or recognized as having infringed the penal law to be treated in a manner consistent with the promotion of the child's sense of dignity and worth, which reinforces the child's respect for the human rights and fundamental freedoms of others and which takes into account the child's age and the desirability of promoting the child's reintegration and the child's assuming a constructive role in society.

2. To this end, and having regard to the relevant provisions of international instruments, States Parties shall, in particular, ensure that:

(a) No child shall be alleged as, be accused of, or recognized as having infringed the penal law by reason of acts or omissions that were not prohibited by national or international law at the time they were committed;

(b) Every child alleged as or accused of having infringed the penal law has at least the following guarantees:

(i) To be presumed innocent until proven guilty according to law;

(ii) To be informed promptly and directly of the charges against him or her, and, if appropriate, through his or her parents or legal guardians, and to have legal or other appropriate assistance in the preparation and presentation of his or her defence;

(iii) To have the matter determined without delay by a competent, independent and impartial authority or judicial body in a fair hearing according to law, in the presence of legal or other appropriate assistance and, unless it is considered not to be in the best interest of the child, in particular, taking into account his or her age or situation, his or her parents or legal guardians;

(iv) Not to be compelled to give testimony or to confess guilt; to examine or have examined adverse witnesses and to obtain the participation and examination of witnesses on his or her behalf under conditions of equality;

(v) If considered to have infringed the penal law, to have this decision and any measures imposed in consequence thereof reviewed by a higher competent, independent and impartial authority or judicial body according to law;

(vi) To have the free assistance of an interpreter if the child cannot understand or speak the language used;

(vii) To have his or her privacy fully respected at all stages of the proceedings.

3. States Parties shall seek to promote the establishment of laws, procedures, authorities and institutions specifically applicable to children alleged as, accused of, or recognized as having infringed the penal law, and, in particular:

(a) The establishment of a minimum age below which children shall be presumed not to have the capacity to infringe the penal law;

(b) Whenever appropriate and desirable, measures for dealing with such children without resorting to judicial proceedings, providing that human rights and legal safeguards are fully respected.

4. A variety of dispositions, such as care, guidance and supervision orders; counselling; probation; foster care; education and vocational training programmes and other alternatives to institutional care shall be available to ensure that children are dealt with in a manner appropriate to their well-being and proportionate both to their circumstances and the offence.

Article 41

Nothing in the present Convention shall affect any provisions which are more conducive to the realization of the rights of the child and which may be contained in:

(a) The law of a State party; or

(b) International law in force for that State.

PART II

Article 42

States Parties undertake to make the principles and provisions of the Convention widely known, by appropriate and active means, to adults and children alike.

Article 43

1. For the purpose of examining the progress made by States Parties in achieving the realization of the obligations undertaken in the present Convention, there shall be established a Committee on the Rights of the Child, which shall carry out the functions hereinafter provided.

2. The Committee shall consist of ten experts of high moral standing and recognized competence in the field covered by this Convention. The members of the Committee shall be elected by States Parties from among their nationals and shall serve in their personal capacity, consideration being given to equitable geographical distribution, as well as to the principal legal systems.

3. The members of the Committee shall be elected by secret ballot from a list of persons nominated by States Parties. Each State Party may nominate one person from among its own nationals.

4. The initial election to the Committee shall be held no later than six months after the date of the entry into force of the present Convention and thereafter every second year. At least four months before the date of each election, the Secretary-General of the United Nations shall address a letter to States Parties inviting them to submit their nominations within two months. The Secretary-General shall subsequently prepare a list in alphabetical order of all persons thus nominated, indicating States Parties which have nominated them, and shall submit it to the States Parties to the present Convention.

5. The elections shall be held at meetings of States Parties convened by the Secretary-General at United Nations Headquarters. At those meetings, for which two thirds of States Parties shall constitute a quorum, the persons elected to the Committee shall be those who obtain the largest number of votes and an absolute majority of the votes of the representatives of States Parties present and voting.

6. The members of the Committee shall be elected for a term of four years. They shall be eligible for re-election if renominated. The term of five of the members elected at the first election shall expire at the end of two years; immediately after the first election, the names of these five members shall be chosen by lot by the Chairman of the meeting.

7. If a member of the Committee dies or resigns or declares that for any other cause he or she can no longer perform the duties of the Committee, the State Party which nominated the member shall appoint another expert from among its nationals to serve for the remainder of the term, subject to the approval of the Committee.

8. The Committee shall establish its own rules of procedure.

9. The Committee shall elect its officers for a period of two years.

10. The meetings of the Committee shall normally be held at United Nations Headquarters or at any other convenient place as determined by the Committee. The Committee shall normally meet annually. The duration of the meetings of the Committee shall be determined, and reviewed, if necessary, by a meeting of the States Parties to the present Convention, subject to the approval of the General Assembly.

11. The Secretary-General of the United Nations shall provide the necessary staff and facilities for the effective performance of the functions of the Committee under the present Convention.

12. With the approval of the General Assembly, the members of the Committee established under the present Convention shall receive emoluments from United Nations resources on such terms and conditions as the Assembly may decide.

Article 44

1. States Parties undertake to submit to the Committee, through the Secretary-General of the United Nations, reports on the measures they have adopted which give effect to the rights recognized herein and on the progress made on the enjoyment of those rights:

(a) Within two years of the entry into force of the Convention for the State Party concerned;

(b) Thereafter every five years.

2. Reports made under the present article shall indicate factors and difficulties, if any, affecting the degree of fulfilment of the obligations under the present Convention. Reports shall also contain sufficient information to provide the Committee with a comprehensive understanding of the implementation of the Convention in the country concerned.

3. A State Party which has submitted a comprehensive initial report to the Committee need not, in its subsequent reports submitted in accordance with paragraph 1 (b) of the present article, repeat basic information previously provided.

4. The Committee may request from States Parties further information relevant to the implementation of the Convention.

5. The Committee shall submit to the General Assembly, through the Economic and Social Council, every two years, reports on its activities.

6. States Parties shall make their reports widely available to the public in their own countries.

Article 45

In order to foster the effective implementation of the Convention and to encourage international co-operation in the field covered by the Convention:

(a) The specialized agencies, the United Nations Children's Fund, and other United Nations organs shall be entitled to be represented at the consideration of the implementation of such provisions of the present Convention as fall within the scope of their mandate. The Committee may invite the specialized agencies, the United Nations Children's Fund and other competent bodies as it may consider appropriate to provide expert advice on the implementation of the Convention in areas falling within the scope of their respective mandates. The Committee may invite the specialized agencies, the United Nations Children's Fund, and other United Nations organs to submit reports on the implementation of the Convention in areas falling within the scope of their activities;

(b) The Committee shall transmit, as it may consider appropriate, to the specialized agencies, the United Nations Children's Fund and other competent bodies, any reports from States Parties that contain a request, or indicate a need, for technical advice or assistance, along with the Committee's observations and suggestions, if any, on these requests or indications;

(c) The Committee may recommend to the General Assembly to request the Secretary-General to undertake on its behalf studies on specific issues relating to the rights of the child;

(d) The Committee may make suggestions and general recommendations based on information received pursuant to articles 44 and 45 of the present Convention. Such suggestions and general recommendations shall be transmitted to any State Party concerned and reported to the General Assembly, together with comments, if any, from States Parties.

[Ed. Note: Part III, Articles 46 to 54, addressing signature, ratification, accession, entry into force, amendment, reservation, denunciation, deposit, and languages of the Convention, is omitted.]

Optional Protocol to the Convention on the Rights of the Child on the Involvement of Children in Armed Conflicts

May 25, 2000, S. Treaty Doc. No. 106-37 (2000), G.A. Res. 54/263,
Annex I, U.N. GAOR. 54th Sess., U.N. Doc. A/54/L.84; A/54/49

[Ed. Note: This Protocol entered into force on February 12, 2002. As of March 2003, 51 nations were parties to the Protocol. Although the United States is not a party to the Convention on the Rights of the Child, it became a party to this Protocol, through ratification deposited on December 23, 2002. The declarations and understandings of the United States follow the text of the Protocol.]

The General Assembly,

Recalling all its previous resolutions on the rights of the child topic, and in particular its resolution 54/149 of 17 December 1999, in which it strongly supported the work of the open-ended inter-sessional working groups and urged them to finalize their work before the tenth anniversary of the entry into force of the Convention on the Rights of the Child,

Expressing its appreciation to the Commission on Human Rights for having finalized the texts of the two optional protocols to the Convention on the Rights of the Child, on the involvement of children in armed conflict and on the sale of children, child prostitution and child pornography,

Conscious of the tenth anniversaries, in the year 2000, of the World Summit for Children and the entry into force of the Convention on the Rights of the Child and of the symbolic and practical importance of the adoption of the two optional protocols to the Convention on the Rights of the Child before the special session of the General Assembly for the follow-up to the World Summit for Children, to be convened in 2001,

Adhering to the principle that the best interests of the child are to be a primary consideration in all actions concerning children,

Reaffirming its commitment to strive for the promotion and protection of the rights of the child in all avenues of life,

Recognizing that the adoption and implementation of the two optional protocols will make a substantial contribution to the promotion and protection of the rights of the child,

1. Adopts and opens for signature, ratification and accession the two optional protocols to the Convention on the Rights of the Child, on the involvement of children in armed conflict and on the sale of children, child prostitution and child pornography, the texts of which are annexed to the present resolution;

2. Invites all States that have signed, ratified or acceded to the Convention on the Rights of the Child to sign and ratify or accede to the annexed optional protocols as soon as possible in order to facilitate their early entry into force;

3. Decides that the two optional protocols to the Convention on the Rights of the Child will be opened for signature at the special session of the General Assembly, entitled "Women 2000: gender equality, development and peace for the twenty-first century", to be convened from 5 to 9 June 2000 in New York, and thereafter at United Nations Headquarters, at the special session of the General Assembly, entitled "World Summit for Social Development and beyond: achieving social development for all in a globalizing world", to be convened from 26 to 30 June 2000 in Geneva, and at the Millennium Summit of the United Nations, to be convened from 6 to 8 September 2000 in New York;

4. Requests the Secretary-General to include information on the status of the two optional protocols in his regular report to the General Assembly on the status of the Convention on the Rights of the Child.

The States Parties to the present Protocol,

Encouraged by the overwhelming support for the Convention on the Rights of the Child, demonstrating the widespread commitment that exists to strive for the promotion and protection of the rights of the child,

Reaffirming that the rights of children require special protection, and calling for continuous improvement of the situation of children without distinction, as well as for their development and education in conditions of peace and security,

Disturbed by the harmful and widespread impact of armed conflict on children and the long-term consequences this has for durable peace, security and development,

Condemning the targeting of children in situations of armed conflict and direct attacks on objects protected under international law, including places generally having a significant presence of children, such as schools and hospitals,

Noting the adoption of the Statute of the International Criminal Court and, in particular, its inclusion as a war crime of conscripting or enlisting children under the age of 15 years or using them to participate actively in hostilities in both international and non-international armed conflicts,

Considering, therefore, that to strengthen further the implementation of rights recognized in the Convention on the Rights of the Child there is a need to increase the protection of children from involvement in armed conflict,

Noting that article 1 of the Convention on the Rights of the Child specifies that, for the purposes of that Convention, a child means every human being below the age of 18 years unless, under the law applicable to the child, majority is attained earlier,

Convinced that an optional protocol to the Convention raising the age of possible recruitment of persons into armed forces and their participation in hostilities will contribute effectively to the implementation of the principle that the best interests of the child are to be a primary consideration in all actions concerning children,

Noting that the twenty-sixth international Conference of the Red Cross and Red Crescent in December 1995 recommended, inter alia, that parties to conflict take every feasible step to ensure that children under the age of 18 years do not take part in hostilities,

Welcoming the unanimous adoption, in June 1999, of International Labour Organization Convention No. 182 on the Prohibition and Immediate Action for the Elimination of the Worst Forms of Child Labour, which prohibits, inter alia, forced or compulsory recruitment of children for use in armed conflict,

Condemning with the gravest concern the recruitment, training and use within and across national borders of children in hostilities by armed groups distinct from the armed forces of a State, and recognizing the responsibility of those who recruit, train and use children in this regard,

Recalling the obligation of each party to an armed conflict to abide by the provisions of international humanitarian law,

Stressing that this Protocol is without prejudice to the purposes and principles contained in the Charter of the United Nations, including Article 51, and relevant norms of humanitarian law,

Bearing in mind that conditions of peace and security based on full respect of the purposes and principles contained in the Charter and observance of applicable human rights instruments are indispensable for the full protection of children, in particular during armed conflicts and foreign occupation,

Recognizing the special needs of those children who are particularly vulnerable to recruitment or use in hostilities contrary to this Protocol owing to their economic or social status or gender,

Mindful of the necessity of taking into consideration the economic, social and political root causes of the involvement of children in armed conflicts,

Convinced of the need to strengthen international cooperation in the implementation of this Protocol, as well as the physical and psychosocial rehabilitation and social reintegration of children who are victims of armed conflict,

Encouraging the participation of the community and, in particular, children and child victims in the dissemination of informational and educational programmes concerning the implementation of the Protocol,

Have agreed as follows:

Article 1

States Parties shall take all feasible measures to ensure that members of their armed forces who have not attained the age of 18 years do not take a direct part in hostilities.

Article 2

States Parties shall ensure that persons who have not attained the age of 18 years are not compulsorily recruited into their armed forces.

Article 3

1. States Parties shall raise the minimum age for the voluntary recruitment of persons into their national armed forces from that set out in article 38, paragraph 3, of the Convention on the Rights of the Child, taking account of the principles contained in that article and recognizing that under the Convention persons under 18 are entitled to special protection.

2. Each State Party shall deposit a binding declaration upon ratification of or accession to this Protocol that sets forth the minimum age at which it will permit voluntary recruitment into its national armed forces and a description of the safeguards that it has adopted to ensure that such recruitment is not forced or coerced.

3. States Parties that permit voluntary recruitment into their national armed forces under the age of 18 shall maintain safeguards to ensure, as a minimum, that:

(a) Such recruitment is genuinely voluntary;

(b) Such recruitment is done with the informed consent of the person's parents or legal guardians;

(c) Such persons are fully informed of the duties involved in such military service;

(d) Such persons provide reliable proof of age prior to acceptance into national military service.

4. Each State Party may strengthen its declaration at any time by notification to that effect addressed to the Secretary-General of the United Nations, who shall inform all States Parties. Such notification shall take effect on the date on which it is received by the Secretary-General.

5. The requirement to raise the age in paragraph 1 of the present article does not apply to schools operated by or under the control of the armed forces of the States Parties, in keeping with articles 28 and 29 of the Convention on the Rights of the Child.

Article 4

1. Armed groups that are distinct from the armed forces of a State should not, under any circumstances, recruit or use in hostilities persons under the age of 18 years.

2. States Parties shall take all feasible measures to prevent such recruitment and use, including the adoption of legal measures necessary to prohibit and criminalize such practices.

3. The application of the present article under this Protocol shall not affect the legal status of any party to an armed conflict.

Article 5

Nothing in the present Protocol shall be construed as precluding provisions in the law of a State Party or in international instruments and international humanitarian law that are more conducive to the realization of the rights of the child.

Article 6

1. Each State Party shall take all necessary legal, administrative and other measures to ensure the effective implementation and enforcement of the provisions of this Protocol within its jurisdiction.

2. States Parties undertake to make the principles and provisions of the present Protocol widely known and promoted by appropriate means, to adults and children alike.

3. States Parties shall take all feasible measures to ensure that persons within their jurisdiction recruited or used in hostilities contrary to this Protocol are demobilized or otherwise released from service. States Parties shall, when necessary, accord to these persons all appropriate assistance for their physical and psychological recovery and their social reintegration.

Article 7

1. States Parties shall cooperate in the implementation of the present Protocol, including in the prevention of any activity contrary to the Protocol and in the rehabilitation and social reintegration of persons who are victims of acts contrary to this Protocol, including through technical cooperation and financial assistance. Such assistance and cooperation will be undertaken in consultation with concerned States Parties and relevant international organizations.

2. States Parties in a position to do so shall provide such assistance through existing multilateral, bilateral or other programmes, or, inter alia, through a voluntary fund established in accordance with the rules of the General Assembly.

Article 8

1. Each State Party shall submit, within two years following the entry into force of the Protocol for that State Party, a report to the Committee on the Rights of the Child providing comprehensive information on the measures it has taken to implement the provisions of the Protocol, including the measures taken to implement the provisions on participation and recruitment.

2. Following the submission of the comprehensive report, each State Party shall include in the reports they submit to the Committee on the Rights of the Child, in accordance with article 44 of the Convention, any further information with respect to the implementation of the Protocol. Other States Parties to the Protocol shall submit a report every five years.

3. The Committee on the Rights of the Child may request from States Parties further information relevant to the implementation of this Protocol.

[Ed. Note: Articles 9 to 13, addressing the signature, ratification and accession, entry into force, denunciation, amendment, and deposit of the Optional Protocol, have been omitted.]

Declaration and Understandings of the United States
Declaration:

"The Government of the United States of America declares, pursuant to Article 3 (2) of the Optional Protocol to the Convention on the Rights of the Child on the Involvement of Children in Armed Conflict that—

(A) the minimum age at which the United States permits voluntary recruitment into the Armed Forces of the United States is 17 years of age;

(B) The United States has established safeguards to ensure that such recruitment is not forced or coerced, including a requirement in section 505 (a) of title 10, United States Code, that no person under 18 years of age may be originally enlisted in the Armed Forces of the United States without the written consent of the person's parent or guardian, if the parent or guardian is entitled to the person's custody and control;

(C) each person recruited into the Armed Forces of the United States receives a comprehensive briefing and must sign an enlistment contract that, taken together, specify the duties involved in military service; and

(D) all persons recruited into the Armed Forces of the United States must provide reliable proof of age before their entry into military service."

Understandings:

(1) No assumption of obligations under the Convention on the Rights of the Child—

The United States understands that the United States assumes no obligations under the Convention on the Rights of the Child by becoming a party to the Protocol.

(2) Implementation of Obligation not to Permit Children to Take Direct Part in Hostilities—

The United States understands that, with respect to Article 1 of the Protocol—

(A) the term "feasible measures" means those measures that are practical or practically possible, taking into account all the circumstances ruling at the time, including humanitarian and military considerations;

(B) the phrase "direct part in hostilities"—

(i) means immediate and actual action on the battlefield likely to cause harm to the enemy because there is a direct causal relationship between the activity engaged in and the harm done to the enemy; and

(ii) does not mean indirect participation in hostilities, such as gathering and transmitting military information, transporting weapons, munitions, or other supplies, or forward deployment; and

(C) any decision by any military commander, military personnel, or other person responsible for planning, authorizing, or executing military action, including the assignment of military personnel, shall only be judged on the basis of all the relevant circumstances and on the basis of that person's assessment of the information reasonably available to the person at the time the person planned, authorized, or executed the action under review, and shall not be judged on the basis of information that comes to light after the action under review was taken.

(3) Minimum Age for Voluntary Recruitment—

The United States understands that Article 3 of the Protocol obligates States Parties to the Protocol to raise the minimum age for voluntary recruitment into their national armed forces from the current international standard of 15 years of age.

(4) Armed Groups—

The United States understands that the term "armed groups" in Article 4 of the Protocol means nongovernmental armed groups such as rebel groups, dissident armed forces, and other insurgent groups.

(5) No Basis for Jurisdiction by any International Tribunal—

The United States understands that nothing in the Protocol establishes a basis for jurisdiction by any international tribunal, including the International Criminal Court."

Optional Protocol to the Convention on the Rights of the Child on the Sale of Children, Child Prostitution and Child Pornography

May 25, 2000, S. Treaty Doc. No. 106-37 (2000), G.A. Res. 54/263, Annex II, U.N. GAOR. 54th Sess., U.N. Doc. A/54/L.84; A/54/49

[Ed. Note: This Protocol entered into force on January 18, 2002. As of March 2003, 49 nations were parties to the Protocol.

Although the United States is not a party to the Convention on the Rights of the Child, it became a party to this Protocol through ratification deposited on December 23, 2002. The reservation of the United States follows the text of the Protocol.

The General Assembly's introduction to the Optional Protocol on the Involvement of Children in Armed Conflict, set forth above, is identical to the introduction to this Optional Protocol, and has therefore been omitted here.]

The States Parties to the present Protocol,

Considering that, in order further to achieve the purposes of the Convention on the Rights of the Child and the implementation of its provisions, especially articles 1, 11, 21, 32, 33, 34, 35 and 36, it would be appropriate to extend the measures that States Parties should undertake in order to guarantee the protection of the child from the sale of children, child prostitution and child pornography,

Considering also that the Convention on the Rights of the Child recognizes the right of the child to be protected from economic exploitation and from performing any work that is likely to be hazardous or to interfere with the child's education, or to be harmful to the child's health or physical, mental, spiritual, moral or social development,

Gravely concerned at the significant and increasing international traffic of children for the purpose of the sale of children, child prostitution and child pornography,

Deeply concerned at the widespread and continuing practice of sex tourism, to which children are especially vulnerable, as it directly promotes the sale of children, child prostitution and child pornography,

Recognizing that a number of particularly vulnerable groups, including girl children, are at greater risk of sexual exploitation, and that girl children are disproportionately represented among the sexually exploited,

Concerned about the growing availability of child pornography on the Internet and other evolving technologies, and recalling the International Conference on Combating Child Pornography on the Internet (Vienna, 1999) and, in particular, its conclusion calling for the worldwide criminalization of the production, distribution, exportation, transmission, importation, intentional possession and advertising of child pornography, and stressing the importance of closer cooperation and partnership between Governments and the Internet industry,

Believing that the elimination of the sale of children, child prostitution and child pornography will be facilitated by adopting a holistic approach, addressing the contributing factors, including underdevelopment, poverty, economic disparities, inequitable socio-economic structure, dysfunctioning families, lack of education, urban-rural migration, gender discrimination, irresponsible adult sexual behaviour, harmful traditional practices, armed conflicts and trafficking of children,

Believing that efforts to raise public awareness are needed to reduce consumer demand for the sale of children, child prostitution and child pornography, and also believing in the importance of strengthening global partnership among all actors and of improving law enforcement at the national level,

Noting the provisions of international legal instruments relevant to the protection of children, including the Hague Convention on the Protection of Children and Cooperation with Respect to Inter-Country Adoption, the Hague Convention on the Civil Aspects of International Child Abduction, the Hague Convention on Jurisdiction, Applicable Law, Recognition, Enforcement and Cooperation in Respect of Parental Responsibility and Measures for the Protection of Children, and International Labour Organization Convention No. 182 on the Prohibition and Immediate Action for the Elimination of the Worst Forms of Child Labour,

Encouraged by the overwhelming support for the Convention on the Rights of the Child, demonstrating the widespread commitment that exists for the promotion and protection of the rights of the child,

Recognizing the importance of the implementation of the provisions of the Programme of Action for the Prevention of the Sale of Children, Child Prostitution and Child Pornography and the Declaration and Agenda for Action adopted at the World Congress against Commercial Sexual Exploitation of Children, held at Stockholm from 27 to 31 August 1996, and the other relevant decisions and recommendations of pertinent international bodies,

Taking due account of the importance of the traditions and cultural values of each people for the protection and harmonious development of the child,

Have agreed as follows:

Article 1

States Parties shall prohibit the sale of children, child prostitution and child pornography as provided for by the present Protocol.

Article 2

For the purpose of the present Protocol:

(a) Sale of children means any act or transaction whereby a child is transferred by any person or group of persons to another for remuneration or any other consideration;

(b) Child prostitution means the use of a child in sexual activities for remuneration or any other form of consideration;

(c) Child pornography means any representation, by whatever means, of a child engaged in real or simulated explicit sexual activities or any representation of the sexual parts of a child for primarily sexual purposes.

Article 3

1. Each State Party shall ensure that, as a minimum, the following acts and activities are fully covered under its criminal or penal law, whether these offences are committed domestically or transnationally or on an individual or organized basis:

(a) In the context of sale of children as defined in article 2:

(i) The offering, delivering or accepting, by whatever means, a child for the purpose of:

    a. Sexual exploitation of the child;

    b. Transfer of organs of the child for profit;

    c. Engagement of the child in forced labour;

(ii) Improperly inducing consent, as an intermediary, for the adoption of a child in violation of applicable international legal instruments on adoption;

(b) Offering, obtaining, procuring or providing a child for child prostitution, as defined in article 2;

(c) Producing, distributing, disseminating, importing, exporting, offering, selling or possessing for the above purposes child pornography as defined in article 2.

2. Subject to the provisions of a State Party's national law, the same shall apply to an attempt to commit any of these acts and to complicity or participation in any of these acts.

3. Each State Party shall make these offences punishable by appropriate penalties that take into account their grave nature.

4. Subject to the provisions of its national law, each State Party shall take measures, where appropriate, to establish the liability of legal persons for offences established in paragraph 1 of the present article. Subject to the legal principles of the State Party, this liability of legal persons may be criminal, civil or administrative.

5. States Parties shall take all appropriate legal and administrative measures to ensure that all persons involved in the adoption of a child act in conformity with applicable international legal instruments.

Article 4

1. Each State Party shall take such measures as may be necessary to establish its jurisdiction over the offences referred to in article 3, paragraph 1, when the offences are commited in its territory or on board a ship or aircraft registered in that State.

2. Each State Party may take such measures as may be necessary to establish its jurisdiction over the offences referred to in article 3, paragraph 1, in the following cases:

(a) When the alleged offender is a national of that State or a person who has his habitual residence in its territory;

(b) When the victim is a national of that State.

3. Each State Party shall also take such measures as may be necessary to establish its jurisdiction over the above-mentioned offences when the alleged offender is present in its territory and it does not extradite him or her to another State Party on the ground that the offence has been committed by one of its nationals.

4. This Protocol does not exclude any criminal jurisdiction exercised in accordance with internal law.

Article 5

1. The offences referred to in article 3, paragraph 1, shall be deemed to be included as extraditable offences in any extradition treaty existing between States Parties and shall be included as extraditable offences in every extradition treaty subsequently concluded between them, in accordance with the conditions set forth in those treaties.

2. If a State Party that makes extradition conditional on the existence of a treaty receives a request for extradition from another State Party with which it has no extradition treaty, it may consider this Protocol as a legal basis for extradition in respect of such offences. Extradition shall be subject to the conditions provided by the law of the requested State.

3. States Parties that do not make extradition conditional on the existence of a treaty shall recognize such offences as extraditable offences between themselves subject to the conditions provided by the law of the requested State.

4. Such offences shall be treated, for the purpose of extradition between States Parties, as if they had been committed not only in the place in which they occurred but also in the territories of the States required to establish their jurisdiction in accordance with article 4.

5. If an extradition request is made with respect to an offence described in article 3, paragraph 1, and if the requested State Party does not or will not extradite on the basis of the nationality of the offender, that State shall take suitable measures to submit the case to its competent authorities for the purpose of prosecution.

Article 6

1. States Parties shall afford one another the greatest measure of assistance in connection with investigations or criminal or extradition proceedings brought in respect of the offences set forth in article 3, paragraph 1, including assistance in obtaining evidence at their disposal necessary for the proceedings.

2. States Parties shall carry out their obligations under paragraph 1 of the present article in conformity with any treaties or other arrangements on mutual legal assistance that may exist between them. In the absence of such treaties or arrangements, States Parties shall afford one another assistance in accordance with their domestic law.

Article 7

States Parties shall, subject to the provisions of their national law:

(a) Take measures to provide for the seizure and confiscation, as appropriate, of:

(i) Goods such as materials, assets and other instrumentalities used to commit or facilitate offences under the present protocol;

(ii) Proceeds derived from such offences;

(b) Execute requests from another State Party for seizure or confiscation of goods or proceeds referred to in subparagraph (a) (i);

(c) Take measures aimed at closing, on a temporary or definitive basis, premises used to commit such offences.

Article 8

1. States Parties shall adopt appropriate measures to protect the rights and interests of child victims of the practices prohibited under the present Protocol at all stages of the criminal justice process, in particular by:

(a) Recognizing the vulnerability of child victims and adapting procedures to recognize their special needs, including their special needs as witnesses;

(b) Informing child victims of their rights, their role and the scope, timing and progress of the proceedings and of the disposition of their cases;

(c) Allowing the views, needs and concerns of child victims to be presented and considered in proceedings where their personal interests are affected, in a manner consistent with the procedural rules of national law;

(d) Providing appropriate support services to child victims throughout the legal process;

(e) Protecting, as appropriate, the privacy and identity of child victims and taking measures in accordance with national law to avoid the inappropriate dissemination of information that could lead to the identification of child victims;

(f) Providing, in appropriate cases, for the safety of child victims, as well as that of their families and witnesses on their behalf, from intimidation and retaliation;

(g) Avoiding unnecessary delay in the disposition of cases and the execution of orders or decrees granting compensation to child victims.

2. States Parties shall ensure that uncertainty as to the actual age of the victim shall not prevent the initiation of criminal investigations, including investigations aimed at establishing the age of the victim.

3. States Parties shall ensure that, in the treatment by the criminal justice system of children who are victims of the offences described in the present Protocol, the best interest of the child shall be a primary consideration.

4. States Parties shall take measures to ensure appropriate training, in particular legal and psychological training, for the persons who work with victims of the offences prohibited under the present Protocol.

5. States Parties shall, in appropriate cases, adopt measures in order to protect the safety and integrity of those persons and/or organizations involved in the prevention and/or protection and rehabilitation of victims of such offences.

6. Nothing in the present article shall be construed as prejudicial to or inconsistent with the rights of the accused to a fair and impartial trial.

Article 9

1. States Parties shall adopt or strengthen, implement and disseminate laws, administrative measures, social policies and programmes to prevent the offences referred to in the present Protocol. Particular attention shall be given to protect children who are especially vulnerable to these practices.

2. States Parties shall promote awareness in the public at large, including children, through information by all appropriate means, education and training, about the preventive measures and harmful effects of the offences referred to in the present Protocol. In fulfilling their obligations under this article, States Parties shall encourage the participation of the community and, in particular, children and child victims, in such information and education and training programmes, including at the international level.

3. States Parties shall take all feasible measures with the aim of ensuring all appropriate assistance to victims of such offences, including their full social reintegration and their full physical and psychological recovery.

4. States Parties shall ensure that all child victims of the offences described in the present Protocol have access to adequate procedures to seek, without discrimination, compensation for damages from those legally responsible.

5. States Parties shall take appropriate measures aimed at effectively prohibiting the production and dissemination of material advertising the offences described in the present Protocol.

Article 10

1. States Parties shall take all necessary steps to strengthen international cooperation by multilateral, regional and bilateral arrangements for the prevention, detection, investigation, prosecution and punishment of those responsible for acts involving the sale of children, child prostitution, child pornography and child sex tourism. States Parties shall also promote international cooperation and coordination between their authorities, national and international non-governmental organizations and international organizations.

2. States Parties shall promote international cooperation to assist child victims in their physical and psychological recovery, social reintegration and repatriation.

3. States Parties shall promote the strengthening of international cooperation in order to address the root causes, such as poverty and underdevelopment, contributing to the vulnerability of children to the sale of children, child prostitution, child pornography and child sex tourism.

4. States Parties in a position to do so shall provide financial, technical or other assistance through existing multilateral, regional, bilateral or other programmes.

Article 11

Nothing in the present Protocol shall affect any provisions that are more conducive to the realization of the rights of the child and that may be contained in:

(a) The law of a State Party;

(b) International law in force for that State.

Article 12

1. Each State Party shall submit, within two years following the entry into force of the Protocol for that State Party, a report to the Committee on the Rights of the Child providing comprehensive information on the measures it has taken to implement the provisions of the Protocol.

2. Following the submission of the comprehensive report, each State Party shall include in the reports they submit to the Committee on the Rights of the Child, in accordance with article 44 of the Convention, any further information with respect to the implementation of the Protocol. Other States Parties to the Protocol shall submit a report every five years.

3. The Committee on the Rights of the Child may request from States Parties further information relevant to the implementation of this Protocol.

[Ed. Note: Articles 13 to 17, addressing signature, ratification and accession, entry into force, denunciation, amendment, languages, and deposit of the Convention, are omitted.]

Reservation of the United States

"To the extent that the domestic law of the United States does not provide for jurisdiction over an offense described in Article 3 (1) of the Protocol if the offense is committed on board a ship or aircraft registered in the United States, the obligation with respect to jurisdiction over that offense shall not apply to the United States until such time as the United States may notify the Secretary-General of the United Nations that United States domestic law is in full conformity with the requirements of Article 4 (1) of the Protocol.

The Senate's advice and consent is subject to the following understandings:

(1) No Assumption of Obligations under the Convention on the Rights of the Child—

The United States understands that the United States assumes no obligations under the Convention on the Rights of the Child by becoming a party to the Protocol.

(2) The Term "Sale of Children" —

The United States understands that the term "sale of children" as defined in Article 2(a) of the Protocol, is intended to cover any transaction in which remuneration or other consideration is given and received under circumstances in which a person who does not have a lawful right to custody of the child thereby obtains de facto control over the child.

(3) The Term "Child Pornography" —

The United States understands the term "child pornography," as defined in Article 2(c) of the Protocol, to mean the visual representation of a child engaged in real or simulated sexual activities or of the genitalia of a child where the dominant characteristic is depiction for a sexual purpose.

(4) The Term "Transfer of Organs for Profit" —

The United States understands that—

(A) the term "transfer of organs for profit," as used in Article 3(1)(a)(i) of the Protocol, does not cover any situation in which a child donates an organ pursuant to lawful consent; and

(B) the term "profit," as used in Article 3(1)(a)(i) of the Protocol, does not include the lawful payment of a reasonable amount associated with the transfer of organs, including any payment for the expense of travel, housing, lost wages, or medical costs.

(5) The Terms "Applicable International Legal Instruments" and "Improperly Inducing Consent" —

(A) Understanding of "Applicable International Legal Instruments" —

The United States understands that the term "applicable international legal instruments" in Articles 3 (1)(a)(ii) and 3(5) of the Protocol refers to the Convention on Protection of Children and Co-operation in Respect of Intercountry Adoption done at The Hague on May 29, 1993 (in this paragraph referred to as "The Hague Convention").

(B) No Obligation to Take Certain Action—

The United States is not a party to The Hague Convention, but expects to become a party. Accordingly, until such time as the United States becomes a party to The Hague Convention, it understands that it is not obligated to criminalize conduct proscribed by Article 3(1)(a)(ii) of the Protocol or to take all appropriate legal and administrative measures required by Article 3(5) of the Protocol.

(C) Understanding of "Improperly Inducing Consent"—

The United States understands that the term "improperly inducing consent" in Article 3(1)(a)(ii) of the Protocol means knowingly and willfully inducing consent by offering or giving compensation for the relinquishment of parental rights.

(6) Implementation of the Protocol in the Federal System of the United States—

The United States understands that the Protocol shall be implemented by the Federal Government to the extent that it exercises jurisdiction over the matters covered therein, and otherwise by the State and local governments. To the extent that State and local governments exercise jurisdiction over such matters, the Federal Government shall as necessary, take appropriate measures to ensure the fulfillment of the Protocol.

Part II

Selected Conventions of the Hague Conference on Private International Law

A. Marriage and Dissolution

Convention on Celebration and Recognition of the Validity of Marriages

Mar. 14, 1978, 16 I.L.M. 18

Hague Conf. Priv. Int'l L. Collection of Conventions (1951–1996) at 243

available at http://www.hcch.net

[Ed. Note: This Convention entered into force on May 1, 1991. As of March 2003, only Australia, Luxembourg, and Netherlands were parties to the Convention. The only other signatories, Egypt, Finland, and Portugal, signed the Convention over 20 years ago, but have never ratified it.]

The States signatory to the present Convention,

Desiring to facilitate the celebration of marriages and the recognition of the validity of marriages,

Have resolved to conclude a Convention to this effect, and have agreed on the following provisions—

Chapter I — Celebration of Marriages

Article 1

This Chapter shall apply to the requirements in a Contracting State for celebration of marriages.

Article 2

The formal requirements for marriages shall be governed by the law of the State of celebration.

Article 3

A marriage shall be celebrated—

(1) where the future spouses meet the substantive requirements of the internal law of the State of celebration and one of them has the nationality of that State or habitually resides there; or

(2) where each of the future spouses meets the substantive requirements of the internal law designated by the choice of law rules of the State of celebration.

Article 4

The State of celebration may require the future spouses to furnish any necessary evidence as to the content of any foreign law which is applicable under the preceding Articles.

Article 5

The application of a foreign law declared applicable by this Chapter may be refused only if such application is manifestly incompatible with the public policy ("ordre public") of the State of celebration.

Article 6

A Contracting State may reserve the right, by way of derogation from Article 3, subparagraph 1, not to apply its internal law to the substantive requirements for marriage in respect of a future spouse who neither is a national of that State nor habitually resides there.

Chapter II — Recognition of the Validity of Marriages

Article 7

This Chapter shall apply to the recognition in a Contracting State of the validity of marriages entered into in other States.

Article 8

This Chapter shall not apply to—

(1) marriages celebrated by military authorities;

(2) marriages celebrated aboard ships or aircraft;

(3) proxy marriages;

(4) posthumous marriages;

(5) informal marriages.

Article 9

A marriage validly entered into under the law of the State of celebration or which subsequently becomes valid under that law shall be considered as such in all Contracting States, subject to the provisions of this Chapter.

A marriage celebrated by a diplomatic agent or consular official in accordance with his law shall similarly be considered valid in all Contracting States, provided that the celebration is not prohibited by the State of celebration.

Article 10

Where a marriage certificate has been issued by a competent authority, the marriage shall be presumed to be valid until the contrary is established.

Article 11

A Contracting State may refuse to recognize the validity of a marriage only where, at the time of the marriage, under the law of that State—

(1) one of the spouses was already married; or

(2) the spouses were related to one another, by blood or by adoption, in the direct line or as brother and sister; or

(3) one of the spouses had not attained the minimum age required for marriage, nor had obtained the necessary dispensation; or

(4) one of the spouses did not have the mental capacity to consent; or

(5) one of the spouses did not freely consent to the marriage.

However, recognition may not be refused where, in the case mentioned in sub-paragraph 1 of the preceding paragraph, the marriage has subsequently become valid by reason of the dissolution or annulment of the prior marriage.

Article 12

The rules of this Chapter shall apply even where the recognition of the validity of a marriage is to be dealt with as an incidental question in the context of another question.

However, these rules need not be applied where that other question, under the choice of law rules of the forum, is governed by the law of a non-Contracting State.

Article 13

This Convention shall not prevent the application in a Contracting State of rules of law more favourable to the recognition of foreign marriages.

Article 14

A Contracting State may refuse to recognize the validity of a marriage where such recognition is manifestly incompatible with its public policy ("ordre public").

Article 15

This Chapter shall apply regardless of the date on which the marriage was celebrated.

However, a Contracting State may reserve the right not to apply this Chapter to a marriage celebrated before the date on which, in relation to that State, the Convention enters into force.

Chapter III — General Clauses

Article 16

A Contracting State may reserve the right to exclude the application of Chapter I.

Article 17

Where a State has two or more territorial units in which different systems of law apply in relation to marriage, any reference to the law of the State of celebration shall be construed as referring to the law of the territorial unit in which the marriage is or was celebrated.

Article 18

Where a State has two or more territorial units in which different systems of law apply in relation to marriage, any reference to the law of that State in connection with the recognition of the validity of a marriage shall be construed as referring to the law of the territorial unit in which recognition is sought.

Article 19

Where a State has two or more territorial units in which different systems of law apply in relation to marriage, this Convention need not be applied to the recognition in one territorial unit of the validity of a marriage entered into in another territorial unit.

Article 20

Where a State has, in relation to marriage, two or more systems of law applicable to different categories of persons, any reference to the law of that State shall be construed as referring to the system of law designated by the rules in force in that State.

Article 21

The Convention shall not affect the application of any convention containing provisions on the celebration or recognition of the validity of marriages to which a Contracting State is a Party at the time this Convention enters into force for that State.

This Convention shall not affect the right of a Contracting State to become a Party to a convention, based on special ties of a regional or other nature, containing provisions on the celebration or recognition of validity of marriages.

Article 22

This Convention shall replace, in the relations between the States who are Parties to it, the Convention Governing Conflicts of Laws Concerning Marriage, concluded at The Hague, the 12th of June 1902.

[Ed. Note: Articles 23 to 31, addressing provision of information regarding authorities competent to issue marriage certificates, signature, ratification, accession, deposit of instruments, territorial application, reservations, entry into force, denunciation, and notification, are omitted.]

Convention on the Recognition
of Divorces and Legal Separations
June 1, 1970, 978 U.N.T.S. 393
Hague Conf. Priv. Int'l L. Collection of Conventions (1951–1996) at 129
available at http://www.hcch.net

[Ed. Note: This Convention entered into force on August 24, 1975. As of March 2003, 18 nations were parties to the Convention. The United States is not a party to this Convention.]

The States signatory to the present Convention,

Desiring to facilitate the recognition of divorces and legal separations obtained in their respective territories,

Have resolved to conclude a Convention to this effect, and have agreed on the following provisions:

Article 1

The present Convention shall apply to the recognition in one Contracting State of divorces and legal separations obtained in another Contracting State which follow judicial or other proceedings officially recognized in that State and which are legally effective there.

The Convention does not apply to findings of fault or to ancillary orders pronounced on the making of a decree of divorce or legal separation; in particular, it does not apply to orders relating to pecuniary obligations or to the custody of children.

Article 2

Such divorces and legal separations shall be recognized in all other Contracting States, subject to the remaining terms of this Convention, if, at the date of the institution of the proceedings in the State of the divorce or legal separation (hereinafter called "the State of origin") —

(1) the respondent had his habitual residence there; or

(2) the petitioner had his habitual residence there and one of the following further conditions was fulfilled —

a) such habitual residence had continued for not less than one year immediately prior to the institution of proceedings;

b) the spouses last habitually resided there together; or

(3) both spouses were nationals of that State; or

(4) the petitioner was a national of that State and one of the following further conditions was fulfilled —

a) the petitioner had his habitual residence there; or

b) he had habitually resided there for a continuous period of one year falling, at least in part, within the two years preceding the institution of the proceedings; or

(5) the petitioner for divorce was a national of that State and both the following further conditions were fulfilled —

a) the petitioner was present in that State at the date of institution of the proceedings and

b) the spouses last habitually resided together in a State whose law, at the date of institution of the proceedings, did not provide for divorce.

Article 3

Where the State of origin uses the concept of domicile as a test of jurisdiction in matters of divorce or legal separation, the expression "habitual residence" in Article 2 shall be deemed to include domicile as the term is used in that State.

Nevertheless, the preceding paragraph shall not apply to the domicile of dependence of a wife.

Article 4

Where there has been a cross-petition, a divorce or legal separation following upon the petition or cross-petition shall be recognized if either falls within the terms of Articles 2 or 3.

Article 5

Where a legal separation complying with the terms of this Convention has been converted into a divorce in the State of origin, the recognition of the divorce shall not be refused for the reason that the conditions stated in Articles 2 or 3 were no longer fulfilled at the time of the institution of the divorce proceedings.

Article 6

Where the respondent has appeared in the proceedings, the authorities of the State in which recognition of a divorce or legal separation is sought shall be bound by the findings of fact on which jurisdiction was assumed.

The recognition of a divorce or legal separation shall not be refused—

a) because the internal law of the State in which such recognition is sought would not allow divorce or, as the case may be, legal separation upon the same facts, or,

b) because a law was applied other than that applicable under the rules of private international law of that State.

Without prejudice to such review as may be necessary for the application of other provisions of this Convention, the authorities of the State in which recognition of a divorce or legal separation is sought shall not examine the merits of the decision.

Article 7

Contracting States may refuse to recognize a divorce when, at the time it was obtained, both the parties were nationals of States which did not provide for divorce and of no other State.

Article 8

If, in the light of all the circumstances, adequate steps were not taken to give notice of the proceedings for a divorce or legal separation to the respondent, or if he was not afforded a sufficient opportunity to present his case, the divorce or legal separation may be refused recognition.

Article 9

Contracting States may refuse to recognize a divorce or legal separation if it is incompatible with a previous decision determining the matrimonial status of the spouses and that decision either was rendered in the State in which recognition is sought, or is recognized, or fulfils the conditions required for recognition, in that State.

Article 10

Contracting States may refuse to recognize a divorce or legal separation if such recognition is manifestly incompatible with their public policy ("ordre public").

Article 11

A State which is obliged to recognize a divorce under this Convention may not preclude either spouse from remarrying on the ground that the law of another State does not recognize that divorce.

Article 12

Proceedings for divorce or legal separation in any Contracting State may be suspended when proceedings relating to the matrimonial status of either party to the marriage are pending in another Contracting State.

Article 13

In the application of this Convention to divorces or legal separations obtained or sought to be recognized in Contracting States having, in matters of divorce or legal separation, two or more legal systems applying in different territorial units—

(1) any reference to the law of the State of origin shall be construed as referring to the law of the territory in which the divorce or separation was obtained;

(2) any reference to the law of the State in which recognition is sought shall be construed as referring to the law of the forum; and

(3) any reference to domicile or residence in the State of origin shall be construed as referring to domicile or residence in the territory in which the divorce or separation was obtained.

Article 14

For the purposes of Articles 2 and 3, where the State of origin has in matters of divorce or legal separation two or more legal systems applying in different territorial units—

(1) Article 2, sub-paragraph (3), shall apply where both spouses were nationals of the State of which the territorial unit where the divorce or legal separation was obtained forms a part, and that regardless of the habitual residence of the spouses;

(2) Article 2, sub-paragraphs (4) and (5), shall apply where the petitioner was a national of the State of which the territorial unit where the divorce or legal separation was obtained forms a part.

Article 15

In relation to a Contracting State having, in matters of divorce or legal separation, two or more legal systems applicable to different categories of persons, any reference to the law of that State shall be construed as referring to the legal system specified by the law of that State.

Article 16

When, for the purposes of this Convention, it is necessary to refer to the law of a State, whether or not it is a Contracting State, other than the State of origin or the State in which recognition is sought, and having in matters of divorce or legal separation two or more legal systems of territorial or personal application, reference shall be made to the system specified by the law of that State.

Article 17

This Convention shall not prevent the application in a Contracting State of rules of law more favourable to the recognition of foreign divorces and legal separations.

Article 18

This Convention shall not affect the operation of other conventions to which one or several Contracting States are or may in the future become Parties and which contain provisions relating to the subject-matter of this Convention.

Contracting States, however, should refrain from concluding other conventions on the same matter incompatible with the terms of this Convention, unless for special reasons based on regional or other ties; and, notwithstanding the terms of such conventions, they undertake to recognize in accordance with this Convention divorces and legal separations granted in Contracting States which are not Parties to such other conventions.

Article 19

Contracting States may, not later than the time of ratification or accession, reserve the right—

(1) to refuse to recognize a divorce or legal separation between two spouses who, at the time of the divorce or legal separation, were nationals of the State in which recogni-

tion is sought, and of no other State, and a law other than that indicated by the rules of private international law of the State of recognition was applied, unless the result reached is the same as that which would have been reached by applying the law indicated by those rules;

(2) to refuse to recognize a divorce when, at the time it was obtained, both parties habitually resided in States which did not provide for divorce. A State which utilizes the reservation stated in this paragraph may not refuse recognition by the application of Article 7.

Article 20

Contracting States whose law does not provide for divorce may, not later than the time of ratification or accession, reserve the right not to recognize a divorce if, at the date it was obtained, one of the spouses was a national of a State whose law did not provide for divorce.

This reservation shall have effect only so long as the law of the State utilizing it does not provide for divorce.

Article 21

Contracting States whose law does not provide for legal separation may, not later than the time of ratification or accession, reserve the right to refuse to recognize a legal separation when, at the time it was obtained, one of the spouses was a national of a Contracting State whose law did not provide for legal separation.

Article 22

Contracting States may, from time to time, declare that certain categories of persons having their nationality need not be considered their nationals for the purposes of this Convention.

Article 23

If a Contracting State has more than one legal system in matters of divorce or legal separation, it may, at the time of signature, ratification or accession, declare that this Convention shall extend to all its legal systems or only to one or more of them, and may modify its declaration by submitting another declaration at anytime thereafter.

These declarations shall be notified to the Ministry of Foreign Affairs of the Netherlands, and shall state expressly the legal systems to which the Convention applies.

Contracting States may decline to recognize a divorce or legal separation if, at the date on which recognition is sought, the Convention is not applicable to the legal system under which the divorce or legal separation was obtained.

Article 24

This Convention applies regardless of the date on which the divorce or legal separation was obtained.

Nevertheless a Contracting State may, not later than the time of ratification or accession, reserve the right not to apply this Convention to a divorce or to a legal separation obtained before the date on which, in relation to that State, the Convention comes into force.

[Ed. Note: Articles 25 to 31, addressing reservations, signature and ratification, entry into force, accession, territorial application, denunciation, and notification, are omitted.]

Convention on the Recognition and Enforcement of Decisions Relating to Maintenance Obligations

Oct. 2, 1973, 1021 U.N.T.S. 209

Hague Conf. Priv. Int'l L. Collection of Conventions (1951–1996) at 203

available at http://www.hcch.net

[Ed. Note: This Convention entered into force on August 1, 1976. As of March 2003, 20 nations were parties to the Convention. All member nations were European, with the exception of Australia, one of the newer contracting parties, for which the Convention entered into force on February 1, 2002. The United States is not a party to this Convention.]

The States signatory to this Convention,

Desiring to establish common provisions to govern the reciprocal recognition and enforcement of decisions relating to maintenance obligations in respect of adults,

Desiring to coordinate these provisions and those of the Convention of the 15th of April 1958 on the Recognition and Enforcement of Decisions Relating to Maintenance Obligations in Respect of Children,

Have resolved to conclude a Convention for this purpose and have agreed upon the following provisions:

Chapter I — Scope of the Convention

Article 1

This Convention shall apply to a decision rendered by a judicial or administrative authority in a Contracting State in respect of a maintenance obligation arising from a family relationship, parentage, marriage or affinity, including a maintenance obligation towards an infant who is not legitimate, between—

(1) a maintenance creditor and a maintenance debtor; or

(2) a maintenance debtor and a public body which claims reimbursement of benefits given to a maintenance creditor.

It shall also apply to a settlement made by or before such an authority ("transaction") in respect of the said obligations and between the same parties (hereafter referred to as a "settlement").

Article 2

This Convention shall apply to a decision or settlement however described.

It shall also apply to a decision or settlement modifying a previous decision or settlement, even in the case where this originates from a non-Contracting State.

It shall apply irrespective of the international or internal character of the maintenance claim and whatever may be the nationality or habitual residence of the parties.

Article 3

If a decision or settlement does not relate solely to a maintenance obligation, the effect of the Convention is limited to the parts of the decision or settlement which concern maintenance obligations.

Chapter II — Conditions for Recognition and Enforcement of Decisions

Article 4

A decision rendered in a Contracting State shall be recognised or enforced in another Contracting State —

(1) if it was rendered by an authority considered to have jurisdiction under Article 7 or 8; and

(2) if it is no longer subject to ordinary forms of review in the State of origin.

Provisionally enforceable decisions and provisional measures shall, although subject to ordinary forms of review, be recognised or enforced in the State addressed if similar decisions may be rendered and enforced in that State.

Article 5

Recognition or enforcement of a decision may, however, be refused —

(1) if recognition or enforcement of the decision is manifestly incompatible with the public policy ("ordre public") of the State addressed; or

(2) if the decision was obtained by fraud in connection with a matter of procedure; or

(3) if proceedings between the same parties and having the same purpose are pending before an authority of the State addressed and those proceedings were the first to be instituted; or

(4) if the decision is incompatible with a decision rendered between the same parties and having the same purpose, either in the State addressed or in another State, provided that this latter decision fulfils the conditions necessary for its recognition and enforcement in the State addressed.

Article 6

Without prejudice to the provisions of Article 5, a decision rendered by default shall be recognised or enforced only if notice of the institution of the proceedings, including notice of the substance of the claim, has been served on the defaulting party in accordance with the law of the State of origin and if, having regard to the circumstances, that party has had sufficient time to enable him to defend the proceedings.

Article 7

An authority in the State of origin shall be considered to have jurisdiction for the purposes of this Convention —

(1) if either the maintenance debtor or the maintenance creditor had his habitual residence in the State of origin at the time when the proceedings were instituted; or

(2) if the maintenance debtor and the maintenance creditor were nationals of the State of origin at the time when the proceedings were instituted; or

(3) if the defendant had submitted to the jurisdiction of the authority, either expressly or by defending on the merits of the case without objecting to the jurisdiction.

Article 8

Without prejudice to the provisions of Article 7, the authority of a Contracting State which has given judgment on a maintenance claim shall be considered to have jurisdiction for the purposes of this Convention if the maintenance is due by reason of a divorce or a legal separation, or a declaration that a marriage is void or annulled, obtained from an authority of that State recognised as having jurisdiction in that matter, according to the law of the State addressed.

Article 9

The authority of the State addressed shall be bound by the findings of fact on which the authority of the State of origin based its jurisdiction.

Article 10

If a decision deals with several issues in an application for maintenance and if recognition or enforcement cannot be granted for the whole of the decision, the authority of the State addressed shall apply this Convention to that part of the decision which can be recognised or enforced.

Article 11

If a decision provided for the periodical payment of maintenance, enforcement shall be granted in respect of payments already due and in respect of future payments.

Article 12

There shall be no review by the authority of the State addressed of the merits of a decision, unless this Convention otherwise provides.

Chapter III — Procedure for Recognition and Enforcement of Decisions

Article 13

The procedure for the recognition or enforcement of a decision shall be governed by the law of the State addressed, unless this Convention otherwise provides.

Article 14

Partial recognition or enforcement of a decision can always be applied for.

Article 15

A maintenance creditor, who, in the State of origin, has benefited from complete or partial legal aid or exemption from costs or expenses, shall be entitled, in any proceedings for recognition or enforcement, to benefit from the most favourable legal aid or the most extensive exemption from costs or expenses provided for by the law of the State addressed.

Article 16

No security, bond or deposit, however described, shall be required to guarantee the payment of costs and expenses in the proceedings to which the Convention refers.

Article 17

The party seeking recognition or applying for enforcement of a decision shall furnish —

(1) a complete and true copy of the decision;

(2) any document necessary to prove that the decision is no longer subject to the ordinary forms of review in the State of origin and, where necessary, that it is enforceable;

(3) if the decision was rendered by default, the original or a certified true copy of any document required to prove that the notice of the institution of proceedings, including notice of the substance of claim, has been properly served on the defaulting party according to the law of the State of origin;

(4) where appropriate, any document necessary to prove that he obtained legal aid or exemption from costs or expenses in the State of origin;

(5) a translation, certified as true, of the above-mentioned documents unless the authority of the State addressed dispenses with such translation.

If there is a failure to produce the documents mentioned above or if the contents of the decision do not permit the authority of the State addressed to verify whether the conditions of this Convention have been fulfilled, the authority shall allow a specified period of time for the production of the necessary documents.

No legalisation or other like formality may be required.

Chapter IV — Additional Provisions Relating to Public Bodies

Article 18

A decision rendered against a maintenance debtor on the application of a public body which claims reimbursement of benefits provided for a maintenance creditor shall be recognised and enforced in accordance with this Convention —

(1) if reimbursement can be obtained by the public body under the law to which it is subject; and

(2) if the existence of a maintenance obligation between the creditor and the debtor is provided for by the internal law applicable under the rules of private international law of the State addressed.

Article 19

A public body may seek recognition or claim enforcement of a decision rendered between a maintenance creditor and maintenance debtor to the extent of the benefits provided for the creditor if it is entitled *ipso jure*, under the law to which it is subject, to seek recognition or claim enforcement of the decision in place of the creditor.

Article 20

Without prejudice to the provisions of Article 17, the public body seeking recognition or claiming enforcement of a decision shall furnish any document necessary to prove that it fulfils the conditions of sub-paragraph 1, of Article 18 or Article 19, and that benefits have been provided for the maintenance creditor.

Chapter V — Settlements

Article 21

A settlement which is enforceable in the State of origin shall be recognised and enforced subject to the same conditions as a decision so far as such conditions are applicable to it.

Chapter VI — Miscellaneous Provisions

Article 22

A Contracting State, under whose law the transfer of funds is restricted, shall accord the highest priority to the transfer of funds payable as maintenance or to cover costs and expenses in respect of any claim under this Convention.

Article 23

This Convention shall not restrict the application of an international instrument in force between the State of origin and the State addressed or other law of the State addressed for the purposes of obtaining recognition or enforcement of a decision or settlement.

Article 24

This Convention shall apply irrespective of the date on which a decision was rendered.

Where a decision has been rendered prior to the entry into force of the Convention between the State of origin and the State addressed, it shall be enforced in the latter State only for payments falling due after such entry into force.

Article 25

Any Contracting State may, at any time, declare that the provisions of this Convention will be extended, in relation to other States making a declaration under this Article, to an official deed ("acte authentique") drawn up by or before an authority or public official and directly enforceable in the State of origin insofar as these provisions can be applied to such deeds.

Article 26

Any Contracting State may, in accordance with Article 34, reserve the right not to recognise or enforce—

(1) a decision or settlement insofar as it relates to a period of time after a maintenance creditor attains the age of twenty-one years or marries, except when the creditor is or was the spouse of the maintenance debtor;

(2) a decision or settlement in respect of maintenance obligations

a) between persons related collaterally;

b) between persons related by affinity;

(3) a decision or settlement unless it provides for the periodical payment of maintenance.

A Contracting State which has made a reservation shall not be entitled to claim the application of this Convention to such decisions or settlements as are excluded by its reservation.

Article 27

If a Contracting State has, in matters of maintenance obligations, two or more legal systems applicable to different categories of persons, any reference to the law of that State shall be construed as referring to the legal system which its law designates as applicable to a particular category of persons.

Article 28

If a Contracting State has two or more territorial units in which different systems of law apply in relation to the recognition and enforcement of maintenance decisions—

(1) any reference to the law or procedure or authority of the State of origin shall be construed as referring to the law or procedure or authority of the territorial unit in which the decision was rendered;

(2) any reference to the law or procedure or authority of the State addressed shall be construed as referring to the law or procedure or authority of the territorial unit in which recognition or enforcement is sought;

(3) any reference made in the application of sub-paragraph 1 or 2 to the law or procedure of the State of origin or to the law or procedure of the State addressed shall be construed as including any relevant legal rules and principles of the Contracting State which apply to the territorial units comprising it;

(4) any reference to the habitual residence of the maintenance creditor or the maintenance debtor in the State of origin shall be construed as referring to his habitual residence in the territorial unit in which the decision was rendered.

Any Contracting State may, at any time, declare that it will not apply any one or more of the foregoing rules to one or more of the provisions of this Convention.

Article 29

This Convention shall replace, as regards the States who are Parties to it, the Convention on the Recognition and Enforcement of Decisions Relating to Maintenance Obligations in Respect of Children, concluded at The Hague on the 15th of April 1958.

[Ed. Note: Articles 30 to 37, addressing signature, ratification, deposit, accession, territorial application, reservations, entry into force, denunciation, and notification, are omitted.]

Convention on the Law Applicable to Maintenance Obligations

Oct. 2, 1973, 1056 U.N.T.S. 199

Hague Conf. Priv. Int'l L. Collection of Conventions (1951–1996) at 219

available at http://www.hcch.net

[Ed. Note: This Convention entered into force on October 1, 1977. As of March 2003, 13 nations were parties to the Convention. The United States is not a party to this Convention.]

The States signatory to this Convention,

Desiring to establish common provisions concerning the law applicable to maintenance obligations in respect of adults,

Desiring to coordinate these provisions and those of the Convention of the 24th of October 1956 on the Law Applicable to Maintenance Obligations in Respect of Children,

Have resolved to conclude a Convention for this purpose and have agreed upon the following provisions:

Chapter I — Scope of the Convention

Article 1

This Convention shall apply to maintenance obligations arising from a family relationship, parentage, marriage or affinity, including a maintenance obligation in respect of a child who is not legitimate.

Article 2

This Convention shall govern only conflicts of laws in respect of maintenance obligations.

Decisions rendered in application of this Convention shall be without prejudice to the existence of any of the relationships referred to in Article 1.

Article 3

The law designated by this Convention shall apply irrespective of any requirement of reciprocity and whether or not it is the law of a Contracting State.

Chapter II — Applicable Law

Article 4

The internal law of the habitual residence of the maintenance creditor shall govern the maintenance obligations referred to in Article 1.

In the case of a change in the habitual residence of the creditor, the internal law of the new habitual residence shall apply as from the moment when the change occurs.

Article 5

If the creditor is unable, by virtue of the law referred to in Article 4, to obtain maintenance from the debtor, the law of their common nationality shall apply.

Article 6

If the creditor is unable, by virtue of the laws referred to in Articles 4 and 5, to obtain maintenance from the debtor, the internal law of the authority seized shall apply.

Article 7

In the case of a maintenance obligation between persons related collaterally or by affinity, the debtor may contest a request from the creditor on the ground that there is no such obligation under the law of their common nationality or, in the absence of a common nationality, under the internal law of the debtor's habitual residence.

Article 8

Notwithstanding the provisions of Articles 4 to 6, the law applied to a divorce shall, in a Contracting State in which the divorce is granted or recognised, govern the maintenance obligations between the divorced spouses and the revision of decisions relating to these obligations.

The preceding paragraph shall apply also in the case of a legal separation and in the case of a marriage which has been declared void or annulled.

Article 9

The right of a public body to obtain reimbursement of benefits provided for the maintenance creditor shall be governed by the law to which the body is subject.

Article 10

The law applicable to a maintenance obligation shall determine *inter alia* —

(1) whether, to what extent and from whom a creditor may claim maintenance;

(2) who is entitled to institute maintenance proceedings and the time limits for their institution;

(3) the extent of the obligation of a maintenance debtor, where a public body seeks reimbursement of benefits provided for a creditor.

Article 11

The application of the law designated by this Convention may be refused only if it is manifestly incompatible with public policy ("ordre public").

However, even if the applicable law provides otherwise, the needs of the creditor and the resources of the debtor shall be taken into account in determining the amount of maintenance.

Chapter III — Miscellaneous Provisions

Article 12

This Convention shall not apply to maintenance claimed in a Contracting State relating to a period prior to its entry into force in that State.

Article 13

Any Contracting State may, in accordance with Article 24, reserve the right to apply this Convention only to maintenance obligations—

(1) between spouses and former spouses;

(2) in respect of a person who has not attained the age of twenty-one years and has not been married.

Article 14

Any Contracting State may, in accordance with Article 24, reserve the right not to apply this Convention to maintenance obligations—

(1) between persons related collaterally;

(2) between persons related by affinity;

(3) between divorced or legally separated spouses or spouses whose marriage has been declared void or annulled if the decree of divorce, legal separation, nullity or annulment has been rendered by default in a State in which the defaulting party did not have his habitual residence.

Article 15

Any Contracting State may, in accordance with Article 24, make a reservation to the effect that its authorities shall apply its internal law if the creditor and the debtor are both nationals of that State and if the debtor has his habitual residence there.

Article 16

Where the law of a State, having in matters of maintenance obligations two or more systems of law of territorial or personal application, must be taken into consideration — as may be the case if a reference is made to the law of the habitual residence of the creditor or the debtor or to the law of common nationality, reference shall be made to the system designated by the rules in force in that State or, if there are no such rules, to the system with which the persons concerned are most closely connected.

Article 17

A Contracting State within which different territorial units have their own rules of law in matters of maintenance obligations is not bound to apply this Convention to conflicts of law concerned solely with its territorial units.

Article 18

This Convention shall replace, in the relations between the States who are Parties to it, the Convention on the Law Applicable to Maintenance Obligations in Respect of Children, concluded at The Hague, the 24th of October 1956.

However, the preceding paragraph shall not apply to a State which, by virtue of the reservation provided for in Article 13, has excluded the application of this Convention to maintenance obligations in respect of a person who has not attained the age of twenty-one years and has not been married.

Article 19

This Convention shall not affect any other international instrument containing provisions on matters governed by this Convention to which a Contracting State is, or becomes, a Party.

[Ed. Note: Articles 20 to 27, addressing signature, ratification, deposit, accession, territorial application, reservations, entry into force, denunciation, and notification, are omitted.]

Convention on the Law Applicable to Matrimonial Property Regimes
Mar. 14, 1978, 16 I.L.M. 14
Hague Conf. Priv. Int'l L. Collection of Conventions (1951–1996) at 229
available at http://www.hcch.net

[Ed. Note: This Convention entered into force on September 1, 1992. As of March 2003, only three nations were parties to the Convention: France, Luxembourg, and Netherlands. Austria and Portugal signed the Convention in 1978, but have not ratified it.]

The States signatory to this Convention,

Desiring to establish common provisions concerning the law applicable to matrimonial property regimes,

Have resolved to conclude a Convention for this purpose and have agreed upon the following provisions—

Chapter I—Scope of the Convention

Article 1

This Convention determines the law applicable to matrimonial property regimes.

The Convention does not apply to—

(1) maintenance obligations between spouses;

(2) succession rights of a surviving spouse;

(3) the capacity of the spouses.

Article 2

The Convention applies even if the nationality or the habitual residence of the spouses or the law to be applied by virtue of the following Articles is not that of a Contracting State.

Chapter II — Applicable Law

Article 3

The matrimonial property regime is governed by the internal law designated by the spouses before marriage.

The spouses may designate only one of the following laws —

(1) the law of any State of which either spouse is a national at the time of designation;

(2) the law of the State in which either spouse has his habitual residence at the time of designation;

(3) the law of the first State where one of the spouses establishes a new habitual residence after marriage.

The law thus designated applies to the whole of their property.

Nonetheless, the spouses, whether or not they have designated a law under the previous paragraphs, may designate with respect to all or some of the immovables, the law of the place where these immovables are situated. They may also provide that any immovables which may subsequently be acquired shall be governed by the law of the place where such immovables are situated.

Article 4

If the spouses, before marriage, have not designated the applicable law, their matrimonial property regime is governed by the internal law of the State in which both spouses establish their first habitual residence after marriage.

Nonetheless, in the following cases, the matrimonial property regime is governed by the internal law of the State of the common nationality of the spouses —

(1) where the declaration provided for in Article 5 has been made by that State and its application to the spouses is not excluded by the provisions of the second paragraph of that Article;

(2) where that State is not a Party to the Convention and according to the rules of private international law of that State its internal law is applicable, and the spouses establish their first habitual residence after marriage —

a) in a State which has made the declaration provided for in Article 5, or

b) in a State which is not a Party to the Convention and whose rules of private international law also provide for the application of the law of their nationality;

(3) where the spouses do not establish their first habitual residence after marriage in the same State.

If the spouses do not have their habitual residence in the same State, nor have a common nationality, their matrimonial property regime is governed by the internal law of the State with which, taking all circumstances into account, it is most closely connected.

Article 5

Any State may, not later than the moment of ratification, acceptance, approval or accession, make a declaration requiring the application of its internal law according to sub-paragraph 1 of the second paragraph of Article 4.

This declaration shall not apply to spouses who both retain their habitual residence in the State in which they have both had their habitual residence at the time of marriage for a period of not less than five years, unless that State is a Contracting State which has made the declaration provided for in the first paragraph of this Article, or is a State which is not a Party to the Convention and whose rules of private international law require the application of the national law.

Article 6

During marriage the spouses may subject their matrimonial property regime to an internal law other than that previously applicable.

The spouses may designate only one of the following laws—

(1) the law of any State of which either spouse is a national at the time of designation;

(2) the law of the State in which either spouse has his habitual residence at the time of designation.

The law thus designated applies to the whole of their property.

Nonetheless, the spouses, whether or not they have designated a law under the previous paragraphs or under Article 3, may designate with respect to all or some of the immovables, the law of the place where these immovables are situated. They may also provide that any immovables which may subsequently be acquired shall be governed by the law of the place where such immovables are situated.

Article 7

The law applicable under the Convention continues to apply so long as the spouses have not designated a different applicable law and notwithstanding any change of their nationality or habitual residence.

Nonetheless, if the spouses have neither designated the applicable law nor concluded a marriage contract, the internal law of the State in which they both have their habitual residence shall become applicable, in place of the law previously applicable—

(1) when that habitual residence is established in that State, if the nationality of that State is their common nationality, or otherwise from the moment they become nationals of that State, or

(2) when, after the marriage, that habitual residence has endured for a period of not less than ten years, or

(3) when that habitual residence is established, in cases when the matrimonial property regime was subject to the law of the State of the common nationality solely by virtue of sub-paragraph 3 of the second paragraph of Article 4.

Article 8

A change of applicable law pursuant to the second paragraph of Article 7 shall have effect only for the future, and property belonging to the spouses before the change is not subject to the new applicable law.

Nonetheless, the spouses may at any time, employing the forms available under Article 13, subject the whole of their property to the new law, without prejudice, with respect to immovables, to the provisions of the fourth paragraph of Article 3 and the fourth paragraph of Article 6. The exercise of this option shall not adversely affect the rights of third parties.

Article 9

The effects of the matrimonial property regime on the legal relations between a spouse and a third party are governed by the law applicable to the matrimonial property regime in accordance with the Convention.

Nonetheless, the law of a Contracting State may provide that the law applicable to the matrimonial property regime may not be relied upon by a spouse against a third party where either that spouse or the third party has his habitual residence in its territory, unless

(1) any requirements of publicity or registration specified by that law have been complied with, or

(2) the legal relations between that spouse and the third party arose at a time when the third party either knew or should have known of the law applicable to the matrimonial property regime.

The law of a Contracting State where an immovable is situated may provide an analogous rule for the legal relations between a spouse and a third party as regards that immovable.

A Contracting State may specify by declaration the scope of the second and third paragraphs of this Article.

Article 10

Any requirements relating to the consent of the spouses to the law designated as applicable shall be determined by that law.

Article 11

The designation of the applicable law shall be by express stipulation, or arise by necessary implication from the provisions of a marriage contract.

Article 12

The marriage contract is valid as to form if it complies either with the internal law applicable to the matrimonial property regime, or with the internal law of the place where it was made. In any event, the marriage contract shall be in writing, dated and signed by both spouses.

Article 13

The designation of the applicable law by express stipulation shall comply with the form prescribed for marriage contracts, either by the internal law designated by the spouses, or by the internal law of the place where it is made. In any event, the designation shall be in writing, dated and signed by both spouses.

Article 14

The application of the law determined by the Convention may be refused only if it is manifestly incompatible with public policy ("ordre public").

Chapter III — Miscellaneous Provisions

Article 15

For the purposes of the Convention, a nationality shall be considered the common nationality of the spouses only in the following circumstances —

(1) where both spouses had that nationality before marriage;

(2) where one spouse voluntarily has acquired the nationality of the other at the time of marriage or later, either by a declaration to that effect or by not exercising a right known to him or her to decline the acquisition of the new nationality;

(3) where both spouses voluntarily have acquired that nationality after marriage.

Except in the cases referred to in sub-paragraph 1 of the second paragraph of Article 7, the provisions referring to the common nationality of the spouses are not applicable where the spouses have more than one common nationality.

Article 16

For the purposes of the Convention, where a State has two or more territorial units in which different systems of law apply to matrimonial property regimes, any reference to the national law of such a State shall be construed as referring to the system determined by the rules in force in that State.

In the absence of such rules, a reference to the State of which a spouse is a national shall be construed, for the purposes of sub-paragraph 1 of the second paragraph of Article 3 and sub-paragraph 1 of the second paragraph of Article 6, as referring to the territorial unit where that spouse had his or her last habitual residence; and, for the purposes of the second paragraph of Article 4, a reference to the State of the common nationality of the spouses shall be construed as referring to the last territorial unit, if any, where each has had a habitual residence.

Article 17

For the purposes of the Convention, where a State has two or more territorial units in which different systems of law apply to matrimonial property regimes, any reference to habitual residence in that State shall be construed as referring to habitual residence in a territorial unit of that State.

Article 18

A Contracting State which has two or more territorial units in which different systems of law apply to matrimonial property regimes shall not be bound to apply the rules of the Convention to conflicts between the laws of such units where the law of no other State is applicable by virtue of the Convention.

Article 19

For the purposes of the Convention, where a State has two or more legal systems applicable to the matrimonial property regimes of different categories of persons, any reference to the law of such State shall be construed as referring to the system determined by the rules in force in that State.

In the absence of such rules, the internal law of the State of the common nationality of the spouses applies under the circumstances referred to in the first paragraph of Article 4, and the internal law of the State where each has had a habitual residence continues to apply under the circumstances referred to in sub-paragraph 2 of the second paragraph of Article 7. In the absence of a common nationality of the spouses, the third paragraph of Article 4 applies.

Article 20

The Convention shall not affect any other international instrument containing provisions on matters governed by this Convention to which a Contracting State is, or becomes, a Party.

Article 21

The Convention applies, in each Contracting State, only to spouses who have married or who designate the law applicable to their matrimonial property regime after the Convention enters into force for that State.

A Contracting State may by declaration extend the application of the Convention to other spouses.

[Ed. Note: Articles 22 to 31, addressing signature, ratification, deposit, accession, territorial application, construction of national law, prohibition of reservations, notification of declarations under Article 5, entry into force, denunciation, and notification, are omitted.]

B. Children and Incompetent Adults

Convention on the Civil Aspects of
International Child Abduction
Oct. 25, 1980, T.I.A.S. No. 11,670, 1343 U.N.T.S. 89
Hague Conf. Priv. Int'l L. Collection of Conventions (1951–1996) at 265
available at http://www.hcch.net

[Ed. Note: This Convention entered into force on December 1, 1983. As of March 2003, 73 nations were party to the Convention. The United States became a party to this Convention through ratification on April 29, 1988, and the Convention entered into force for the United States on July 1, 1988. The Central Authority designated for the United States under Article 6 is the Office of Children's Issues in the Bureau of Consular Affairs of the Department of State. The United States made two reservations, which are included following the Convention.]

The States signatory to the present Convention,

Firmly convinced that the interests of children are of paramount importance in matters relating to their custody,

Desiring to protect children internationally from the harmful effects of their wrongful removal or retention and to establish procedures to ensure their prompt return to the State of their habitual residence, as well as to secure protection for rights of access,

Have resolved to conclude a Convention to this effect, and have agreed upon the following provisions—

Chapter I—Scope of the Convention

Article 1
The objects of the present Convention are—

a) to secure the prompt return of children wrongfully removed to or retained in any Contracting State; and

b) to ensure that rights of custody and of access under the law of one Contracting State are effectively respected in the other Contracting States.

Article 2
Contracting States shall take all appropriate measures to secure within their territories the implementation of the objects of the Convention. For this purpose they shall use the most expeditious procedures available.

Article 3
The removal or the retention of a child is to be considered wrongful where—

a) it is in breach of rights of custody attributed to a person, an institution or any other body, either jointly or alone, under the law of the State in which the child was habitually resident immediately before the removal or retention; and

b) at the time of removal or retention those rights were actually exercised, either jointly or alone, or would have been so exercised but for the removal or retention.

The rights of custody mentioned in sub-paragraph *a)* above, may arise in particular by operation of law or by reason of a judicial or administrative decision, or by reason of an agreement having legal effect under the law of that State.

Article 4

The Convention shall apply to any child who was habitually resident in a Contracting State immediately before any breach of custody or access rights. The Convention shall cease to apply when the child attains the age of 16 years.

Article 5

For the purposes of this Convention —

a) "rights of custody" shall include rights relating to the care of the person of the child and, in particular, the right to determine the child's place of residence;

b) "rights of access" shall include the right to take a child for a limited period of time to a place other than the child's habitual residence.

Chapter II — Central Authorities

Article 6

A Contracting State shall designate a Central Authority to discharge the duties which are imposed by the Convention upon such authorities.

Federal States, States with more than one system of law or States having autonomous territorial organizations shall be free to appoint more than one Central Authority and to specify the territorial extent of their powers. Where a State has appointed more than one Central Authority, it shall designate the Central Authority to which applications may be addressed for transmission to the appropriate Central Authority within that State.

Article 7

Central Authorities shall co-operate with each other and promote co-operation amongst the competent authorities in their respective State to secure the prompt return of children and to achieve the other objects of this Convention.

In particular, either directly or through any intermediary, they shall take all appropriate measures —

a) to discover the whereabouts of a child who has been wrongfully removed or retained;

b) to prevent further harm to the child or prejudice to interested parties by taking or causing to be taken provisional measures;

c) to secure the voluntary return of the child or to bring about an amicable resolution of the issues;

d) to exchange, where desirable, information relating to the social background of the child;

e) to provide information of a general character as to the law of their State in connection with the application of the Convention;

f) to initiate or facilitate the institution of judicial or administrative proceedings with a view to obtaining the return of the child and, in a proper case, to make arrangements for organizing or securing the effective exercise of rights of access;

g) where the circumstances so require, to provide or facilitate the provision of legal aid and advice, including the participation of legal counsel and advisers;

h) to provide such administrative arrangements as may be necessary and appropriate to secure the safe return of the child;

i) to keep each other informed with respect to the operation of this Convention and, as far as possible, to eliminate any obstacles to its application.

Chapter III — Return of Children

Article 8

Any person, institution or other body claiming that a child has been removed or retained in breach of custody rights may apply either to the Central Authority of the child's habitual residence or to the Central Authority of any other Contracting State for assistance in securing the return of the child.

The application shall contain —

a) information concerning the identity of the applicant, of the child and of the person alleged to have removed or retained the child;

b) where available, the date of birth of the child;

c) the grounds on which the applicant's claim for return of the child is based;

d) all available information relating to the whereabouts of the child and the identity of the person with whom the child is presumed to be.

The application may be accompanied or supplemented by —

e) an authenticated copy of any relevant decision or agreement;

f) a certificate or an affidavit emanating from a Central Authority, or other competent authority of the State of the child's habitual residence, or from a qualified person, concerning the relevant law of that State;

g) any other relevant document.

Article 9

If the Central Authority which receives an application referred to in Article 8 has reason to believe that the child is in another Contracting State, it shall directly and without delay transmit the application to the Central Authority of that Contracting State and inform the requesting Central Authority, or the applicant, as the case may be.

Article 10

The Central Authority of the State where the child is shall take or cause to be taken all appropriate measures in order to obtain the voluntary return of the child.

Article 11

The judicial or administrative authorities of Contracting States shall act expeditiously in proceedings for the return of children.

If the judicial or administrative authority concerned has not reached a decision within six weeks from the date of commencement of the proceedings, the applicant or the Central Authority of the requested State, on its own initiative or if asked by the Central Authority of the requesting State, shall have the right to request a statement of the reasons for the delay. If a reply is received by the Central Authority of the requested State, that Authority shall transmit the reply to the Central Authority of the requesting State, or to the applicant, as the case may be.

Article 12

Where a child has been wrongfully removed or retained in terms of Article 3 and, at the date of the commencement of the proceedings before the judicial or administrative authority of the Contracting State where the child is, a period of less than one year has elapsed from the date of the wrongful removal or retention, the authority concerned shall order the return of the child forthwith.

The judicial or administrative authority, even where the proceedings have been commenced after the expiration of the period of one year referred to in the preceding paragraph, shall also order the return of the child, unless it is demonstrated that the child is now settled in its new environment.

Where the judicial or administrative authority in the requested State has reason to believe that the child has been taken to another State, it may stay the proceedings or dismiss the application for the return of the child.

Article 13

Notwithstanding the provisions of the preceding Article, the judicial or administrative authority of the requested State is not bound to order the return of the child if the person, institution or other body which opposes its return establishes that—

a) the person, institution or other body having the care of the person of the child was not actually exercising the custody rights at the time of removal or retention, or had consented to or subsequently acquiesced in the removal or retention; or

b) there is a grave risk that his or her return would expose the child to physical or psychological harm or otherwise place the child in an intolerable situation.

The judicial or administrative authority may also refuse to order the return of the child if it finds that the child objects to being returned and has attained an age and degree of maturity at which it is appropriate to take account of its views.

In considering the circumstances referred to in this Article, the judicial and administrative authorities shall take into account the information relating to the social background of the child provided by the Central Authority or other competent authority of the child's habitual residence.

Article 14

In ascertaining whether there has been a wrongful removal or retention within the meaning of Article 3, the judicial or administrative authorities of the requested State may take notice directly of the law of, and of judicial or administrative decisions, formally recognized or not in the State of the habitual residence of the child, without recourse to the specific procedures for the proof of that law or for the recognition of foreign decisions which would otherwise be applicable.

Article 15

The judicial or administrative authorities of a Contracting State may, prior to the making of an order for the return of the child, request that the applicant obtain from the authorities of the State of the habitual residence of the child a decision or other determination that the removal or retention was wrongful within the meaning of Article 3 of the Convention, where such a decision or determination may be obtained in that State. The Central Authorities of the Contracting States shall so far as practicable assist applicants to obtain such a decision or determination.

Article 16

After receiving notice of a wrongful removal or retention of a child in the sense of Article 3, the judicial or administrative authorities of the Contracting State to which the child has been removed or in which it has been retained shall not decide on the merits of rights of custody until it has been determined that the child is not to be returned under this Convention or unless an application under this Convention is not lodged within a reasonable time following receipt of the notice.

Article 17

The sole fact that a decision relating to custody has been given in or is entitled to recognition in the requested State shall not be a ground for refusing to return a child under this Convention, but the judicial or administrative authorities of the requested State may take account of the reasons for that decision in applying this Convention.

Article 18

The provisions of this Chapter do not limit the power of a judicial or administrative authority to order the return of the child at any time.

Article 19

A decision under this Convention concerning the return of the child shall not be taken to be a determination on the merits of any custody issue.

Article 20

The return of the child under the provisions of Article 12 may be refused if this would not be permitted by the fundamental principles of the requested State relating to the protection of human rights and fundamental freedoms.

Chapter IV — Rights of Access

Article 21

An application to make arrangements for organizing or securing the effective exercise of rights of access may be presented to the Central Authorities of the Contracting States in the same way as an application for the return of a child.

The Central Authorities are bound by the obligations of co-operation which are set forth in Article 7 to promote the peaceful enjoyment of access rights and the fulfilment of any conditions to which the exercise of those rights may be subject. The Central Authorities shall take steps to remove, as far as possible, all obstacles to the exercise of such rights.

The Central Authorities, either directly or through intermediaries, may initiate or assist in the institution of proceedings with a view to organizing or protecting these rights and securing respect for the conditions to which the exercise of these rights may be subject.

Chapter V — General Provisions

Article 22

No security, bond or deposit, however described, shall be required to guarantee the payment of costs and expenses in the judicial or administrative proceedings falling within the scope of this Convention.

Article 23

No legalization or similar formality may be required in the context of this Convention.

Article 24

Any application, communication or other document sent to the Central Authority of the requested State shall be in the original language, and shall be accompanied by a translation into the official language or one of the official languages of the requested State or, where that is not feasible, a translation into French or English.

However, a Contracting State may, by making a reservation in accordance with Article 42, object to the use of either French or English, but not both, in any application, communication or other document sent to its Central Authority.

Article 25

Nationals of the Contracting States and persons who are habitually resident within those States shall be entitled in matters concerned with the application of this Convention to legal aid and advice in any other Contracting State on the same conditions as if they themselves were nationals of and habitually resident in that State.

Article 26

Each Central Authority shall bear its own costs in applying this Convention.

Central Authorities and other public services of Contracting States shall not impose any charges in relation to applications submitted under this Convention. In particular, they may not require any payment from the applicant towards the costs and expenses of the proceedings or, where applicable, those arising from the participation of legal counsel or advisers. However, they may require the payment of the expenses incurred or to be incurred in implementing the return of the child.

However, a Contracting State may, by making a reservation in accordance with Article 42, declare that it shall not be bound to assume any costs referred to in the preceding paragraph resulting from the participation of legal counsel or advisers or from court proceedings, except insofar as those costs may be covered by its system of legal aid and advice.

Upon ordering the return of a child or issuing an order concerning rights of access under this Convention, the judicial or administrative authorities may, where appropriate, direct the person who removed or retained the child, or who prevented the exercise of rights of access, to pay necessary expenses incurred by or on behalf of the applicant, including travel expenses, any costs incurred or payments made for locating the child, the costs of legal representation of the applicant, and those of returning the child.

Article 27

When it is manifest that the requirements of this Convention are not fulfilled or that the application is otherwise not well founded, a Central Authority is not bound to accept the application. In that case, the Central Authority shall forthwith inform the applicant or the Central Authority through which the application was submitted, as the case may be, of its reasons.

Article 28

A Central Authority may require that the application be accompanied by a written authorization empowering it to act on behalf of the applicant, or to designate a representative so to act.

Article 29

This Convention shall not preclude any person, institution or body who claims that there has been a breach of custody or access rights within the meaning of Article 3 or 21 from applying directly to the judicial or administrative authorities of a Contracting State, whether or not under the provisions of this Convention.

Article 30

Any application submitted to the Central Authorities or directly to the judicial or administrative authorities of a Contracting State in accordance with the terms of this Convention, together with documents and any other information appended thereto or provided by a Central Authority, shall be admissible in the courts or administrative authorities of the Contracting States.

Article 31

In relation to a State which in matters of custody of children has two or more systems of law applicable in different territorial units—

a) any reference to habitual residence in that State shall be construed as referring to habitual residence in a territorial unit of that State;

b) any reference to the law of the State of habitual residence shall be construed as referring to the law of the territorial unit in that State where the child habitually resides.

Article 32

In relation to a State which in matters of custody of children has two or more systems of law applicable to different categories of persons, any reference to the law of that State shall be construed as referring to the legal system specified by the law of that State.

Article 33

A State within which different territorial units have their own rules of law in respect of custody of children shall not be bound to apply this Convention where a State with a unified system of law would not be bound to do so.

Article 34

This Convention shall take priority in matters within its scope over the Convention of 5 October 1961 concerning the powers of authorities and the law applicable in respect of the protection of minors, as between parties to both Conventions. Otherwise the present Convention shall not restrict the application of an international instrument in force between the State of origin and the State addressed or other law of the State addressed for the purposes of obtaining the return of a child who has been wrongfully removed or retained or of organizing access rights.

Article 35

This Convention shall apply as between Contracting States only to wrongful removals or retentions occurring after its entry into force in those States.

Where a declaration has been made under Article 39 or 40, the reference in the preceding paragraph to a Contracting State shall be taken to refer to the territorial unit or units in relation to which this Convention applies.

Article 36

Nothing in this Convention shall prevent two or more Contracting States, in order to limit the restrictions to which the return of the child may be subject, from agreeing among themselves to derogate from any provisions of this Convention which may imply such a restriction.

Chapter VI — Final Clauses

Article 37

The Convention shall be open for signature by the States which were Members of the Hague Conference on Private International Law at the time of its Fourteenth Session.

It shall be ratified, accepted or approved and the instruments of ratification, acceptance or approval shall be deposited with the Ministry of Foreign Affairs of the Kingdom of the Netherlands.

Article 38

Any other State may accede to the Convention.

The instrument of accession shall be deposited with the Ministry of Foreign Affairs of the Kingdom of the Netherlands.

The Convention shall enter into force for a State acceding to it on the first day of the third calendar month after the deposit of its instrument of accession.

The accession will have effect only as regards the relations between the acceding State and such Contracting States as will have declared their acceptance of the accession. Such a declaration will also have to be made by any Member State ratifying, accepting or approving the Convention after an accession. Such declaration shall be deposited at the Ministry of Foreign Affairs of the Kingdom of the Netherlands; this Ministry shall forward, through diplomatic channels, a certified copy to each of the Contracting States.

The Convention will enter into force as between the acceding State and the State that has declared its acceptance of the accession on the first day of the third calendar month after the deposit of the declaration of acceptance.

Article 39

Any State may, at the time of signature, ratification, acceptance, approval or accession, declare that the Convention shall extend to all the territories for the international relations of which it is responsible, or to one or more of them. Such a declaration shall take effect at the time the Convention enters into force for that State.

Such declaration, as well as any subsequent extension, shall be notified to the Ministry of Foreign Affairs of the Kingdom of the Netherlands.

Article 40

If a Contracting State has two or more territorial units in which different systems of law are applicable in relation to matters dealt with in this Convention, it may at the time of signature, ratification, acceptance, approval or accession declare that this Convention shall extend to all its territorial units or only to one or more of them and may modify this declaration by submitting another declaration at any time.

Any such declaration shall be notified to the Ministry of Foreign Affairs of the Kingdom of the Netherlands and shall state expressly the territorial units to which the Convention applies.

Article 41

Where a Contracting State has a system of government under which executive, judicial and legislative powers are distributed between central and other authorities within that State, its signature or ratification, acceptance or approval of, or accession to this Convention, or its making of any declaration in terms of Article 40 shall carry no implication as to the internal distribution of powers within that State.

Article 42

Any State may, not later than the time of ratification, acceptance, approval or accession, or at the time of making a declaration in terms of Article 39 or 40, make one or both of the reservations provided for in Article 24 and Article 26, third paragraph. No other reservation shall be permitted.

Any State may at any time withdraw a reservation it has made. The withdrawal shall be notified to the Ministry of Foreign Affairs of the Kingdom of the Netherlands.

The reservation shall cease to have effect on the first day of the third calendar month after the notification referred to in the preceding paragraph.

Article 43

The Convention shall enter into force on the first day of the third calendar month after the deposit of the third instrument of ratification, acceptance, approval or accession referred to in Articles 37 and 38.

Thereafter the Convention shall enter into force—

(1) for each State ratifying, accepting, approving or acceding to it subsequently, on the first day of the third calendar month after the deposit of its instrument of ratification, acceptance, approval or accession;

(2) for any territory or territorial unit to which the Convention has been extended in conformity with Article 39 or 40, on the first day of the third calendar month after the notification referred to in that Article.

Article 44

The Convention shall remain in force for five years from the date of its entry into force in accordance with the first paragraph of Article 43 even for States which subsequently have ratified, accepted, approved it or acceded to it.

If there has been no denunciation, it shall be renewed tacitly every five years.

Any denunciation shall be notified to the Ministry of Foreign Affairs of the Kingdom of the Netherlands at least six months before the expiry of the five year period. It may be limited to certain of the territories or territorial units to which the Convention applies.

The denunciation shall have effect only as regards the State which has notified it. The Convention shall remain in force for the other Contracting States.

Article 45

The Ministry of Foreign Affairs of the Kingdom of the Netherlands shall notify the States Members of the Conference, and the States which have acceded in accordance with Article 38, of the following—

(1) the signatures and ratifications, acceptances and approvals referred to in Article 37;

(2) the accessions referred to in Article 38;

(3) the date on which the Convention enters into force in accordance with Article 43;

(4) the extensions referred to in Article 39;

(5) the declarations referred to in Articles 38 and 40;

(6) the reservations referred to in Article 24 and Article 26, third paragraph, and the withdrawals referred to in Article 42;

(7) the denunciations referred to in Article 44.

In witness whereof the undersigned, being duly authorised thereto, have signed this Convention.

Done at The Hague, on the 25th day of October, 1980, in the English and French languages, both texts being equally authentic, in a single copy which shall be deposited in the archives of the Government of the Kingdom of the Netherlands, and of which a certified copy shall be sent, through diplomatic channels, to each of the States Members of the Hague Conference on Private International Law at the date of its Fourteenth Session.

United States of America — Reservations to the Convention

(1) Pursuant to the second paragraph of Article 24, and Article 42, the United States makes the following reservation: All applications, communications and other documents sent to the U.S. Central Authority should be accompanied by their translation into English.

(2) Pursuant to the third paragraph of Article 26, the United States declares that it will not be bound to assume any costs or expenses resulting from the participation of legal counsel or advisers or from court and legal proceedings in connection with efforts to return children from the United States pursuant to the Convention except insofar as those costs or expenses are covered by a legal aid program.

Convention on Protection of Children and Co-operation in Respect of Intercountry Adoption

May 29, 1993, S. Treaty Doc. No. 105-51, 32 I.L.M. 1134

Hague Conf. Priv. Int'l L. Collection of Conventions (1951–1996) at 357

available at http://www.hcch.net

[Ed. Note: This Convention entered into force on May 1, 1995. As of March 2003, 52 nations were parties by ratification or accession. The United States signed the Convention on March 31, 1994. Implementing legislation, the Intercountry Adoption Act, Pub. L. 106-279, 114 Stat. 844, was passed in October, 2000, and is found in Part IV of this book. Ratification by the United States is anticipated to occur by 2004. The Department of State serves as the U.S. Central Authority for this Convention.]

The States signatory to the present Convention,

Recognizing that the child, for the full and harmonious development of his or her personality, should grow up in a family environment, in an atmosphere of happiness, love and understanding,

Recalling that each State should take, as a matter of priority, appropriate measures to enable the child to remain in the care of his or her family of origin,

Recognizing that intercountry adoption may offer the advantage of a permanent family to a child for whom a suitable family cannot be found in his or her State of origin,

Convinced of the necessity to take measures to ensure that intercountry adoptions are made in the best interests of the child and with respect for his or her fundamental rights, and to prevent the abduction, the sale of, or traffic in children,

Desiring to establish common provisions to this effect, taking into account the principles set forth in international instruments, in particular the United Nations Convention on the Rights of the Child, of 20 November 1989, and the United Nations Declaration on Social and Legal Principles relating to the Protection and Welfare of Children, with Special Reference to Foster Placement and Adoption Nationally and Internationally (General Assembly Resolution 41/85, of 3 December 1986),

Have agreed upon the following provisions—

Chapter I—Scope of the Convention

Article 1

The objects of the present Convention are—

a) to establish safeguards to ensure that intercountry adoptions take place in the best interests of the child and with respect for his or her fundamental rights as recognized in international law;

b) to establish a system of co-operation amongst Contracting States to ensure that those safeguards are respected and thereby prevent the abduction, the sale of, or traffic in children;

c) to secure the recognition in Contracting States of adoptions made in accordance with the Convention.

Article 2

(1) The Convention shall apply where a child habitually resident in one Contracting State ("the State of origin") has been, is being, or is to be moved to another Contracting State ("the receiving State") either after his or her adoption in the State of origin by spouses or a person habitually resident in the receiving State, or for the purposes of such an adoption in the receiving State or in the State of origin.

(2) The Convention covers only adoptions which create a permanent parent-child relationship.

Article 3

The Convention ceases to apply if the agreements mentioned in Article 17, sub-paragraph c, have not been given before the child attains the age of eighteen years.

Chapter II—Requirements for Intercountry Adoptions

Article 4

An adoption within the scope of the Convention shall take place only if the competent authorities of the State of origin—

a) have established that the child is adoptable;

b) have determined, after possibilities for placement of the child within the State of origin have been given due consideration, that an intercountry adoption is in the child's best interests;

c) have ensured that

(1) the persons, institutions and authorities whose consent is necessary for adoption, have been counseled as may be necessary and duly informed of the effects of their consent, in particular whether or not an adoption will result in the termination of the legal relationship between the child and his or her family of origin,

(2) such persons, institutions and authorities have given their consent freely, in the required legal form, and expressed or evidenced in writing,

(3) the consents have not been induced by payment or compensation of any kind and have not been withdrawn, and

(4) the consent of the mother, where required, has been given only after the birth of the child; and

d) have ensured, having regard to the age and degree of maturity of the child, that

(1) he or she has been counseled and duly informed of the effects of the adoption and of his or her consent to the adoption, where such consent is required,

(2) consideration has been given to the child's wishes and opinions,

(3) the child's consent to the adoption, where such consent is required, has been given freely, in the required legal form, and expressed or evidenced in writing, and

(4) such consent has not been induced by payment or compensation of any kind.

Article 5

An adoption within the scope of the Convention shall take place only if the competent authorities of the receiving State—

a) have determined that the prospective adoptive parents are eligible and suited to adopt;

b) have ensured that the prospective adoptive parents have been counselled as may be necessary; and

c) have determined that the child is or will be authorized to enter and reside permanently in that State.

Chapter III—Central Authorities and Accredited Bodies

Article 6

(1) A Contracting State shall designate a Central Authority to discharge the duties which are imposed by the Convention upon such authorities.

(2) Federal States, States with more than one system of law or States having autonomous territorial units shall be free to appoint more than one Central Authority and to specify the territorial or personal extent of their functions. Where a State has appointed more than one Central Authority, it shall designate the Central Authority to which any communication may be addressed for transmission to the appropriate Central Authority within that State.

Article 7

(1) Central Authorities shall co-operate with each other and promote co-operation amongst the competent authorities in their States to protect children and to achieve the other objects of the Convention.

(2) They shall take directly all appropriate measures to—

a) provide information as to the laws of their States concerning adoption and other general information, such as statistics and standard forms;

b) keep one another informed about the operation of the Convention and, as far as possible, eliminate any obstacles to its application.

Article 8

Central Authorities shall take, directly or through public authorities, all appropriate measures to prevent improper financial or other gain in connection with an adoption and to deter all practices contrary to the objects of the Convention.

Article 9

Central Authorities shall take, directly or through public authorities or other bodies duly accredited in their State, all appropriate measures, in particular to—

a) collect, preserve and exchange information about the situation of the child and the prospective adoptive parents, so far as is necessary to complete the adoption;

b) facilitate, follow and expedite proceedings with a view to obtaining the adoption;

c) promote the development of adoption counselling and post-adoption services in their States;

d) provide each other with general evaluation reports about experience with intercountry adoption;

e) reply, in so far as is permitted by the law of their State, to justified requests from other Central Authorities or public authorities for information about a particular adoption situation.

Article 10

Accreditation shall only be granted to and maintained by bodies demonstrating their competence to carry out properly the tasks with which they may be entrusted.

Article 11

An accredited body shall—

a) pursue only non-profit objectives according to such conditions and within such limits as may be established by the competent authorities of the State of accreditation;

b) be directed and staffed by persons qualified by their ethical standards and by training or experience to work in the field of intercountry adoption; and

c) be subject to supervision by competent authorities of that State as to its composition, operation and financial situation.

Article 12

A body accredited in one Contracting State may act in another Contracting State only if the competent authorities of both States have authorized it to do so.

Article 13

The designation of the Central Authorities and, where appropriate, the extent of their functions, as well as the names and addresses of the accredited bodies shall be communicated by each Contracting State to the Permanent Bureau of the Hague Conference on Private International Law.

Chapter IV — Procedural Requirements in Intercountry Adoption

Article 14

Persons habitually resident in a Contracting State, who wish to adopt a child habitually resident in another Contracting State, shall apply to the Central Authority in the State of their habitual residence.

Article 15

(1) If the Central Authority of the receiving State is satisfied that the applicants are eligible and suited to adopt, it shall prepare a report including information about their identity, eligibility and suitability to adopt, background, family and medical history, social environment, reasons for adoption, ability to undertake an intercountry adoption, as well as the characteristics of the children for whom they would be qualified to care.

(2) It shall transmit the report to the Central Authority of the State of origin.

Article 16

(1) If the Central Authority of the State of origin is satisfied that the child is adoptable, it shall—

a) prepare a report including information about his or her identity, adoptability, background, social environment, family history, medical history including that of the child's family, and any special needs of the child;

b) give due consideration to the child's upbringing and to his or her ethnic, religious and cultural background;

c) ensure that consents have been obtained in accordance with Article 4; and

d) determine, on the basis in particular of the reports relating to the child and the prospective adoptive parents, whether the envisaged placement is in the best interests of the child.

(2) It shall transmit to the Central Authority of the receiving State its report on the child, proof that the necessary consents have been obtained and the reasons for its determination on the placement, taking care not to reveal the identity of the mother and the father if, in the State of origin, these identities may not be disclosed.

Article 17

Any decision in the State of origin that a child should be entrusted to prospective adoptive parents may only be made if—

a) the Central Authority of that State has ensured that the prospective adoptive parents agree;

b) the Central Authority of the receiving State has approved such decision, where such approval is required by the law of that State or by the Central Authority of the State of origin;

c) the Central Authorities of both States have agreed that the adoption may proceed; and

d) it has been determined, in accordance with Article 5, that the prospective adoptive parents are eligible and suited to adopt and that the child is or will be authorized to enter and reside permanently in the receiving State.

Article 18

The Central Authorities of both States shall take all necessary steps to obtain permission for the child to leave the State of origin and to enter and reside permanently in the receiving State.

Article 19

(1) The transfer of the child to the receiving State may only be carried out if the requirements of Article 17 have been satisfied.

(2) The Central Authorities of both States shall ensure that this transfer takes place in secure and appropriate circumstances and, if possible, in the company of the adoptive or prospective adoptive parents.

(3) If the transfer of the child does not take place, the reports referred to in Articles 15 and 16 are to be sent back to the authorities who forwarded them.

Article 20

The Central Authorities shall keep each other informed about the adoption process and the measures taken to complete it, as well as about the progress of the placement if a probationary period is required.

Article 21

(1) Where the adoption is to take place after the transfer of the child to the receiving State and it appears to the Central Authority of that State that the continued placement of the child with the prospective adoptive parents is not in the child's best interests, such Central Authority shall take the measures necessary to protect the child, in particular—

a) to cause the child to be withdrawn from the prospective adoptive parents and to arrange temporary care;

b) in consultation with the Central Authority of the State of origin, to arrange without delay a new placement of the child with a view to adoption or, if this is not appropriate, to arrange alternative long-term care; an adoption shall not take place until the Central Authority of the State of origin has been duly informed concerning the new prospective adoptive parents;

c) as a last resort, to arrange the return of the child, if his or her interests so require.

(2) Having regard in particular to the age and degree of maturity of the child, he or she shall be consulted and, where appropriate, his or her consent obtained in relation to measures to be taken under this Article.

Article 22

(1) The functions of a Central Authority under this Chapter may be performed by public authorities or by bodies accredited under Chapter III, to the extent permitted by the law of its State.

(2) Any Contracting State may declare to the depositary of the Convention that the functions of the Central Authority under Articles 15 to 21 may be performed in that State, to the extent permitted by the law and subject to the supervision of the competent authorities of that State, also by bodies or persons who—

a) meet the requirements of integrity, professional competence, experience and accountability of that State; and

b) are qualified by their ethical standards and by training or experience to work in the field of intercountry adoption.

(3) A Contracting State which makes the declaration provided for in paragraph 2 shall keep the Permanent Bureau of the Hague Conference on Private International Law informed of the names and addresses of these bodies and persons.

(4) Any Contracting State may declare to the depositary of the Convention that adoptions of children habitually resident in its territory may only take place if the functions of the Central Authorities are performed in accordance with paragraph 1.

(5) Notwithstanding any declaration made under paragraph 2, the reports provided for in Articles 15 and 16 shall, in every case, be prepared under the responsibility of the Central Authority or other authorities or bodies in accordance with paragraph 1.

Chapter V — Recognition and Effects of the Adoption

Article 23

(1) An adoption certified by the competent authority of the State of the adoption as having been made in accordance with the Convention shall be recognized by operation of law in the other Contracting States. The certificate shall specify when and by whom the agreements under Article 17, sub-paragraph c), were given.

(2) Each Contracting State shall, at the time of signature, ratification, acceptance, approval or accession, notify the depositary of the Convention of the identity and the

functions of the authority or the authorities which, in that State, are competent to make the certification. It shall also notify the depositary of any modification in the designation of these authorities.

Article 24

The recognition of an adoption may be refused in a Contracting State only if the adoption is manifestly contrary to its public policy, taking into account the best interests of the child.

Article 25

Any Contracting State may declare to the depositary of the Convention that it will not be bound under this Convention to recognize adoptions made in accordance with an agreement concluded by application of Article 39, paragraph 2.

Article 26

(1) The recognition of an adoption includes recognition of
a) the legal parent-child relationship between the child and his or her adoptive parents;
b) parental responsibility of the adoptive parents for the child;
c) the termination of a pre-existing legal relationship between the child and his or her mother and father, if the adoption has this effect in the Contracting State where it was made.

(2) In the case of an adoption having the effect of terminating a pre-existing legal parent-child relationship, the child shall enjoy in the receiving State, and in any other Contracting State where the adoption is recognized, rights equivalent to those resulting from adoptions having this effect in each such State.

(3) The preceding paragraphs shall not prejudice the application of any provision more favourable for the child, in force in the Contracting State which recognizes the adoption.

Article 27

(1) Where an adoption granted in the State of origin does not have the effect of terminating a pre-existing legal parent-child relationship, it may, in the receiving State which recognizes the adoption under the Convention, be converted into an adoption having such an effect —
a) if the law of the receiving State so permits; and
b) if the consents referred to in Article 4, sub-paragraphs c and d, have been or are given for the purpose of such an adoption.

(2) Article 23 applies to the decision converting the adoption.

Chapter VI — General Provisions

Article 28

The Convention does not affect any law of a State of origin which requires that the adoption of a child habitually resident within that State take place in that State or which prohibits the child's placement in, or transfer to, the receiving State prior to adoption.

Article 29

There shall be no contact between the prospective adoptive parents and the child's parents or any other person who has care of the child until the requirements of Article 4, sub-paragraphs a) to c), and Article 5, sub-paragraph a), have been met, unless the adoption takes place within a family or unless the contact is in compliance with the conditions established by the competent authority of the State of origin.

Article 30

(1) The competent authorities of a Contracting State shall ensure that information held by them concerning the child's origin, in particular information concerning the identity of his or her parents, as well as the medical history, is preserved.

(2) They shall ensure that the child or his or her representative has access to such information, under appropriate guidance, in so far as is permitted by the law of that State.

Article 31

Without prejudice to Article 30, personal data gathered or transmitted under the Convention, especially data referred to in Articles 15 and 16, shall be used only for the purposes for which they were gathered or transmitted.

Article 32

(1) No one shall derive improper financial or other gain from an activity related to an intercountry adoption.

(2) Only costs and expenses, including reasonable professional fees of persons involved in the adoption, may be charged or paid.

(3) The directors, administrators and employees of bodies involved in an adoption shall not receive remuneration which is unreasonably high in relation to services rendered.

Article 33

A competent authority which finds that any provision of the Convention has not been respected or that there is a serious risk that it may not be respected, shall immediately inform the Central Authority of its State. This Central Authority shall be responsible for ensuring that appropriate measures are taken.

Article 34

If the competent authority of the State of destination of a document so requests, a translation certified as being in conformity with the original must be furnished. Unless otherwise provided, the costs of such translation are to be borne by the prospective adoptive parents.

Article 35

The competent authorities of the Contracting States shall act expeditiously in the process of adoption.

Article 36

In relation to a State which has two or more systems of law with regard to adoption applicable in different territorial units—

a) any reference to habitual residence in that State shall be construed as referring to habitual residence in a territorial unit of that State;

b) any reference to the law of that State shall be construed as referring to the law in force in the relevant territorial unit;

c) any reference to the competent authorities or to the public authorities of that State shall be construed as referring to those authorized to act in the relevant territorial unit;

d) any reference to the accredited bodies of that State shall be construed as referring to bodies accredited in the relevant territorial unit.

Article 37

In relation to a State which with regard to adoption has two or more systems of law applicable to different categories of persons, any reference to the law of that State shall be construed as referring to the legal system specified by the law of that State.

Article 38

A State within which different territorial units have their own rules of law in respect of adoption shall not be bound to apply the Convention where a State with a unified system of law would not be bound to do so.

Article 39

(1) The Convention does not affect any international instrument to which Contracting States are Parties and which contains provisions on matters governed by the Convention, unless a contrary declaration is made by the States Parties to such instrument.

(2) Any Contracting State may enter into agreements with one or more other Contracting States, with a view to improving the application of the Convention in their mutual relations. These agreements may derogate only from the provisions of Articles 14 to 16 and 18 to 21. The States which have concluded such an agreement shall transmit a copy to the depositary of the Convention.

Article 40

No reservation to the Convention shall be permitted.

Article 41

The Convention shall apply in every case where an application pursuant to Article 14 has been received after the Convention has entered into force in the receiving State and the State of origin.

Article 42

The Secretary General of the Hague Conference on Private International Law shall at regular intervals convene a Special Commission in order to review the practical operation of the Convention.

Chapter VII — Final Clauses

Article 43

(1) The Convention shall be open for signature by the States which were Members of the Hague Conference on Private International Law at the time of its Seventeenth Session and by the other States which participated in that Session.

(2) It shall be ratified, accepted or approved and the instruments of ratification, acceptance or approval shall be deposited with the Ministry of Foreign Affairs of the Kingdom of the Netherlands, depositary of the Convention.

Article 44

(1) Any other State may accede to the Convention after it has entered into force in accordance with Article 46, paragraph 1.

(2) The instrument of accession shall be deposited with the depositary.

(3) Such accession shall have effect only as regards the relations between the acceding State and those Contracting States which have not raised an objection to its accession in the six months after the receipt of the notification referred to in sub-paragraph b) of

Article 48. Such an objection may also be raised by States at the time when they ratify, accept or approve the Convention after an accession. Any such objection shall be notified to the depositary.

Article 45

(1) If a State has two or more territorial units in which different systems of law are applicable in relation to matters dealt with in the Convention, it may at the time of signature, ratification, acceptance, approval or accession declare that this Convention shall extend to all its territorial units or only to one or more of them and may modify this declaration by submitting another declaration at any time.

(2) Any such declaration shall be notified to the depositary and shall state expressly the territorial units to which the Convention applies.

(3) If a State makes no declaration under this Article, the Convention is to extend to all territorial units of that State.

Article 46

(1) The Convention shall enter into force on the first day of the month following the expiration of three months after the deposit of the third instrument of ratification, acceptance or approval referred to in Article 43.

(2) Thereafter the Convention shall enter into force—

a) for each State ratifying, accepting or approving it subsequently, or acceding to it, on the first day of the month following the expiration of three months after the deposit of its instrument of ratification, acceptance, approval or accession;

b) for a territorial unit to which the Convention has been extended in conformity with Article 45, on the first day of the month following the expiration of three months after the notification referred to in that Article.

Article 47

(1) A State Party to the Convention may denounce it by a notification in writing addressed to the depositary.

(2) The denunciation takes effect on the first day of the month following the expiration of twelve months after the notification is received by the depositary. Where a longer period for the denunciation to take effect is specified in the notification, the denunciation takes effect upon the expiration of such longer period after the notification is received by the depositary.

Article 48

The depositary shall notify the States Members of the Hague Conference on Private International Law, the other States which participated in the Seventeenth Session and the States which have acceded in accordance with Article 44, of the following—

a) the signatures, ratifications, acceptances and approvals referred to in Article 43;

b) the accessions and objections raised to accessions referred to in Article 44;

c) the date on which the Convention enters into force in accordance with Article 46;

d) the declarations and designations referred to in Articles 22, 23, 25 and 45;

e) the agreements referred to in Article 39;

f) the denunciations referred to in Article 47.

In witness whereof the undersigned, being duly authorized thereto, have signed this Convention.

Done at The Hague, on the 29th day of May 1993, in the English and French languages, both texts being equally authentic, in a single copy which shall be deposited in the archives of the Government of the Kingdom of the Netherlands, and of which a certified copy shall be sent, through diplomatic channels, to each of the States Members of the Hague Conference on Private International Law at the date of its Seventeenth Session and to each of the other States which participated in that Session.

Convention on Jurisdiction, Applicable Law, Recognition, Enforcement and Co-operation in Respect of Parental Responsibility and Measures for the Protection of Children

Oct. 19, 1996, 35 I.L.M. 1391
Hague Conf. Priv. Int'l L. Collection of Conventions (1951–1996) at 379
available at http://www.hcch.net

[Ed. Note: This Convention entered into force on January 1, 2002. As of March 2003, the Czech Republic, Ecuador, Estonia, Latvia, Monaco, Morocco, and Slovakia had ratified or acceded to the Convention, and two other nations, Netherlands and Poland, had signed the Convention. Although representatives of the United States actively participated in drafting the Convention, the United States has not yet signed or ratified it.]

The States signatory to the present Convention,

Considering the need to improve the protection of children in international situations,

Wishing to avoid conflicts between their legal systems in respect of jurisdiction, applicable law, recognition and enforcement of measures for the protection of children,

Recalling the importance of international co-operation for the protection of children,

Confirming that the best interests of the child are to be a primary consideration,

Noting that the Convention of 5 October 1961 concerning the powers of authorities and the law applicable in respect of the protection of minors is in need of revision,

Desiring to establish common provisions to this effect, taking into account the United Nations Convention on the Rights of the Child of 20 November 1989,

Have agreed on the following provisions—

Chapter I—Scope of the Convention

Article 1

1. The objects of the present Convention are—

a. to determine the State whose authorities have jurisdiction to take measures directed to the protection of the person or property of the child;

b. to determine which law is to be applied by such authorities in exercising their jurisdiction;

c. to determine the law applicable to parental responsibility;

d. to provide for the recognition and enforcement of such measures of protection in all Contracting States;

e. to establish such co-operation between the authorities of the Contracting States as may be necessary in order to achieve the purposes of this Convention.

2. For the purposes of this Convention, the term 'parental responsibility' includes parental authority, or any analogous relationship of authority determining the rights, powers and responsibilities of parents, guardians or other legal representatives in relation to the person or the property of the child.

Article 2

The Convention applies to children from the moment of their birth until they reach the age of 18 years.

Article 3

The measures referred to in Article 1 may deal in particular with—

a. the attribution, exercise, termination or restriction of parental responsibility, as well as its delegation;

b. rights of custody, including rights relating to the care of the person of the child and, in particular, the right to determine the child's place of residence, as well as rights of access including the right to take a child for a limited period of time to a place other than the child's habitual residence;

c. guardianship, curatorship and analogous institutions;

d. the designation and functions of any person or body having charge of the child's person or property, representing or assisting the child;

e. the placement of the child in a foster family or in institutional care, or the provision of care by *kafala* or an analogous institution;

f. the supervision by a public authority of the care of a child by any person having charge of the child;

g. the administration, conservation or disposal of the child's property.

Article 4

The Convention does not apply to—

a. the establishment or contesting of a parent-child relationship;

b. decisions on adoption, measures preparatory to adoption, or the annulment or revocation of adoption;

c. the name and forenames of the child;

d. emancipation;

e. maintenance obligations;

f. trusts or succession;

g. social security;

h. public measures of a general nature in matters of education or health;

i. measures taken as a result of penal offences committed by children;

j. decisions on the right of asylum and on immigration.

Chapter II — Jurisdiction

Article 5

1. The judicial or administrative authorities of the Contracting State of the habitual residence of the child have jurisdiction to take measures directed to the protection of the child's person or property.

2. Subject to Article 7, in case of a change of the child's habitual residence to another Contracting State, the authorities of the State of the new habitual residence have jurisdiction.

Article 6

1. For refugee children and children who, due to disturbances occurring in their country, are internationally displaced, the authorities of the Contracting State on the territory of which these children are present as a result of their displacement have the jurisdiction provided for in paragraph 1 of Article 5.

2. The provisions of the preceding paragraph also apply to children whose habitual residence cannot be established.

Article 7

1. In case of wrongful removal or retention of the child, the authorities of the Contracting State in which the child was habitually resident immediately before the removal or retention keep their jurisdiction until the child has acquired a habitual residence in another State, and

a. each person, institution or other body having rights of custody has acquiesced in the removal or retention; or

b. the child has resided in that other State for a period of at least one year after the person, institution or other body having rights of custody has or should have had knowledge of the whereabouts of the child, no request for return lodged within that period is still pending, and the child is settled in his or her new environment.

2. The removal or the retention of a child is to be considered wrongful where _

a. it is in breach of rights of custody attributed to a person, an institution or any other body, either jointly or alone, under the law of the State in which the child was habitually resident immediately before the removal or retention; and

b. at the time of removal or retention those rights were actually exercised, either jointly or alone, or would have been so exercised but for the removal or retention.

The rights of custody mentioned in sub-paragraph *a* above, may arise in particular by operation of law or by reason of a judicial or administrative decision, or by reason of an agreement having legal effect under the law of that State.

3. So long as the authorities first mentioned in paragraph 1 keep their jurisdiction, the authorities of the Contracting State to which the child has been removed or in which he or she has been retained can take only such urgent measures under Article 11 as are necessary for the protection of the person or property of the child.

Article 8

1. By way of exception, the authority of a Contracting State having jurisdiction under Article 5 or 6, if it considers that the authority of another Contracting State would be better placed in the particular case to assess the best interests of the child, may either

– request that other authority, directly or with the assistance of the Central Authority of its State, to assume jurisdiction to take such measures of protection as it considers to be necessary, or

– suspend consideration of the case and invite the parties to introduce such a request before the authority of that other State.

2. The Contracting States whose authorities may be addressed as provided in the preceding paragraph are

a. a State of which the child is a national,

b. a State in which property of the child is located,

c. a State whose authorities are seised of an application for divorce or legal separation of the child's parents, or for annulment of their marriage,

d. a State with which the child has a substantial connection.

3. The authorities concerned may proceed to an exchange of views.

4. The authority addressed as provided in paragraph 1 may assume jurisdiction, in place of the authority having jurisdiction under Article 5 or 6, if it considers that this is in the child's best interests.

Article 9

1. If the authorities of a Contracting State referred to in Article 8, paragraph 2, consider that they are better placed in the particular case to assess the child's best interests, they may either

– request the competent authority of the Contracting State of the habitual residence of the child, directly or with the assistance of the Central Authority of that State, that they be authorised to exercise jurisdiction to take the measures of protection which they consider to be necessary, or

– invite the parties to introduce such a request before the authority of the Contracting State of the habitual residence of the child.

2. The authorities concerned may proceed to an exchange of views.

3. The authority initiating the request may exercise jurisdiction in place of the authority of the Contracting State of the habitual residence of the child only if the latter authority has accepted the request.

Article 10

1. Without prejudice to Articles 5 to 9, the authorities of a Contracting State exercising jurisdiction to decide upon an application for divorce or legal separation of the parents of a child habitually resident in another Contracting State, or for annulment of their marriage, may, if the law of their State so provides, take measures directed to the protection of the person or property of such child if

a. at the time of commencement of the proceedings, one of his or her parents habitually resides in that State and one of them has parental responsibility in relation to the child, and

b. the jurisdiction of these authorities to take such measures has been accepted by the parents, as well as by any other person who has parental responsibility in relation to the child, and is in the best interests of the child.

2. The jurisdiction provided for by paragraph 1 to take measures for the protection of the child ceases as soon as the decision allowing or refusing the application for divorce, legal separation or annulment of the marriage has become final, or the proceedings have come to an end for another reason.

Article 11

1. In all cases of urgency, the authorities of any Contracting State in whose territory the child or property belonging to the child is present have jurisdiction to take any necessary measures of protection.

2. The measures taken under the preceding paragraph with regard to a child habitually resident in a Contracting State shall lapse as soon as the authorities which have jurisdiction under Articles 5 to 10 have taken the measures required by the situation.

3. The measures taken under paragraph 1 with regard to a child who is habitually resident in a non-Contracting State shall lapse in each Contracting State as soon as measures required by the situation and taken by the authorities of another State are recognised in the Contracting State in question.

Article 12

1. Subject to Article 7, the authorities of a Contracting State in whose territory the child or property belonging to the child is present have jurisdiction to take measures of a provisional character for the protection of the person or property of the child which have a territorial effect limited to the State in question, in so far as such measures are not incompatible with measures already taken by authorities which have jurisdiction under Articles 5 to 10.

2. The measures taken under the preceding paragraph with regard to a child habitually resident in a Contracting State shall lapse as soon as the authorities which have jurisdiction under Articles 5 to 10 have taken a decision in respect of the measures of protection which may be required by the situation.

3. The measures taken under paragraph 1 with regard to a child who is habitually resident in a non-Contracting State shall lapse in the Contracting State where the measures were taken as soon as measures required by the situation and taken by the authorities of another State are recognized in the Contracting State in question.

Article 13

1. The authorities of a Contracting State which have jurisdiction under Articles 5 to 10 to take measures for the protection of the person or property of the child must abstain from exercising this jurisdiction if, at the time of the commencement of the proceedings, corresponding measures have been requested from the authorities of another Contracting State having jurisdiction under Articles 5 to 10 at the time of the request and are still under consideration.

2. The provisions of the preceding paragraph shall not apply if the authorities before whom the request for measures was initially introduced have declined jurisdiction.

Article 14

The measures taken in application of Articles 5 to 10 remain in force according to their terms, even if a change of circumstances has eliminated the basis upon which jurisdiction was founded, so long as the authorities which have jurisdiction under the Convention have not modified, replaced or terminated such measures.

Chapter III — Applicable Law

Article 15

1. In exercising their jurisdiction under the provisions of Chapter II, the authorities of the Contracting States shall apply their own law.

2. However, in so far as the protection of the person or the property of the child requires, they may exceptionally apply or take into consideration the law of another State with which the situation has a substantial connection.

3. If the child's habitual residence changes to another Contracting State, the law of that other State governs, from the time of the change, the conditions of application of the measures taken in the State of the former habitual residence.

Article 16

1. The attribution or extinction of parental responsibility by operation of law, without the intervention of a judicial or administrative authority, is governed by the law of the State of the habitual residence of the child.

2. The attribution or extinction of parental responsibility by an agreement or a unilateral act, without intervention of a judicial or administrative authority, is governed by the law of the State of the child's habitual residence at the time when the agreement or unilateral act takes effect.

3. Parental responsibility which exists under the law of the State of the child's habitual residence subsists after a change of that habitual residence to another State.

4. If the child's habitual residence changes, the attribution of parental responsibility by operation of law to a person who does not already have such responsibility is governed by the law of the State of the new habitual residence.

Article 17

The exercise of parental responsibility is governed by the law of the State of the child's habitual residence. If the child's habitual residence changes, it is governed by the law of the State of the new habitual residence.

Article 18

The parental responsibility referred to in Article 16 may be terminated, or the conditions of its exercise modified, by measures taken under this Convention.

Article 19

1. The validity of a transaction entered into between a third party and another person who would be entitled to act as the child's legal representative under the law of the State where the transaction was concluded cannot be contested, and the third party cannot be held liable, on the sole ground that the other person was not entitled to act as the child's legal representative under the law designated by the provisions of this Chapter, unless the third party knew or should have known that the parental responsibility was governed by the latter law.

2. The preceding paragraph applies only if the transaction was entered into between persons present on the territory of the same State.

Article 20

The provisions of this Chapter apply even if the law designated by them is the law of a non-Contracting State.

Article 21

1. In this Chapter the term "law" means the law in force in a State other than its choice of law rules.

2. However, if the law applicable according to Article 16 is that of a non-Contracting State and if the choice of law rules of that State designate the law of another non-Contracting State which would apply its own law, the law of the latter State applies. If that other non-Contracting State would not apply its own law, the applicable law is that designated by Article 16.

Article 22

The application of the law designated by the provisions of this Chapter can be refused only if this application would be manifestly contrary to public policy, taking into account the best interests of the child.

Chapter IV — Recognition and Enforcement

Article 23

1. The measures taken by the authorities of a Contracting State shall be recognised by operation of law in all other Contracting States.

2. Recognition may however be refused—

a. if the measure was taken by an authority whose jurisdiction was not based on one of the grounds provided for in Chapter II;

b. if the measure was taken, except in a case of urgency, in the context of a judicial or administrative proceeding, without the child having been provided the opportunity to be heard, in violation of fundamental principles of procedure of the requested State;

c. on the request of any person claiming that the measure infringes his or her parental responsibility, if such measure was taken, except in a case of urgency, without such person having been given an opportunity to be heard;

d. if such recognition is manifestly contrary to public policy of the requested State, taking into account the best interests of the child;

e. if the measure is incompatible with a later measure taken in the non-Contracting State of the habitual residence of the child, where this later measure fulfils the requirements for recognition in the requested State;

f. if the procedure provided in Article 33 has not been complied with.

Article 24

Without prejudice to Article 23, paragraph 1, any interested person may request from the competent authorities of a Contracting State that they decide on the recognition or non-recognition of a measure taken in another Contracting State. The procedure is governed by the law of the requested State.

Article 25

The authority of the requested State is bound by the findings of fact on which the authority of the State where the measure was taken based its jurisdiction.

Article 26

1. If measures taken in one Contracting State and enforceable there require enforcement in another Contracting State, they shall, upon request by an interested party, be declared enforceable or registered for the purpose of enforcement in that other State according to the procedure provided in the law of the latter State.

2. Each Contracting State shall apply to the declaration of enforceability or registration a simple and rapid procedure.

3. The declaration of enforceability or registration may be refused only for one of the reasons set out in Article 23, paragraph 2.

Article 27

Without prejudice to such review as is necessary in the application of the preceding Articles, there shall be no review of the merits of the measure taken.

Article 28

Measures taken in one Contracting State and declared enforceable, or registered for the purpose of enforcement, in another Contracting State shall be enforced in the latter

State as if they had been taken by the authorities of that State. Enforcement takes place in accordance with the law of the requested State to the extent provided by such law, taking into consideration the best interests of the child.

Chapter V — Co-operation

Article 29

1. A Contracting State shall designate a Central Authority to discharge the duties which are imposed by the Convention on such authorities.

2. Federal States, States with more than one system of law or States having autonomous territorial units shall be free to appoint more than one Central Authority and to specify the territorial or personal extent of their functions. Where a State has appointed more than one Central Authority, it shall designate the Central Authority to which any communication may be addressed for transmission to the appropriate Central Authority within that State.

Article 30

1. Central Authorities shall co-operate with each other and promote co-operation amongst the competent authorities in their States to achieve the purposes of the Convention.

2. They shall, in connection with the application of the Convention, take appropriate steps to provide information as to the laws of, and services available in, their States relating to the protection of children.

Article 31

The Central Authority of a Contracting State, either directly or through public authorities or other bodies, shall take all appropriate steps to —

a. facilitate the communications and offer the assistance provided for in Articles 8 and 9 and in this Chapter;

b. facilitate, by mediation, conciliation or similar means, agreed solutions for the protection of the person or property of the child in situations to which the Convention applies;

c. provide, on the request of a competent authority of another Contracting State, assistance in discovering the whereabouts of a child where it appears that the child may be present and in need of protection within the territory of the requested State.

Article 32

On a request made with supporting reasons by the Central Authority or other competent authority of any Contracting State with which the child has a substantial connection, the Central Authority of the Contracting State in which the child is habitually resident and present may, directly or through public authorities or other bodies,

a. provide a report on the situation of the child;

b. request the competent authority of its State to consider the need to take measures for the protection of the person or property of the child.

Article 33

1. If an authority having jurisdiction under Articles 5 to 10 contemplates the placement of the child in a foster family or institutional care, or the provision of care by *kafala* or an analogous institution, and if such placement or such provision of care is

to take place in another Contracting State, it shall first consult with the Central Authority or other competent authority of the latter State. To that effect it shall transmit a report on the child together with the reasons for the proposed placement or provision of care.

2. The decision on the placement or provision of care may be made in the requesting State only if the Central Authority or other competent authority of the requested State has consented to the placement or provision of care, taking into account the child's best interests.

Article 34

1. Where a measure of protection is contemplated, the competent authorities under the Convention, if the situation of the child so requires, may request any authority of another Contracting State which has information relevant to the protection of the child to communicate such information.

2. A Contracting State may declare that requests under paragraph 1 shall be communicated to its authorities only through its Central Authority.

Article 35

1. The competent authorities of a Contracting State may request the authorities of another Contracting State to assist in the implementation of measures of protection taken under this Convention, especially in securing the effective exercise of rights of access as well as of the right to maintain direct contacts on a regular basis.

2. The authorities of a Contracting State in which the child does not habitually reside may, on the request of a parent residing in that State who is seeking to obtain or to maintain access to the child, gather information or evidence and may make a finding on the suitability of that parent to exercise access and on the conditions under which access is to be exercised. An authority exercising jurisdiction under Articles 5 to 10 to determine an application concerning access to the child, shall admit and consider such information, evidence and finding before reaching its decision.

3. An authority having jurisdiction under Articles 5 to 10 to decide on access may adjourn a proceeding pending the outcome of a request made under paragraph 2, in particular, when it is considering an application to restrict or terminate access rights granted in the State of the child's former habitual residence.

4. Nothing in this Article shall prevent an authority having jurisdiction under Articles 5 to 10 from taking provisional measures pending the outcome of the request made under paragraph 2.

Article 36

In any case where the child is exposed to a serious danger, the competent authorities of the Contracting State where measures for the protection of the child have been taken or are under consideration, if they are informed that the child's residence has changed to, or that the child is present in another State, shall inform the authorities of that other State about the danger involved and the measures taken or under consideration.

Article 37

An authority shall not request or transmit any information under this Chapter if to do so would, in its opinion, be likely to place the child's person or property in danger, or constitute a serious threat to the liberty or life of a member of the child's family.

Article 38

1. Without prejudice to the possibility of imposing reasonable charges for the provision of services, Central Authorities and other public authorities of Contracting States shall bear their own costs in applying the provisions of this Chapter.

2. Any Contracting State may enter into agreements with one or more other Contracting States concerning the allocation of charges.

Article 39

Any Contracting State may enter into agreements with one or more other Contracting States with a view to improving the application of this Chapter in their mutual relations. The States which have concluded such an agreement shall transmit a copy to the depositary of the Convention.

Chapter VI — General Provisions

Article 40

1. The authorities of the Contracting State of the child's habitual residence, or of the Contracting State where a measure of protection has been taken, may deliver to the person having parental responsibility or to the person entrusted with protection of the child's person or property, at his or her request, a certificate indicating the capacity in which that person is entitled to act and the powers conferred upon him or her.

2. The capacity and powers indicated in the certificate are presumed to be vested in that person, in the absence of proof to the contrary.

3. Each Contracting State shall designate the authorities competent to draw up the certificate.

Article 41

Personal data gathered or transmitted under the Convention shall be used only for the purposes for which they were gathered or transmitted.

Article 42

The authorities to whom information is transmitted shall ensure its confidentiality, in accordance with the law of their State.

Article 43

All documents forwarded or delivered under this Convention shall be exempt from legalisation or any analogous formality.

Article 44

Each Contracting State may designate the authorities to which requests under Articles 8, 9 and 33 are to be addressed.

Article 45

1. The designations referred to in Articles 29 and 44 shall be communicated to the Permanent Bureau of the Hague Conference on Private International Law.

2. The declaration referred to in Article 34, paragraph 2, shall be made to the depositary of the Convention.

Article 46

A Contracting State in which different systems of law or sets of rules of law apply to the protection of the child and his or her property shall not be bound to apply the rules of the Convention to conflicts solely between such different systems or sets of rules of law.

Article 47

In relation to a State in which two or more systems of law or sets of rules of law with regard to any matter dealt with in this Convention apply in different territorial units—

1. any reference to habitual residence in that State shall be construed as referring to habitual residence in a territorial unit;

2. any reference to the presence of the child in that State shall be construed as referring to presence in a territorial unit;

3. any reference to the location of property of the child in that State shall be construed as referring to location of property of the child in a territorial unit;

4. any reference to the State of which the child is a national shall be construed as referring to the territorial unit designated by the law of that State or, in the absence of relevant rules, to the territorial unit with which the child has the closest connection;

5. any reference to the State whose authorities are seised of an application for divorce or legal separation of the child's parents, or for annulment of their marriage, shall be construed as referring to the territorial unit whose authorities are seised of such application;

6. any reference to the State with which the child has a substantial connection shall be construed as referring to the territorial unit with which the child has such connection;

7. any reference to the State to which the child has been removed or in which he or she has been retained shall be construed as referring to the relevant territorial unit to which the child has been removed or in which he or she has been retained;

8. any reference to bodies or authorities of that State, other than Central Authorities, shall be construed as referring to those authorised to act in the relevant territorial unit;

9. any reference to the law or procedure or authority of the State in which a measure has been taken shall be construed as referring to the law or procedure or authority of the territorial unit in which such measure was taken;

10. any reference to the law or procedure or authority of the requested State shall be construed as referring to the law or procedure or authority of the territorial unit in which recognition or enforcement is sought.

Article 48

For the purpose of identifying the applicable law under Chapter III, in relation to a State which comprises two or more territorial units each of which has its own system of law or set of rules of law in respect of matters covered by this Convention, the following rules apply—

a. if there are rules in force in such a State identifying which territorial unit's law is applicable, the law of that unit applies;

b. in the absence of such rules, the law of the relevant territorial unit as defined in Article 47 applies.

Article 49

For the purpose of identifying the applicable law under Chapter III, in relation to a State which has two or more systems of law or sets of rules of law applicable to different categories of persons in respect of matters covered by this Convention, the following rules apply—

a. if there are rules in force in such a State identifying which among such laws applies, that law applies;

b. in the absence of such rules, the law of the system or the set of rules of law with which the child has the closest connection applies.

Article 50

This Convention shall not affect the application of the *Convention of 25 October 1980 on the Civil Aspects of International Child Abduction*, as between Parties to both Conventions. Nothing, however, precludes provisions of this Convention from being invoked for the purposes of obtaining the return of a child who has been wrongfully removed or retained or of organizing access rights.

Article 51

In relations between the Contracting States this Convention replaces the *Convention of 5 October 1961 concerning the powers of authorities and the law applicable in respect of the protection of minors*, and the *Convention governing the guardianship of minors*, signed at The Hague 12 June 1902, without prejudice to the recognition of measures taken under the Convention of 5 October 1961 mentioned above.

Article 52

1. This Convention does not affect any international instrument to which Contracting States are Parties and which contains provisions on matters governed by the Convention, unless a contrary declaration is made by the States Parties to such instrument.

2. This Convention does not affect the possibility for one or more Contracting States to conclude agreements which contain, in respect of children habitually resident in any of the States Parties to such agreements, provisions on matters governed by this Convention.

3. Agreements to be concluded by one or more Contracting States on matters within the scope of this Convention do not affect, in the relationship of such States with other Contracting States, the application of the provisions of this Convention.

4. The preceding paragraphs also apply to uniform laws based on special ties of a regional or other nature between the States concerned.

Article 53

1. The Convention shall apply to measures only if they are taken in a State after the Convention has entered into force for that State.

2. The Convention shall apply to the recognition and enforcement of measures taken after its entry into force as between the State where the measures have been taken and the requested State.

Article 54

1. Any communication sent to the Central Authority or to another authority of a Contracting State shall be in the original language, and shall be accompanied by a translation into the official language or one of the official languages of the other State or, where that is not feasible, a translation into French or English.

2. However, a Contracting State may, by making a reservation in accordance with Article 60, object to the use of either French or English, but not both.

Article 55

1. A Contracting State may, in accordance with Article 60,

a. reserve the jurisdiction of its authorities to take measures directed to the protection of property of a child situated on its territory;

b. reserve the right not to recognise any parental responsibility or measure in so far as it is incompatible with any measure taken by its authorities in relation to that property.

2. The reservation may be restricted to certain categories of property.

Article 56

The Secretary General of the Hague Conference on Private International Law shall at regular intervals convoke a Special Commission in order to review the practical operation of the Convention.

Chapter VII — Final Clauses

[Ed. Note: Articles 57, 58, and 59, addressing signature, ratification, accession, and territorial application, are omitted.]

Article 60

1. Any state may, not later than the time of ratification, acceptance, approval or accession, or at the time of making a declaration in terms of Article 59, make one or both of the reservations provided for in Articles 54, paragraph 2, and 55. No other reservation shall be permitted.

2. Any State may at any time withdraw a reservation it has made. The withdrawal shall be notified to the depositary.

3. The reservation shall cease to have effect on the first day of the third calendar month after the notification referred to in the preceding paragraph.

[Ed. Note: Articles 61, 62, and 63, addressing entry into force, denunciation and notification, are omitted.]

Convention on the International Protection of Adults

Oct. 2, 1999, 39 I.L.M. 4
available at http://www.hcch.net

[Ed. Note: This Convention has not yet entered into force. As of March 2003, no nations were as yet parties to the Convention, and only France and Netherlands had signed the Convention. Although representatives of the United States actively participated in drafting the Convention, the United States has not yet signed or ratified it.]

The States signatory to the present Convention,

Considering the need to provide for the protection in international situations of adults who, by reason of an impairment or insufficiency of their personal faculties, are not in a position to protect their interests,

Wishing to avoid conflicts between their legal systems in respect of jurisdiction, applicable law, recognition and enforcement of measures for the protection of adults,

Recalling the importance of international co-operation for the protection of adults,

Affirming that the interests of the adult and respect for his or her dignity and autonomy are to be primary considerations,

Have agreed on the following provisions—

Chapter I — Scope of the Convention

Article 1

1. This Convention applies to the protection in international situations of adults who, by reason of an impairment or insufficiency of their personal faculties, are not in a position to protect their interests.

2. Its objects are—

a) to determine the State whose authorities have jurisdiction to take measures directed to the protection of the person or property of the adult;

b) to determine which law is to be applied by such authorities in exercising their jurisdiction;

c) to determine the law applicable to representation of the adult;

d) to provide for the recognition and enforcement of such measures of protection in all Contracting States;

e) to establish such co-operation between the authorities of the Contracting States as may be necessary in order to achieve the purposes of this Convention.

Article 2

1. For the purposes of this Convention, an adult is a person who has reached the age of 18 years.

2. The Convention applies also to measures in respect of an adult who had not reached the age of 18 years at the time the measures were taken.

Article 3

The measures referred to in Article 1 may deal in particular with—

a) the determination of incapacity and the institution of a protective regime;

b) the placing of the adult under the protection of a judicial or administrative authority;

c) guardianship, curatorship and analogous institutions;

d) the designation and functions of any person or body having charge of the adult's person or property, representing or assisting the adult;

e) the placement of the adult in an establishment or other place where protection can be provided;

f) the administration, conservation or disposal of the adult's property;

g) the authorisation of a specific intervention for the protection of the person or property of the adult.

Article 4

1. The Convention does not apply to—

a) maintenance obligations;

b) the formation, annulment and dissolution of marriage or any similar relationship, as well as legal separation;

c) property regimes in respect of marriage or any similar relationship;

d) trusts or succession;

e) social security;

f) public measures of a general nature in matters of health;

g) measures taken in respect of a person as a result of penal offences committed by that person;

h) decisions on the right of asylum and on immigration;

i) measures directed solely to public safety.

2. Paragraph 1 does not affect, in respect of the matters referred to therein, the entitlement of a person to act as the representative of the adult.

Chapter II — Jurisdiction

Article 5

1. The judicial or administrative authorities of the Contracting State of the habitual residence of the adult have jurisdiction to take measures directed to the protection of the adult's person or property.

2. In case of a change of the adult's habitual residence to another Contracting State, the authorities of the State of the new habitual residence have jurisdiction.

Article 6

1. For adults who are refugees and those who, due to disturbances occurring in their country, are internationally displaced, the authorities of the Contracting State on the territory of which these adults are present as a result of their displacement have the jurisdiction provided for in Article 5, paragraph 1.

2. The provisions of the preceding paragraph also apply to adults whose habitual residence cannot be established.

Article 7

1. Except for adults who are refugees or who, due to disturbances occurring in their State of nationality, are internationally displaced, the authorities of a Contracting State of which the adult is a national have jurisdiction to take measures for the protection of the person or property of the adult if they consider that they are in a better position to assess the interests of the adult, and after advising the authorities having jurisdiction under Article 5 or Article 6, paragraph 2.

2. This jurisdiction shall not be exercised if the authorities having jurisdiction under Article 5, Article 6, paragraph 2, or Article 8 have informed the authorities of the State of which the adult is a national that they have taken the measures required by the situation or have decided that no measures should be taken or that proceedings are pending before them.

3. The measures taken under paragraph 1 shall lapse as soon as the authorities having jurisdiction under Article 5, Article 6, paragraph 2, or Article 8 have taken measures required by the situation or have decided that no measures are to be taken. These authorities shall inform accordingly the authorities which have taken measures in accordance with paragraph 1.

Article 8

1. The authorities of a Contracting State having jurisdiction under Article 5 or Article 6, if they consider that such is in the interests of the adult, may, on their own motion or on an application by the authority of another Contracting State, request the authorities of one of the States mentioned in paragraph 2 to take measures for the protection of the person or property of the adult. The request may relate to all or some aspects of such protection.

2. The Contracting States whose authorities may be addressed as provided in the preceding paragraph are —

a) a State of which the adult is a national;

b) the State of the preceding habitual residence of the adult;

c) a State in which property of the adult is located;

d) the State whose authorities have been chosen in writing by the adult to take measures directed to his or her protection;

e) the State of the habitual residence of a person close to the adult prepared to undertake his or her protection;

f) the State in whose territory the adult is present, with regard to the protection of the person of the adult.

3. In case the authority designated pursuant to the preceding paragraphs does not accept its jurisdiction, the authorities of the Contracting State having jurisdiction under Article 5 or Article 6 retain jurisdiction.

Article 9

The authorities of a Contracting State where property of the adult is situated have jurisdiction to take measures of protection concerning that property, to the extent that such measures are compatible with those taken by the authorities having jurisdiction under Articles 5 to 8.

Article 10

1. In all cases of urgency, the authorities of any Contracting State in whose territory the adult or property belonging to the adult is present have jurisdiction to take any necessary measures of protection.

2. The measures taken under the preceding paragraph with regard to an adult habitually resident in a Contracting State shall lapse as soon as the authorities which have jurisdiction under Articles 5 to 9 have taken the measures required by the situation.

3. The measures taken under paragraph 1 with regard to an adult who is habitually resident in a non-Contracting State shall lapse in each Contracting State as soon as measures required by the situation and taken by the authorities of another State are recognised in the Contracting State in question.

4. The authorities which have taken measures under paragraph 1 shall, if possible, inform the authorities of the Contracting State of the habitual residence of the adult of the measures taken.

Article 11

1. By way of exception, the authorities of a Contracting State in whose territory the adult is present have jurisdiction to take measures of a temporary character for the protection of the person of the adult which have a territorial effect limited to the State in question, in so far as such measures are compatible with those already taken by the authorities which have jurisdiction under Articles 5 to 8, and after advising the authorities having jurisdiction under Article 5.

2. The measures taken under the preceding paragraph with regard to an adult habitually resident in a Contracting State shall lapse as soon as the authorities which have jurisdiction under Articles 5 to 8 have taken a decision in respect of the measures of protection which may be required by the situation.

Article 12

Subject to Article 7, paragraph 3, the measures taken in application of Articles 5 to 9 remain in force according to their terms, even if a change of circumstances has eliminated the basis upon which jurisdiction was founded, so long as the authorities which have jurisdiction under the Convention have not modified, replaced or terminated such measures.

Chapter III — Applicable Law

Article 13

1. In exercising their jurisdiction under the provisions of Chapter II, the authorities of the Contracting States shall apply their own law.

2. However, in so far as the protection of the person or the property of the adult requires, they may exceptionally apply or take into consideration the law of another State with which the situation has a substantial connection.

Article 14

Where a measure taken in one Contracting State is implemented in another Contracting State, the conditions of its implementation are governed by the law of that other State.

Article 15

1. The existence, extent, modification and extinction of powers of representation granted by an adult, either under an agreement or by a unilateral act, to be exercised when such adult is not in a position to protect his or her interests, are governed by the law of the State of the adult's habitual residence at the time of the agreement or act, unless one of the laws mentioned in paragraph 2 has been designated expressly in writing.

2. The States whose laws may be designated are—

a) a State of which the adult is a national;

b) the State of a former habitual residence of the adult;

c) a State in which property of the adult is located, with respect to that property.

3. The manner of exercise of such powers of representation is governed by the law of the State in which they are exercised.

Article 16

Where powers of representation referred to in Article 15 are not exercised in a manner sufficient to guarantee the protection of the person or property of the adult, they may be withdrawn or modified by measures taken by an authority having jurisdiction under the Convention. Where such powers of representation are withdrawn or modified, the law referred to in Article 15 should be taken into consideration to the extent possible.

Article 17

1. The validity of a transaction entered into between a third party and another person who would be entitled to act as the adult's representative under the law of the State where the transaction was concluded cannot be contested, and the third party cannot be held liable, on the sole ground that the other person was not entitled to act as the adult's representative under the law designated by the provisions of this Chapter, unless the third party knew or should have known that such capacity was governed by the latter law.

2. The preceding paragraph applies only if the transaction was entered into between persons present on the territory of the same State.

Article 18

The provisions of this Chapter apply even if the law designated by them is the law of a non-Contracting State.

Article 19

In this Chapter the term "law" means the law in force in a State other than its choice of law rules.

Article 20

This Chapter does not prevent the application of those provisions of the law of the State in which the adult is to be protected where the application of such provisions is mandatory whatever law would otherwise be applicable.

Article 21

The application of the law designated by the provisions of this Chapter can be refused only if this application would be manifestly contrary to public policy.

Chapter IV — Recognition and Enforcement

Article 22

1. The measures taken by the authorities of a Contracting State shall be recognised by operation of law in all other Contracting States.

2. Recognition may however be refused—

a) if the measure was taken by an authority whose jurisdiction was not based on, or was not in accordance with, one of the grounds provided for by the provisions of Chapter II;

b) if the measure was taken, except in a case of urgency, in the context of a judicial or administrative proceeding, without the adult having been provided the opportunity to be heard, in violation of fundamental principles of procedure of the requested State;

c) if such recognition is manifestly contrary to public policy of the requested State, or conflicts with a provision of the law of that State which is mandatory whatever law would otherwise be applicable;

d) if the measure is incompatible with a later measure taken in a non-Contracting State which would have had jurisdiction under Articles 5 to 9, where this later measure fulfils the requirements for recognition in the requested State;

e) if the procedure provided in Article 33 has not been complied with.

Article 23

Without prejudice to Article 22, paragraph 1, any interested person may request from the competent authorities of a Contracting State that they decide on the recognition or non-recognition of a measure taken in another Contracting State. The procedure is governed by the law of the requested State.

Article 24

The authority of the requested State is bound by the findings of fact on which the authority of the State where the measure was taken based its jurisdiction.

Article 25

1. If measures taken in one Contracting State and enforceable there require enforcement in another Contracting State, they shall, upon request by an interested party, be

declared enforceable or registered for the purpose of enforcement in that other State according to the procedure provided in the law of the latter State.

2. Each Contracting State shall apply to the declaration of enforceability or registration a simple and rapid procedure.

3. The declaration of enforceability or registration may be refused only for one of the reasons set out in Article 22, paragraph 2.

Article 26

Without prejudice to such review as is necessary in the application of the preceding Articles, there shall be no review of the merits of the measure taken.

Article 27

Measures taken in one Contracting State and declared enforceable, or registered for the purpose of enforcement, in another Contracting State shall be enforced in the latter State as if they had been taken by the authorities of that State. Enforcement takes place in accordance with the law of the requested State to the extent provided by such law.

Chapter V — Co-operation

Article 28

1. A Contracting State shall designate a Central Authority to discharge the duties which are imposed by the Convention on such authorities.

2. Federal States, States with more than one system of law or States having autonomous territorial units shall be free to appoint more than one Central Authority and to specify the territorial or personal extent of their functions. Where a State has appointed more than one Central Authority, it shall designate the Central Authority to which any communication may be addressed for transmission to the appropriate Central Authority within that State.

Article 29

1. Central Authorities shall co-operate with each other and promote co-operation amongst the competent authorities in their States to achieve the purposes of the Convention.

2. They shall, in connection with the application of the Convention, take appropriate steps to provide information as to the laws of, and services available in, their States relating to the protection of adults.

Article 30

The Central Authority of a Contracting State, either directly or through public authorities or other bodies, shall take all appropriate steps to —

a) facilitate communications, by every means, between the competent authorities in situations to which the Convention applies;

b) provide, on the request of a competent authority of another Contracting State, assistance in discovering the whereabouts of an adult where it appears that the adult may be present and in need of protection within the territory of the requested State.

Article 31

The competent authorities of a Contracting State may encourage, either directly or through other bodies, the use of mediation, conciliation or similar means to achieve agreed solutions for the protection of the person or property of the adult in situations to which the Convention applies.

Article 32

1. Where a measure of protection is contemplated, the competent authorities under the Convention, if the situation of the adult so requires, may request any authority of another Contracting State which has information relevant to the protection of the adult to communicate such information.

2. A Contracting State may declare that requests under paragraph 1 shall be communicated to its authorities only through its Central Authority.

3. The competent authorities of a Contracting State may request the authorities of another Contracting State to assist in the implementation of measures of protection taken under this Convention.

Article 33

1. If an authority having jurisdiction under Articles 5 to 8 contemplates the placement of the adult in an establishment or other place where protection can be provided, and if such placement is to take place in another Contracting State, it shall first consult with the Central Authority or other competent authority of the latter State. To that effect it shall transmit a report on the adult together with the reasons for the proposed placement.

2. The decision on the placement may not be made in the requesting State if the Central Authority or other competent authority of the requested State indicates its opposition within a reasonable time.

Article 34

In any case where the adult is exposed to a serious danger, the competent authorities of the Contracting State where measures for the protection of the adult have been taken or are under consideration, if they are informed that the adult's residence has changed to, or that the adult is present in, another State, shall inform the authorities of that other State about the danger involved and the measures taken or under consideration.

Article 35

An authority shall not request or transmit any information under this Chapter if to do so would, in its opinion, be likely to place the adult's person or property in danger, or constitute a serious threat to the liberty or life of a member of the adult's family.

Article 36

1. Without prejudice to the possibility of imposing reasonable charges for the provision of services, Central Authorities and other public authorities of Contracting States shall bear their own costs in applying the provisions of this Chapter.

2. Any Contracting State may enter into agreements with one or more other Contracting States concerning the allocation of charges.

Article 37

Any Contracting State may enter into agreements with one or more other Contracting States with a view to improving the application of this Chapter in their mutual relations. The States which have concluded such an agreement shall transmit a copy to the depositary of the Convention.

Chapter VI—General Provisions

Article 38

1. The authorities of the Contracting State where a measure of protection has been taken or a power of representation confirmed may deliver to the person entrusted with protection of the adult's person or property, on request, a certificate indicating the capacity in which that person is entitled to act and the powers conferred.

2. The capacity and powers indicated in the certificate are presumed to be vested in that person as of the date of the certificate, in the absence of proof to the contrary.

3. Each Contracting State shall designate the authorities competent to draw up the certificate.

Article 39

Personal data gathered or transmitted under the Convention shall be used only for the purposes for which they were gathered or transmitted.

Article 40

The authorities to whom information is transmitted shall ensure its confidentiality, in accordance with the law of their State.

Article 41

All documents forwarded or delivered under this Convention shall be exempt from legalisation or any analogous formality.

Article 42

Each Contracting State may designate the authorities to which requests under Article 8 and Article 33 are to be addressed.

Article 43

1. The designations referred to in Article 28 and Article 42 shall be communicated to the Permanent Bureau of the Hague Conference on Private International Law not later than the date of the deposit of the instrument of ratification, acceptance or approval of the Convention or of accession thereto. Any modifications thereof shall also be communicated to the Permanent Bureau.

2. The declaration referred to in Article 32, paragraph 2, shall be made to the depositary of the Convention.

Article 44

A Contracting State in which different systems of law or sets of rules of law apply to the protection of the person or property of the adult shall not be bound to apply the rules of the Convention to conflicts solely between such different systems or sets of rules of law.

Article 45

In relation to a State in which two or more systems of law or sets of rules of law with regard to any matter dealt with in this Convention apply in different territorial units—

a) any reference to habitual residence in that State shall be construed as referring to habitual residence in a territorial unit;

b) any reference to the presence of the adult in that State shall be construed as referring to presence in a territorial unit;

c) any reference to the location of property of the adult in that State shall be construed as referring to location of property of the adult in a territorial unit;

d) any reference to the State of which the adult is a national shall be construed as referring to the territorial unit designated by the law of that State or, in the absence of relevant rules, to the territorial unit with which the adult has the closest connection;

e) any reference to the State whose authorities have been chosen by the adult shall be construed

  – as referring to the territorial unit if the adult has chosen the authorities of this territorial unit;

  – as referring to the territorial unit with which the adult has the closest connection if the adult has chosen the authorities of the State without specifying a particular territorial unit within the State;

f) any reference to the law of a State with which the situation has a substantial connection shall be construed as referring to the law of a territorial unit with which the situation has a substantial connection;

g) any reference to the law or procedure or authority of the State in which a measure has been taken shall be construed as referring to the law or procedure in force in such territorial unit or authority of the territorial unit in which such measure was taken;

h) any reference to the law or procedure or authority of the requested State shall be construed as referring to the law or procedure in force in such territorial unit or authority of the territorial unit in which recognition or enforcement is sought;

i) any reference to the State where a measure of protection is to be implemented shall be construed as referring to the territorial unit where the measure is to be implemented;

j) any reference to bodies or authorities of that State, other than Central Authorities, shall be construed as referring to those authorised to act in the relevant territorial unit.

Article 46

For the purpose of identifying the applicable law under Chapter III, in relation to a State which comprises two or more territorial units each of which has its own system of law or set of rules of law in respect of matters covered by this Convention, the following rules apply—

a) if there are rules in force in such a State identifying which territorial unit's law is applicable, the law of that unit applies;

b) in the absence of such rules, the law of the relevant territorial unit as defined in Article 45 applies.

Article 47

For the purpose of identifying the applicable law under Chapter III, in relation to a State which has two or more systems of law or sets of rules of law applicable to different categories of persons in respect of matters covered by this Convention, the following rules apply—

a) if there are rules in force in such a State identifying which among such laws applies, that law applies;

b) in the absence of such rules, the law of the system or the set of rules of law with which the adult has the closest connection applies.

Article 48

In relations between the Contracting States this Convention replaces the Convention concernant l'interdiction et les mesures de protection analogues, signed at The Hague 17 July 1905.

Article 49

1. The Convention does not affect any other international instrument to which Contracting States are Parties and which contains provisions on matters governed by this Convention, unless a contrary declaration is made by the States Parties to such instrument.

2. This Convention does not affect the possibility for one or more Contracting States to conclude agreements which contain, in respect of adults habitually resident in any of the States Parties to such agreements, provisions on matters governed by this Convention.

3. Agreements to be concluded by one or more Contracting States on matters within the scope of this Convention do not affect, in the relationship of such States with other Contracting States, the application of the provisions of this Convention.

4. The preceding paragraphs also apply to uniform laws based on special ties of a regional or other nature between the States concerned.

Article 50

1. The Convention shall apply to measures only if they are taken in a State after the Convention has entered into force for that State.

2. The Convention shall apply to the recognition and enforcement of measures taken after its entry into force as between the State where the measures have been taken and the requested State.

3. The Convention shall apply from the time of its entry into force in a Contracting State to powers of representation previously granted under conditions corresponding to those set out in Article 15.

Article 51

1. Any communication sent to the Central Authority or to another authority of a Contracting State shall be in the original language, and shall be accompanied by a translation into the official language or one of the official languages of the other State or, where that is not feasible, a translation into French or English.

2. However, a Contracting State may, by making a reservation in accordance with Article 56, object to the use of either French or English, but not both.

Article 52

The Secretary General of the Hague Conference on Private International Law shall at regular intervals convoke a Special Commission in order to review the practical operation of the Convention.

[Ed. Note: Articles 53 to 59, addressing signature, ratification, accession, territorial application, limitations on reservations, entry into force, denunciation, and notification, are omitted.]

Part III

Selected Regional Conventions

A. European Conventions

1. European Union Documents

Charter of Fundamental Rights of the European Union
Dec. 7, 2000, 2000 O.J. (C 364) 1

[Ed. Note: In 1999, the European Council convened a convention to draft the Charter. The European Council unanimously approved the draft in October 2000. The European Parliament and Commission gave their approval almost immediately thereafter. The document was signed by the Presidents of the European Parliament, the Council, and the Commission for their respective institutions on December 7, 2000. *See generally* http://www.europarl.eu.int/charter/default_en.htm. The European Union currently has fifteen member states.]

SOLEMN PROCLAMATION

The European Parliament, the Council and the Commission solemnly proclaim the text below as the Charter of fundamental rights of the European Union....

PREAMBLE

The peoples of Europe, in creating an ever closer union among them, are resolved to share a peaceful future based on common values.

Conscious of its spiritual and moral heritage, the Union is founded on the indivisible, universal values of human dignity, freedom, equality and solidarity; it is based on the principles of democracy and the rule of law. It places the individual at the heart of its activities, by establishing the citizenship of the Union and by creating an area of freedom, security and justice.

The Union contributes to the preservation and to the development of these common values while respecting the diversity of the cultures and traditions of the peoples of Europe as well as the national identities of the Member States and the organisation of their public authorities at national, regional and local levels; it seeks to promote balanced and sustainable development and ensures free movement of persons, goods, services and capital, and the freedom of establishment.

To this end, it is necessary to strengthen the protection of fundamental rights in the light of changes in society, social progress and scientific and technological developments by making those rights more visible in a Charter.

This Charter reaffirms, with due regard for the powers and tasks of the Community and the Union and the principle of subsidiarity, the rights as they result, in particular, from the constitutional traditions and international obligations common to the Member States, the Treaty on European Union, the Community Treaties, the European Convention for the Protection of Human Rights and Fundamental Freedoms, the Social Charters adopted by the Community and by the Council of Europe and the case-law of the Court of Justice of the European Communities and of the European Court of Human Rights

Enjoyment of these rights entails responsibilities and duties with regard to other persons, to the human community and to future generations.

The Union therefore recognizes the rights, freedoms and principles set out hereafter.

CHAPTER I—DIGNITY

Article 1—Human dignity
Human dignity is inviolable. It must be respected and protected.

Article 2—Right to life
1. Everyone has the right to life.
2. No one shall be condemned to the death penalty, or executed.

Article 3—Right to the integrity of the person
1. Everyone has the right to respect for his or her physical and mental integrity.
2. In the fields of medicine and biology, the following must be respected in particular:
– the free and informed consent of the person concerned, according to the procedures laid down by law,
– the prohibition of eugenic practices, in particular those aiming at the selection of persons,
– the prohibition on making the human body and its parts as such a source of financial gain,
– the prohibition of the reproductive cloning of human beings.

Article 4—Prohibition of torture and inhuman or degrading treatment or punishment
No one shall be subjected to torture or to inhuman or degrading treatment or punishment.

Article 5—Prohibition of slavery and forced labour
1. No one shall be held in slavery or servitude.
2. No one shall be required to perform forced or compulsory labour.
3. Trafficking in human beings is prohibited.

CHAPTER II—FREEDOMS

Article 6—Right to liberty and security
Everyone has the right to liberty and security of person.

Article 7 — Respect for private and family life

Everyone has the right to respect for his or her private and family life, home and communications.

Article 8 — Protection of personal data

1. Everyone has the right to the protection of personal data concerning him or her.

2. Such data must be processed fairly for specified purposes and on the basis of the consent of the person concerned or some other legitimate basis laid down by law. Everyone has the right of access to data which has been collected concerning him or her, and the right to have it ratified.

3. Compliance with these rules shall be subject to control by an independent authority.

Article 9 — Right to marry and right to found a family

The right to marry and the right to found a family shall be guaranteed in accordance with the national laws governing the exercise of these rights.

Article 10 — Freedom of thought, conscience and religion

1. Everyone has the right to freedom of thought, conscience and religion. This right includes freedom to change religion or belief and freedom, either alone or in community with others and in public or in private, to manifest religion or belief, in worship, teaching, practice and observance.

2. The right to conscientious objection is recognised, in accordance with the national laws governing the exercise of this right.

Article 11 — Freedom of expression and information

1. Everyone has the right to freedom of expression. This right shall include freedom to hold opinions and to receive and impart information and ideas without interference by public authority and regardless of frontiers.

2. The freedom and pluralism of the media shall be respected.

Article 12 — Freedom of assembly and of association

1. Everyone has the right to freedom of peaceful assembly and to freedom of association at all levels, in particular in political, trade union and civic matters, which implies the right of everyone to form and to join trade unions for the protection of his or her interests.

2. Political parties at Union level contribute to expressing the political will of the citizens of the Union.

Article 13 — Freedom of the arts and sciences

The arts and scientific research shall be free of constraint. Academic freedom shall be respected.

Article 14 — Right to education

1. Everyone has the right to education and to have access to vocational and continuing training.

2. This right includes the possibility to receive free compulsory education.

3. The freedom to found educational establishments with due respect for democratic principles and the right of parents to ensure the education and teaching of their children in conformity with their religious, philosophical and pedagogical convictions shall be respected, in accordance with the national laws governing the exercise of such freedom and right.

Article 15 — Freedom to choose an occupation and right to engage in work

1. Everyone has the right to engage in work and to pursue a freely chosen or accepted occupation.

2. Every citizen of the Union has the freedom to seek employment, to work, to exercise the right of establishment and to provide services in any Member State.

3. Nationals of third countries who are authorized to work in the territories of the Member States are entitled to working conditions equivalent to those of citizens of the Union.

Article 16 — Freedom to conduct a business

The freedom to conduct a business in accordance with Community law and national laws and practices is recognised.

Article 17 — Right to property

1. Everyone has the right to own, use, dispose of and bequeath his or her lawfully acquired possessions. No one may be deprived of his or her possessions, except in the public interest and in the cases and under the conditions provided for by law, subject to fair compensation being paid in good time for their loss. The use of property may be regulated by law in so far as is necessary for the general interest.

2. Intellectual property shall be protected.

Article 18 — Right to asylum

The right to asylum shall be guaranteed with due respect for the rules of the Geneva Convention of 28 July 1951 and the Protocol of 31 January 1967 relating to the status of refugees and in accordance with the Treaty establishing the European Community.

Article 19 — Protection in the event of removal, expulsion or extradition

1. Collective expulsions are prohibited.

2. No one may be removed, expelled or extradited to a State where there is a serious risk that he or she would be subjected to the death penalty, torture or other inhuman or degrading treatment or punishment.

CHAPTER III — EQUALITY

Article 20 — Equality before the law

Everyone is equal before the law.

Article 21 — Non-discrimination

1. Any discrimination based on any ground such as sex, race, colour, ethnic or social origin, genetic features, language, religion or belief, political or any other opinion, membership of a national minority, property, birth, disability, age or sexual orientation shall be prohibited.

2. Within the scope of application of the Treaty establishing the European Community and of the Treaty on European Union, and without prejudice to the special provisions of those Treaties, any discrimination on grounds of nationality shall be prohibited.

Article 22 — Cultural, religious and linguistic diversity

The Union shall respect cultural, religious and linguistic diversity.

Article 23 — Equality between men and women

Equality between men and women must be ensured in all areas, including employment, work and pay.

The principle of equality shall not prevent the maintenance or adoption of measures providing for specific advantages in favour of the under-represented sex.

Article 24 — The rights of the child

1. Children shall have the right to such protection and care as is necessary for their well-being. They may express their views freely. Such views shall be taken into consideration on matters which concern them in accordance with their age and maturity.

2. In all actions relating to children, whether taken by public authorities or private institutions, the child's best interests must be a primary consideration.

3. Every child shall have the right to maintain on a regular basis a personal relationship and direct contact with both his or her parents, unless that is contrary to his or her interests.

Article 25 — The rights of the elderly

The Union recognizes and respects the rights of the elderly to lead a life of dignity and independence and to participate in social and cultural life.

Article 26 — Integration of persons with disabilities

The Union recognizes and respects the right of persons with disabilities to benefit from measures designed to ensure their independence, social and occupational integration and participation in the life of the community.

CHAPTER IV — SOLIDARITY

Article 27 — Workers' right to information and consultation within the undertaking

Workers or their representatives must, at the appropriate levels, be guaranteed information and consultation in good time in the cases and under the conditions provided for by Community law and national laws and practices.

Article 28 — Right of collective bargaining and action

Workers and employers, or their respective organisations, have, in accordance with Community law and national laws and practices, the right to negotiate and conclude collective agreements at the appropriate levels and, in cases of conflicts of interest, to take collective action to defend their interests, including strike action.

Article 29 — Right of access to placement services

Everyone has the right of access to a free placement service.

Article 30 — Protection in the event of unjustified dismissal

Every worker has the right to protection against unjustified dismissal, in accordance with Community law and national laws and practices.

Article 31 — Fair and just working conditions

1. Every worker has the right to working conditions which respect his or her health, safety and dignity.

2. Every worker has the right to limitation of maximum working hours, to daily and weekly rest periods and to an annual period of paid leave.

Article 32 — Prohibition of child labour and protection of young people at work

The employment of children is prohibited. The minimum age of admission to employment may not be lower than the minimum school-leaving age, without prejudice to such rules as may be more favourable to young people and except for limited derogations.

Young people admitted to work must have working conditions appropriate to their age and be protected against economic exploitation and any work likely to harm their safety, health or physical, mental, moral or social development or to interfere with their education.

Article 33 — Family and professional life

1. The family shall enjoy legal, economic and social protection.

2. To reconcile family and professional life, everyone shall the right to protection from dismissal for a reason connected with maternity and the right to paid maternity leave and to parental leave following the birth or adoption of a child.

Article 34 — Social security and social assistance

1. The Union recognizes and respects the entitlement to social security benefits and social services providing protection in cases such as maternity, illness, industrial accidents, dependency or old age, and in the case of loss of employment, in accordance with the rules laid down by Community law and national laws and practices.

2. Everyone residing and moving legally within the European Union is entitled to social security benefits and social advantages in accordance with Community law and national laws and practices.

3. In order to combat social exclusion and poverty, the Union recognises and respects the right to social and housing assistance so as to ensure a decent existence for all those who lack sufficient resources, in accordance with the rules laid down by Community law and national laws and practices.

Article 35 — Health care

Everyone has the right of access to preventive health care and the right to benefit from medical treatment under the conditions established by national laws and practices. A high level of human health protection shall be ensured in the definition and implementation of all Union policies and activities.

Article 36 — Access to services of general economic interest

The Union recognizes and respects access to services of general economic interest as provided for in national laws and practices, in accordance with the Treaty establishing the European Community, in order to promote the social and territorial cohesion of the Union.

Article 37 — Environmental protection

A high level of environmental protection and the improvement of the quality of the environment must be integrated into the policies of the Union and ensured in accordance with the principle of sustainable development.

Article 38—Consumer protection

Union policies shall ensure a high level of consumer protection.

CHAPTER V—CITIZENS' RIGHTS

Article 39—Right to vote and to stand as a candidate at elections to the European Parliament

1. Every citizen of the Union has the right to vote and to stand as a candidate at elections to the European Parliament in the Member State in which he or she resides, under the same conditions as nationals of that State.

2. Members of the European Parliament shall be elected by direct universal suffrage in a free and secret ballot.

Article 40—Right to vote and to stand as a candidate at municipal election

Every citizen of the Union has the right to vote and to stand as a candidate at municipal elections in the Member State in which he or she resides under the same conditions as nationals of that State.

Article 41—Right to good administration

1. Every person has the right to have his or her affairs handled impartially, fairly and within a reasonable time by the institutions and bodies of the Union.

2. This right includes:
– the right of every person to be heard, before any individual measure which would affect him or her adversely is taken;
– the right of every person to have access to his or her file, while respecting the legitimate interests of confidentiality and of professional and business secrecy;
– the obligation of the administration to give reasons for its decisions.

3. Every person has the right to have the Community make good any damage caused by its institutions or by its servants in the performance of their duties, in accordance with the general principles common to the laws of the Member States.

4. Every person may write to the institutions of the Union in one of the languages of the Treaties and must have an answer in the same language.

Article 42—Right of access to documents

Any citizen of the Union, and any natural or legal person residing or having its registered office in a Member State, has a right of access to European Parliament, Council and Commission documents.

Article 43—Ombudsman

Any citizen of the Union and any natural or legal person residing or having its registered office in a Member State has the right to refer to the Ombudsman of the Union cases of maladministration in the activities of the Community institutions or bodies, with the exception of the Court of Justice and the Court of First Instance acting in their judicial role.

Article 44—Right to petition

Any citizen of the Union and any natural or legal person residing or having its registered office in a Member State has the right to petition the European Parliament.

Article 45 — Freedom of movement and of residence

1. Every citizen of the Union has the right to move and reside freely within the territory of the Member States.

2. Freedom of movement and residence may be granted, in accordance with the Treaty establishing the European Community, to nationals of third countries legally resident in the territory of a Member State.

Article 46 — Diplomatic and consular protection

Every citizen of the Union shall, in the territory of a third country in which the Member State of which he or she is a national is not represented, be entitled to protection by the diplomatic or consular authorities of any Member State, on the same conditions as the nationals of that Member State.

CHAPTER VI — JUSTICE

Article 47 — Right to an effective remedy and to a fair trial

Everyone whose rights and freedoms guaranteed by the law of the Union are violated has the right to an effective remedy before a tribunal in compliance with the conditions laid down in this Article.

Everyone is entitled to a fair and public hearing within a reasonable time by in independent and impartial tribunal previously established by law. Everyone shall have the possibility of being advised, defended and represented.

Legal aid shall be made available to those who lack sufficient resources in so far as such aid is necessary to ensure effective access to justice.

Article 48 — Presumption of innocence and right of defence

1. Everyone who has been charged shall be presumed innocent until proved guilty according to law.

2. Respect for the rights of the defence of anyone who has been charged shall be guaranteed.

Article 49 — Principles of legality and proportionality of criminal offences and penalties

1. No one shall be held guilty of any criminal offence on account of any act or omission which did not constitute a criminal offence under national law or international law at the time when it was committed. Nor shall a heavier penalty be imposed than that which, was applicable at the time the criminal offence was committed. if, subsequent to the commission of a criminal offence, the law provides for a lighter penalty, that penalty shall be applicable.

2. This Article shall not prejudice the trial and punishment of any person for any act or omission which, at the time when it was committed, was criminal according to the general principles recognised by the community of nations.

3. The severity of penalties must not be disproportionate to the criminal offence.

Article 50 — Right not to be tried or punished twice in criminal proceedings for the same criminal offence

No one shall be liable to be tried or punished again in criminal proceedings for an offence for which he or she has already been finally acquitted or convicted within the Union in accordance with the law.

CHAPTER VII—GENERAL PROVISIONS

Article 51—Scope

1. The provisions of this Charter are addressed to the institutions and bodies of the Union with due regard for the principle of subsidiarity and to the Member States only when they are implementing Union law. They shall therefore respect the rights, observe the principles and promote the application thereof in accordance with their respective powers.

2. This Charter does not establish any new power or task for the Community or the Union, or modify powers and tasks defined by the Treaties.

Article 52—Scope of guaranteed rights

1. Any limitation on the exercise of the rights and freedoms recognised by this Charter must be provided for by law and respect the essence of those rights and freedoms. Subject to the principle of proportionality, limitations may be made only if they are necessary and genuinely meet objectives of general interest recognised by the Union or the need to protect the rights and freedoms of others.

2. Rights recognised by this Charter which are based on the Community Treaties or the Treaty on European Union shall be exercised under the conditions and within the limits defined by those Treaties.

3. In so far as this Charter contains rights which correspond to rights guaranteed by the Convention for the Protection of Human Rights and Fundamental Freedoms, the meaning and scope of those rights shall be the same as those laid down by the said Convention. This provision shall not prevent Union law providing more extensive protection.

Article 53—Level of protection

Nothing in this Charter shall be interpreted as restricting or adversely affecting human rights and fundamental freedoms as recognised, in their respective fields of application, by Union law and international law and by international agreements to which the Union, the Community or all the Member States are party, including the European Convention for the Protection of Human Rights and Fundamental Freedoms, and by the Member States' constitutions.

Article 54—Prohibition of abuse of rights

Nothing in this Charter shall be interpreted as implying any right to engage in any activity or to perform any act aimed at the destruction of any of the rights and freedoms recognised in this Charter or at their limitation to a greater extent than is provided for herein.

Council Regulation No. 1347/2000 on Jurisdiction and the Recognition and Enforcement of Judgments in Matrimonial Matters and in Matters of Parental Responsibility for Children of Both Spouses
2000 O.J. (L 160) 19

[Ed. Note: This regulation was designed to expedite implementation of Brussels II Convention. This regulation entered into force on March 1, 2001. Sweden and Finland entered a declaration pursuant to Article 36(2)(a). *See generally* Judicial Cooperation in Civil Matters, *at* http://europa.eu.iat.scadplus/leg/en/lvb/l33082.htm.

In May 2002, the European Commission proposed a new Council Regulation that would replace Regulation No. 1347/2000 (above) and amend Regulation No. 44/2001. The proposed new regulation is entitled, "Council Regulation Concerning Jurisdiction and the Recognition and Enforcement of Judgments in Matrimonial Matters and in Matters of Parental Responsibility Repealing Regulation (EC) No. 1347/2000 and amending Regulation (EC) No. 44/2001 in Matters related to Maintenance," COM (2002) 222/final/2.]

THE COUNCIL OF THE EUROPEAN UNION,

Having regard to the Treaty establishing the European Community, and in particular Article 61(c) and Article 67(1) thereof,

Having regard to the proposal from the Commission,

Having regard to the opinion of the European Parliament,

Having regard to the opinion of the Economic and Social Committee,

Whereas:

1. The Member States have set themselves the objective of maintaining and developing the Union as an area of freedom, security and justice, in which the free movement of persons is assured. To establish such an area, the Community is to adopt, among others, the measures in the field of judicial cooperation in civil matters needed for the proper functioning of the internal market.

2. The proper functioning of the internal market entails the need to improve and simplify the free movement of judgments in civil matters.

3. This is a subject now falling within the ambit of Article 65 of the Treaty.

4. Differences between certain national rules governing jurisdiction and enforcement hamper the free movement of persons and the sound operation of the internal market. There are accordingly grounds for enacting provisions to unify the rules of conflict of jurisdiction in matrimonial matters and in matters of parental responsibility so as to simplify the formalities for rapid and automatic recognition and enforcement of judgments.

5. In accordance with the principles of subsidiarity and proportionality as set out in Article 5 of the Treaty, the objectives of this Regulation cannot be sufficiently achieved by the Member States and can therefore be better achieved by the Community. This Regulation does not go beyond what is necessary to achieve those objectives.

6. The Council, by an Act dated 28 May 1998, drew up a Convention on jurisdiction and the recognition and enforcement of judgments in matrimonial matters and recommended it for adoption by the Member States in accordance with their respective constitutional rules. Continuity in the results of the negotiations for conclusion of the Convention should be ensured. The content of this Regulation is substantially taken over from the Convention, but this Regulation contains a number of new provisions not in the Convention in order to secure consistency with certain provisions of the proposed regulation on jurisdiction and the recognition and enforcement of judgments in civil and commercial matters.

7. In order to attain the objective of free movement of judgments in matrimonial matters and in matters of parental responsibility within the Community, it is necessary and appropriate that the cross-border recognition of jurisdiction and judgments in relation to the dissolution of matrimonial ties and to parental responsibility for the children of both spouses be governed by a mandatory, and directly applicable, Community legal instrument.

8. The measures laid down in this Regulation should be consistent and uniform, to enable people to move as widely as possible. Accordingly, it should also apply to nation-

als of non-member States whose links with the territory of a Member State are sufficiently close, in keeping with the grounds of jurisdiction laid down in the Regulation.

9. The scope of this Regulation should cover civil proceedings and non-judicial proceedings in matrimonial matters in certain States, and exclude purely religious procedures. It should therefore be provided that the reference to "courts" includes all the authorities, judicial or otherwise, with jurisdiction in matrimonial matters.

10. This Regulation should be confined to proceedings relating to divorce, legal separation or marriage annulment. The recognition of divorce and annulment rulings affects only the dissolution of matrimonial ties; despite the fact that they may be interrelated, the Regulation does not affect issues such as the fault of the spouses, property consequences of the marriage, the maintenance obligation or any other ancillary measures.

11. This Regulation covers parental responsibility for children of both spouses on issues that are closely linked to proceedings for divorce, legal separation or marriage annulment.

12. The grounds of jurisdiction accepted in this Regulation are based on the rule that there must be a real link between the party concerned and the Member State exercising jurisdiction; the decision to include certain grounds corresponds to the fact that they exist in different national legal systems and are accepted by the other Member States.

13. One of the risks to be considered in relation to the protection of the children of both spouses in a marital crisis is that one of the parents will take the child to another country. The fundamental interests of the children must therefore be protected, in accordance with, in particular, the Hague Convention of 25 October 1980 on the Civil Aspects of the International Abduction of Children. The lawful habitual residence is accordingly maintained as the grounds of jurisdiction in cases where, because the child has been moved or has not been returned without lawful reason, there has been a de facto change in the habitual residence.

14. This Regulation does not prevent the courts of a Member State from taking provisional, including protective, measures, in urgent cases, with regard to persons or property situated in that State.

15. The word "judgment" refers only to decisions that lead to divorce, legal separation or marriage annulment. Those documents which have been formally drawn up or registered as authentic instruments and are enforceable in one Member State are treated as equivalent to such "judgments."

16. The recognition and enforcement of judgments given in a Member State are based on the principle of mutual trust. The grounds for non-recognition are kept to the minimum required. Those proceedings should incorporate provisions to ensure observance of public policy in the State addressed and to safeguard the rights of the defence and those of the parties, including the individual rights of any child involved, and so as to withhold recognition of irreconcilable judgments.

17. The State addressed should review neither the jurisdiction of the State of origin nor the findings of fact.

18. No procedures may be required for the updating of civil-status documents in one Member State on the basis of a final judgment given in another Member State.

19. The Convention concluded by the Nordic States in 1931 should be capable of application within the limits set by this Regulation.

20. Spain, Italy and Portugal had concluded Concordats before the matters covered by this Regulation were brought within the ambit of the Treaty: It is necessary to ensure that these States do not breach their international commitments in relation to the Holy See.

21. The Member States should remain free to agree among themselves on practical measures for the application of the Regulation as long as no Community measures have been taken to that end.

22. Annexes I to III relating to the courts and redress procedures should be amended by the Commission on the basis of amendments transmitted by the Member State concerned. Amendments to Annexes IV and V should be adopted in accordance with Council Decision 1999/468/EC of 28 June 1999 laying down the procedures for the exercise of implementing powers conferred on the Commission.

23. No later than five years after the date of the entry into force of this Regulation, the Commission is to review its application and propose such amendments as may appear necessary.

24. The United Kingdom and Ireland, in accordance with Article 3 of the Protocol on the position of the United Kingdom and Ireland annexed to the Treaty on European Union and the Treaty establishing the European Community, have given notice of their wish to take part in the adoption and application of this Regulation.

25. Denmark, in accordance with Articles 1 and 2 of the Protocol on the position of Denmark annexed to the Treaty on European Union and the Treaty establishing the European Community, is not participating in the adoption of this Regulation, and is therefore not bound by it nor subject to its application,

HAS ADOPTED THIS REGULATION:

CHAPTER I — SCOPE

Article 1

1. This Regulation shall apply to:

a. civil proceedings relating to divorce, legal separation or marriage annulment;

b. or civil proceedings relating to parental responsibility for the children of both spouses on the occasion of the matrimonial proceedings referred to in (a).

2. or other proceedings officially recognised in a Member State shall be regarded as equivalent to judicial proceedings. The term "court" shall cover all the authorities with jurisdiction in these matters in the Member States.

3. In this Regulation, the term "Member State" shall mean all Member States with the exception of Denmark.

CHAPTER II — JURISDICTION

SECTION 1 — GENERAL PROVISIONS

Article 2 — Divorce, legal separation and marriage annulment

1. In matters relating to divorce, legal separation or marriage annulment, jurisdiction shall lie with the courts of the Member State:

a. in whose territory:

– the spouses are habitually resident, or

– the spouses were last habitually resident, in so far as one of them still resides there, or

– the respondent is habitually resident, or

– in the event of a joint application, either of the spouses is habitually resident, or

– the applicant is habitually resident if he or she resided there for at least a year immediately before the application was made, or

– the applicant is habitually resident if he or she resided there for at least six months immediately before the application was made and is either a national of the Member State in question or, in the case of the United Kingdom and Ireland, has his "domicile" there;

b. of the nationality of both spouses or, in the case of the United Kingdom and Ireland, of the "domicile" of both spouses.

2. For the purpose of this Regulation, "domicile" shall have the same meaning as it has under the legal systems of the United Kingdom and Ireland.

Article 3 — Parental responsibility

1. The Courts of a Member State exercising jurisdiction by virtue of Article 2 on an application for divorce, legal separation or marriage annulment shall have jurisdiction in a matter relating to parental responsibility over a child of both spouses where the child is habitually resident in that Member State.

2. Where the child is not habitually resident in the Member State referred to in paragraph 1, the courts of that State shall have jurisdiction in such a matter if the child is habitually resident in one of the Member States and:

a. at least one of the spouses has parental responsibility in relation to the child; and

b. the jurisdiction of the courts has been accepted by the spouses and is in the best interests of the child.

3. The jurisdiction conferred by paragraphs 1 and 2 shall cease as soon as:

a. the judgment allowing or refusing the application for divorce, legal separation or marriage annulment has become final; or

b. in those cases where proceedings in relation to parental responsibility are still pending on the date referred to in (a), a judgment in these proceedings has become final; or

c. the proceedings referred to in (a) and (b) have come to an end for another reason.

Article 4 — Child abduction

The courts with jurisdiction within the meaning of Article 3 shall exercise their jurisdiction in conformity with the Hague Convention of 25 October 1980 on the Civil Aspects of International Child Abduction, and in particular Articles 3 and 16 thereof.

Article 5 — Counterclaim

The court in which proceedings are pending on the basis of Articles 2 to 4 shall also have jurisdiction to examine a counterclaim, in so far as the latter comes within the scope of this Regulation.

Article 6 — Conversion of legal separation into divorce

Without prejudice to Article 2, a court of a Member State which has given a judgment on a legal separation shall also have jurisdiction for converting that judgment into a divorce, if the law of that Member State so provides.

Article 7 — Exclusive nature of jurisdiction under Articles 2 to 6

A spouse who:

a. is habitually resident in the territory of a Member State; or

b. is a national of a Member State, or, in the case of the United Kingdom and Ireland, has his or her "domicile" in the territory of one of the latter Member States, may be sued in another Member State only in accordance with Articles 2 to 6.

Article 8 — Residual jurisdiction

1. Where no court of a Member State has jurisdiction pursuant to Articles 2 to 6, jurisdiction shall be determined, in each Member State, by the laws of that State.

2. As against a respondent who is not habitually resident and is not either a national of a Member State or, in the case of the United Kingdom and Ireland, does not have his "domicile" within the territory of one of the latter Member States, any national of a Member State who is habitually resident within the territory of another Member State may, like the nationals of that State, avail himself of the rules of jurisdiction applicable in that State.

SECTION 2 — EXAMINATION AS TO JURISDICTION AND ADMISSIBILITY

Article 9 — Examination as to jurisdiction

Where a court of a Member State is seised of a case over which it has no jurisdiction under this Regulation and over which a court of another Member State has jurisdiction by virtue of this Regulation, it shall declare of its own motion that it has no jurisdiction.

Article 10 — Examination as to admissibility

1. Where a respondent habitually resident in a State other than the Member State where the action was brought does not enter an appearance, the court with jurisdiction shall stay the proceedings so long as it is not shown that the respondent has been able to receive the document instituting the proceedings or an equivalent document in sufficient time to enable him to arrange for his defence, or that all necessary steps have been taken to this end.

2. Article 19 of Council Regulation (EC) No 1348/2000 of 29 May 2000 on the service in the Member States of judicial and extrajudicial documents in civil or commercial matters, shall apply instead of the provisions of paragraph 1 of this Article if the document instituting the proceedings or an equivalent document had to be transmitted from one Member State to another pursuant to that Regulation.

3. Where the provisions of Council Regulation (EC) No 1348/2000 are not applicable, Article 15 of the Hague Convention of 15 November 1965 on the service abroad of judicial and extrajudicial documents in civil or commercial matters shall apply if the document instituting the proceedings or an equivalent document had to be transmitted abroad pursuant to that Convention.

SECTION 3 — LIS PENDENS AND DEPENDENT ACTIONS

Article 11

1. Where proceedings involving the same cause of action and between the same parties are brought before courts of different Member States, the court second seised shall of its own motion stay its proceedings until such time as the jurisdiction of the court first seised is established.

2. Where proceedings for divorce, legal separation or marriage annulment not involving the same cause of action and between the same parties are brought before courts of different Member States, the court second seised shall of its own motion stay its proceedings until such time as the jurisdiction of the court first seised is established.

3. Where the jurisdiction of the court first seised is established, the court second seised shall decline jurisdiction in favour of that court.

In that case, the party who brought the relevant action before the court second seised may bring that action before the court first seised.

4. For the purposes of this Article, a court shall be deemed to be seised:

a. at the time when the document instituting the proceedings or an equivalent document is lodged with the court, provided that the applicant has not subsequently failed to take the steps he was required to take to have service effected on the respondent; or

b. if the document has to be served before being lodged with the court, at the time when it is received by the authority responsible for service, provided that the applicant has not subsequently failed to take the steps he was required to take to have the document lodged with the court.

SECTION 4—PROVISIONAL, INCLUDING PROTECTIVE, MEASURES

Article 12

In urgent cases, the provisions of this Regulation shall not prevent the courts of a Member State from taking such provisional, including protective, measures in respect of persons or assets in that State as may be available under the law of that Member State, even if, under this Regulation, the court of another Member State has jurisdiction as to the substance of the matter.

CHAPTER III—RECOGNITION AND ENFORCEMENT

Article 13—Meaning of "judgment"

1. For the purposes of this Regulation, "judgment" means a divorce, legal separation or marriage annulment pronounced by a court of a Member State, as well as a judgment relating to the parental responsibility of the spouses given on the occasion of such matrimonial proceedings, whatever the judgment may be called, including a decree, order or decision.

2. The provisions of this chapter shall also apply to the determination of the amount of costs and expenses of proceedings under this Regulation and to the enforcement of any order concerning such costs and expenses.

3. For the purposes of implementing this Regulation, documents which have been formally drawn up or registered as authentic instruments and are enforceable in one Member State and also settlements which have been approved by a court in the course of proceedings and are enforceable in the Member State in which they were concluded shall be recognised and declared enforceable under the same conditions as the judgments referred to in paragraph 1.

SECTION 1—RECOGNITION

Article 14—Recognition of a judgment

1. A judgment given in a Member State shall be recognised in the other Member States without any special procedure being required.

2. In particular, and without prejudice to paragraph 3, no special procedure shall be required for up-dating the civil-status records of a Member State on the basis of a judgment relating to divorce, legal separation or marriage annulment given in another member State, and against which no further appeal lies under the law of that Member State.

3. Any interested party may, in accordance with the procedures provided for in Sections 2 and 3 of this Chapter, apply for a decision that the judgment be or not be recognised.

4. Where the recognition of a judgment is raised as an incidental question in a court of a Member State, that court may determine that issue.

Article 15 — Grounds of non-recognition

1. A judgment relating to a divorce, legal separation or marriage annulment shall not be recognised:

a. if such recognition is manifestly contrary to the public policy of the Member State in which recognition is sought;

b. where it was given in default of appearance, if the respondent was not served with the document which instituted the proceedings or with an equivalent document in sufficient time and in such a way as to enable the respondent to arrange for his or her defence unless it is determined that the respondent has accepted the judgment unequivocally;

c. it is irreconcilable with a judgment given in proceedings between the same parties in the Member State in which recognition is sought; or

d. if it is irreconcilable with an earlier judgment given in another Member State or in a non-member State between the same parties, provided that the earlier judgment fulfils the conditions necessary for its recognition in the Member State in which recognition is sought.

2. A judgment relating to the parental responsibility of the spouses given on the occasion of matrimonial proceedings as referred to in Article 13 shall not be recognised:

a. if such recognition is manifestly contrary to the public policy of the Member State in which recognition is sought taking into account the best interests of the child;

b. if it was given, except in case of urgency, without the child having been given an opportunity to be heard, in violation of fundamental principles of procedure of the Member State in which recognition is sought;

c. where it was given in default of appearance if the person in default was not served with the document which instituted the proceedings or with an equivalent document in sufficient time and in such a way as to enable that person to arrange for his or her defence unless it is determined that such person has accepted the judgment unequivocally;

d. on the request of any person claiming that the judgment infringes his or her parental responsibility, if it was given without such person having been given an opportunity to be heard;

e. if it is irreconcilable with a later judgment relating to parental responsibility given in the Member State in which recognition is sought; or

f. if it is irreconcilable with a later judgment relating to parental responsibility given in another Member State or in the non-member State of the habitual residence of the child provided that the later judgment fulfils the conditions necessary for its recognition in the Member State in which recognition is sought.

Article 16 — Agreement with third States

A court of a Member State may, on the basis of an agreement on the recognition and enforcement of judgments, not recognise a judgment given in another Member State where, in cases provided for in Article 8, the judgment could only be founded on grounds of jurisdiction other than those specified in Articles 2 to 7.

Article 17 — Prohibition of review of jurisdiction of court of origin

The jurisdiction of the court of the Member State of origin may not be reviewed. The test of public policy referred to in Article 15(1)(a) and (2)(a) may not be applied to the rules relating to jurisdiction set out in Articles 2 to 8.

Article 18—Differences in applicable law

The recognition of a judgment relating to a divorce, legal separation or a marriage annulment may not be refused because the law of the Member State in which such recognition is sought would not allow divorce, legal separation or marriage annulment on the same facts.

Article 19—Differences in applicable law

Under no circumstances may a judgment be reviewed as to its substance.

Article 20—Stay of proceedings

1. A court of a Member State in which recognition is sought of a judgment given in another Member State may stay the proceedings if an ordinary appeal against the judgment has been lodged.

2. A court of a Member State in which recognition is sought of a judgment given in Ireland or the United Kingdom may stay the proceedings if enforcement is suspended in the Member State of origin by reason of an appeal.

SECTION 2—ENFORCEMENT

Article 21—Enforceable judgments

1. A judgment on the exercise of parental responsibility in respect of a child of both parties given in a Member State which is enforceable in that Member State and has been served shall be enforced in another Member State when, on the application of any interested party, it has been declared enforceable there.

2. However, in the United Kingdom, such a judgment shall be enforced in England and Wales, in Scotland or in Northern Ireland when, on the application of any interested party, it has been registered for enforcement in that part of the United Kingdom.

Article 22—Jurisdiction of local courts

1. An application for a declaration of enforceability shall be submitted to the court appearing in the list in Annex I.

2. The local jurisdiction shall be determined by reference to the place of the habitual residence of the person against whom enforcement is sought or by reference to the habitual residence of any child to whom the application relates.

Where neither of the places referred to in the first subparagraph can be found in the Member State where enforcement is sought, the local jurisdiction shall be determined by reference to the place of enforcement.

3. In relation to procedures referred to in Article 14(3), the local jurisdiction shall be determined by the internal law of the Member State in which proceedings for recognition or non-recognition are brought.

Article 23—Procedure for enforcement

1. The procedure for making the application shall be governed by the law of the Member State in which enforcement is sought.

2. The applicant must give an address for service within the area of jurisdiction of the court applied to. However, if the law of the Member State in which enforcement is sought does not provide for the furnishing of such an address, the applicant shall appoint a representative ad litem.

3. The documents referred to in Articles 32 and 33 shall be attached to the application.

Article 24 — Decision of the court

1. The court applied to shall give its decision without delay. The person against whom enforcement is sought shall not at this stage of the proceedings be entitled to make any submissions on the application.

2. The application may be refused only for one of the reasons specified in Articles 15, 16 and 17.

3. Under no circumstances may a judgment be reviewed as to its substance.

Article 25 — Notice of the decision

The appropriate officer of the court shall without delay bring to the notice of the applicant the decision given on the application in accordance with the procedure laid down by the law of the Member State in which enforcement is sought.

Article 26 — Appeal against the enforcement decision

1. The decision on the application for a declaration of enforceability may be appealed against by either party.

2. The appeal shall be lodged with the court appearing in the list in Annex II.

3. The appeal shall be dealt with in accordance with the rules governing procedure in contradictory matters.

4. If the appeal is brought by the applicant for a declaration of enforceability, the party against whom enforcement is sought shall be summoned to appear before the appellate court. If such person fails to appear, the provisions of Article 10 shall apply.

5. An appeal against a declaration of enforceability must be lodged within one month of service thereof. If the party against whom enforcement is sought is habitually resident in a Member State other than that in which the declaration of enforceability was given, the time for appealing shall be two months and shall run from the date of service, either on him or at his residence. No extension of time may be granted on account of distance.

Article 27 — Courts of appeal and means of contest

The judgment given on appeal may be contested only by the proceedings referred to in Annex III.

Article 28 — Stay of proceedings

1. The court with which the appeal is lodged under Articles 26 or 27 may, on the application of the party against whom enforcement is sought, stay the proceedings if an ordinary appeal has been lodged in the Member State of origin or if the time for such appeal has not yet expired. In the latter case, the court may specify the time within which an appeal is to be lodged.

2. Where the judgment was given in Ireland or the United Kingdom, any form of appeal available in the Member State of origin shall be treated as an ordinary appeal for the purposes of paragraph 1.

Article 29 — Partial enforcement

1. Where a judgment has been given in respect of several matters and enforcement cannot be authorised for all of them, the court shall authorise enforcement for one or more of them.

2. An applicant may request partial enforcement of a judgment.

Article 30 — Legal aid

An applicant who, in the Member State of origin, has benefited from complete or partial legal aid or exemption from costs or expenses shall be entitled, in the procedures provided for in Articles 22 to 25, to benefit from the most favourable legal aid or the most extensive exemption from costs and expenses provided for by the law of the Member State addressed.

Article 31 — Security, bond or deposit

No security, bond or deposit, however described, shall be required of a party who in one Member State applies for enforcement of a judgment given in another Member State on the following grounds:

a. that he or she is not habitually resident in the Member State in which enforcement is sought; or

b. that he or she is either a foreign national or, where enforcement is sought in either the United Kingdom or Ireland, does not have his or her "domicile" in either of those Member States.

SECTION 3 — COMMON PROVISIONS

Article 32 — Documents

1. A party seeking or contesting recognition or applying for a declaration of enforceability shall produce:

a. a copy of the judgment which satisfies the conditions necessary to establish its authenticity; and

b. a certificate referred to in Article 33.

2. In addition, in the case of a judgment given in default, the party seeking recognition or applying for a declaration of enforceability shall produce:

a. the original or certified true copy of the document which establishes that the defaulting party was served with the document instituting the proceedings or with an equivalent document; or

b. any document indicating that the defendant has accepted the judgment unequivocally.

Article 33 — Other documents

The competent court or authority of a Member State where a judgment was given shall issue, at the request of any interested party, a certificate using the standard form in Annex IV (judgments in matrimonial matters) or Annex V (judgments on parental responsibility).

Article 34 — Absence of documents

1. If the documents specified in Article 32(1)(b) or (2) are not produced, the court may specify a time for their production, accept equivalent documents or, if it considers that it has sufficient information before it, dispense with their production.

2. If the Court so requires, a translation of such documents shall be furnished. The translation shall be certified by a person qualified to do so in one of the Member States.

Article 35 — Legalisation or other similar formality

No legalisation or other similar formality shall be required in respect of the documents referred to in Articles 32, 33 and 34(2) or in respect of a document appointing a representative ad litem.

CHAPTER IV — GENERAL PROVISIONS

Article 36 — Relation with other instruments

1. Subject to the provisions of Articles 38, 42 and paragraph 2 of this Article, this Regulation shall, for the Member States, supersede conventions existing at the time of entry into force of this Regulation which have been concluded between two or more Member States and relate to matters governed by this Regulation.

2.

a. Finland and Sweden shall have the option of declaring that the Convention of 6 February 1931 between Denmark, Finland, Iceland, Norway and Sweden comprising international private law provisions on marriage, adoption and guardianship, together with the Final Protocol thereto, will apply, in whole or in part, in their mutual relations, in place of the rules of this Regulation. Such declarations shall be annexed to this Regulation and published in the Official Journal of the European Communities. They may be withdrawn, in whole or in part, at any moment by the said Member States.

b. The principle of non-discrimination on the grounds of nationality between citizens of the Union shall be respected.

c. The rules of jurisdiction in any future agreement to be concluded between the Member States referred to in subparagraph (a) which relate to matters governed by this Regulation shall be in line with those laid down in this Regulation.

d. Judgments handed down in any of the Nordic States which have made the declaration provided for in subparagraph (a) under a forum of jurisdiction corresponding to one of those laid down in Chapter II, shall be recognised and enforced in the other Member States under the rules laid down in Chapter III.

3. Member States shall send to the Commission:

a. a copy of the agreements and uniform laws implementing these agreements referred to in paragraphs 2(a) and (c);

b. any denunciations of, or amendments to, those agreements or uniform laws.

Article 37 — Relations with certain multilateral conventions

In relations between Member States, this Regulation shall take precedence over the following Conventions in so far as they concern matters governed by this Regulation:

– the Hague Convention of 5 October 1961 concerning the Powers of Authorities and the Law Applicable in respect of the Protection of Minors,

– the Luxembourg Convention of 8 September 1967 on the Recognition of Decisions Relating to the Validity of Marriages,

– the Hague Convention of 1 June 1970 on the Recognition of Divorces and Legal Separations,

– the European Convention of 20 May 1980 on Recognition and Enforcement of Decisions concerning Custody of Children and on Restoration of Custody of Children,

– the Hague Convention of 19 October 1996 on Jurisdiction, Applicable law, Recognition, Enforcement and Cooperation in Respect of Parental Responsibility and Measures for the Protection of Children, provided that the child concerned is habitually resident in a Member State.

Article 38 — Extent of effects

1. The agreements and conventions referred to in Articles 36(1) and 37 shall continue to have effect in relation to matters to which this Regulation does not apply.

2. They shall continue to have effect in respect of judgments given and documents formally drawn up or registered as authentic before the entry into force of this Regulation.

Article 39—Agreements between Member States

1. Two or more Member States may conclude agreements or arrangements to amplify this Regulation or to facilitate its application. Member States shall send to the Commission:
   a. a copy of the draft agreements; and
   b. any denunciations of, or amendments to, these agreements.

2. In no circumstances may the agreements or arrangements derogate from Chapters II or III.

Article 40—Treaties with the Holy See

1. This Regulation shall apply without prejudice to the International Treaty (Concordat) between the Holy See and Portugal, signed at the Vatican City on 7 May 1940.

2. Any decision as to the invalidity of a marriage taken under the Treaty referred to in paragraph 1 shall be recognised in the Member States on the conditions laid down in Chapter III.

3. The provisions laid down in paragraphs 1 and 2 shall also apply to the following international treaties (Concordats) with the Holy See:
   a. Concordato lateranense of 11 February 1929 between Italy and the Holy See, modified by the agreement, with additional Protocol signed in Rome on 18 February 1984;
   b. Agreement between the Holy See and Spain on legal affairs of 3 January 1979.

4. Recognition of the decisions provided for in paragraph 2 may, in Italy or in Spain, be subject to the same procedures and the same checks as are applicable to decisions of the ecclesiastical courts handed down in accordance with the international treaties concluded with the Holy See referred to in paragraph 3.

5. Member States shall send to the Commission:
   a. a copy of the Treaties referred to in paragraphs 1 and 3;
   b. any denunciations of or amendments to those Treaties.

Article 41—Member States with two or more legal systems

With regard to a Member State in which two or more systems of law or sets of rules concerning matters governed by this Regulation apply in different territorial units:
   a. any reference to habitual residence in that Member State shall refer to habitual residence in a territorial unit;
   b. any reference to nationality, or in the case of the United Kingdom "domicile," shall refer to the territorial unit designated by the law of that State;
   c. any reference to the authority of a Member State having received an application for divorce or legal separation or for marriage annulment shall refer to the authority of a territorial unit which has received such an application;
   d. any reference to the rules of the requested Member State shall refer to the rules of the territorial unit in which jurisdiction, recognition or enforcement is invoked.

CHAPTER V—TRANSITIONAL PROVISIONS

Article 42

1. The provisions of this Regulation shall apply only to legal proceedings instituted, to documents formally drawn up or registered as authentic instruments and to settle-

ments which have been approved by a court in the course of proceedings after its entry into force.

2. Judgments given after the date of entry into force of this Regulation in proceedings instituted before that date shall be recognised and enforced in accordance with the provisions of Chapter III if jurisdiction was founded on rules which accorded with those provided for either in Chapter II of this Regulation or in a convention concluded between the Member State of origin and the Member State addressed which was in force when the proceedings were instituted.

CHAPTER VI—FINAL PROVISIONS

Article 43—Review
No later than 1 March 2006, and every five years thereafter, the Commission shall present to the European Parliament, the Council and the Economic and Social Committee a report on the application of this Regulation, and in particular Articles 36, 39 and 40(2) thereof. The report shall be accompanied if need be by proposals for adaptations.

Article 44—Amendment to lists of courts and redress procedures
1. Member States shall notify the Commission of the texts amending the lists of courts and redress procedures set out in Annexes I to III. The Commission shall adapt the Annexes concerned accordingly.

2. The updating or making of technical amendments to the standard forms set out in Annexes IV and V shall be adopted in accordance with the advisory procedure set out in Article 45(2).

Article 45
1. The Commission shall be assisted by a committee.

2. Where reference is made to this paragraph, Articles 3 and 7 of Decision 1999/468 EC shall apply.

3. The committee shall adopt its rules of procedure.

Article 46—Entry into force

This Regulation shall enter into force on 1 March 2001. This Regulation shall be binding in its entirety and directly applicable in the Member States in accordance with the Treaty establishing the European Community.

[Ed. Note: Annex I, which lists the courts in each country to which the applications provided for by Article 22 shall be submitted, Annex II, which lists the courts in each country to which appeals provided for by Article 26 shall be lodged, and Annex III, which provides the courts in each country to which appeals provided for by Article 27 may be brought, are omitted. In addition Annex IV and V are omitted. Annex IV was the certificate referred to in Article 33 concerning judgments in matrimonial matters. Annex V was the certificate referred to in Article 33 concerning judgments on parental responsibility.]

Council Regulation No. 44/2001 on Jurisdiction and the Recognition and Enforcement of Judgments in Civil and Commercial Matters (Selected Portions)

2001 O.J. (L 12) 1

[Ed. Note: Council Regulation 44/2001 entered into force on March 1, 2002. For all European Union (EU) member nations except Denmark, the regulation replaces the EU Convention on Jurisdiction and Enforcement of Judgments in Civil and Commercial Matters, commonly referred to as "Brussels I." Denmark continues to be governed in its relations with other European Union members by the "Brussels I" Convention. Although the regulation addresses jurisdiction, recognition, and enforcement of civil and commercial judgments generally, it is relevant to international family law because it also governs jurisdiction over maintenance proceedings as well as recognition and enforcement of maintenance judgments. Only those articles most directly relevant are included here. However, other articles may be of interest as well. The full Regulation can be found at the European Union's official website, *at* http://www.europa.eu.int/eur-lex/en/search/search_lif.html.

In May 2002, the European Commission proposed an amendment to this Regulation. It would add to the end of the paragraph in article 5.2 the following language: "or, if the matter is ancillary to proceedings concerning parental responsibility, in the court which according to Council Regulation...[on jurisdiction and the recognition and enforcement of judgments in matrimonial matters and in matters of parental responsibility], has jurisdiction to entertain those proceedings." *See* Council Regulation Concerning Jurisdiction and the Recognition and Enforcement of Judgments in Matrimonial Matters and in Matters of Parental Responsibility Repealing Regulation (EC) No. 1347/2000 and amending Regulation (EC) No. 44/2001 in Matters related to Maintenance, COM (02) 222 final/2 at art. 70. If the proposed regulation is adopted without amendment, this addition shall apply from July 1, 2004.]

[Ed. Note: The preamble has been omitted.]

CHAPTER I—SCOPE

Article 1

1. This Regulation shall apply in civil and commercial matters whatever the nature of the court or tribunal. It shall not extend, in particular, to revenue, customs or administrative matters.

2. The Regulation shall not apply to:

a. the status or legal capacity of natural persons, rights in property arising out of a matrimonial relationship, wills and succession;

b. bankruptcy, proceedings relating to the winding-up of insolvent companies or other legal persons, judicial arrangements, compositions and analogous proceedings;

c. social security;

d. arbitration.

3. In this Regulation, the term 'Member State' shall mean Member States with the exception of Denmark.

CHAPTER II — JURISDICTION

SECTION I — GENERAL PROVISIONS

Article 2

1. Subject to this Regulation, persons domiciled in a Member State shall, whatever their nationality, be sued in the courts of that Member State.

2. Persons who are not nationals of the Member State in which they are domiciled shall be governed by the rules of jurisdiction applicable to nationals of that State.

Article 3

1. Persons domiciled in a Member State may be sued in the courts of another Member State only by virtue of the rules set out in Sections 2 to 7 of this Chapter.

2. In particular the rules of national jurisdiction set out in Annex I shall not be applicable as against them.

Article 4

1. If the defendant is not domiciled in a Member State, the jurisdiction of the courts of each Member State shall, subject to Articles 22 and 23, be determined by the law of that Member State.

2. As against such a defendant, any person domiciled in a Member State may, whatever his nationality, avail himself in that State of the rules of jurisdiction there in force, and in particular those specified in Annex I, in the same way as the nationals of that State.

SECTION 2 — SPECIAL JURISDICTION

Article 5

A person domiciled in a Member State may, in another Member State, be sued:...

2. In matters relating to maintenance, in the courts for the place where the maintenance creditor is domiciled or habitually resident or, if the matter is ancillary to proceedings concerning the status of a person, in the court which, according to its own law, has jurisdiction to entertain those proceedings, unless that jurisdiction is based solely on the nationality of one of the parties....

SECTION 7 — PROROGATION OF JURISDICTION

Article 23

1. If the parties, one or more of whom is domiciled in a Member State, have agreed that a court or the courts of a Member State are to have jurisdiction to settle any disputes which have arisen or which may arise in connection with a particular legal relationship, that court or those courts shall have jurisdiction. Such jurisdiction shall be exclusive unless the parties have agreed otherwise. Such an agreement conferring jurisdiction shall be either:

a. in writing or evidenced in writing; or

b. in a form which accords with practices which the parties have established between themselves; or

c. in international trade or commerce, in a form which accords with a usage of which the parties are or ought to have been aware and which in such trade or commerce is widely known to, and regularly observed by, parties to contracts of the type involved in the particular trade or commerce concerned.

2. Any communication by electronic means which provides a durable record of the agreement shall be equivalent to 'writing.'

3. Where such an agreement is concluded by parties, none of whom is domiciled in a Member State, the courts of other Member States shall have no jurisdiction over their disputes unless the court or courts chosen have declined jurisdiction.

4. The court or courts of a Member State on which a trust instrument has conferred jurisdiction shall have exclusive jurisdiction in any proceedings brought against a settlor, trustee or beneficiary, if relations between these persons or their rights or obligations under the trust are involved.

5. Agreements or provisions of a trust instrument conferring jurisdiction shall have no legal force if they are contrary to Articles 13, 17 or 21, or if the courts whose jurisdiction they purport to exclude have exclusive jurisdiction by virtue of Article 22.

Article 24

Apart from jurisdiction derived from other provisions of this Regulation, a court of a Member State before which a defendant enters an appearance shall have jurisdiction. This rule shall not apply where appearance was entered to contest the jurisdiction, or where another court has exclusive jurisdiction by virtue of Article 22....

CHAPTER III — RECOGNITION AND ENFORCEMENT

Article 32

For the purposes of this Regulation, 'judgment' means any judgment given by a court or tribunal of a Member State, whatever the judgment may be called, including a decree, order, decision or writ of execution, as well as the determination of costs or expenses by an office of the court.

SECTION 1 — RECOGNITION

Article 33

1. A judgment given in a Member State shall be recognised in the other Member States without any special procedure being required.

2. Any interested party who raises the recognition of a judgment as the principal issue in a dispute may, in accordance with the procedures provided for in Sections 2 and 3 of this Chapter, apply for a decision that the judgment by recognised.

3. If the outcome of proceedings in a court of a Member State depends on the determination of an incidental question of recognition that court shall have jurisdiction over that question.

Article 34

A judgment shall not be recognised:

1. if such recognition is manifestly contrary to public policy in the Member State in which recognition is sought;

2. where it was given in default of appearance, if the defendant was not served with the document which instituted the proceedings or with an equivalent document in sufficient time and in such a way as to enable him to arrange for his defence, unless the defendant failed to commence proceedings to challenge the judgment when it was possible for him to do so;

3. if it is irreconcilable with a judgment given in a dispute between the same parties in the Member State in which recognition is sought;

4. if it is irreconcilable with an earlier judgment given in another Member State or in a third State involving the same cause of action and between the same parties, provided that the earlier judgment fulfils the conditions necessary for its recognition in the Member State addressed.

Article 35

1. Moreover, a judgment shall not be recognised if it conflicts with Sections 3, 4 or 6 of Chapter II, or in a case provided for in Article 72.

2. In its examination of the grounds of jurisdiction referred to in the foregoing paragraph, the court or authority applied to shall be bound by the findings of fact on which the court of the Member State of origin based its jurisdiction.

3. Subject to the paragraph 1, the jurisdiction of the court of the Member State of origin may not be reviewed. The test of public policy referred to in point 1 of Article 34 may not be applied to the rules relating to jurisdiction.

Article 36

Under no circumstances may a foreign judgment be reviewed as to its substance.

Article 37

1. A court of a Member State in which recognition is sought of a judgment given in another Member State may stay the proceedings if an ordinary appeal against the judgment has been lodged.

2. A court of a Member State in which recognition is sought of a judgment given in Ireland or the United Kingdom may stay the proceedings if enforcement is suspended in the State of origin, by reason of an appeal.

SECTION 2 — ENFORCEMENT

Article 38

1. A judgment given in a Member State and enforceable in that State shall be enforced in another Member State when, on the application of any interested party, it has been declared enforceable there.

2. However, in the United Kingdom, such a judgment shall be enforced in England and Wales, in Scotland, or in Northern Ireland when, on the application of any interested party, it has been registered for enforcement in that part of the United Kingdom.

Article 39

1. The application shall be submitted to the court or competent authority indicated in the list in Annex II.

2. The local jurisdiction shall be determined by reference to the place of domicile of the party against whom enforcement is sought, or to the place of enforcement.

Article 40

1. The procedure for making the application shall be governed by the law of the Member State in which enforcement is sought.

2. The applicant must give an address for service of process within the area of jurisdiction of the court applied to. However, if the law of the Member State in which enforcement is sought does not provide for the furnishing of such an address, the applicant shall appoint a representative *ad litem*.

3. The documents referred to in Article 53 shall be attached to the application.

Article 41

The judgment shall be declared enforceable immediately on completion of the formalities in Article 53 without any review under Articles 34 and 35. The party against whom enforcement is sought shall not at this stage of the proceedings be entitled to make any submissions on the application.

Article 42

1. The decision on the application for a declaration of enforceability shall forthwith be brought to the notice of the applicant in accordance with the procedure laid down by the law of the Member State in which enforcement is sought.

2. The declaration of enforceability shall be served on the party against whom enforcement is sought, accompanied by the judgment, if not already served on that party.

Article 43

1. The decision on the application for a declaration of enforceability may be appealed against by either party.

2. The appeal is to be lodged with the court indicated in the list in Annex III.

3. The appeal shall be dealt with in accordance with the rules governing procedure in contradictory matters.

4. If the party against whom enforcement is sought fails to appear before the appellate court in proceedings concerning an appeal brought by the applicant, Article 26(2) to (4) shall apply even where the party against whom enforcement is sought is not domiciled in any of the Member States.

5. An appeal against the declaration of enforceability is to be lodged within one month of service thereof. If the party against whom enforcement is sought is domiciled in a Member State other than that in which the declaration of enforceability was given, the time for appealing shall be two months and shall run from the date of service, either on him in person or at his residence. No extension of time may be granted on account of distance.

Article 44

The judgment given on appeal may be contested only by the appeal referred to in Annex IV.

Article 45

1. The court with which an appeal is lodged under Article 43 or Article 44 shall refuse or revoke a declaration of enforceability only on one of the grounds specified in Articles 34 and 35. It shall give its decision without delay.

2. Under no circumstances may the foreign judgment be reviewed as to its substance.

Article 46

1. The court with which an appeal is lodged under Article 43 or Article 44 may, on the application of the party against whom enforcement is sought, stay the proceedings if an ordinary appeal has been lodged against the judgment in the Member State of origin or if the time for such an appeal has not yet expired; in the latter case, the court may specify the time within which such an appeal is to be lodged.

2. Where the judgment was given in Ireland or the United Kingdom, any form of appeal available in the Member State of origin shall be treated as an ordinary appeal for the purposes of paragraph 1.

3. The court may also make enforcement conditional on the provision of such security as it shall determine.

Article 47

1. When a judgment must be recognised in accordance with this Regulation, nothing shall prevent the applicant from availing himself of provisional, including protective, measures in accordance with the law of the Member State requested without a declaration of enforceability under Article 41 being required.

2. The declaration of enforceability shall carry with it the power to proceed to any protective measures.

3. During the time specified for an appeal pursuant to Article 43(5) against the declaration of enforceability and until any such appeal has been determined, no measures of enforcement may be taken other than protective measures against the property of the party against whom enforcement is sought.

Article 48

1. Where a foreign judgment has been given in respect of several matters and the declaration of enforceability cannot be given for all of them, the court or competent authority shall give it for one or more of them.

2. An applicant may request a declaration of enforceability limited to parts of a judgment.

Article 49

A foreign judgment which orders a periodic payment by way of a penalty shall be enforceable in the Member State in which enforcement is sought only if the amount of the payment has been finally determined by the courts of the Member State of origin.

Article 50

An applicant who, in the Member State of origin has benefited from complete or partial legal aid or exemption from costs or expenses, shall be entitled, in the procedure provided for in this Section, to benefit from the most favourable legal aid or the most extensive exemption from costs or expenses provided for by the law of the Member State addressed.

Article 51

No security, bond or deposit, however described, shall be required of a party who in one Member State applies for enforcement of a judgment given in another Member State on the ground that he is a foreign national or that he is not domiciled or resident in the State in which enforcement is sought.

Article 52

In proceedings for the issue of a declaration of enforceability, no charge, duty or fee calculated by reference to the value of the matter at issue may be levied in the Member State in which enforcement is sought.

SECTION 3 — COMMON PROVISIONS

Article 53

1. A party seeking recognition or applying for a declaration of enforceability shall produce a copy of the judgment which satisfies the conditions necessary to establish its authenticity.

2. A party applying for a declaration of enforceability shall also produce the certificate referred to in Article 54, without prejudice to Article 55.

Article 54

The court or competent authority of a Member State where a judgment was given shall issue, at the request of any interested party, a certificate using the standard form in Annex V to this Regulation.

Article 55

1. If the certificate referred to in Article 54 is not produced, the court or competent authority may specify a time for its production or accept an equivalent document or, if it considers that it has sufficient information before it, dispense with its production.

2. If the court or competent authority so requires, a translation of the documents shall be produced. The translation shall be certified by a person qualified to do so in one of the Member States.

Article 56

No legalisation or other similar formality shall be required in respect of the documents referred to in Article 53 or Article 55(2), or in respect of a document appointing a representative *ad litem*.

CHAPTER IV — AUTHENTIC INSTRUMENTS AND COURT SETTLEMENTS

Article 57

1. A document which has been formally drawn up or registered as an authentic instrument and is enforceable in one Member State shall, in another Member State, be declared enforceable there, on application made in accordance with the procedures provided for in Article 38, et seq. The court with which an appeal is lodged under Article 43 or Article 44 shall refuse or revoke a declaration of enforceability only if enforcement of the instrument is manifestly contrary to public policy in the Member State addressed.

2. Arrangements relating to maintenance obligations concluded with administrative authorities or authenticated by them shall also be regarded as authentic instruments within the meaning of paragraph 1.

3. The instrument produced must satisfy the conditions necessary to establish its authenticity in the Member State of origin.

4. Section 3 of Chapter III shall apply as appropriate. The competent authority of a Member State where an authentic instrument was drawn up or registered shall issue, at the request of any interested party, a certificate using the standard form in Annex VI to this Regulation.

Article 58

A settlement which has been approved by a court in the course of proceedings and is enforceable in the Member State in which it was concluded shall be enforceable in the State addressed under the same conditions as authentic instruments. The court or competent authority of a Member State where a court settlement was approved shall issue, at the request of any interested party, a certificate using the standard form in Annex V to this Regulation.

CHAPTER V — GENERAL PROVISIONS

Article 59

1. In order to determine whether a party is domiciled in the Member State whose courts are seised of a matter, the court shall apply its internal law.

2. If a party is not domiciled in the Member State whose courts are seised of the matter, then, in order to determine whether the party is domiciled in another Member State, the courts shall apply the law of that Member State....

[Ed. Note: Articles 60–76 and Annexes I–VI are omitted.]

2. Council of Europe Documents

Convention for the Protection of Human Rights and Fundamental Freedoms, as amended by Protocol No. 11
Nov. 4, 1950, 213 U.N.T.S. 221

[Ed. Note: The Convention entered into force on September 3, 1953. Protocol No. 11 (ETS. No. 155) entered into force on November 1, 1998. It replaced Protocols No. 2 (ETS. No. 44), No. 3 (ETS No. 45), No. 5 (ETS. No. 55), and No. 8 (ETS. No. 118), amended Protocol No. 1 (ETS No. 9), No. 4 (ETS No. 46), No. 6 (ETS No. 114), No. 7 (ETS No. 117), and repealed Protocol No. 9 (ETS. No. 140). Protocol No. 10 (ETS. No. 146) is no longer relevant. *See generally* http://conventions.coe.int/Treaty/EN/Treaties/html/005.htm. As of February 17, 2002, the Convention had been ratified or acceded to by forty-one countries. *See* http://conventions.coe.int/Treaty/EN/cadreprincipal.htm.]

The governments signatory hereto, being members of the Council of Europe,

Considering the Universal Declaration of Human Rights proclaimed by the General Assembly of the United Nations on 10th December 1948;

Considering that this Declaration aims at securing the universal and effective recognition and observance of the Rights therein declared;

Considering that the aim of the Council of Europe is the achievement of greater unity between its members and that one of the methods by which that aim is to be pursued is the maintenance and further realisation of human rights and fundamental freedoms;

Reaffirming their profound belief in those fundamental freedoms which are the foundation of justice and peace in the world and are best maintained on the one hand by an effective political democracy and on the other by a common understanding and observance of the human rights upon which they depend;

Being resolved, as the governments of European countries which are like-minded and have a common heritage of political traditions, ideals, freedom and the rule of law, to take the first steps for the collective enforcement of certain of the rights stated in the Universal Declaration,

Have agreed as follows:

Article 1 — Obligation to respect human rights

The High Contracting Parties shall secure to everyone within their jurisdiction the rights and freedoms defined in Section I of this Convention.

SECTION I—RIGHTS AND FREEDOMS

Article 2—Right to life

1. Everyone's right to life shall be protected by law. No one shall be deprived of his life intentionally save in the execution of a sentence of a court following his conviction of a crime for which this penalty is provided by law.

2. Deprivation of life shall not be regarded as inflicted in contravention of this article when it results from the use of force which is no more than absolutely necessary:

a. in defence of any person from unlawful violence;

b. in order to effect a lawful arrest or to prevent the escape of a person lawfully detained;

c. in action lawfully taken for the purpose of quelling a riot or insurrection.

Article 3—Prohibition of torture

No one shall be subjected to torture or to inhuman or degrading treatment or punishment.

Article 4—Prohibition of slavery and forced labour

1. No one shall be held in slavery or servitude.

2. No one shall be required to perform forced or compulsory labour.

3. For the purpose of this article the term "forced or compulsory labour" shall not include:

a. any work required to be done in the ordinary course of detention imposed according to the provisions of Article 5 of this Convention or during conditional release from such detention;

b. any service of a military character or, in case of conscientious objectors in countries where they are recognised, service exacted instead of compulsory military service;

c. any service exacted in case of an emergency or calamity threatening the life or well-being of the community;

d. any work or service which forms part of normal civic obligations.

Article 5—Right to liberty and security

1. Everyone has the right to liberty and security of person. No one shall be deprived of his liberty save in the following cases and in accordance with a procedure prescribed by law:

a. the lawful detention of a person after conviction by a competent court;

b. the lawful arrest or detention of a person for non-compliance with the lawful order of a court or in order to secure the fulfilment of any obligation prescribed by law;

c. the lawful arrest or detention of a person effected for the purpose of bringing him before the competent legal authority on reasonable suspicion of having committed an offence or when it is reasonably considered necessary to prevent his committing an offence or fleeing after having done so;

d. the detention of a minor by lawful order for the purpose of educational supervision or his lawful detention for the purpose of bringing him before the competent legal authority;

e. the lawful detention of persons for the prevention of the spreading of infectious diseases, of persons of unsound mind, alcoholics or drug addicts or vagrants;

f. the lawful arrest or detention of a person to prevent his effecting an unauthorised entry into the country or of a person against whom action is being taken with a view to deportation or extradition.

2. Everyone who is arrested shall be informed promptly, in a language which he understands, of the reasons for his arrest and of any charge against him.

3. Everyone arrested or detained in accordance with the provisions of paragraph 1.c of this article shall be brought promptly before a judge or other officer authorised by law to exercise judicial power and shall be entitled to trial within a reasonable time or to release pending trial. Release may be conditioned by guarantees to appear for trial.

4. Everyone who is deprived of his liberty by arrest or detention shall be entitled to take proceedings by which the lawfulness of his detention shall be decided speedily by a court and his release ordered if the detention is not lawful.

5. Everyone who has been the victim of arrest or detention in contravention of the provisions of this article shall have an enforceable right to compensation.

Article 6 — Right to a fair trial

1. In the determination of his civil rights and obligations or of any criminal charge against him, everyone is entitled to a fair and public hearing within a reasonable time by an independent and impartial tribunal established by law. Judgment shall be pronounced publicly but the press and public may be excluded from all or part of the trial in the interests of morals, public order or national security in a democratic society, where the interests of juveniles or the protection of the private life of the parties so require, or to the extent strictly necessary in the opinion of the court in special circumstances where publicity would prejudice the interests of justice.

2. Everyone charged with a criminal offence shall be presumed innocent until proved guilty according to law.

3. Everyone charged with a criminal offence has the following minimum rights:

a. to be informed promptly, in a language which he understands and in detail, of the nature and cause of the accusation against him;

b. to have adequate time and facilities for the preparation of his defence;

c. to defend himself in person or through legal assistance of his own choosing or, if he has not sufficient means to pay for legal assistance, to be given it free when the interests of justice so require;

d. to examine or have examined witnesses against him and to obtain the attendance and examination of witnesses on his behalf under the same conditions as witnesses against him;

e. to have the free assistance of an interpreter if he cannot understand or speak the language used in court.

Article 7 — No punishment without law

1. No one shall be held guilty of any criminal offence on account of any act or omission which did not constitute a criminal offence under national or international law at the time when it was committed. Nor shall a heavier penalty be imposed than the one that was applicable at the time the criminal offence was committed.

2. This article shall not prejudice the trial and punishment of any person for any act or omission which, at the time when it was committed, was criminal according to the general principles of law recognised by civilised nations.

Article 8 — Right to respect for private and family life

1. Everyone has the right to respect for his private and family life, his home and his correspondence.

2. There shall be no interference by a public authority with the exercise of this right except such as is in accordance with the law and is necessary in a democratic society in the interests of national security, public safety or the economic well-being of the country, for the prevention of disorder or crime, for the protection of health or morals, or for the protection of the rights and freedoms of others.

Article 9 — Freedom of thought, conscience and religion

1. Everyone has the right to freedom of thought, conscience and religion; this right includes freedom to change his religion or belief and freedom, either alone or in community with others and in public or private, to manifest his religion or belief, in worship, teaching, practice and observance.

2. Freedom to manifest one's religion or beliefs shall be subject only to such limitations as are prescribed by law and are necessary in a democratic society in the interests of public safety, for the protection of public order, health or morals, or for the protection of the rights and freedoms of others.

Article 10 — Freedom of expression

1. Everyone has the right to freedom of expression. This right shall include freedom to hold opinions and to receive and impart information and ideas without interference by public authority and regardless of frontiers. This article shall not prevent States from requiring the licensing of broadcasting, television or cinema enterprises.

2. The exercise of these freedoms, since it carries with it duties and responsibilities, may be subject to such formalities, conditions, restrictions or penalties as are prescribed by law and are necessary in a democratic society, in the interests of national security, territorial integrity or public safety, for the prevention of disorder or crime, for the protection of health or morals, for the protection of the reputation or rights of others, for preventing the disclosure of information received in confidence, or for maintaining the authority and impartiality of the judiciary.

Article 11 — Freedom of assembly and association

1. Everyone has the right to freedom of peaceful assembly and to freedom of association with others, including the right to form and to join trade unions for the protection of his interests.

2. No restrictions shall be placed on the exercise of these rights other than such as are prescribed by law and are necessary in a democratic society in the interests of national security or public safety, for the prevention of disorder or crime, for the protection of health or morals or for the protection of the rights and freedoms of others. This article shall not prevent the imposition of lawful restrictions on the exercise of these rights by members of the armed forces, of the police or of the administration of the State.

Article 12 — Right to marry

Men and women of marriageable age have the right to marry and to found a family, according to the national laws governing the exercise of this right.

Article 13 — Right to an effective remedy

Everyone whose rights and freedoms as set forth in this Convention are violated shall have an effective remedy before a national authority notwithstanding that the violation has been committed by persons acting in an official capacity.

Article 14 — Prohibition of discrimination

The enjoyment of the rights and freedoms set forth in this Convention shall be secured without discrimination on any ground such as sex, race, colour, language, religion, political or other opinion, national or social origin, association with a national minority, property, birth or other status.

Article 15 — Derogation in time of emergency

1. In time of war or other public emergency threatening the life of the nation any High Contracting Party may take measures derogating from its obligations under this Convention to the extent strictly required by the exigencies of the situation, provided that such measures are not inconsistent with its other obligations under international law.

2. No derogation from Article 2, except in respect of deaths resulting from lawful acts of war, or from Articles 3, 4 (paragraph 1) and 7 shall be made under this provision.

3. Any High Contracting Party availing itself of this right of derogation shall keep the Secretary General of the Council of Europe fully informed of the measures which it has taken and the reasons therefor. It shall also inform the Secretary General of the Council of Europe when such measures have ceased to operate and the provisions of the Convention are again being fully executed.

Article 16 — Restrictions on political activity of aliens

Nothing in Articles 10, 11 and 14 shall be regarded as preventing the High Contracting Parties from imposing restrictions on the political activity of aliens.

Article 17 — Prohibition of abuse of rights

Nothing in this Convention may be interpreted as implying for any State, group or person any right to engage in any activity or perform any act aimed at the destruction of any of the rights and freedoms set forth herein or at their limitation to a greater extent than is provided for in the Convention.

Article 18 — Limitation on use of restrictions on rights

The restrictions permitted under this Convention to the said rights and freedoms shall not be applied for any purpose other than those for which they have been prescribed.

SECTION II — EUROPEAN COURT OF HUMAN RIGHTS

Article 19 — Establishment of the Court

To ensure the observance of the engagements undertaken by the High Contracting Parties in the Convention and the Protocols thereto, there shall be set up a European Court of Human Rights, hereinafter referred to as "the Court." It shall function on a permanent basis.

Article 20 — Number of judges

The Court shall consist of a number of judges equal to that of the High Contracting Parties.

Article 21 — Criteria for office

1. The judges shall be of high moral character and must either possess the qualifications required for appointment to high judicial office or be jurisconsults of recognised competence.

2. The judges shall sit on the Court in their individual capacity.

3. During their term of office the judges shall not engage in any activity which is incompatible with their independence, impartiality or with the demands of a full-time office; all questions arising from the application of this paragraph shall be decided by the Court.

Article 22 — Election of judges

1. The judges shall be elected by the Parliamentary Assembly with respect to each High Contracting Party by a majority of votes cast from a list of three candidates nominated by the High Contracting Party.

2. The same procedure shall be followed to complete the Court in the event of the accession of new High Contracting Parties and in filling casual vacancies.

Article 23 — Terms of office

1. The judges shall be elected for a period of six years. They may be re-elected. However, the terms of office of one-half of the judges elected at the first election shall expire at the end of three years.

2. The judges whose terms of office are to expire at the end of the initial period of three years shall be chosen by lot by the Secretary General of the Council of Europe immediately after their election.

3. In order to ensure that, as far as possible, the terms of office of one-half of the judges are renewed every three years, the Parliamentary Assembly may decide, before proceeding to any subsequent election, that the term or terms of office of one or more judges to be elected shall be for a period other than six years but not more than nine and not less than three years.

4. In cases where more than one term of office is involved and where the Parliamentary Assembly applies the preceding paragraph, the allocation of the terms of office shall be effected by a drawing of lots by the Secretary General of the Council of Europe immediately after the election.

5. A judge elected to replace a judge whose term of office has not expired shall hold office for the remainder of his predecessor's term.

6. The terms of office of judges shall expire when they reach the age of 70.

7. The judges shall hold office until replaced. They shall, however, continue to deal with such cases as they already have under consideration.

Article 24 — Dismissal

No judge may be dismissed from his office unless the other judges decide by a majority of two-thirds that he has ceased to fulfil the required conditions.

Article 25 — Registry and legal secretaries

The Court shall have a registry, the functions and organisation of which shall be laid down in the rules of the Court. The Court shall be assisted by legal secretaries.

Article 26 — Plenary Court

The plenary Court shall:

1. elect its President and one or two Vice-Presidents for a period of three years; they may be re-elected;

2. set up Chambers, constituted for a fixed period of time;

3. elect the Presidents of the Chambers of the Court; they may be re-elected;

4. adopt the rules of the Court, and

5. elect the Registrar and one or more Deputy Registrars.

Article 27 — Committees, Chambers and Grand Chamber

1. To consider cases brought before it, the Court shall sit in committees of three judges, in Chambers of seven judges and in a Grand Chamber of seventeen judges. The Court's Chambers shall set up committees for a fixed period of time.

2. There shall sit as an *ex officio* member of the Chamber and the Grand Chamber the judge elected in respect of the State Party concerned or, if there is none or if he is unable to sit, a person of its choice who shall sit in the capacity of judge.

3. The Grand Chamber shall also include the President of the Court, the Vice-Presidents, the Presidents of the Chambers and other judges chosen in accordance with the rules of the Court. When a case is referred to the Grand Chamber under Article 43, no judge from the Chamber which rendered the judgment shall sit in the Grand Chamber, with the exception of the President of the Chamber and the judge who sat in respect of the State Party concerned.

Article 28 — Declarations of inadmissibility by committees

A committee may, by a unanimous vote, declare inadmissible or strike out of its list of cases an application submitted under Article 34 where such a decision can be taken without further examination. The decision shall be final.

Article 29 — Decisions by Chambers on admissibility and merits

1. If no decision is taken under Article 28, a Chamber shall decide on the admissibility and merits of individual applications submitted under Article 34.

2. A Chamber shall decide on the admissibility and merits of inter-State applications submitted under Article 33.

3. The decision on admissibility shall be taken separately unless the Court, in exceptional cases, decides otherwise.

Article 30 — Relinquishment of jurisdiction to the Grand Chamber

Where a case pending before a Chamber raises a serious question affecting the interpretation of the Convention or the protocols thereto, or where the resolution of a question before the Chamber might have a result inconsistent with a judgment previously delivered by the Court, the Chamber may, at any time before it has rendered its judgment, relinquish jurisdiction in favour of the Grand Chamber, unless one of the parties to the case objects.

Article 31 — Powers of the Grand Chamber

The Grand Chamber shall:

1. determine applications submitted either under Article 33 or Article 34 when a Chamber has relinquished jurisdiction under Article 30 or when the case has been referred to it under Article 43; and

2. consider requests for advisory opinions submitted under Article 47.

Article 32 — Jurisdiction of the Court

1. The jurisdiction of the Court shall extend to all matters concerning the interpretation and application of the Convention and the protocols thereto which are referred to it as provided in Articles 33, 34 and 47.

2. In the event of dispute as to whether the Court has jurisdiction, the Court shall decide.

Article 33 — Inter-State cases

Any High Contracting Party may refer to the Court any alleged breach of the provisions of the Convention and the protocols thereto by another High Contracting Party.

Article 34 — Individual applications

The Court may receive applications from any person, non-governmental organisation or group of individuals claiming to be the victim of a violation by one of the High Contracting Parties of the rights set forth in the Convention or the protocols thereto. The High Contracting Parties undertake not to hinder in any way the effective exercise of this right.

Article 35 — Admissibility criteria

1. The Court may only deal with the matter after all domestic remedies have been exhausted, according to the generally recognised rules of international law, and within a period of six months from the date on which the final decision was taken.

2. The Court shall not deal with any application submitted under Article 34 that:

a. is anonymous; or

b. is substantially the same as a matter that has already been examined by the Court or has already been submitted to another procedure of international investigation or settlement and contains no relevant new information.

3. The Court shall declare inadmissible any individual application submitted under Article 34 which it considers incompatible with the provisions of the Convention or the protocols thereto, manifestly ill-founded, or an abuse of the right of application.

4. The Court shall reject any application which it considers inadmissible under this Article. It may do so at any stage of the proceedings.

Article 36 — Third party intervention

1. In all cases before a Chamber or the Grand Chamber, a High Contracting Party one of whose nationals is an applicant shall have the right to submit written comments and to take part in hearings.

2. The President of the Court may, in the interest of the proper administration of justice, invite any High Contracting Party which is not a party to the proceedings or any person concerned who is not the applicant to submit written comments or take part in hearings.

Article 37 — Striking out applications

1. The Court may at any stage of the proceedings decide to strike an application out of its list of cases where the circumstances lead to the conclusion that:

a. the applicant does not intend to pursue his application; or

b. the matter has been resolved; or

c. for any other reason established by the Court, it is no longer justified to continue the examination of the application.

However, the Court shall continue the examination of the application if respect for human rights as defined in the Convention and the protocols thereto so requires.

2. The Court may decide to restore an application to its list of cases if it considers that the circumstances justify such a course.

Article 38 — Examination of the case and friendly settlement proceedings

1. If the Court declares the application admissible, it shall:

a. pursue the examination of the case, together with the representatives of the parties, and if need be, undertake an investigation, for the effective conduct of which the States concerned shall furnish all necessary facilities;

b. place itself at the disposal of the parties concerned with a view to securing a friendly settlement of the matter on the basis of respect for human rights as defined in the Convention and the protocols thereto.

2. Proceedings conducted under paragraph 1.b shall be confidential.

Article 39 — Finding of a friendly settlement

If a friendly settlement is effected, the Court shall strike the case out of its list by means of a decision which shall be confined to a brief statement of the facts and of the solution reached.

Article 40 — Public hearings and access to documents

1. Hearings shall be in public unless the Court in exceptional circumstances decides otherwise.

2. Documents deposited with the Registrar shall be accessible to the public unless the President of the Court decides otherwise.

Article 41 — Just satisfaction

If the Court finds that there has been a violation of the Convention or the protocols thereto, and if the internal law of the High Contracting Party concerned allows only partial reparation to be made, the Court shall, if necessary, afford just satisfaction to the injured party.

Article 42 — Judgments of Chambers

Judgments of Chambers shall become final in accordance with the provisions of Article 44, paragraph 2.

Article 43 — Referral to the Grand Chamber

1. Within a period of three months from the date of the judgment of the Chamber, any party to the case may, in exceptional cases, request that the case be referred to the Grand Chamber.

2. A panel of five judges of the Grand Chamber shall accept the request if the case raises a serious question affecting the interpretation or application of the Convention or the protocols thereto, or a serious issue of general importance.

3. If the panel accepts the request, the Grand Chamber shall decide the case by means of a judgment.

Article 44 — Final judgments

1. The judgment of the Grand Chamber shall be final.

2. The judgment of a Chamber shall become final:

a. when the parties declare that they will not request that the case be referred to the Grand Chamber; or

b. three months after the date of the judgment, if reference of the case to the Grand Chamber has not been requested; or

c. when the panel of the Grand Chamber rejects the request to refer under Article 43.

3. The final judgment shall be published.

Article 45 — Reasons for judgments and decisions

1. Reasons shall be given for judgments as well as for decisions declaring applications admissible or inadmissible.

2. If a judgment does not represent, in whole or in part, the unanimous opinion of the judges, any judge shall be entitled to deliver a separate opinion.

Article 46 — Binding force and execution of judgments

1. The High Contracting Parties undertake to abide by the final judgment of the Court in any case to which they are parties.

2. The final judgment of the Court shall be transmitted to the Committee of Ministers, which shall supervise its execution.

Article 47 — Advisory opinions

1. The Court may, at the request of the Committee of Ministers, give advisory opinions on legal questions concerning the interpretation of the Convention and the protocols thereto.

2. Such opinions shall not deal with any question relating to the content or scope of the rights or freedoms defined in Section I of the Convention and the protocols thereto, or with any other question which the Court or the Committee of Ministers might have to consider in consequence of any such proceedings as could be instituted in accordance with the Convention.

3. Decisions of the Committee of Ministers to request an advisory opinion of the Court shall require a majority vote of the representatives entitled to sit on the Committee.

Article 48 — Advisory jurisdiction of the Court

The Court shall decide whether a request for an advisory opinion submitted by the Committee of Ministers is within its competence as defined in Article 47.

Article 49 — Reasons for advisory opinions

1. Reasons shall be given for advisory opinions of the Court.

2. If the advisory opinion does not represent, in whole or in part, the unanimous opinion of the judges, any judge shall be entitled to deliver a separate opinion.

3. Advisory opinions of the Court shall be communicated to the Committee of Ministers.

Article 50 — Expenditure on the Court

The expenditure on the Court shall be borne by the Council of Europe.

Article 51 — Privileges and immunities of judges

The judges shall be entitled, during the exercise of their functions, to the privileges and immunities provided for in Article 40 of the Statute of the Council of Europe and in the agreements made thereunder.

SECTION III — MISCELLANEOUS PROVISIONS

Article 52 — Inquiries by the Secretary General

On receipt of a request from the Secretary General of the Council of Europe any High Contracting Party shall furnish an explanation of the manner in which its internal law ensures the effective implementation of any of the provisions of the Convention.

Article 53 — Safeguard for existing human rights

Nothing in this Convention shall be construed as limiting or derogating from any of the human rights and fundamental freedoms which may be ensured under the laws of any High Contracting Party or under any other agreement to which it is a Party.

Article 54 — Powers of the Committee of Ministers

Nothing in this Convention shall prejudice the powers conferred on the Committee of Ministers by the Statute of the Council of Europe.

Article 55 — Exclusion of other means of dispute settlement

The High Contracting Parties agree that, except by special agreement, they will not avail themselves of treaties, conventions or declarations in force between them for the purpose of submitting, by way of petition, a dispute arising out of the interpretation or application of this Convention to a means of settlement other than those provided for in this Convention.

Article 56 — Territorial application

1. Any State may at the time of its ratification or at any time thereafter declare by notification addressed to the Secretary General of the Council of Europe that the present Convention shall, subject to paragraph 4 of this Article, extend to all or any of the territories for whose international relations it is responsible.

2. The Convention shall extend to the territory or territories named in the notification as from the thirtieth day after the receipt of this notification by the Secretary General of the Council of Europe.

3. The provisions of this Convention shall be applied in such territories with due regard, however, to local requirements.

4. Any State which has made a declaration in accordance with paragraph 1 of this article may at any time thereafter declare on behalf of one or more of the territories to which the declaration relates that it accepts the competence of the Court to receive applications from individuals, non-governmental organisations or groups of individuals as provided by Article 34 of the Convention.

Article 57 — Reservations

1. Any State may, when signing this Convention or when depositing its instrument of ratification, make a reservation in respect of any particular provision of the Convention to the extent that any law then in force in its territory is not in conformity with the provision. Reservations of a general character shall not be permitted under this article.

2. Any reservation made under this article shall contain a brief statement of the law concerned.

Article 58 — Denunciation

1. A High Contracting Party may denounce the present Convention only after the expiry of five years from the date on which it became a party to it and after six months' notice contained in a notification addressed to the Secretary General of the Council of Europe, who shall inform the other High Contracting Parties.

2. Such a denunciation shall not have the effect of releasing the High Contracting Party concerned from its obligations under this Convention in respect of any act which,

being capable of constituting a violation of such obligations, may have been performed by it before the date at which the denunciation became effective.

3. Any High Contracting Party which shall cease to be a member of the Council of Europe shall cease to be a Party to this Convention under the same conditions.

4. The Convention may be denounced in accordance with the provisions of the preceding paragraphs in respect of any territory to which it has been declared to extend under the terms of Article 56.

Article 59 — Signature and ratification

1. This Convention shall be open to the signature of the members of the Council of Europe. It shall be ratified. Ratifications shall be deposited with the Secretary General of the Council of Europe.

2. The present Convention shall come into force after the deposit of ten instruments of ratification.

3. As regards any signatory ratifying subsequently, the Convention shall come into force at the date of the deposit of its instrument of ratification.

4. The Secretary General of the Council of Europe shall notify all the members of the Council of Europe of the entry into force of the Convention, the names of the High Contracting Parties who have ratified it, and the deposit of all instruments of ratification which may be effected subsequently.

Protocol No. 1, as amended by Protocol No. 11
Mar. 20, 1952, 213 U.N.T.S. 2621

[Ed. Note: This Protocol entered into force on May 18, 1954. As of February 17, 2002, thirty-eight countries had ratified or acceded to the Protocol. *See* http://conventions. coe.int/Treaty/EN/cadreprincipal.htm.]

The governments signatory hereto,

Being members of the Council of Europe,

Being resolved to take steps to ensure the collective enforcement of certain rights and freedoms other than those already included in Section I of the Convention for the Protection of Human Rights and Fundamental Freedoms signed at Rome on 4 November 1950 (hereinafter referred to as "the Convention"),

Have agreed as follows:

Article 1 — Protection of property

Every natural or legal person is entitled to the peaceful enjoyment of his possessions. No one shall be deprived of his possessions except in the public interest and subject to the conditions provided for by law and by the general principles of international law. The preceding provisions shall not, however, in any way impair the right of a State to enforce such laws as it deems necessary to control the use of property in accordance with the general interest or to secure the payment of taxes or other contributions or penalties.

Article 2 — Right to education

No person shall be denied the right to education. In the exercise of any functions which it assumes in relation to education and to teaching, the State shall respect the right of parents to ensure such education and teaching in conformity with their own religious and philosophical convictions.

Article 3 — Right to free elections

The High Contracting Parties undertake to hold free elections at reasonable intervals by secret ballot, under conditions which will ensure the free expression of the opinion of the people in the choice of the legislature.

Article 4 — Territorial application

Any High Contracting Party may at the time of signature or ratification or at any time thereafter communicate to the Secretary General of the Council of Europe a declaration stating the extent to which it undertakes that the provisions of the present Protocol shall apply to such of the territories for the international relations of which it is responsible as are named therein. Any High Contracting Party which has communicated a declaration in virtue of the preceding paragraph may from time to time communicate a further declaration modifying the terms of any former declaration or terminating the application of the provisions of this Protocol in respect of any territory. A declaration made in accordance with this article shall be deemed to have been made in accordance with paragraph 1 of Article 56 of the Convention.

Article 5 — Relationship to the Convention

As between the High Contracting Parties the provisions of Articles 1, 2, 3 and 4 of this Protocol shall be regarded as additional articles to the Convention and all the provisions of the Convention shall apply accordingly.

Article 6 — Signature and ratification

This Protocol shall be open for signature by the members of the Council of Europe, who are the signatories of the Convention; it shall be ratified at the same time as or after the ratification of the Convention. It shall enter into force after the deposit of ten instruments of ratification. As regards any signatory ratifying subsequently, the Protocol shall enter into force at the date of the deposit of its instrument of ratification.

The instruments of ratification shall be deposited with the Secretary General of the Council of Europe, who will notify all members of the names of those who have ratified....

Protocol No. 4, as amended by Protocol No. 11

Sept. 16, 1963, Europ. T.S. No. 46

[Ed. Note: This Protocol entered into force on September 21, 1970. As of February 17, 2002, forty countries had ratified or acceded to the Protocol. *See* http://conventions.coe.int/Treaty/EN/cadreprincipal.htm.]

The governments signatory hereto,

Being members of the Council of Europe,

Being resolved to take steps to ensure the collective enforcement of certain rights and freedoms other than those already included in Section 1 of the Convention for the Protection of Human Rights and Fundamental Freedoms signed at Rome on 4th November 1950 (hereinafter referred to as the "Convention") and in Articles 1 to 3 of the First Protocol to the Convention, signed at Paris on 20th March 1952,

Have agreed as follows:

Article 1 — Prohibition of imprisonment for debt

No one shall be deprived of his liberty merely on the ground of inability to fulfil a contractual obligation.

Article 2 — Freedom of movement

Everyone lawfully within the territory of a State shall, within that territory, have the right to liberty of movement and freedom to choose his residence. Everyone shall be free to leave any country, including his own.

No restrictions shall be placed on the exercise of these rights other than such as are in accordance with law and are necessary in a democratic society in the interests of national security or public safety, for the maintenance of *ordre public*, of the prevention of crime, for the protection of health or morals, or for the protection of the rights and freedoms of others. The rights set forth in paragraph 1 may also be subject, in particular areas, to restrictions imposed in accordance with law and justified by the public interest in a democratic society.

Article 3 — Prohibition of expulsion of nationals

No one shall be expelled, by means either of an individual or of a collective measure, from the territory of the State of which he is a national.

No one shall be deprived of the right to enter the territory of the state of which he is a national.

No restrictions shall be placed on the exercise of these rights other than such as are in accordance with law and are necessary in a democratic society in the interests of national security or public safety, for the maintenance of *ordre public*, of the prevention of crime, for the protection of health or morals, or for the protection of the rights and freedoms of others. The rights set forth in paragraph 1 may also be subject, in particular areas, to restrictions imposed in accordance with law and justified by the public interest in a democratic society.

Article 4 — Prohibition of collective expulsion of aliens

Collective expulsion of aliens is prohibited.

{Ed. Note: Article 5 on territorial application has been omitted.]

Article 6 — Relationship to the Convention

As between the High Contracting Parties the provisions of Articles 1 to 5 of this Protocol shall be regarded as additional articles to the Convention, and all the provisions of the Convention shall apply accordingly.

Article 7 — Signature and ratification

This Protocol shall be open for signature by the members of the Council of Europe who are the signatories of the Convention; it shall be ratified at the same time as or after the ratification of the Convention. It shall enter into force after the deposit of five instruments of ratification. As regards any signatory ratifying subsequently, the Protocol shall enter into force at the date of the deposit of its instrument of ratification.

The instruments of ratification shall be deposited with the Secretary General of the Council of Europe, who will notify all Members of the names of those who have ratified.

Protocol No. 6, as amended by Protocol No. 11
Apr. 29, 1983, Europ. T.S. No. 114

[Ed. Note: The Protocol entered into force on March 1, 1985. As of February 17, 2002, thirty-nine countries ratified or acceded to the Protocol. *See* http://conventions.coe. int/Treaty/EN/cadreprincipal.htm.]

The member States of the Council of Europe, signatory to this Protocol to the Convention for the Protection of Human Rights and Fundamental Freedoms, signed at Rome on 4 November 1950 (hereinafter referred to as "the Convention"),

Considering that the evolution that has occurred in several member States of the Council of Europe expresses a general tendency in favour of abolition of the death penalty,

Have agreed as follows:

Article 1 — Abolition of the death penalty

The death penalty shall be abolished. No-one shall be condemned to such penalty or executed.

Article 2 — Death penalty in time of war

A State may make provision in its law for the death penalty in respect of acts committed in time of war or of imminent threat of war; such penalty shall be applied only in the instances laid down in the law and in accordance with its provisions. The State shall communicate to the Secretary General of the Council of Europe the relevant provisions of that law.

Article 3 — Prohibition of derogations

No derogation from the provisions of this Protocol shall be made under Article 15 of the Convention.

Article 4 — Prohibition of reservations

No reservation may be made under Article 57 of the Convention in respect of the provisions of this Protocol.

Article 5 — Territorial application

1. Any State may at the time of signature or when depositing its instrument of ratification, acceptance or approval, specify the territory or territories to which this Protocol shall apply.

2. Any State may at any later date, by a declaration addressed to the Secretary General of the Council of Europe, extend the application of this Protocol to any other territory specified in the declaration. In respect of such territory the Protocol shall enter into force on the first day of the month following the date of receipt of such declaration by the Secretary General.

3. Any declaration made under the two preceding paragraphs may, in respect of any territory specified in such declaration, be withdrawn by a notification addressed to the Secretary General. The withdrawal shall become effective on the first day of the month following the date of receipt of such notification by the Secretary General.

Article 6—Relationship to the Convention

As between the States Parties the provisions of Articles 1 and 5 of this Protocol shall be regarded as additional articles to the Convention and all the provisions of the Convention shall apply accordingly.

Article 7—Signature and ratification

The Protocol shall be open for signature by the member States of the Council of Europe, signatories to the Convention. It shall be subject to ratification, acceptance or approval. A member State of the Council of Europe may not ratify, accept or approve this Protocol unless it has, simultaneously or previously, ratified the Convention. Instruments of ratification, acceptance or approval shall be deposited with the Secretary General of the Council of Europe.

Article 8—Entry into force

1. This Protocol shall enter into force on the first day of the month following the date on which five member States of the Council of Europe have expressed their consent to be bound by the Protocol in accordance with the provisions of Article 7.

2. In respect of any member State which subsequently expresses its consent to be bound by it, the Protocol shall enter into force on the first day of the month following the date of the deposit of the instrument of ratification, acceptance or approval.

Article 9—Depositary functions

The Secretary General of the Council of Europe shall notify the member States of the Council of:

a. any signature;

b. the deposit of any instrument of ratification, acceptance or approval;

c. any date of entry into force of this Protocol in accordance with Articles 5 and 8;

d. any other act, notification or communication relating to this Protocol.

Protocol No. 7, as amended by Protocol No. 11

Nov. 22, 1984, Europ. T.S. No. 117

[Ed. Note: Protocol No. 7 entered into force on November 1, 1988. As of February 17, 2002, thirty countries had signed or acceded to the Protocol. *See* http://conventions. coe.int/Treaty/EN/cadreprincipal.htm.]

The member States of the Council of Europe signatory hereto,

Being resolved to take further steps to ensure the collective enforcement of certain rights and freedoms by means of the Convention for the Protection of Human Rights and Fundamental Freedoms signed at Rome on 4 November 1950 (hereinafter referred to as "the Convention"),

Have agreed as follows:

[Ed. Note: Article 1 (procedural safeguards relating to expulsion of aliens), article 2 (right of appeal in criminal matters), article 3 (compensation for wrongful conviction), and article 4 (right not to be tried or punished twice) have been omitted.]

Article 5 — Equality between spouses

Spouses shall enjoy equality of rights and responsibilities of a private law character between them, and in their relations with their children, as to marriage, during marriage and in the event of its dissolution. This Article shall not prevent States from taking such measures as are necessary in the interests of the children.

Article 6 — Territorial application

1. Any State may at the time of signature or when depositing its instrument of ratification, acceptance or approval, specify the territory or territories to which the Protocol shall apply and state the extent to which it undertakes that the provisions of this Protocol shall apply to such territory or territories.

2. Any State may at any later date, by a declaration addressed to the Secretary General of the Council of Europe, extend the application of this Protocol to any other territory specified in the declaration. In respect of such territory the Protocol shall enter into force on the first day of the month following the expiration of a period of two months after the date of receipt by the Secretary General of such declaration.

3. Any declaration made under the two preceding paragraphs may, in respect of any territory specified in such declaration, be withdrawn or modified by a notification addressed to the Secretary General. The withdrawal or modification shall become effective on the first day of the month following the expiration of a period of two months after the date of receipt of such notification by the Secretary General.

4. A declaration made in accordance with this Article shall be deemed to have been made in accordance with paragraph 1 of Article 56 of the Convention.

5. The territory of any State to which this Protocol applies by virtue of ratification, acceptance or approval by that State, and each territory to which this Protocol is applied by virtue of a declaration by that State under this Article, may be treated as separate territories for the purpose of the reference in Article 1 to the territory of a State.

6. Any State which has made a declaration in accordance with paragraph 1 or 2 of this Article may at any time thereafter declare on behalf of one or more of the territories to which the declaration relates that it accepts the competence of the Court to receive applications from individuals, non-governmental organisations or groups of individuals as provided in Article 34 of the Convention in respect of Articles 1 to 5 of this Protocol.

Article 7 — Relationship to the Convention

As between the States Parties, the provisions of Articles 1 to 6 of this Protocol shall be regarded as additional Articles to the Convention, and all the provisions of the Convention shall apply accordingly.

Article 8 — Signature and ratification

This Protocol shall be open for signature by member States of the Council of Europe which have signed the Convention. It is subject to ratification, acceptance or approval. A member State of the Council of Europe may not ratify, accept or approve this Protocol without previously or simultaneously ratifying the Convention. Instruments of ratification, acceptance or approval shall be deposited with the Secretary General of the Council of Europe.

[Ed. Note: Article 9 (entry into force) and article 10 (depositary functions) have been omitted.]

Protocol No. 12

Nov. 4, 2000, Europ. T.S. No. 177

[Ed. Note: As of February 17, 2002, Protocol No. 12 had not yet entered into force. While twenty-six states had signed it, only one had ratified or acceded to it. Ten states must ratify this Protocol for it to enter into force. *See* http://conventions.coe.int/Treaty/EN/cadreprincipal.htm.]

The member States of the Council of Europe signatory hereto,

Having regard to the fundamental principle according to which all persons are equal before the law and are entitled to the equal protection of the law;

Being resolved to take further steps to promote the equality of all persons through the collective enforcement of a general prohibition of discrimination by means of the Convention for the Protection of Human Rights and Fundamental Freedoms signed at Rome on 4 November 1950 (hereinafter referred to as "the Convention");

Reaffirming that the principle of non-discrimination does not prevent States Parties from taking measures in order to promote full and effective equality, provided that there is an objective and reasonable justification for those measures,

Have agreed as follows:

Article 1 — General prohibition of discrimination

1. The enjoyment of any right set forth by law shall be secured without discrimination on any ground such as sex, race, colour, language, religion, political or other opinion, national or social origin, association with a national minority, property, birth or other status.

2. No one shall be discriminated against by any public authority on any ground such as those mentioned in paragraph 1.

Article 2 — Territorial application

1. Any State may, at the time of signature or when depositing its instrument of ratification, acceptance or approval, specify the territory or territories to which this Protocol shall apply.

2. Any State may at any later date, by a declaration addressed to the Secretary General of the Council of Europe, extend the application of this Protocol to any other territory specified in the declaration. In respect of such territory the Protocol shall enter into force on the first day of the month following the expiration of a period of three months after the date of receipt by the Secretary General of such declaration.

3. Any declaration made under the two preceding paragraphs may, in respect of any territory specified in such declaration, be withdrawn or modified by a notification addressed to the Secretary General of the Council of Europe. The withdrawal or modification shall become effective on the first day of the month following the expiration of a period of three months after the date of receipt of such notification by the Secretary General.

4. A declaration made in accordance with this article shall be deemed to have been made in accordance with paragraph 1 of Article 56 of the Convention.

5. Any State which has made a declaration in accordance with paragraph 1 or 2 of this article may at any time thereafter declare on behalf of one or more of the territories to which the declaration relates that it accepts the competence of the Court to receive applications from individuals, non-governmental organisations or groups of individuals as provided by Article 34 of the Convention in respect of Article 1 of this Protocol.

Article 3 — Relationship to the Convention

As between the States Parties, the provisions of Articles 1 and 2 of this Protocol shall be regarded as additional articles to the Convention, and all the provisions of the Convention shall apply accordingly.

Article 4 — Signature and ratification

This Protocol shall be open for signature by member States of the Council of Europe which have signed the Convention. It is subject to ratification, acceptance or approval. A member State of the Council of Europe may not ratify, accept or approve this Protocol without previously or simultaneously ratifying the Convention. Instruments of ratification, acceptance or approval shall be deposited with the Secretary General of the Council of Europe.

Article 5 — Entry into force

1. This Protocol shall enter into force on the first day of the month following the expiration of a period of three months after the date on which ten member States of the Council of Europe have expressed their consent to be bound by the Protocol in accordance with the provisions of Article 4.

2. In respect of any member State which subsequently expresses its consent to be bound by it, the Protocol shall enter into force on the first day of the month following the expiration of a period of three months after the date of the deposit of the instrument of ratification, acceptance or approval.

[Ed. Note: Article 6 (depositary functions) has been omitted.]

European Social Charter (revised) (Selected Portions)
May 3, 1996, Europ. T.S. No. 163

[Ed. Note: The European Social Charter was originally signed in 1961. Protocols were added to the Charter in 1988, 1991, and 1995. The Charter was then revised in 1996, and entered into force on July 1, 1999. According to the Preamble, the intent is for the revised Charter to "progressively replace the First Charter." As of July 2002, the 1961 Charter had been ratified by nineteen of the forty-three states that comprise the Council of Europe. The 1996 revised Charter had been ratified by twelve states. An additional twelve states have signed, but not ratified, either the 1961 or 1996 Charter. *See* Council of Europe, Directorate General of Human Rights, Presentation of the European Social Charter, *at* http://www.humanrights.coe.int/cseweb/GB/GBl/GBl.htm. The Preamble suggests that the Revised Charter was crafted to embody "the rights guaranteed by the Charter as amended, the rights guaranteed by the Additional Protocol of 1988 and to add new rights." The 1961 European Social Charter can be found at http://conventions.coe.int/treaty/en/treaties/html/035.htm.]

Preamble

The governments signatory hereto, being members of the Council of Europe,

Considering that the aim of the Council of Europe is the achievement of greater unity between its members for the purpose of safeguarding and realizing the ideals and principles which are their common heritage and of facilitating their economic and social progress, in particular by the maintenance and further realization of human rights and fundamental freedoms;

Considering that in the Convention for the Protection of Human Rights and Fundamental Freedoms signed at Rome on 4 November 1950, and the Protocols thereto, the member States of the Council of Europe agreed to secure to their populations the civil and political rights and freedoms therein specified;

Considering that in the European Social Charter opened for signature in Turin on 18 October 1961 and the Protocols thereto, the member States of the Council of Europe agreed to secure to their populations the social rights specified therein in order to improve their standard of living and their social well-being;

Recalling that the Ministerial Conference on Human Rights held in Rome on 5 November 1990 stressed the need, on the one hand, to preserve the indivisible nature of all human rights, be they civil, political, economic, social or cultural and, on the other hand, to give the European Social Charter fresh impetus;

Resolved, as was decided during the Ministerial Conference held in Turin on 21 and 22 October 1991, to update and adapt the substantive contents of the Charter in order to take account in particular of the fundamental social changes which have occurred since the text was adopted;

Recognizing the advantage of embodying in a Revised Charter, designed progressively to take the place of the European Social Charter, the rights guaranteed by the Charter as amended, the rights guaranteed by the Additional Protocol of 1988 and to add new rights,

Have agreed as follows:

PART I

The Parties accept as the aim of their policy, to be pursued by all appropriate means both national and international in character, the attainment of conditions in which the following rights and principles may be effectively realised:...

4. All workers have the right to a fair remuneration sufficient for a decent standard of living for themselves and their families....

7. Children and young persons have the right to a special protection against the physical and moral hazards to which they are exposed.

8. Employed women, in case of maternity, have the right to a special protection....

11. Everyone has the right to benefit from any measures enabling him to enjoy the highest possible standard of health attainable.

12. All workers and their dependents have the right to social security.

13. Anyone without adequate resources has the right to social and medical assistance.

14. Everyone has the right to benefit from social welfare services....

16. The family as a fundamental unit of society has the right to appropriate social, legal and economic protection to ensure its full development.

17. Children and young persons have the right to appropriate social, legal and economic protection.

18. The nationals of any one of the Parties have the right to engage in any gainful occupation in the territory of any one of the others on a footing of equality with the nationals of the latter, subject to restrictions based on cogent economic or social reasons.

19. Migrant workers who are nationals of a Party and their families have the right to protection and assistance in the territory of any other Party.

20. All workers have the right to equal opportunities and equal treatment in matters of employment and occupation without discrimination on the grounds of sex....

23. Every elderly person has the right to social protection....

27. All persons with family responsibilities and who are engaged or wish to engage in employment have a right to do so without being subject to discrimination and as far as possible without conflict between their employment and family responsibilities....

30. Everyone has the right to protection against poverty and social exclusion.

31. Everyone has the right to housing.

PART II

The Parties undertake, as provided for in Part III, to consider themselves bound by the obligations laid down in the following articles and paragraphs....

Article 4—The right to a fair remuneration

With a view to ensuring the effective exercise of the right to a fair remuneration, the Parties undertake:

1. to recognise the right of workers to a remuneration such as will give them and their families a decent standard of living;

2. to recognise the right of workers to an increased rate of remuneration for overtime work, subject to exceptions in particular cases;

3. to recognise the right of men and women workers to equal pay for work of equal value;

4. to recognise the right of all workers to a reasonable period of notice for termination of employment;

5. to permit deductions from wages only under conditions and to the extent prescribed by national laws or regulations or fixed by collective agreements or arbitration awards.

The exercise of these rights shall be achieved by freely concluded collective agreements, by statutory wage-fixing machinery, or by other means appropriate to national conditions....

Article 7—The right of children and young persons to protection

With a view to ensuring the effective exercise of the right of children and young persons to protection, the Parties undertake:

1. to provide that the minimum age of admission to employment shall be 15 years, subject to exceptions for children employed in prescribed light work without harm to their health, morals or education;

2. to provide that the minimum age of admission to employment shall be 18 years with respect to prescribed occupations regarded as dangerous or unhealthy;

3. to provide that persons who are still subject to compulsory education shall not be employed in such work as would deprive them of the full benefit of their education;

4. to provide that the working hours of persons under 18 years of age shall be limited in accordance with the needs of their development, and particularly with their need for vocational training;

5. to recognise the right of young workers and apprentices to a fair wage or other appropriate allowances;

6. to provide that the time spent by young persons in vocational training during the normal working hours with the consent of the employer shall be treated as forming part of the working day;

7. to provide that employed persons of under 18 years of age shall be entitled to a minimum of four weeks' annual holiday with pay;

8. to provide that persons under 18 years of age shall not be employed in night work with the exception of certain occupations provided for by national laws or regulations;

9. to provide that persons under 18 years of age employed in occupations prescribed by national laws or regulations shall be subject to regular medical control;

10. to ensure special protection against physical and moral dangers to which children and young persons are exposed, and particularly against those resulting directly or indirectly from their work.

Article 8 — The right of employed women to protection of maternity

With a view to ensuring the effective exercise of the right of employed women to the protection of maternity, the Parties undertake:

1. to provide either by paid leave, by adequate social security benefits or by benefits from public funds for employed women to take leave before and after childbirth up to a total of at least fourteen weeks;

2. to consider it as unlawful for an employer to give a woman notice of dismissal during the period from the time she notifies her employer that she is pregnant until the end of her maternity leave, or to give her notice of dismissal at such a time that the notice would expire during such a period;

3. to provide that mothers who are nursing their infants shall be entitled to sufficient time off for this purpose;

4. to regulate the employment in night work of pregnant women, women who have recently given birth and women nursing their infants;

5. to prohibit the employment of pregnant women, women who have recently given birth or who are nursing their infants in underground mining and all other work which is unsuitable by reason of its dangerous, unhealthy or arduous nature and to take appropriate measures to protect the employment rights of these women....

Article 11 — The right to protection of health

With a view to ensuring the effective exercise of the right to protection of health, the Parties undertake, either directly or in cooperation with public or private organisations, to take appropriate measures designed inter alia:

1. to remove as far as possible the causes of ill-health;

2. to provide advisory and educational facilities for the promotion of health and the encouragement of individual responsibility in matters of health;

3. to prevent as far as possible epidemic, endemic and other diseases, as well as accidents.

Article 12 — The right to social security

With a view to ensuring the effective exercise of the right to social security, the Parties undertake:

1. to establish or maintain a system of social security;

2. to maintain the social security system at a satisfactory level at least equal to that necessary for the ratification of the European Code of Social Security;

3. to endeavour to raise progressively the system of social security to a higher level;

4. to take steps, by the conclusion of appropriate bilateral and multilateral agreements or by other means, and subject to the conditions laid down in such agreements, in order to ensure:

a. equal treatment with their own nationals of the nationals of other Parties in respect of social security rights, including the retention of benefits arising out of social security legislation, whatever movements the persons protected may undertake between the territories of the Parties;

b. the granting, maintenance and resumption of social security rights by such means as the accumulation of insurance or employment periods completed under the legislation of each of the Parties.

Article 13—The right to social and medical assistance

With a view to ensuring the effective exercise of the right to social and medical assistance, the Parties undertake:

1. to ensure that any person who is without adequate resources and who is unable to secure such resources either by his own efforts or from other sources, in particular by benefits under a social security scheme, be granted adequate assistance, and, in case of sickness, the care necessitated by his condition;

2. to ensure that persons receiving such assistance shall not, for that reason, suffer from a diminution of their political or social rights;

3. to provide that everyone may receive by appropriate public or private services such advice and personal help as may be required to prevent, to remove, or to alleviate personal or family want;

4. to apply the provisions referred to in paragraphs 1, 2 and 3 of this article on an equal footing with their nationals to nationals of other Parties lawfully within their territories, in accordance with their obligations under the European Convention on Social and Medical Assistance, signed at Paris on 11 December 1953.

Article 14—The right to benefit from social welfare services

With a view to ensuring the effective exercise of the right to benefit from social welfare services, the Parties undertake:

1. to promote or provide services which, by using methods of social work, would contribute to the welfare and development of both individuals and groups in the community, and to their adjustment to the social environment;

2. to encourage the participation of individuals and voluntary or other organisations in the establishment and maintenance of such services....

Article 16—The right of the family to social, legal and economic protection

With a view to ensuring the necessary conditions for the full development of the family, which is a fundamental unit of society, the Parties undertake to promote the economic, legal and social protection of family life by such means as social and family benefits, fiscal arrangements, provision of family housing, benefits for the newly married and other appropriate means.

Article 17—The right of children and young persons to social, legal and economic protection

With a view to ensuring the effective exercise of the right of children and young persons to grow up in an environment which encourages the full development of their personality and of their physical and mental capacities, the Parties undertake, either directly or in co-operation with public and private organisations, to take all appropriate and necessary measures designed:

1.

a. to ensure that children and young persons, taking account of the rights and duties of their parents, have the care, the assistance, the education and the training they need, in particular by providing for the establishment or maintenance of institutions and services sufficient and adequate for this purpose;

b. to protect children and young persons against negligence, violence or exploitation;

c. to provide protection and special aid from the state for children and young persons temporarily or definitively deprived of their family's support;

2. to provide to children and young persons a free primary and secondary education as well as to encourage regular attendance at schools....

[Ed. Note: Article 18, on the right to work in the territory of other parties, and Article 19, on the rights of migrant workers and their families, have been omitted.]

Article 20 — The right to equal opportunities and equal treatment in matters of employment and occupation without discrimination on the grounds of sex

With a view to ensuring the effective exercise of the right to equal opportunities and equal treatment in matters of employment and occupation without discrimination on the grounds of sex, the Parties undertake to recognise that right and to take appropriate measures to ensure or promote its application in the following fields:

a. access to employment, protection against dismissal and occupational reintegration;

b. vocational guidance, training, retraining and rehabilitation;

c. terms of employment and working conditions, including remuneration;

d. career development, including promotion...

[Ed. Note: Article 21, the right of workers to information and consultation, and article 22, the right to take part in the determination and improvement of the working conditions and working environment, have been omitted.]

Article 23 — The right of elderly persons to social protection

With a view to ensuring the effective exercise of the right of elderly persons to social protection, the Parties undertake to adopt or encourage, either directly or in co-operation with public or private organizations, appropriate measures designed in particular:

— to enable elderly persons to remain full members of society for as long as possible, by means of:

a. adequate resources enabling them to lead a decent life and play an active part in public, social and cultural life;

b. provision of information about services and facilities available for elderly persons and their opportunities to make use of them;

— to enable elderly persons to choose their life-style freely and to lead independent lives in their familiar surroundings for as long as they wish and are able, by means of:

a. provision of housing suited to their needs and their state of health or of adequate support for adapting their housing;

b. the health care and the services necessitated by their state;

— to guarantee elderly persons living in institutions appropriate support, while respecting their privacy, and participation in decisions concerning living conditions in the institution.

[Ed. Note: Article 24, the right to protection in cases of termination of employment, and article 25, the right of workers to the protection of their claims in the event of the insolvency of their employer, have been omitted.]

Article 26—The right to dignity at work

With a view to ensuring the effective exercise of the right of all workers to protection of their dignity at work, the Parties undertake, in consultation with employers' and workers' organizations:

1. to promote awareness, information and prevention of sexual harassment in the workplace or in relation to work and to take all appropriate measures to protect workers from such conduct;

2. to promote awareness, information and prevention of recurrent reprehensible or distinctly negative and offensive actions directed against individual workers in the workplace or in relation to work and to take all appropriate measures to protect workers from such conduct.

Article 27—The right of workers with family responsibilities to equal opportunities and equal treatment

With a view to ensuring the exercise of the right to equality of opportunity and treatment for men and women workers with family responsibilities and between such workers and other workers, the Parties undertake:

1. to take appropriate measures:

a. to enable workers with family responsibilities to enter and remain in employment, as well as to reenter employment after an absence due to those responsibilities, including measures in the field of vocational guidance and training;

b. to take account of their needs in terms of conditions of employment and social security;

c. to develop or promote services, public or private, in particular child daycare services and other childcare arrangements;

2. to provide a possibility for either parent to obtain, during a period after maternity leave, parental leave to take care of a child, the duration and conditions of which should be determined by national legislation, collective agreements or practice;

3. to ensure that family responsibilities shall not, as such, constitute a valid reason for termination of employment....

Article 30—The right to protection against poverty and social exclusion

With a view to ensuring the effective exercise of the right to protection against poverty and social exclusion, the Parties undertake:

a. to take measures within the framework of an overall and co-ordinated approach to promote the effective access of persons who live or risk living in a situation of social exclusion or poverty, as well as their families, to, in particular, employment, housing, training, education, culture and social and medical assistance;

b. to review these measures with a view to their adaptation if necessary.

Article 31—The right to housing

With a view to ensuring the effective exercise of the right to housing, the Parties undertake to take measures designed:

1. to promote access to housing of an adequate standard;

2. to prevent and reduce homelessness with a view to its gradual elimination;

3. to make the price of housing accessible to those without adequate resources.

PART III

Article A — Undertakings

1. Subject to the provisions of Article B below, each of the Parties undertakes:

a. to consider Part I of this Charter as a declaration of the aims which it will pursue by all appropriate means, as stated in the introductory paragraph of that part;

b. to consider itself bound by at least six of the following nine articles of Part II of this Charter: Articles 1, 5, 6, 7, 12, 13, 16, 19 and 20;

c. to consider itself bound by an additional number of articles or numbered paragraphs of Part II of the Charter which it may select, provided that the total number of articles or numbered paragraphs by which it is bound is not less than sixteen articles or sixty-three numbered paragraphs.

2. The articles or paragraphs selected in accordance with sub-paragraphs b and c of paragraph 1 of this article shall be notified to the Secretary General of the Council of Europe at the time when the instrument of ratification, acceptance or approval is deposited.

3. Any Party may, at a later date, declare by notification addressed to the Secretary General that it considers itself bound by any articles or any numbered paragraphs of Part II of the Charter which it has not already accepted under the terms of paragraph 1 of this article. Such undertakings subsequently given shall be deemed to be an integral part of the ratification, acceptance or approval and shall have the same effect as from the first day of the month following the expiration of a period of one month after the date of the notification.

4. Each Party shall maintain a system of labour inspection appropriate to national conditions.

Article B — Links with the European Social Charter and the 1988 Additional Protocol

1. No Contracting Party to the European Social Charter or Party to the Additional Protocol of 5 May 1988 may ratify, accept or approve this Charter without considering itself bound by at least the provisions corresponding to the provisions of the European Social Charter and, where appropriate, of the Additional Protocol, to which it was bound.

2. Acceptance of the obligations of any provision of this Charter shall, from the date of entry into force of those obligations for the Party concerned, result in the corresponding provision of the European Social Charter and, where appropriate, of its Additional Protocol of 1988, ceasing to apply to the Party concerned in the event of that Party being bound by the first of those instruments or by both instruments.

PART IV

Article C — Supervision of the implementation of the undertakings contained in this Charter

The implementation of the legal obligations contained in this Charter shall be submitted to the same supervision as the European Social Charter.

[Ed. Note: "An international system of supervision monitors the implementation of the Charter by the 28 states which have ratified it. Governments must regularly submit reports on the application of the provisions of the Charter that they have accepted. These are examined by the European Committee of Social Rights — made up of independent experts — which gives a legal assessment of the conformity of the situation with the

Charter. In the light of these conclusions, the Committee of Ministers issues recommendations to governments asking them to change their national legislation or practice to ensure conformity with the Charter. Its decisions are prepared by the Governmental Committee on which the contracting parties are represented along with employers' and trade union representatives as observers." Council of Europe, Communication and Research, The European Social Charter, *available at* http://www.coe.int/T/E/ Communication_and_Research/Contacts_with_the_public/About_Council_of_Europe/ An_overview/European_social_charter/default.asp#TopOfPage (last visited March 7, 2003).]

Article D—Collective complaints

1. The provisions of the Additional Protocol to the European Social Charter providing for a system of collective complaints shall apply to the undertakings given in this Charter for the States which have ratified the said Protocol.

[Ed. Note: The Additional Protocol to the European Social Charter Providing for a System of Collective Complaints, Nov. 9, 1995, is available at http://conventions.coe.int/ treaty/en/treaties/html/158.htm. The Protocol gives certain organizations standing to submit complaints alleging unsatisfactory application of the Charter, including workers' and employers' organizations and NGOs which have consultative status with the Council of Europe. The list of NGOs with standing can be expanded with a Contracting State's agreement. *See* art. 2(1). A Committee of Independent Experts decides upon the admissibility of the complaint. *See* art. 7(1). The report of the Committee is transmitted to the Committee of Ministers for an appropriate resolution. *See* art. 9. The State Party them must report on the measures it has taken to implement the Committee of Ministers' Recommendation. *See* art. 10.]

2. Any State which is not bound by the Additional Protocol to the European Social Charter providing for a system of collective complaints may when depositing its instrument of ratification, acceptance or approval of this Charter or at any time thereafter, declare by notification addressed to the Secretary General of the Council of Europe, that it accepts the supervision of its obligations under this Charter following the procedure provided for in the said Protocol.

PART V

Article E—Non-discrimination

The enjoyment of the rights set forth in this Charter shall be secured without discrimination on any ground such as race, colour, sex, language, religion, political or other opinion, national extraction or social origin, health, association with a national minority, birth or other status.

Article F—Derogations in time of war or public emergency

1. In time of war or other public emergency threatening the life of the nation any Party may take measures derogating from its obligations under this Charter to the extent strictly required by the exigencies of the situation, provided that such measures are not inconsistent with its other obligations under international law.

2. Any Party which has availed itself of this right of derogation shall, within a reasonable lapse of time, keep the Secretary General of the Council of Europe fully informed

of the measures taken and of the reasons therefor. It shall likewise inform the Secretary General when such measures have ceased to operate and the provisions of the Charter which it has accepted are again being fully executed.

Article G — Restrictions

1. The rights and principles set forth in Part I when effectively realised, and their effective exercise as provided for in Part II, shall not be subject to any restrictions or limitations not specified in those parts, except such as are prescribed by law and are necessary in a democratic society for the protection of the rights and freedoms of others or for the protection of public interest, national security, public health, or morals.

2. The restrictions permitted under this Charter to the rights and obligations set forth herein shall not be applied for any purpose other than that for which they have been prescribed.

Article H — Relations between the Charter and domestic law or international agreements

The provisions of this Charter shall not prejudice the provisions of domestic law or of any bilateral or multilateral treaties, conventions or agreements which are already in force, or may come into force, under which more favourable treatment would be accorded to the persons protected.

Article I — Implementation of the undertakings given

1. Without prejudice to the methods of implementation foreseen in these articles, the relevant provisions of Articles 1 to 31 of Part II of this Charter shall be implemented by:
   a. laws or regulations;
   b. agreements between employers or employers' organisations and workers' organisations;
   c. a combination of those two methods;
   d. other appropriate means.

2. Compliance with the undertakings deriving from the provisions of paragraphs 1, 2, 3, 4, 5 and 7 of Article 2, paragraphs 4, 6 and 7 of Article 7, paragraphs 1, 2, 3 and 5 of Article 10 and Articles 21 and 22 of Part II of this Charter shall be regarded as effective if the provisions are applied, in accordance with paragraph 1 of this article, to the great majority of the workers concerned....

Article N — Appendix

The appendix to this Charter shall form an integral part of it.

[Ed. Note: Article J (amendments), article K (signature, ratification and entry into force), article L (territorial application), article M (denunciation), and article O (notifications) have been omitted.]

Appendix to the Revised European Social Charter

Scope of the Revised European Social Charter in terms of persons protected.

1. Without prejudice to Article 12, paragraph 4, and Article 13, paragraph 4, the persons covered by Articles 1 to 17 and 20 to 31 include foreigners only in so far as they are nationals of other Parties lawfully resident or working regularly within the territory of

the Party concerned, subject to the understanding that these articles are to be interpreted in the light of the provisions of Articles 18 and 19.

This interpretation would not prejudice the extension of similar facilities to other persons by any of the Parties.

2. Each Party will grant to refugees as defined in the Convention relating to the Status of Refugees, signed in Geneva on 28 July 1951 and in the Protocol of 31 January 1967, and lawfully staying in its territory, treatment as favourable as possible, and in any case not less favourable than under the obligations accepted by the Party under the said convention and under any other existing international instruments applicable to those refugees.

3. Each Party will grant to stateless persons as defined in the Convention on the Status of Stateless Persons done in New York on 28 September 1954 and lawfully staying in its territory, treatment as favourable as possible and in any case not less favourable than under the obligations accepted by the Party under the said instrument and under any other existing international instruments applicable to those stateless persons....

PART II...

Article 4, paragraph 4

This provision shall be so understood as not to prohibit immediate dismissal for any serious offence.

Article 4, paragraph 5

It is understood that a Party may give the undertaking required in this paragraph if the great majority of workers are not permitted to suffer deductions from wages either by law or through collective agreements or arbitration awards, the exceptions being those persons not so covered.

Article 7, paragraph 2

This provision does not prevent Parties from providing in their legislation that young persons not having reached the minimum age laid down may perform work in so far as it is absolutely necessary for their vocational training where such work is carried out in accordance with conditions prescribed by the competent authority and measures are taken to protect the health and safety of these young persons.

Article 7, paragraph 8

It is understood that a Party may give the undertaking required in this paragraph if it fulfils the spirit of the undertaking by providing by law that the great majority of persons under eighteen years of age shall not be employed in night work.

Article 8, paragraph 2

This provision shall not be interpreted as laying down an absolute prohibition. Exceptions could be made, for instance, in the following cases:

a. if an employed woman has been guilty of misconduct which justifies breaking off the employment relationship;

b. if the undertaking concerned ceases to operate;

c. if the period prescribed in the employment contract has expired.

Article 12, paragraph 4

The words "and subject to the conditions laid down in such agreements" in the introduction to this paragraph are taken to imply inter alia that with regard to benefits which are available independently of any insurance contribution, a Party may require the completion of a prescribed period of residence before granting such benefits to nationals of other Parties.

Article 13, paragraph 4

Governments not Parties to the European Convention on Social and Medical Assistance may ratify the Charter in respect of this paragraph provided that they grant to nationals of other Parties a treatment which is in conformity with the provisions of the said convention.

Article 16

It is understood that the protection afforded in this provision covers single-parent families.

Article 17

It is understood that this provision covers all persons below the age of 18 years, unless under the law applicable to the child majority is attained earlier, without prejudice to the other specific provisions provided by the Charter, particularly Article 7.

This does not imply an obligation to provide compulsory education up to the above-mentioned age....

Article 20

1. It is understood that social security matters, as well as other provisions relating to unemployment benefit, old age benefit and survivor's benefit, may be excluded from the scope of this article.

2. Provisions concerning the protection of women, particularly as regards pregnancy, confinement and the post-natal period, shall not be deemed to be discrimination as referred to in this article.

3. This article shall not prevent the adoption of specific measures aimed at removing de facto inequalities.

4. Occupational activities which, by reason of their nature or the context in which they are carried out, can be entrusted only to persons of a particular sex may be excluded from the scope of this article or some of its provisions. This provision is not to be interpreted as requiring the Parties to embody in laws or regulations a list of occupations which, by reason of their nature or the context in which they are carried out, may be reserved to persons of a particular sex....

Article 27

It is understood that this article applies to men and women workers with family responsibilities in relation to their dependent children as well as in relation to other members of their immediate family who clearly need their care or support where such responsibilities restrict their possibilities of preparing for, entering, participating in or advancing in economic activity. The terms "dependent children" and "other members of their immediate family who clearly need their care and support" mean persons defined as such by the national legislation of the Party concerned....

PART V

Article E

A differential treatment based on an objective and reasonable justification shall not be deemed discriminatory.

Article F

The terms "in time of war or other public emergency" shall be so understood as to cover also the threat of war....

European Convention on the Adoption of Children
Apr. 24, 1967, 634 U.N.T.S. 255

[Ed. Note: The Convention entered into force on April 26, 1968. As of February 17, 2002, seventeen countries had ratified or acceded to it. *See* http://conventions.coe. int/Treaty/EN/cadreprincipal.htm.]

Preamble

The member States of the Council of Europe, signatory hereto,

Considering that the aim of the Council of Europe is to achieve a greater unity between its members for the purpose, among others, of facilitating their social progress;

Considering that, although the institution of the adoption of children exists in all member countries of the Council of Europe, there are in those countries differing views as to the principles which should govern adoption and differences in the procedure for effecting, and the legal consequences of, adoption; and

Considering that the acceptance of common principles and practices with respect to the adoption of children would help to reduce the difficulties caused by those differences and at the same time promote the welfare of children who are adopted,

Have agreed as follows:

PART I—UNDERTAKINGS AND FIELD OF APPLICATION

Article 1

Each Contracting Party undertakes to ensure the conformity of its law with the provisions of Part II of this Convention and to notify the Secretary General of the Council of Europe of the measures taken for that purpose.

Article 2

Each Contracting Party undertakes to give consideration to the provisions set out in Part III of this Convention, and if it gives effect, or if, having given effect, it ceases to give effect to any of these provisions, it shall notify the Secretary General of the Council of Europe.

Article 3

This Convention applies only to legal adoption of a child who, at the time when the adopter applies to adopt him, has not attained the age of 18, is not and has not been married, and is not deemed in law to have come of age.

PART II—ESSENTIAL PROVISIONS

Article 4

An adoption shall be valid only if it is granted by a judicial or administrative authority (hereinafter referred to as the "competent authority").

Article 5

1. Subject to paragraphs 2 to 4 of this article, an adoption shall not be granted unless at least the following consents to the adoption have been given and not withdrawn:

a. the consent of the mother and, where the child is legitimate, the father; or if there is neither father nor mother to consent, the consent of any person or body who may be entitled in their place to exercise their parental rights in that respect;

b. the consent of the spouse of the adopter.

2. The competent authority shall not:

a. dispense with the consent of any person mentioned in paragraph 1 of this article, or

b. overrule the refusal to consent of any person or body mentioned in the said paragraph 1, save on exceptional grounds determined by law.

3. If the father or mother is deprived of his or her parental rights in respect of the child, or at least of the right to consent to an adoption, the law may provide that it shall not be necessary to obtain his or her consent.

4. A mother's consent to the adoption of her child shall not be accepted unless it is given at such time after the birth of the child, not being less than six weeks, as may be prescribed by law, or, if no such time has been prescribed, at such time as, in the opinion of the competent authority, will have enabled her to recover sufficiently from the effects of giving birth to the child.

5. For the purposes of this article "father" and "mother" mean the persons who are according to law the parents of the child.

Article 6

1. The law shall not permit a child to be adopted except by either two persons married to each other, whether they adopt simultaneously or successively, or by one person.

2. The law shall not permit a child to be again adopted save in one or more of the following circumstances:

a. where the child is adopted by the spouse of the adopter;

b. where the former adopter has died;

c. where the former adoption has been annulled;

d. where the former adoption has come to an end.

Article 7

1. A child may be adopted only if the adopter has attained the minimum age prescribed for the purpose, this age being neither less than 21 nor more than 35 years.

2. The law may, however, permit the requirement as to the minimum age to be waived:

a. when the adopter is the child's father or mother, or

b. by reason of exceptional circumstances.

Article 8

1. The competent authority shall not grant an adoption unless it is satisfied that the adoption will be in the interest of the child.

2. In each case the competent authority shall pay particular attention to the importance of the adoption providing the child with a stable and harmonious home.

3. As a general rule, the competent authority shall not be satisfied as aforesaid if the difference in age between the adopter and the child is less than the normal difference in age between parents and their children.

Article 9

1. The competent authority shall not grant an adoption until appropriate enquiries have been made concerning the adopter, the child and his family.

2. The enquiries, to the extent appropriate in each case, shall concern, inter alia, the following matters:

a. the personality, health and means of the adopter, particulars of his home and household and his ability to bring up the child;

b. why the adopter wishes to adopt the child;

c. where only one of two spouses of the same marriage applies to adopt a child, why the other spouse does not join in the application;

d. the mutual suitability of the child and the adopter, and the length of time that the child has been in his care and possession;

e. the personality and health of the child, and subject to any limitations imposed by law, his antecedents;

f. the views of the child with respect to the proposed adoption;

g. the religious persuasion, if any, of the adopter and of the child.

3. These enquiries shall be entrusted to a person or body recognised for that purpose by law or by a judicial or administrative body. They shall, as far as practicable, be made by social workers who are qualified in this field as a result of either their training or their experience.

4. The provisions of this article shall not affect the power or duty of the competent authority to obtain any information or evidence, whether or not within the scope of these enquiries, which it considers likely to be of assistance.

Article 10

1. Adoption confers on the adopter in respect of the adopted person the rights and obligations of every kind that a father or mother has in respect of a child born in lawful wedlock.

Adoption confers on the adopted person in respect of the adopter the rights and obligations of every kind that a child born in lawful wedlock has in respect of his father or mother.

2. When the rights and obligations referred to in paragraph 1 of this article are created, any rights and obligations of the same kind existing between the adopted person and his father or mother or any other person or body shall cease to exist. Nevertheless, the law may provide that the spouse of the adopter retains his rights and obligations in respect of the adopted person if the latter is his legitimate, illegitimate or adopted child. In addition the law may preserve the obligation of the parents to maintain (in the sense of l'obligation d'entretenir and l'obligation alimentaire) or set up in life or provide a dowry for the adopted person if the adopter does not discharge any such obligation.

3. As a general rule, means shall be provided to enable the adopted person to acquire the surname of the adopter either in substitution for, or in addition to, his own.

4. If the parent of a child born in lawful wedlock has a right to the enjoyment of that child's property, the adopter's right to the enjoyment of the adopted person's property may, notwithstanding paragraph 1 of this article, be restricted by law.

5. In matters of succession, in so far as the law of succession gives a child born in lawful wedlock a right to share in the estate of his father or mother, an adopted child shall, for the like purposes, be treated as if he were a child of the adopter born in lawful wedlock.

Article 11

1. Where the adopted child does not have, in the case of an adoption by one person, the same nationality as the adopter, or in the case of an adoption by a married couple, their common nationality, the Contracting Party of which the adopter or adopters are nationals shall facilitate acquisition of its nationality by the child.

2. A loss of nationality which could result from an adoption shall be conditional upon possession or acquisition of another nationality.

Article 12

1. The number of children who may be adopted by an adopter shall not be restricted by law.

2. A person who has, or is able to have, a child born in lawful wedlock, shall not on that account be prohibited by law from adopting a child.

3. If adoption improves the legal position of a child, a person shall not be prohibited by law from adopting his own child not born in lawful wedlock.

Article 13

1. Before an adopted person comes of age the adoption may be revoked only by a decision of a judicial or administrative authority on serious grounds, and only if revocation on that ground is permitted by law.

2. The preceding paragraph shall not affect the case of:

a. an adoption which is null and void;

b. an adoption coming to an end where the adopted person becomes the legitimated child of the adopter.

Article 14

When the enquiries made pursuant to Articles 8 and 9 of this Convention relate to a person who lives or has lived in the territory of another Contracting Party, that Contracting Party shall, if a request for information is made, promptly endeavour to secure that the information requested is provided. The authorities may communicate directly with each other for this purpose.

Article 15

Provision shall be made to prohibit any improper financial advantage arising from a child being given up for adoption.

Article 16

Each Contracting Party shall retain the option of adopting provisions more favourable to the adopted child.

PART III—SUPPLEMENTARY PROVISIONS

Article 17

An adoption shall not be granted until the child has been in the care of the adopters for a period long enough to enable a reasonable estimate to be made by the competent authority as to their future relations if the adoption were granted.

Article 18

The public authorities shall ensure the promotion and proper functioning of public or private agencies to which those who wish to adopt a child or to cause a child to be adopted may go for help and advice.

Article 19

The social and legal aspects of adoption shall be included in the curriculum for the training of social workers.

Article 20

1. Provision shall be made to enable an adoption to be completed without disclosing to the child's family the identity of the adopter.

2. Provision shall be made to require or permit adoption proceedings to take place in camera.

3. The adopter and the adopted person shall be able to obtain a document which contains extracts from the public records attesting the fact, date and place of birth of the adopted person, but not expressly revealing the fact of adoption or the identity of his former parents.

4. Public records shall be kept and, in any event, their contents reproduced in such a way as to prevent persons who do not have a legitimate interest from learning the fact that a person has been adopted or, if that is disclosed, the identity of his former parents.

PART IV — FINAL CLAUSES

Article 21

1. This Convention shall be open to signature by the member States of the Council of Europe. It shall be subject to ratification or acceptance. Instruments of ratification or acceptance shall be deposited with the Secretary General of the Council of Europe.

2. This Convention shall enter into force three months after the date of the deposit of the third instrument of ratification or acceptance.

3. In respect of a signatory State ratifying or accepting subsequently, the Convention shall come into force three months after the date of the deposit of its instrument of ratification or acceptance.

Article 22

1. After the entry into force of this Convention, the Committee of Ministers of the Council of Europe may invite any non-member State to accede thereto.

2. Such accession shall be effected by depositing with the Secretary General of the Council of Europe an instrument of accession which shall take effect three months after the date of its deposit.

Article 23

1. Any Contracting Party may, at the time of signature or when depositing its instrument of ratification, acceptance or accession, specify the territory or territories to which this Convention shall apply.

2. Any Contracting Party may, when depositing its instrument of ratification, acceptance or accession or at any later date, by declaration addressed to the Secretary General of the Council of Europe, extend this Convention to any other territory or territories

specified in the declaration and for whose international relations it is responsible or on whose behalf it is authorised to give undertakings.

3. Any declaration made in pursuance of the preceding paragraph may, in respect of any territory mentioned in such declaration, be withdrawn according to the procedure laid down in Article 27 of this Convention.

Article 24

1. Any Contracting Party whose law provides more than one form of adoption shall have the right to apply the provisions of Article 10, paragraphs 1, 2, 3 and 4, and Article 12, paragraphs 2 and 3, of this Convention to one only of such forms.

2. The Contracting Party exercising this right, shall, at the time of signature or when depositing its instrument of ratification, acceptance or accession, or when making a declaration in accordance with paragraph 2 of Article 23 of this Convention, notify the Secretary General of the Council of Europe thereof and indicate the way in which it has been exercised.

3. Such Contracting Party may terminate the exercise of this right and shall give notice thereof to the Secretary General of the Council of Europe.

Article 25

1. Any Contracting Party may, at the time of signature or when depositing its instrument of ratification, acceptance or accession, or when making a declaration in accordance with paragraph 2 of Article 23 of this Convention, make not more than two reservations in respect of the provisions of Part II of the Convention.

Reservations of a general nature shall not be permitted; each reservation may not affect more than one provision. A reservation shall be valid for five years from the entry into force of this Convention for the Contracting Party concerned. It may be renewed for successive periods of five years by means of a declaration addressed to the Secretary General of the Council of Europe before the expiration of each period.

2. Any Contracting Party may wholly or partly withdraw a reservation it has made in accordance with the foregoing paragraph by means of a declaration addressed to the Secretary General of the Council of Europe, which shall become effective as from the date of its receipt.

Article 26

Each Contracting Party shall notify the Secretary General of the Council of Europe of the names and addresses of the authorities to which requests under Article 14 may be addressed.

Article 27

1. This Convention shall remain in force indefinitely.

2. Any Contracting Party may, in so far as it is concerned, denounce this Convention by means of a notification addressed to the Secretary General of the Council of Europe.

3. Such denunciation shall take effect six months after the date of receipt by the Secretary General of such notification.

[Ed. Note: Article 28, setting forth the obligation of the parties of various occurrences with respect to the Convention, has been omitted.]

European Convention on the Legal Status
of Children Born Out of Wedlock
Oct. 15, 1975, 1138 U.N.T.S. 303

[Ed. Note: This Convention entered into force on August 11, 1978. As of February 17, 2002, seventeen countries had ratified or acceded to the Convention. *See* http:// conventions.coe.int/Treaty/EN/cadreprincipal.htm.]

The member States of the Council of Europe, signatory hereto,

Considering that the aim of the Council of Europe is to achieve a greater unity between its members, in particular by the adoption of common rules in the field of law;

Noting that in a great number of member States efforts have been, or are being, made to improve the legal status of children born out of wedlock by reducing the differences between their legal status and that of children born in wedlock which are to the legal or social disadvantage of the former;

Recognising that wide disparities in the laws of member States in this field still exist;

Believing that the situation of children born out of wedlock should be improved and that the formulation of certain common rules concerning their legal status would assist this objective and at the same time would contribute to a harmonisation of the laws of the member States in this field;

Considering however that it is necessary to allow progressive stages for those States which consider themselves unable to adopt immediately certain rules of this Convention,

Have agreed as follows :

Article 1

Each Contracting Party undertakes to ensure the conformity of its law with the provisions of this Convention and to notify the Secretary General of the Council of Europe of the measures taken for that purpose.

Article 2

Maternal affiliation of every child born out of wedlock shall be based solely on the fact of the birth of the child.

Article 3

Paternal affiliation of every child born out of wedlock may be evidenced or established by voluntary recognition or by judicial decision.

Article 4

The voluntary recognition of paternity may not be opposed or contested insofar as the internal law provides for these procedures unless the person seeking to recognise or having recognised the child is not the biological father.

Article 5

In actions relating to paternal affiliation scientific evidence which may help to establish or disprove paternity shall be admissible.

Article 6

1. The father and mother of a child born out of wedlock shall have the same obligation to maintain the child as if it were born in wedlock.

2. Where a legal obligation to maintain a child born in wedlock falls on certain members of the family of the father or mother, this obligation shall also apply for the benefit of a child born out of wedlock.

Article 7

1. Where the affiliation of a child born out of wedlock has been established as regards both parents, parental authority may not be attributed automatically to the father alone.

2. There shall be power to transfer parental authority; cases of transfer shall be governed by the internal law.

Article 8

Where the father or mother of a child born out of wedlock does not have parental authority over or the custody of the child, that parent may obtain a right of access to the child in appropriate cases.

Article 9

A child born out of wedlock shall have the same right of succession in the estate of its father and its mother and of a member of its father's or mother's family, as if it had been born in wedlock.

Article 10

The marriage between the father and mother of a child born out of wedlock shall confer on the child the legal status of a child born in wedlock.

Article 11

1. This Convention shall be open to signature by the member States of the Council of Europe. It shall be subject to ratification, acceptance or approval. Instruments of ratification, acceptance or approval shall be deposited with the Secretary General of the Council of Europe.

2. This Convention shall enter into force three months after the date of the deposit of the third instrument of ratification, acceptance or approval.

3. In respect of a signatory State ratifying, accepting or approving subsequently, the Convention shall come into force three months after the date of the deposit of its instrument of ratification, acceptance or approval.

Article 12

1. After the entry into force of this Convention, the Committee of Ministers of the Council of Europe may invite any non-member State to accede to this Convention.

2. Such accession shall be effected by depositing with the Secretary General of the Council of Europe an instrument of accession which shall take effect three months after the date of its deposit.

Article 13

1. Any State may, at the time of signature, or when depositing its instrument of ratification, acceptance, approval or accession, specify the territory or territories to which this Convention shall apply.

2. Any State may, when depositing its instrument of ratification, acceptance, approval or accession or at any later date, by declaration addressed to the Secretary General of the Council of Europe, extend this Convention to any other territory or territo-

ries specified in the declaration and for whose international relations it is responsible or on whose behalf it is authorised to give undertakings.

3. Any declaration made in pursuance of the preceding paragraph may, in respect of any territory mentioned in such declaration, be withdrawn according to the procedure laid down in Article 15 of this Convention.

Article 14

1. Any State may, at the time of signature, or when depositing its instrument of ratification, acceptance, approval or accession or when making a declaration in accordance with paragraph 2 of Article 13 of this Convention, make not more than three reservations in respect of the provisions of Articles 2 to 10 of the Convention. Reservations of a general nature shall not be permitted; each reservation may not affect more than one provision.

2. A reservation shall be valid for five years from the entry into force of this Convention for the Contracting Party concerned. It may be renewed for successive periods of five years by means of a declaration addressed to the Secretary General of the Council of Europe before the expiration of each period.

3. Any Contracting Party may wholly or partly withdraw a reservation it has made in accordance with the foregoing paragraphs by means of a declaration addressed to the Secretary General of the Council of Europe, which shall become effective as from the date of its receipt.

Article 15

1. Any Contracting Party may, insofar as it is concerned, denounce this Convention by means of a notification addressed to the Secretary General of the Council of Europe.

2. Such denunciation shall take effect six months after the date of receipt by the Secretary General of such notification.

[Ed. Note: Article 16, setting forth the obligation of the Secretary General of the Council of Europe to notify parties of various occurrences with respect to the Convention, has been omitted.]

European Convention on Recognition and Enforcement of Decisions Concerning Custody of Children and on Restoration of Custody of Children
May 20, 1980, Europ. T.S. No. 105

[Ed. Note: The Convention entered into force on September 1, 1983. As of February 17, 2002, twenty-seven countries had ratified or acceded to the Convention. *See* http://conventions.coe.int/Treaty/EN/cadreprincipal.htm.]

The member States of the Council of Europe, signatory hereto,

Recognising that in the member States of the Council of Europe the welfare of the child is of overriding importance in reaching decisions concerning his custody;

Considering that the making of arrangements to ensure that decisions concerning the custody of a child can be more widely recognised and enforced will provide greater protection of the welfare of children;

Considering it desirable, with this end in view, to emphasise that the right of access of parents is a normal corollary to the right of custody;

Noting the increasing number of cases where children have been improperly removed across an international frontier and the difficulties of securing adequate solutions to the problems caused by such cases;

Desirous of making suitable provision to enable the custody of children which has been arbitrarily interrupted to be restored;

Convinced of the desirability of making arrangements for this purpose answering to different needs and different circumstances;

Desiring to establish legal co-operation between their authorities,

Have agreed as follows:

Article 1

For the purposes of this Convention:

a. child means a person of any nationality, so long as he is under 16 years of age and has not the right to decide on his own place of residence under the law of his habitual residence, the law of his nationality or the internal law of the State addressed;

b. authority means a judicial or administrative authority;

c. decision relating to custody means a decision of an authority in so far as it relates to the care of the person of the child, including the right to decide on the place of his residence, or to the right of access to him;

d. improper removal means the removal of a child across an international frontier in breach of a decision relating to his custody which has been given in a Contracting State and which is enforceable in such a State; improper removal also includes:

i. the failure to return a child across an international frontier at the end of a period of the exercise of the right of access to this child or at the end of any other temporary stay in a territory other than that where the custody is exercised;

ii. a removal which is subsequently declared unlawful within the meaning of Article 12.

Part 1 — Central authorities

Article 2

1. Each Contracting State shall appoint a central authority to carry out the functions provided for by this Convention.

2. Federal States and States with more than one legal system shall be free to appoint more than one central authority and shall determine the extent of their competence.

3. The Secretary General of the Council of Europe shall be notified of any appointment under this Article.

Article 3

1. The central authorities of the Contracting States shall co-operate with each other and promote co-operation between the competent authorities in their respective countries. They shall act with all necessary despatch.

2. With a view to facilitating the operation of this Convention, the central authorities of the Contracting States:

a. shall secure the transmission of requests for information coming from competent authorities and relating to legal or factual matters concerning pending proceedings;

b. shall provide each other on request with information about their law relating to the custody of children and any changes in that law;

c. shall keep each other informed of any difficulties likely to arise in applying the Convention and, as far as possible, eliminate obstacles to its application.

Article 4

1. Any person who has obtained in a Contracting State a decision relating to the custody of a child and who wishes to have that decision recognised or enforced in another Contracting State may submit an application for this purpose to the central authority in any Contracting State.

2. The application shall be accompanied by the documents mentioned in Article 13.

3. The central authority receiving the application, if it is not the central authority in the State addressed, shall send the documents directly and without delay to that central authority.

4. The central authority receiving the application may refuse to intervene where it is manifestly clear that the conditions laid down by this Convention are not satisfied.

5. The central authority receiving the application shall keep the applicant informed without delay of the progress of his application.

Article 5

1. The central authority in the State addressed shall take or cause to be taken without delay all steps which it considers to be appropriate, if necessary by instituting proceedings before its competent authorities, in order:

a. to discover the whereabouts of the child;

b. to avoid, in particular by any necessary provisional measures, prejudice to the interests of the child or of the applicant;

c. to secure the recognition or enforcement of the decision;

d. to secure the delivery of the child to the applicant where enforcement is granted;

e. to inform the requesting authority of the measures taken and their results.

2. Where the central authority in the State addressed has reason to believe that the child is in the territory of another Contracting State it shall send the documents directly and without delay to the central authority of that State.

3. With the exception of the cost of repatriation, each Contracting State undertakes not to claim any payment from an applicant in respect of any measures taken under paragraph 1 of this Article by the central authority of that State on the applicant's behalf, including the costs of proceedings and, where applicable, the costs incurred by the assistance of a lawyer.

4. If recognition or enforcement is refused, and if the central authority of the State addressed considers that it should comply with a request by the applicant to bring in that State proceedings concerning the substance of the case, that authority shall use its best endeavours to secure the representation of the applicant in the proceedings under conditions no less favourable than those available to a person who is resident in and a national of that State and for this purpose it may, in particular, institute proceedings before its competent authorities.

Article 6

1. Subject to any special agreements made between the central authorities concerned and to the provisions of paragraph 3 of this Article:

a. communications to the central authority of the State addressed shall be made in the official language or in one of the official languages of that State or be accompanied by a translation into that language;

b. the central authority of the State addressed shall nevertheless accept communications made in English or in French or accompanied by a translation into one of these languages.

2. Communications coming from the central authority of the State addressed, including the results of enquiries carried out, may be made in the official language or one of the official languages of that State or in English or French.

3. A Contracting State may exclude wholly or partly the provisions of paragraph 1.b of this Article. When a Contracting State has made this reservation any other Contracting State may also apply the reservation in respect of that State.

Part II — Recognition and enforcement of decisions and restoration of custody of children

Article 7

A decision relating to custody given in a Contracting State shall be recognised and, where it is enforceable in the State of origin, made enforceable in every other Contracting State.

Article 8

1. In the case of an improper removal, the central authority of the State addressed shall cause steps to be taken forthwith to restore the custody of the child where:

a. at the time of the institution of the proceedings in the State where the decision was given or at the time of the improper removal, if earlier, the child and his parents had as their sole nationality the nationality of that State and the child had his habitual residence in the territory of that State, and

b. a request for the restoration was made to a central authority within a period of six months from the date of the improper removal.

2. If, in accordance with the law of the State addressed, the requirements of paragraph 1 of this Article cannot be complied with without recourse to a judicial authority, none of the grounds of refusal specified in this Convention shall apply to the judicial proceedings.

3. Where there is an agreement officially confirmed by a competent authority between the person having the custody of the child and another person to allow the other person a right of access, and the child, having been taken abroad, has not been restored at the end of the agreed period to the person having the custody, custody of the child shall be restored in accordance with paragraphs 1.b and 2 of this Article. The same shall apply in the case of a decision of the competent authority granting such a right to a person who has not the custody of the child.

Article 9

1. In cases of improper removal, other than those dealt with in Article 8, in which an application has been made to a central authority within a period of six months from the date of the removal, recognition and enforcement may be refused only if:

a. in the case of a decision given in the absence of the defendant or his legal representative, the defendant was not duly served with the document which instituted the proceedings or an equivalent document in sufficient time to enable him to arrange his defence; but such a failure to effect service cannot constitute a ground for refusing recognition or enforcement where service was not effected because the defendant had concealed his whereabouts from the person who instituted the proceedings in the State of origin;

b. in the case of a decision given in the absence of the defendant or his legal representative, the competence of the authority giving the decision was not founded:

i. on the habitual residence of the defendant, or

ii. on the last common habitual residence of the child's parents, at least one parent being still habitually resident there, or

iii. on the habitual residence of the child;

c. the decision is incompatible with a decision relating to custody which became enforceable in the State addressed before the removal of the child, unless the child has had his habitual residence in the territory of the requesting State for one year before his removal.

2. Where no application has been made to a central authority, the provisions of paragraph 1 of this Article shall apply equally, if recognition and enforcement are requested within six months from the date of the improper removal.

3. In no circumstances may the foreign decision be reviewed as to its substance.

Article 10

1. In cases other than those covered by Articles 8 and 9, recognition and enforcement may be refused not only on the grounds provided for in Article 9 but also on any of the following grounds:

a. if it is found that the effects of the decision are manifestly incompatible with the fundamental principles of the law relating to the family and children in the State addressed;

b. if it is found that by reason of a change in the circumstances including the passage of time but not including a mere change in the residence of the child after an improper removal, the effects of the original decision are manifestly no longer in accordance with the welfare of the child;

c. if at the time when the proceedings were instituted in the State of origin:

i.the child was a national of the State addressed or was habitually resident there and no such connection existed with the State of origin;

ii. the child was a national both of the State of origin and of the State addressed and was habitually resident in the State addressed;

d. if the decision is incompatible with a decision given in the State addressed or enforceable in that State after being given in a third State, pursuant to proceedings begun before the submission of the request for recognition or enforcement, and if the refusal is in accordance with the welfare of the child.

2. In the same cases, proceedings for recognition or enforcement may be adjourned on any of the following grounds:

a. if an ordinary form of review of the original decision has been commenced;

b. if proceedings relating to the custody of the child, commenced before the proceedings in the State of origin were instituted, are pending in the State addressed;

c. if another decision concerning the custody of the child is the subject of proceedings for enforcement or of any other proceedings concerning the recognition of the decision.

Article 11

1. Decisions on rights of access and provisions of decisions relating to custody which deal with the right of access shall be recognised and enforced subject to the same conditions as other decisions relating to custody.

2. However, the competent authority of the State addressed may fix the conditions for the implementation and exercise of the right of access taking into account, in particular, undertakings given by the parties on this matter.

3. Where no decision on the right of access has been taken or where recognition or enforcement of the decision relating to custody is refused, the central authority of the State addressed may apply to its competent authorities for a decision on the right of access, if the person claiming a right of access so requests.

Article 12

Where, at the time of the removal of a child across an international frontier, there is no enforceable decision given in a Contracting State relating to his custody, the provisions of this Convention shall apply to any subsequent decision, relating to the custody of that child and declaring the removal to be unlawful, given in a Contracting State at the request of any interested person.

Part III — Procedure

Article 13

1. A request for recognition or enforcement in another Contracting State of a decision relating to custody shall be accompanied by:

a. a document authorising the central authority of the State addressed to act on behalf of the applicant or to designate another representative for that purpose;

b. a copy of the decision which satisfies the necessary conditions of authenticity;

c. in the case of a decision given in the absence of the defendant or his legal representative, a document which establishes that the defendant was duly served with the document which instituted the proceedings or an equivalent document;

d. if applicable, any document which establishes that, in accordance with the law of the State of origin, the decision is enforceable;

e. if possible, a statement indicating the whereabouts or likely whereabouts of the child in the State addressed;

f. proposals as to how the custody of the child should be restored.

2. The documents mentioned above shall, where necessary, be accompanied by a translation according to the provisions laid down in Article 6.

Article 14

Each Contracting State shall apply a simple and expeditious procedure for recognition and enforcement of decisions relating to the custody of a child. To that end it shall ensure that a request for enforcement may be lodged by simple application.

Article 15

1. Before reaching a decision under paragraph 1.b of Article 10, the authority concerned in the State addressed:

a. shall ascertain the child's views unless this is impracticable having regard in particular to his age and understanding; and

b. may request that any appropriate enquiries be carried out.

2. The cost of enquiries in any Contracting State shall be met by the authorities of the State where they are carried out.

3. Request for enquiries and the results of enquiries may be sent to the authority concerned through the central authorities.

Article 16

For the purposes of this Convention, no legalisation or any like formality may be required.

Part IV — Reservations

Article 17

1. A Contracting State may make a reservation that, in cases covered by Articles 8 and 9 or either of these Articles, recognition and enforcement of decisions relating to custody may be refused on such of the grounds provided under Article 10 as may be specified in the reservation.

2. Recognition and enforcement of decisions given in a Contracting State which has made the reservation provided for in paragraph 1 of this Article may be refused in any other Contracting State on any of the additional grounds referred to in that reservation.

Article 18

A Contracting State may make a reservation that it shall not be bound by the provisions of Article 12. The provisions of this Convention shall not apply to decisions referred to in Article 12 which have been given in a Contracting State which has made such a reservation.

Part V — Other instruments

Article 19

This Convention shall not exclude the possibility of relying on any other international instrument in force between the State of origin and the State addressed or on any other law of the State addressed not derived from an international agreement for the purpose of obtaining recognition or enforcement of a decision.

Article 20

1. This Convention shall not affect any obligations which a Contracting State may have towards a non-Contracting State under an international instrument dealing with matters governed by this Convention.

2. When two or more Contracting States have enacted uniform laws in relation to custody of children or created a special system of recognition or enforcement of decisions in this field, or if they should do so in the future, they shall be free to apply, between themselves, those laws or that system in place of this Convention or any part of it. In order to avail themselves of this provision the State shall notify their decision to the Secretary General of the Council of Europe. Any alteration or revocation of this decision must also be notified.

Part VI — Final clauses

Article 21

This Convention shall be open for signature by the member States of the Council of Europe. It is subject to ratification, acceptance or approval. Instruments of ratification, acceptance or approval shall be deposited with the Secretary General of the Council of Europe.

Article 22

1. This Convention shall enter into force on the first day of the month following the expiration of a period of three months after the date on which three member States of the Council of Europe have expressed their consent to be bound by the Convention in accordance with the provisions of Article 21.

2. In respect of any member State which subsequently expresses its consent to be bound by it, the Convention shall enter into force on the first day of the month following the expiration of a period of three months after the date of the deposit of the instrument of ratification, acceptance or approval.

Article 23

1. After the entry into force of this Convention, the Committee of Ministers of the Council of Europe may invite any State not a member of the Council to accede to this Convention, by a decision taken by the majority provided for by Article 20.d of the Statute and by the unanimous vote of the representatives of the Contracting States entitled to sit on the Committee.

2. In respect of any acceding State, the Convention shall enter into force on the first day of the month following the expiration of a period of three months after the date of deposit of the instrument of accession with the Secretary General of the Council of Europe.

Article 24

1. Any State may at the time of signature or when depositing its instrument of ratification, acceptance, approval or accession, specify the territory or territories to which this Convention shall apply.

2. Any State may at any later date, by a declaration addressed to the Secretary General of the Council of Europe, extend the application of this Convention to any other territory specified in the declaration. In respect of such territory, the Convention shall enter into force on the first day of the month following the expiration of a period of three months after the date of receipt by the Secretary General of such declaration.

3. Any declaration made under the two preceding paragraphs may, in respect of any territory specified in such declaration, be withdrawn by a notification addressed to the Secretary General. The withdrawal shall become effective on the first day of the month following the expiration of a period of six months after the date of receipt of such notification by the Secretary General.

Article 25

1. A State which has two or more territorial units in which different systems of law apply in matters of custody of children and of recognition and enforcement of decisions relating to custody may, at the time of signature or when depositing its instrument of ratification, acceptance, approval or accession, declare that this Convention shall apply to all its territorial units or to one or more of them.

2. Such a State may at any later date, by a declaration addressed to the Secretary General of the Council of Europe, extend the application of this Convention to any other territorial unit specified in the declaration. In respect of such territorial unit the Convention shall enter into force on the first day of the month following the expiration of a period of three months after the date of receipt by the Secretary General of such declaration.

3. Any declaration made under the two preceding paragraphs may, in respect of any territorial unit specified in such declaration, be withdrawn by notification addressed to the Secretary General. The withdrawal shall become effective on the first day of the month following the expiration of a period of six months after the date of receipt of such notification by the Secretary General.

Article 26

1. In relation to a State which has in matters of custody two or more systems of law of territorial application:

a. reference to the law of a person's habitual residence or to the law of a person's nationality shall be construed as referring to the system of law determined by the rules in force in that State or, if there are no such rules, to the system of law with which the person concerned is most closely connected;

b. reference to the State of origin or to the State addressed shall be construed as referring, as the case may be, to the territorial unit where recognition or enforcement of the decision or restoration of custody is requested.

2. Paragraph 1.a of this Article also applies mutatis mutandis to States which have in matters of custody two or more systems of law of personal application.

Article 27

1. Any State may, at the time of signature or when depositing its instrument of ratification, acceptance, approval or accession, declare that it avails itself of one or more of the reservations provided for in paragraph 3 of Article 6, Article 17 and Article 18 of this Convention. No other reservation may be made.

2. Any Contracting State which has made a reservation under the preceding paragraph may wholly or partly withdraw it by means of a notification addressed to the Secretary General of the Council of Europe. The withdrawal shall take effect on the date of receipt of such notification by the Secretary General.

Article 28

At the end of the third year following the date of the entry into force of this Convention and, on his own initiative, at any time after this date, the Secretary General of the Council of Europe shall invite the representatives of the central authorities appointed by the Contracting States to meet in order to study and to facilitate the functioning of the Convention. Any member State of the Council of Europe not being a party to the Convention may be represented by an observer. A report shall be prepared on the work of each of these meetings and forwarded to the Committee of Ministers of the Council of Europe for information.

[Ed. Note: Article 29, on denunciation, and Article 30, on the administrative obligations of the Secretary General of the Council of Europe, have been omitted.]

European Convention on the Exercise of Children's Rights
Jan. 25, 1996, Europ. T.S. No. 160

[Ed. Note: The Convention entered into force on July 1, 2000. Five countries have ratified or acceded to it. *See* http://conventions.coe.int/Treaty/EN/cadreprincipal.htm.]

Preamble

The member States of the Council of Europe and the other States signatory hereto,

Considering that the aim of the Council of Europe is to achieve greater unity between its members;

Having regard to the United Nations Convention on the Rights of the Child and in particular Article 4 which requires States Parties to undertake all appropriate legislative, administrative and other measures for the implementation of the rights recognised in the said Convention;

Noting the contents of Recommendation 1121 (1990) of the Parliamentary Assembly on the rights of the child;

Convinced that the rights and best interests of children should be promoted and to that end children should have the opportunity to exercise their rights, in particular in family proceedings affecting them;

Recognising that children should be provided with relevant information to enable such rights and best interests to be promoted and that due weight should be given to the views of children;

Recognising the importance of the parental role in protecting and promoting the rights and best interests of children and considering that, where necessary, States should also engage in such protection and promotion;

Considering, however, that in the event of conflict it is desirable for families to try to reach agreement before bringing the matter before a judicial authority,

Have agreed as follows:

CHAPTER I — SCOPE AND OBJECT OF THE CONVENTION AND DEFINITIONS

Article 1 — Scope and object of the Convention

1. This Convention shall apply to children who have not reached the age of 18 years.

2. The object of the present Convention is, in the best interests of children, to promote their rights, to grant them procedural rights and to facilitate the exercise of these rights by ensuring that children are, themselves or through other persons or bodies, informed and allowed to participate in proceedings affecting them before a judicial authority.

3. For the purposes of this Convention, proceedings before a judicial authority affecting children are family proceedings, in particular those involving the exercise of parental responsibilities such as residence and access to children.

4. Every State shall, at the time of signature or when depositing its instrument of ratification, acceptance, approval or accession, by a declaration addressed to the Secretary General of the Council of Europe, specify at least three categories of family cases before a judicial authority to which this Convention is to apply.

5. Any Party may, by further declaration, specify additional categories of family cases to which this Convention is to apply or provide information concerning the application of Article 5, paragraph 2 of Article 9, paragraph 2 of Article 10 and Article 11.

6. Nothing in this Convention shall prevent Parties from applying rules more favourable to the promotion and the exercise of children's rights.

Article 2 — Definitions

For the purposes of this Convention:

a. the term "judicial authority" means a court or an administrative authority having equivalent powers;

b. the term "holders of parental responsibilities" means parents and other persons or bodies entitled to exercise some or all parental responsibilities;

c. the term "representative" means a person, such as a lawyer, or a body appointed to act before a judicial authority on behalf of a child;

d. the term "relevant information" means information which is appropriate to the age and understanding of the child, and which will be given to enable the child to exercise his or her rights fully unless the provision of such information were contrary to the welfare of the child.

CHAPTER II — PROCEDURAL MEASURES TO PROMOTE THE EXERCISE OF CHILDREN'S RIGHTS

A. Procedural rights of a child

Article 3 — Right to be informed and to express his or her views in proceedings

A child considered by internal law as having sufficient understanding, in the case of proceedings before a judicial authority affecting him or her, shall be granted, and shall be entitled to request, the following rights:

a. to receive all relevant information;

b. to be consulted and express his or her views;

c. to be informed of the possible consequences of compliance with these views and the possible consequences of any decision.

Article 4 — Right to apply for the appointment of a special representative

1. Subject to Article 9, the child shall have the right to apply, in person or through other persons or bodies, for a special representative in proceedings before a judicial authority affecting the child where internal law precludes the holders of parental responsibilities from representing the child as a result of a conflict of interest with the latter.

2. States are free to limit the right in paragraph 1 to children who are considered by internal law to have sufficient understanding.

Article 5 — Other possible procedural rights

Parties shall consider granting children additional procedural rights in relation to proceedings before a judicial authority affecting them, in particular:

a. the right to apply to be assisted by an appropriate person of their choice in order to help them express their views;

b. the right to apply themselves, or through other persons or bodies, for the appointment of a separate representative, in appropriate cases a lawyer;

c. the right to appoint their own representative;

d. the right to exercise some or all of the rights of parties to such proceedings.

B. Role of judicial authorities

Article 6 — Decision-making process

In proceedings affecting a child, the judicial authority, before taking a decision, shall:

a. consider whether it has sufficient information at its disposal in order to take a decision in the best interests of the child and, where necessary, it shall obtain further information, in particular from the holders of parental responsibilities;

b. in a case where the child is considered by internal law as having sufficient understanding:

- ensure that the child has received all relevant information;
- consult the child in person in appropriate cases, if necessary privately, itself or
  through other persons or bodies, in a manner appropriate to his or her understanding, unless this would be manifestly contrary to the best interests of the child;
- allow the child to express his or her views; give due weight to the views expressed by the child.

Article 7 — Duty to act speedily

In proceedings affecting a child the judicial authority shall act speedily to avoid any
unnecessary delay and procedures shall be available to ensure that its decisions are
rapidly enforced. In urgent cases the judicial authority shall have the power, where appropriate, to take decisions which are immediately enforceable.

Article 8 — Acting on own motion

In proceedings affecting a child the judicial authority shall have the power to act on
its own motion in cases determined by internal law where the welfare of a child is in serious danger.

Article 9 — Appointment of a representative

1. In proceedings affecting a child where, by internal law, the holders of parental responsibilities are precluded from representing the child as a result of a conflict of interest between them and the child, the judicial authority shall have the power to appoint a
special representative for the child in those proceedings.

2. Parties shall consider providing that, in proceedings affecting a child, the judicial
authority shall have the power to appoint a separate representative, in appropriate cases
a lawyer, to represent the child.

C. Role of representatives

Article 10

1. In the case of proceedings before a judicial authority affecting a child the representative shall, unless this would be manifestly contrary to the best interests of the child:

a. provide all relevant information to the child, if the child is considered by internal law as having sufficient understanding;

b. provide explanations to the child if the child is considered by internal law as
having sufficient understanding, concerning the possible consequences of compliance
with his or her views and the possible consequences of any action by the representative;

c. determine the views of the child and present these views to the judicial authority.

2. Parties shall consider extending the provisions of paragraph 1 to the holders of
parental responsibilities.

D. Extension of certain provisions

Article 11

Parties shall consider extending the provisions of Articles 3, 4 and 9 to proceedings
affecting children before other bodies and to matters affecting children which are not
the subject of proceedings.

E. National bodies

Article 12

1. Parties shall encourage, through bodies which perform, inter alia, the functions set out in paragraph 2, the promotion and the exercise of children's rights.

2. The functions are as follows:

a. to make proposals to strengthen the law relating to the exercise of children's rights;

b. to give opinions concerning draft legislation relating to the exercise of children's rights;

c. to provide general information concerning the exercise of children's rights to the media, the public and persons and bodies dealing with questions relating to children;

d. to seek the views of children and provide them with relevant information.

F. Other matters

Article 13 — Mediation or other processes to resolve disputes

In order to prevent or resolve disputes or to avoid proceedings before a judicial authority affecting children, Parties shall encourage the provision of mediation or other processes to resolve disputes and the use of such processes to reach agreement in appropriate cases to be determined by Parties.

Article 14 — Legal aid and advice

Where internal law provides for legal aid or advice for the representation of children in proceedings before a judicial authority affecting them, such provisions shall apply in relation to the matters covered by Articles 4 and 9.

Article 15 — Relations with other international instruments

This Convention shall not restrict the application of any other international instrument which deals with specific issues arising in the context of the protection of children and families, and to which a Party to this Convention is, or becomes, a Party.

CHAPTER III — STANDING COMMITTEE

Article 16 — Establishment and functions of the Standing Committee

1. A Standing Committee is set up for the purposes of this Convention.

2. The Standing Committee shall keep under review problems relating to this Convention. It may, in particular:

a. consider any relevant questions concerning the interpretation or implementation of the Convention. The Standing Committee's conclusions concerning the implementation of the Convention may take the form of a recommendation; recommendations shall be adopted by a three-quarters majority of the votes cast;

b. propose amendments to the Convention and examine those proposed in accordance with Article 20;

c. provide advice and assistance to the national bodies having the functions under paragraph 2 of Article 12 and promote international co-operation between them.

Article 17 — Composition

1. Each Party may be represented on the Standing Committee by one or more delegates. Each Party shall have one vote.

2. Any State referred to in Article 21, which is not a Party to this Convention, may be represented in the Standing Committee by an observer. The same applies to any other State or to the European Community after having been invited to accede to the Convention in accordance with the provisions of Article 22.

3. Unless a Party has informed the Secretary General of its objection, at least one month before the meeting, the Standing Committee may invite the following to attend as observers at all its meetings or at one meeting or part of a meeting:
- any State not referred to in paragraph 2 above;
- the United Nations Committee on the Rights of the Child;
- the European Community;
- any international governmental body;
- any international non-governmental body with one or more functions mentioned under paragraph 2 of Article 12;
- any national governmental or non-governmental body with one or more functions mentioned under paragraph 2 of Article 12.

4. The Standing Committee may exchange information with relevant organisations dealing with the exercise of children's rights.

Article 18 — Meetings

1. At the end of the third year following the date of entry into force of this Convention and, on his or her own initiative, at any time after this date, the Secretary General of the Council of Europe shall invite the Standing Committee to meet.

2. Decisions may only be taken in the Standing Committee if at least one-half of the Parties are present.

3. Subject to Articles 16 and 20 the decisions of the Standing Committee shall be taken by a majority of the members present.

4. Subject to the provisions of this Convention, the Standing Committee shall draw up its own rules of procedure and the rules of procedure of any working party it may set up to carry out all appropriate tasks under the Convention.

Article 19 — Reports of the Standing Committee

After each meeting, the Standing Committee shall forward to the Parties and the Committee of Ministers of the Council of Europe a report on its discussions and any decisions taken.

CHAPTER IV — AMENDMENTS TO THE CONVENTION

Article 20

1. Any amendment to the articles of this Convention proposed by a Party or the Standing Committee shall be communicated to the Secretary General of the Council of Europe and forwarded by him or her, at least two months before the next meeting of the Standing Committee, to the member States of the Council of Europe, any signatory, any Party, any State invited to sign this Convention in accordance with the provisions of Article 21 and any State or the European Community invited to accede to it in accordance with the provisions of Article 22.

2. Any amendment proposed in accordance with the provisions of the preceding paragraph shall be examined by the Standing Committee which shall submit the text adopted by a three-quarters majority of the votes cast to the Committee of Ministers for approval. After its approval, this text shall be forwarded to the Parties for acceptance.

3. Any amendment shall enter into force on the first day of the month following the expiration of a period of one month after the date on which all Parties have informed the Secretary General that they have accepted it.

CHAPTER V — FINAL CLAUSES

Article 21 — Signature, ratification and entry into force

1. This Convention shall be open for signature by the member States of the Council of Europe and the non-member States which have participated in its elaboration.

2. This Convention is subject to ratification, acceptance or approval. Instruments of ratification, acceptance or approval shall be deposited with the Secretary General of the Council of Europe.

3. This Convention shall enter into force on the first day of the month following the expiration of a period of three months after the date on which three States, including at least two member States of the Council of Europe, have expressed their consent to be bound by the Convention in accordance with the provisions of the preceding paragraph.

4. In respect of any signatory which subsequently expresses its consent to be bound by it, the Convention shall enter into force on the first day of the month following the expiration of a period of three months after the date of the deposit of its instrument of ratification, acceptance or approval.

Article 22 — Non-member States and the European Community

1. After the entry into force of this Convention, the Committee of Ministers of the Council of Europe may, on its own initiative or following a proposal from the Standing Committee and after consultation of the Parties, invite any non-member State of the Council of Europe, which has not participated in the elaboration of the Convention, as well as the European Community to accede to this Convention by a decision taken by the majority provided for in Article 20, sub-paragraph d of the Statute of the Council of Europe, and by the unanimous vote of the representatives of the contracting States entitled to sit on the Committee of Ministers.

2. In respect of any acceding State or the European Community, the Convention shall enter into force on the first day of the month following the expiration of a period of three months after the date of deposit of the instrument of accession with the Secretary General of the Council of Europe.

Article 23 — Territorial application

1. Any State may, at the time of signature or when depositing its instrument of ratification, acceptance, approval or accession, specify the territory or territories to which this Convention shall apply.

2. Any Party may, at any later date, by a declaration addressed to the Secretary General of the Council of Europe, extend the application of this Convention to any other territory specified in the declaration and for whose international relations it is responsible or on whose behalf it is authorised to give undertakings. In respect of such territory the Convention shall enter into force on the first day of the month following the expiration of a period of three months after the date of receipt of such declaration by the Secretary General.

3. Any declaration made under the two preceding paragraphs may, in respect of any territory specified in such declaration, be withdrawn by a notification addressed to the Secretary General. The withdrawal shall become effective on the first day of the month

following the expiration of a period of three months after the date of receipt of such notification by the Secretary General.

Article 24 — Reservations

No reservation may be made to the Convention.

[Ed. Note: Article 25 on denunciation, and Article, 26 on notifications, have been omitted.]

B. Inter-American Conventions

American Declaration of the Rights and Duties of Man

O.A.S. Res. XXX, Int'l Conf. Am. States,
9th Conf., 43 Am. J. Int'l L. 133 (May 2, 1948)

[Ed. Note: The American Declaration was adopted by the Ninth International Conference of American States in Bogotá, Colombia, in 1948. Twenty-one States participated in that Conference, including the United States of America.

Today thirty-five States are members of the Organization of American States, having ratified its Charter. The Inter-American Commission on Human Rights has held that as a consequence of articles 3j, 16, 51e, 112 and 150 of the OAS Charter, the Declaration has binding force on OAS members. *See* The Baby Boy Case, Resolution 23/81, Case 2141, Inter-Am. C.H.R. 25, OEA.ser.L/V/II.54, doc. 9 rev. 1 (1981). The United States disputes that the American Declaration has binding force since the revised OAS Charter does not explicitly incorporate the American Declaration. *See* Memorandum of the United States at 6 n.6, Case 9647, Inter-Am. C.H.R. 147, OEA/ser. L./V/II.71, doc. 9 rev. 1 (1987). *See also* Case 11.139 (Andrews v. United States), Inter-Am. C.H.R. ¶59, OEA/ser.L/V/II.98 doc. 6 rev. (1998) (The United States government "categorically rejects...that the American Declaration...has acquired legally binding force for all OAS countries."). The United States has stated, "The American Declaration of the Rights and Duties of Man represents a noble statement of the human rights aspirations of the American States. Unlike the American Convention, however, it was not drafted as a legal instrument and lacks the precision necessary to resolve complex legal questions. Its normative value lies as a declaration of basic moral principles and broad political commitments and as a basis to review the general human rights performance of member states, not as a binding set of obligations." Advisory Opinion OC-10/89, Interpretation of the American Declaration of the Rights and Duties of Man Within the Framework of Article 64 of the American Convention on Human Rights, 1989 Inter-Am. Ct. H.R. (ser. A) No. 10 at ¶12. *See also id.* at ¶17.

Courts in the United States have held that the American Declaration is not self-executing, but merely aspirational. *See, e.g.,* Buell v. Mitchell, 274 F.3d 337, 372 (6th Cir. 2001); Garza v. Lappin, 253 F.3d 918, 923 (7th Cir. 2001). Congress has never enacted implementing legislation. In addition, in 2001, a U.S. court of appeals held for the first time that the Inter-American Commission's decisions do not create judicially-cognizable rights in the United States for individuals. *See Garza,* 253 F.3d at 925.]

WHEREAS:

The American peoples have acknowledged the dignity of the individual, and their national constitutions recognize that juridical and political institutions, which regulate life in human society, have as their principal aim the protection of the essential rights of man and the creation of circumstances that will permit him to achieve spiritual and material progress and attain happiness;

The American States have on repeated occasions recognized that the essential rights of man are not derived from the fact that he is a national of a certain state, but are based upon attributes of his human personality;

The international protection of the rights of man should be the principal guide of an evolving American law;

The affirmation of essential human rights by the American States together with the guarantees given by the internal regimes of the states establish the initial system of protection considered by the American States as being suited to the present social and juridical conditions, not without a recognition on their part that they should increasingly strengthen that system in the international field as conditions become more favorable,

The Ninth International Conference of American States AGREES:

To adopt the following....

PREAMBLE

All men are born free and equal, in dignity and in rights, and, being endowed by nature with reason and conscience, they should conduct themselves as brothers one to another.

The fulfillment of duty by each individual is a prerequisite to the rights of all. Rights and duties are interrelated in every social and political activity of man. While rights exalt individual liberty, duties express the dignity of that liberty.

Duties of a juridical nature presuppose others of a moral nature which support them in principle and constitute their basis.

Inasmuch as spiritual development is the supreme end of human existence and the highest expression thereof, it is the duty of man to serve that end with all his strength and resources.

Since culture is the highest social and historical expression of that spiritual development, it is the duty of man to preserve, practice and foster culture by every means within his power.

And, since moral conduct constitutes the noblest flowering of culture, it is the duty of every man always to hold it in high respect.

CHAPTER ONE—RIGHTS

Article I—Right to life, liberty and personal security

Every human being has the right to life, liberty and the security of his person.

Article II—Right to equality before law

All persons are equal before the law and have the rights and duties established in this Declaration, without distinction as to race, sex, language, creed or any other factor.

Article III—Right to religious freedom and worship

Every person has the right freely to profess a religious faith, and to manifest and practice it both in public and in private.

Article IV — Right to freedom of investigation, opinion, expression and dissemination

Every person has the right to freedom of investigation, of opinion, and of the expression and dissemination of ideas, by any medium whatsoever.

Article V — Right to protection of honor, personal reputation, and private and family life

Every person has the right to the protection of the law against abusive attacks upon his honor, his reputation, and his private and family life.

Article VI — Right to a family and to protection thereof

Every person has the right to establish a family, the basic element of society, and to receive protection therefor.

Article VII — Right to protection for mothers and children

All women, during pregnancy and the nursing period, and all children have the right to special protection, care and aid.

Article VIII — Right to residence and movement

Every person has the right to fix his residence within the territory of the state of which he is a national, to move about freely within such territory, and not to leave it except by his own will.

Article IX — Right to inviolability of the home

Every person has the right to the inviolability of his home.

Article X — Right to the inviolability and transmission of correspondence

Every person has the right to the inviolability and transmission of his correspondence.

Article XI — Right to the preservation of health and to well-being

Every person has the right to the preservation of his health through sanitary and social measures relating to food, clothing, housing and medical care, to the extent permitted by public and community resources.

Article XII — Right to education

Every person has the right to an education, which should be based on the principles of liberty, morality and human solidarity.

Likewise every person has the right to an education that will prepare him to attain a decent life, to raise his standard of living, and to be a useful member of society.

The right to an education includes the right to equality of opportunity in every case, in accordance with natural talents, merit and the desire to utilize the resources that the state or the community is in a position to provide.

Every person has the right to receive, free, at least a primary education.

Article XIII — Right to the benefits of culture

Every person has the right to take part in the cultural life of the community, to enjoy the arts, and to participate in the benefits that result from intellectual progress, especially scientific discoveries.

He likewise has the right to the protection of his moral and material interests as regards his inventions or any literary, scientific or artistic works of which he is the author.

Article XIV — Right to work and to fair remuneration

Every person has the right to work, under proper conditions, and to follow his vocation freely, in so far as existing conditions of employment permit.

Every person who works has the right to receive such remuneration as will, in proportion to his capacity and skill, assure him a standard of living suitable for himself and for his family.

Article XV — Right to leisure time and to the use thereof

Every person has the right to leisure time, to wholesome recreation, and to the opportunity for advantageous use of his free time to his spiritual, cultural and physical benefit.

Article XVI — Right to social security

Every person has the right to social security which will protect him from the consequences of unemployment, old age, and any disabilities arising from causes beyond his control that make it physically or mentally impossible for him to earn a living.

Article XVII — Right to recognition of juridical personality and of civil rights

Every person has the right to be recognized everywhere as a person having rights and obligations, and to enjoy the basic civil rights.

Article XVIII — Right to a fair trial

Every person may resort to the courts to ensure respect for his legal rights. There should likewise be available to him a simple, brief procedure whereby the courts will protect him from acts of authority that, to his prejudice, violate any fundamental constitutional rights.

Article XIX — Right to nationality

Every person has the right to the nationality to which he is entitled by law and to change it, if he so wishes, for the nationality of any other country that is willing to grant it to him.

Article XX — Right to vote and to participate in government

Every person having legal capacity is entitled to participate in the government of his country, directly or through his representatives, and to take part in popular elections, which shall be by secret ballot, and shall be honest, periodic and free.

Article XXI — Right of assembly

Every person has the right to assemble peaceably with others in a formal public meeting or an informal gathering, in connection with matters of common interest of any nature.

Article XXII — Right of association

Every person has the right to associate with others to promote, exercise and protect his legitimate interests of a political, economic, religious, social, cultural, professional, labor union or other nature.

Article XXIII — Right to property

Every person has a right to own such private property as meets the essential needs of decent living and helps to maintain the dignity of the individual and of the home.

Article XXIV — Right of petition

Every person has the right to submit respectful petitions to any competent authority, for reasons of either general or private interest, and the right to obtain a prompt decision thereon.

Article XXV — Right of protection from arbitrary arrest

No person may be deprived of his liberty except in the cases and according to the procedures established by pre-existing law.

No person may be deprived of liberty for nonfulfillment of obligations of a purely civil character.

Every individual who has been deprived of his liberty has the right to have the legality of his detention ascertained without delay by a court, and the right to be tried without undue delay or, otherwise, to be released. He also has the right to humane treatment during the time he is in custody.

Article XXVI — Right to due process of law

Every accused person is presumed to be innocent until proved guilty.

Every person accused of an offense has the right to be given an impartial and public hearing, and to be tried by courts previously established in accordance with pre-existing laws, and not to receive cruel, infamous or unusual punishment.

Article XXVII — Right of asylum

Every person has the right, in case of pursuit not resulting from ordinary crimes, to seek and receive asylum in foreign territory, in accordance with the laws of each country and with international agreements.

Article XXVIII — Scope of the rights of man

The rights of man are limited by the rights of others, by the security of all, and by the just demands of the general welfare and the advancement of democracy.

CHAPTER TWO — DUTIES

Article XXIX — Duties to society

It is the duty of the individual so to conduct himself in relation to others that each and every one may fully form and develop his personality.

Article XXX — Duties toward children and parents

It is the duty of every person to aid, support, educate and protect his minor children, and it is the duty of children to honor their parents always and to aid, support and protect them when they need it.

Article XXXI — Duty to receive instruction

It is the duty of every person to acquire at least an elementary education.

Article XXXII.—Duty to vote

It is the duty of every person to vote in the popular elections of the country of which he is a national, when he is legally capable of doing so.

Article XXXIII—Duty to obey the law

It is the duty of every person to obey the law and other legitimate commands of the authorities of his country and those of the country in which he may be.

Article XXXIV—Duty to serve the community and the nation

It is the duty of every able-bodied person to render whatever civil and military service his country may require for its defense and preservation, and, in case of public disaster, to render such services as may be in his power.

It is likewise his duty to hold any public office to which he may be elected by popular vote in the state of which he is a national.

Article XXXV—Duties with respect to social security and welfare

It is the duty of every person to cooperate with the state and the community with respect to social security and welfare, in accordance with his ability and with existing circumstances.

Article XXXVI—Duty to pay taxes

It is the duty of every person to pay the taxes established by law for the support of public services.

Article XXXVII—Duty to work

It is the duty of every person to work, as far as his capacity and possibilities permit, in order to obtain the means of livelihood or to benefit his community.

Article XXXVIII—Duty to refrain from political activities in a foreign country

It is the duty of every person to refrain from taking part in political activities that, according to law, are reserved exclusively to the citizens of the state in which he is an alien.

American Convention on Human Rights, "Pact of San Jose, Costa Rica"
Nov. 22. 1969, S. Exec. Doc. F, 95-2, 1144 U.N.T.S. 123

[Ed. Note: The Convention entered into force July 18, 1978. As of March 7, 2003, twenty-five countries have ratified or acceded to the Convention. Twenty-two countries have accepted the jurisdiction of the Inter-American Court of Human Rights, pursuant to article 62. Pursuant to article 45, nine states have accepted the Commission's competence to adjudicate disputes between states on alleged violations of the Convention. The United States signed the Convention on June 1, 1977, but has not ratified the Convention. *See* http://www.cidh.oas.org/Basicos/basic4.htm.]

PREAMBLE

The American states signatory to the present Convention,

Reaffirming their intention to consolidate in this hemisphere, within the framework of democratic institutions, a system of personal liberty and social justice based on respect for the essential rights of man;

Recognizing that the essential rights of man are not derived from one's being a national of a certain state, but are based upon attributes of the human personality, and that they therefore justify international protection in the form of a convention reinforcing or complementing the protection provided by the domestic law of the American states;

Considering that these principles have been set forth in the Charter of the Organization of American States, in the American Declaration of the Rights and Duties of Man, and in the Universal Declaration of Human Rights, and that they have been reaffirmed and refined in other international instruments, worldwide as well as regional in scope;

Reiterating that, in accordance with the Universal Declaration of Human Rights, the ideal of free men enjoying freedom from fear and want can be achieved only if conditions are created whereby everyone may enjoy his economic, social, and cultural rights, as well as his civil and political rights; and

Considering that the Third Special Inter-American Conference (Buenos Aires, 1967) approved the incorporation into the Charter of the Organization itself of broader standards with respect to economic, social, and educational rights and resolved that an inter-American convention on human rights should determine the structure, competence, and procedure of the organs responsible for these matters,

Have agreed upon the following:

PART I—STATE OBLIGATIONS AND RIGHTS PROTECTED

CHAPTER I—GENERAL OBLIGATIONS

Article 1—Obligation to Respect Rights
1. The States Parties to this Convention undertake to respect the rights and freedoms recognized herein and to ensure to all persons subject to their jurisdiction the free and full exercise of those rights and freedoms, without any discrimination for reasons of race, color, sex, language, religion, political or other opinion, national or social origin, economic status, birth, or any other social condition.

2. For the purposes of this Convention, "person" means every human being.

Article 2—Domestic Legal Effects
Where the exercise of any of the rights or freedoms referred to in Article 1 is not already ensured by legislative or other provisions, the States Parties undertake to adopt, in accordance with their constitutional processes and the provisions of this Convention, such legislative or other measures as may be necessary to give effect to those rights or freedoms.

CHAPTER II—CIVIL AND POLITICAL RIGHTS

Article 3—Right to Juridical Personality
Every person has the right to recognition as a person before the law.

Article 4—Right to Life
1. Every person has the right to have his life respected. This right shall be protected by law and, in general, from the moment of conception. No one shall be arbitrarily deprived of his life.

2. In countries that have not abolished the death penalty, it may be imposed only for the most serious crimes and pursuant to a final judgment rendered by a competent

court and in accordance with a law establishing such punishment, enacted prior to the commission of the crime. The application of such punishment shall not be extended to crimes to which it does not presently apply.

3. The death penalty shall not be reestablished in states that have abolished it.

4. In no case shall capital punishment be inflicted for political offenses or related common crimes.

5. Capital punishment shall not be imposed upon persons who, at the time the crime was committed, were under 18 years of age or over 70 years of age; nor shall it be applied to pregnant women.

6. Every person condemned to death shall have the right to apply for amnesty, pardon, or commutation of sentence, which may be granted in all cases. Capital punishment shall not be imposed while such a petition is pending decision by the competent authority.

Article 5 — Right to Humane Treatment

1. Every person has the right to have his physical, mental, and moral integrity respected.

2. No one shall be subjected to torture or to cruel, inhuman, or degrading punishment or treatment. All persons deprived of their liberty shall be treated with respect for the inherent dignity of the human person.

3. Punishment shall not be extended to any person other than the criminal.

4. Accused persons shall, save in exceptional circumstances, be segregated from convicted persons, and shall be subject to separate treatment appropriate to their status as unconvicted persons.

5. Minors while subject to criminal proceedings shall be separated from adults and brought before specialized tribunals, as speedily as possible, so that they may be treated in accordance with their status as minors.

6. Punishments consisting of deprivation of liberty shall have as an essential aim the reform and social readaptation of the prisoners.

Article 6 — Freedom from Slavery

1. No one shall be subject to slavery or to involuntary servitude, which are prohibited in all their forms, as are the slave trade and traffic in women.

2. No one shall be required to perform forced or compulsory labor. This provision shall not be interpreted to mean that, in those countries in which the penalty established for certain crimes is deprivation of liberty at forced labor, the carrying out of such a sentence imposed by a competent court is prohibited. Forced labor shall not adversely affect the dignity or the physical or intellectual capacity of the prisoner.

3. For the purposes of this article, the following do not constitute forced or compulsory labor:

a. work or service normally required of a person imprisoned in execution of a sentence or formal decision passed by the competent judicial authority. Such work or service shall be carried out under the supervision and control of public authorities, and any persons performing such work or service shall not be placed at the disposal of any private party, company, or juridical person;

b. military service and, in countries in which conscientious objectors are recognized, national service that the law may provide for in lieu of military service;

c. service exacted in time of danger or calamity that threatens the existence or the well-being of the community; or

d. work or service that forms part of normal civic obligations.

Article 7 — Right to Personal Liberty

1. Every person has the right to personal liberty and security.

2. No one shall be deprived of his physical liberty except for the reasons and under the conditions established beforehand by the constitution of the State Party concerned or by a law established pursuant thereto.

3. No one shall be subject to arbitrary arrest or imprisonment.

4. Anyone who is detained shall be informed of the reasons for his detention and shall be promptly notified of the charge or charges against him.

5. Any person detained shall be brought promptly before a judge or other officer authorized by law to exercise judicial power and shall be entitled to trial within a reasonable time or to be released without prejudice to the continuation of the proceedings. His release may be subject to guarantees to assure his appearance for trial.

6. Anyone who is deprived of his liberty shall be entitled to recourse to a competent court, in order that the court may decide without delay on the lawfulness of his arrest or detention and order his release if the arrest or detention is unlawful. In States Parties whose laws provide that anyone who believes himself to be threatened with deprivation of his liberty is entitled to recourse to a competent court in order that it may decide on the lawfulness of such threat, this remedy may not be restricted or abolished. The interested party or another person in his behalf is entitled to seek these remedies.

7. No one shall be detained for debt. This principle shall not limit the orders of a competent judicial authority issued for nonfulfillment of duties of support.

[Ed. Note: Article 8 (right to a fair trial), article 9 (freedom from ex post facto laws), and article 10 (right to compensation) have been omitted.]

Article 11 — Right to Privacy

1. Everyone has the right to have his honor respected and his dignity recognized.

2. No one may be the object of arbitrary or abusive interference with his private life, his family, his home, or his correspondence, or of unlawful attacks on his honor or reputation.

3. Everyone has the right to the protection of the law against such interference or attacks.

Article 12 — Freedom of Conscience and Religion

1. Everyone has the right to freedom of conscience and of religion. This right includes freedom to maintain or to change one's religion or beliefs, and freedom to profess or disseminate one's religion or beliefs, either individually or together with others, in public or in private.

2. No one shall be subject to restrictions that might impair his freedom to maintain or to change his religion or beliefs.

3. Freedom to manifest one's religion and beliefs may be subject only to the limitations prescribed by law that are necessary to protect public safety, order, health, or morals, or the rights or freedoms of others.

4. Parents or guardians, as the case may be, have the right to provide for the religious and moral education of their children or wards that is in accord with their own convictions.

Article 13 — Freedom of Thought and Expression

1. Everyone has the right to freedom of thought and expression. This right includes freedom to seek, receive, and impart information and ideas of all kinds, regardless of

frontiers, either orally, in writing, in print, in the form of art, or through any other medium of one's choice.

2. The exercise of the right provided for in the foregoing paragraph shall not be subject to prior censorship but shall be subject to subsequent imposition of liability, which shall be expressly established by law to the extent necessary to ensure:

a. respect for the rights or reputations of others; or

b. the protection of national security, public order, or public health or morals.

3. The right of expression may not be restricted by indirect methods or means, such as the abuse of government or private controls over newsprint, radio broadcasting frequencies, or equipment used in the dissemination of information, or by any other means tending to impede the communication and circulation of ideas and opinions.

4. Notwithstanding the provisions of paragraph 2 above, public entertainments may be subject by law to prior censorship for the sole purpose of regulating access to them for the moral protection of childhood and adolescence.

5. Any propaganda for war and any advocacy of national, racial, or religious hatred that constitute incitements to lawless violence or to any other similar action against any person or group of persons on any grounds including those of race, color, religion, language, or national origin shall be considered as offenses punishable by law.

[Ed. Note: Article 14 (right of reply) and article 15 (right of assembly) have been omitted.]

Article 16 — Freedom of Association

1. Everyone has the right to associate freely for ideological, religious, political, economic, labor, social, cultural, sports, or other purposes.

2. The exercise of this right shall be subject only to such restrictions established by law as may be necessary in a democratic society, in the interest of national security, public safety or public order, or to protect public health or morals or the rights and freedoms of others.

3. The provisions of this article do not bar the imposition of legal restrictions, including even deprivation of the exercise of the right of association, on members of the armed forces and the police.

Article 17 — Rights of the Family

1. The family is the natural and fundamental group unit of society and is entitled to protection by society and the state.

2. The right of men and women of marriageable age to marry and to raise a family shall be recognized, if they meet the conditions required by domestic laws, insofar as such conditions do not affect the principle of nondiscrimination established in this Convention.

3. No marriage shall be entered into without the free and full consent of the intending spouses.

4. The States Parties shall take appropriate steps to ensure the equality of rights and the adequate balancing of responsibilities of the spouses as to marriage, during marriage, and in the event of its dissolution. In case of dissolution, provision shall be made for the necessary protection of any children solely on the basis of their own best interests.

5. The law shall recognize equal rights for children born out of wedlock and those born in wedlock.

Article 18 — Right to a Name

Every person has the right to a given name and to the surnames of his parents or that of one of them. The law shall regulate the manner in which this right shall be ensured for all, by the use of assumed names if necessary.

Article 19 — Rights of the Child

Every minor child has the right to the measures of protection required by his condition as a minor on the part of his family, society, and the state.

Article 20 — Right to Nationality

1. Every person has the right to a nationality.

2. Every person has the right to the nationality of the state in whose territory he was born if he does not have the right to any other nationality.

3. No one shall be arbitrarily deprived of his nationality or of the right to change it.

Article 21 — Right to Property

1. Everyone has the right to the use and enjoyment of his property. The law may subordinate such use and enjoyment to the interest of society.

2. No one shall be deprived of his property except upon payment of just compensation, for reasons of public utility or social interest, and in the cases and according to the forms established by law.

3. Usury and any other form of exploitation of man by man shall be prohibited by law.

Article 22 — Freedom of Movement and Residence

1. Every person lawfully in the territory of a State Party has the right to move about in it, and to reside in it subject to the provisions of the law.

2. Every person has the right to leave any country freely, including his own.

3. The exercise of the foregoing rights may be restricted only pursuant to a law to the extent necessary in a democratic society to prevent crime or to protect national security, public safety, public order, public morals, public health, or the rights or freedoms of others.

4. The exercise of the rights recognized in paragraph 1 may also be restricted by law in designated zones for reasons of public interest.

5. No one can be expelled from the territory of the state of which he is a national or be deprived of the right to enter it.

6. An alien lawfully in the territory of a State Party to this Convention may be expelled from it only pursuant to a decision reached in accordance with law.

7. Every person has the right to seek and be granted asylum in a foreign territory, in accordance with the legislation of the state and international conventions, in the event he is being pursued for political offenses or related common crimes.

8. In no case may an alien be deported or returned to a country, regardless of whether or not it is his country of origin, if in that country his right to life or personal freedom is in danger of being violated because of his race, nationality, religion, social status, or political opinions.

9. The collective expulsion of aliens is prohibited.

Article 23 — Right to Participate in Government

1. Every citizen shall enjoy the following rights and opportunities:

a. to take part in the conduct of public affairs, directly or through freely chosen representatives;

b. to vote and to be elected in genuine periodic elections, which shall be by universal and equal suffrage and by secret ballot that guarantees the free expression of the will of the voters; and

c. to have access, under general conditions of equality, to the public service of his country.

2. The law may regulate the exercise of the rights and opportunities referred to in the preceding paragraph only on the basis of age, nationality, residence, language, education, civil and mental capacity, or sentencing by a competent court in criminal proceedings.

Article 24 — Right to Equal Protection

All persons are equal before the law. Consequently, they are entitled, without discrimination, to equal protection of the law.

Article 25 — Right to Judicial Protection

1. Everyone has the right to simple and prompt recourse, or any other effective recourse, to a competent court or tribunal for protection against acts that violate his fundamental rights recognized by the constitution or laws of the state concerned or by this Convention, even though such violation may have been committed by persons acting in the course of their official duties.

2. The States Parties undertake:

a. to ensure that any person claiming such remedy shall have his rights determined by the competent authority provided for by the legal system of the state;

b. to develop the possibilities of judicial remedy; and

c. to ensure that the competent authorities shall enforce such remedies when granted.

CHAPTER III — ECONOMIC, SOCIAL, AND CULTURAL RIGHTS

Article 26 — Progressive Development

The States Parties undertake to adopt measures, both internally and through international cooperation, especially those of an economic and technical nature, with a view to achieving progressively, by legislation or other appropriate means, the full realization of the rights implicit in the economic, social, educational, scientific, and cultural standards set forth in the Charter of the Organization of American States as amended by the Protocol of Buenos Aires.

CHAPTER IV — SUSPENSION OF GUARANTEES, INTERPRETATION, AND APPLICATION

Article 27 — Suspension of Guarantees

1. In time of war, public danger, or other emergency that threatens the independence or security of a State Party, it may take measures derogating from its obligations under the present Convention to the extent and for the period of time strictly required by the exigencies of the situation, provided that such measures are not inconsistent with its other obligations under international law and do not involve discrimination on the ground of race, color, sex, language, religion, or social origin.

2. The foregoing provision does not authorize any suspension of the following articles: Article 3 (Right to Juridical Personality), Article 4 (Right to Life), Article 5 (Right to Humane Treatment), Article 6 (Freedom from Slavery), Article 9 (Freedom from Ex

Post Facto Laws), Article 12 (Freedom of Conscience and Religion), Article 17 (Rights of the Family), Article 18 (Right to a Name), Article 19 (Rights of the Child), Article 20 (Right to Nationality), and Article 23 (Right to Participate in Government), or of the judicial guarantees essential for the protection of such rights.

3. Any State Party availing itself of the right of suspension shall immediately inform the other States Parties, through the Secretary General of the Organization of American States, of the provisions the application of which it has suspended, the reasons that gave rise to the suspension, and the date set for the termination of such suspension.

Article 28 — Federal Clause

1. Where a State Party is constituted as a federal state, the national government of such State Party shall implement all the provisions of the Convention over whose subject matter it exercises legislative and judicial jurisdiction.

2. With respect to the provisions over whose subject matter the constituent units of the federal state have jurisdiction, the national government shall immediately take suitable measures, in accordance with its constitution and its laws, to the end that the competent authorities of the constituent units may adopt appropriate provisions for the fulfillment of this Convention.

3. Whenever two or more States Parties agree to form a federation or other type of association, they shall take care that the resulting federal or other compact contains the provisions necessary for continuing and rendering effective the standards of this Convention in the new state that is organized.

Article 29 — Restrictions Regarding Interpretation

No provision of this Convention shall be interpreted as:

a. permitting any State Party, group, or person to suppress the enjoyment or exercise of the rights and freedoms recognized in this Convention or to restrict them to a greater extent than is provided for herein;

b. restricting the enjoyment or exercise of any right or freedom recognized by virtue of the laws of any State Party or by virtue of another convention to which one of the said states is a party;

c. precluding other rights or guarantees that are inherent in the human personality or derived from representative democracy as a form of government; or

d. excluding or limiting the effect that the American Declaration of the Rights and Duties of Man and other international acts of the same nature may have.

Article 30 — Scope of Restrictions

The restrictions that, pursuant to this Convention, may be placed on the enjoyment or exercise of the rights or freedoms recognized herein may not be applied except in accordance with laws enacted for reasons of general interest and in accordance with the purpose for which such restrictions have been established.

Article 31 — Recognition of Other Rights

Other rights and freedoms recognized in accordance with the procedures established in Articles 76 and 77 may be included in the system of protection of this Convention.

CHAPTER V — PERSONAL RESPONSIBILITIES

Article 32 — Relationship between Duties and Rights

1. Every person has responsibilities to his family, his community, and mankind.

2. The rights of each person are limited by the rights of others, by the security of all, and by the just demands of the general welfare, in a democratic society.

PART II—MEANS OF PROTECTION

CHAPTER VI—COMPETENT ORGANS

Article 33

The following organs shall have competence with respect to matters relating to the fulfillment of the commitments made by the States Parties to this Convention:

a. the Inter-American Commission on Human Rights, referred to as "The Commission;" and

b. the Inter-American Court of Human Rights, referred to as "The Court."

CHAPTER VII—INTER-AMERICAN COMMISSION ON HUMAN RIGHTS

Section 1—Organization

Article 34

The Inter-American Commission on Human Rights shall be composed of seven members, who shall be persons of high moral character and recognized competence in the field of human rights.

Article 35

The Commission shall represent all the member countries of the Organization of American States.

Article 36

1. The members of the Commission shall be elected in a personal capacity by the General Assembly of the Organization from a list of candidates proposed by the governments of the member states.

2. Each of those governments may propose up to three candidates, who may be nationals of the states proposing them or of any other member state of the Organization of American States. When a slate of three is proposed, at least one of the candidates shall be a national of a state other than the one proposing the slate.

Article 37

1. The members of the Commission shall be elected for a term of four years and may be reelected only once, but the terms of three of the members chosen in the first election shall expire at the end of two years. Immediately following that election the General Assembly shall determine the names of those three members by lot.

2. No two nationals of the same state may be members of the Commission.

Article 38

Vacancies that may occur on the Commission for reasons other than the normal expiration of a term shall be filled by the Permanent Council of the Organization in accordance with the provisions of the Statute of the Commission.

Article 39

The Commission shall prepare its Statute, which it shall submit to the General Assembly for approval. It shall establish its own Regulations.

Article 40

Secretariat services for the Commission shall be furnished by the appropriate specialized unit of the General Secretariat of the Organization. This unit shall be provided with the resources required to accomplish the tasks assigned to it by the Commission.

Section 2—Functions

Article 41

The main function of the Commission shall be to promote respect for and defense of human rights. In the exercise of its mandate, it shall have the following functions and powers:

a. to develop an awareness of human rights among the peoples of America;

b. to make recommendations to the governments of the member states, when it considers such action advisable, for the adoption of progressive measures in favor of human rights within the framework of their domestic law and constitutional provisions as well as appropriate measures to further the observance of those rights;

c. to prepare such studies or reports as it considers advisable in the performance of its duties;

d. to request the governments of the member states to supply it with information on the measures adopted by them in matters of human rights;

e. to respond, through the General Secretariat of the Organization of American States, to inquiries made by the member states on matters related to human rights and, within the limits of its possibilities, to provide those states with the advisory services they request;

f. to take action on petitions and other communications pursuant to its authority under the provisions of Articles 44 through 51 of this Convention; and

g. to submit an annual report to the General Assembly of the Organization of American States.

Article 42

The States Parties shall transmit to the Commission a copy of each of the reports and studies that they submit annually to the Executive Committees of the Inter-American Economic and Social Council and the Inter-American Council for Education, Science, and Culture, in their respective fields, so that the Commission may watch over the promotion of the rights implicit in the economic, social, educational, scientific, and cultural standards set forth in the Charter of the Organization of American States as amended by the Protocol of Buenos Aires.

Article 43

The States Parties undertake to provide the Commission with such information as it may request of them as to the manner in which their domestic law ensures the effective application of any provisions of this Convention.

Section 3—Competence

Article 44

Any person or group of persons, or any nongovernmental entity legally recognized in one or more member states of the Organization, may lodge petitions with the Commission containing denunciations or complaints of violation of this Convention by a State Party.

Article 45

1. Any State Party may, when it deposits its instrument of ratification of or adherence to this Convention, or at any later time, declare that it recognizes the competence of the Commission to receive and examine communications in which a State Party alleges that another State Party has committed a violation of a human right set forth in this Convention.

2. Communications presented by virtue of this article may be admitted and examined only if they are presented by a State Party that has made a declaration recognizing the aforementioned competence of the Commission. The Commission shall not admit any communication against a State Party that has not made such a declaration.

3. A declaration concerning recognition of competence may be made to be valid for an indefinite time, for a specified period, or for a specific case.

4. Declarations shall be deposited with the General Secretariat of the Organization of American States, which shall transmit copies thereof to the member states of that Organization.

Article 46

1. Admission by the Commission of a petition or communication lodged in accordance with Articles 44 or 45 shall be subject to the following requirements:

a. that the remedies under domestic law have been pursued and exhausted in accordance with generally recognized principles of international law;

b. that the petition or communication is lodged within a period of six months from the date on which the party alleging violation of his rights was notified of the final judgment;

c. that the subject of the petition or communication is not pending in another international proceeding for settlement; and

d. that, in the case of Article 44, the petition contains the name, nationality, profession, domicile, and signature of the person or persons or of the legal representative of the entity lodging the petition.

2. The provisions of paragraphs 1.a and 1.b of this article shall not be applicable when:

a. the domestic legislation of the state concerned does not afford due process of law for the protection of the right or rights that have allegedly been violated;

b. the party alleging violation of his rights has been denied access to the remedies under domestic law or has been prevented from exhausting them; or

c. there has been unwarranted delay in rendering a final judgment under the aforementioned remedies.

Article 47

The Commission shall consider inadmissible any petition or communication submitted under Articles 44 or 45 if:

a. any of the requirements indicated in Article 46 has not been met;

b. the petition or communication does not state facts that tend to establish a violation of the rights guaranteed by this Convention;

c. the statements of the petitioner or of the state indicate that the petition or communication is manifestly groundless or obviously out of order; or

d. the petition or communication is substantially the same as one previously studied by the Commission or by another international organization.

Section 4—Procedure

Article 48

1. When the Commission receives a petition or communication alleging violation of any of the rights protected by this Convention, it shall proceed as follows:

a. If it considers the petition or communication admissible, it shall request information from the government of the state indicated as being responsible for the alleged violations and shall furnish that government a transcript of the pertinent portions of the petition or communication. This information shall be submitted within a reasonable period to be determined by the Commission in accordance with the circumstances of each case.

b. After the information has been received, or after the period established has elapsed and the information has not been received, the Commission shall ascertain whether the grounds for the petition or communication still exist. If they do not, the Commission shall order the record to be closed.

c. The Commission may also declare the petition or communication inadmissible or out of order on the basis of information or evidence subsequently received.

d. If the record has not been closed, the Commission shall, with the knowledge of the parties, examine the matter set forth in the petition or communication in order to verify the facts. If necessary and advisable, the Commission shall carry out an investigation, for the effective conduct of which it shall request, and the states concerned shall furnish to it, all necessary facilities.

e. The Commission may request the states concerned to furnish any pertinent information and, if so requested, shall hear oral statements or receive written statements from the parties concerned.

f. The Commission shall place itself at the disposal of the parties concerned with a view to reaching a friendly settlement of the matter on the basis of respect for the human rights recognized in this Convention.

2. However, in serious and urgent cases, only the presentation of a petition or communication that fulfills all the formal requirements of admissibility shall be necessary in order for the Commission to conduct an investigation with the prior consent of the state in whose territory a violation has allegedly been committed.

Article 49

If a friendly settlement has been reached in accordance with paragraph 1.f of Article 48, the Commission shall draw up a report, which shall be transmitted to the petitioner and to the States Parties to this Convention, and shall then be communicated to the Secretary General of the Organization of American States for publication. This report shall contain a brief statement of the facts and of the solution reached. If any party in the case so requests, the fullest possible information shall be provided to it.

Article 50

1. If a settlement is not reached, the Commission shall, within the time limit established by its Statute, draw up a report setting forth the facts and stating its conclusions. If the report, in whole or in part, does not represent the unanimous agreement of the members of the Commission, any member may attach to it a separate opinion. The written and oral statements made by the parties in accordance with paragraph 1.e of Article 48 shall also be attached to the report.

2. The report shall be transmitted to the states concerned, which shall not be at liberty to publish it.

3. In transmitting the report, the Commission may make such proposals and recommendations as it sees fit.

Article 51

1. If, within a period of three months from the date of the transmittal of the report of the Commission to the states concerned, the matter has not either been settled or submitted by the Commission or by the state concerned to the Court and its jurisdiction accepted, the Commission may, by the vote of an absolute majority of its members, set forth its opinion and conclusions concerning the question submitted for its consideration.

2. Where appropriate, the Commission shall make pertinent recommendations and shall prescribe a period within which the state is to take the measures that are incumbent upon it to remedy the situation examined.

3. When the prescribed period has expired, the Commission shall decide by the vote of an absolute majority of its members whether the state has taken adequate measures and whether to publish its report.

CHAPTER VIII—INTER-AMERICAN COURT OF HUMAN RIGHTS

Section 1—Organization

Article 52

1. The Court shall consist of seven judges, nationals of the member states of the Organization, elected in an individual capacity from among jurists of the highest moral authority and of recognized competence in the field of human rights, who possess the qualifications required for the exercise of the highest judicial functions in conformity with the law of the state of which they are nationals or of the state that proposes them as candidates.

2. No two judges may be nationals of the same state.

Article 53

1. The judges of the Court shall be elected by secret ballot by an absolute majority vote of the States Parties to the Convention, in the General Assembly of the Organization, from a panel of candidates proposed by those states.

2. Each of the States Parties may propose up to three candidates, nationals of the state that proposes them or of any other member state of the Organization of American States. When a slate of three is proposed, at least one of the candidates shall be a national of a state other than the one proposing the slate.

Article 54

1. The judges of the Court shall be elected for a term of six years and may be re-elected only once. The term of three of the judges chosen in the first election shall ex-

pire at the end of three years. Immediately after the election, the names of the three judges shall be determined by lot in the General Assembly.

2. A judge elected to replace a judge whose term has not expired shall complete the term of the latter.

3. The judges shall continue in office until the expiration of their term. However, they shall continue to serve with regard to cases that they have begun to hear and that are still pending, for which purposes they shall not be replaced by the newly elected judges.

Article 55

1. If a judge is a national of any of the States Parties to a case submitted to the Court, he shall retain his right to hear that case.

2. If one of the judges called upon to hear a case should be a national of one of the States Parties to the case, any other State Party in the case may appoint a person of its choice to serve on the Court as an ad hoc judge.

3. If among the judges called upon to hear a case none is a national of any of the States Parties to the case, each of the latter may appoint an ad hoc judge.

4. An ad hoc judge shall possess the qualifications indicated in Article 52.

5. If several States Parties to the Convention should have the same interest in a case, they shall be considered as a single party for purposes of the above provisions. In case of doubt, the Court shall decide.

Article 56

Five judges shall constitute a quorum for the transaction of business by the Court.

Article 57

The Commission shall appear in all cases before the Court.

Article 58

1. The Court shall have its seat at the place determined by the States Parties to the Convention in the General Assembly of the Organization; however, it may convene in the territory of any member state of the Organization of American States when a majority of the Court considers it desirable, and with the prior consent of the state concerned. The seat of the Court may be changed by the States Parties to the Convention in the General Assembly by a two-thirds vote.

2. The Court shall appoint its own Secretary.

3. The Secretary shall have his office at the place where the Court has its seat and shall attend the meetings that the Court may hold away from its seat.

Article 59

The Court shall establish its Secretariat, which shall function under the direction of the Secretary of the Court, in accordance with the administrative standards of the General Secretariat of the Organization in all respects not incompatible with the independence of the Court. The staff of the Court's Secretariat shall be appointed by the Secretary General of the Organization, in consultation with the Secretary of the Court.

Article 60

The Court shall draw up its Statute which it shall submit to the General Assembly for approval. It shall adopt its own Rules of Procedure.

Section 2 — Jurisdiction and Functions

Article 61

1. Only the States Parties and the Commission shall have the right to submit a case to the Court.

2. In order for the Court to hear a case, it is necessary that the procedures set forth in Articles 48 and 50 shall have been completed.

Article 62

1. A State Party may, upon depositing its instrument of ratification or adherence to this Convention, or at any subsequent time, declare that it recognizes as binding, ipso facto, and not requiring special agreement, the jurisdiction of the Court on all matters relating to the interpretation or application of this Convention.

2. Such declaration may be made unconditionally, on the condition of reciprocity, for a specified period, or for specific cases. It shall be presented to the Secretary General of the Organization, who shall transmit copies thereof to the other member states of the Organization and to the Secretary of the Court.

3. The jurisdiction of the Court shall comprise all cases concerning the interpretation and application of the provisions of this Convention that are submitted to it, provided that the States Parties to the case recognize or have recognized such jurisdiction, whether by special declaration pursuant to the preceding paragraphs, or by a special agreement.

Article 63

1. If the Court finds that there has been a violation of a right or freedom protected by this Convention, the Court shall rule that the injured party be ensured the enjoyment of his right or freedom that was violated. It shall also rule, if appropriate, that the consequences of the measure or situation that constituted the breach of such right or freedom be remedied and that fair compensation be paid to the injured party.

2. In cases of extreme gravity and urgency, and when necessary to avoid irreparable damage to persons, the Court shall adopt such provisional measures as it deems pertinent in matters it has under consideration. With respect to a case not yet submitted to the Court, it may act at the request of the Commission.

Article 64

1. The member states of the Organization may consult the Court regarding the interpretation of this Convention or of other treaties concerning the protection of human rights in the American states. Within their spheres of competence, the organs listed in Chapter X of the Charter of the Organization of American States, as amended by the Protocol of Buenos Aires, may in like manner consult the Court.

2. The Court, at the request of a member state of the Organization, may provide that state with opinions regarding the compatibility of any of its domestic laws with the aforesaid international instruments.

Article 65

To each regular session of the General Assembly of the Organization of American States the Court shall submit, for the Assembly's consideration, a report on its work during the previous year. It shall specify, in particular, the cases in which a state has not complied with its judgments, making any pertinent recommendations.

Section 3 — Procedure

Article 66

1. Reasons shall be given for the judgment of the Court.

2. If the judgment does not represent in whole or in part the unanimous opinion of the judges, any judge shall be entitled to have his dissenting or separate opinion attached to the judgment.

Article 67

The judgment of the Court shall be final and not subject to appeal. In case of disagreement as to the meaning or scope of the judgment, the Court shall interpret it at the request of any of the parties, provided the request is made within ninety days from the date of notification of the judgment.

Article 68

1. The States Parties to the Convention undertake to comply with the judgment of the Court in any case to which they are parties.

2. That part of a judgment that stipulates compensatory damages may be executed in the country concerned in accordance with domestic procedure governing the execution of judgments against the state.

Article 69

The parties to the case shall be notified of the judgment of the Court and it shall be transmitted to the States Parties to the Convention.

[Ed. Note: Chapter IX, entitled common provisions, has been omitted. It contained articles 70–73, which addressed the privileges and responsibilities of judges and Commission members.]

PART III — GENERAL AND TRANSITORY PROVISIONS

[Ed. Note: Chapter X, which included article 74 (signature & ratification), article 75 (reservations), article 76 (amendment), article 77 (protocols), and article 78 (denunciation), has been omitted. In addition, Chapter XI, entitled transitory provisions, has been omitted. It contained articles 79–82, addressing the initial composition of the Court and Commission.]

Additional Protocol to the American Convention on Human Rights in the Area of Economic, Social and Cultural Rights, "Protocol of San Salvador"

November 17, 1988, O.A.S. Treaty Series No. 69, 28 I.L.M. 161

[Ed. Note: The treaty entered into force on Nov. 16, 1999. As of March 7, 2003, twelve countries have deposited their instruments of ratification, and an additional seven countries are signatories. *See* http://www.oas.org/juridico/english/sigs/9-82.html. The U.S. could not become a party to this protocol since the U.S. is not a State Party to the American Convention on Human Rights. *See* art. 21 *infra*.]

PREAMBLE

The States Parties to the American Convention on Human Rights "Pact San José, Costa Rica,"

Reaffirming their intention to consolidate in this hemisphere, within the framework of democratic institutions, a system of personal liberty and social justice based on respect for the essential rights of man;

Recognizing that the essential rights of man are not derived from one's being a national of a certain State, but are based upon attributes of the human person, for which reason they merit international protection in the form of a convention reinforcing or complementing the protection provided by the domestic law of the American States;

Considering the close relationship that exists between economic, social and cultural rights, and civil and political rights, in that the different categories of rights constitute an indivisible whole based on the recognition of the dignity of the human person, for which reason both require permanent protection and promotion if they are to be fully realized, and the violation of some rights in favor of the realization of others can never be justified;

Recognizing the benefits that stem from the promotion and development of cooperation among States and international relations;

Recalling that, in accordance with the Universal Declaration of Human Rights and the American Convention on Human Rights, the ideal of free human beings enjoying freedom from fear and want can only be achieved if conditions are created whereby everyone may enjoy his economic, social and cultural rights as well as his civil and political rights;

Bearing in mind that, although fundamental economic, social and cultural rights have been recognized in earlier international instruments of both world and regional scope, it is essential that those rights be reaffirmed, developed, perfected and protected in order to consolidate in America, on the basis of full respect for the rights of the individual, the democratic representative form of government as well as the right of its peoples to development, self-determination, and the free disposal of their wealth and natural resources; and

Considering that the American Convention on Human Rights provides that draft additional protocols to that Convention may be submitted for consideration to the States Parties, meeting together on the occasion of the General Assembly of the Organization of American States, for the purpose of gradually incorporating other rights and freedoms into the protective system thereof,

Have agreed upon the following Additional Protocol to the American Convention on Human Rights "Protocol of San Salvador:"

Article 1 — Obligation to Adopt Measures

The States Parties to this Additional Protocol to the American Convention on Human Rights undertake to adopt the necessary measures, both domestically and through international cooperation, especially economic and technical, to the extent allowed by their available resources, and taking into account their degree of development, for the purpose of achieving progressively and pursuant to their internal legislations, the full observance of the rights recognized in this Protocol.

Article 2 — Obligation to Enact Domestic Legislation

If the exercise of the rights set forth in this Protocol is not already guaranteed by legislative or other provisions, the States Parties undertake to adopt, in accordance with their constitutional processes and the provisions of this Protocol, such legislative or other measures as may be necessary for making those rights a reality.

Article 3 — Obligation of nondiscrimination

The State Parties to this Protocol undertake to guarantee the exercise of the rights set forth herein without discrimination of any kind for reasons related to race, color, sex, language, religion, political or other opinions, national or social origin, economic status, birth or any other social condition.

Article 4 — Inadmissibility of Restrictions

A right which is recognized or in effect in a State by virtue of its internal legislation or international conventions may not be restricted or curtailed on the pretext that this Protocol does not recognize the right or recognizes it to a lesser degree.

Article 5 — Scope of Restrictions and Limitations

The State Parties may establish restrictions and limitations on the enjoyment and exercise of the rights established herein by means of laws promulgated for the purpose of preserving the general welfare in a democratic society only to the extent that they are not incompatible with the purpose and reason underlying those rights.

Article 6 — Right to Work

1. Everyone has the right to work, which includes the opportunity to secure the means for living a dignified and decent existence by performing a freely elected or accepted lawful activity.

2. The State Parties undertake to adopt measures that will make the right to work fully effective, especially with regard to the achievement of full employment, vocational guidance, and the development of technical and vocational training projects, in particular those directed to the disabled. The States Parties also undertake to implement and strengthen programs that help to ensure suitable family care, so that women may enjoy a real opportunity to exercise the right to work.

Article 7 — Just, Equitable, and Satisfactory Conditions of Work

The States Parties to this Protocol recognize that the right to work to which the foregoing article refers presupposes that everyone shall enjoy that right under just, equitable, and satisfactory conditions, which the States Parties undertake to guarantee in their internal legislation, particularly with respect to:

a. Remuneration which guarantees, as a minimum, to all workers dignified and decent living conditions for them and their families and fair and equal wages for equal work, without distinction;

b. The right of every worker to follow his vocation and to devote himself to the activity that best fulfills his expectations and to change employment in accordance with the pertinent national regulations;

c. The right of every worker to promotion or upward mobility in his employment, for which purpose account shall be taken of his qualifications, competence, integrity and seniority;

d. Stability of employment, subject to the nature of each industry and occupation and the causes for just separation. In cases of unjustified dismissal, the worker shall have the right to indemnity or to reinstatement on the job or any other benefits provided by domestic legislation;

e. Safety and hygiene at work;

f. The prohibition of night work or unhealthy or dangerous working conditions and, in general, of all work which jeopardizes health, safety, or morals, for persons under 18 years of age. As regards minors under the age of 16, the work day shall be subordinated to the provisions regarding compulsory education and in no case shall work constitute an impediment to school attendance or a limitation on benefiting from education received;

g. A reasonable limitation of working hours, both daily and weekly. The days shall be shorter in the case of dangerous or unhealthy work or of night work;

h. Rest, leisure and paid vacations as well as remuneration for national holidays.

Article 8 — Trade Union Rights

1. The States Parties shall ensure:

a. The right of workers to organize trade unions and to join the union of their choice for the purpose of protecting and promoting their interests. As an extension of that right, the States Parties shall permit trade unions to establish national federations or confederations, or to affiliate with those that already exist, as well as to form international trade union organizations and to affiliate with that of their choice. The States Parties shall also permit trade unions, federations and confederations to function freely;

b. The right to strike.

2. The exercise of the rights set forth above may be subject only to restrictions established by law, provided that such restrictions are characteristic of a democratic society and necessary for safeguarding public order or for protecting public health or morals or the rights and freedoms of others. Members of the armed forces and the police and of other essential public services shall be subject to limitations and restrictions established by law.

3. No one may be compelled to belong to a trade union.

Article 9 — Right to Social Security

1. Everyone shall have the right to social security protecting him from the consequences of old age and of disability which prevents him, physically or mentally, from securing the means for a dignified and decent existence. In the event of the death of a beneficiary, social security benefits shall be applied to his dependents.

2. In the case of persons who are employed, the right to social security shall cover at least medical care and an allowance or retirement benefit in the case of work accidents or occupational disease and, in the case of women, paid maternity leave before and after childbirth.

Article 10 — Right to Health

1. Everyone shall have the right to health, understood to mean the enjoyment of the highest level of physical, mental and social well-being.

2. In order to ensure the exercise of the right to health, the States Parties agree to recognize health as a public good and, particularly, to adopt the following measures to ensure that right:

a. Primary health care, that is, essential health care made available to all individuals and families in the community;

b. Extension of the benefits of health services to all individuals subject to the State's jurisdiction;

c. Universal immunization against the principal infectious diseases;

d. Prevention and treatment of endemic, occupational and other diseases;

e. Education of the population on the prevention and treatment of health problems, and

f. Satisfaction of the health needs of the highest risk groups and of those whose poverty makes them the most vulnerable.

Article 11 — Right to a Healthy Environment

1. Everyone shall have the right to live in a healthy environment and to have access to basic public services.

2. The States Parties shall promote the protection, preservation, and improvement of the environment.

Article 12 — Right to Food

1. Everyone has the right to adequate nutrition which guarantees the possibility of enjoying the highest level of physical, emotional and intellectual development.

2. In order to promote the exercise of this right and eradicate malnutrition, the States Parties undertake to improve methods of production, supply and distribution of food, and to this end, agree to promote greater international cooperation in support of the relevant national policies.

Article 13 — Right to Education

1. Everyone has the right to education.

2. The States Parties to this Protocol agree that education should be directed towards the full development of the human personality and human dignity and should strengthen respect for human rights, ideological pluralism, fundamental freedoms, justice and peace. They further agree that education ought to enable everyone to participate effectively in a democratic and pluralistic society and achieve a decent existence and should foster understanding, tolerance and friendship among all nations and all racial, ethnic or religious groups and promote activities for the maintenance of peace.

3. The States Parties to this Protocol recognize that in order to achieve the full exercise of the right to education:

    a. Primary education should be compulsory and accessible to all without cost;

    b. Secondary education in its different forms, including technical and vocational secondary education, should be made generally available and accessible to all by every appropriate means, and in particular, by the progressive introduction of free education;

    c. Higher education should be made equally accessible to all, on the basis of individual capacity, by every appropriate means, and in particular, by the progressive introduction of free education;

    d. Basic education should be encouraged or intensified as far as possible for those persons who have not received or completed the whole cycle of primary instruction;

    e. Programs of special education should be established for the handicapped, so as to provide special instruction and training to persons with physical disabilities or mental deficiencies.

4. In conformity with the domestic legislation of the States Parties, parents should have the right to select the type of education to be given to their children, provided that it conforms to the principles set forth above.

5. Nothing in this Protocol shall be interpreted as a restriction of the freedom of individuals and entities to establish and direct educational institutions in accordance with the domestic legislation of the States Parties.

Article 14 — Right to the Benefits of Culture

1. The States Parties to this Protocol recognize the right of everyone:

a. To take part in the cultural and artistic life of the community;

b. To enjoy the benefits of scientific and technological progress;

c. To benefit from the protection of moral and material interests deriving from any scientific, literary or artistic production of which he is the author.

2. The steps to be taken by the States Parties to this Protocol to ensure the full exercise of this right shall include those necessary for the conservation, development and dissemination of science, culture and art.

3. The States Parties to this Protocol undertake to respect the freedom indispensable for scientific research and creative activity.

4. The States Parties to this Protocol recognize the benefits to be derived from the encouragement and development of international cooperation and relations in the fields of science, arts and culture, and accordingly agree to foster greater international cooperation in these fields.

Article 15 — Right to the Formation and the Protection of Families

1. The family is the natural and fundamental element of society and ought to be protected by the State, which should see to the improvement of its spiritual and material conditions.

2. Everyone has the right to form a family, which shall be exercised in accordance with the provisions of the pertinent domestic legislation.

3. The States Parties hereby undertake to accord adequate protection to the family unit and in particular:

a. To provide special care and assistance to mothers during a reasonable period before and after childbirth;

b. To guarantee adequate nutrition for children at the nursing stage and during school attendance years;

c. To adopt special measures for the protection of adolescents in order to ensure the full development of their physical, intellectual and moral capacities;

d. To undertake special programs of family training so as to help create a stable and positive environment in which children will receive and develop the values of understanding, solidarity, respect and responsibility.

Article 16 — Rights of Children

Every child, whatever his parentage, has the right to the protection that his status as a minor requires from his family, society and the State. Every child has the right to grow under the protection and responsibility of his parents; save in exceptional, judicially-recognized circumstances, a child of young age ought not to be separated from his mother. Every child has the right to free and compulsory education, at least in the elementary phase, and to continue his training at higher levels of the educational system.

Article 17 — Protection of the Elderly

Everyone has the right to special protection in old age. With this in view the States Parties agree to take progressively the necessary steps to make this right a reality and, particularly, to:

a. Provide suitable facilities, as well as food and specialized medical care, for elderly individuals who lack them and are unable to provide them for themselves;

b. Undertake work programs specifically designed to give the elderly the opportunity to engage in a productive activity suited to their abilities and consistent with their vocations or desires;

c. Foster the establishment of social organizations aimed at improving the quality of life for the elderly.

Article 18 — Protection of the Handicapped

Everyone affected by a diminution of his physical or mental capacities is entitled to receive special attention designed to help him achieve the greatest possible development of his personality. The States Parties agree to adopt such measures as may be necessary for this purpose and, especially, to:

a. Undertake programs specifically aimed at providing the handicapped with the resources and environment needed for attaining this goal, including work programs consistent with their possibilities and freely accepted by them or their legal representatives, as the case may be;

b. Provide special training to the families of the handicapped in order to help them solve the problems of coexistence and convert them into active agents in the physical, mental and emotional development of the latter;

c. Include the consideration of solutions to specific requirements arising from needs of this group as a priority component of their urban development plans;

d. Encourage the establishment of social groups in which the handicapped can be helped to enjoy a fuller life.

Article 19 — Means of Protection

1. Pursuant to the provisions of this article and the corresponding rules to be formulated for this purpose by the General Assembly of the Organization of American States, the States Parties to this Protocol undertake to submit periodic reports on the progressive measures they have taken to ensure due respect for the rights set forth in this Protocol.

2. All reports shall be submitted to the Secretary General of the OAS, who shall transmit them to the Inter-American Economic and Social Council and the Inter-American Council for Education, Science and Culture so that they may examine them in accordance with the provisions of this article. The Secretary General shall send a copy of such reports to the Inter-American Commission on Human Rights.

3. The Secretary General of the Organization of American States shall also transmit to the specialized organizations of the inter-American system of which the States Parties to the present Protocol are members, copies or pertinent portions of the reports submitted, insofar as they relate to matters within the purview of those organizations, as established by their constituent instruments.

4. The specialized organizations of the inter-American system may submit reports to the Inter-American Economic and Social Council and the Inter-American Council for Education, Science and Culture relative to compliance with the provisions of the present Protocol in their fields of activity.

5. The annual reports submitted to the General Assembly by the Inter-American Economic and Social Council and the Inter-American Council for Education, Science and Culture shall contain a summary of the information received from the States Parties to the present Protocol and the specialized organizations concerning the progressive measures adopted in order to ensure respect for the rights acknowledged in the Protocol itself and the general recommendations they consider to be appropriate in this respect.

6. Any instance in which the rights established in paragraph a) of Article 8 and in Article 13 are violated by action directly attributable to a State Party to this Protocol may give rise, through participation of the Inter-American Commission on Human Rights

and, when applicable, of the Inter-American Court of Human Rights, to application of the system of individual petitions governed by Article 44 through 51 and 61 through 69 of the American Convention on Human Rights.

7. Without prejudice to the provisions of the preceding paragraph, the Inter-American Commission on Human Rights may formulate such observations and recommendations as it deems pertinent concerning the status of the economic, social and cultural rights established in the present Protocol in all or some of the States Parties, which it may include in its Annual Report to the General Assembly or in a special report, whichever it considers more appropriate.

8. The Councils and the Inter-American Commission on Human Rights, in discharging the functions conferred upon them in this article, shall take into account the progressive nature of the observance of the rights subject to protection by this Protocol.

Article 20 — Reservations

The States Parties may, at the time of approval, signature, ratification or accession, make reservations to one or more specific provisions of this Protocol, provided that such reservations are not incompatible with the object and purpose of the Protocol.

Article 21 — Signature, Ratification or Accession (Entry into Effect)

1. This Protocol shall remain open to signature and ratification or accession by any State Party to the American Convention on Human Rights.

2. Ratification of or accession to this Protocol shall be effected by depositing an instrument of ratification or accession with the General Secretariat of the Organization of American States.

3. The Protocol shall enter into effect when eleven States have deposited their respective instruments of ratification or accession.

4. The Secretary General shall notify all the member states of the Organization of American States of the entry of the Protocol into effect.

Article 22 — Inclusion of other Rights and Expansion of those Recognized

1. Any State Party and the Inter-American Commission on Human Rights may submit for the consideration of the States Parties meeting on the occasion of the General Assembly proposed amendments to include the recognition of other rights or freedoms or to extend or expand rights or freedoms recognized in this Protocol.

2. Such amendments shall enter into effect for the States that ratify them on the date of deposit of the instrument of ratification corresponding to the number representing two thirds of the States Parties to this Protocol. For all other States Parties they shall enter into effect on the date on which they deposit their respective instrument of ratification.

Protocol to the American Convention on Human Rights to Abolish the Death Penalty
June 8, 1990, O.A.S. Treaty Series 73, 29 I.L.M. 1447.

[Ed. Note: Eight countries have ratified this Convention as of February 17, 2002. The U.S. has not signed the protocol, *see* http://www.cidh.oas.org/Basicos/basic8.htm, nor could it since the U.S. is not a State Party to the American Convention on Human Rights. *See* art. 3 *infra*. The Convention entered into force immediately for those countries that ratified it.]

PREAMBLE

THE STATES PARTIES TO THIS PROTOCOL, CONSIDERING:

That Article 4 of the American Convention on Human Rights recognizes the right to life and restricts the application of the death penalty;

That everyone has the inalienable right to respect for his life, a right that cannot be suspended for any reason;

That the tendency among the American States is to be in favor of abolition of the death penalty;

That application of the death penalty has irrevocable consequences, forecloses the correction of judicial error, and precludes any possibility of changing or rehabilitating those convicted;

That the abolition of the death penalty helps to ensure more effective protection of the right to life;

That an international agreement must be arrived at that will entail a progressive development of the American Convention on Human Rights, and

That States Parties to the American Convention on Human Rights have expressed their intention to adopt an international agreement with a view to consolidating the practice of not applying the death penalty in the Americas,

HAVE AGREED TO SIGN THE FOLLOWING PROTOCOL TO THE AMERICAN CONVENTION ON HUMAN RIGHTS TO ABOLISH THE DEATH PENALTY

Article 1

The States Parties to this Protocol shall not apply the death penalty in their territory to any person subject to their jurisdiction.

Article 2

1. No reservations may be made to this Protocol. However, at the time of ratification or accession, the States Parties to this instrument may declare that they reserve the right to apply the death penalty in wartime in accordance with international law, for extremely serious crimes of a military nature.

2. The State Party making this reservation shall, upon ratification or accession, inform the Secretary General of the Organization of American States of the pertinent provisions of its national legislation applicable in wartime, as referred to in the preceding paragraph.

3. Said State Party shall notify the Secretary General of the Organization of American States of the beginning or end of any state of war in effect in its territory.

Article 3

1. This Protocol shall be open for signature and ratification or accession by any State Party to the American Convention on Human Rights.

2. Ratification of this Protocol or accession thereto shall be made through the deposit of an instrument of ratification or accession with the General Secretariat of the Organization of American States.

Article 4

This Protocol shall enter into force among the States that ratify or accede to it when they deposit their respective instruments of ratification or accession with the General Secretariat of the Organization of American States.

Inter-American Convention on the Granting of Civil Rights to Women

May 2, 1948, 1438 U.N.T.S. 51

[Ed. Note: This Convention entered into force for each country on the date that country deposited its instrument of ratification. As of February 17, 2002, twenty-one countries had ratified the Convention. The U.S. has not signed or ratified it. *See* http://www. oas.org/juridico/english/sigs/a-45.html]

The governments represented at the Ninth International Conference of American States, Considering:

That the majority of the American Republics, inspired by lofty principles of justice, have granted civil rights to women;

That it has been a constant aspiration of the American community of nations to equalize the status for men and women in the enjoyment and exercise of civil rights;

That Resolution XX of the Eighth International Conference of American States expressly declares: "That women have the right to the enjoyment of equality as to civil status";

That long before the women of America demanded their rights they were able to carry out nobly all their responsibilities side by side with men;

That the principle of equality of human rights for men and women is contained in the Charter of the United Nations,

Have Resolved:

To authorize their respective Representatives, whose Full Powers have been found to be in good and due form, to sign the following articles:

Article 1.

The American States agree to grant to women the same civil rights that men enjoy.

Article 2.

The present Convention shall be open for signature by the American States and shall be ratified in accordance with their respective constitutional procedures. The original instrument, the Spanish, English, Portuguese and French texts of which are equally authentic, shall be deposited with the General Secretariat of the Organization of American States, which shall transmit certified copies to the Governments for the purpose of ratification. The instruments of ratification shall be deposited with the General Secretariat of the Organization of American States, which shall notify the signatory governments of the said deposit. Such notification shall serve as an exchange of ratifications.

Inter-American Convention on the Granting of Political Rights to Women

May 2, 1948, 1438 U.N.T.S. 63

[Ed. Note: This Convention entered into force for each country on the date that country deposited its instrument of ratification. As of February 17, 2002, twenty-four countries ratified or acceded to the Convention. The U.S. deposited its instrument of ratification on May 24, 1976. *See* http://www.oas.org/juridico/english/sigs/a-44.html]

The governments represented at the Ninth International Conference of American States, Considering:

That the majority of the American Republics, inspired by lofty principles of justice, have granted political rights to women;

That it has been a constant aspiration of the American community of nations to equalize the status for men and women in the enjoyment and exercise of political rights;

That Resolution XX of the Eighth International Conference of American States expressly declares: "That women have the right to political treatment on the basis of equality with men";

That long before the women of America demanded their rights they were able to carry out nobly all their responsibilities side by side with men;

That the principle of equality of human rights for men and women is contained in the Charter of the United Nations,

Have Resolved:

To authorize their respective Representatives, whose Full Powers have been found to be in good and due form, to sign the following articles:

Article 1

The High Contracting Parties agree that the right to vote and to be elected to national office shall not be denied or abridged by reason of sex.

Article 2

The present Convention shall be open for signature by the American States and shall be ratified in accordance with their respective constitutional procedures. The original instrument, the Spanish, English, Portuguese and French texts of which are equally authentic, shall be deposited with the General Secretariat of the Organization of American States, which shall transmit certified copies to the Governments for the purpose of ratification. The instruments of ratification shall be deposited with the General Secretariat of the Organization of American States, which shall notify the signatory governments of the said deposit. Such notification shall serve as an exchange of ratifications.

Inter-American Convention on Conflict of Laws Concerning the Adoption of Minors

May 24, 1984, O.A.S. Treaty Series No. 62, 24 I.L.M. 460

[Ed. Note: This Convention entered into force on May 26, 1988. As of March 7, 2003, six countries had ratified the Convention. The U.S. has not signed the Convention. *See* http://www.oas.org/juridico/english/sigs/b-48.html]

The Governments of the Member States of the Organization of American States, desirous of concluding a convention on conflict of laws concerning the adoption of minors, have agreed as follows:

Article 1

This Convention shall apply to the adoption of minors in the form of full adoption, adoptive legitimation and other similar institutions that confer on the adoptee a legally established filiation, when the domicile of the adopter (or of the adopters) is in one State Party and the habitual residence of the adoptee is in another State Party.

Article 2

When signing, ratifying or acceding to this Convention, any State Party may declare that it applies to any other form of international adoption of minors.

Article 3

The law of the habitual residence of the minor shall govern capacity, consent, and other requirements for adoption, as well as those procedures and formalities that are necessary for creating the relationship.

Article 4

The law of the domicile of the adopter (or adopters) shall govern:
a. The capacity to be an adopter;
b. The age and marital status requirement to be met by an adopter;
c. The consent of an adopter's spouse, if required, and
d. The other requirements for being an adopter.

If, however, the requirements of the last of the adopter (or adopters) are manifestly less strict than those of the law of the adoptee's habitual residence, the law of the adoptee shall govern.

Article 5

Adoptions that are in conformity with this Convention shall produce their effects unconditionally in the States Parties, and the exception of the unknown institution may not be invoked.

Article 6

The requirements of publication and registration of adoption shall be subject to the law of the State in which they are to be satisfied.

The particular features and type of adoption shall be stated in the registration.

Article 7

Where called for, the secrecy of the adoption shall be guaranteed. However, whenever possible, medical background information on the minor and on the birth parents, if it is known, shall be communicated to the legally appropriate person, without mention of their names or of other data whereby they may be identified.

Article 8

In adoptions governed by this Convention, the authorities granting the adoption may require the adopter (or adopters) to provide evidence of his physical, moral, psychological and economic capacity, through public or private institutions, the specific purpose is to protect minors. These institutions must be specifically authorized by some State or by some international organization.

The institutions that certify the capacity referred to above shall undertake to report to the authority granting the adoption on the conditions under which the adoption has developed over a period of one year. To this end, the authority granting the adoption shall inform the certifying institution that the adoption has been granted.

Article 9

In case of full adoption, adoptive legitimation, and similar institutions:

a. The relations between the adopter (or adopters) and the adoptee, including support relations, and the relations between the adoptee and the family of the adopter (or adopters), shall be governed by the same law as would govern the relations between the adopter (or adopters) and his legitimate family;

b. Ties between the adoptee and his family of origin shall be considered dissolved. However, impediments to marriage shall continue.

Article 10

In the case of adoptions other than full adoption, adoptive legitimation, and similar institutions, relations between the adopter (or adopters) and the adoptee shall be governed by the law of the domicile of the adopter (or adopters).

The relations between the adoptee and his family of origin shall be governed by the law of his habitual residence at the time of adoption.

Article 11

The rights of succession of the adoptee or the adopter (or adopters) shall be governed by the rules applicable to the respective successions.

In case of full adoption, adoptive legitimation, and similar institutions, the adoptee, and the adopter (or adopters) and the family thereof, shall have the same rights of succession as those of legitimate family members.

Article 12

Adoptions referred to in Article 1 are irrevocable. Revocation of adoptions referred to in Article 2 shall be governed by the law of the habitual residence of the adoptee at the time of adoption.

Article 13

Where it is permitted, conversion of simple adoption into full adoption, adoptive legitimation, or similar institutions shall be governed, at the choice of the petitioner, by the law of the habitual residence of the adoptee at the time of the adoption, or by that of the State in which the adopter (or adopters) has his domicile at the time the conversion is requested.

If the adoptee is more than 14 years of age, his consent shall be required.

Article 14

Annulment of the adoption shall be governed by the law under which it was granted. An annulment shall be decreed only by judicial authorities, and the interests of the minor shall be protected in accordance with Article 19 of this Convention.

Article 15

The authorities of the State of the habitual residence of the adoptee shall be competent to grant the adoptions referred to in this Convention.

Article 16

The judges of the State where the adoptee was habitually resident at the time the adoption was granted shall be competent to decide on annulment or revocation of the adoption.

The authorities of the State of habitual residence of the adoptee at the time of the adoption; those of the State of domicile of the adopter (or adopters); or those of the

State of domicile of the adoptee, if he has a domicile of his own at the time the conversion is requested, shall be competent, at the option of the petitioner, to decide on the conversion, where it is permitted, of simple adoption into full adoption, adoptive legitimation, or similar institutions.

Article 17

The judges of the State of the domicile of the adopter (or adopters) shall be competent to rule on matters concerning the relations between the adoptee and the adopter (or adopters) and the family thereof until the adoptee has a domicile of his own.

As soon as the adoptee has his own domicile, the judge of the domicile of the adoptee or that of the adopter (or adopters) shall, at the option of the petitioner, have jurisdiction.

Article 18

The authorities of a State Party may refuse to apply the law declared applicable under this Convention when the law is manifestly contrary to its public policy (ordre public).

Article 19

The terms of this Convention and the laws applicable under it shall be interpreted consistently and in favor of the validity of the adoption and the best interests of the adoptee.

Article 20

A State Party may at any time declare that this Convention applies to adoptions of minors habitually resident in it by persons also habitually resident in it when, in the opinion of the authority concerned, the circumstances of a given case indicate that the adopter (or adopters) plans to establish his domicile in another State Party after the adoption has been granted.

Article 21

This Convention shall be open for signature by the Member States of the organization of American States.

Article 22

This Convention is subject to ratification. The instruments of ratification shall be deposited with the General Secretariat of the Organization of American States.

Article 23

This Convention shall remain open for accession by any other State. The instruments of accession shall be deposited with the General Secretariat of the Organization of American States.

Article 24

Each State may, at the time of signature, ratification or accession, make reservations to this Convention, provided that each reservation concerns one or more specific provisions.

Article 25

Adoptions granted according to domestic law when the adoptee and the adopter (or adopters) have their domicile or habitual residence in the same State Party shall produce their effects unconditionally in the other States Parties, without prejudice to their being governed by the law of the new domicile of the adopter (or adopters).

Article 26

This Convention shall enter into force on the thirtieth day following the date of deposit of the second instrument of ratification.

For each State ratifying or acceding to the Convention after the deposit of the second instrument of ratification, the Convention shall enter into force on the thirtieth day after deposit by such State of its instrument of ratification or accession.

Article 27

If a State Party has two or more territorial units in which different systems of law apply in relation to the matters dealt with in this Convention, it may, at the time of signature, ratification or accession, declare that this Convention shall extend to all its territorial units or to only one or more of them.

Such declaration may be modified by subsequent declarations, which shall expressly indicate the territorial unit or units to which the Convention applies. Such subsequent declarations shall be transmitted to the General Secretariat of the Organization of American States, and shall become effective thirty days after the date of their receipt.

Article 28

This Convention shall remain in force indefinitely, but any of the States Parties may denounce it. The instrument of denunciation shall be deposited with the General Secretariat of the Organization of American States. After one year from the date of deposit of the instrument of denunciation, the Convention shall no longer be in effect for the denouncing State, but shall remain in effect for the other States Parties.

Article 29

The original instrument of this Convention, the English, French, Portuguese and Spanish texts of which are equally authentic, shall be deposited with the General Secretariat of the Organization of American States, which shall forward an authenticated copy of its text to the Secretariat of the United Nations for registration and publication in accordance with Article 102 of its Charter. The General Secretariat of the Organization of American States shall notify the Member States of that Organization and the States that have acceded to the Convention of the signatures, deposits of instruments of ratification, accession and denunciation as well as of reservations, if any. It shall also transmit the declarations provided for in Articles 2, 20, and 27 of this Convention.

Inter-American Convention on Support Obligations

July 15, 1989, O.A.S. Treaty Series No. 71, 29 I.L.M. 73

[Ed. Note: The Convention entered into force on March 6, 1996. As of March 7, 2003, eleven countries had ratified or acceded to the Convention. The U.S. has not signed the treaty. *See* http://www.oas.org/juridico/english/sigs/b-54.html]

SCOPE

Article 1

The purpose of this Convention is to establish the law applicable to support obligations and to jurisdiction and international procedural cooperation when the support creditor is domiciled or habitually resides in one State Party and the debtor is domiciled or habitually resides or has property or income in another State Party.

This Convention shall apply to child support obligations owed because of the child's minority and to spousal support obligations arising from the matrimonial relationship between spouses or former spouses.

When signing, ratifying, or acceding to this Convention, a State may declare that it restricts the scope of the Convention to child support obligations.

Article 2

For the purposes of this Convention, a child shall be any person below the age of eighteen years. However, the benefits of this Convention shall also apply to those who, having attained that age, continue to be entitled to support under the applicable law prescribed by Articles 6 and 7.

Article 3

When signing, ratifying or acceding to this Convention or after it has taken effect, a State may declare that it shall apply to support obligations in favor of other creditors, and may indicate the degree of kinship or other legal relationship required by its law for a person to be a support creditor or debtor.

Article 4

Any person without regard to nationality, race, sex, religion, parentage, place of origin, immigration status or any other distinction, is entitled to receive support.

Article 5

Decisions rendered pursuant to this Convention shall be without prejudice to questions of parentage and family relationships between support creditors and debtors. Where relevant, however, such decisions may be used as evidence.

APPLICABLE LAW

Article 6

Support obligations, as well as the definition of support creditor and debtor, shall be governed by whichever of the following laws the competent authority finds the most favorable to the creditor:
   a. That of the State of domicile or habitual residence of the creditor;
   b. That of the State of domicile or habitual residence of the debtor.

Article 7

The applicable law pursuant to Article 6 shall determine:
   a. The amount of support due and the timing of and conditions for payment;
   b. Who may bring a support claim on behalf of the creditor; and
   c. Any other condition necessary for enjoyment of the right to support.

JURISDICTION

Article 8

At the motion of the creditor, support claims may be heard by the following judicial or administrative authorities:

a. Those of the State of domicile or habitual residence of the creditor;

b. Those of the State of domicile or habitual residence of the debtor; or

c. Those of the State to which the debtor is connected by personal links such as possessing property, receiving income or obtaining financial benefits.

Notwithstanding the provisions of this article, a judicial or administrative authority of another State shall also have jurisdiction if the defendant appears before it without challenging its jurisdiction.

Article 9

Actions to increase the amount of support may be heard by any of the authorities mentioned in Article 8. Actions to discontinue or reduce support shall be heard by the authorities of the State that set the amount of support.

Article 10

Support shall be commensurate with both the need of the creditor and the financial resources of the debtor.

Should a judicial or administrative authority responsible for enforcing or securing the effectiveness of a judgment order provisional measures or provide for execution of judgment in an amount lower than requested, the rights of the creditor shall not thereby be impaired.

INTERNATIONAL PROCEDURAL COOPERATION

Article 11

Support orders of one State Party shall be enforced in other States Parties if they meet the following requirements:

a. The judicial or administrative authority issuing the order had jurisdiction under Articles 8 and 9 of this Convention to hear and decide the matter;

b. The order and the documents attached thereto required under this Convention have been duly translated into the official language of the State in which the order is to be enforced;

c. As necessary, the order and the documents attached thereto have been certified in accordance with the law of the State in which the order is to be enforced;

d. They have been certified in accordance with the law of the State of origin;

e. The defendant was served with notice or was summoned to appear in due legal form substantially equivalent to that established by the law of the State in which the order is to be enforced;

f. The parties had the opportunity to present their defense;

g. The orders are final in the State in which they were rendered. A pending appeal from such order shall not delay its enforcement.

Article 12

A request for enforcement of an order shall include the following:

a. A certified copy of the order;

b. Certified copies of the documents needed to prove compliance with Article 11.e and 11.f;

c. A certified copy of a document showing that the support order is final or is being appealed.

Article 13

Compliance with the above requirements shall be ascertained directly by the competent authority from which enforcement is sought, which shall proceed summarily, giving notice to the debtor and, where necessary, to the appropriate public agency and holdings a hearing without reopening the merits. Should the enforcement decision be appealable, the appeal shall not suspend provisional measures or such collection or enforcement orders as may be in effect.

Article 14

No security of any kind may be required from the support creditor because of his foreign nationality or his domicile or habitual residence in another State.

An in forma pauperis waiver of court costs granted to a support creditor in the State Party where he brought his action for support shall be recognized in the State Party where recognition or enforcement is sought. The States Parties undertake to provide free legal assistance to the beneficiaries of such waivers.

Article 15

The judicial or administrative authorities of the States Parties shall order and carry out, pursuant to a well-founded request of a party or through the respective diplomatic agent or consular officer, provisional or urgent measures that are territorial in nature and whose purpose is to secure the outcome of a pending or anticipated support claim.

These provisions shall apply [to] whatever authorities may have jurisdiction, so long as the property or income concerned is to be found within the territory where the action is brought.

Article 16

The granting of a request for provisional or precautionary measures shall imply neither recognition of jurisdiction of the requesting authority nor a commitment to recognize the validity of, or enforce, a support order presented for enforcement.

Article 17

Temporary support orders and interlocutory support judgments, including those rendered by courts hearing annulment, divorce, separation and similar cases, shall be enforced by the competent authority, although they may be subject to appeal in the State where rendered.

Article 18

Upon signing, ratifying or acceding to the Convention, a State may declare that its procedural law will govern jurisdiction of the courts and the proceedings for recognition of a foreign support order.

GENERAL PROVISIONS

Article 19

The States Parties shall endeavor to provide, as far as they are able, temporary support to children from other States abandoned in their territory.

Article 20

The States Parties undertake to facilitate the transfer of funds required for compliance with this Convention.

Article 21

The provisions of this Convention may not be construed in such a way as to restrict the rights of the support creditor under the law of the forum.

Article 22

The enforcement of foreign judgments or application of foreign law prescribed by this Convention may be refused when the requested State Party considers such enforcement or application manifestly contrary to its fundamental principles of public policy (ordre public).

FINAL PROVISIONS

Article 23

This Convention shall be open for signature by the Member States of the Organization of American States.

Article 24

This Convention is subject to ratification. The instruments of ratification shall be deposited with the General Secretariat of the Organization of American States.

Article 25

This Convention shall remain open for accession by any other State. The instruments of accession shall be deposited with the General Secretariat of the Organization of American States.

Article 26

Each State may, at the time of signature, ratification or accession, make reservations to this Convention, provided that the reservation concerns one or more specific provisions and is not incompatible with the purpose and fundamental objectives of this Convention.

Article 27

If a State has two or more territorial units in which different systems of law apply in relation to the matters dealt with in this Convention, it may, at the time of signature, ratification or accession, declare that this Convention shall extend to all its territorial units or only to one or more of them.

Such declaration may be modified by subsequent declarations, which shall expressly indicate the territorial unit or units to which the Convention applies. Such subsequent declarations shall be transmitted to the General Secretariat of the Organization of American States, and shall become effective thirty days after the date of their receipt.

Article 28

In the case of a State that, with respect to child support obligations, has two or more systems of law applicable in different territorial units:

a. Any reference to the domicile or habitual residence in that State refers to domicile or habitual residence in a territorial unit of that State;

b. Any reference to the law of the State of domicile or habitual residence refers to the law of the territorial unit in which the child has its domicile or habitual residence.

Article 29

Among Member States of the Organization of American States that are parties to this Convention and to the Hague Conventions of October 2, 1973 on the recognition and enforcement of decisions relating to maintenance obligations and on the law applicable to maintenance obligations, this Convention shall prevail.

However, States Parties may enter into bilateral agreements to give priority to the application of the Hague Conventions of October 2, 1973.

Article 30

This Convention shall limit neither the provisions of existing or future bilateral or multilateral conventions on this subject entered into by the States Parties, nor the more favorable practices that those States may observe in this area.

Article 31

This Convention shall enter into force on the thirtieth day following the date of deposit of the second instrument of ratification.

For each State ratifying or acceding to the Convention after the deposit of the second instrument of ratification, the Convention shall enter into force on the thirtieth day after deposit by such State of its instrument of ratification or accession.

Article 32

This Convention shall remain in force indefinitely, but any of the States Parties may denounce it. The instrument of denunciation shall be deposited with the General Secretariat of the Organization of American States. After one year from the date of deposit of the instrument of denunciation, the Convention shall no longer be in force for the denouncing State, but shall remain in force for the other States Parties.

Article 33

The original instrument of this Convention, the English, French, Portuguese and Spanish texts of which are equally authentic, shall be deposited with the General Secretariat of the Organization of American States, which shall forward an authenticated copy of its text to the Secretariat of the United Nations for registration and publication in accordance with Article 102 of its Charter. The General Secretariat of the Organization of American States shall notify the Member States of the Organization and the States that have acceded to the Convention of the signatures, deposits of instruments of ratification, accession and denunciation, as well as of reservations, if any. It shall also transmit the declarations provided for in this Convention.

Inter-American Convention on the International Return of Children

July 15, 1989, O.A.S. Treaty Series No. 70, 29 I.L.M. 63

[Ed. Note: The Convention entered into force on November 4, 1989. As of March 7, 2003, ten countries have ratified it. The U.S. is not a signatory. See http://www.oas.org/juridico/english/sigs/b-53.html]

SCOPE

Article 1
The purpose of this Convention is to secure the prompt return of children habitually resident in one State Party who have been wrongfully removed from any State to a State Party or who, having been lawfully removed, have been wrongfully retained. This Convention further seeks to secure enforcement of visitation and custody rights of parties entitled to them.

Article 2
For the purposes of this Convention, a child shall be any person below the age of sixteen years.

Article 3
For the purposes of this Convention:

a. Rights of custody include rights relating to the care of the child and, in particular, the right to determine the child's place of residence;

b. Rights of visitation include the right to take a child for a limited period of time to a place other than the child's habitual residence.

Article 4
The removal or retention of a child shall be considered wrongful whenever it is in breach of the custody rights that parents, institutions or others having such rights individually or jointly exercise over the child under the law of the child's habitual residence immediately prior to the removal or retention.

Article 5
Any party designated by Article 4 may, in the exercise of custody or similar rights, bring an action for the child's return.

Article 6
Judicial or administrative authorities of the State Party in which the child habitually resided immediately before the removal or retention shall have jurisdiction to consider a petition for the child's return.

In urgent cases, the applicant may choose, instead, to file a request for the child's return directly with authorities of the State Party in whose territory the wrongfully removed or retained child is or is thought to be when the request is made, or with the authorities of the State Party in which the wrongful act giving rise to the request took place.

Making a request in the manner described in the preceding paragraph shall in no way alter the jurisdiction authorized by the first paragraph of this article.

THE CENTRAL AUTHORITY

Article 7
For the purposes of this Convention, each State Party shall designate a central authority to ensure fulfillment of the obligations established under this Convention and shall inform the General Secretariat of the Organization of American States of that designation.

Specifically the Central Authority shall assist the applicant and competent authorities of the respective States in locating and returning the child. It shall also facilitate the prompt return and delivery of the child to the applicant and assist the parties in obtaining the necessary documents for proceedings under this Convention.

The Central Authorities of the States Parties shall cooperate with one another and exchange information on the operation of the Convention in order to secure the prompt return of children and to achieve the other purposes of this Convention.

RETURN PROCEEDINGS

Article 8

A party seeking a child's return may file an application or petition with the competent authorities in accordance with Article 6:

a. By a letter rogatory;

b. By filing a request with a central authority; or

c. Directly, or through diplomatic or consular channels.

Article 9

1. The application or petition referred to in Article 8 shall contain:

a. An account of the removal or retention and sufficient information to identify the applicant, the removed or retained child and, where possible, the person alleged to have removed or retained the child;

b. Information on the presumed location of the child and on the circumstances and dates of the removal to a foreign country or of the expiration of the authorized length of stay; and

c. The legal grounds for the child's return.

2. The application or petition shall be accompanied by:

a. A full and certified copy of a judicial or administrative opinion, if any, or of a determination on which the request is based; concise evidence of the existing situation or, if appropriate, a statement of the pertinent applicable law;

b. Certified documents establishing the standing of the applicant;

c. Certification of or information on the applicable law of the State of the child's habitual residence issued by the Central Authority of, or by any other competent source in, that State;

d. Where necessary, translations into the official language of the requested State of all documents referred to in this article; and

e. A statement of the measures required to effect the return of the child.

3. A competent authority may dispense with any of the requirements of the presentation of documents called for by this article if, in its opinion, the child's return is justified.

4. Letters rogatory or requests, and the documents attached thereto, shall not require certification if they are transmitted through diplomatic or consular channels or through the Central Authority.

Article 10

The requested court, Central Authority, or other competent authorities of the State where the child is found shall, where appropriate, take all measures conducive to the voluntary return of the child.

Should a voluntary return not take place, the judicial or administrative authorities, after verifying compliance with Article 9, shall forthwith meet with the child and take such measures to provide for its temporary custody or care as the circumstances may dictate, and shall, where appropriate, immediately order its return. Further, the agency charged by domestic law with protecting the child's welfare shall be notified.

In addition, while the application for return is pending, the competent authorities shall take the necessary steps to prevent the child from leaving their jurisdiction.

Article 11

A judicial or administrative authority of the requested State is not required to order the child's return if the party raising objections to the return establishes that:

a. The party seeking the child's return was not actually exercising its rights at the time of the removal or retention, or had consented to or subsequently acquiesced in such removal or retention; or

b. There is a grave risk that the child's return would expose the child to physical or psychological danger.

The requested authority may also refuse to order the child's return if it finds that the child is opposed to it and if, in the judgment of the requested authority, the child's age and maturity warrant taking its views into account.

Article 12

The objections mentioned in Article 11 shall be raised within a period of eight working days from the time the authorities meet with the child and bring such period to the attention of the person retaining the child.

The judicial or administrative authorities shall assess the circumstances and the evidence furnished by the opposing party to support its objections to the child's return, shall ascertain the applicable law and judicial or administrative precedents of the State of the child's habitual residence, and, if necessary, shall request assistance from Central Authorities, diplomatic agents or consular officers of the States Parties.

The judicial or administrative authority shall issue its decision within sixty calendar days after receipt of the objection.

Article 13

If within forty-five calendar days after the requesting authority has received notice of a decision to return the child, the steps necessary for the child's return have not been taken, the return order shall become inoperative and any measures taken shall be lifted.

Costs of the return shall be borne by the claimant; should the claimant lack the means, the authorities of a requesting State may defray the costs, which may be recovered from the person responsible for the wrongful removal or retention.

Article 14

Proceedings under this Convention shall be commenced within one calendar year of the wrongful removal or retention.

As to children whose location is unknown, the period shall run from the time they are located.

Nevertheless, expiration of the one-year period shall not bar the child's return if, in the opinion of the requested authority, the circumstances so warrant, unless it is demonstrated that the child is settled in its new environment.

Article 15

The fact of a child's return shall not prejudge the ultimate custody decision.

Article 16

After receiving notice of a child's wrongful removal or retention as defined in Article 4, the judicial or administrative authorities of the State Party to which the child has been removed or where it is retained shall refrain from deciding on the merits of custody claims until it is determined either that the child is not to be returned under this Convention or that no request pursuant to this Convention has been lodged within a reasonable time following receipt of such notice.

Article 17

The foregoing provisions shall not limit the power of a judicial or administrative authority to order the child's return at any time.

LOCATING MINORS

Article 18

Any person mentioned in Article 5 may directly, through the Central Authority, or through the judicial or administrative authorities of one State Party request the competent authorities of another State Party to locate children whose habitual residence is in the State of the requesting authority and who are thought to be wrongfully in the requested State.

The request shall be accompanied by any information supplied by the person making the request or gathered by the requesting authority relevant to the locating of the child and the identity of the person with whom the child is presumed to be.

Article 19

The Central Authority or judicial or administrative authorities of one State Party which, upon learning from a request pursuant to Article 18 that a child wrongfully outside its habitual residence is located within their jurisdiction, shall immediately take all appropriate measures to safeguard its health and prevent its concealment or removal to another jurisdiction.

The location of the child shall be reported to the authorities of the requesting State.

Article 20

The measures adopted pursuant to Article 19 may be lifted if the child's return is not requested within sixty calendar days after the authorities of the requesting State have been informed of the location of the child.

A lifting of such measures shall not preclude exercise of the right to request the child's return in accordance with the procedures and time limits specified in this Convention.

VISITATION RIGHTS

Article 21

Any person with visitation rights may, pursuant to Article 6, address a request for their enforcement to the competent authorities of any State Party. The same procedures shall be followed as those governing a request for a child's return under this Convention.

GENERAL PROVISIONS

Article 22

Letters rogatory and requests for the return or the locating of children may be transmitted, as appropriate, to the requested authority by the parties themselves, or through judicial, diplomatic, or consular channels, or through the Central Authority of the requesting or the requested State.

Article 23

The processing of letters rogatory or requests under this Convention and the measures arising therefrom shall be free of charge and exempt from any tax, deposit or bond, however named.

The parties initiating a letter rogatory or request that have appointed a person to represent them in the requested forum shall bear any expenses incurred in connection with such representation.

Nevertheless, upon ordering a child's return under this Convention, the competent authorities may, where appropriate, direct the person who wrongfully removed or retained the child to pay the necessary expenses incurred by the applicant, those incurred in locating the minor, and the costs of return.

Article 24

The arrangements and measures necessary to give effect to letters rogatory shall not require the intervention of the petitioner, and shall be implemented directly by the requested authority. This procedure, however, shall not bar any party from intervening either personally or through a duly appointed representative.

Article 25

A child's return under this Convention may be refused where it would be manifestly in violation of the fundamental principles of the requested State recognized by universal and regional instruments on human rights or on the rights of children.

Article 26

This Convention shall not bar the competent authorities from ordering the child's immediate return when its removal or retention is a criminal offense.

Article 27

As a Specialized Organization of the Organization of American States, the Inter-American Children's Institute shall be responsible for coordinating the activities of the Central Authorities within the scope of the Convention and for receiving and evaluating information from the States Parties in respect of application of the Convention.

It shall also be responsible for cooperating with other international organizations competent in the matter.

FINAL PROVISIONS

[Ed. Note: Article 28 (signatures), article 29 (ratification), article 30 (accession), article 31 (reservations), article 32 (declaration regarding territorial units), and article 33 (law in territorial units) have been omitted.]

Article 34

Among the Member States of the Organization of American States that are parties to this Convention and to the Hague Convention of October 25, 1980 on the civil aspects of international child abduction, this Convention shall prevail.

However, States Parties may enter into bilateral agreements to give priority to the application of the Hague Convention.

Article 35

This Convention shall limit neither the provisions of existing or future bilateral or multilateral conventions on this subject entered into by the States Parties, nor the more favorable practices that those States may observe in this area.

[Ed. Note: Article 36 (entry into force), article 37 (denunciation), and article 38 (authentic texts) have been omitted.]

Inter-American Convention on International Traffic in Minors

Mar. 18, 1994, O.A.S. Treaty Series No. 79, 33 I.L.M. 721

[Ed. Note: The Convention entered into force on August 15, 1997. Eight countries have acceded or ratified the treaty. The U.S. is not a signatory. *See* http://www.oas.org/juridico/english/sigs/b-57.html]

The States Parties to this Convention,

CONSIDERING the importance of ensuring comprehensive and effective protection for minors, through appropriate mechanisms to guarantee respect for their rights;

AWARE that the international traffic in minors is a universal concern;

TAKING INTO CONSIDERATION conventions on international protection of minors, particularly the provisions of Articles 11 and 35 of the Convention on the Rights of the Child, adopted by the United Nations General Assembly on November 20, 1989;

CONVINCED of the need to regulate civil and penal aspects of the international traffic in minors; and

REAFFIRMING the importance of international cooperation to achieve effective protection of the best interests of minors,

Have agreed upon the following:

CHAPTER ONE—GENERAL PROVISIONS

Article 1

The purpose of the present Convention, with a view to protection of the fundamental rights of minors and their best interests, is the prevention and punishment of the international traffic in minors as well as the regulation of its civil and penal aspects.

Accordingly, the States Parties to this Convention undertake to:

a) ensure the protection of minors in consideration of their best interests;

b) institute a system of mutual legal assistance among the States Parties, dedicated to the prevention and punishment of the international traffic in minors, as well as adopt related administrative and legal provisions to that effect; and

c) ensure the prompt return of minors who are victims of international traffic to the State of their habitual residence, bearing in mind the best interests of the minors.

Article 2

This Convention shall apply to any minor who is habitually resident in a State Party or is located in a State Party at the time when an act of international traffic occurs in respect of him or her.

For the purpose of the present Convention:

a) "Minor" means any human being below the age of eighteen.

b) "International traffic in minors" means the abduction, removal or retention, or attempted abduction, removal or retention, of a minor for unlawful purposes or by unlawful means.

c) "Unlawful purpose" includes, among others, prostitution, sexual exploitation, servitude or any other purpose unlawful in either the State of the minor's habitual residence or the State Party where the minor is located.

d) "Unlawful means" includes, among others, kidnapping, fraudulent or coerced consent, the giving or receipt of unlawful payments or benefits to achieve the consent of the parents, persons or institution having care of the child, or any other means unlawful in either the State of the minor's habitual residence or the State Party where the minor is located.

Article 3

This Convention shall also cover the civil aspects of the wrongful removal, transfer, or retention of minors internationally, not dealt with by other international conventions on this subject.

Article 4

To the extent possible, States Parties shall cooperate with States that are not Parties in preventing and punishing international traffic in minors, and in protecting and caring for minors who are victims of that wrongful act.

The competent authorities of a State Party are to notify the competent authorities of a State that is not a Party whenever a minor is within its territory who has been a victim of international traffic in minors in a State Party.

Article 5

For the purposes of the present Convention, each State Party shall designate a Central Authority and shall inform the General Secretariat of the Organization of American States of that designation.

A federal State, or a State in which several legal systems apply, or a State with autonomous territorial units may designate more than one Central Authority, specifying the legal or territorial area covered by each of them. The State making use of this possibility shall designate the Central Authority to which all communications should be addressed.

Should a State Party designate more than one Central Authority, it shall so inform the General Secretariat of the Organization of American States.

Article 6

States Parties shall protect the minor's interests with a view to ensuring that all procedures applied pursuant to the present Convention shall remain confidential.

CHAPTER TWO — PENAL ASPECTS

Article 7
The States Parties undertake to adopt effective measures, under their domestic law, to prevent and severely punish the international traffic in minors defined in this Convention.

Article 8
The States Parties to the present Convention undertake to:

a) assist each other promptly and expeditiously through their Central Authorities, as permitted by the domestic laws of each State and by applicable international treaties, to conduct judicial and administrative proceedings, to take evidence, and to take any other procedural steps that may be necessary for fulfilling the objectives of this Convention;

b) establish through their Central Authorities mechanisms for the exchange of information about any domestic statute, case law, administrative practices, statistics and modalities regarding international traffic in minors in their States; and

c) order such measures as may be necessary to remove any obstacles that might affect the enforcement of this Convention in their States.

Article 9
The following shall have competence in cases of crimes involving international traffic in minors:

a) the State Party where the wrongful conduct occurred;

b) the State Party that is the habitual residence of the minor;

c) the State Party in which the alleged offender is located if said offender has not been extradited;

d) the State Party in which the minor who is a victim of said traffic is located.

For the purposes of the preceding paragraph, the State Party that first conducted formal proceedings concerning the wrongful act shall have preference.

Article 10
If one of the States Parties where extradition is subject to the existence of a treaty receives a request for extradition from a State Party with which it has no such treaty, or if it has such a treaty, this crime is not among the extraditable offenses, it may consider the present Convention as the legal grounds needed to grant extradition in the case of the international traffic in minors.

Further, States Parties that do not make extradition conditional on the existence of a treaty shall recognize the international traffic in minors as a basis for extradition between them. Where no extradition treaty exists, extradition shall be subject to the other conditions required by the domestic laws of the requested State.

Article 11
The actions taken in accordance with the provisions of this chapter shall not prevent the competent authorities of the State Party where the minor is located from ordering, at any time, said minor's immediate return to the State of his or her habitual residence, bearing in mind the best interests of the minor.

CHAPTER THREE—CIVIL ASPECTS

Article 12

A request for locating and returning a minor under the present Convention shall be lodged by those entitled to do so by the laws of the State where the minor habitually resides.

Article 13

The judicial or administrative authorities of the State Party of the minor's habitual residence, or those of the State Party where the minor is or is assumed to be retained, shall be competent to hear the request for the minor's location and return, at the option of the complainants.

When the complainants view there are urgent reasons, the request may be submitted to the judicial or administrative authorities of the State Party where the wrongful act occurred.

Article 14

The request for locating and returning shall not require authentication and shall be processed through the Central Authorities or directly through the competent authorities referred to in Article 13 of the present Convention. The requested authorities shall decide upon the most expeditious procedures for effecting it.

After receiving the request, the requested authorities shall order the necessary steps taken in accordance with their domestic laws to initiate, facilitate, and assist the judicial and administrative procedures involved in locating and returning the minor. In addition, steps shall be taken to ensure the immediate return of the minor, and where necessary, to ensure his or her care, custody or provisional guardianship, depending on the circumstances, and, as a preventive measure, to bar the minor from being wrongfully removed to another State.

The request, stating grounds for location and return of the minor, shall be lodged within one hundred and twenty days after the wrongful removal or retention of the minor has been detected. If the request for location and return is lodged by a State Party, the latter shall do so within one hundred and eighty days.

When it is necessary to take action before locating the minor, the above-mentioned period shall run from the day on which a person or authority entitled to file the request is informed that the minor has been located.

Irrespective of the above, the authorities of the State Party where the minor is retained may at any time order his or her return if it is in the minor's best interests.

Article 15

The authentication or similar formalities otherwise required shall be unnecessary when requests for cooperation encompassed by this Convention are transmitted via consular or diplomatic channels or via the Central Authorities, and when conveyed directly from one tribunal to another in the border area of the States Parties. No authentication in the requesting State Party shall be required in the case of related documents returned via the same channels.

Where necessary, the requests shall be translated into the official language or languages of the State Party to which they are addressed. With respect to attachments, a translation of the summary of the essential information shall suffice.

Article 16

Having confirmed that a victim of traffic in minors is present within their jurisdiction, the competent authorities of a State Party shall take such immediate measures as may be necessary for the minor's protection, including those of a preventive nature to ensure that the minor is not improperly removed to another State.

The Central Authorities shall inform the competent authorities of the State of the minor's previous habitual residence of all such measures. The intervening authorities shall take such steps as may be necessary to keep the persons or authorities seeking the minor's location and return duly informed of the measures adopted.

Article 17

In keeping with the purposes of this Convention, the Central Authorities of the States Parties shall exchange information and cooperate with their competent judicial and administrative authorities on all matters concerning control of the entry of minors into and departure from their territories.

Article 18

Adoptions and other similar legal proceedings performed in a State Party shall be subject to annulment if they had their origin or purpose in international traffic in minors.

In such annulment, the minor's best interests shall be taken into account at all times.

The annulment shall be subject to the law and the competent authorities of the State where the adoption or legal proceedings concerned took place.

Article 19

Care or custody of a minor may be revoked whenever it has its origin or purpose in the international traffic in minors, under the same conditions provided for in the preceding article.

Article 20

A request for locating and returning a minor may be lodged without prejudice to the annulment and revocation actions provided for in Articles 18 and 19.

Article 21

In any proceeding provided for under this chapter, the competent authority may order the person or organization responsible for international traffic in minors to pay the costs and expenses of locating and returning the minor if such person or organization is a party to the proceeding.

A person or authority lodging a request for the return or, where applicable, the competent authority may bring a civil action to recover costs, including legal fees and the expenses of locating and returning the minor, unless said costs were already assessed in a criminal proceeding or a proceeding under this chapter.

The competent authority or any injured person or authority may bring a civil action for damages against the persons or organizations responsible for the international traffic in minors involving the minor.

Article 22

The States Parties shall adopt the measures needed to ensure that no costs are charged for proceedings to secure the return of the minor, in accordance with their laws and shall advise persons legitimately interested in the return of the minor of the public defender services, benefits to the needy and other forms of free legal aid to which they may be entitled under the laws and regulations of the respective States Parties.

CHAPTER FOUR—FINAL CLAUSES

Article 23
Each State Party may, at the time of signature, ratification, or accession to the present Convention or at any time thereafter, declare that it will recognize and execute criminal judgments handed down in other States Parties in respect of awards of damages resulting from the international traffic in minors.

[Ed. Note: Article 24 (law in territorial units) and article 25 (declaration regarding territorial units) have been omitted.]

Article 26
Each State Party may, at the time of signature, ratification or accession to the present Convention or at any time thereafter, declare that it will not entertain in any civil suit a challenge to the existence of the facts of the crime or the guilt of the person convicted when a conviction has been handed down for this crime in another State Party.

Article 27
The competent authorities in border areas of the States Parties may, at any time, directly agree on more expeditious procedures to locate and return minors than those provided for in the present Convention and without prejudice thereto.

None of the provisions in the present Convention shall be interpreted as restricting the more favorable practices that the competent authorities of the States Parties may agree to follow for the matters covered by this Convention.

[Ed. Note: Article 28 (signature), article 29 (ratification), article 30 (accession), article 31 (reservations), article 32 (existing treaties), article 33 (entry into force), article 34 (denounciation), and article 35 (authentic copies) have been omitted.]

Inter-American Convention on the Prevention, Punishment, and Eradication of Violence against Women, "Convention of Belém Do Pará"
June 9, 1994, 33 I.L.M. 1534

[Ed. Note: The Convention entered into force on March 5, 1995. As of March 20, 2003, thirty-one countries have ratified the Convention. The U.S. has not signed it. *See* http://www.oas.org/cim/English/Laws.Rat.Belem.htm.]

THE STATES PARTIES TO THIS CONVENTION,

RECOGNIZING that full respect for human rights has been enshrined in the American Declaration of the Rights and Duties of Man and the Universal Declaration of Human Rights, and reaffirmed in other international and regional instruments;

AFFIRMING that violence against women constitutes a violation of their human rights and fundamental freedoms, and impairs or nullifies the observance, enjoyment and exercise of such rights and freedoms;

CONCERNED that violence against women is an offense against human dignity and a manifestation of the historically unequal power relations between women and men;

RECALLING the Declaration on the Elimination of Violence against Women, adopted by the Twenty-fifth Assembly of Delegates of the Inter-American Commission of Women, and affirming that violence against women pervades every sector of society regardless of class, race or ethnic group, income, culture, level of education, age or religion and strikes at its very foundations:

CONVINCED that the elimination of violence against women is essential for their individual and social development and their full and equal participation in all walks of life; and

CONVINCED that the adoption of a convention on the prevention, punishment and eradication of all forms of violence against women within the framework of the Organization of American States is a positive contribution to protecting the rights of women and eliminating violence against them,

HAVE AGREED to the following:

CHAPTER I — DEFINITION AND SCOPE OF APPLICATION

Article 1

For the purposes of this Convention, violence against women shall be understood as any act or conduct, based on gender, which causes death or physical, sexual or psychological harm or suffering to women, whether in the public or the private sphere.

Article 2

Violence against women shall be understood to include physical, sexual and psychological violence:

a. that occurs within the family or domestic unit or within any other interpersonal relationship, whether or not the perpetrator shares or has shared the same residence with the woman, including, among others, rape, battery and sexual abuse;

b. that occurs in the community and is perpetrated by any person, including, among others, rape, sexual abuse, torture, trafficking in persons, forced prostitution, kidnapping and sexual harassment in the workplace, as well as in educational institutions, health facilities or any other place; and

c. that is perpetrated or condoned by the state or its agents regardless of where it occurs.

CHAPTER II — RIGHTS PROTECTED

Article 3

Every woman has the right to be free from violence in both the public and private spheres.

Article 4

Every woman has the right to the recognition, enjoyment, exercise and protection of all human rights and freedoms embodied in regional and international human rights instruments.

These rights include, among others:

a. The right to have her life respected;

b. The right to have her physical, mental and moral integrity respected;

c. The right to personal liberty and security;

d. The right not to be subjected to torture;

e. The rights to have the inherent dignity of her person respected and her family protected;

f. The right to equal protection before the law and of the law;

g. The right to simple and prompt recourse to a competent court for protection against acts that violate her rights;

h. The right to associate freely;

i. The right of freedom to profess her religion and beliefs within the law; and

j. The right to have equal access to the public service of her country and to take part in the conduct of public affairs, including decision-making.

Article 5

Every woman is entitled to the free and full exercise of her civil, political, economic, social and cultural rights, and may rely on the full protection of those rights as embodied in regional and international instruments on human rights. The States Parties recognize that violence against women prevents and nullifies the exercise of these rights.

Article 6

The right of every woman to be free from violence includes, among others:

a. The right of women to be free from all forms of discrimination; and

b. The right of women to be valued and educated free of stereotyped patterns of behavior and social and cultural practices based on concepts of inferiority or subordination.

CHAPTER III—DUTIES OF THE STATES

Article 7

The States Parties condemn all forms of violence against women and agree to pursue, by all appropriate means and without delay, policies to prevent, punish and eradicate such violence and undertake to:

a. refrain from engaging in any act or practice of violence against women and to ensure that their authorities, officials, personnel, agents, and institutions act in conformity with this obligation;

b. apply due diligence to prevent, investigate and impose penalties for violence against women;

c. include in their domestic legislation penal, civil, administrative and any other type of provisions that may be needed to prevent, punish and eradicate violence against women and to adopt appropriate administrative measures where necessary;

d. adopt legal measures to require the perpetrator to refrain from harassing, intimidating or threatening the woman or using any method that harms or endangers her life or integrity, or damages her property;

e. take all appropriate measures, including legislative measures, to amend or repeal existing laws and regulations or to modify legal or customary practices which sustain the persistence and tolerance of violence against women;

f. establish fair and effective legal procedures for women who have been subjected to violence which include, among others, protective measures, a timely hearing and effective access to such procedures;

g. establish the necessary legal and administrative mechanisms to ensure that women subjected to violence have effective access to restitution, reparations or other just and effective remedies; and

h. adopt such legislative or other measures as may be necessary to give effect to this Convention.

Article 8

The States Parties agree to undertake progressively specific measures, including programs:

a. to promote awareness and observance of the right of women to be free from violence, and the right of women to have their human rights respected and protected;

b. to modify social and cultural patterns of conduct of men and women, including the development of formal and informal educational programs appropriate to every level of the educational process, to counteract prejudices, customs and all other practices which are based on the idea of the inferiority or superiority of either of the sexes or on the stereotyped roles for men and women which legitimize or exacerbate violence against women;

c. to promote the education and training of all those involved in the administration of justice, police and other law enforcement officers as well as other personnel responsible for implementing policies for the prevention, punishment and eradication of violence against women;

d. to provide appropriate specialized services for women who have been subjected to violence, through public and private sector agencies, including shelters, counseling services for all family members where appropriate, and care and custody of the affected children;

e. to promote and support governmental and private sector education designed to raise the awareness of the public with respect to the problems of and remedies for violence against women;

f. to provide women who are subjected to violence access to effective readjustment and training programs to enable them to fully participate in public, private and social life;

g. to encourage the communications media to develop appropriate media guidelines in order to contribute to the eradication of violence against women in all its forms, and to enhance respect for the dignity of women;

h. to ensure research and the gathering of statistics and other relevant information relating to the causes, consequences and frequency of violence against women, in order to assess the effectiveness of measures to prevent, punish and eradicate violence against women and to formulate and implement the necessary changes; and

i. to foster international cooperation for the exchange of ideas and experiences and the execution of programs aimed at protecting women who are subjected to violence.

Article 9

With respect to the adoption of the measures in this Chapter, the States Parties shall take special account of the vulnerability of women to violence by reason of, among others, their race or ethnic background or their status as migrants, refugees or displaced persons. Similar consideration shall be given to women subjected to violence while pregnant or who are disabled, of minor age, elderly, socioeconomically disadvantaged, affected by armed conflict or deprived of their freedom.

CHAPTER IV—INTER-AMERICAN MECHANISMS OF PROTECTION

Article 10

In order to protect the rights of every woman to be free from violence, the States Parties shall include in their national reports to the Inter-American Commission of Women information on measures adopted to prevent and prohibit violence against women, and to assist women affected by violence, as well as on any difficulties they observe in applying those measures, and the factors that contribute to violence against women.

Article 11

The States Parties to this Convention and the Inter-American Commission of Women may request of the Inter-American Court of Human Rights advisory opinions on the interpretation of this Convention.

Article 12

Any person or group of persons, or any nongovernmental entity legally recognized in one or more member states of the Organization, may lodge petitions with the Inter-American Commission on Human Rights containing denunciations or complaints of violations of Article 7 of this Convention by a State Party, and the Commission shall consider such claims in accordance with the norms and procedures established by the American Convention on Human Rights and the Statutes and Regulations of the Inter-American Commission on Human Rights for lodging and considering petitions.

CHAPTER V—GENERAL PROVISIONS

Article 13

No part of this Convention shall be understood to restrict or limit the domestic law of any State Party that affords equal or greater protection and guarantees of the rights of women and appropriate safeguards to prevent and eradicate violence against women.

Article 14

No part of this Convention shall be understood to restrict or limit the American Convention on Human Rights or any other international convention on the subject that provides for equal or greater protection in this area.

Article 15

This Convention is open to signature by all the member states of the Organization of American States.

Article 16

This Convention is subject to ratification. The instruments of ratification shall be deposited with the General Secretariat of the Organization of American States.

Article 17

This Convention is open to accession by any other state. Instruments of accession shall be deposited with the General Secretariat of the Organization of American States.

Article 18

Any State may, at the time of approval, signature, ratification, or accession, make reservations to this Convention provided that such reservations are:

a. not incompatible with the object and purpose of the Convention, and

b. not of a general nature and relate to one or more specific provisions.

Article 19

Any State Party may submit to the General Assembly, through the Inter-American Commission of Women, proposals for the amendment of this Convention. Amendments shall enter into force for the states ratifying them on the date when two-thirds of the States Parties to this Convention have deposited their respective instruments of ratification. With respect to the other States Parties, the amendments shall enter into force on the dates on which they deposit their respective instruments of ratification.

[Ed. Note: Article 20 (declaration regarding territorial units), article 21 (entry into force), article 22 (notification), article 23 (annual report), article 24 (denunciation), and article 25 (authentic texts) have been omitted.]

C. African Conventions

African [Banjul] Charter on Human and Peoples' Rights
June 27, 1981, OAU Doc. CAB/LEG/67/3 rev. 5,
reprinted in 21 I.L.M. 58 (1982)

[Ed. Note: The Charter was adopted by the eighteenth Assembly of Heads of State and Government on June 27, 1981 in Nairobi, Kenya. The Charter entered into force on October 21, 1986. As of 1999, fifty-two countries had ratified the Charter. *See* http://www.up.ac.za/chr/ahrdb/statorat_2.htm (last updated 7/22/02).]

PREAMBLE

The African States members of the Organization of African Unity, parties to the present convention entitled "African Charter on Human and Peoples' Rights",

Recalling Decision 115 (XVI) of the Assembly of Heads of State and Government at its Sixteenth Ordinary Session held in Monrovia, Liberia, from 17 to 20 July 1979 on the preparation of a "preliminary draft on an African Charter on Human and Peoples' Rights providing *inter alia* for the establishment of bodies to promote and protect human and peoples' rights";

Considering the Charter of the Organization of African Unity, which stipulates that "freedom, equality, justice and dignity are essential objectives for the achievement of the legitimate aspirations of the African peoples";

Reaffirming the pledge they solemnly made in Article 2 of the said Charter to eradicate all forms of colonialism from Africa, to coordinate and intensify their cooperation and efforts to achieve a better life for the peoples of Africa and to promote international cooperation having due regard to the Charter of the United Nations and the Universal Declaration of Human Rights;

Taking into consideration the virtues of their historical tradition and the values of African civilization which should inspire and characterize their reflection on the concept of human and peoples' rights;

Recognizing on the one hand, that fundamental human rights stem from the attributes of human beings which justifies their national and international protection and on the other hand that the reality and respect of peoples rights should necessarily guarantee human rights;

Considering that the enjoyment of rights and freedoms also implies the performance of duties on the part of everyone;

Convinced that it is henceforth essential to pay a particular attention to the right to development and that civil and political rights cannot be dissociated from economic, social and cultural rights in their conception as well as universality and that the satisfaction of economic, social and cultural rights is a guarantee for the enjoyment of civil and political rights;

Conscious of their duty to achieve the total liberation of Africa, the peoples of which are still struggling for their dignity and genuine independence, and undertaking to eliminate colonialism, neo-colonialism, apartheid, zionism and to dismantle aggressive foreign military bases and all forms of discrimination, particularly those based on race, ethnic group, color, sex, language, religion or political opinions;

Reaffirming their adherence to the principles of human and peoples' rights and freedoms contained in the declarations, conventions and other instruments adopted by the Organization of African Unity, the Movement of Non-Aligned Countries and the United Nations;

Firmly convinced of their duty to promote and protect human and people' rights and freedoms taking into account the importance traditionally attached to these rights and freedoms in Africa;

Have agreed as follows:

PART I—RIGHTS AND DUTIES

CHAPTER I—HUMAN AND PEOPLES' RIGHTS

Article 1

The Member States of the Organization of African Unity parties to the present Charter shall recognize the rights, duties and freedoms enshrined in this Charter and shall undertake to adopt legislative or other measures to give effect to them.

Article 2

Every individual shall be entitled to the enjoyment of the rights and freedoms recognized and guaranteed in the present Charter without distinction of any kind such as race, ethnic group, color, sex, language, religion, political or any other opinion, national and social origin, fortune, birth or other status.

Article 3

1. Every individual shall be equal before the law.
2. Every individual shall be entitled to equal protection of the law.

Article 4

Human beings are inviolable. Every human being shall be entitled to respect for his life and the integrity of his person. No one may be arbitrarily deprived of this right.

Article 5

Every individual shall have the right to the respect of the dignity inherent in a human being and to the recognition of his legal status. All forms of exploitation and degradation of man particularly slavery, slave trade, torture, cruel, inhuman or degrading punishment and treatment shall be prohibited.

Article 6

Every individual shall have the right to liberty and to the security of his person. No one may be deprived of his freedom except for reasons and conditions previously laid down by law. In particular, no one may be arbitrarily arrested or detained.

Article 7

1. Every individual shall have the right to have his cause heard. This comprises:

   a. the right to an appeal to competent national organs against acts of violating his fundamental rights as recognized and guaranteed by conventions, laws, regulations and customs in force;

   b. the right to be presumed innocent until proved guilty by a competent court or tribunal;

   c. the right to defence, including the right to be defended by counsel of his choice;

   d. the right to be tried within a reasonable time by an impartial court or tribunal.

2. No one maybe condemned for an act or omission which did not constitute a legally punishable offence at the time it was committed. No penalty may be inflicted for an offence for which no provision was made at the time it was committed. Punishment is personal and can be imposed only on the offender.

Article 8

Freedom of conscience, the profession and free practice of religion shall be guaranteed. No one may, subject to law and order, be submitted to measures restricting the exercise of these freedoms.

Article 9

1. Every individual shall have the right to receive information.

2. Every individual shall have the right to express and disseminate his opinions within the law.

Article 10

1. Every individual shall have the right to free association provided that he abides by the law.

2. Subject to the obligation of solidarity provided for in Article 29 no one may be compelled to join an association.

Article 11

Every individual shall have the right to assemble freely with others. The exercise of this right shall be subject only to necessary restrictions provided for by law in particular those enacted in the interest of national security, the safety, health, ethics and rights and freedoms of others.

Article 12

1. Every individual shall have the right to freedom of movement and residence within the borders of a State provided he abides by the law.

2. Every individual shall have the right to leave any country including his own, and to return to his country. This right may only be subject to restrictions, provided

for by law for the protection of national security, law and order, public health or morality.

3. Every individual shall have the right, when persecuted, to seek and obtain asylum in other countries in accordance with laws of those countries and international conventions.

4. A non-national legally admitted in a territory of a State Party to the present Charter, may only be expelled from it by virtue of a decision taken in accordance with the law.

5. The mass expulsion of non-nationals shall be prohibited. Mass expulsion shall be that which is aimed at national, racial, ethnic or religious groups.

Article 13

1. Every citizen shall have the right to participate freely in the government of his country, either directly or through freely chosen representatives in accordance with the provisions of the law.

2. Every citizen shall have the right of equal access to the public service of his country.

3. Every individual shall have the right of access to public property and services in strict equality of all persons before the law.

Article 14

The right to property shall be guaranteed. It may only be encroached upon in the interest of public need or in the general interest of the community and in accordance with the provisions of appropriate laws.

Article 15

Every individual shall have the right to work under equitable and satisfactory conditions, and shall receive equal pay for equal work.

Article 16

1. Every individual shall have the right to enjoy the best attainable state of physical and mental health.

2. States Parties to the present Charter shall take the necessary measures to protect the health of their people and to ensure that they receive medical attention when they are sick.

Article 17

1. Every individual shall have the right to education.

2. Every individual may freely take part in the cultural life of his community.

3. The promotion and protection of morals and traditional values recognized by the community shall be the duty of the State.

Article 18

1. The family shall be the natural unit and basis of society. It shall be protected by the State which shall take care of its physical health and moral.

2. The State shall have the duty to assist the family which is the custodian of morals and traditional values recognized by the community.

3. The State shall ensure the elimination of every discrimination against women and also ensure the protection of the rights of the woman and the child as stipulated in international declarations and conventions.

4. The aged and the disabled shall also have the right to special measures of protection in keeping with their physical or moral needs.

Article 19

All peoples shall be equal; they shall enjoy the same respect and shall have the same rights. Nothing shall justify the domination of a people by another.

Article 20

1. All peoples shall have the right to existence. They shall have the unquestionable and inalienable right to self-determination. They shall freely determine their political status and shall pursue their economic and social development according to the policy they have freely chosen.

2. Colonized or oppressed peoples shall have the right to free themselves from the bonds of domination by resorting to any means recognized by the international community.

3. All peoples shall have the right to the assistance of the States parties to the present Charter in their liberation struggle against foreign domination, be it political, economic or cultural.

Article 21

1. All peoples shall freely dispose of their wealth and natural resources. This right shall be exercised in the exclusive interest of the people. In no case shall a people be deprived of it.

2. In case of spoliation the dispossessed people shall have the right to the lawful recovery of its property as well as to an adequate compensation.

3. The free disposal of wealth and natural resources shall be exercised without prejudice to the obligation of promoting international economic cooperation based on mutual respect, equitable exchange and the principles of international law.

4. States parties to the present Charter shall individually and collectively exercise the right to free disposal of their wealth and natural resources with a view to strengthening African unity and solidarity.

5. States parties to the present Charter shall undertake to eliminate all forms of foreign economic exploitation particularly that practiced by international monopolies so as to enable their peoples to fully benefit from the advantages derived from their national resources.

Article 22

1. All peoples shall have the right to their economic, social and cultural development with due regard to their freedom and identity and in the equal enjoyment of the common heritage of mankind.

2. States shall have the duty, individually or collectively, to ensure the exercise of the right to development.

Article 23

1. All peoples shall have the right to national and international peace and security. The principles of solidarity and friendly relations implicitly affirmed by the Charter of the United Nations and reaffirmed by that of the Organization of African Unity shall govern relations between States.

2. For the purpose of strengthening peace, solidarity and friendly relations, States parties to the present Charter shall ensure that:

a. any individual enjoying the right of asylum under Article 12 of the present Charter shall not engage in subversive activities against his country of origin or any other State party to the present Charter;

b. their territories shall not be used as bases for subversive or terrorist activities against the people of any other State party to the present Charter.

Article 24

All peoples shall have the right to a general satisfactory environment favorable to their development.

Article 25

States parties to the present Charter shall have the duty to promote and ensure through teaching, education and publication, the respect of the rights and freedoms contained in the present Charter and to see to it that these freedoms and rights as well as corresponding obligations and duties are understood.

Article 26

States parties to the present Charter shall have the duty to guarantee the independence of the Courts and shall allow the establishment and improvement of appropriate national institutions entrusted with the promotion and protection of the rights and freedoms guaranteed by the present Charter.

CHAPTER II—DUTIES

Article 27

1. Every individual shall have duties towards his family and society, the State and other legally recognized communities and the international community.

2. The rights and freedoms of each individual shall be exercised with due regard to the rights of others, collective security, morality and common interest.

Article 28

Every individual shall have the duty to respect and consider his fellow beings without discrimination, and to maintain relations aimed at promoting, safeguarding and reinforcing mutual respect and tolerance.

Article 29

The individual shall also have the duty:

1. To preserve the harmonious development of the family and to work for the cohesion and respect of the family; to respect his parents at all times, to maintain them in case of need;

2. To serve his national community by placing his physical and intellectual abilities at its service;

3. Not to compromise the security of the State whose national or resident he is;

4. To preserve and strengthen social and national solidarity, particularly when the latter is threatened;

5. To preserve and strengthen the national independence and the territorial integrity of his country and to contribute to its defence in accordance with the law;

6. To work to the best of his abilities and competence, and to pay taxes imposed by law in the interest of the society;

7. To preserve and strengthen positive African cultural values in his relations with other members of the society, in the spirit of tolerance, dialogue and consultation and, in general, to contribute to the promotion of the moral well being of society;

8. To contribute to the best of his abilities, at all times and at all levels, to the promotion and achievement of African unity.

PART II—MEASURES OF SAFEGUARD

CHAPTER I—ESTABLISHMENT AND ORGANIZATION OF THE AFRICAN COMMISSION ON HUMAN AND PEOPLES' RIGHTS

Article 30

An African Commission on Human and Peoples' Rights, hereinafter called "the Commission," shall be established within the Organization of African Unity to promote human and peoples' rights and ensure their protection in Africa.

Article 31

1. The Commission shall consist of eleven members chosen from amongst African personalities of the highest reputation, known for their high morality, integrity, impartiality and competence in matters of human and peoples' rights; particular consideration being given to persons having legal experience.

2. The members of the Commission shall serve in their personal capacity.

Article 32

The Commission shall not include more than one national of the same State.

Article 33

The members of the Commission shall be elected by secret ballot by the Assembly of Heads of State and Government, from a list of persons nominated by the States parties to the present Charter.

Article 34

Each State party to the present Charter may not nominate more than two candidates. The candidates must have the nationality of one of the States parties to the present Charter. When two candidates are nominated by a State, one of them may not be a national of that State.

Article 35

1. The Secretary General of the Organization of African Unity shall invite States parties to the present Charter at least four months before the elections to nominate candidates;

2. The Secretary General of the Organization of African Unity shall make an alphabetical list of the persons thus nominated and communicate it to the Heads of State and Government at least one month before the elections.

Article 36

The members of the Commission shall be elected for a six year period and shall be eligible for re-election. However, the term of office of four of the members elected at the first election shall terminate after two years and the term of office of three others, at the end of four years.

Article 37

Immediately after the first election, the Chairman of the Assembly of Heads of State and Government of the Organization of African Unity shall draw lots to decide the names of those members referred to in Article 36.

Article 38

After their election, the members of the Commission shall make a solemn declaration to discharge their duties impartially and faithfully.

Article 39

1. In the case of death or resignation of a member of the Commission the Chairman of the Commission shall immediately inform the Secretary General of the Organization of African Unity, who shall declare the seat vacant from the date of death or from the date on which the resignation takes effect.

2. If, in the unanimous opinion of other members of the Commission, a member has stopped discharging his duties for any reason other than temporary absence, the Chairman of the Commission shall inform the Secretary General of the Organization of African Unity, who shall then declare the seat vacant.

3. In each of the cases anticipated above, the Assembly of Heads of State and Government shall replace the member whose seat became vacant for the remaining period of his term unless the period is less than six months.

Article 40

Every member of the Commission shall be in office until the date his successor assumes office.

Article 41

The Secretary-General of the Organization of African Unity shall appoint the Secretary of the Commission. He shall also provide the staff and services necessary for the effective discharge of the duties of the Commission. The Organization of African Unity shall bear the costs of the staff and services.

Article 42

1. The Commission shall elect its Chairman and Vice Chairman for a two-year period. They shall be eligible for re-election.

2. The Commission shall lay down its rules of procedure.

3. Seven members shall form the quorum.

4. In case of an equality of votes, the Chairman shall have a casting vote.

5. The Secretary General may attend the meetings of the Commission. He shall neither participate in the deliberations nor shall he be entitled to vote. The Chairman of the Commission may, however, invite him to speak.

Article 43

In discharging their duties, members of the Commission shall enjoy diplomatic privileges and immunities provided for in the General Convention on the Privileges and Immunities of the Organization of African Unity.

Article 44

Provision shall be made for the emoluments and allowances of the members of the Commission in the Regular Budget of the Organization of African Unity.

CHAPTER II—MANDATE OF THE COMMISSION

Article 45

The functions of the Commission shall be:

1. To promote Human and Peoples' Rights and in particular:

   a. to collect documents, undertake studies and researches on African problems in the field of human and peoples' rights, organize seminars, symposia and conferences, disseminate information, encourage national and local institutions concerned with human and peoples' rights, and should the case arise, give its views or make recommendations to Governments.

   b. to formulate and lay down, principles and rules aimed at solving legal problems relating to human and peoples' rights and fundamental freedoms upon which African Governments may base their legislations.

   c. [to] co-operate with other African and international institutions concerned with the promotion and protection of human and peoples' rights.

2. Ensure the protection of human and peoples' rights under conditions laid down by the present Charter.

3. Interpret all the provisions of the present Charter at the request of a State party, an institution of the OAU or an African Organization recognized by the OAU.

4. Perform any other tasks which may be entrusted to it by the Assembly of Heads of State and Government.

CHAPTER III—PROCEDURE OF THE COMMISSION

Article 46

The Commission may resort to any appropriate method of investigation; it may hear from the Secretary General of the Organization of African Unity or any other person capable of enlightening it.

Communication From States

Article 47

If a State party to the present Charter has good reasons to believe that another State party to this Charter has violated the provisions of the Charter, it may draw, by written communication, the attention of that State to the matter. This communication shall also be addressed to the Secretary General of the OAU and to the Chairman of the Commission. Within three months of the receipt of the communication, the State to which the communication is addressed shall give the enquiring State, written explanation or statement elucidating the matter. This should include as much as possible relevant information relating to the laws and rules of procedure applied and applicable, and the redress already given or course of action available.

Article 48

If within three months from the date on which the original communication is received by the State to which it is addressed, the issue is not settled to the satisfaction of the two States involved through bilateral negotiation or by any other peaceful procedure, either State shall have the right to submit the matter to the Commission through the Chairman and shall notify the other States involved.

Article 49

Notwithstanding the provisions of Article 47, if a State party to the present Charter considers that another State party has violated the provisions of the Charter, it may refer the matter directly to the Commission by addressing a communication to the Chairman, to the Secretary General of the Organization of African Unity and the State concerned.

Article 50

The Commission can only deal with a matter submitted to it after making sure that all local remedies, if they exist, have been exhausted, unless it is obvious to the Commission that the procedure of achieving these remedies would be unduly prolonged.

Article 51

1. The Commission may ask the States concerned to provide it with all relevant information.

2. When the Commission is considering the matter, States concerned may be represented before it and submit written or oral representation.

Article 52

After having obtained from the States concerned and from other sources all the information it deems necessary and after having tried all appropriate means to reach an amicable solution based on the respect of Human and Peoples' Rights, the Commission shall prepare, within a reasonable period of time from the notification referred to in Article 48, a report stating the facts and its findings. This report shall be sent to the States concerned and communicated to the Assembly of Heads of State and Government.

Article 53

While transmitting its report, the Commission may make to the Assembly of Heads of State and Government such recommendations as it deems useful.

Article 54

The Commission shall submit to each ordinary Session of the Assembly of Heads of State and Government a report on its activities.

Other Communications

Article 55

1. Before each Session, the Secretary of the Commission shall make a list of the communications other than those of States parties to the present Charter and transmit them to the members of the Commission, who shall indicate which communications should be considered by the Commission.

2. A communication shall be considered by the Commission if a simple majority of its members so decide.

Article 56

Communications relating to human and peoples' rights referred to in Article 55 received by the Commission, shall be considered if they:

1. Indicate their authors even if the latter request anonymity,

2. Are compatible with the Charter of the Organization of African Unity or with the present Charter,

3. Are not written in disparaging or insulting language directed against the State concerned and its institutions or to the Organization of African Unity,

4. Are not based exclusively on news discriminated [sic] through the mass media,

5. Are sent after exhausting local remedies, if any, unless it is obvious that this procedure is unduly prolonged,

6. Are submitted within a reasonable period from the time local remedies are exhausted or from the date the Commission is seized of the matter, and

7. Do not deal with cases which have been settled by these States involved in accordance with the principles of the Charter of the United Nations, or the Charter of the Organization of African Unity or the provisions of the present Charter.

Article 57

Prior to any substantive consideration, all communications shall be brought to the knowledge of the State concerned by the Chairman of the Commission.

Article 58

1. When it appears after deliberations of the Commission that one or more communications apparently relate to special cases which reveal the existence of a series of serious or massive violations of human and peoples' rights, the Commission shall draw the attention of the Assembly of Heads of State and Government to these special cases.

2. The Assembly of Heads of State and Government may then request the Commission to undertake an in-depth study of these cases and make a factual report, accompanied by its findings and recommendations.

3. A case of emergency duly noticed by the Commission shall be submitted by the latter to the Chairman of the Assembly of Heads of State and Government who may request an in-depth study.

Article 59

1. All measures taken within the provisions of the present Chapter shall remain confidential until such a time as the Assembly of Heads of State and Government shall otherwise decide.

2. However, the report shall be published by the Chairman of the Commission upon the decision of the Assembly of Heads of State and Government.

3. The report on the activities of the Commission shall be published by its Chairman after it has been considered by the Assembly of Heads of State and Government.

CHAPTER IV — APPLICABLE PRINCIPLES

Article 60

The Commission shall draw inspiration from international law on human and peoples' rights, particularly from the provisions of various African instruments on human and peoples' rights, the Charter of the United Nations, the Charter of the Organization of African Unity, the Universal Declaration of Human Rights, other instruments adopted by the United Nations and by African countries in the field of human and peoples' rights as well as from the provisions of various instruments adopted within the Specialized Agencies of the United Nations of which the parties to the present Charter are members.

Article 61

The Commission shall also take into consideration, as subsidiary measures to determine the principles of law, other general or special international conventions, laying down rules expressly recognized by member states of the Organization of African Unity, African practices consistent with international norms on human and people's rights, customs generally accepted as law, general principles of law recognized by African states as well as legal precedents and doctrine.

Article 62

Each state party shall undertake to submit every two years, from the date the present Charter comes into force, a report on the legislative or other measures taken with a view to giving effect to the rights and freedoms recognized and guaranteed by the present Charter.

[Ed. Note: Article 63 (signature, ratification, and entry into force), article 64 (selection and convocation of Commission), article 65 (entry into force for countries that ratify or accede later), article 66 (special agreements allowed), article 67 (notification), and article 68 (amendments) have been omitted.]

Protocol to the African Charter on Human and Peoples' Rights on the Establishment of an African Court on Human and Peoples' Rights

June 9, 1998, OAU/LEG/EXP/AFCHPR/PROTII, *available at* http://www.africa-union.org/en/docs/Protocol%20African%20court.pdf.

[Ed. Note: As of May 2002, this Protocol had not come into force. Thirty-six States have signed the Protocol. Fifteen instruments of ratification or accession are required for the Protocol to come into force, and only five have been received. *See* Resolution on the Ratification of the Protocol to the African Charter on Human and People's Rights on the Establishment of an African Court on Human and Peoples' Rights, African Commission on Human and Peoples' Rights, May 2002 (Pretoria, South Africa), *available at* http://www1.umn.edu/humanrts/africa/courtresolution-2002.html.]

The Member States of the Organization of African Unity hereinafter referred to as the OAU, States Parties to the African Charter on Human and Peoples' Rights.

Considering that the Charter of the Organization of African Unity recognizes that freedom, equality, justice, peace and dignity are essential objectives for the achievement of the legitimate aspirations of the African Peoples;

Noting that the African Charter on Human and Peoples' Rights reaffirms adherence to the principles of Human and Peoples' Rights, freedoms and duties contained in the declarations, conventions and other instruments adopted by the Organization of African Unity, and other international organizations;

Recognizing that the two-fold objective of the African Commission on Human and Peoples' Rights is to ensure on the one hand promotion and on the other protection of Human and Peoples' Rights, freedom and duties;

Recognizing further, the efforts of the African Charter on Human and Peoples' Rights in the promotion and protection of Human and Peoples' Rights since its inception in 1987;

Recalling resolution AHGéRes.230 (XXX) adopted by the Assembly of Heads of State and Government in June 1994 in Tunis, Tunisia, requesting the Secretary-General to convene a Government experts' meeting to ponder, in conjunction with the African Commission, over the means to enhance the efficiency of the African commission and to consider in particular the establishment of an African Court on Human and Peoples' Rights;

Noting the first and second Government legal experts' meeting held respectively in Cape Town, South Africa (September 1995) and Nouakchott, Mauritania (April 1997), and the third Government Legal Experts meeting held in Addis Ababa, Ethiopia (December 1997), which was enlarged to include Diplomats;

Firmly convinced that the attainment of the objectives of the African Charter on Human and Peoples' Rights requires the establishment of an African Court on Human and Peoples' Rights to complement and reinforce the functions of the African Commission on Human and Peoples' Rights.

HAVE AGREED AS FOLLOWS:

Article 1 — Establishment of the Court

There shall be established within the Organization of African Unity an African Court Human and Peoples' Rights hereinafter referred to as "the Court," the organization, jurisdiction and functioning of which shall be governed by the present Protocol.

Article 2 — Relationship Between the Court and the Commission

The Court shall, bearing in mind the provisions of this Protocol, complement the protective mandate of the African Commission on Human and Peoples' Rights hereinafter referred to as "the Commission," conferred upon it by the African Charter on Human and Peoples' Rights, hereinafter referred to as "the Charter."

Article 3 — Jurisdiction

1. The jurisdiction of the Court shall extend to all cases and disputes submitted to it concerning the interpretation and application of the Charter, this Protocol and any other relevant Human Rights instrument ratified by the States concerned.

2. In the event of a dispute as to whether the Court has jurisdiction, the Court shall decide.

Article 4 — Advisory Opinions

1. At the request of a Member State of the OAU, the OAU, any of its organs, or any African organization recognized by the OAU, the Court may provide an opinion on any legal matter relating to the Charter or any other relevant human rights instruments, provided that the subject matter of the opinion is not related to a matter being examined by the Commission.

2. The Court shall give reasons for its advisory opinions provided that every judge shall be entitled to deliver a separate or dissenting decision.

Article 5 — Access to the Court

1. The following are entitled to submit cases to the Court:

a. The Commission;

b. The State Party, which had lodged a complaint to the Commission;

c. The State Party against which the complaint has been lodged at the Commission;

d. The State Party whose citizen is a victim of human rights violation;

e. African Intergovernmental Organizations.

2. When a State Party has an interest in a case, it may submit a request to the Court to be permitted to join.

3. The Court may entitle relevant Non-Governmental organizations (NGOs) with observer status before the Commission, and individuals to institute cases directly before it, in accordance with article 34(6) of this Protocol.

Article 6 — Admissibility of Cases

1. The Court, when deciding on the admissibility of a case instituted under article 5(3) of this Protocol, may request the opinion of the Commission which shall give it as soon as possible.

2. The Court shall rule on the admissibility of cases taking into account the provisions of article 56 of the Charter.

3. The Court may consider cases or transfer them to the Commission.

Article 7 — Sources of Law

The Court shall apply the provision of the Charter and any other relevant human rights instruments ratified by the States concerned.

Article 8 — Consideration of Cases

The Rules of Procedure of the Court shall lay down the detailed conditions under which the Court shall consider cases brought before it, bearing in mind the complementarity between the Commission and the Court.

Article 9 — Amicable Settlement

The Court may try to reach an amicable settlement in a case pending before it in accordance with the provisions of the Charter.

Article 10 — Hearings and Representation

1. The Court shall conduct its proceedings in public. The Court may, however, conduct proceedings in camera as may be provided for in the Rules of Procedure.

2. Any party to a case shall be entitled to be represented by a legal representative of the party's choice. Free legal representation may be provided where the interests of justice so require.

3. Any person, witness or representative of the parties, who appears before the Court, shall enjoy protection and all facilities, in accordance with international law, necessary for the discharging of their functions, tasks and duties in relation to the Court.

Article 11 — Composition

1. The Court shall consist of eleven judges, nationals of Member States of the OAU, elected in an individual capacity from among jurists of high moral character and of recognized practical, judicial or academic competence and experience in the field of human and peoples' rights.

2. No two judges shall be nationals of the same State.

Article 12 — Nominations

1. States Parties to the Protocol may each propose up to three candidates, at least two of whom shall be nationals of that State.

2. Due consideration shall be given to adequate gender representation in nomination process.

Article 13 — List of Candidates

1. Upon entry into force of this Protocol, the Secretary-general of the OAU shall request each State Party to the Protocol to present, within ninety (90) days of such a request, its nominees for the office of judge of the Court.

2. The Secretary-General of the OAU shall prepare a list in alphabetical order of the candidates nominated and transmit it to the Member States of the OAU at least thirty

days prior to the next session of the Assembly of Heads of State and Government of the OAU, hereinafter referred to as "the Assembly."

Article 14 — Elections

1. The judges of the Court shall be elected by secret ballot by the Assembly from the list referred to in Article 13(2) of the present Protocol.

2. The Assembly shall ensure that in the Court as a whole there is representation of the main regions of Africa and of their principal legal traditions.

3. In the election of the judges, the Assembly shall ensure that there is adequate gender representation.

Article 15 — Term of Office

1. The judges of the Court shall be elected for a period of six years and may be re-elected only once. The terms of four judges elected at the first election shall expire at the end of two years, and the terms of four more judges shall expire at the end of four years.

2. The judges whose terms are to expire at the end of the initial periods of two and four years shall be chosen by lot to be drawn by the Secretary-General of the OAU immediately after the first election has been completed.

3. A judge elected to replace a judge whose term of office has not expired shall hold office for the remainder of the predecessor's term.

4. All judges except the President shall perform their functions on a part-time basis. However, the Assembly may change this arrangement as it deems appropriate.

Article 16 — Oath of Office

After their election, the judges of the Court shall make a solemn declaration to discharge their duties impartially and faithfully.

Article 17 — Independence

1. The independence of the judges shall be fully ensured in accordance with international law.

2. No judge may hear any case in which the same judge has previously taken part as agent, counsel or advocate for one of the parties or as a member of a national or international court or a commission of enquiry or in any other capacity. Any doubt on this point shall be settled by decision of the Court.

3. The judges of the Court shall enjoy, from the moment of their election and throughout their term of office, the immunities extended to diplomatic agents in accordance with international law.

4. At no time shall the judges of the Court be held liable for any decision or opinion issued in the exercise of their functions.

Article 18 — Incompatibility

The position of judge of the court is incompatible with any activity that might interfere with the independence or impartiality of such a judge or the demands of the office as determined in the Rules of Procedure of the Court.

Article 19 — Cessation of Office

1. A judge shall not be suspended or removed from office unless, by the unanimous decision of the other judges of the Court, the judge concerned has been found to be no longer fulfilling the required conditions to be a judge of the Court.

2. Such a decision of the Court shall become final unless it is set aside by the Assembly at its next session.

Article 20 — Vacancies

1. In case of death or resignation of a judge of the Court, the President of the Court shall immediately inform the Secretary General of the Organization of African Unity, who shall declare the seat vacant from the date of death or from the date on which the resignation takes effect.

2. The Assembly shall replace the judge whose office became vacant unless the remaining period of the term is less than one hundred and eighty (180) days.

3. The same procedure and considerations as set out in Articles 12, 13 and 14 shall be followed for the filling of vacancies.

Article 21 — Presidency of the Court

1. The Court shall elect its President and one Vice-President for a period of two years. They may be re-elected only once.

2. The President shall perform judicial functions on a full-time basis and shall reside at the seat of the Court.

3. The functions of the President and the Vice-President shall be set out in the Rules of Procedure of the Court.

Article 22 — Exclusion

If the judge is a national of any State, which is a party to a case, submitted to the Court, that judge shall not hear the case.

Article 23 — Quorum

The Court shall examine cases brought before it, if it has a quorum of at least seven judges.

Article 24 — Registry of the Court

1. The Court shall appoint its own Registrar and other staff of the registry from among nationals of Member States of the OAU according to the Rules of Procedure.

2. The office and residence of the Registrar shall be at the place where the Court has its seat.

Article 25 — Seat of the Court

1. The Court shall have its seat at the place determined by the Assembly from among States parties to this Protocol. However, it may convene in the territory of any Member State of the OAU when the majority of the Court considers it desirable, and with the prior consent of the State concerned.

2. The seat of the Court may be changed by the Assembly after due consultation with the Court.

Article 26 — Evidence

1. The Court shall hear submissions by all parties and if deemed necessary, hold an enquiry. The States concerned shall assist by providing relevant facilities for the efficient handling of the case.

2. The Court may receive written and oral evidence including expert testimony and shall make its decision on the basis of such evidence.

Article 27 — Findings

1. If the Court finds that there has been violation of a human or peoples' rights, it shall make appropriate orders to remedy the violation, including the payment of fair compensation or reparation.

2. In cases of extreme gravity and urgency, and when necessary to avoid irreparable harm to persons, the Court shall adopt such provisional measures as it deems necessary.

Article 28 — Judgment

1. The Court shall render its judgment within ninety (90) days of having completed its deliberations.

2. The judgment of the Court decided by majority shall be final and not subject to appeal.

3. Without prejudice to sub-article 2 above, the Court may review its decision in the light of new evidence under conditions to be set out in the Rules of Procedure.

4. The Court may interpret its own decision.

5. The judgment of the Court shall be read in open court, due notice having been given to the parties.

6. Reasons shall be given for the judgment of the Court.

7. If the judgment of the court does not represent, in whole or in part, the unanimous decision of the judges, any judge shall be entitled to deliver a separate or dissenting opinion.

Article 29 — Notification of Judgment

1. The parties to the case shall be notified of the judgment of the Court and it shall be transmitted to the Member States of the OAU and the Commission.

2. The Council of Ministers shall also be notified of the judgment and shall monitor its execution on behalf of the Assembly.

Article 30 — Execution of Judgment

The States Parties to the present Protocol undertake to comply with the judgment in any case to which they are parties within the time stipulated by the Court and to guarantee its execution.

Article 31 — Report

The Court shall submit to each regular session of the Assembly, a report on its work during the previous year. The report shall specify, in particular, the cases in which a State has not complied with the Court's judgment.

Article 32 — Budget

Expenses of the Court, emoluments and allowances for judges and the budget of its registry, shall be determined and borne by the OAU, in accordance with criteria laid down by the OAU in consultation with the Court.

Article 33 — Rules of Procedure

The Court shall draw up its Rules and determine its own procedures. The Court shall consult the Commission as appropriate.

Article 34 — Ratification

1. This Protocol shall be open for signature and ratification or accession by any State Party to the Charter.

2. The instrument of ratification or accession to the present Protocol shall be deposited with the Secretary-General of the OAU.

3. The Protocol shall come into force thirty days after fifteen instruments of ratification or accession have been deposited.

4. For any State Party ratifying or acceding subsequently, the present Protocol shall come into force in respect of that State on the date of the deposit of its instrument of ratification or accession.

5. The Secretary-General of the OAU shall inform all Member States of the entry into force of the present Protocol.

6. At the time of the ratification of this Protocol or any time thereafter, the State shall make a declaration accepting the competence of the Court to receive cases under article 5(3) of this Protocol. The Court shall not receive any petition under article 5(3) involving a State Party which has not made such a declaration.

7. Declarations made under sub-article (6) above shall be deposited with the Secretary-General, who shall transmit copies thereof to the State parties.

Article 35 — Amendments

1. The present Protocol may be amended if a State Party to the Protocol makes a written request to that effect to the Secretary-General of the OAU. The Assembly may adopt, by simple majority, the draft amendment after all the State Parties to the present Protocol have been duly informed of it and the Court has given its opinion on the amendment.

2. The Court shall also be entitled to propose such amendments to the present Protocol, as it may deem necessary, through the Secretary-General of the OAU.

3. The amendment shall come into force for each State Party, which has accepted it thirty days after the Secretary-General of the OAU has received notice of the acceptance.

Draft Protocol to the African Charter on Human and Peoples' Rights on the Rights of Women in Africa
Sept. 13, 2000, OAU Doc. CAB/LEG/66.6

[Ed. Note: The Protocol was first drafted in 1997, at the Experts Meeting on the Preparation of a Draft Protocol to the African Charter on Human and People's Rights. The African Commission on Human and Peoples' Rights adopted the draft Protocol and sent it to the OAU General Secretariat for appropriate action. As of June 2002, a Second Experts Meeting on the Protocol was planned. Before being submitted to countries for possible ratification, the Draft Protocol will have to be approved by the Assembly of Heads of State and Government of the African Union.]

The State Parties to this Protocol,

CONSIDERING that Article 66 of the African Charter on Human and Peoples' Rights provides for special protocols or agreements, if necessary, to supplement the provisions of the African Charter, and that the OAU Assembly of Heads of State and Government meeting in its Thirty-first Ordinary Session in Addis Ababa, Ethiopia, in June 1995, endorsed by resolution AHG/Res.240 (XXXI) the recommendation of the African Commission on Human and Peoples' Rights to elaborate a Protocol on the Rights of Women in Africa;

CONSIDERING that Article 2 of the African Charter on Human and Peoples' Rights enshrines the principle of non-discrimination on the grounds of race, ethnic group, colour, sex, language, religion, political or any other opinion, national and social origin, fortune, birth or other status;

FURTHER CONSIDERING that Article 18 of the African Charter on Human and Peoples' Rights calls on all Member States to eliminate every discrimination against women and to ensure the protection of the rights of women as stipulated in international declarations and conventions;

NOTING that Articles 60 and 61 of the African Charter on Human and Peoples' Rights recognise regional and international human rights instruments and African practices consistent with international norms on human and peoples' rights as being important reference points for the application and interpretation of the African Charter;

RECALLING that women's rights have been recognised and guaranteed in all international human rights instruments, notably the Universal Declaration of Human Rights, the International Covenant on Civil and Political Rights, the International Covenant on Economic, Social and Cultural Rights, the Convention on the Elimination of All Forms of Discrimination Against Women and all other international conventions and covenants relating to the rights of women as being inalienable, interdependent and indivisible human rights;

NOTING that women's rights and women's essential role in development have been reaffirmed in the United Nations Plans of Action on the Environment and Development in 1992, on Human Rights in 1993, on Population and Development in 1994 and on Social Development in 1995;

FURTHER NOTING that the Plans of Action adopted in Dakar and in Beijing call on all Member States of the United Nations, which have made a solemn commitment to implement them, to take concrete steps to give greater attention to the human rights of women in order to eliminate all forms of discrimination and of gender-based violence against women;

BEARING IN MIND related Resolutions, Declarations, Recommendations, Decisions and other Conventions aimed at eliminating all forms of discrimination and at promoting equality between men and women;

CONCERNED that despite the ratification of the African Charter on Human and Peoples' Rights and other international human rights instruments by the majority of Member States, and their solemn commitment to eliminate all forms of discrimination and harmful practices against women, women in Africa still continue to be victims of discrimination and harmful practices;

FIRMLY CONVINCED that any practice that hinders or endangers the normal growth and affects the physical, emotional and psychological development of women and girls should be condemned and eliminated, and

DETERMINED to ensure that the rights of women are protected in order to enable them to enjoy fully all their human rights;

HAVE AGREED AS FOLLOWS:

Article 1 — Definitions

For the purpose of the present Protocol

a. "African Charter" shall mean the African Charter on Human and Peoples' Rights;

b. "African Commission" shall mean the African Commission on Human and Peoples' Rights;

c. "Assembly" shall mean the Assembly of Heads of State and Government of the OAU;

d. "Discrimination against women" shall mean any distinction, exclusion or restriction based on sex, or any differential treatment whose objective or effects compromise or destroy the recognition, enjoyment or the exercise by women, regardless of their marital status, of human rights and fundamental freedoms in all spheres of life.

e. "Harmful Practices (HPs)" shall mean all behaviour, attitudes and/or practices which negatively affect the fundamental rights of women and girls, such as their right to life, health and bodily integrity.

f. "OAU" shall mean the Organization of African Unity.

g. "State Parties" shall mean the State Parties to this Protocol.

h. "Violence against women" shall mean all acts directed against women which cause or could cause them physical, sexual, or psychological harm, including the threat of such acts; or the imposition of arbitrary restrictions on or deprivation of fundamental freedoms in private or public life in peace time and during situations of conflict/war.

Article 2 — Elimination of Discrimination Against Women

1. State Parties shall combat all forms of discrimination against women through appropriate legislative measures. In this regard they shall:

a. include in their national constitutions and other legislative instruments the principle of equality between men and women and ensure its effective application;

b. enact and effectively implement appropriate national legislative measures to prohibit all forms of harmful practices which endanger the health and general well-being of women and girls;

c. integrate a gender perspective in their policy decisions, legislation, development plans, activities and all other spheres of life;

d. take positive action in those areas where discrimination against women in law and in fact continues to exist.

2. State Parties shall modify the social and cultural patterns of conduct of men and women through specific actions, such as:

a. public education, with a view to achieving the elimination of harmful cultural and traditional practices and all other practices which are based on the idea of the inferiority or the superiority of either of the sexes, or on stereotyped roles for men and women;

b. support local, national, regional and continental initiatives directed at eradicating all forms of discrimination against women.

Article 3 — Respect for Dignity

Women contribute to the preservation of those African values that are based on the principles of equality, dignity, justice and democracy. In this regard, the State Parties shall:

a. ensure that women enjoy rights and dignity inherent in all human beings;

b. adopt appropriate measures to prohibit any exploitation and degradation of women.

Article 4 — Right to Physical and Emotional Security

Women shall be entitled to respect of their lives and the integrity of their person. Accordingly, the State Parties shall:

a. not pronounce or carry out death sentences on pregnant women;

b. prohibit medical or scientific experiments on women without their informed consent;

c. protect girls and women against rape and all other forms of violence, including the trafficking of girls and women;

d. ensure that in times of conflict and/or war, rape, sexual abuse and violence against girls and women are considered a war crime and are punished as such.

Article 5 — Elimination of Violence Against Women

State Parties shall take appropriate measures to:

a. prohibit all forms of violence against women whether physical, mental, verbal or sexual, domestic and family, whether they take place in the private sphere or in society and public life;

b. identify the cause of violence against women and take appropriate measures to prevent and eliminate such acts of violence;

c. punish the perpetrators of such violence committed against women and ensure that the perpetrators pay adequate compensation;

d. establish mechanisms to ensure effective rehabilitation and reparation for victims of such violence.

Article 6 — Elimination of Harmful Practices

State Parties shall condemn all harmful practices which affect the fundamental human rights of women and girls and which are contrary to recognised international standards, and undertake to take all the necessary measures, inter alia:

a. to create public awareness regarding harmful practices through information, formal and informal education, communication campaigns and outreach programmes targeting all stakeholders;

b. to prohibit the amelioration or preservation of harmful practices such as the medicalisation and para-medicalisation of female genital mutilation and scarification, in order to effect a total elimination of such practices;

c. to rehabilitate victims of harmful practices by providing them with social support services such as health services to meet their health-care needs, emotional and psychological counselling and skills training aimed at making them self-supporting in order to facilitate their re-integration into their families, communities and in other sectors of the society;

d. to protect and grant asylum to those women and girls who are at risk of, have been, or are being subjected to harmful practices and all other forms of intolerance.

Article 7 — Marriage

State Parties shall ensure that man and women enjoy equal rights and are regarded as equal partners in marriage. They shall enact appropriate national legislative measures to ensure that:

a. no marriage shall take place without the informed consent of both parties;

b. the minimum age of marriage for men and women shall be 18 years;

c. polygamy shall be prohibited;

d. every marriage shall be recorded where possible in writing, as soon as possible, and registered in accordance with national laws, in order to be legally recognised;

e. the husband and wife shall by mutual agreement choose their place of residence;

f. a married woman shall have the right to keep her maiden name, to use it as she pleases, jointly or separately with her husband's surname. By mutual agreement the children of a married couple may use their mother's maiden name either separately from or jointly with that of their father's;

g. a married woman shall have the right to retain or change her nationality;

h. a man and a woman shall have the same rights and responsibilities towards their children;

i. during her marriage, the women shall have the right to acquire her own property and to administer and manage it freely; and in cases of joint ownership of property the husband and wife shall have the same rights.

Article 8 — Separation and Termination of Marriage

State Parties shall enact appropriate national legislative measures to ensure that men and women enjoy the same rights in case of separation and termination of marriage. In this regard, they shall ensure that:

a. divorce and annulment of a marriage shall be effected only by judicial order;

b. women and men shall have the same rights to seek divorce or annulment of a marriage;

c. after divorce or annulment, women and men shall have the same rights and responsibilities with respect to the children and property of the marriage;

d. in the event of separation women and men shall have equal rights and responsibilities with respect to the children and property of the marriage.

Article 9 — Right to Information and Legal Aid

Women shall have the right to have their cause heard and State Parties shall have the duty to promote and ensure that the rights of women are protected in this respect. They shall:

a. take all appropriate measures to facilitate the access of women to legal aid services;

b. support local, national, regional and continental initiatives directed at giving women access to legal aid services;

c. put in place adequate structures including appropriate education programmes to inform women and make them aware of their rights.

Article 10 — Right to Participation in Political Process and Decision Making

1. State Parties shall take specific positive action to promote the equal participation of women in the political life of their countries, ensuring that:

a. women do participate without any discrimination in all elections;

b. women are represented equally at all levels with men in all electoral and candidate lists;

c. women are partners with men at all levels of development and implementation of state policy;

2. State Parties shall ensure women's effective representation and participation at all levels of decision-making.

Article 11 — Right to Peace

1. Women shall have the right to participate in the promotion and maintainance of peace, and to live in a peaceful environment.

2. State Parties shall take all appropriate measures to involve women:

a. in programmes of education for peace and a culture of peace;

b. in the structures for conflict prevention, management and resolution at local, national, regional, continental and international levels;

c. in the local, national, sub-regional, regional, continental and international decision making structures to ensure physical, psychological, social and legal protection of refugee, returnee and displaced women;

d. in all levels of the structures established for the management of camps and asylum areas.

3. State Parties additionally shall reduce military expenditure significantly in favour of spending on social development, while guaranteeing the effective participation of women in the distribution of these resources.

4. State Parties shall take special measures to ensure:

a. effective protection of women and children in emergency and conflict situations;

b. effective protection of refugee, returnee and displaced women and children.

Article 12 — Right to Education and Training

1. State Parties shall take all appropriate measures to:

a. eliminate all forms of discrimination against women and girls in the sphere of education and training;

b. eliminate all references in textbooks and syllabuses to the stereotypes which perpetuate such discrimination;

2. State Parties shall take specific positive action to:

a. increase literacy among women;

b. promote education and training for women and girls at all levels and in all disciplines;

c. promote the retention of girls in schools and other training institutions.

Article 13 — Economic and Social Welfare Rights

State Parties shall guarantee women equal opportunities to work. In this respect, they shall:

a. promote equality in access to employment;

b. promote the right to equal remuneration for jobs of equal value for men and women;

c. ensure transparency in employment and dismissal relating to women in order to address issues of sexual harassment in the workplace;

d. allow women freedom to choose their occupation, and protect them from exploitation by their employers;

e. create conditions to promote and support the occupations and economic activities dominated by women, in particular, within the informal sector;

f. encourage the establishment of a system of protection and social insurance for women working in the informal sector;

g. introduce a minimum age of work and prohibit children below that age from working, and prohibit the exploitation of children, especially the girl-child;

h. take the necessary measures to recognise the economic value of the work of women in the home;

i. guarantee adequate pre and post-natal maternity leave;

j. ensure equality in taxation for men and women;

k. recognise the right of salaried women to the same allowances and entitlements as those granted to salaried men for their spouses and children;

l. recognise motherhood and the upbringing of children as a social function for which the State, the private sector and both parents must take responsibility.

Article 14 — Health and Reproductive Rights

1. State Parties shall ensure that the right to health of women are respected and promoted. These rights include:

a. the right to control their fertility;

b. the right to decide whether to have children;

c. the right to space their children;

d. the right to choose any method of contraception;

e. the right to protect themselves against sexually transmitted diseases, including HIV/AIDs;

f. the right to be informed on one's health status and on the health status of one's partner.

2. State Parties shall take appropriate measures to:

a. provide adequate, affordable and accessible health services to women especially those in rural areas;

b. establish pre-and post-natal health and nutritional services for women during pregnancy and while they are breast-feeding;

c. protect the reproductive rights of women particularly by authorising medical abortion in cases of rape and incest.

Article 15 — Right to Food Security

State Parties shall ensure that women have the right to nutritious and adequate food. In this regard, they shall take appropriate measures to:

a. provide women with access to clean drinking water, sources of domestic fuel, land, and the means of producing nutritious food;

b. establish adequate systems of supply and storage to ensure food security.

Article 16 — Right to Adequate Housing

Women shall have the right to equal access to housing and to acceptable living conditions in a healthy environment. To ensure this right, State Parties shall grant to women, whatever their marital status, access to adequate housing.

Article 17 — Right to Positive Cultural Context

1. Women shall have the right to live in a positive cultural context and to participate at all levels in the determination of cultural policies.

2. State Parties shall take all appropriate measures to enhance the participation of women in the conception of cultural policies at all levels.

Article 18 — Right to a Healthy and Sustainable Environment

1. Women shall have the right to live in a healthy and sustainable environment.

2. State Parties shall take all appropriate measures to:

a. involve women in the management of the environment at all levels;

b. promote research into renewable energy sources and facilitate women's access to them;

c. regulate the management, processing and storage of domestic waste;

d. ensure that proper standards are followed for the storage, transportation and destruction of toxic waste.

Article 19 — Right to Sustainable Development

1. Women shall have the right to fully enjoy their right to sustainable development.

2. State Parties shall take all appropriate measures to:

a. ensure that women participate fully at all levels in the conceptualisation, decision-making, implementation and evaluation of development policies and programmes;

b. facilitate women's access to land and guarantee their right to property, whatever their marital status;

c. facilitate women's access to credit and natural resources through flexible mechanisms;

d. take into account indicators of human development specifically relating to women in the elaboration of development policies and programmes;

e. and ensure that in the implementation of trade and economic policies and programmes such as globalisation, the negative effects on women are minimised.

Article 20—Widows' Rights

State Parties shall take appropriate measures to ensure effective implementation of the following provisions:

a. prohibit that widows be subjected to inhuman, humiliating and degrading treatment;

b. widows shall become the guardians of their children, after the death of the husband;

c. widows shall have the right to marry a person of their choice.

Article 21—Right to Inheritance

1. A widow/widower shall have the right to inherit each other's property. In the event of death, the surviving spouse has the right, whatever the matrimonial regime, to continue living in the matrimonial house.

2. Women and girls shall have the same rights as men and boys to inherit, in equal shares, their parents' properties.

Article 22—Special Protection of Elderly Women and Women with Disability

Elderly women and women with disability have the right to specific measures of protection commensurate with their physical and moral needs.

Article 23—Interpretation

The African Court on Human and Peoples' Rights shall be seized with matters of interpretation arising from the application or implementation of this Protocol.

Article 24—Signature, Ratification and Accession

1. This Protocol shall be open to signature, ratification and accession by the State Parties, in accordance with their respective constitutional procedures.

2. The instruments of ratification or accession shall be deposited with the Secretary General of the OAU.

Article 25—Entry into Force

1. This Protocol shall enter into force thirty (30) days after the deposit of the fifteenth (15) instrument of ratification.

2. For each of the State Party that accedes to this Protocol after its coming into force, the Protocol shall come into force at the date of deposit of the instrument of accession.

3. The Secretary General of the OAU shall inform the State Parties of the coming into force of this Protocol.

Article 26—Amendment and Revision

1. Any State Party may submit proposals for the amendment or revision of this Protocol.

2. Proposals for amendment or revision shall be submitted, in writing, to the Secretary General of the OAU who shall transmit same to the State Parties within thirty (30) days of receipt thereof.

3. The Assembly, upon advice of the African Commission, shall examine these proposals within a period of one (1) year following notification of State Parties, in accordance with the provisions of paragraph 2 of this article.

4. Amendments or revision shall be adopted by the Assembly by consensus or, failing which, by a simple majority.

5. The Commission may also, through the Secretary General of the OAU, propose amendments to this Protocol.

6. The amendment shall come into force for each State Party which has accepted it thirty (30) days after the Secretary General of the OAU has received notice of the acceptance.

Article 27 — Status of the Present Protocol

None of the provisions of the present Protocol shall affect more favourable provisions for the realisation of rights of women contained in the national legislation of State Parties or in any other regional, sub-regional, continental or international conventions, treaties or agreements applicable in these State Parties.

African Charter on the Rights and Welfare of the Child

July 1, 1990, OAU Doc. CAB/LEG/153/Rev. 2 (1990)

[Ed. Note: The treaty entered into force November 29, 1999. As of August 2000, twenty-one countries had deposited their instruments of ratification. Another eighteen countries had signed the Charter. *See* http://www1.umn.edu/humanrts/instree/afchildratifications.html]

PREAMBLE

The African Member States of the Organization of African Unity, Parties to the present Charter entitled 'African Charter on the Rights and Welfare of the Child,'

Considering that the Charter of the Organization of African Unity recognizes the paramountcy of Human Rights and the African Charter on Human and People's Rights proclaimed and agreed that everyone is entitled to all the rights and freedoms recognized and guaranteed therein, without distinction of any kind such as race, ethnic group, colour, sex, language, religion, political or any other opinion, national and social origin, fortune, birth or other status,

Recalling the Declaration on the Rights and Welfare of the African Child (AHG/ST.4 Rev.l) adopted by the Assembly of Heads of State and Government of the Organization of African Unity, at its Sixteenth Ordinary Session in Monrovia, Liberia, from 17 to 20 July 1979, recognized the need to take appropriate measures to promote and protect the rights and welfare of the African Child,

Noting with concern that the situation of most African children, remains critical due to the unique factors of their socio-economic, cultural, traditional and developmental circumstances, natural disasters, armed conflicts, exploitation and hunger, and on account of the child's physical and mental immaturity he/she needs special safeguards and care,

Recognizing that the child occupies a unique and privileged position in the African society and that for the full and harmonious development of his personality. the child should grow up in a family environment in an atmosphere of happiness, love and understanding,

Recognizing that the child, due to the needs of his physical and mental development requires particular care with regard to health, physical, mental, moral and social development, and requires legal protection in conditions of freedom, dignity and security,

Taking into consideration the virtues of their cultural heritage, historical background and the values of the African civilization which should inspire and characterize their reflection on the concept of the rights and welfare of the child,

Considering that the promotion and protection of the rights and welfare of the child also implies the performance of duties on the part of everyone,

Reaffirming adherence to the principles of the rights and welfare of the child contained in the declaration, conventions and other instruments of the Organization of African Unity and in the United Nations and in particular the United Nations Convention on the Rights of the Child, and the OAU Heads of State and Government's Declaration on the Rights and Welfare of the African Child:

HAVE AGREED AS FOLLOWS:

PART I: RIGHTS AND DUTIES

CHAPTER ONE—RIGHTS AND WELFARE OF THE CHILD

Article I—Obligation of States Parties

1. The Member States of the Organization of African Unity Parties to the present Charter shall recognize the rights, freedoms and duties enshrined in this Charter and shall undertake the necessary steps, in accordance with their Constitutional processes and with the provisions of the present Charter, to adopt such legislative or other measures as may be necessary to give effect to the provisions of this Charter.

2. Nothing in this Charter shall affect any provisions that are more conducive to the realization of the rights and welfare of the child contained in the law of a State Party or in any other international Convention or agreement in force in that State.

3. Any custom, tradition, cultural or religious practice that is inconsistent with the rights, duties and obligations contained in the present Charter shall to the extent of such inconsistency be discouraged.

Article II—Definition of a Child

For the purposes of this Charter, a child means every human being below the age of 18 years.

Article III—Non-Discrimination

Every child shall be entitled to the enjoyment of the rights and freedoms recognized and guaranteed in this Charter irrespective of the child's or his/her parents' or legal guardians' race, ethnic group, colour, sex, language, relation [sic], political or other opinion, national and social origin, fortune, birth or other status.

Article IV—Best Interests of the Child

1. In all actions concerning the child undertaken by any person or authority the best interests of the child shall be the primary consideration.

2. In all judicial or administrative proceedings affecting a child who is capable of communicating his/her own views, an opportunity shall be provided for the views of the child to be heard either directly or through an impartial representative as a party to the proceedings, and those views shall be taken into consideration by the relevant authority in accordance with the provisions of appropriate law.

Article V—Survival and Development

1. Every child has an inherent right to life. This right shall be protected by law.

2. States Parties to the present Charter shall ensure, to the maximum extent possible, the survival, protection and development of the child.

3. Death sentence shall not be pronounced for crimes committed by children.

Article VI — Name and Nationality

1. Every child shall have the right from his birth to a name.
2. Every child shall be registered immediately after birth.
3. Every child has the right to acquire a nationality.
4. States Parties to the present Charter shall undertake to ensure that their constitutional legislations recognize the principles according to which a child shall acquire the nationality of the State in the territory of which he has been born if, at the time of the child's birth, he is not granted nationality by any other State in accordance with its laws.

Article VII — Freedom of Expression

Every child who is capable of communicating his or her own views shall be assured the rights to express his opinions freely in all matters and to disseminate his opinions subject to such restrictions as are prescribed by laws.

Article VIII — Freedom of Association

Every child shall have the right to free association and freedom of peaceful assembly in conformity with the law.

Article IX — Freedom of Thought, Conscience and Religion

1. Every child shall have the right to freedom of thought, conscience and relation [sic].
2. Parents and, where applicable, legal guardians shall have a duty to provide guidance and direction in the exercise of these rights having regard to the evolving capacities, and best interests of the child.
3. States Parties shall respect the duty of parents and, where applicable, legal guardians to provide guidance and direction in the enjoyment of these rights subject to the national laws and policies.

Article X — Protection of Privacy

No child shall be subject to arbitrary or unlawful interference with his privacy, family, home or correspondence, or to the attacks upon his honour or reputation, provided that parents or legal guardians shall have the right to exercise reasonable supervision over the conduct of their children. The child has the right to the protection of the law against such interference or attacks.

Article XI — Education

1. Every child shall have the right to an education.
2. The education of the child shall be directed to:

   a. the promotion and development of the child's personality, talents and mental and physical abilities to their fullest potential;

   b. fostering respect for human rights and fundamental freedoms with particular reference to those set out in the provisions of various African instruments on human and peoples' rights and international human rights declarations and conventions;

   c. the preservation and strengthening of positive African morals, traditional values and cultures;

   d. the preparation of the child for responsible life in a free society, in the spirit of understanding, tolerance, dialogue, mutual respect and friendship among all peoples ethnic, tribal and religious groups;

   e. the preservation of national independence and territorial integrity;

f. the promotion and achievement of African unity and solidarity;

g. the development of respect for the environment and natural resources;

h. the promotion of the child's understanding of primary health care.

3. States Parties to the present Charter shall take all appropriate measures with a view to achieving the full realization of this right and shall in particular:

a. provide free and compulsory basic education;

b. encourage the development of secondary education in its different forms and to progressively make it free and accessible to all;

c. make the higher education accessible to all on the basis of capacity and ability by every appropriate means;

d. take measures to encourage regular attendance at schools and the reduction of drop-out rate;

e. take special measures in respect of female, gifted and disadvantaged children, to ensure equal access to education for all sections of the community.

4. States Parties to the present Charter shall respect the rights and duties of parents, and where applicable, of legal guardians to choose for their children schools, other than those established by public authorities, which conform to such minimum standards as may be approved by the State, to ensure the religious and moral education of the child in a manner consistent with the evolving capacities of the child.

5. States Parties to the present Charter shall take all appropriate measures to ensure that a child who is subjected to schools or parental discipline shall be treated with humanity and with respect for the inherent dignity of the child and in conformity with the present Charter.

6. States Parties to the present Charter shall take all appropriate measures to ensure that children who become pregnant before completing their education shall have an opportunity to continue with their education on the basis of their individual ability.

7. No part of this Article shall be construed as to interfere with the liberty of individuals and bodies to establish and direct educational institutions subject to the observance of the principles set out in paragraph 1 of this Article and the requirement that the education given in such institutions shall conform to such minimum standards as may be laid down by the States.

Article XII — Leisure, Recreation and Cultural Activities

1. States Parties recognize the right of the child to rest and leisure, to engage in play and recreational activities appropriate to the age of the child and to participate freely in cultural life and the arts.

2. States Parties shall respect and promote the right of the child to fully participate in cultural and artistic life and shall encourage the provision of appropriate and equal opportunities for cultural, artistic, recreational and leisure activity.

Article XIII — Handicapped Children

1. Every child who is mentally or physically disabled shall have the right to special measures of protection in keeping with his physical and moral needs and under conditions which ensure his dignity, promote his self-reliance and active participation in the community.

2. States Parties to the present Charter shall ensure, subject to available resources, to a disabled child and to those responsible for his care, of assistance for which application is made and which is appropriate to the child's condition and in particular shall

ensure that the disabled child has effective access to training, preparation for employment and recreation opportunities in a manner conducive to the child achieving the fullest possible social integration, individual development and his cultural and moral development.

3. The States Parties to the present Charter shall use their available resources with a view to achieving progressively the full convenience of the mentally and physically disabled person to movement and access to public highway, buildings and other places to which the disabled may legitimately want to have access to.

Article XIV — Health and Health Services

1. Every child shall have the right to enjoy the best attainable state of physical, mental and spiritual health.

2. States Parties to the present Charter shall undertake to pursue the full implementation of this right and in particular shall take measures:

    a. to reduce infant and child morality rate;

    b. to ensure the provision of necessary medical assistance and health care to all children with emphasis on the development of primary health care;

    c. to ensure the provision of adequate nutrition and safe drinking water;

    d. to combat disease and malnutrition within the framework of primary health care through the application of appropriate technology;

    e. to ensure appropriate health care for expectant and nursing mothers;

    f. to develop preventive health care and family life education and provision of service;

    g. to integrate basic health service programmes in national development plans;

    h. to ensure that all sectors of the society, in particular, parents, children, community leaders and community workers are informed and supported in the use of basic knowledge of child health and nutrition, the advantages of breastfeeding, hygiene and environmental sanitation and the prevention of domestic and other accidents;

    i. to ensure the meaningful participation of non-governmental organizations, local communities and the beneficiary population in the planning and management of a basic service programme for children;

    j. to support through technical and financial means, the mobilization of local community resources in the development of primary health care for children.

Article XV — Child Labour

1. Every child shall be protected from all forms of economic exploitation and from performing any work that is likely to be hazardous or to interfere with the child's physical, mental, spiritual, moral, or social development.

2. States Parties to the present Charter take all appropriate legislative and administrative measures to ensure the full implementation of this Article which covers both the formal and informal sectors of employment and having regard to the relevant provisions of the International Labour Organization's instruments relating to children, States Parties shall in particular:

    a. provide through legislation, minimum wages for admission to every employment;

    b. provide for appropriate regulation of hours and conditions of employment;

    c. provide for appropriate penalties or other sanctions to ensure the effective enforcement of this Article;

    d. promote the dissemination of information on the hazards of child labour to all sectors of the community.

Article XVI — Protection against Child Abuse and Torture

1. States Parties to the present Charter shall take specific legislative, administrative, social and educational measures to protect the child from all forms of torture, inhuman or degrading treatment and especially physical or mental injury or abuse, neglect or maltreatment including sexual abuse, while in the care of a parent, legal guardian or school authority or any other person who has the care of the child.

2. Protective measures under this Article shall include effective procedures for the establishment of special monitoring units to provide necessary support for the child and for those who have the care of the child, as well as other forms of prevention and for identification, reporting referral investigation, treatment, and follow-up of instances of child abuse and neglect.

Article XVII — Administration of Juvenile Justice

1. Every child accused or found guilty of having infringed penal law shall have the right to special treatment in a manner consistent with the child's sense of dignity and worth and which reinforces the child['s] respect for human rights and fundamental freedoms of others.

2. States Parties to the present Charter shall in particular:

a. ensure that no child who is detained or imprisoned or otherwise deprived of his/her liberty is subjected to torture, inhuman or degrading treatment or punishment;

b. ensure that children are separated from adults in their place of detention or imprisonment;

c. ensure that every child accused of infringing the penal law:

i. shall be presumed innocent until duly recognized guilty;

ii. shall be informed promptly in a language that he understands and in detail of the charge against him, and shall be entitled to the assistance of an interpreter if he or she cannot understand the language used;

iii. shall be afforded legal and other appropriate assistance in the preparation and presentation of his defence;

iv. shall have the matter determined as speedily as possible by an impartial tribunal and if found guilty, be entitled to an appeal by a higher tribunal;

d. prohibit the press and the public from trial.

3. The essential aim of treatment of every child during the trial and also if found guilty of infringing the penal law shall be his or her reformation, re-integration into his or her family and social rehabilitation.

4. There shall be a minimum age below which children shall be presumed not to have the capacity to infringe the penal law.

Article XVIII — Protection of the Family

1. The family shall be the natural unit and basis of society. It shall enjoy the protection and support of the State for its establishment and development.

2. States Parties to the present Charter shall take appropriate steps to ensure equality of rights and responsibilities of spouses with regard to children during marriage and in the event of its dissolution. In case of dissolution, provision shall be made for the necessary protection of the child.

3. No child shall be deprived of maintenance by reference to the parents' marital status.

Article XIX — Parent Care and Protection

1. Every child shall be entitled to the enjoyment of parental care and protection and shall, whenever possible, have the right to reside with his or her parents. No child shall be separated from his parents against his will, except when a judicial authority determines in accordance with the appropriate law, that such separation is in the best interest of the child.

2. Every child who is separated from one or both parents shall have the right to maintain personal relations and direct contact with both parents on a regular basis.

3. Where separation results from the action of a State Party, the State Party shall provide the child, or if appropriate, another member of the family with essential information concerning the whereabouts of the absent member or members of the family. States Parties shall also ensure that the submission of such a request shall not entail any adverse consequences for the person or persons in whose respects [sic] it is made.

4. Where a child is apprehended by a State Party, his/her parents or guardians shall, as soon as possible, be notified of such apprehension by that State Party.

Article XX — Parental Reponsibilities

1. Parents or other persons responsible for the child shall have the primary responsibility of the upbringing and development of the child and shall have the duty:

    a. to ensure that the best interests of the child are their basic concern at all times;

    b. to secure, within their abilities and financial capacities, conditions of living necessary to the child's development; and

    c. to ensure that domestic discipline is administered with humanity and in a manner consistent with the inherent dignity of the child.

2. States Parties to the present Charter shall in accordance with their means and national conditions take all appropriate measures:

    a. to assist parents and other persons responsible for the child and in case of need provide material assistance and support programmes particularly with regard to nutrition, health, education, clothing and housing;

    b. to assist parents and others responsible for the child in the performance of child-rearing and ensure the development of institutions responsible for providing care of children; and

    c. to ensure that the children of working parents are provided with care services and facilities.

Article XXI — Protection against Harmful Social and Cultural Practices

1. States Parties to the present Charter shall take all appropriate measures to eliminate harmful social and cultural practices affecting the welfare, dignity, normal growth and development of the child and in particular:

    a. those customs and practices prejudicial to the health or life of the child; and

    b. those customs and practices discriminatory to the child on the grounds of sex or other status.

2. Child marriage and the betrothal of girls and boys shall be prohibited and effective action, including legislation, shall be taken to specify the minimum age of marriage to be 18 years and make registration of all marriages in an official registry compulsory.

Article XXII — Armed Conflicts

1. States Parties to this Charter shall undertake to respect and ensure respect for rules of international humanitarian law applicable in armed conflicts which affect the child.

2. States Parties to the present Charter shall take all necessary measures to ensure that no child shall take a direct part in hostilities and refrain in particular, from recruiting any child.

3. States Parties to the present Charter shall, in accordance with their obligations under international humanitarian law, protect the civilian population in armed conflicts and shall take all feasible measures to ensure the protection and care of children who are affected by armed conflicts. Such rules shall also apply to children in situations of internal armed conflicts, tension and strife.

Article XXIII — Refugee Children

1. States Parties to the present Charter shall take all appropriate measures to ensure that a child who is seeking refugee status or who is considered a refugee in accordance with applicable international or domestic law shall, whether unaccompanied or accompanied by parents, legal guardians or close relatives, receive appropriate protection and humanitarian assistance in the enjoyment of the rights set out in this Charter and other international human right[s] and humanitarian instruments to which the States are Parties.

2. States Parties shall undertake to cooperate with existing international organizations which protect and assist refugees in their efforts to protect and assist such a child and to trace the parents or other close relatives of an unaccompanied refugee child in order to obtain information necessary for reunification with the family.

3. Where no parents, legal guardians or close relatives can be found, the child shall be accorded the same protection as any other child permanently or temporarily deprived of his family environment for any reason.

4. The provisions of this Article apply *mutatis mulandis* to internally displaced children whether through natural disaster, internal armed conflicts, civil strife, breakdown of economic and social order or howsoever caused.

Article XXIV — Adoption

States Parties which recognize the system of adoption shall ensure that the best interest of the child shall be the paramount consideration and they shall:

a. establish competent authorities to determine matters of adoption and ensure that the adoption is carried out in conformity with applicable laws and procedures and on the basis of all relevant and reliable information, that the adoption is permissible in view of the child's status concerning parents, relatives and guardians and that, if necessary, the appropriate persons concerned have given their informed consent to the adoption on the basis of appropriate counselling;

b. recognize that inter-country adoption in those States who have ratified or adhered to the International Convention on the Rights of the Child or this Charter, may, as the last resort, be considered as an alternative means of a child's care, if the child cannot be placed in a foster or an adoptive family or cannot in any suitable manner be cared for in the child's country of origin;

c. ensure that the child affected by inter-country adoption enjoys safeguards and standards equivalent to those existing in the case of national adoption;

d. take all appropriate measures to ensure that, in inter-country adoption, the placement does not result in trafficking or improper financial gain for those who try to adopt a child;

e. promote, where appropriate, the objectives of this Article by concluding bilateral or multilateral arrangements or agreements, and endeavour, within this framework, to ensure that the placement of the child in another country is carried out by competent authorities or organs;

f. establish a machinery to monitor the well-being of the adopted child.

Article XXV — Separation from Parents

1. Any child who is permanently or temporarily deprived of his family environment for any reason shall be entitled to special protection and assistance.

2. States Parties to the present Charter:

a. shall ensure that a child who is parentless, or who is temporarily or permanently deprived of his or her family environment, or who in his or her best interest cannot be brought up or allowed to remain in that environment shall be provided with alternative family care, which could include, among others, foster placement, or placement in suitable institutions for the care of children;

b. shall take all necessary measures to trace and re-unite children with parents or relatives where separation is caused by internal and external displacement arising from armed conflicts or natural disasters.

3. When considering alternative family care of the child and the best interests of the child, due regard shall be paid to the desirability of continuity in a child's up-bringing and to the child's ethnic, religious or linguistic background.

Article XXVI — Protection Against Apartheid and Discrimination

1. States Parties to the present Charter shall individually and collectively undertake to accord the highest priority to the special needs of children living under *Apartheid* and in States subject to military destabilization by the *Apartheid* regime.

2. States Parties to the present Charter shall individually and collectively undertake to accord the highest priority to the special needs of children living under regimes practicing racial, ethnic, religious or other forms of discrimination as well as in States subject to military destabilization.

3. States Parties shall undertake to provide whenever possible, material assistance to such children and to direct their efforts towards the elimination of all forms of discrimination and *Apartheid* on the African Continent.

Article XXVII — Sexual Exploitation

1. States Parties to the present Charter shall undertake to protect the child from all forms of sexual exploitation and sexual abuse and shall in particular take measures to prevent:

a. the inducement, coercion or encouragement of a child to engage in any sexual activity;

b. the use of children in prostitution or other sexual practices;

c. the use of children in pornographic activities, performances and materials.

Article XXVIII — Drug Abuse

States Parties to the present Charter shall take all appropriate measures to protect the child from the use of narcotics and illicit use of psychotropic substances as defined in the relevant international treaties, and to prevent the use of children in the production and trafficking of such substances.

Article XXIX — Sale, Trafficking and Abduction

States Parties to the present Charter shall take appropriate measures to prevent:

a. the abduction, the sale of, or traffic in children for any purpose or in any form, by any person including parents or legal guardians of the child;

b. the use of children in all forms of begging.

Article XXX — Children of Imprisoned Mothers

States Parties to the present Charter shall undertake to provide special treatment to expectant mothers and to mothers of infants and young children who have been accused or found guilty of infringing the penal law and shall in particular:

a. ensure that a non-custodial sentence will always be first considered when sentencing such mothers;

b. establish and promote measures alternative to institutional confinement for the treatment of such mothers;

c. establish special alternative institutions for holding such mothers;

d. ensure that a mother shall not be imprisoned with her child;

e. ensure that a death sentence shall not be imposed on such mothers;

f. the essential aim of the penitentiary system will be the reformation, the integration of the mother to the family and social rehabilitation.

Article XXXI — Responsibility of the Child

Every child shall have responsibilities towards his family and society, the State and other legally recognized communities and the international community. The child, subject to his age and ability, and such limitations as may be contained in the present Charter, shall have the duty;

a. to work for the cohesion of the family, to respect his parents, superiors and elders at all times and to assist them in case of need;

b. to serve his national community by placing his physical and intellectual abilities at its service;

c. to preserve and strengthen social and national solidarity;

d. to preserve and strengthen African cultural values in his relations with other members of the society, in the spirit of tolerance, dialogue and consultation and to contribute to the moral well-being of society;

e. to preserve and strengthen the independence and the integrity of his country;

f. to contribute to the best of his abilities, at all times and at all levels, to the promotion and achievement of Afncan Unity.

PART II

CHAPTER TWO — ESTABLISHMENT AND ORGANIZATION OF THE COMMITTEE ON THE RIGHTS AND WELFARE OF THE CHILD

Article XXXII — The Committee

An African Committee of Experts on the Rights and Welfare of the Child[,] hereinafter called 'the Committee[,]' shall be established within the Organization of African Unity to promote and protect the rights and welfare of the child.

Article XXXIII — Composition

1. The Committee shall consist of 11 members of high moral standing, integrity, impartiality and competence in matters of the rights and welfare of the child.

2. The members of the Committee shall serve in their personal capacity.

3. The Committee shall not include more than one national of the same State.

Article XXXIV — Election

As soon as this Charter shall enter into force the members of the Committee shall be elected by secret ballot by the Assembly of Heads of State and Government from a list of persons nominated by the States Parties to the present Charter.

Article XXXV — Candidates

Each State Party to the present Charter may nominate not more than two candidates. The candidates must have one of the nationalities of the States Parties to the present Charter. When two candidates are nominated by a State, one of them shall not be a national of that State.

Article XXXVI

1. The Secretary-General of the Organization of African Unity shall invite States Parties to the present Charter to nominate candidates at least six months before the elections.

2. The Secretary-General of the Organization of African Unity shall draw up in alphabetical order, a list of persons nominated and communicate it to the Heads of State and Government at least two months before the elections.

Article XXXVII — Term of Office

1. The members of the Committee shall be elected for a term of five years and may not be re-elected, however, the term of four of the members elected at the first election shall expire after two years and the term of six others, after four years.

2. Immediately after the first election, the Chairman of the Assembly of Heads of State and Government of the Organization of African Unity shall draw lots to determine the names of those members referred to in sub-paragraph 1 of this Article.

3. The Secretary-General of the Organization of African Unity shall convene the first meeting of Committee at the Headquarters of the Organization within six months of the election of the members of the Committee, and thereafter the Committee shall be convened by its Chairman whenever necessary, at least once a year.

Article XXXVIII — Bureau

1. The Committee shall establish its own Rules of Procedure.

2. The Committee shall elect its officers for a period of two years.

3. Seven Committee members shall form the quorum.

4. In case of an equality of votes, the Chairman shall have a casting vote.

5. The working languages of the Committee shall be the official languages of the OAU.

Article XXXIX — Vacancy

If a member of the Committee vacates his office for any reason other than the normal expiration of a term, the State which nominated that member shall appoint another member from among its nationals to serve for the remainder of the term — subject to the approval of the Assembly.

Article XL — Secretariat

The Secretary-General of the Organization of African Unity shall appoint a Secretary for the Committee.

Article XLI — Privileges and Immunities

In discharging their duties, members of the Committee shall enjoy the privileges and immunities provided for in the General Convention on the Privileges and Immunities of the Organization of African Unity.

CHAPTER THREE — MANDATE AND PROCEDURE OF THE COMMITTEE

Article XLII — Mandate

The functions of the Committee shall be:

a. To promote and protect the rights enshrined in this Charter and in particular to:

i. collect and document information, commission inter-disciplinary assessment of situations on African problems in the fields of the rights and welfare of the child, organize meetings, encourage national and local institutions concerned with the rights and welfare of the child, and where necessary give its views and make recommendations to Governments;

ii. formulate and lay down principles and rules aimed at protecting the rights and welfare of children in Africa;

iii. cooperate with other African, International and Regional Institutions and Organizations concerned with the promotion and protection of the rights and welfare of the child.

b. To monitor the implementation and ensure protection of the rights enshrined in this Charter.

c. To interpret the provisions of the present Charter at the request of a State Party, an Institution of the Organization of African Unity or any other person or Institution recognized by the Organization of African Unity, or any State Party.

d. Perform such other task as may be entrusted to it by the Assembly of Heads of State and Government, Secretary-General of the OAU and any other organs of the OAU or the United Nations.

Article XLIII — Reporting Procedure

1. Every State Party to the present Charter shall undertake to submit to the Committee through the Secretary-General of the Organization of African Unity, reports on the measures they have adopted which give effect to the provisions of this Charter and on the progress made in the enjoyment of these rights:

a. within two years of the entry into force of the Charter for the State Party concerned; and

b. and thereafter, every three years.

2. Every report made under this Article shall:

a. contain sufficient information on the implementation of the present Charter to provide the Committee with comprehensive understanding of the implementation of the Charter in the relevant country; and

b. ... indicate factors and difficulties, if any, affecting the fullfilment of the obligations contained in the Charter.

3. A State Party which has submitted a comprehensive first report to the Committee need not, in its subsequent reports submitted in accordance with paragraph 1(a) of this Article, repeat the basic information previously provided.

Article XLIV — Communications

1. The Committee may receive communication, from any person, group or non-governmental organization recognized by the Organization of African Unity, by a Member State, or the United Nations relating to any matter covered by this Charter.

2. Every communication to the Committee shall contain the name and address of the author and shall be treated in confidence.

Article XLV — Investigations by the Committee

1. The Committee may... resort to any appropriate method of investigating any matter falling within the ambit of the present Charter, request from the States Parties any information relevant to the implementation of the Charter and may also resort to any appropriate method of investigating the measures the State Party has adopted to implement the Charter.

2. The Committee shall submit to each Ordinary Session of the Assembly of Heads of State and Government every two years, a report on its activities and on any communication made under Article 46 [sic] of this Charter.

3. The Committee shall publish its report after it has been considered by the Assembly of Heads of State and Government.

4. States Parties shall make the Committee's reports widely available to the public in their own countries.

CHAPTER FOUR — MISCELLANEOUS PROVISIONS

Article XLVI — Sources of Inspiration

The Committee shall draw inspiration from international law on Human Rights, particularly from the provisions of the African Charter on Human and Peoples' Rights, the Charter of the Organization of African Unity, the Universal Declaration on Human Rights, the International Convention on the Rights of the Child, and other instruments adopted by the United Nations and by African countries in the field of human rights, and from African values and traditions.

[Ed. Note: Article 47 (signature, ratification or adherence) and article 48 (amendment and revision of the Charter) have been omitted.]

D. League of Arab States Conventions

Arab Charter on Human Rights

Sept. 15, 1994, Res. 5437 Council of the League of Arab States, 102 Sess., *reprinted in* 18 Hum. Rts. L.J. 151 (1997).

[Ed. Note: The twenty-two member States of the League of Arab States are Jordan, United Arab Emirates, Bahrain, Tunisia, Algeria, Djibouti, Saudi Arabia, Sudan, Syrian Arab Republic, Somalia, Iraq, Oman, Palestine, Qatar, Comoros, Kuwait, Lebanon, Libyan Arab Jamahiriya, Egypt, Morocco, Mauritania, and Yemen. The Arab Charter was adopted in 1994, but as of 2003 it had not yet entered into force. In fact, it has not been ratified by any members of the League of Arab States. *See*

William A. Schabas, *Islam and the Death Penalty*, 9 Wm. & Mary Bill Rts. J. 223, 233 (2000).]

PREAMBLE

Given the Arab nation's belief in human dignity since God honoured it by making the Arab World the cradle of religions and the birthplace of civilizations which confirmed its right to a life of dignity based on freedom, justice and peace,

Pursuant to the eternal principles of brotherhood and equality among all human beings which were firmly established by the Islamic Shari'a and the other divinely-revealed religions,

Being proud of the humanitarian values and principles which it firmly established in the course of its long history and which played a major role in disseminating centres of learning between the East and the West, thereby making it an international focal point for seekers of knowledge, culture and wisdom,

Conscious of the fact that the entire Arab World has always worked together to preserve its faith, believing in its unity, struggling to protect its freedom, defending the right of nations to self-determination and to safeguard their resources, believing in the rule of law and that every individual's enjoyment of freedom, justice and equality of opportunity is the yardstick by which the merits of any society are gauged,

Rejecting racism and zionism, which constitute a violation of human rights and pose a threat to world peace,

Acknowledging the close interrelationship between human rights and world peace,

Reaffirming the principles of the Charter of the United Nations and the Universal Declaration of Human Rights, as well as the provisions of the United Nations International Covenants on Civil and Political Rights and Economic, Social and Cultural Rights and the Cairo Declaration on Human Rights in Islam.

In confirmation of all the above, have agreed as follows:

PART I

Article 1

a. All peoples have the right of self-determination and control over their natural wealth and resources and, accordingly, have the right to freely determine the form of their political structure and to freely pursue their economic, social and cultural development.

b. Racism, zionism, occupation and foreign domination pose a challenge to human dignity and constitute a fundamental obstacle to the realization of the basic rights of peoples. There is a need to condemn and endeavour to eliminate all such practices.

PART II

Article 2

Each State Party to the present Charter undertakes to ensure to all individuals within its territory and subject to its jurisdiction the right to enjoy all the rights and freedoms recognized herein, without any distinction on grounds of race, colour, sex, language, religion, political opinion, national or social origin, property, birth or other status and without any discrimination between men and women.

Article 3

a. No restriction upon or derogation from any of the fundamental human rights recognized or existing in any State Party to the present Charter in virtue of law, conventions or custom shall be admitted on the pretext that the present Charter does not recognize such rights or that it recognizes them to a lesser extent.

b. No State Party to the present Charter shall derogate from the fundamental freedoms recognized herein and which are enjoyed by the nationals of another State that shows less respect for those freedoms.

Article 4

a. No restrictions shall be placed on the rights and freedoms recognized in the present Charter except where such is provided by law and deemed necessary to protect the national security and economy, public order, health or morals or the rights and freedoms of others.

b. In time of public emergency which threatens the life of the nation, the States Parties may take measures derogating from their obligations under the present Charter to the extent strictly required by the exigencies of the situation.

c. Such measures or derogations shall under no circumstances affect or apply to the rights and special guarantees concerning the prohibition of torture and degrading treatment, return to one's country, political asylum, trial, the inadmissibility of retrial for the same act, and the legal status of crime and punishment.

Article 5

Every individual has the right to life, liberty and security of person. These rights shall be protected by law.

Article 6

There shall be no crime or punishment except as provided by law and there shall be no punishment in respect of an act preceding the promulgation of that provision. The accused shall benefit from subsequent legislation if it is in his favour.

Article 7

The accused shall be presumed innocent until proved guilty at a lawful trial in which he has enjoyed the guarantees necessary for his defence.

Article 8

Everyone has the right to liberty and security of person and no one shall be arrested, held in custody or detained without a legal warrant and without being brought promptly before a judge.

Article 9

All persons are equal before the law and everyone within the territory of the State has a guaranteed right to [a] legal remedy.

Article 10

The death penalty may be imposed only for the most serious crimes and anyone sentenced to death shall have the right to seek [a] pardon or commutation of the sentence.

Article 11

The death penalty shall under no circumstances be imposed for a political offence.

Article 12

The death penalty shall not be inflicted on a person under 18 years of age, on a pregnant woman prior to her delivery or on a nursing mother within two years from the date on which she gave birth.

Article 13

a. The States parties shall protect every person in their territory from being subjected to physical or mental torture or cruel, inhuman or degrading treatment. They shall take effective measures to prevent such acts and shall regard the practice thereof, or participation therein, as a punishable offence.

b. No medical or scientific experimentation shall be carried out on any person without his free consent.

Article 14

No one shall be imprisoned on the ground of his proven inability to meet a debt or fulfil any civil obligation.

Article 15

Persons sentenced to a penalty of deprivation of liberty shall be treated with humanity.

Article 16

No one shall be tried twice for the same offence.

Anyone against whom such proceedings are brought shall have the right to challenge their legality and to demand his release.

Anyone who is the victim of unlawful arrest or detention shall be entitled to compensation.

Article 17

Privacy shall be inviolable and any infringement thereof shall constitute an offence. This privacy includes private family affairs, the inviolability of the home and the confidentiality of correspondence and other private means of communication.

Article 18

Everyone shall have the inherent right to recognition as a person before the law.

Article 19

The people are the source of authority and every citizen of full legal age shall have the right of political participation, which he shall exercise in accordance with the law.

Article 20

Every individual residing within the territory of a State shall have the right to liberty of movement and freedom to choose his place of residence in any part of the said territory, within the limits of the law.

Article 21

No citizen shall be arbitrarily or unlawfully prevented from leaving any Arab country, including his own, nor prohibited from residing, or compelled to reside, in any part of his country.

Article 22
No citizen shall be expelled from his country or prevented from returning thereto.

Article 23
Every citizen shall have the right to seek political asylum in other countries in order to escape persecution. This right shall not be enjoyed by persons facing prosecution for an offence under the ordinary law. Political refugees shall not be extraditable.

Article 24
No citizen shall be arbitrarily deprived of his original nationality, nor shall his right to acquire another nationality be denied without a legally valid reason.

Article 25
Every citizen has a guaranteed right to own private property. No citizen shall under any circumstances be divested of all or any part of his property in an arbitrary or unlawful manner.

Article 26
Everyone has a guaranteed right to freedom of belief, thought and opinion.

Article 27
Adherents of every religion have the right to practise their religious observances and to manifest their views through expression, practice or teaching, without prejudice to the rights of others. No restrictions shall be imposed on the exercise of freedom of belief, thought and opinion except as provided by law.

Article 28
All citizens have the right to freedom of peaceful assembly and association. No restrictions shall be placed on the exercise of this right unless so required by the exigencies of national security, public safety or the need to protect the rights and freedoms of others.

Article 29
The State guarantees the right to form trade unions and the right to strike within the limits laid down by law.

Article 30
The State guarantees every citizen's right to work in order to secure for himself a standard of living that meets the basic requirements of life. The State also guarantees every citizen's right to comprehensive social security.

Article 31
Free choice of work is guaranteed and forced labour is prohibited. Compelling a person to perform work under the terms of a court judgement shall not be deemed to constitute forced labour.

Article 32
The State shall ensure that its citizens enjoy equality of opportunity in regard to work, as well as a fair wage and equal remuneration for work of equal value.

Article 33

Every citizen shall have the right of access to public office in his country.

Article 34

The eradication of illiteracy is a binding obligation and every citizen has a right to education. Primary education, at the very least, shall be compulsory and free and both secondary and university education shall be made easily accessible to all.

Article 35

Citizens have a right to live in an intellectual and cultural environment in which Arab nationalism is a source of pride, in which human rights are sanctified and in which racial, religious and other forms of discrimination are rejected and international cooperation and the cause of world peace are supported.

Article 36

Everyone has the right to participate in cultural life, as well as the right to enjoy literary and artistic works and to be given opportunities to develop his artistic, intellectual and creative talents.

Article 37

Minorities shall not be deprived of their right to enjoy their culture or to follow the teachings of their religions.

Article 38

a. The family is the basic unit of society, whose protection it shall enjoy.

b. The State undertakes to provide outstanding care and special protection for the family, mothers, children and the aged.

Article 39

Young persons have the right to be afforded the most ample opportunities for physical and mental development.

PART III

Article 40

a. The States members of the League's Council which are parties to the Charter shall elect a Committee of Experts on Human Rights by secret ballot.

b. The Committee shall consist of seven members nominated by the member States Parties to the Charter. The initial elections to the Committee shall be held six months after the Charter's entry into force. The Committee shall not include more than one person from the same State.

c. The Secretary-General shall request the member States to submit their candidates two months before the scheduled date of the elections.

d. The candidates, who must be highly experienced and competent in the Committee's field of work, shall serve in their personal capacity with full impartiality and integrity.

e. The Committee's members shall be elected for a three-year term which, in the case of three of them, shall be renewable for one further term, their names being selected by lot. The principle of rotation shall be observed as far as possible.

f. The Committee shall elect its chairman and shall draw up its rules of procedure specifying its method of operation.

g. Meetings of the Committee shall be convened by the Secretary-General at the Headquarters of the League's Secretariat. With the Secretary-General's approval, the Committee may also meet in another Arab country if the exigencies of its work so require.

Article 41

1. The States Parties shall submit reports to the Committee of Experts on Human Rights in the following manner:

   a. An initial report one year after the date of the Charter's entry into force.

   b. Periodic reports every three years.

   c. Reports containing the replies of States to the Committee's questions.

2. The Committee shall consider the reports submitted by the member States Parties to the Charter in accordance with the provisions of paragraph 1 of this article.

3. The Committee shall submit a report, together with the views and comments of the States, to the Standing Committee on Human Rights at the Arab League.

PART IV

Article 42

a. The Secretary-General of the League of Arab States shall submit the present Charter, after its approval by the Council of the League, to the member States for signature and ratification or accession.

b. The present Charter shall enter into effect two months after the date of deposit of the seventh instrument of ratification or accession with the Secretariat of the League of Arab States.

Article 43

Following its entry into force, the present Charter shall become binding on each State two months after the date of the deposit of its instrument of ratification or accession with the Secretariat. The Secretary-General shall notify the member States of the deposit of each instrument of ratification or accession.

Part IV

Selected U.S. Federal Statutes and Regulations

A. United States Code

Title 8. Aliens and Nationality

Chapter 12 — Immigration and Nationality

Subchapter I — General Provisions

Sec. 1101. Definitions

[Ed. Note: Amendments to Subsection (b) of this Act, which were passed as part of the Intercountry Adoption Act in 2000 and will take effect when the Hague Convention on Protection of Children and Co-operation in Respect of Intercounty Adoption enters into force for the United States, are set forth at the end of this Section.]

(a) As used in this chapter—

(1) The term "administrator" means the official designated by the Secretary of State pursuant to section 1104(b) of this title.

(2) The term "advocates" includes, but is not limited to, advises, recommends, furthers by overt act, and admits belief in.

(3) The term "alien" means any person not a citizen or national of the United States.

(4) The term "application for admission" has reference to the application for admission into the United States and not to the application for the issuance of an immigrant or nonimmigrant visa.

(5) The term "Attorney General" means the Attorney General of the United States.

(6) The term "border crossing identification card" means a document of identity bearing that designation issued to an alien who is lawfully admitted for permanent residence, or to an alien who is a resident in foreign contiguous territory, by a consular officer or an immigration officer for the purpose of crossing over the borders between the United States and foreign contiguous territory in accordance with such conditions for its issuance and use as may be prescribed by regulations. Such regulations shall provide that

(A) each such document include a biometric identifier (such as the fingerprint or handprint of the alien) that is machine readable and

(B) an alien presenting a border crossing identification card is not permitted to cross over the border into the United States unless the biometric identifier contained on the card matches the appropriate biometric characteristic of the alien.

(7) The term "clerk of court" means a clerk of a naturalization court.

(8) The terms "Commissioner" and "Deputy Commissioner" mean the Commissioner of Immigration and Naturalization and a Deputy Commissioner of Immigration and Naturalization, respectively.

(9) The term "consular officer" means any consular, diplomatic, or other officer or employee of the United States designated under regulations prescribed under authority contained in this chapter, for the purpose of issuing immigrant or nonimmigrant visas or, when used in subchapter III of this chapter, for the purpose of adjudicating nationality.

(10) The term "crewman" means a person serving in any capacity on board a vessel or aircraft.

(11) The term "diplomatic visa" means a nonimmigrant visa bearing that title and issued to a nonimmigrant in accordance with such regulations as the Secretary of State may prescribe.

(12) The term "doctrine" includes, but is not limited to, policies, practices, purposes, aims, or procedures.

(13)(A) The terms "admission" and "admitted" mean, with respect to an alien, the lawful entry of the alien into the United States after inspection and authorization by an immigration officer.

(B) An alien who is paroled under section 1182(d)(5) of this title or permitted to land temporarily as an alien crewman shall not be considered to have been admitted.

(C) An alien lawfully admitted for permanent residence in the United States shall not be regarded as seeking an admission into the United States for purposes of the immigration laws unless the alien —

(i) has abandoned or relinquished that status,

(ii) has been absent from the United States for a continuous period in excess of 180 days,

(iii) has engaged in illegal activity after having departed the United States,

(iv) has departed from the United States while under legal process seeking removal of the alien from the United States, including removal proceedings under this chapter and extradition proceedings,

(v) has committed an offense identified in section 1182(a)(2) of this title, unless since such offense the alien has been granted relief under section 1182(h) or 1229b(a) of this title, or

(vi) is attempting to enter at a time or place other than as designated by immigration officers or has not been admitted to the United States after inspection and authorization by an immigration officer.

(14) The term "foreign state" includes outlying possessions of a foreign state, but self-governing dominions or territories under mandate or trusteeship shall be regarded as separate foreign states.

(15) The term "immigrant" means every alien except an alien who is within one of the following classes of nonimmigrant aliens—

[Ed. Note: The classes of nonimmigrant aliens are omitted.]

(16) The term "immigrant visa" means an immigrant visa required by this chapter and properly issued by a consular officer at his office outside of the United States to an eligible immigrant under the provisions of this chapter

(17) The term "immigration laws" includes this chapter and all laws, conventions, and treaties of the United States relating to the immigration, exclusion, deportation, expulsion, or removal of aliens.

(18) The term "immigration officer" means any employee or class of employees of the Service or of the United States designated by the Attorney General, individually or by regulation, to perform the functions of an immigration officer specified by this chapter or any section of this title.

(19) The term "ineligible to citizenship," when used in reference to any individual, means, notwithstanding the provisions of any treaty relating to military service, an individual who is, or was at any time, permanently debarred from becoming a citizen of the United States under section 3(a) of the Selective Training and Service Act of 1940, as amended (54 Stat. 885; 55 Stat. 844), or under section 4(a) of the Selective Service Act of 1948, as amended (62 Stat. 605; 65 Stat. 76), or under any section of this chapter, or any other Act, or under any law amendatory of, supplementary to, or in substitution for, any of such sections or Acts.

(20) The term "lawfully admitted for permanent residence" means the status of having been lawfully accorded the privilege of residing permanently in the United States as an immigrant in accordance with the immigration laws, such status not having changed.

(21) The term "national" means a person owing permanent allegiance to a state.

(22) The term "national of the United States" means

(A) a citizen of the United States, or

(B) a person who, though not a citizen of the United States, owes permanent allegiance to the United States.

(23) The term "naturalization" means the conferring of nationality of a state upon a person after birth, by any means whatsoever.

(24) Repealed. Pub.L. 102-232, Title III, § 305(m)(1), Dec. 12, 1991, 105 Stat. 1750.

(25) The term "noncombatant service" shall not include service in which the individual is not subject to military discipline, court martial, or does not wear the uniform of any branch of the armed forces.

(26) The term "nonimmigrant visa" means a visa properly issued to an alien as an eligible nonimmigrant by a competent officer as provided in this chapter.

(27) The term "special immigrant" means—

(A) an immigrant, lawfully admitted for permanent residence, who is returning from a temporary visit abroad;

(B) an immigrant who was a citizen of the United States and may, under section 1435(a) or 1438 of this title, apply for reacquisition of citizenship;

[Ed. Note: Categories C through I are omitted.]

(J) an immigrant who is present in the United States—

(i) who has been declared dependent on a juvenile court located in the United States or whom such a court has legally committed to, or placed under the custody of, an agency or department of a State and who has been deemed eligible by that court for long-term foster care due to abuse, neglect, or abandonment;

(ii) for whom it has been determined in administrative or judicial proceedings that it would not be in the alien's best interest to be returned to the alien's or parent's previous country of nationality or country of last habitual residence; and

(iii) in whose case the Attorney General expressly consents to the dependency order serving as a precondition to the grant of special immigrant juvenile status; except that—

(I) no juvenile court has jurisdiction to determine the custody status or placement of an alien in the actual or constructive custody of the Attorney General unless the Attorney General specifically consents to such jurisdiction; and

(II) no natural parent or prior adoptive parent of any alien provided special immigrant status under this subparagraph shall thereafter, by virtue of such parentage, be accorded any right, privilege, or status under this chapter;

[Ed. Note: Categories K through M are omitted.]

(28) The term "organization" means, but is not limited to, an organization, corporation, company, partnership, association, trust, foundation or fund; and includes a group of persons, whether or not incorporated, permanently or temporarily associated together with joint action on any subject or subjects.

(29) The term "outlying possessions of the United States" means American Samoa and Swains Island.

(30) The term "passport" means any travel document issued by competent authority showing the bearer's origin, identity, and nationality if any, which is valid for the admission of the bearer into a foreign country.

(31) The term "permanent" means a relationship of continuing or lasting nature, as distinguished from temporary, but a relationship may be permanent even though it is one that may be dissolved eventually at the instance either of the United States or of the individual, in accordance with law.

(32) The term "profession" shall include but not be limited to architects, engineers, lawyers, physicians, surgeons, and teachers in elementary or secondary schools, colleges, academies, or seminaries.

(33) The term "residence" means the place of general abode; the place of general abode of a person means his principal, actual dwelling place in fact, without regard to intent.

(34) The term "Service" means the Immigration and Naturalization Service of the Department of Justice.

(35) The term "spouse", "wife", or "husband" do not include a spouse, wife, or husband by reason of any marriage ceremony where the contracting parties thereto are not physically present in the presence of each other, unless the marriage shall have been consummated.

(36) The term "State" includes the District of Columbia, Puerto Rico, Guam, and the Virgin Islands of the United States.

(37) The term "totalitarian party" means an organization which advocates the establishment in the United States of a totalitarian dictatorship or totalitarianism. The terms "totalitarian dictatorship" and "totalitarianism" mean and refer to systems of government not representative in fact, characterized by

(A) the existence of a single political party, organized on a dictatorial basis, with so close an identity between such party and its policies and the governmental policies of the country in which it exists, that the party and the government constitute an indistinguishable unit, and

(B) the forcible suppression of opposition to such party.

(38) The term "United States", except as otherwise specifically herein provided, when used in a geographical sense, means the continental United States, Alaska, Hawaii, Puerto Rico, Guam, and the Virgin Islands of the United States.

(39) The term "unmarried", when used in reference to any individual as of any time, means an individual who at such time is not married, whether or not previously married.

(40) The term "world communism" means a revolutionary movement, the purpose of which is to establish eventually a Communist totalitarian dictatorship in any or all the countries of the world through the medium of an internationally coordinated Communist political movement.

(41) [Ed. Note: The definition of "graduates of a medical school" is omitted.]

(42) The term "refugee" means

(A) any person who is outside any country of such person's nationality or, in the case of a person having no nationality, is outside any country in which such person last habitually resided, and who is unable or unwilling to return to, and is unable or unwilling to avail himself or herself of the protection of, that country because of persecution or a well-founded fear of persecution on account of race, religion, nationality, membership in a particular social group, or political opinion, or

(B) in such special circumstances as the President after appropriate consultation (as defined in section 1157(e) of this title) may specify, any person who is within the country of such person's nationality or, in the case of a person having no nationality, within the country in which such person is habitually residing, and who is persecuted or who has a well-founded fear of persecution on account of race, religion, nationality, membership in a particular social group, or political opinion.

The term "refugee" does not include any person who ordered, incited, assisted, or otherwise participated in the persecution of any person on account of race, religion, nationality, membership in a particular social group, or political opinion. For purposes of determinations under this chapter, a person who has been forced to abort a pregnancy or to undergo involuntary sterilization, or who has been persecuted for failure or refusal to undergo such a procedure or for other resistance to a coercive population control program, shall be deemed to have been persecuted on account of political opinion, and a person who has a well founded fear that he or she will be forced to undergo such a procedure or subject to persecution for such failure, refusal, or resistance shall be deemed to have a well founded fear of persecution on account of political opinion.

(43) [Ed. Note: The definition of aggravated felony, set forth in Subsections (A)–(U), is omitted.]

(44) [Ed. Note: The definitions of managerial capacity and executive capacity are omitted.]

(45) The term "substantial" means, for purposes of paragraph (15)(E) with reference to trade or capital, such an amount of trade or capital as is established by the Secretary of State, after consultation with appropriate agencies of Government.

(46) The term "extraordinary ability" means, for purposes of subsection (a)(15)(O)(i) of this section, in the case of the arts, distinction.

(47)(A) The term "order of deportation" means the order of the special inquiry officer, or other such administrative officer to whom the Attorney General has delegated the responsibility for determining whether an alien is deportable, concluding that the alien is deportable or ordering deportation.

(B) The order described under subparagraph (A) shall become final upon the earlier of—

(i) a determination by the Board of Immigration Appeals affirming such order; or

(ii) the expiration of the period in which the alien is permitted to seek review of such order by the Board of Immigration Appeals.

(48)(A) The term "conviction" means, with respect to an alien, a formal judgment of guilt of the alien entered by a court or, if adjudication of guilt has been withheld, where—

(i) a judge or jury has found the alien guilty or the alien has entered a plea of guilty or nolo contendere or has admitted sufficient facts to warrant a finding of guilt, and

(ii) the judge has ordered some form of punishment, penalty, or restraint on the alien's liberty to be imposed.

(B) Any reference to a term of imprisonment or a sentence with respect to an offense is deemed to include the period of incarceration or confinement ordered by a court of law regardless of any suspension of the imposition or execution of that imprisonment or sentence in whole or in part.

(49) The term "stowaway" means any alien who obtains transportation without the consent of the owner, charterer, master or person in command of any vessel or aircraft through concealment aboard such vessel or aircraft. A passenger who boards with a valid ticket is not to be considered a stowaway.

(50) The term "intended spouse" means any alien who meets the criteria set forth in section 1154(a)(1)(A)(iii)(II)(aa)(BB), 1154(a)(1)(B)(ii)(II)(aa)(BB), or 1229b(b)(2)(A)(i)(III) of this title.

(b) As used in subchapters I and II of this chapter—

(1) The term "child" means an unmarried person under twenty-one years of age who is—

(A) a child born in wedlock;

(B) a stepchild, whether or not born out of wedlock, provided the child had not reached the age of eighteen years at the time the marriage creating the status of stepchild occurred;

(C) a child legitimated under the law of the child's residence or domicile, or under the law of the father's residence or domicile, whether in or outside the United States, if such legitimation takes place before the child reaches the age of eighteen years and the child is in the legal custody of the legitimating parent or parents at the time of such legitimation;

(D) a child born out of wedlock, by, through whom, or on whose behalf a status, privilege, or benefit is sought by virtue of the relationship of the child to its natural mother or to its natural father if the father has or had a bona fide parent-child relationship with the person;

(E)(i) a child adopted while under the age of sixteen years if the child has been in the legal custody of, and has resided with, the adopting parent or parents for at least two years: Provided, That no natural parent of any such adopted child shall thereafter, by virtue of such parentage, be accorded any right, privilege, or status under this chapter; or

(ii) subject to the same proviso as in clause (i), a child who:

(I) is a natural sibling of a child described in clause (i) or subparagraph (F)(i);

(II) was adopted by the adoptive parent or parents of the sibling described in such clause or subparagraph; and

(III) is otherwise described in clause (i), except that the child was adopted while under the age of 18 years; or

(F)(i) a child, under the age of sixteen at the time a petition is filed in his behalf to accord a classification as an immediate relative under section 1151(b) of this title, who is an orphan because of the death or disappearance of, abandonment or desertion by, or separation or loss from, both parents, or for whom the sole or surviving parent is incapable of providing the proper care and has in writing irrevocably released the child for emigration and adoption; who has been adopted abroad by a United States citizen and spouse jointly, or by an unmarried United States citizen at least twenty-five years of age, who personally saw and observed the child prior to or during the adoption proceedings; or who is coming to the United States for adoption by a United States citizen and spouse jointly, or by an unmarried United States citizen at least twenty-five years of age, who have or has complied with the preadoption requirements, if any, of the child's proposed residence: Provided, That the Attorney General is satisfied that proper care will be furnished the child if admitted to the United States: Provided further, That no natural parent or prior adoptive parent of any such child shall thereafter, by virtue of such parentage, be accorded any right, privilege, or status under this chapter; or

(ii) subject to the same provisos as in clause (i), a child who:

(I) is a natural sibling of a child described in clause (i) or subparagraph (E)(i);

(II) has been adopted abroad, or is coming to the United States for adoption, by the adoptive parent (or prospective adoptive parent) or parents of the sibling described in such clause or subparagraph; and

(III) is otherwise described in clause (i), except that the child is under the age of 18 at the time a petition is filed in his or her behalf to accord a classification as an immediate relative under section 1151(b) of this title.

(2) The terms "parent", "father", or "mother" mean a parent, father, or mother only where the relationship exists by reason of any of the circumstances set forth in subdivision (1) of this subsection, except that, for purposes of paragraph (1)(F) (other than the second proviso therein) in the case of a child born out of wedlock described in paragraph (1)(D) (and not described in paragraph (1)(C)), the term "parent" does not include the natural father of the child if the father has disappeared or abandoned or deserted the child or if the father has in writing irrevocably released the child for emigration and adoption.

(3) The term "person" means an individual or an organization.

(4) The term "immigration judge" means an attorney whom the Attorney General appoints as an administrative judge within the Executive Office for Immigration Review, qualified to conduct specified classes of proceedings, including a hearing under section 1229a of this title. An immigration judge shall be subject to such supervision and shall perform such duties as the Attorney General shall prescribe, but shall not be employed by the Immigration and Naturalization Service.

(5) The term "adjacent islands" includes Saint Pierre, Miquelon, Cuba, the Dominican Republic, Haiti, Bermuda, the Bahamas, Barbados, Jamaica, the Windward and Leeward Islands, Trinidad, Martinique, and other British, French, and Netherlands territory or possessions in or bordering on the Caribbean Sea.

(c) As used in subchapter III of this chapter—

(1) The term "child" means an unmarried person under twenty-one years of age and includes a child legitimated under the law of the child's residence or domicile, or under the law of the father's residence or domicile, whether in the United States or elsewhere, and, except as otherwise provided in sections 1431 and 1432 of this title, a child adopted in the United States, if such legitimation or adoption takes place before the child reaches the age of 16 years (except to the extent that the child is described in subparagraph (E)(ii) or (F)(ii) of subsection (b)(1) of this section), and the child is in the legal custody of the legitimating or adopting parent or parents at the time of such legitimation or adoption.

(2) The terms "parent", "father", and "mother" include in the case of a posthumous child a deceased parent, father, and mother.

(d) Repealed. Pub.L. 100-525, § 9(a)(3), Oct. 24, 1988, 102 Stat. 2619.

(e) For the purposes of this chapter—

(1) The giving, loaning, or promising of support or of money or any other thing of value to be used for advocating any doctrine shall constitute the advocating of such doctrine; but nothing in this paragraph shall be construed as an exclusive definition of advocating.

(2) The giving, loaning, or promising of support or of money or any other thing of value for any purpose to any organization shall be presumed to constitute affiliation therewith; but nothing in this paragraph shall be construed as an exclusive definition of affiliation.

(3) Advocating the economic, international, and governmental doctrines of world communism means advocating the establishment of a totalitarian Communist dictatorship in any or all of the countries of the world through the medium of an internationally coordinated Communist movement.

(f) For the purposes of this chapter —

No person shall be regarded as, or found to be, a person of good moral character who, during the period for which good moral character is required to be established, is, or was —

(1) a habitual drunkard;

(2) Repealed. Pub.L. 97-116, § 2(c)(1), Dec. 29, 1981, 95 Stat. 1611.

(3) a member of one or more of the classes of persons, whether inadmissible or not, described in paragraphs (2)(D), (6)(E), and (9)(A) of section 1182(a) of this title; or subparagraphs (A) and (B) of section 1182(a)(2) of this title and subparagraph (C) thereof of such section (except as such paragraph relates to a single offense of simple possession of 30 grams or less of marihuana), if the offense described therein, for which such person was convicted or of which he admits the commission, was committed during such period;

(4) one whose income is derived principally from illegal gambling activities;

(5) one who has been convicted of two or more gambling offenses committed during such period;

(6) one who has given false testimony for the purpose of obtaining any benefits under this chapter;

(7) one who during such period has been confined, as a result of conviction, to a penal institution for an aggregate period of one hundred and eighty days or more, regardless of whether the offense, or offenses, for which he has been confined were committed within or without such period;

(8) one who at any time has been convicted of an aggravated felony (as defined in subsection (a)(43) of this section).

The fact that any person is not within any of the foregoing classes shall not preclude a finding that for other reasons such person is or was not of good moral character.

In the case of an alien who makes a false statement or claim of citizenship, or who registers to vote or votes in a Federal, State, or local election (including an initiative, recall, or referendum) in violation of a lawful restriction of such registration or voting to citizens, if each natural parent of the alien (or, in the case of an adopted alien, each adoptive parent of the alien) is or was a citizen (whether by birth or naturalization), the alien permanently resided in the United States prior to attaining the age of 16, and the alien reasonably believed at the time of such statement, claim, or violation that he or she was a citizen, no finding that the alien is, or was, not of good moral character may be made based on it.

(g) For the purposes of this chapter any alien ordered deported or removed (whether before or after the enactment of this chapter) who has left the United States, shall be considered to have been deported or removed in pursuance of law, irrespective of the source from which the expenses of his transportation were defrayed or of the place to which he departed.

(h) For purposes of section 1182(a)(2)(E) of this title, the term "serious criminal offense" means—

(1) any felony;

(2) any crime of violence, as defined in section 16 of Title 18; or

(3) any crime of reckless driving or of driving while intoxicated or under the influence of alcohol or of prohibited substances if such crime involves personal injury to another.

(i) With respect to each nonimmigrant alien described in subsection (a)(15)(T)(i) of this section—

(1) the Attorney General and other Government officials, where appropriate, shall provide the alien with a referral to a nongovernmental organization that would advise the alien regarding the alien's options while in the United States and the resources available to the alien; and

(2) the Attorney General shall, during the period the alien is in lawful temporary resident status under that subsection, grant the alien authorization to engage in employment in the United States and provide the alien with an "employment authorized" endorsement or other appropriate work permit.

(June 27, 1952, c. 477, Title I, §101, 66 Stat. 166; [intervening amendments omitted]; Nov. 2, 2002, Pub.L. 107-274, §2(a), (b), 116 Stat. 1923.)

[Ed. Note: Subsection (b)(1) of Sec. 1101 was amended in Pub.L. 106-279, Title III, §302(a), Title V, §505(a)(2), (b), Oct. 6, 2000, 114 Stat. 838, 844, which provides that:

Effective upon entry into force for the United States of the Convention on Protection of Children and Co-operation in Respect of Intercountry Adoption, pursuant to Article 46(2)(a) of the Convention, with transition rule, subsection (b) is amended in paragraph (1) by striking out "or" at the end of subparagraph (E), by striking the period at the end of subparagraph (F) and inserting "; or", and by inserting a new subparagraph (G), as follows:

(G) a child, under the age of sixteen at the time a petition is filed on the child's behalf to accord a classification as an immediate relative under section 1151(b) of this title, who has been adopted in a foreign state that is a party to the Convention on Protection of Children and Co-operation in Respect of Intercountry Adoption done at The Hague on May 29, 1993, or who is emigrating from such a foreign state to be adopted in the United States, by a United States citizen and spouse jointly, or by an unmarried United States citizen at least 25 years of age—>

(i) if—

(I) the Attorney General is satisfied that proper care will be furnished the child if admitted to the United States;

(II) the child's natural parents (or parent, in the case of a child who has one sole or surviving parent because of the death or disappearance of, abandonment or desertion by, the other parent), or other persons or institutions that retain legal custody of the child, have freely given their written irrevocable consent to the termination of their legal relationship with the child, and to the child's emigration and adoption;

(III) in the case of a child having two living natural parents, the natural parents are incapable of providing proper care for the child;

(IV) the Attorney General is satisfied that the purpose of the adoption is to form a bona fide parent-child relationship, and the parent-child relationship of the child and the natural parents has been terminated (and in carrying out both obligations under this subclause the Attorney General may consider whether there is a petition pending to confer immigrant status on one or both of such natural parents); and

(V) in the case of a child who has not been adopted—

(aa) the competent authority of the foreign state has approved the child's emigration to the United States for the purpose of adoption by the prospective adoptive parent or parents; and

(bb) the prospective adoptive parent or parents has or have complied with any pre-adoption requirements of the child's proposed residence; and

(ii) except that no natural parent or prior adoptive parent of any such child shall thereafter, by virtue of such parentage, be accorded any right, privilege, or status under this chapter.

Pub.L. 106-279, Title III, § 302(c), Title V, § 505(a)(2), (b), Oct. 6, 2000, 114 Stat. 839, 844, also provides that, effective upon entry into force for the United States of the Convention on Protection of Children and Co-operation in Respect of Intercountry Adoption, pursuant to Article 46(2)(a) of the Convention, with transition rule, subsection (b) is amended in paragraph (2) by inserting "and paragraph (1)(G)(i)" after "second proviso therein.)".]

Subchapter II—Immigration
Part I—Selection System

Sec. 1151. Worldwide level of immigration

(a) In general

Exclusive of aliens described in subsection (b) of this section, aliens born in a foreign state or dependent area who may be issued immigrant visas or who may otherwise acquire the status of an alien lawfully admitted to the United States for permanent residence are limited to—

(1) family-sponsored immigrants described in section 1153(a) of this title (or who are admitted under section 1181(a) of this title on the basis of a prior issuance of a visa to their accompanying parent under section 1153(a) of this title) in a number not to exceed in any fiscal year the number specified in subsection (c) of this section for that year, and not to exceed in any of the first 3 quarters of any fiscal year 27 percent of the worldwide level under such subsection for all of such fiscal year;

(2) employment-based immigrants described in section 1153(b) of this title (or who are admitted under section 1181(a) of this title on the basis of a prior issuance of a visa to their accompanying parent under section 1153(b) of this title), in a number not to exceed in any fiscal year the number specified in subsection (d) of this section for that year, and not to exceed in any of the first 3 quarters of any fiscal year 27 percent of the worldwide level under such subsection for all of such fiscal year; and

(3) for fiscal years beginning with fiscal year 1995, diversity immigrants described in section 1153(c) of this title (or who are admitted under section 1181(a) of this title on the

basis of a prior issuance of a visa to their accompanying parent under section 1153(c) of this title) in a number not to exceed in any fiscal year the number specified in subsection (e) of this section for that year, and not to exceed in any of the first 3 quarters of any fiscal year 27 percent of the worldwide level under such subsection for all of such fiscal year.

(b) Aliens not subject to direct numerical limitations

Aliens described in this subsection, who are not subject to the worldwide levels or numerical limitations of subsection (a) of this section, are as follows:

(1)(A) Special immigrants described in subparagraph (A) or (B) of section 1101(a)(27) of this title.

(B) Aliens who are admitted under section 1157 of this title or whose status is adjusted under section 1159 of this title.

(C) Aliens whose status is adjusted to permanent residence under section 1160 or 1255a of this title.

(D) Aliens whose removal is canceled under section 1229b(a) of this title.

(E) Aliens provided permanent resident status under section 1259 of this title.

(2)(A)(i) Immediate relatives. — For purposes of this subsection, the term "immediate relatives" means the children, spouses, and parents of a citizen of the United States, except that, in the case of parents, such citizens shall be at least 21 years of age. In the case of an alien who was the spouse of a citizen of the United States for at least 2 years at the time of the citizen's death and was not legally separated from the citizen at the time of the citizen's death, the alien (and each child of the alien) shall be considered, for purposes of this subsection, to remain an immediate relative after the date of the citizen's death but only if the spouse files a petition under section 1154(a)(1)(A)(ii) of this title within 2 years after such date and only until the date the spouse remarries. For purposes of this clause, an alien who has filed a petition under clause (iii) or (iv) of section 1154(a)(1)(A) of this title remains an immediate relative in the event that the United States citizen spouse or parent loses United States citizenship on account of the abuse.

(ii) Aliens admitted under section 1181(a) of this title on the basis of a prior issuance of a visa to their accompanying parent who is such an immediate relative.

(B) Aliens born to an alien lawfully admitted for permanent residence during a temporary visit abroad.

(c) Worldwide level of family-sponsored immigrants

(1)(A) The worldwide level of family-sponsored immigrants under this subsection for a fiscal year is, subject to subparagraph (B), equal to—

(i) 480,000, minus

(ii) the sum of the number computed under paragraph (2) and the number computed under paragraph (4), plus

(iii) the number (if any) computed under paragraph (3).

(B)(i) For each of fiscal years 1992, 1993, and 1994, 465,000 shall be substituted for 480,000 in subparagraph (A)(i).

(ii) In no case shall the number computed under subparagraph (A) be less than 226,000.

(2) The number computed under this paragraph for a fiscal year is the sum of the number of aliens described in subparagraphs (A) and (B) of subsection (b)(2) of this section who were issued immigrant visas or who otherwise acquired the status of aliens lawfully admitted to the United States for permanent residence in the previous fiscal year.

(3)(A) The number computed under this paragraph for fiscal year 1992 is zero.

(B) The number computed under this paragraph for fiscal year 1993 is the difference (if any) between the worldwide level established under paragraph (1) for the previous fiscal year and the number of visas issued under section 1153(a) of this title during that fiscal year.

(C) The number computed under this paragraph for a subsequent fiscal year is the difference (if any) between the maximum number of visas which may be issued under section 1153(b) of this title (relating to employment-based immigrants) during the previous fiscal year and the number of visas issued under that section during that year.

(4) The number computed under this paragraph for a fiscal year (beginning with fiscal year 1999) is the number of aliens who were paroled into the United States under section 1182(d)(5) of this title in the second preceding fiscal year—

(A) who did not depart from the United States (without advance parole) within 365 days; and

(B) who

(i) did not acquire the status of aliens lawfully admitted to the United States for permanent residence in the two preceding fiscal years, or

(ii) acquired such status in such years under a provision of law (other than subsection (b) of this section) which exempts such adjustment from the numerical limitation on the worldwide level of immigration under this section.

(5) If any alien described in paragraph (4) (other than an alien described in paragraph (4)(B)(ii)) is subsequently admitted as an alien lawfully admitted for permanent residence, such alien shall not again be considered for purposes of paragraph (1).

(d) Worldwide level of employment-based immigrants

(1) The worldwide level of employment-based immigrants under this subsection for a fiscal year is equal to—

(A) 140,000, plus

(B) the number computed under paragraph (2).

(2)(A) The number computed under this paragraph for fiscal year 1992 is zero.

(B) The number computed under this paragraph for fiscal year 1993 is the difference (if any) between the worldwide level established under paragraph (1) for the previous fiscal year and the number of visas issued under section 1153(b) of this title during that fiscal year.

(C) The number computed under this paragraph for a subsequent fiscal year is the difference (if any) between the maximum number of visas which may be issued under section 1153(a) of this title (relating to family-sponsored immigrants) during the previous fiscal year and the number of visas issued under that section during that year.

(e) Worldwide level of diversity immigrants

The worldwide level of diversity immigrants is equal to 55,000 for each fiscal year.

(f) Rules for determining whether certain aliens are immediate relatives

(1) Age on petition filing date

Except as provided in paragraphs (2) and (3), for purposes of subsection (b)(2)(A)(i) of this section, a determination of whether an alien satisfies the age requirement in the matter preceding subparagraph (A) of section 1101(b)(1) of this title shall be made using the age of the alien on the date on which the petition is filed with the Attorney General under section 1154 of this title to classify the alien as an immediate relative under subsection (b)(2)(A)(i) of this section.

(2) Age on parent's naturalization date

In the case of a petition under section 1154 of this title initially filed for an alien child's classification as a family-sponsored immigrant under section 1153(a)(2)(A) of this title, based on the child's parent being lawfully admitted for permanent residence, if the petition is later converted, due to the naturalization of the parent, to a petition to classify the alien as an immediate relative under subsection (b)(2)(A)(i) of this section, the determination described in paragraph (1) shall be made using the age of the alien on the date of the parent's naturalization.

(3) Age on marriage termination date

In the case of a petition under section 1154 of this title initially filed for an alien's classification as a family-sponsored immigrant under section 1153(a)(3) of this title, based on the alien's being a married son or daughter of a citizen, if the petition is later converted, due to the legal termination of the alien's marriage, to a petition to classify the alien as an immediate relative under subsection (b)(2)(A)(i) of this section or as an unmarried son or daughter of a citizen under section 1153(a)(1) of this title, the determination described in paragraph (1) shall be made using the age of the alien on the date of the termination of the marriage.

(June 27, 1952, c. 477, Title II, ch. 1, § 201, 66 Stat. 175; [intervening amendments omitted]; Aug. 6, 2002, Pub.L. 107-268, § 2, 116 Stat. 927.)

[Ed. Note: Sec. 1152, Numerical Limitations on individual foreign states, is omitted.]

Sec. 1153. Allocation of immigrant visas

(a) Preference allocation for family-sponsored immigrants

Aliens subject to the worldwide level specified in section 1151(c) of this title for family-sponsored immigrants shall be allotted visas as follows:

(1) Unmarried sons and daughters of citizens

Qualified immigrants who are the unmarried sons or daughters of citizens of the United States shall be allocated visas in a number not to exceed 23,400, plus any visas not required for the class specified in paragraph (4).

(2) Spouses and unmarried sons and unmarried daughters of permanent resident aliens

Qualified immigrants—

(A) who are the spouses or children of an alien lawfully admitted for permanent residence, or

(B) who are the unmarried sons or unmarried daughters (but are not the children) of an alien lawfully admitted for permanent residence,

shall be allocated visas in a number not to exceed 114,200, plus the number (if any) by which such worldwide level exceeds 226,000, plus any visas not required for the class specified in paragraph (1); except that not less than 77 percent of such visa numbers shall be allocated to aliens described in subparagraph (A).

(3) Married sons and married daughters of citizens

Qualified immigrants who are the married sons or married daughters of citizens of the United States shall be allocated visas in a number not to exceed 23,400, plus any visas not required for the classes specified in paragraphs (1) and (2).

(4) Brothers and sisters of citizens

Qualified immigrants who are the brothers or sisters of citizens of the United States, if such citizens are at least 21 years of age, shall be allocated visas in a number not to exceed 65,000, plus any visas not required for the classes specified in paragraphs (1) through (3).

[Ed. Note: Subsection (b), addressing preference allocation for employment-based immigrants, and Subsection (c), addressing diversity immigrants, are omitted.]

(d) Treatment of family members

A spouse or child as defined in subparagraph (A), (B), (C), (D), or (E) of section 1101(b)(1) of this title shall, if not otherwise entitled to an immigrant status and the immediate issuance of a visa under subsection (a), (b), or (c) of this section, be entitled to the same status, and the same order of consideration provided in the respective subsection, if accompanying or following to join, the spouse or parent.

(e) Order of consideration

(1) Immigrant visas made available under subsection (a) or (b) of this section shall be issued to eligible immigrants in the order in which a petition in behalf of each such immigrant is filed with the Attorney General (or in the case of special immigrants under section 1101(a)(27)(D) of this title, with the Secretary of State) as provided in section 1154(a) of this title.

(2) Immigrant visa numbers made available under subsection (c) of this section (relating to diversity immigrants) shall be issued to eligible qualified immigrants strictly in a random order established by the Secretary of State for the fiscal year involved.

(3) Waiting lists of applicants for visas under this section shall be maintained in accordance with regulations prescribed by the Secretary of State.

(f) Authorization for issuance

In the case of any alien claiming in his application for an immigrant visa to be described in section 1151(b)(2) of this title or in subsection (a), (b), or (c) of this section, the consular officer shall not grant such status until he has been authorized to do so as provided by section 1154 of this title.

(g) Lists

For purposes of carrying out the Secretary's responsibilities in the orderly administration of this section, the Secretary of State may make reasonable estimates of the anticipated numbers of visas to be issued during any quarter of any fiscal year within each of the categories under subsections (a), (b), and (c) of this section and to rely upon such estimates in authorizing the issuance of visas. The Secretary of State shall terminate the registration of any alien who fails to apply for an immigrant visa within one year following notification to the alien of the availability of such visa, but the Secretary shall reinstate the registration of any such alien who establishes within 2 years following the date of notification of the availability of such visa that such failure to apply was due to circumstances beyond the alien's control.

(h) Rules for determining whether certain aliens are children

(1) In general

For purposes of subsections (a)(2)(A) and (d) of this section, a determination of whether an alien satisfies the age requirement in the matter preceding subparagraph (A) of section 1101(b)(1) of this title shall be made using—

(A) the age of the alien on the date on which an immigrant visa number becomes available for such alien (or, in the case of subsection (d) of this section, the date on which an immigrant visa number became available for the alien's parent), but only if the alien has sought to acquire the status of an alien lawfully admitted for permanent residence within one year of such availability; reduced by

(B) the number of days in the period during which the applicable petition described in paragraph (2) was pending.

(2) Petitions described

The petition described in this paragraph is—

(A) with respect to a relationship described in subsection (a)(2)(A) of this section, a petition filed under section 1154 of this title for classification of an alien child under subsection (a)(2)(A) of this section; or

(B) with respect to an alien child who is a derivative beneficiary under subsection (d) of this section, a petition filed under section 1154 of this title for classification of the alien's parent under subsection (a), (b), or (c) of this section.

(3) Retention of priority date

If the age of an alien is determined under paragraph (1) to be 21 years of age or older for the purposes of subsections (a)(2)(A) and (d) of this section, the alien's petition shall automatically be converted to the appropriate category and the alien shall retain the original priority date issued upon receipt of the original petition.

(June 27, 1952, c. 477, Title II, ch. 1, § 203, 66 Stat. 178; [intervening amendments omitted]; Nov. 2, 2002, Pub.L. 107-273, Div. C, Title I, §§ 11035, 11036(a), 116 Stat. 1846.)

Sec. 1154. Procedure for granting immigrant status

[Ed. Note: Amendments to Subsection (d) of this Act, which were passed as part of the Intercountry Adoption Act in 2000 and will take effect when the Hague Convention on Protection of Children and Co-operation in Respect of Intercounty Adoption enters into force for the United States, are set forth at the end of this Section.]

(a) Petitioning procedure

(1)(A)(i) Any citizen of the United States claiming that an alien is entitled to classification by reason of a relationship described in paragraph (1), (3), or (4) of section 1153(a) of this title or to an immediate relative status under section 1151(b)(2)(A)(i) of this title may file a petition with the Attorney General for such classification.

(ii) An alien spouse described in the second sentence of section 1151(b)(2)(A)(i) of this title also may file a petition with the Attorney General under this subparagraph for classification of the alien (and the alien's children) under such section.

(iii)(I) An alien who is described in subclause (II) may file a petition with the Attorney General under this clause for classification of the alien (and any child of the alien) if the alien demonstrates to the attorney general that

(aa) the marriage or the intent to marry the United States citizen was entered into in good faith by the alien; and

(bb) during the marriage or relationship intended by the alien to be legally a marriage, the alien or a child of the alien has been battered or has been the subject of extreme cruelty perpetrated by the alien's spouse or intended spouse.

(II) For purposes of subclause (I), an alien described in this subclause is an alien

(aa)(AA) who is the spouse of a citizen of the United States;

(BB) who believed that he or she had married a citizen of the United States and with whom a marriage ceremony was actually performed and who otherwise meets any applicable requirements under this chapter to establish the existence of and bona fides of a marriage, but whose marriage is not legitimate solely because of the bigamy of such citizen of the United States; or

(CC) who was a bona fide spouse of a United States citizen within the past 2 years and—

(aaa) whose spouse died within the past 2 years;

(bbb) whose spouse lost or renounced citizenship status within the past 2 years related to an incident of domestic violence; or

(ccc) who demonstrates a connection between the legal termination of the marriage within the past 2 years and battering or extreme cruelty by the United States citizen spouse;

(bb) who is a person of good moral character;

(cc) who is eligible to be classified as an immediate relative under section 1151(b)(2)(A)(i) of this title or who would have been so classified but for the bigamy of the citizen of the United States that the alien intended to marry; and

(dd) who has resided with the alien's spouse or intended spouse.

(iv) An alien who is the child of a citizen of the United States, or who was a child of a United States citizen parent who within the past 2 years lost or renounced citizenship status related to an incident of domestic violence, and who is a person of good moral character, who is eligible to be classified as an immediate relative under section 1151(b)(2)(A)(i) of this title, and who resides, or has resided in the past, with the citizen parent may file a petition with the Attorney General under this subparagraph for classification of the alien (and any child of the alien) under such section if the alien demonstrates to the Attorney General that the alien has been battered by or has been the subject of extreme cruelty perpetrated by the alien's citizen parent. For purposes of this clause, residence includes any period of visitation.

(v) An alien who—

(I) is the spouse, intended spouse, or child living abroad of a citizen who—

(aa) is an employee of the United States Government;

(bb) is a member of the uniformed services (as defined in section 101(a) of Title 10); or (cc) has subjected the alien or the alien's child to battery or extreme cruelty in the United States; and

(II) is eligible to file a petition under clause (iii) or (iv), shall file such petition with the Attorney General under the procedures that apply to self-petitioners under clause (iii) or (iv), as applicable.

(vi) For the purposes of any petition filed under clause (iii) or (iv), the denaturalization, loss or renunciation of citizenship, death of the abuser, divorce, or changes to the abuser's citizenship status after filing of the petition shall not adversely affect the approval of the petition, and for approved petitions shall not preclude the classification of the eligible self-petitioning spouse or child as an immediate relative or affect the alien's ability to adjust status under subsections (a) and (c) of section 1255 of this title or obtain status as a lawful permanent resident based on the approved self-petition under such clauses.

(B)(i) Any alien lawfully admitted for permanent residence claiming that an alien is entitled to a classification by reason of the relationship described in section 1153(a)(2) of this title may file a petition with the Attorney General for such classification.

(ii)(I) An alien who is described in subclause (II) may file a petition with the Attorney General under this clause for classification of the alien (and any child of the alien) if such a child has not been classified under clause (iii) of section 1153(a)(2)(A) of this title and if the alien demonstrates to the attorney general that

(aa) the marriage or the intent to marry the lawful permanent resident was entered into in good faith by the alien; and (bb) during the marriage or relationship intended by the alien to be legally a marriage, the alien or a child of the alien has been battered or has been the subject of extreme cruelty perpetrated by the alien's spouse or intended spouse.

(II) For purposes of subclause (I), an alien described in this paragraph is an alien

(aa)(AA) who is the spouse of a lawful permanent resident of the United States; or

(BB) who believed that he or she had married a lawful permanent resident of the United States and with whom a marriage ceremony was actually performed and who otherwise meets any applicable requirements under this Chapter to establish the existence of and bona fides of a marriage, but whose marriage is not legitimate solely because of the bigamy of such lawful permanent resident of the United States; or

(CC) who was a bona fide spouse of a lawful permanent resident within the past 2 years and—

(aaa) whose spouse lost status within the past 2 years due to an incident of domestic violence; or

(bbb) who demonstrates a connection between the legal termination of the marriage within the past 2 years and battering or extreme cruelty by the lawful permanent resident spouse;

(bb) who is a person of good moral character;

(cc) who is eligible to be classified as a spouse of an alien lawfully admitted for permanent residence under section 1153(a)(2)(A) of this title or who would have been so classified but for the bigamy of the lawful permanent resident of the United States that the alien intended to marry; and

(dd) who has resided with the alien's spouse or intended spouse.

(iii) An alien who is the child of an alien lawfully admitted for permanent residence, or who was the child of a lawful permanent resident who within the past 2 years lost lawful permanent resident status due to an incident of domestic violence, and who is a person of good moral character, who is eligible for classification under section 1153(a)(2)(A) of this title, and who resides, or has resided in the past, with the alien's permanent resident alien parent may file a petition with the Attorney General under this subparagraph for classification of the alien (and any child of the alien) under such section if the alien demonstrates to the Attorney General that the alien has been battered by or has been the subject of extreme cruelty perpetrated by the alien's permanent resident parent.

(iv) An alien who

(I) is the spouse, intended spouse, or child living abroad of a lawful permanent resident who—

(aa) is an employee of the United States Government;

(bb) is a member of the uniformed services (as defined in section 101(a) of Title 10); or (cc) has subjected the alien or the alien's child to battery or extreme cruelty in the United States; and

(II) is eligible to file a petition under clause (ii) or (iii), shall file such petition with the Attorney General under the procedures that apply to self-petitioners under clause (ii) or (iii), as applicable.

(v)(I) For the purposes of any petition filed or approved under clause (ii) or (iii), divorce, or the loss of lawful permanent resident status by a spouse or parent after the filing of a petition under that clause shall not adversely affect approval of the petition, and, for an approved petition, shall not affect the alien's ability to adjust status under subsections (a) and (c) of section 1255 of this title or obtain status as a lawful permanent resident based on an approved self-petition under clause (ii) or (iii).

(II) Upon the lawful permanent resident spouse or parent becoming or establishing the existence of United States citizenship through naturalization, acquisition of citizenship, or other means, any petition filed with the Immigration and Naturalization Service and pending or approved under clause (ii) or (iii) on behalf of an alien who has been battered or subjected to extreme cruelty shall be deemed reclassified as a petition filed under subparagraph (A) even if the acquisition of citizenship occurs after divorce or termination of parental rights.

(C) Notwithstanding section 1101(f) of this title, an act or conviction that is waivable with respect to the petitioner for purposes of a determination of the petitioner's admissibility under section 1182(a) of this title or deportability under section 1227(a) of this title shall not bar the Attorney General from finding the petitioner to be of good moral character under subparagraph (A)(iii), (A)(iv), (B)(ii), or (B)(iii) if the Attorney General finds that the act or conviction was connected to the alien's having been battered or subjected to extreme cruelty.

(D)(i)(I) Any child who attains 21 years of age who has filed a petition under clause (iv) of subsection (a)(1)(A) of this section that was filed or approved before the date on which the child attained 21 years of age shall be considered (if the child has not been admitted or approved for lawful permanent residence by the date the child attained 21 years of age) a petitioner for preference status under paragraph (1), (2), or (3) of section 1153(a) of this title, whichever paragraph is applicable, with the same priority date assigned to the self-petition filed under clause (iv) of subsection (a)(1)(A) of this section. No new petition shall be required to be filed.

(II) Any individual described in subclause (I) is eligible for deferred action and work authorization.

(III) Any derivative child who attains 21 years of age who is included in a petition described in clause (ii) that was filed or approved before the date on which the child attained 21 years of age shall be considered (if the child has not been admitted or approved for lawful permanent residence by the date the child attained 21 years of age) a petitioner for preference status under paragraph (1), (2), or (3) of section 1153(a) of this title, whichever paragraph is applicable, with the same priority date as that assigned to the petitioner in any petition described in clause (ii). No new petition shall be required to be filed.

(IV) Any individual described in subclause (III) and any derivative child of a petition described in clause (ii) is eligible for deferred action and work authorization.

(ii) The petition referred to in clause (i)(III) is a petition filed by an alien under subparagraph (A)(iii), (A)(iv), (B)(ii) or (B)(iii) in which the child is included as a derivative beneficiary.

(iii) Nothing in the amendments made by the Child Status Protection Act shall be construed to limit or deny any right or benefit provided under this subparagraph.

(E) Any alien desiring to be classified under section 1153(b)(1)(A) of this title, or any person on behalf of such an alien, may file a petition with the Attorney General for such classification.

(F) Any employer desiring and intending to employ within the United States an alien entitled to classification under section 1153(b)(1)(B), 1153(b)(1)(C), 1153(b)(2), or 1153(b)(3) of this title may file a petition with the Attorney General for such classification.

(G)(i) Any alien (other than a special immigrant under section 1101(a)(27)(D) of this title) desiring to be classified under section 1153(b)(4) of this title, or any person on behalf of such an alien, may file a petition with the Attorney General for such classification.

(ii) Aliens claiming status as a special immigrant under section 1101(a)(27)(D) of this title may file a petition only with the Secretary of State and only after notification by the Secretary that such status has been recommended and approved pursuant to such section.

(H) Any alien desiring to be classified under section 1153(B)(5) of this title may file a petition with the Attorney General for such classification.

(I)(i) Any alien desiring to be provided an immigrant visa under section 1153(c) of this title may file a petition at the place and time determined by the Secretary of State by regulation. Only one such petition may be filed by an alien with respect to any petitioning period established. If more than one petition is submitted all such petitions submitted for such period by the alien shall be voided.

(ii)(I) The Secretary of State shall designate a period for the filing of petitions with respect to visas which may be issued under section 1153(c) of this title for the fiscal year beginning after the end of the period.

(II) Aliens who qualify, through random selection, for a visa under section 1153(c) of this title shall remain eligible to receive such visa only through the end of the specific fiscal year for which they were selected.

(III) The Secretary of State shall prescribe such regulations as may be necessary to carry out this clause.

(iii) A petition under this subparagraph shall be in such form as the Secretary of State may by regulation prescribe and shall contain such information and be supported by such documentary evidence as the Secretary of State may require.

(J) In acting on petitions filed under clause (iii) or (iv) of subparagraph (A) or clause (ii) or (iii) of subparagraph (B), or in making determinations under subparagraphs (C) and (D), the Attorney General shall consider any credible evidence relevant to the petition. The determination of what evidence is credible and the weight to be given that evidence shall be within the sole discretion of the Attorney General.

(2)(A) The Attorney General may not approve a spousal second preference petition for the classification of the spouse of an alien if the alien, by virtue of a prior marriage, has been accorded the status of an alien lawfully admitted for permanent residence as the spouse of a citizen of the United States or as the spouse of an alien lawfully admitted for permanent residence, unless—

(i) a period of 5 years has elapsed after the date the alien acquired the status of an alien lawfully admitted for permanent residence, or

(ii) the alien establishes to the satisfaction of the Attorney General by clear and convincing evidence that the prior marriage (on the basis of which the alien obtained the status of an alien lawfully admitted for permanent residence) was not entered into for the purpose of evading any provision of the immigration laws.

In this subparagraph, the term "spousal second preference petition" refers to a petition, seeking preference status under section 1153(a)(2) of this title, for an alien as a spouse of an alien lawfully admitted for permanent residence.

(B) Subparagraph (A) shall not apply to a petition filed for the classification of the spouse of an alien if the prior marriage of the alien was terminated by the death of his or her spouse.

(b) Investigation; consultation; approval; authorization to grant preference status

After an investigation of the facts in each case, and after consultation with the Secretary of Labor with respect to petitions to accord a status under section 1153(b)(2) or 1153(b)(3) of this title, the Attorney General shall, if he determines that the facts stated in the petition are true and that the alien in behalf of whom the petition is made is an immediate relative specified in section 1151(b) of this title, or is eligible for preference under subsection (a) or (b) of section 1153 of this title, approve the petition and forward one copy thereof to the Department of State. The Secretary of State shall then authorize the consular officer concerned to grant the preference status.

(c) Limitation on orphan petitions approved for a single petitioner; prohibition against approval in cases of marriages entered into in order to evade immigration laws; restriction on future entry of aliens involved with marriage fraud

Notwithstanding the provisions of subsection (b) of this section no petition shall be approved if

(1) the alien has previously been accorded, or has sought to be accorded, an immediate relative or preference status as the spouse of a citizen of the United States or the spouse of an alien lawfully admitted for permanent residence, by reason of a marriage determined by the Attorney General to have been entered into for the purpose of evading the immigration laws, or

(2) the Attorney General has determined that the alien has attempted or conspired to enter into a marriage for the purpose of evading the immigration laws.

(d) Recommendation of valid home-study

Notwithstanding the provisions of subsections (a) and (b) of this section no petition may be approved on behalf of a child defined in section 1101(b)(1)(F) of this title unless a valid home-study has been favorably recommended by an agency of the State of the child's proposed residence, or by an agency authorized by that State to conduct such a study, or, in the case of a child adopted abroad, by an appropriate public or private adoption agency which is licensed in the United States.

(e) Subsequent finding of non-entitlement to preference classification

Nothing in this section shall be construed to entitle an immigrant, in behalf of whom a petition under this section is approved, to be admitted [sic] the United States as an immigrant under subsection (a), (b), or (c) of section 1153 of this title or as an immediate relative under section 1151(b) of this title if upon his arrival at a port of entry in the United States he is found not to be entitled to such classification.

(f) Preferential treatment for children fathered by United States citizens and born in Korea, Vietnam, Laos, Kampuchea, or Thailand after 1950 and before October 22, 1982

(1) Any alien claiming to be an alien described in paragraph (2)(A) of this subsection (or any person on behalf of such an alien) may file a petition with the Attorney General for classification under section 1151(b), 1153(a)(1), or 1153(a)(3) of this title, as appropriate. After an investigation of the facts of each case the Attorney General shall, if the conditions described in paragraph (2) are met, approve the petition and forward one copy to the Secretary of State.

(2) The Attorney General may approve a petition for an alien under paragraph (1) if—

(A) he has reason to believe that the alien

(i) was born in Korea, Vietnam, Laos, Kampuchea, or Thailand after 1950 and before October 22, 1982, and

(ii) was fathered by a United States citizen;

(B) he has received an acceptable guarantee of legal custody and financial responsibility described in paragraph (4); and

(C) in the case of an alien under eighteen years of age,

(i) the alien's placement with a sponsor in the United States has been arranged by an appropriate public, private, or State child welfare agency licensed in the United States and actively involved in the intercountry placement of children and

(ii) the alien's mother or guardian has in writing irrevocably released the alien for emigration.

(3) In considering petitions filed under paragraph (1), the Attorney General shall—

(A) consult with appropriate governmental officials and officials of private voluntary organizations in the country of the alien's birth in order to make the determinations described in subparagraphs (A) and (C)(ii) of paragraph (2); and

(B) consider the physical appearance of the alien and any evidence provided by the petitioner, including birth and baptismal certificates, local civil records, photographs of, and letters or proof of financial support from, a putative father who is a citizen of the United States, and the testimony of witnesses, to the extent it is relevant or probative.

(4)(A) A guarantee of legal custody and financial responsibility for an alien described in paragraph (2) must—

(i) be signed in the presence of an immigration officer or consular officer by an individual (hereinafter in this paragraph referred to as the "sponsor") who is twenty-one years of age or older, is of good moral character, and is a citizen of the United States or alien lawfully admitted for permanent residence, and

(ii) provide that the sponsor agrees

(I) in the case of an alien under eighteen years of age, to assume legal custody for the alien after the alien's departure to the United States and until the alien becomes eighteen years of age, in accordance with the laws of the State where the alien and the sponsor will reside, and

(II) to furnish, during the five-year period beginning on the date of the alien's acquiring the status of an alien lawfully admitted for permanent residence, or during the period beginning on the date of the alien's acquiring the status of an alien lawfully admitted for permanent residence and ending on the date on which the alien becomes twenty-one years of age, whichever period is longer, such financial support as is necessary to maintain the family in the United States of which the alien is a member at a level equal to at least 125 per centum of the current official poverty line (as established by the Director of the Office of Management and Budget, under section 9902(2) of title 42 and as revised by the Secretary of Health and Human Services under the second and third sentences of such section) for a family of the same size as the size of the alien's family.

(B) A guarantee of legal custody and financial responsibility described in subparagraph (A) may be enforced with respect to an alien against his sponsor in a civil suit brought by the Attorney General in the United States district court for the district in which the sponsor resides, except that a sponsor or his estate shall not be liable under such a guarantee if the sponsor dies or is adjudicated a bankrupt under title 11.

(g) Restriction on petitions based on marriages entered while in exclusion or deportation proceedings

Notwithstanding subsection (a) of this section, except as provided in section 1255(e)(3) of this title, a petition may not be approved to grant an alien immediate relative status or preference status by reason of a marriage which was entered into during the period described in section 1255(e)(2) of this title, until the alien has resided outside the United States for a 2-year period beginning after the date of the marriage.

(h) Survival of rights to petition

The legal termination of a marriage may not be the sole basis for revocation under section 1155 of this title of a petition filed under subsection (a)(1)(A)(iii) of this section or a petition filed under subsection (a)(1)(B)(ii) of this section pursuant to conditions described in subsection (a)(1)(A)(iii)(I) of this section. Remarriage of an alien whose petition was approved under subsection (a)(1)(B)(ii) or (a)(1)(A)(iii) of this section or marriage of an alien described in clause (iv) or (vi) of subsection (a)(1)(A) of this section or in subsection (a)(1)(B)(iii) of this section shall not be the basis for revocation of a petition approval under section 1155 of this title.

[Ed. Note: Subsections (i) Professional Athletes; (j) Job flexibility for long delayed applicants for adjustment of status to permanent residence; and (k) Procedures for unmarried sons and daughters of citizens, are omitted.]

(June 27, 1952, c. 477, Title II, ch. 1, §204, 66 Stat. 179; [intervening amendments omitted]; Aug. 6, 2002, Pub.L. 107-208, §§6, 7, 116 Stat. 929.)

Pub.L. 106-279, Title III, §302(b), Title V, §505(a)(2), (b), Oct. 6, 2000, 114 Stat. 839, 844, provides that, effective upon entry into force for the United States of the Convention on Protection of Children and Co-operation in Respect of Intercountry Adoption, pursuant to Article 46(2)(a) of the Convention, subsection (d) is amended by striking out "(d)" and inserting "(d)(1)", by striking out "section 1101(b)(1)(F)" and inserting "subparagraph (F) or (G) of section 1101(b)(1)", and by adding a new paragraph (2), as follows:

(2) Notwithstanding the provisions of subsections (a) and (b), no petition may be approved on behalf of a child defined in section 1101(b)(1)(G) of this title unless the Secretary of State has certified that the central authority of the child's country of origin has notified the United States central authority under the convention referred to in such section 1101(b)(1)(G) of this title that a United States citizen habitually resident in the United States has effected final adoption of the child, or has been granted custody of the child for the purpose of emigration and adoption, in accordance with such convention and the Intercountry Adoption Act of 2000.

Part II—Admission Qualifications for Aliens; Travel Control of Citizens and Aliens

Sec. 1182. Inadmissible aliens

(a) Classes of aliens ineligible for visas or admission

Except as otherwise provided in this chapter, aliens who are inadmissible under the following paragraphs are ineligible to receive visas and ineligible to be admitted to the United States:

(1) Health-related grounds

(A) In general

Any alien—

(i) who is determined (in accordance with regulations prescribed by the Secretary of Health and Human Services) to have a communicable disease of public health significance, which shall include infection with the etiologic agent for acquired immune deficiency syndrome,

(ii) except as provided in subparagraph (C), who seeks admission as an immigrant, or who seeks adjustment of status to the status of an alien lawfully admitted for permanent residence, and who has failed to present documentation of having received vaccination against vaccine-preventable diseases, which shall include at least the following diseases: mumps, measles, rubella, polio, tetanus and diphtheria toxoids, pertussis, influenza type B and hepatitis B, and any other vaccinations against vaccine-preventable diseases recommended by the Advisory Committee for Immunization Practices,

(iii) who is determined (in accordance with regulations prescribed by the Secretary of Health and Human Services in consultation with the Attorney General)—

(I) to have a physical or mental disorder and behavior associated with the disorder that may pose, or has posed, a threat to the property, safety, or welfare of the alien or others, or

(II) to have had a physical or mental disorder and a history of behavior associated with the disorder, which behavior has posed a threat to the property, safety, or welfare of the alien or others and which behavior is likely to recur or to lead to other harmful behavior, or

(iv) who is determined (in accordance with regulations prescribed by the Secretary of Health and Human Services) to be a drug abuser or addict, is inadmissible.

(B) Waiver authorized

For provision authorizing waiver of certain clauses of subparagraph (A), see subsection (g) of this section.

(C) Exception from immunization requirement for adopted children 10 years of age or younger

Clause (ii) of subparagraph (A) shall not apply to a child who—

(i) is 10 years of age or younger,

(ii) is described in section 1101(b)(1)(F) of this title, and

(iii) is seeking an immigrant visa as an immediate relative under section 1151(b) of this title,

if, prior to the admission of the child, an adoptive parent or prospective adoptive parent of the child, who has sponsored the child for admission as an immediate relative, has executed an affidavit stating that the parent is aware of the provisions of subparagraph (A)(ii) and will ensure that, within 30 days of the child's admission, or at the earliest time that is medically appropriate, the child will receive the vaccinations identified in such subparagraph.

[Ed. Note: Subsections (2) Criminal and related grounds; and (3) Security and related grounds, are omitted.]

(4) Public charge

(A) In general

Any alien who, in the opinion of the consular officer at the time of application for a visa, or in the opinion of the Attorney General at the time of application for admission or adjustment of status, is likely at any time to become a public charge is inadmissible.

(B) Factors to be taken into account

(i) In determining whether an alien is inadmissible under this paragraph, the consular officer or the Attorney General shall at a minimum consider the alien's—

(I) age;

(II) health;

(III) family status;

(IV) assets, resources, and financial status; and

(V) education and skills.

(ii) In addition to the factors under clause (i), the consular officer or the Attorney General may also consider any affidavit of support under section 1183a of this title for purposes of exclusion under this paragraph.

(C) Family-sponsored immigrants

Any alien who seeks admission or adjustment of status under a visa number issued under section 1151(b)(2) or 1153(a) of this title is inadmissible under this paragraph unless—

(i) the alien has obtained—

(I) status as a spouse or a child of a United States citizen pursuant to clause (ii), (iii), or (iv) of section 1154(a)(1)(A) of this title or

(II) classification pursuant to clause (ii) or (iii) of section 1154(a)(1)(B) of this title; or

(ii) the person petitioning for the alien's admission (and any additional sponsor required under section 1183a(f) of this title or any alternative sponsor permitted under paragraph (5)(B) of such section) has executed an affidavit of support described in section 1183a of this title with respect to such alien.

(D) Certain employment-based immigrants

Any alien who seeks admission or adjustment of status under a visa number issued under section 1153(b) of this title by virtue of a classification petition filed by a relative of the alien (or by an entity in which such relative has a significant ownership interest) is inadmissible under this paragraph unless such relative has executed an affidavit of support described in section 1183a of this title with respect to such alien.

[Ed. Note: Subsection (5) Labor certification and qualifications for certain immigrants, is omitted.]

(6) Illegal entrants and immigration violators

(A) Aliens present without admission or parole

(i) In general

An alien present in the United States without being admitted or paroled, or who arrives in the United States at any time or place other than as designated by the Attorney General, is inadmissible.

(ii) Exception for certain battered women and children

Clause (i) shall not apply to an alien who demonstrates that—

(I) the alien qualifies for immigrant status under subparagraph (A)(iii), (A)(iv), (B)(ii), or (B)(iii) of section 1134(a)(1) of this title),

(II) (a) the alien has been battered or subjected to extreme cruelty by a spouse or parent, or by a member of the spouse's or parent's family residing in the same household as the alien and the spouse or parent consented or acquiesced to such battery or cruelty, or

(b) the alien's child has been battered or subjected to extreme cruelty by a spouse or parent of the alien (without the active participation of the alien in the battery or cruelty) or by a member of the spouse's or parent's family residing in the same household as the alien when the spouse or parent consented to or acquiesced in such battery or cruelty and the alien did not actively participate in such battery or cruelty, and

(III) there was a substantial connection between the battery or cruelty described in subclause (I) or (II) and the alien's unlawful entry into the United States.

[Ed. Note: Subsections (B) Failure to attend removal proceeding, (C) Misrepresentation, (D) Stowaways, (E) Smugglers, (F) Subject of civil penalty, and (G) Student visa abusers, of Subsection (6); and Subsections (7) Documentation requirements; (8) Ineligible for citizenship; and (9) Aliens previously removed; are omitted.]

(10) Miscellaneous

(A) Practicing polygamists

Any immigrant who is coming to the United States to practice polygamy is inadmissible.

[Ed. Note: Subsection (B) Guardian required to accompany helpless alien, is omitted.]

(C) International child abduction

(i) In general

Except as provided in clause (ii), any alien who, after entry of an order by a court in the United States granting custody to a person of a United States citizen child who detains or retains the child, or withholds custody of the child, outside the United States from the person granted custody by that order, is inadmissible until the child is surrendered to the person granted custody by that order.

(ii) Aliens supporting abductors and relatives of abductors

Any alien who—

(I) is known by the Secretary of State to have intentionally assisted an alien in the conduct described in clause (i),

(II) is known by the Secretary of State to be intentionally providing material support or safe haven to an alien described in clause (i), or

(III) is a spouse (other than the spouse who is the parent of the abducted child), child (other than the abducted child), parent, sibling, or agent of an alien described in clause (i), if such person has been designated by the Secretary of State at the Secretary's sole and unreviewable discretion, is inadmissible until the child described in clause (i) is surrendered to the person granted custody by the order described in that clause, and such person and child are permitted to return to the United States or such person's place of residence.

(iii) Exceptions

Clauses (i) and (ii) shall not apply—

(I) to a government official of the United States who is acting within the scope of his or her official duties;

(II) to a government official of any foreign government if the official has been designated by the Secretary of State at the Secretary's sole and unreviewable discretion; or

(III) so long as the child is located in a foreign state that is a party to the Convention on the Civil Aspects of International Child Abduction, done at The Hague on October 25, 1980.

(D) Unlawful voters [Ed. Note: omitted]

(E) Former citizens who renounced citizenship to avoid taxation [Ed. Note: omitted]

(b) Notices of denials

(1) Subject to paragraphs (2) and (3), if an alien's application for a visa, for admission to the United States, or for adjustment of status is denied by an immigration or consular officer because the officer determines the alien to be inadmissible under subsection (a) of this section, the officer shall provide the alien with a timely written notice that—

(A) states the determination, and

(B) lists the specific provision or provisions of law under which the alien is inadmissible or ineligible for entry or adjustment of status.

(2) The Secretary of State may waive the requirements of paragraph (1) with respect to a particular alien or any class or classes of inadmissible aliens.

(3) Paragraph (1) does not apply to any alien inadmissible under paragraph (2) or (3) of subsection (a) of this section.

[Ed. Note: Subsection (c) has been repealed. Subsection (d), addressing temporary admission of nonimmigrants; subsection (e), addressing educational visitor status, foreign residence requirement and waiver; subsection (f), addressing suspension of entry or imposition of restrictions by President; subsection (g), addressing bond and conditions for admission of alien inadmissible on health-related grounds; subsection (h), addressing waiver of subsection (a)(2)(A)(i)(I), (II), (B), (D), and (E); subsection (i), addressing admission of immigrant inadmissible for fraud or willful misrepresentation of material fact; subsection (j), addressing limitation on immigration of foreign medical graduates; subsection (k), addressing Attorney General's discretion to admit otherwise inadmissible aliens who possess immigrant visas; and subsections (l) through (r), addressing Guam, nurses, labor condition applications, computation of wage levels, academic honoraria, and certification of alien nurses, are omitted.]
(June 27, 1952, c. 477, Title II, ch. 2, §212, 66 Stat. 182; [intervening amendments are omitted]; Nov. 2, 2002, Pub.L. 107-273, Div. C, Title I, §11018(c), 116 Stat. 1825.)

Part III — Issuance of Entry Documents

Sec. 1201. Issuance of Visas
(a) Immigrants; nonimmigrants

(1) Under the conditions hereinafter prescribed and subject to the limitations prescribed in this chapter or regulations issued thereunder, a consular officer may issue

(A) to an immigrant who has made proper application therefor, an immigrant visa which shall consist of the application provided for in section 1202 of this title, visaed by such consular officer, and shall specify the foreign state, if any, to which the immigrant is charged, the immigrant's particular status under such foreign state, the preference, immediate relative, or special immigrant classification to which the alien is charged, the date on which the validity of the visa shall expire, and such additional information as may be required; and

(B) to a nonimmigrant who has made proper application therefor, a nonimmigrant visa, which shall specify the classification under section 1101(a)(15) of this title of the nonimmigrant, the period during which the nonimmigrant visa shall be valid, and such additional information as may be required.

(2) The Secretary of State shall provide to the Service an electronic version of the visa file of each alien who has been issued a visa to ensure that the data in that visa file is available to immigration inspectors at the United States ports of entry before the arrival of the alien at such a port of entry.

(b) Registration; photographs; waiver of requirement
Each alien who applies for a visa shall be registered in connection with his application, and shall furnish copies of his photograph signed by him for such use as may be by regulations required. The requirements of this subsection may be waived in the discre-

tion of the Secretary of State in the case of any alien who is within that class of nonimmigrants enumerated in sections 1101(a)(15)(A), and 1101(a)(15)(G) of this title, or in the case of any alien who is granted a diplomatic visa on a diplomatic passport or on the equivalent thereof.

(c) Period of validity; requirement of visa

An immigrant visa shall be valid for such period, not exceeding six months, as shall be by regulations prescribed, except that any visa issued to a child lawfully adopted by a United States citizen and spouse while such citizen is serving abroad in the United States Armed Forces, or is employed abroad by the United States Government, or is temporarily abroad on business, shall be valid until such time, for a period not to exceed three years, as the adoptive citizen parent returns to the United States in due course of his service, employment, or business. A nonimmigrant visa shall be valid for such periods as shall be by regulations prescribed. In prescribing the period of validity of a nonimmigrant visa in the case of nationals of any foreign country who are eligible for such visas, the Secretary of State shall, insofar as practicable, accord to such nationals the same treatment upon a reciprocal basis as such foreign country accords to nationals of the United States who are within a similar class; except that in the case of aliens who are nationals of a foreign country and who either are granted refugee status and firmly resettled in another foreign country or are granted permanent residence and residing in another foreign country, the Secretary of State may prescribe the period of validity of such a visa based upon the treatment granted by that other foreign country to alien refugees and permanent residents, respectively, in the United States. An immigrant visa may be replaced under the original number during the fiscal year in which the original visa was issued for an immigrant who establishes to the satisfaction of the consular officer that he was unable to use the original immigrant visa during the period of its validity because of reasons beyond his control and for which he was not responsible: Provided, That the immigrant is found by the consular officer to be eligible for an immigrant visa and the immigrant pays again the statutory fees for an application and an immigrant visa.

(d) Physical examination

Prior to the issuance of an immigrant visa to any alien, the consular officer shall require such alien to submit to a physical and mental examination in accordance with such regulations as may be prescribed. Prior to the issuance of a nonimmigrant visa to any alien, the consular officer may require such alien to submit to a physical or mental examination, or both, if in his opinion such examination is necessary to ascertain whether such alien is eligible to receive a visa.

(e) Surrender of visa

Each immigrant shall surrender his immigrant visa to the immigration officer at the port of entry, who shall endorse on the visa the date and the port of arrival, the identity of the vessel or other means of transportation by which the immigrant arrived, and such other endorsements as may be by regulations required.

(f) Surrender of documents

Each nonimmigrant shall present or surrender to the immigration officer at the port of entry such documents as may be by regulation required. In the case of an alien crewman not in possession of any individual documents other than a passport and until such time as it becomes practicable to issue individual documents, such alien crewman may be admitted, subject to the provisions of this part, if his name appears in the crew list of the vessel or aircraft on which he arrives and the crew list is visaed by a consular officer, but the consular officer shall have the right to deny admission to any alien crewman from the crew list visa.

(g) Nonissuance of visas or other documents

No visa or other documentation shall be issued to an alien if

(1) it appears to the consular officer, from statements in the application, or in the papers submitted therewith, that such alien is ineligible to receive a visa or such other documentation under section 1182 of this title, or any other provision of law,

(2) the application fails to comply with the provisions of this chapter, or the regulations issued thereunder, or

(3) the consular officer knows or has reason to believe that such alien is ineligible to receive a visa or such other documentation under section 1182 of this title, or any other provision of law:

Provided, That a visa or other documentation may be issued to an alien who is within the purview of section 1182(a)(4) of this title, if such alien is otherwise entitled to receive a visa or other documentation, upon receipt of notice by the consular officer from the Attorney General of the giving of a bond or undertaking providing indemnity as in the case of aliens admitted under section 1183 of this title:

Provided further, That a visa may be issued to an alien defined in section 1101(a)(15)(B) or (F) of this title, if such alien is otherwise entitled to receive a visa, upon receipt of a notice by the consular officer from the Attorney General of the giving of a bond with sufficient surety in such sum and containing such conditions as the consular officer shall prescribe, to insure that at the expiration of the time for which such alien has been admitted by the Attorney General, as provided in section 1184(a) of this title, or upon failure to maintain the status under which he was admitted, or to maintain any status subsequently acquired under section 1258 of this title, such alien will depart from the United States.

(h) Nonadmission upon arrival

Nothing in this chapter shall be construed to entitle any alien, to whom a visa or other documentation has been issued, to be admitted [sic] the United States, if, upon arrival at a port of entry in the United States, he is found to be inadmissible under this chapter, or any other provision of law. The substance of this subsection shall appear upon every visa application.

(i) Revocation of visas or documents

After the issuance of a visa or other documentation to any alien, the consular officer or the Secretary of State may at any time, in his discretion, revoke such visa or other documentation. Notice of such revocation shall be communicated to the Attorney General, and such revocation shall invalidate the visa or other documentation from the date of issuance: Provided, That carriers or transportation companies, and masters, commanding officers, agents, owners, charterers, or consignees, shall not be penalized under section 1323(b) of this title for action taken in reliance on such visas or other documentation, unless they received due notice of such revocation prior to the alien's embarkation.

(June 27, 1952, c. 477, Title II, ch. 3, § 221, 66 Stat. 191; [intervening amendments are omitted]; amended May 14, 2002, Pub.L. 107-173, Title III, § 301, 116 Stat. 552.)

Part IX. Miscellaneous

Sec. 1374 Information regarding female genital mutilation

(a) Provision of information regarding female genital mutilation

The Immigration and Naturalization Service (in cooperation with the Department of State) shall make available for all aliens who are issued immigrant or nonimmigrant visas, prior to or at the time of entry into the United States, the following information:

(1) Information on the severe harm to physical and psychological health caused by female genital mutilation which is compiled and presented in a manner which is limited to the practice itself and respectful to the cultural values of the societies in which such practice takes place.

(2) Information concerning potential legal consequences in the United States for (A) performing female genital mutilation, or (B) allowing a child under his or her care to be subjected to female genital mutilation, under criminal or child protection statutes or as a form of child abuse.

(b) Limitation

In consultation with the Secretary of State, the Commissioner of Immigration and Naturalization shall identify those countries in which female genital mutilation is commonly practiced and, to the extent practicable, limit the provision of information under subsection (a) of this section to aliens from such countries.

(c) "Female genital mutilation" defined

For purposes of this section, the term "female genital mutilation" means the removal or infibulation (or both) of the whole or part of the clitoris, the labia minora, or labia majora. (Pub.L. 104-208, Div. C, Title VI, s 644, Sept. 30, 1996, 110 Stat. 3009-708.)

Sec. 1375 Mail-order bride business

(a) Findings

The Congress finds as follows:

(1) There is a substantial "mail-order bride" business in the United States. With approximately 200 companies in the United States, an estimated 2,000 to 3,500 men in the United States find wives through mail-order bride catalogs each year. However, there are no official statistics available on the number of mail-order brides entering the United States each year.

(2) The companies engaged in the mail-order bride business earn substantial profits.

(3) Although many of these mail-order marriages work out, in many other cases, anecdotal evidence suggests that mail-order brides find themselves in abusive relationships. There is also evidence to suggest that a substantial number of mail-order marriages are fraudulent under United States law.

(4) Many mail-order brides come to the United States unaware or ignorant of United States immigration law. Mail-order brides who are battered often think that if they flee an abusive marriage, they will be deported. Often the citizen spouse threatens to have them deported if they report the abuse.

(5) The Immigration and Naturalization Service estimates that the rate of marriage fraud between foreign nationals and United States citizens or aliens lawfully admitted for permanent residence is 8 percent. It is unclear what percentage of these marriage fraud cases originate as mail-order marriages.

(b) Information dissemination

(1) Requirement

Each international matchmaking organization doing business in the United States shall disseminate to recruits, upon recruitment, such immigration and naturalization information as the Immigration and Naturalization Service deems appropriate, in the recruit's native language, including information regarding conditional permanent residence status and the battered spouse waiver under such status, permanent resident status, marriage fraud penalties, the unregulated nature of the business engaged in by such organizations, and the study required under subsection (c) of this section.

(2) Civil penalty

(A) Violation

Any international matchmaking organization that the Attorney General determines has violated this subsection shall be subject, in addition to any other penalties that may be prescribed by law, to a civil money penalty of not more than $20,000 for each such violation.

(B) Procedures for imposition of penalty

Any penalty under subparagraph (A) may be imposed only after notice and opportunity for an agency hearing on the record in accordance with sections 554 through 557 of Title 5.

(c) Study

The Attorney General, in consultation with the Commissioner of Immigration and Naturalization and the Director of the Violence Against Women Initiative of the Department of Justice, shall conduct a study of mail-order marriages to determine, among other things—

(1) the number of such marriages;

(2) the extent of marriage fraud in such marriages, including an estimate of the extent of marriage fraud arising from the services provided by international matchmaking organizations;

(3) the extent to which mail-order spouses utilize section 1254a(a)(3) of this title (providing for suspension of deportation in certain cases involving abuse) [Ed. Note: Westlaw suggests this citation should be to § 1229b(b)(2)], or section 1154(a)(1)(A)(iii) of this title (providing for certain aliens who have been abused to file a classification petition on their own behalf);

(4) the extent of domestic abuse in mail-order marriages; and

(5) the need for continued or expanded regulation and education to implement the objectives of the Violence Against Women Act of 1994 and the Immigration Marriage Fraud Amendments of 1986 with respect to mail-order marriages.

(d) Report

Not later than 1 year after September 30, 1996, the Attorney General shall submit a report to the Committees on the Judiciary of the House of Representatives and of the Senate setting forth the results of the study conducted under subsection (c) of this section.

(e)Definitions

As used in this section:

(1) International matchmaking organization

(A) In general

The term "international matchmaking organization" means a corporation, partnership, business, or other legal entity, whether or not organized under the laws of the United States or any State, that does business in the United States and for profit offers to United States citizens or aliens lawfully admitted for permanent residence, dating, matrimonial, or social referral services to nonresident noncitizens, by—

(i) an exchange of names, telephone numbers, addresses, or statistics;

(ii) selection of photographs; or

(iii) a social environment provided by the organization in a country other than the United States.

(B) Exception

Such term does not include a traditional matchmaking organization of a religious nature that otherwise operates in compliance with the laws of the countries of the recruits of such organization and the laws of the United States.

(2) Recruit

The term "recruit" means a noncitizen, nonresident person, recruited by the international matchmaking organization for the purpose of providing dating, matrimonial, or social referral services to United States citizens or aliens lawfully admitted for permanent residence.

(Pub.L. 104-208, Div. C, Title VI, s 652, Sept. 30, 1996, 110 Stat. 3009-712.)

Subchapter III—Nationality and Naturalization
Part II—Nationality Through Naturalization

Sec. 1431. Children born outside the United States and residing permanently in the United States, Conditions under which citizenship automatically acquired

(a) A child born outside of the United States automatically becomes a citizen of the United States when all of the following conditions have been fulfilled:

(1) At least one parent of the child is a citizen of the United States, whether by birth or naturalization.

(2) The child is under the age of eighteen years.

(3) The child is residing in the United States in the legal and physical custody of the citizen parent pursuant to a lawful admission for permanent residence.

(b) Subsection (a) shall apply to a child adopted by a United States citizen parent if the child satisfies the requirements applicable to adopted children under section 1101(b)(1) of this title.

(June 27, 1952, c. 477, Title III, ch. 2, §320, 66 Stat. 245; Oct. 5, 1978, Pub.L. 95-417, §4, 92 Stat. 917; Dec. 29, 1981, Pub.L. 97-116, §18(m), 95 Stat. 1620; Nov. 14, 1986, Pub.L. 99-653, §14, 100 Stat. 3657; Oct. 24, 1988, Pub.L. 100-525, §§8(1), 9(w), 102 Stat. 2618, 2621; amended Oct. 30, 2000, Pub.L.106-395, Title I, §101(a), 114 Stat. 1631.)

Sec. 1432. Repealed. Pub.L. 106-395, Title I, §103(a), Oct. 30, 2000, 114 Stat. 1632

Sec. 1433. Child born and residing outside United States; conditions for acquiring certificate of citizenship

(a) Application by citizen parents; requirements

A parent who is a citizen of the United States (or, if the citizen parent has died during the preceding 5 years, a citizen grandparent or citizen legal guardian) may apply for naturalization on behalf of a child born outside of the United States who has not acquired citizenship automatically under section 1431 of this title. The Attorney General shall issue a certificate of citizenship to such applicant upon proof, to the satisfaction of the Attorney General, that the following conditions have been fulfilled:

(1) At least one parent (or, at the time of his or her death, was) is (sic)a citizen of the United States, whether by birth or naturalization.

(2) The United States citizen parent—

(A) has (or at the time of his or her death, had) been physically present in the United States or its outlying possessions for a period or periods totaling not less than five years, at least two of which were after attaining the age of fourteen years; or

(B) has (or at the time of his or her death, had) a citizen parent who has been physically present in the United States or its outlying possessions for a period or periods totaling not less than five years, at least two of which were after attaining the age of fourteen years.

(3) The child is under the age of eighteen years.

(4) The child is residing outside of the United States in the legal and physical custody of the applicant (or, if the citizen parent is deceased, an individual who does not object to the application).

(5) The child is temporarily present in the United States pursuant to a lawful admission, and is maintaining such lawful status.

(b) Attainment of citizenship status; receipt of certificate

Upon approval of the application (which may be filed from abroad) and, except as provided in the last sentence of section 1448(a) of this title, upon taking and subscribing before an officer of the Service within the United States to the oath of allegiance required by this Chapter of an applicant for naturalization, the child shall become a citizen of the United States and shall be furnished by the Attorney General with a certificate of citizenship.

(c) Adopted children

Subsections (a) and (b) of this section shall apply to a child adopted by a United States citizen parent if the child satisfies the requirements applicable to adopted children under section 1101(b)(1)of this title.

(June 27, 1952, c. 477, Title III, ch. 2, § 322, 66 Stat. 246; [intervening amendments omitted]; Nov. 2, 2002, Pub.L. 107-273, Div. C, Title I, § 11030B, 116 Stat. 1837.]

Title 18. Crimes and Criminal Procedure

Part I—Crimes
Chapter 55—Kidnapping

Sec. 1204. International parental kidnapping

(a) Whoever removes a child from the United States, or attempts to do so, or retains a child (who has been in the United States) outside the United States with intent to obstruct the lawful exercise of parental rights shall be fined under this title or imprisoned not more than 3 years, or both.

(b) As used in this section—

(1) the term "child" means a person who has not attained the age of 16 years; and

(2) the term "parental rights", with respect to a child, means the right to physical custody of the child—

(A) whether joint or sole (and includes visiting rights); and

(B) whether arising by operation of law, court order, or legally binding agreement of the parties.

(c) It shall be an affirmative defense under this section that—

(1) the defendant acted within the provisions of a valid court order granting the defendant legal custody or visitation rights and that order was obtained pursuant to the Uniform Child Custody Jurisdiction Act or the Uniform Child Custody Jurisdiction and Enforcement Act and was in effect at the time of the offense;

(2) the defendant was fleeing an incidence or pattern of domestic violence; or

(3) the defendant had physical custody of the child pursuant to a court order granting legal custody or visitation rights and failed to return the child as a result of circumstances beyond the defendant's control, and the defendant notified or made reasonable attempts to notify the other parent or lawful custodian of the child of such circumstances within 24 hours after the visitation period had expired and returned the child as soon as possible.

(d) This section does not detract from The Hague Convention on the Civil Aspects of International Parental Child Abduction, done at The Hague on October 25, 1980.
(Pub.L. 103-173, § 2(a), Dec. 2, 1993, 107 Stat. 1998; Pub.L. 108-21, Title I, § 107, Apr. 30, 2003, 117 Stat. 655.)

Title 22. Foreign Relations and Intercourse

Chapter 78—Trafficking Victims Protection Act

Sec. 7101. Purposes and findings

(a) Purposes

The purposes of this chapter are to combat trafficking in persons, a contemporary manifestation of slavery whose victims are predominantly women and children, to ensure just and effective punishment of traffickers, and to protect their victims.

(b) Findings

Congress finds that:

(1) As the 21st century begins, the degrading institution of slavery continues throughout the world. Trafficking in persons is a modern form of slavery, and it is the largest manifestation of slavery today. At least 700,000 persons annually, primarily women and children, are trafficked within or across international borders. Approximately 50,000 women and children are trafficked into the United States each year.

(2) Many of these persons are trafficked into the international sex trade, often by force, fraud, or coercion. The sex industry has rapidly expanded over the past several decades. It involves sexual exploitation of persons, predominantly women and girls, involving activities related to prostitution, pornography, sex tourism, and other commercial sexual services. The low status of women in many parts of the world has contributed to a burgeoning of the trafficking industry.

(3) Trafficking in persons is not limited to the sex industry. This growing transnational crime also includes forced labor and involves significant violations of labor, public health, and human rights standards worldwide.

(4) Traffickers primarily target women and girls, who are disproportionately affected by poverty, the lack of access to education, chronic unemployment, discrimination, and the lack of economic opportunities in countries of origin. Traffickers lure women and girls into their networks through false promises of decent working conditions at relatively good pay as nannies, maids, dancers, factory workers, restaurant workers, sales

clerks, or models. Traffickers also buy children from poor families and sell them into prostitution or into various types of forced or bonded labor.

(5) Traffickers often transport victims from their home communities to unfamiliar destinations, including foreign countries away from family and friends, religious institutions, and other sources of protection and support, leaving the victims defenseless and vulnerable.

(6) Victims are often forced through physical violence to engage in sex acts or perform slavery-like labor. Such force includes rape and other forms of sexual abuse, torture, starvation, imprisonment, threats, psychological abuse, and coercion.

(7) Traffickers often make representations to their victims that physical harm may occur to them or others should the victim escape or attempt to escape. Such representations can have the same coercive effects on victims as direct threats to inflict such harm.

(8) Trafficking in persons is increasingly perpetrated by organized, sophisticated criminal enterprises. Such trafficking is the fastest growing source of profits for organized criminal enterprises worldwide. Profits from the trafficking industry contribute to the expansion of organized crime in the United States and worldwide. Trafficking in persons is often aided by official corruption in countries of origin, transit, and destination, thereby threatening the rule of law.

(9) Trafficking includes all the elements of the crime of forcible rape when it involves the involuntary participation of another person in sex acts by means of fraud, force, or coercion.

(10) Trafficking also involves violations of other laws, including labor and immigration codes and laws against kidnapping, slavery, false imprisonment, assault, battery, pandering, fraud, and extortion.

(11) Trafficking exposes victims to serious health risks. Women and children trafficked in the sex industry are exposed to deadly diseases, including HIV and AIDS. Trafficking victims are sometimes worked or physically brutalized to death.

(12) Trafficking in persons substantially affects interstate and foreign commerce. Trafficking for such purposes as involuntary servitude, peonage, and other forms of forced labor has an impact on the nationwide employment network and labor market. Within the context of slavery, servitude, and labor or services which are obtained or maintained through coercive conduct that amounts to a condition of servitude, victims are subjected to a range of violations.

(13) Involuntary servitude statutes are intended to reach cases in which persons are held in a condition of servitude through nonviolent coercion. In United States v. Kozminski, 487 U.S. 931 (1988), the Supreme Court found that section 1584 of Title 18, should be narrowly interpreted, absent a definition of involuntary servitude by Congress. As a result, that section was interpreted to criminalize only servitude that is brought about through use or threatened use of physical or legal coercion, and to exclude other conduct that can have the same purpose and effect.

(14) Existing legislation and law enforcement in the United States and other countries are inadequate to deter trafficking and bring traffickers to justice, failing to reflect the gravity of the offenses involved. No comprehensive law exists in the United States that penalizes the range of offenses involved in the trafficking scheme. Instead, even the most brutal instances of trafficking in the sex industry are often punished under laws that also apply to lesser offenses, so that traffickers typically escape deserved punishment.

(15) In the United States, the seriousness of this crime and its components is not reflected in current sentencing guidelines, resulting in weak penalties for convicted traffickers.

(16) In some countries, enforcement against traffickers is also hindered by official indifference, by corruption, and sometimes even by official participation in trafficking.

(17) Existing laws often fail to protect victims of trafficking, and because victims are often illegal immigrants in the destination country, they are repeatedly punished more harshly than the traffickers themselves.

(18) Additionally, adequate services and facilities do not exist to meet victims' needs regarding health care, housing, education, and legal assistance, which safely reintegrate trafficking victims into their home countries.

(19) Victims of severe forms of trafficking should not be inappropriately incarcerated, fined, or otherwise penalized solely for unlawful acts committed as a direct result of being trafficked, such as using false documents, entering the country without documentation, or working without documentation.

(20) Because victims of trafficking are frequently unfamiliar with the laws, cultures, and languages of the countries into which they have been trafficked, because they are often subjected to coercion and intimidation including physical detention and debt bondage, and because they often fear retribution and forcible removal to countries in which they will face retribution or other hardship, these victims often find it difficult or impossible to report the crimes committed against them or to assist in the investigation and prosecution of such crimes.

(21) Trafficking of persons is an evil requiring concerted and vigorous action by countries of origin, transit or destination, and by international organizations.

(22) One of the founding documents of the United States, the Declaration of Independence, recognizes the inherent dignity and worth of all people. It states that all men are created equal and that they are endowed by their Creator with certain unalienable rights. The right to be free from slavery and involuntary servitude is among those unalienable rights. Acknowledging this fact, the United States outlawed slavery and involuntary servitude in 1865, recognizing them as evil institutions that must be abolished. Current practices of sexual slavery and trafficking of women and children are similarly abhorrent to the principles upon which the United States was founded.

(23) The United States and the international community agree that trafficking in persons involves grave violations of human rights and is a matter of pressing international concern. The international community has repeatedly condemned slavery and involuntary servitude, violence against women, and other elements of trafficking, through declarations, treaties, and United Nations resolutions and reports, including the Universal Declaration of Human Rights; the 1956 Supplementary Convention on the Abolition of Slavery, the Slave Trade, and Institutions and Practices Similar to Slavery; the 1948 American Declaration on the Rights and Duties of Man; the 1957 Abolition of Forced Labor Convention; the International Covenant on Civil and Political Rights; the Convention Against Torture and Other Cruel, Inhuman or Degrading Treatment or Punishment; United Nations General Assembly Resolutions 50/167, 51/66, and 52/98; the Final Report of the World Congress against Sexual Exploitation of Children (Stockholm, 1996); the Fourth World Conference on Women (Beijing, 1995); and the 1991 Moscow Document of the Organization for Security and Cooperation in Europe.

(24) Trafficking in persons is a transnational crime with national implications. To deter international trafficking and bring its perpetrators to justice, nations including the United States must recognize that trafficking is a serious offense. This is done by prescribing appropriate punishment, giving priority to the prosecution of trafficking offenses, and protecting rather than punishing the victims of such offenses. The

United States must work bilaterally and multilaterally to abolish the trafficking industry by taking steps to promote cooperation among countries linked together by international trafficking routes. The United States must also urge the international community to take strong action in multilateral for a (sic) to engage recalcitrant countries in serious and sustained efforts to eliminate trafficking and protect trafficking victims.

(Pub.L. 106-386, Div. A, § 102, Oct. 28, 2000, 114 Stat. 1466.)

Sec. 7102. Definitions

In this chapter:

(1) Appropriate Congressional committees

The term "appropriate congressional committees" means the Committee on Foreign Relations and the Committee on the Judiciary of the Senate and the Committee on International Relations and the Committee on the Judiciary of the House of Representatives.

(2) Coercion

The term "coercion" means—

(A) threats of serious harm to or physical restraint against any person;

(B) any scheme, plan, or pattern intended to cause a person to believe that failure to perform an act would result in serious harm to or physical restraint against any person; or

(C) the abuse or threatened abuse of the legal process.

(3) Commercial sex act

The term "commercial sex act" means any sex act on account of which anything of value is given to or received by any person.

(4) Debt bondage

The term "debt bondage" means the status or condition of a debtor arising from a pledge by the debtor of his or her personal services or of those of a person under his or her control as a security for debt, if the value of those services as reasonably assessed is not applied toward the liquidation of the debt or the length and nature of those services are not respectively limited and defined.

(5) Involuntary servitude

The term "involuntary servitude" includes a condition of servitude induced by means of—

(A) any scheme, plan, or pattern intended to cause a person to believe that, if the person did not enter into or continue in such condition, that person or another person would suffer serious harm or physical restraint; or

(B) the abuse or threatened abuse of the legal process.

(6) Minimum standards for the elimination of trafficking

The term "minimum standards for the elimination of trafficking" means the standards set forth in section 7106 of this title.

(7) Nonhumanitarian, nontrade-related foreign assistance

The term "nonhumanitarian, nontrade-related foreign assistance" means—

(A) any assistance under the Foreign Assistance Act of 1961, other than—

(i) assistance under chapter 4 of part II of that Act that is made available for any program, project, or activity eligible for assistance under chapter 1 of part I of that Act;

(ii) assistance under chapter 8 of part I of that Act;

(iii) any other narcotics-related assistance under part I of that Act or under chapter 4 or 5 part II of that Act, but any such assistance provided under this clause shall be subject to the prior notification procedures applicable to reprogrammings pursuant to section 634A of that Act;

(iv) disaster relief assistance, including any assistance under chapter 9 of part I of that Act;

(v) antiterrorism assistance under chapter 8 of part II of that Act;

(vi) assistance for refugees;

(vii) humanitarian and other development assistance in support of programs of nongovernmental organizations under chapters 1 and 10 of that Act;

(viii) programs under title IV of chapter 2 of part I of that Act, relating to the Overseas Private Investment Corporation; and

(ix) other programs involving trade-related or humanitarian assistance; and

(B) sales, or financing on any terms, under the Arms Export Control Act, other than sales or financing provided for narcotics-related purposes following notification in accordance with the prior notification procedures applicable to reprogrammings pursuant to section 634A of the Foreign Assistance Act of 1961.

(8) Severe forms of trafficking in persons

The term "severe forms of trafficking in persons" means—

(A) sex trafficking in which a commercial sex act is induced by force, fraud, or coercion, or in which the person induced to perform such act has not attained 18 years of age; or

(B) the recruitment, harboring, transportation, provision, or obtaining of a person for labor or services, through the use of force, fraud, or coercion for the purpose of subjection to involuntary servitude, peonage, debt bondage, or slavery.

(9) Sex trafficking

The term "sex trafficking" means the recruitment, harboring, transportation, provision, or obtaining of a person for the purpose of a commercial sex act.

(10) State

The term "State" means each of the several States of the United States, the District of Columbia, the Commonwealth of Puerto Rico, the United States Virgin Islands, Guam, American Samoa, the Commonwealth of the Northern Mariana Islands, and territories and possessions of the United States.

(11) Task Force

The term "Task Force" means the Interagency Task Force to Monitor and Combat Trafficking established under section 7103 of this title.

(12) United States

The term "United States" means the fifty States of the United States, the District of Columbia, the Commonwealth of Puerto Rico, the Virgin Islands, American Samoa, Guam, the Commonwealth of the Northern Mariana Islands, and the territories and possessions of the United States.

(13) Victim of a severe form of trafficking

The term "victim of a severe form of trafficking" means a person subject to an act or practice described in paragraph (8).

(14) Victim of trafficking

The term "victim of trafficking" means a person subjected to an act or practice described in paragraph (8) or (9).

(Pub.L. 106-386, Div. A, § 103, Oct. 28, 2000, 114 Stat. 1469.)

Sec. 7103. Interagency Task Force to Monitor and Combat Trafficking

(a) Establishment

The President shall establish an Interagency Task Force to Monitor and Combat Trafficking.

(b) Appointment

The President shall appoint the members of the Task Force, which shall include the Secretary of State, the Administrator of the United States Agency for International Development, the Attorney General, the Secretary of Labor, the Secretary of Health and Human Services, the Director of Central Intelligence, and such other officials as may be designated by the President.

(c) Chairman

The Task Force shall be chaired by the Secretary of State.

(d) Activities of the Task Force

The Task Force shall carry out the following activities:

(1) Coordinate the implementation of this chapter.

(2) Measure and evaluate progress of the United States and other countries in the areas of trafficking prevention, protection, and assistance to victims of trafficking, and prosecution and enforcement against traffickers, including the role of public corruption in facilitating trafficking. The Task Force shall have primary responsibility for assisting the Secretary of State in the preparation of the reports described in section 7107 of this title.

(3) Expand interagency procedures to collect and organize data, including significant research and resource information on domestic and international trafficking. Any data collection procedures established under this subsection shall respect the confidentiality of victims of trafficking.

(4) Engage in efforts to facilitate cooperation among countries of origin, transit, and destination. Such efforts shall aim to strengthen local and regional capacities to prevent trafficking, prosecute traffickers and assist trafficking victims, and shall include initiatives to enhance cooperative efforts between destination countries and countries of origin and assist in the appropriate reintegration of stateless victims of trafficking.

(5) Examine the role of the international "sex tourism" industry in the trafficking of persons and in the sexual exploitation of women and children around the world.

(6) Engage in consultation and advocacy with governmental and nongovernmental organizations, among other entities, to advance the purposes of this division.

(e) Support for the Task Force

The Secretary of State is authorized to establish within the Department of State an Office to Monitor and Combat Trafficking, which shall provide assistance to the Task Force. Any such Office shall be headed by a Director. The Director shall have the primary responsibility for assisting the Secretary of State in carrying out the purposes of this chapter and may have additional responsibilities as determined by the Secretary. The Director shall consult with nongovernmental organizations and multilateral organizations, and with trafficking victims or other affected persons. The Director shall have the authority to take evidence in public hearings or by other means. The agencies represented on the Task Force are authorized to provide staff to the Office on a nonreimbursable basis.
(Pub.L. 106-386, Div. A, § 105, Oct. 28, 2000, 114 Stat. 1473.)

Sec. 7104. Prevention of trafficking

(a) Economic alternatives to prevent and deter trafficking

The President shall establish and carry out international initiatives to enhance economic opportunity for potential victims of trafficking as a method to deter trafficking. Such initiatives may include—

(1) microcredit lending programs, training in business development, skills training, and job counseling;

(2) programs to promote women's participation in economic decisionmaking;

(3) programs to keep children, especially girls, in elementary and secondary schools, and to educate persons who have been victims of trafficking;

(4) development of educational curricula regarding the dangers of trafficking; and

(5) grants to nongovernmental organizations to accelerate and advance the political, economic, social, and educational roles and capacities of women in their countries.

(b) Public awareness and information

The President, acting through the Secretary of Labor, the Secretary of Health and Human Services, the Attorney General, and the Secretary of State, shall establish and carry out programs to increase public awareness, particularly among potential victims of trafficking, of the dangers of trafficking and the protections that are available for victims of trafficking.

(c) Consultation requirement

The President shall consult with appropriate nongovernmental organizations with respect to the establishment and conduct of initiatives described in subsections (a) and (b) of this section.
(Pub.L. 106-386, Div. A, § 106, Oct. 28, 2000, 114 Stat. 1474.)

Sec. 7105. Protection and assistance for victims of trafficking

(a) Assistance for victims in other countries

(1) In general

The Secretary of State and the Administrator of the United States Agency for International Development, in consultation with appropriate nongovernmental organizations, shall establish and carry out programs and initiatives in foreign countries to assist in the safe integration, reintegration, or resettlement, as appropriate, of victims of trafficking. Such programs and initiatives shall be designed to meet the appropriate assistance needs of such persons and their children, as identified by the Task Force. In addition, such programs and initiatives shall, to the maximum extent practicable, include the following:

(A) Support for local in-country nongovernmental organization-operated hotlines, culturally and linguistically appropriate protective shelters, and regional and international nongovernmental organization networks and databases on trafficking, including support to assist nongovernmental organizations in establishing service centers and systems that are mobile and extend beyond large cities.

(B) Support for nongovernmental organizations and advocates to provide legal, social, and other services and assistance to trafficked individuals, particularly those individuals in detention.

(C) Education and training for trafficked women and girls.

(D) The safe integration or reintegration of trafficked individuals into an appropriate community or family, with full respect for the wishes, dignity, and safety of the trafficked individual.

(E) Support for developing or increasing programs to assist families of victims in locating, repatriating, and treating their trafficked family members, in assisting the voluntary repatriation of these family members or their integration or resettlement into appropriate communities, and in providing them with treatment.

(2) Additional requirement

In establishing and conducting programs and initiatives described in paragraph (1), the Secretary of State and the Administrator of the United States Agency for International Development shall take all appropriate steps to enhance cooperative efforts among foreign countries, including countries of origin of victims of trafficking, to assist in the integration, reintegration, or resettlement, as appropriate, of victims of trafficking, including stateless victims.

(b) Victims in the United States

(1) Assistance

(A) Eligibility for benefits and services

Notwithstanding title IV of the Personal Responsibility and Work Opportunity Reconciliation Act of 1996, an alien who is a victim of a severe form of trafficking in persons shall be eligible for benefits and services under any Federal or State program or activity funded or administered by any official or agency described in subparagraph (B) to the same extent as an alien who is admitted to the United States as a refugee under section 1157 of Title 8.

(B) Requirement to expand benefits and services

Subject to subparagraph (C) and, in the case of nonentitlement programs, to the availability of appropriations, the Secretary of Health and Human Services, the Secretary of Labor, the Board of Directors of the Legal Services Corporation, and the heads of other Federal agencies shall expand benefits and services to victims of severe forms of trafficking in persons in the United States, without regard to the immigration status of such victims.

(C) Definition of victim of a severe form of trafficking in persons

For the purposes of this paragraph, the term "victim of a severe form of trafficking in persons" means only a person—

(i) who has been subjected to an act or practice described in section 7102(8) of this title as in effect on October 28, 2000; and

(ii)(I) who has not attained 18 years of age; or

(II) who is the subject of a certification under subparagraph (E).

(D) Annual report

Not later than December 31 of each year, the Secretary of Health and Human Services, in consultation with the Secretary of Labor, the Board of Directors of the Legal Services Corporation, and the heads of other appropriate Federal agencies shall submit a report, which includes information on the number of persons who received benefits or other services under this paragraph in connection with programs or activities funded or administered by such agencies or officials during the preceding fiscal year, to the Committee on Ways and Means, the Committee on International Relations, and the Committee on the Judiciary of the House of Representatives and the Committee on Finance, the Committee on Foreign Relations, and the Committee on the Judiciary of the Senate.

(E) Certification

(i) In general

Subject to clause (ii), the certification referred to in subparagraph (C) is a certification by the Secretary of Health and Human Services, after consultation with the Attorney General, that the person referred to in subparagraph (C)(ii)(II)—

(I) is willing to assist in every reasonable way in the investigation and prosecution of severe forms of trafficking in persons; and

(II)(aa) has made a bona fide application for a visa under section 1101(a)(15)(T) of Title 8, that has not been denied; or

(bb) is a person whose continued presence in the United States the Attorney General is ensuring in order to effectuate prosecution of traffickers in persons.

(ii) Period of effectiveness

A certification referred to in subparagraph (C), with respect to a person described in clause (i)(II)(bb), shall be effective only for so long as the Attorney General determines that the continued presence of such person is necessary to effectuate prosecution of traffickers in persons.

(iii) Investigation and prosecution defined

For the purpose of a certification under this subparagraph, the term "investigation and prosecution" includes—

(I) identification of a person or persons who have committed severe forms of trafficking in persons;

(II) location and apprehension of such persons; and

(III) testimony at proceedings against such persons.

(2) Grants

(A) In general

Subject to the availability of appropriations, the Attorney General may make grants to States, Indian tribes, units of local government, and nonprofit, nongovernmental victims' service organizations to develop, expand, or strengthen victim service programs for victims of trafficking.

(B) Allocation of grant funds

Of amounts made available for grants under this paragraph, there shall be set aside—

(i) three percent for research, evaluation, and statistics;

(ii) two percent for training and technical assistance; and

(iii) one percent for management and administration.

(C) Limitation on Federal share

The Federal share of a grant made under this paragraph may not exceed 75 percent of the total costs of the projects described in the application submitted.

(c) Trafficking victim regulations

Not later than 180 days after October 28, 2000, the Attorney General and the Secretary of State shall promulgate regulations for law enforcement personnel, immigration officials, and Department of State officials to implement the following:

(1) Protections while in custody

Victims of severe forms of trafficking, while in the custody of the Federal Government and to the extent practicable, shall—

(A) not be detained in facilities inappropriate to their status as crime victims;

(B) receive necessary medical care and other assistance; and

(C) be provided protection if a victim's safety is at risk or if there is danger of additional harm by recapture of the victim by a trafficker, including—

(i) taking measures to protect trafficked persons and their family members from intimidation and threats of reprisals and reprisals from traffickers and their associates; and

(ii) ensuring that the names and identifying information of trafficked persons and their family members are not disclosed to the public.

(2) Access to information

Victims of severe forms of trafficking shall have access to information about their rights and translation services.

(3) Authority to permit continued presence in the United States

Federal law enforcement officials may permit an alien individual's continued presence in the United States, if after an assessment, it is determined that such individual is a victim of a severe form of trafficking and a potential witness to such trafficking, in order to effectuate prosecution of those responsible, and such officials in investigating and prosecuting traffickers shall protect the safety of trafficking victims, including taking measures to protect trafficked persons and their family members from intimidation, threats of reprisals, and reprisals from traffickers and their associates.

(4) Training of Government personnel

Appropriate personnel of the Department of State and the Department of Justice shall be trained in identifying victims of severe forms of trafficking and providing for the protection of such victims.

(d) Construction

Nothing in subsection (c) of this section shall be construed as creating any private cause of action against the United States or its officers or employees.

(e) Protection from removal for certain crime victims

(1) to (4) Omitted [in original. Ed.]

(5) Statutory construction

Nothing in this section, or in the amendments made by this section, shall be construed as prohibiting the Attorney General from instituting removal proceedings under section 1229a of Title 8 against an alien admitted as a nonimmigrant under section 1101(a)(15)(T)(i) of Title 8, as added by subsection (e) of this section, for conduct committed after the alien's admission into the United States, or for conduct or a condition that was not disclosed to the Attorney General prior to the alien's admission as a nonimmigrant under such section 1101(a)(15)(T)(i) of Title (sic.).

(f) Omitted [in original. Ed.]

(g) Annual reports

On or before October 31 of each year, the Attorney General shall submit a report to the appropriate congressional committees setting forth, with respect to the preceding fiscal year, the number, if any, of otherwise eligible applicants who did not receive visas under section 1101(a)(15)(T) of Title 8, as added by subsection (e) of this section, or who were unable to adjust their status under section 1255(l) of Title 8, solely on account of the unavailability of visas due to a limitation imposed by section 1184(n)(1) or 1255(l)(4)(A) of Title 8.

(Pub.L. 106-386, Div. A, § 107, Oct. 28, 2000, 114 Stat. 1474; Pub.L. 107-228, Div. A, Title VI, § 682(a), Sept. 30, 2002, 116 Stat. 1409.)

Sec. 7106. Minimum standards for the elimination of trafficking

(a) Minimum standards

For purposes of this chapter, the minimum standards for the elimination of trafficking applicable to the government of a country of origin, transit, or destination for a significant number of victims of severe forms of trafficking are the following:

(1) The government of the country should prohibit severe forms of trafficking in persons and punish acts of such trafficking.

(2) For the knowing commission of any act of sex trafficking involving force, fraud, coercion, or in which the victim of sex trafficking is a child incapable of giving meaningful consent, or of trafficking which includes rape or kidnapping or which causes a death, the government of the country should prescribe punishment commensurate with that for grave crimes, such as forcible sexual assault.

(3) For the knowing commission of any act of a severe form of trafficking in persons, the government of the country should prescribe punishment that is sufficiently stringent to deter and that adequately reflects the heinous nature of the offense.

(4) The government of the country should make serious and sustained efforts to eliminate severe forms of trafficking in persons.

(b) Criteria

In determinations under subsection (a)(4) of this section, the following factors should be considered as indicia of serious and sustained efforts to eliminate severe forms of trafficking in persons:

(1) Whether the government of the country vigorously investigates and prosecutes acts of severe forms of trafficking in persons that take place wholly or partly within the territory of the country.

(2) Whether the government of the country protects victims of severe forms of trafficking in persons and encourages their assistance in the investigation and prosecution of such trafficking, including provisions for legal alternatives to their removal to countries in which they would face retribution or hardship, and ensures that victims are not inappropriately incarcerated, fined, or otherwise penalized solely for unlawful acts as a direct result of being trafficked.

(3) Whether the government of the country has adopted measures to prevent severe forms of trafficking in persons, such as measures to inform and educate the public, including potential victims, about the causes and consequences of severe forms of trafficking in persons.

(4) Whether the government of the country cooperates with other governments in the investigation and prosecution of severe forms of trafficking in persons.

(5) Whether the government of the country extradites persons charged with acts of severe forms of trafficking in persons on substantially the same terms and to substantially the same extent as persons charged with other serious crimes (or, to the extent such extradition would be inconsistent with the laws of such country or with international agreements to which the country is a party, whether the government is taking all appropriate measures to modify or replace such laws and treaties so as to permit such extradition).

(6) Whether the government of the country monitors immigration and emigration patterns for evidence of severe forms of trafficking in persons and whether law enforcement agencies of the country respond to any such evidence in a manner that is consistent with the vigorous investigation and prosecution of acts of such trafficking, as well as with the protection of human rights of victims and the internationally recognized human right to leave any country, including one's own, and to return to one's own country.

(7) Whether the government of the country vigorously investigates and prosecutes public officials who participate in or facilitate severe forms of trafficking in persons, and takes all appropriate measures against officials who condone such trafficking. (Pub.L. 106-386, Div. A, § 108, Oct. 28, 2000, 114 Stat. 1480.)

Sec. 7107. Actions against governments failing to meet minimum standards

(a) Statement of policy

It is the policy of the United States not to provide nonhumanitarian, nontrade-related foreign assistance to any government that—

(1) does not comply with minimum standards for the elimination of trafficking; and

(2) is not making significant efforts to bring itself into compliance with such standards.

(b) Reports to Congress

(1) Annual report

Not later than June 1 of each year, the Secretary of State shall submit to the appropriate congressional committees a report with respect to the status of severe forms of trafficking in persons that shall include —

(A) a list of those countries, if any, to which the minimum standards for the elimination of trafficking are applicable and whose governments fully comply with such standards;

(B) a list of those countries, if any, to which the minimum standards for the elimination of trafficking are applicable and whose governments do not yet fully comply with such standards but are making significant efforts to bring themselves into compliance; and

(C) a list of those countries, if any, to which the minimum standards for the elimination of trafficking are applicable and whose governments do not fully comply with such standards and are not making significant efforts to bring themselves into compliance.

(2) Interim reports

In addition to the annual report under paragraph (1), the Secretary of State may submit to the appropriate congressional committees at any time one or more interim reports with respect to the status of severe forms of trafficking in persons, including information about countries whose governments —

(A) have come into or out of compliance with the minimum standards for the elimination of trafficking; or

(B) have begun or ceased to make significant efforts to bring themselves into compliance, since the transmission of the last annual report.

(3) Significant efforts

In determinations under paragraph (1) or (2) as to whether the government of a country is making significant efforts to bring itself into compliance with the minimum standards for the elimination of trafficking, the Secretary of State shall consider —

(A) the extent to which the country is a country of origin, transit, or destination for severe forms of trafficking;

(B) the extent of noncompliance with the minimum standards by the government and, particularly, the extent to which officials or employees of the government have participated in, facilitated, condoned, or are otherwise complicit in severe forms of trafficking; and

(C) what measures are reasonable to bring the government into compliance with the minimum standards in light of the resources and capabilities of the government.

(c) Notification

Not less than 45 days or more than 90 days after the submission, on or after January 1, 2003, of an annual report under subsection (b)(1), or an interim report under subsection (b)(2) of this section, the President shall submit to the appropriate congressional committees a notification of one of the determinations listed in subsection (d) of this section with respect to each foreign country whose government, according to such report —

(A) does not comply with the minimum standards for the elimination of trafficking; and

(B) is not making significant efforts to bring itself into compliance, as described in subsection (b)(1)(C) of this section.

(d) Presidential determinations

The determinations referred to in subsection (c) of this section are the following:

(1) Withholding of nonhumanitarian, nontrade-related assistance

The President has determined that—

(A)(i) the United States will not provide nonhumanitarian, nontrade-related foreign assistance to the government of the country for the subsequent fiscal year until such government complies with the minimum standards or makes significant efforts to bring itself into compliance; or

(ii) in the case of a country whose government received no nonhumanitarian, non-trade-related foreign assistance from the United States during the previous fiscal year, the United States will not provide funding for participation by officials or employees of such governments in educational and cultural exchange programs for the subsequent fiscal year until such government complies with the minimum standards or makes significant efforts to bring itself into compliance; and

(B) the President will instruct the United States Executive Director of each multilateral development bank and of the International Monetary Fund to vote against, and to use the Executive Director's best efforts to deny, any loan or other utilization of the funds of the respective institution to that country (other than for humanitarian assistance, for trade-related assistance, or for development assistance which directly addresses basic human needs, is not administered by the government of the sanctioned country, and confers no benefit to that government) for the subsequent fiscal year until such government complies with the minimum standards or makes significant efforts to bring itself into compliance.

(2) Ongoing, multiple, broad-based restrictions on assistance in response to human rights violations

The President has determined that such country is already subject to multiple, broad-based restrictions on assistance imposed in significant part in response to human rights abuses and such restrictions are ongoing and are comparable to the restrictions provided in paragraph (1). Such determination shall be accompanied by a description of the specific restriction or restrictions that were the basis for making such determination.

(3) Subsequent compliance

The Secretary of State has determined that the government of the country has come into compliance with the minimum standards or is making significant efforts to bring itself into compliance.

(4) Continuation of assistance in the National interest

Notwithstanding the failure of the government of the country to comply with minimum standards for the elimination of trafficking and to make significant efforts to bring itself into compliance, the President has determined that the provision to the country of nonhumanitarian, nontrade-related foreign assistance, or the multilateral assistance described in paragraph (1)(B), or both, would promote the purposes of this chapter or is otherwise in the national interest of the United States.

(5) Exercise of waiver authority

(A) In general

The President may exercise the authority under paragraph (4) with respect to—

(i) all nonhumanitarian, nontrade-related foreign assistance to a country;

(ii) all multilateral assistance described in paragraph (1)(B) to a country; or

(iii) one or more programs, projects, or activities of such assistance.

(B) Avoidance of significant adverse effects

The President shall exercise the authority under paragraph (4) when necessary to avoid significant adverse effects on vulnerable populations, including women and children.

(6) Definition of multilateral development bank

In this subsection, the term "multilateral development bank" refers to any of the following institutions: the International Bank for Reconstruction and Development, the International Development Association, the International Finance Corporation, the Inter-American Development Bank, the Asian Development Bank, the Inter-American Investment Corporation, the African Development Bank, the African Development Fund, the European Bank for Reconstruction and Development, and the Multilateral Investment Guaranty Agency.

(e) Certification

Together with any notification under subsection (c) of this section, the President shall provide a certification by the Secretary of State that, with respect to any assistance described in clause (ii), (iii), or (v) of section 7102(7)(A) of this title, or with respect to any assistance described in section 7102(7)(B) of this title, no assistance is intended to be received or used by any agency or official who has participated in, facilitated, or condoned a severe form of trafficking in persons.
(Pub.L. 106-386, Div. A, §110, Oct. 28, 2000, 114 Stat. 1482.)

Sec. 7108. Actions against significant traffickers in persons

(a) Authority to sanction significant traffickers in persons

(1) In general

The President may exercise the authorities set forth in section 1702 of Title 50 without regard to section 1701 of Title 50 in the case of any of the following persons:

(A) Any foreign person that plays a significant role in a severe form of trafficking in persons, directly or indirectly in the United States.

(B) Foreign persons that materially assist in, or provide financial or technological support for or to, or provide goods or services in support of, activities of a significant foreign trafficker in persons identified pursuant to subparagraph (A).

(C) Foreign persons that are owned, controlled, or directed by, or acting for or on behalf of, a significant foreign trafficker identified pursuant to subparagraph (A).

(2) Penalties

The penalties set forth in section 1705 of Title 50 apply to violations of any license, order, or regulation issued under this section.

(b) Report to Congress on identification and sanctioning of significant traffickers in persons

(1) In general

Upon exercising the authority of subsection (a) of this section, the President shall report to the appropriate congressional committees—

(A) identifying publicly the foreign persons that the President determines are appropriate for sanctions pursuant to this section and the basis for such determination; and

(B) detailing publicly the sanctions imposed pursuant to this section.

(2) Removal of sanctions

Upon suspending or terminating any action imposed under the authority of subsection (a) of this section, the President shall report to the committees described in paragraph (1) on such suspension or termination.

(3) Submission of classified information

Reports submitted under this subsection may include an annex with classified information regarding the basis for the determination made by the President under paragraph (1)(A).

(c) Law enforcement and intelligence activities not affected

Nothing in this section prohibits or otherwise limits the authorized law enforcement or intelligence activities of the United States, or the law enforcement activities of any State or subdivision thereof.

(d) Omitted [in original. Ed.]

(e) Implementation

(1) Delegation of authority

The President may delegate any authority granted by this section, including the authority to designate foreign persons under paragraphs (1)(B) and (1)(C) of subsection (a) of this section.

(2) Promulgation of rules and regulations

The head of any agency, including the Secretary of Treasury, is authorized to take such actions as may be necessary to carry out any authority delegated by the President pursuant to paragraph (1), including promulgating rules and regulations.

(3) Opportunity for review

Such rules and regulations shall include procedures affording an opportunity for a person to be heard in an expeditious manner, either in person or through a representative, for the purpose of seeking changes to or termination of any determination, order, designation or other action associated with the exercise of the authority in subsection (a) of this section.

(f) "Foreign persons" defined

In this section, the term " foreign person" means any citizen or national of a foreign state or any entity not organized under the laws of the United States, including a foreign government official, but does not include a foreign state.

(g) Construction

Nothing in this section shall be construed as precluding judicial review of the exercise of the authority described in subsection (a) of this section.
(Pub.L. 106-386, Div. A, § 111, Oct. 28, 2000, 114 Stat. 1484.)

Sec. 7109. Strengthening prosecution and punishment of traffickers

(a) Omitted [in original. Ed.]

(b) Amendment to the sentencing guidelines

(1) Pursuant to its authority under section 994 of Title 28, and in accordance with this section, the United States Sentencing Commission shall review and, if appropriate, amend the sentencing guidelines and policy statements applicable to persons convicted of offenses involving the trafficking of persons including component or related crimes of peonage, involuntary servitude, slave trade offenses, and possession, transfer or sale of false immigration documents in furtherance of trafficking, and the Fair Labor Standards Act and the Migrant and Seasonal Agricultural Worker Protection Act.

(2) In carrying out this subsection, the Sentencing Commission shall—

(A) take all appropriate measures to ensure that these sentencing guidelines and policy statements applicable to the offenses described in paragraph (1) of this subsection are sufficiently stringent to deter and adequately reflect the heinous nature of such offenses;

(B) consider conforming the sentencing guidelines applicable to offenses involving trafficking in persons to the guidelines applicable to peonage, involuntary servitude, and slave trade offenses; and

(C) consider providing sentencing enhancements for those convicted of the offenses described in paragraph (1) of this subsection that—

(i) involve a large number of victims;

(ii) involve a pattern of continued and flagrant violations;

(iii) involve the use or threatened use of a dangerous weapon; or

(iv) result in the death or bodily injury of any person.

(3) The Commission may promulgate the guidelines or amendments under this subsection in accordance with the procedures set forth in section 21(a) of the Sentencing Act of 1987, as though the authority under that Act had not expired.
(Pub.L. 106-386, Div. A, § 112, Oct. 28, 2000, 114 Stat. 1486.)

Sec. 7110. Authorizations of appropriations

(a) Authorization of appropriations in support of the Task Force

To carry out the purposes of section 104, and sections 7103 and 7107 of this title, there are authorized to be appropriated to the Secretary of State $1,500,000 for fiscal year 2001 and $3,000,000 for fiscal years 2002 and 2003.

(b) Authorization of appropriations to the Secretary of Health and Human Services

To carry out the purposes of section 7105(b) of this title, there are authorized to be appropriated to the Secretary of Health and Human Services $5,000,000 for fiscal year 2001 and $10,000,000 for fiscal year 2002.

(c) Authorization of appropriations to the Secretary of State

(1) Assistance for victims in other countries

To carry out the purposes of section 7105(a) of this title, there are authorized to be appropriated to the Secretary of State $5,000,000 for fiscal year 2001, $10,000,000 for fiscal year 2002, and $15,000,000 for the fiscal year 2003.

(2) Voluntary contributions to OSCE

To carry out the purposes of section 2152d of this title, there is authorized to be appropriated to the Secretary of State for each of the fiscal years 2001, 2002, and 2003 $300,000 for voluntary contributions to advance projects aimed at preventing trafficking, promoting respect for human rights of trafficking victims, and assisting the Organization for Security and Cooperation in Europe participating states in related legal reform for such fiscal year.

(3) Preparation of annual country reports on human rights

To carry out the purposes of section 104, there are authorized to be appropriated to the Secretary of State such sums as may be necessary to include the additional information required by that section in the annual Country Reports on Human Rights Practices, including the preparation and publication of the list described in subsection (a)(1) of that section.

(d) Authorization of appropriations to Attorney General

To carry out the purposes of section 7105(b) of this title, there are authorized to be appropriated to the Attorney General $5,000,000 for fiscal year 2001 and $10, 000,000 for fiscal year 2002.

(e) Authorization of appropriations to President

(1) Foreign victim assistance

To carry out the purposes of section 7104 of this title, there are authorized to be appropriated to the President $5,000,000 for fiscal year 2001, $10,000,000 for fiscal year 2002, and $15,000,000 for fiscal year 2003.

(2) Assistance to foreign countries to meet minimum standards

To carry out the purposes of section 2152d of this title, there are authorized to be appropriated to the President $5,000,000 for fiscal year 2001, $10,000,000 for fiscal year 2002, and $15,000,000 for fiscal year 2003.

(f) Authorization of appropriations to the Secretary of Labor

To carry out the purposes of section 7105(b) of this title, there are authorized to be appropriated to the Secretary of Labor $5,000,000 for fiscal year 2001 and $10,000,000 for fiscal year 2002.
(Pub.L. 106-386, Div. A, § 113, Oct. 28, 2000, 114 Stat. 1490; Pub.L. 107-228, Div. A, Title VI, § 682(b), Sept. 30, 2002, 116 Stat. 1410.)

Title 42. The Public Health and Welfare

Chapter 7 — Social Security
Subchapter IV — Grants to States for Aid and Services to Needy Families
with Children and for Child Welfare Services
Part D — Child Support and Establishment of Paternity

Sec. 654. State plan for child and spousal support
A State plan for child and spousal support must —

* * *

(32)(A) provide that any request for services under this part by a foreign reciprocating country or a foreign country with which the State has an arrangement described in section 659a(d) of this title shall be treated as a request by a State;

(B) provide, at State option, notwithstanding paragraph (4) or any other provision of this part, for services under the plan for enforcement of a spousal support order not described in paragraph (4)(B) entered by such a country (or subdivision); and

(C) provide that no applications will be required from, and no costs will be assessed for such services against, the foreign reciprocating country or foreign obligee (but costs may at State option be assessed against the obligor);

* * *

(Aug. 14, 1935, c. 531, Title IV, § 454, as added Jan. 4, 1975, Pub.L. 93-647, § 101(a), 88 Stat. 2354; [intervening amendments omitted, Ed.]; Dec. 14, 1999, Pub.L. 106-169, Title IV, § 401(g), (h), 113 Stat. 1858.)

Sec. 659a. International support enforcement
(a) Authority for declarations
(1) Declaration

The Secretary of State, with the concurrence of the Secretary of Health and Human Services, is authorized to declare any foreign country (or a political subdivision thereof) to be a foreign reciprocating country if the foreign country has established, or undertakes to establish, procedures for the establishment and enforcement of duties of support owed to obligees who are residents of the United States, and such procedures are substantially in conformity with the standards prescribed under subsection (b) of this section.

(2) Revocation

A declaration with respect to a foreign country made pursuant to paragraph (1) may be revoked if the Secretaries of State and Health and Human Services determine that—

(A) the procedures established by the foreign country regarding the establishment and enforcement of duties of support have been so changed, or the foreign country's implementation of such procedures is so unsatisfactory, that such procedures do not meet the criteria for such a declaration; or

(B) continued operation of the declaration is not consistent with the purposes of this part.

(3) Form of declaration

A declaration under paragraph (1) may be made in the form of an international agreement, in connection with an international agreement or corresponding foreign declaration, or on a unilateral basis.

(b) Standards for foreign support enforcement procedures

(1) Mandatory elements

Support enforcement procedures of a foreign country which may be the subject of a declaration pursuant to subsection (a)(1) of this section shall include the following elements:

(A) The foreign country (or political subdivision thereof) has in effect procedures, available to residents of the United States—

(i) for establishment of paternity, and for establishment of orders of support for children and custodial parents; and

(ii) for enforcement of orders to provide support to children and custodial parents, including procedures for collection and appropriate distribution of support payments under such orders.

(B) The procedures described in subparagraph (A), including legal and administrative assistance, are provided to residents of the United States at no cost.

(C) An agency of the foreign country is designated as a Central Authority responsible for—

(i) facilitating support enforcement in cases involving residents of the foreign country and residents of the United States; and

(ii) ensuring compliance with the standards established pursuant to this subsection.

(2) Additional elements

The Secretary of Health and Human Services and the Secretary of State, in consultation with the States, may establish such additional standards as may be considered necessary to further the purposes of this section.

(c) Designation of United States Central Authority

It shall be the responsibility of the Secretary of Health and Human Services to facilitate support enforcement in cases involving residents of the United States and residents of foreign countries that are the subject of a declaration under this section, by activities including—

(1) development of uniform forms and procedures for use in such cases;

(2) notification of foreign reciprocating countries of the State of residence of individuals sought for support enforcement purposes, on the basis of information provided by the Federal Parent Locator Service; and

(3) such other oversight, assistance, and coordination activities as the Secretary may find necessary and appropriate.

(d) Effect on other laws

States may enter into reciprocal arrangements for the establishment and enforcement of support obligations with foreign countries that are not the subject of a declaration pursuant to subsection (a) of this section, to the extent consistent with Federal law. (Aug. 14, 1935, c. 531, Title IV, §459A, as added Aug. 22, 1996, Pub.L. 104-193, Title III, §371(a), 110 Stat. 2252.)

Chapter 121 — International Child Abduction Remedies

Sec. 11601. Findings and declarations

(a) Findings

The Congress makes the following findings:

(1) The international abduction or wrongful retention of children is harmful to their well-being.

(2) Persons should not be permitted to obtain custody of children by virtue of their wrongful removal or retention.

(3) International abductions and retentions of children are increasing, and only concerted cooperation pursuant to an international agreement can effectively combat this problem.

(4) The Convention on the Civil Aspects of International Child Abduction, done at The Hague on October 25, 1980, establishes legal rights and procedures for the prompt return of children who have been wrongfully removed or retained, as well as for securing the exercise of visitation rights. Children who are wrongfully removed or retained within the meaning of the Convention are to be promptly returned unless one of the narrow exceptions set forth in the Convention applies. The Convention provides a sound treaty framework to help resolve the problem of international abduction and retention of children and will deter such wrongful removals and retentions.

(b) Declarations

The Congress makes the following declarations:

(1) It is the purpose of this chapter to establish procedures for the implementation of the Convention in the United States.

(2) The provisions of this chapter are in addition to and not in lieu of the provisions of the Convention.

(3) In enacting this chapter the Congress recognizes—

(A) the international character of the Convention; and

(B) the need for uniform international interpretation of the Convention.

(4) The Convention and this chapter empower courts in the United States to determine only rights under the Convention and not the merits of any underlying child custody claims.

(Pub.L. 100-300, s 2, Apr. 29, 1988, 102 Stat. 437.)

Sec. 11602. Definitions

For the purposes of this chapter—

(1) the term "applicant" means any person who, pursuant to the Convention, files an application with the United States Central Authority or a Central Authority of any other

party to the Convention for the return of a child alleged to have been wrongfully removed or retained or for arrangements for organizing or securing the effective exercise of rights of access pursuant to the Convention;

(2) the term "Convention" means the Convention on the Civil Aspects of International Child Abduction, done at The Hague on October 25, 1980;

(3) the term "Parent Locator Service" means the service established by the Secretary of Health and Human Services under section 653 of this title;

(4) the term "petitioner" means any person who, in accordance with this chapter, files a petition in court seeking relief under the Convention;

(5) the term "person" includes any individual, institution, or other legal entity or body;

(6) the term "respondent" means any person against whose interests a petition is filed in court, in accordance with this chapter, which seeks relief under the Convention;

(7) the term "rights of access" means visitation rights;

(8) the term "State" means any of the several States, the District of Columbia, and any commonwealth, territory, or possession of the United States; and

(9) the term "United States Central Authority" means the agency of the Federal Government designated by the President under section 11606(a) of this title.
(Pub.L. 100-300, s 3, Apr. 29, 1988, 102 Stat. 437.)

Sec. 11603. Judicial remedies

(a) Jurisdiction of courts

The courts of the States and the United States district courts shall have concurrent original jurisdiction of actions arising under the Convention.

(b) Petitions

Any person seeking to initiate judicial proceedings under the Convention for the return of a child or for arrangements for organizing or securing the effective exercise of rights of access to a child may do so by commencing a civil action by filing a petition for the relief sought in any court which has jurisdiction of such action and which is authorized to exercise its jurisdiction in the place where the child is located at the time the petition is filed.

(c) Notice

Notice of an action brought under subsection (b) of this section shall be given in accordance with the applicable law governing notice in interstate child custody proceedings.

(d) Determination of case

The court in which an action is brought under subsection (b) of this section shall decide the case in accordance with the Convention.

(e) Burdens of proof

(1) A petitioner in an action brought under subsection (b) of this section shall establish by a preponderance of the evidence—

(A) in the case of an action for the return of a child, that the child has been wrongfully removed or retained within the meaning of the Convention; and

(B) in the case of an action for arrangements for organizing or securing the effective exercise of rights of access, that the petitioner has such rights.

(2) In the case of an action for the return of a child, a respondent who opposes the return of the child has the burden of establishing—

(A) by clear and convincing evidence that one of the exceptions set forth in article 13b or 20 of the Convention applies; and

(B) by a preponderance of the evidence that any other exception set forth in article 12 or 13 of the Convention applies.

(f) Application of Convention

For purposes of any action brought under this chapter—

(1) the term "authorities", as used in article 15 of the Convention to refer to the authorities of the state of the habitual residence of a child, includes courts and appropriate government agencies;

(2) the terms "wrongful removal or retention" and "wrongfully removed or retained", as used in the Convention, include a removal or retention of a child before the entry of a custody order regarding that child; and

✱ (3) the term "commencement of proceedings", as used in article 12 of the Convention, means, with respect to the return of a child located in the United States, the filing of a petition in accordance with subsection (b) of this section.

(g) Full faith and credit

Full faith and credit shall be accorded by the courts of the States and the courts of the United States to the judgment of any other such court ordering or denying the return of a child, pursuant to the Convention, in an action brought under this chapter.

(h) Remedies under Convention not exclusive

The remedies established by the Convention and this chapter shall be in addition to remedies available under other laws or international agreements.
(Pub.L. 100-300, s 4, Apr. 29, 1988, 102 Stat. 438.)

Sec. 11604. Provisional remedies

(a) Authority of courts

In furtherance of the objectives of article 7(b) and other provisions of the Convention, and subject to the provisions of subsection (b) of this section, any court exercising jurisdiction of an action brought under section 11603(b) of this title may take or cause to be taken measures under Federal or State law, as appropriate, to protect the well-being of the child involved or to prevent the child's further removal or concealment before the final disposition of the petition.

(b) Limitation on authority

No court exercising jurisdiction of an action brought under section 11603(b) of this title may, under subsection (a) of this section, order a child removed from a person having physical control of the child unless the applicable requirements of State law are satisfied.
(Pub.L. 100-300, s 5, Apr. 29, 1988, 102 Stat. 439.)

Sec. 11605. Admissibility of documents

With respect to any application to the United States Central Authority, or any petition to a court under section 11603 of this title, which seeks relief under the Convention, or any other documents or information included with such application or petition or provided after such submission which relates to the application or petition, as the case may be, no authentication of such application, petition, document, or information shall be required in order for the application, petition, document, or information to be admissible in court.
(Pub.L. 100-300, s 6, Apr. 29, 1988, 102 Stat. 439.)

Sec. 11606. United States Central Authority

(a) Designation

The President shall designate a Federal agency to serve as the Central Authority for the United States under the Convention.

(b) Functions

The functions of the United States Central Authority are those ascribed to the Central Authority by the Convention and this chapter.

(c) Regulatory authority

The United States Central Authority is authorized to issue such regulations as may be necessary to carry out its functions under the Convention and this chapter.

(d) Obtaining information from Parent Locator Service

The United States Central Authority may, to the extent authorized by the Social Security Act, obtain information from the Parent Locator Service.

(e) Grant Authority

The United States Central Authority is authorized to make grants to, or enter into contracts or agreements with, any individual, corporation, other Federal, State, or local agency, or private entity or organization in the United States for purposes of accomplishing its responsibilities under the Convention and this chapter.
(Pub.L. 100-300, s 7, Apr. 29, 1988, 102 Stat. 439; Pub.L. 105-277, Div. G, Title XXII, s 2213, 112 Stat. 2681-812.)

Sec. 11607. Costs and fees

(a) Administrative costs

No department, agency, or instrumentality of the Federal Government or of any State or local government may impose on an applicant any fee in relation to the administrative processing of applications submitted under the Convention.

(b) Costs incurred in civil actions

(1) Petitioners may be required to bear the costs of legal counsel or advisors, court costs incurred in connection with their petitions, and travel costs for the return of the child involved and any accompanying persons, except as provided in paragraphs (2) and (3).

(2) Subject to paragraph (3), legal fees or court costs incurred in connection with an action brought under section 11603 of this title shall be borne by the petitioner unless they are covered by payments from Federal, State, or local legal assistance or other programs.

(3) Any court ordering the return of a child pursuant to an action brought under section 11603 of this title shall order the respondent to pay necessary expenses incurred by or on behalf of the petitioner, including court costs, legal fees, foster home or other care during the course of proceedings in the action, and transportation costs related to the return of the child, unless the respondent establishes that such order would be clearly inappropriate.
(Pub.L. 100-300, s 8, Apr. 29, 1988, 102 Stat. 440.)

Sec. 11608. Collection, maintenance, and dissemination of information

(a) In general

In performing its functions under the Convention, the United States Central Authority may, under such conditions as the Central Authority prescribes by regulation, but subject to subsection (c) of this section, receive from or transmit to any department, agency, or instrumentality of the Federal Government or of any State or foreign government, and receive from or transmit to any applicant, petitioner, or respondent, information necessary to locate a child or for the purpose of otherwise implementing the Convention with respect to a child, except that the United States Central Authority—

(1) may receive such information from a Federal or State department, agency, or instrumentality only pursuant to applicable Federal and State statutes; and

(2) may transmit any information received under this subsection notwithstanding any provision of law other than this chapter.

(b) Requests for information

Requests for information under this section shall be submitted in such manner and form as the United States Central Authority may prescribe by regulation and shall be accompanied or supported by such documents as the United States Central Authority may require.

(c) Responsibility of government entities

Whenever any department, agency, or instrumentality of the United States or of any State receives a request from the United States Central Authority for information authorized to be provided to such Central Authority under subsection (a) of this section, the head of such department, agency, or instrumentality shall promptly cause a search to be made of the files and records maintained by such department, agency, or instrumentality in order to determine whether the information requested is contained in any such files or records. If such search discloses the information requested, the head of such department, agency, or instrumentality shall immediately transmit such information to the United States Central Authority, except that any such information the disclosure of which—

(1) would adversely affect the national security interests of the United States or the law enforcement interests of the United States or of any State; or

(2) would be prohibited by section 9 of Title 13;

shall not be transmitted to the Central Authority. The head of such department, agency, or instrumentality shall, immediately upon completion of the requested search, notify the Central Authority of the results of the search, and whether an exception set forth in paragraph (1) or (2) applies. In the event that the United States Central Authority receives information and the appropriate Federal or State department, agency, or instrumentality thereafter notifies the Central Authority that an exception set forth in paragraph (1) or (2) applies to that information, the Central Authority may not disclose that information under subsection (a) of this section.

(d) Information available from Parent Locator Service

To the extent that information which the United States Central Authority is authorized to obtain under the provisions of subsection (c) of this section can be obtained through the Parent Locator Service, the United States Central Authority shall first seek to obtain such information from the Parent Locator Service, before requesting such information directly under the provisions of subsection (c) of this section.

(e) Recordkeeping

The United States Central Authority shall maintain appropriate records concerning its activities and the disposition of cases brought to its attention.
(Pub.L. 100-300, s 9, Apr. 29, 1988, 102 Stat. 440.)

Sec. 11608a. Office of Children's Issues

(a) Director requirements

The Secretary of State shall fill the position of Director of the Office of Children's Issues of the Department of State (in this section referred to as the "Office") with an individual of senior rank who can ensure long-term continuity in the management and policy matters of the Office and has a strong background in consular affairs.

(b) Case officer staffing

Effective April 1, 2000, there shall be assigned to the Office of Children's Issues of the Department of State a sufficient number of case officers to ensure that the average caseload for each officer does not exceed 75.

(c) Embassy contact

The Secretary of State shall designate in each United States diplomatic mission an employee who shall serve as the point of contact for matters relating to international abductions of children by parents. The Director of the Office shall regularly inform the designated employee of children of United States citizens abducted by parents to that country.

(d) Reports to parents

(1) In general

Except as provided in paragraph (2), beginning 6 months after November 29, 1999, and at least once every 6 months thereafter, the Secretary of State shall report to each parent who has requested assistance regarding an abducted child overseas. Each such report shall include information on the current status of the abducted child's case and the efforts by the Department of State to resolve the case.

(2) Exception

The requirement in paragraph (1) shall not apply in a case of an abducted child if—

(A) the case has been closed and the Secretary of State has reported the reason the case was closed to the parent who requested assistance; or

(B) the parent seeking assistance requests that such reports not be provided.

(Pub.L. 106-113, Div. B, s 1000(a)(7) [Div. A, Title II, s 201], Nov. 29, 1999, 113 Stat. 1536, 1501A-419.)

Sec. 11609. Interagency coordinating group

The Secretary of State, the Secretary of Health and Human Services, and the Attorney General shall designate Federal employees and may, from time to time, designate private citizens to serve on an interagency coordinating group to monitor the operation of the Convention and to provide advice on its implementation to the United States Central Authority and other Federal agencies. This group shall meet from time to time at the request of the United States Central Authority. The agency in which the United States Central Authority is located is authorized to reimburse such private citizens for travel and other expenses incurred in participating at meetings of the interagency coordinating group at rates not to exceed those authorized under subchapter I of chapter 57 of Title 5 for employees of agencies.

(Pub.L. 100-300, s 10, Apr. 29, 1988, 102 Stat. 441.)

Sec. 11610. Authorization of appropriations

There are authorized to be appropriated for each fiscal year such sums as may be necessary to carry out the purposes of the Convention and this chapter.

(Pub.L. 100-300, s 12, Apr. 29, 1988, 102 Stat. 442.)

Sec. 11611. Report on compliance with the Hague Convention on International Child Abduction

(a) In general

Beginning 6 months after October 21, 1998 and every 12 months thereafter, the Secretary of State shall submit a report to the appropriate congressional committees on the compliance with the provisions of the Convention on the Civil Aspects of International Child Abduction, done at The Hague on October 25, 1980, by the signatory countries of the Convention. Each such report shall include the following information:

(1) The number of applications for the return of children submitted by applicants in the United States to the Central Authority for the United States that remain unresolved more than 18 months after the date of filing.

(2) A list of the countries to which children in unresolved applications described in paragraph (1) are alleged to have been abducted, are being wrongfully retained in violation of United States court orders, or which have failed to comply with any of their obligations under such convention with respect to applications for the return of children, access to children, or both, submitted by applicants in the United States.

(3) A list of the countries that have demonstrated a pattern of noncompliance with the obligations of the Convention with respect to applications for the return of children, access to children, or both, submitted by applicants in the United States to the Central Authority for the United States.

(4) Detailed information on each unresolved case described in paragraph (1) and on actions taken by the Department of State to resolve each such case, including the specific actions taken by the United States chief of mission in the country to which the child is alleged to have been abducted.

(5) Information on efforts by the Department of State to encourage other countries to become signatories of the Convention.

(6) A list of the countries that are parties to the Convention in which, during the reporting period, parents who have been left-behind in the United States have not been able to secure prompt enforcement of a final return or access order under a Hague proceeding, of a United States custody, access, or visitation order, or of an access or visitation order by authorities in the country concerned, due to the absence of a prompt and effective method for enforcement of civil court orders, the absence of a doctrine of comity, or other factors.

(7) A description of the efforts of the Secretary of State to encourage the parties to the Convention to facilitate the work of nongovernmental organizations within their countries that assist parents seeking the return of children under the Convention.

(b) Definition

In this section, the term "Central Authority for the United States" has the meaning given the term in Article 6 of the Convention on the Civil Aspects of International Child Abduction, done at The Hague on October 25, 1980.

(Pub.L. 105-277, Div. G, Title XXVIII, § 2803, Oct. 21, 1998, 112 Stat. 2681-846, as amended Pub.L. 106-113, Div. B, § 1000(a)(7) [Div. A, Title II, § 202], Nov. 29, 1999, 113 Stat. 1536, 1501A-420; Pub.L. 107-228, Div. A, Title II, § 212, Sept. 30, 2002, 116 Stat. 1365.)

Chapter 143 — Intercountry Adoptions

[Ed. Note: The following chapter was enacted as part of the Intercountry Adoption Act of 2000. Pub.L. 106-279, Title V, s 505, Oct. 6, 2000, 114 Stat. 844, provided that sections 14901, 14902, 14911 through 14913, 14922 through 14924, 14941(a), 14943 and 14953 entered into effect on Oct. 6, 2000. The remaining sections are to take effect upon the entry into force for the United States of the Convention on Protection of Children and Co-operation in Respect of Intercountry Adoption, pursuant to Article 46(2)(a) of the Convention.

Pub.L. 106-279, Title V, s 505, Oct. 6, 2000, 114 Stat. 844 further provided that the Convention and the Intercountry Adoption Act of 2000 would not apply:
(1) in the case of a child immigrating to the United States, if the application for advance processing of an orphan petition or petition to classify an orphan as an immediate relative for the child is filed before... [the entry into force of the Convention for the United States, pursuant to Article 46(2)(a) of the Convention]; or
(2) in the case of a child emigrating from the United States, if the prospective adoptive parents of the child initiated the adoption process in their country of residence with the filing of an appropriate application before... [the entry into force of the Convention for the United States, pursuant to Article 46(2)(a) of the Convention].

Sec. 14901. Findings and purposes

(a) Findings
Congress recognizes—
(1) the international character of the Convention on Protection of Children and Co-operation in Respect of Intercountry Adoption (done at The Hague on May 29, 1993); and
(2) the need for uniform interpretation and implementation of the Convention in the United States and abroad,
and therefore finds that enactment of a Federal law governing adoptions and prospective adoptions subject to the Convention involving United States residents is essential.

(b) Purposes
The purposes of this chapter are
(1) to provide for implementation by the United States of the Convention;
(2) to protect the rights of, and prevent abuses against, children, birth families, and adoptive parents involved in adoptions (or prospective adoptions) subject to the Convention, and to ensure that such adoptions are in the children's best interests; and
(3) to improve the ability of the Federal Government to assist United States citizens seeking to adopt children from abroad and residents of other countries party to the Convention seeking to adopt children from the United States.
(Pub.L. 106-279, s 2, Oct. 6, 2000, 114 Stat. 825.)

Sec. 14902. Definitions

As used in this chapter:
(1) Accredited agency
The term "accredited agency" means an agency accredited under subchapter II to provide adoption services in the United States in cases subject to the Convention.
(2) Accrediting entity
The term "accrediting entity" means an entity designated under section 14922(a) of this title to accredit agencies and approve persons under subchapter II.

(3) Adoption service

The term "adoption service" means—

(A) identifying a child for adoption and arranging an adoption;

(B) securing necessary consent to termination of parental rights and to adoption;

(C) performing a background study on a child or a home study on a prospective adoptive parent, and reporting on such a study;

(D) making determinations of the best interests of a child and the appropriateness of adoptive placement for the child;

(E) post-placement monitoring of a case until final adoption; and

(F) where made necessary by disruption before final adoption, assuming custody and providing child care or any other social service pending an alternative placement.

The term "providing", with respect to an adoption service, includes facilitating the provision of the service.

(4) Agency

The term "agency" means any person other than an individual.

(5) Approved person

The term "approved person" means a person approved under subchapter II to provide adoption services in the United States in cases subject to the Convention.

(6) Attorney General

Except as used in section 14944 of this title, the term "Attorney General" means the Attorney General, acting through the Commissioner of Immigration and Naturalization.

(7) Central authority

The term "central authority" means the entity designated as such by any Convention country under Article 6(1) of the Convention.

(8) Central authority function

The term "central authority function" means any duty required to be carried out by a central authority under the Convention.

(9) Convention

The term "Convention" means the Convention on Protection of Children and Co-operation in Respect of Intercountry Adoption, done at The Hague on May 29, 1993.

(10) Convention adoption

The term "Convention adoption" means an adoption of a child resident in a foreign country party to the Convention by a United States citizen, or an adoption of a child resident in the United States by an individual residing in another Convention country.

(11) Convention record

The term "Convention record" means any item, collection, or grouping of information contained in an electronic or physical document, an electronic collection of data, a photograph, an audio or video tape, or any other information storage medium of any type whatever that contains information about a specific past, current, or prospective Convention adoption (regardless of whether the adoption was made final) that has been preserved in accordance with section 14941(a) of this title by the Secretary of State or the Attorney General.

(12) Convention country

The term "Convention country" means a country party to the Convention.

(13) Other Convention country

The term "other Convention country" means a Convention country other than the United States.

(14) Person

The term "person" shall have the meaning provided in section 1 of Title 1, and shall not include any agency of government or tribal government entity.

(15) Person with an ownership or control interest

The term "person with an ownership or control interest" has the meaning given such term in section 1320a-3(a)(3) of this title.

(16) Secretary

The term "Secretary" means the Secretary of State.

(17) State

The term "State" means the 50 States, the District of Columbia, the Commonwealth of Puerto Rico, the Commonwealth of the Northern Mariana Islands, Guam, and the Virgin Islands.

(Pub.L. 106-279, s 3, Oct. 6, 2000, 114 Stat. 826.)

Subchapter I—United States Central Authority

Sec. 14911. Designation of central authority

(a) In general

For purposes of the Convention and this chapter—

(1) the Department of State shall serve as the central authority of the United States; and

(2) the Secretary shall serve as the head of the central authority of the United States.

(b) Performance of central authority functions

(1) Except as otherwise provided in this chapter, the Secretary shall be responsible for the performance of all central authority functions for the United States under the Convention and this chapter.

(2) All personnel of the Department of State performing core central authority functions in a professional capacity in the Office of Children's Issues shall have a strong background in consular affairs, personal experience in international adoptions, or professional experience in international adoptions or child services.

(c) Authority to issue regulations

Except as otherwise provided in this chapter, the Secretary may prescribe such regulations as may be necessary to carry out central authority functions on behalf of the United States.

(Pub.L. 106-279, Title I, s 101, Oct. 6, 2000, 114 Stat. 827.)

Sec. 14912. Responsibilities of the Secretary of State

(a) Liaison responsibilities

The Secretary shall have responsibility for—

(1) liaison with the central authorities of other Convention countries; and

(2) the coordination of activities under the Convention by persons subject to the jurisdiction of the United States.

(b) Information exchange

The Secretary shall be responsible for—

(1) providing the central authorities of other Convention countries with information concerning—

(A) accredited agencies and approved persons, agencies and persons whose accreditation or approval has been suspended or canceled, and agencies and persons who have been temporarily or permanently debarred from accreditation or approval;

(B) Federal and State laws relevant to implementing the Convention; and

(C) any other matters necessary and appropriate for implementation of the Convention;

(2) not later than the date of the entry into force of the Convention for the United States (pursuant to Article 46(2)(a) of the Convention) and at least once during each subsequent calendar year, providing to the central authority of all other Convention countries a notice requesting the central authority of each such country to specify any requirements of such country regarding adoption, including restrictions on the eligibility of persons to adopt, with respect to which information on the prospective adoptive parent or parents in the United States would be relevant;

(3) making responses to notices under paragraph (2) available to—

(A) accredited agencies and approved persons; and

(B) other persons or entities performing home studies under section 14921(b)(1) of this title;

(4) ensuring the provision of a background report (home study) on prospective adoptive parent or parents (pursuant to the requirements of section 14923(b)(1)(A)(ii) of this title), through the central authority of each child's country of origin, to the court having jurisdiction over the adoption (or, in the case of a child emigrating to the United States for the purpose of adoption, to the competent authority in the child's country of origin with responsibility for approving the child's emigration) in adequate time to be considered prior to the granting of such adoption or approval;

(5) providing Federal agencies, State courts, and accredited agencies and approved persons with an identification of Convention countries and persons authorized to perform functions under the Convention in each such country; and

(6) facilitating the transmittal of other appropriate information to, and among, central authorities, Federal and State agencies (including State courts), and accredited agencies and approved persons.

(c) Accreditation and approval responsibilities

The Secretary shall carry out the functions prescribed by the Convention with respect to the accreditation of agencies and the approval of persons to provide adoption services in the United States in cases subject to the Convention as provided in subchapter II. Such functions may not be delegated to any other Federal agency.

(d) Additional responsibilities

The Secretary—

(1) shall monitor individual Convention adoption cases involving United States citizens; and

(2) may facilitate interactions between such citizens and officials of other Convention countries on matters relating to the Convention in any case in which an accredited agency or approved person is unwilling or unable to provide such facilitation.

(e) Establishment of registry

The Secretary and the Attorney General shall jointly establish a case registry of all adoptions involving immigration of children into the United States and emigration of children from the United States, regardless of whether the adoption occurs under the Convention. Such registry shall permit tracking of pending cases and retrieval of information on both pending and closed cases.

(f) Methods of performing responsibilities

The Secretary may—

(1) authorize public or private entities to perform appropriate central authority functions for which the Secretary is responsible, pursuant to regulations or under agreements published in the Federal Register; and

(2) carry out central authority functions through grants to, or contracts with, any individual or public or private entity, except as may be otherwise specifically provided in this chapter.

(Pub.L. 106-279, Title I, s 102, Oct. 6, 2000, 114 Stat. 828.)

Sec. 14913. Responsibilities of the Attorney General

In addition to such other responsibilities as are specifically conferred upon the Attorney General by this chapter, the central authority functions specified in Article 14 of the Convention (relating to the filing of applications by prospective adoptive parents to the central authority of their country of residence) shall be performed by the Attorney General.

(Pub.L. 106-279, Title I, s 103, Oct. 6, 2000, 114 Stat. 829.)

Sec. 14914. Annual report on intercountry adoptions

(a) Reports required

Beginning 1 year after the date of the entry into force of the Convention for the United States and each year thereafter, the Secretary, in consultation with the Attorney General and other appropriate agencies, shall submit a report describing the activities of the central authority of the United States under this chapter during the preceding year to the Committee on International Relations, the Committee on Ways and Means, and the Committee on the Judiciary of the House of Representatives and the Committee on Foreign Relations, the Committee on Finance, and the Committee on the Judiciary of the Senate.

(b) Report elements

Each report under subsection (a) shall set forth with respect to the year concerned, the following:

(1) The number of intercountry adoptions involving immigration to the United States, regardless of whether the adoption occurred under the Convention, including the country from which each child emigrated, the State to which each child immigrated, and the country in which the adoption was finalized.

(2) The number of intercountry adoptions involving emigration from the United States, regardless of whether the adoption occurred under the Convention, including the country to which each child immigrated and the State from which each child emigrated.

(3) The number of Convention placements for adoption in the United States that were disrupted, including the country from which the child emigrated, the age of the child, the date of the placement for adoption, the reasons for the disruption, the resolution of the disruption, the agencies that handled the placement for adoption, and the plans for the child, and in addition, any information regarding disruption or dissolution of adoptions of children from other countries received pursuant to section 622(b)(14) of this title.

(4) The average time required for completion of a Convention adoption, set forth by country from which the child emigrated.

(5) The current list of agencies accredited and persons approved under this chapter to provide adoption services.

(6) The names of the agencies and persons temporarily or permanently debarred under this chapter, and the reasons for the debarment.

(7) The range of adoption fees charged in connection with Convention adoptions involving immigration to the United States and the median of such fees set forth by the country of origin.

(8) The range of fees charged for accreditation of agencies and the approval of persons in the United States engaged in providing adoption services under the Convention.
(Pub.L. 106-279, Title I, s 104, Oct. 6, 2000, 114 Stat. 829.)

Subchapter II — Provisions Relating to Accreditation and Approval

Sec. 14921. Accreditation or approval required in order to provide adoption services in cases subject to the Convention

(a) In general

Except as otherwise provided in this subchapter, no person may offer or provide adoption services in connection with a Convention adoption in the United States unless that person—

(1) is accredited or approved in accordance with this subchapter; or

(2) is providing such services through or under the supervision and responsibility of an accredited agency or approved person.

(b) Exceptions

Subsection (a) shall not apply to the following:

(1) Background studies and home studies

The performance of a background study on a child or a home study on a prospective adoptive parent, or any report on any such study by a social work professional or organization who is not providing any other adoption service in the case, if the background or home study is approved by an accredited agency.

(2) Child welfare services

The provision of a child welfare service by a person who is not providing any other adoption service in the case.

(3) Legal services

The provision of legal services by a person who is not providing any adoption service in the case.

(4) Prospective adoptive parents acting on own behalf

The conduct of a prospective adoptive parent on his or her own behalf in the case, to the extent not prohibited by the law of the State in which the prospective adoptive parent resides.
(Pub.L. 106-279, Title II, s 201, Oct. 6, 2000, 114 Stat. 830.)

Sec. 14922. Process for accreditation and approval; role of accrediting entities

(a) Designation of accrediting entities

(1) In general

The Secretary shall enter into agreements with one or more qualified entities under which such entities will perform the duties described in subsection (b) in accordance with the Convention, this subchapter, and the regulations prescribed under section 14923 of this title, and upon entering into each such agreement shall designate the qualified entity as an accrediting entity.

(2) Qualified entities

In paragraph (1), the term "qualified entity" means—

(A) a nonprofit private entity that has expertise in developing and administering standards for entities providing child welfare services and that meets such other criteria as the Secretary may by regulation establish; or

(B) a public entity (other than a Federal entity), including an agency or instrumentality of State government having responsibility for licensing adoption agencies, that—

(i) has expertise in developing and administering standards for entities providing child welfare services;

(ii) accredits only agencies located in the State in which the public entity is located; and

(iii) meets such other criteria as the Secretary may by regulation establish.

(b) Duties of accrediting entities

The duties described in this subsection are the following:

(1) Accreditation and approval

Accreditation of agencies, and approval of persons, to provide adoption services in the United States in cases subject to the Convention.

(2) Oversight

Ongoing monitoring of the compliance of accredited agencies and approved persons with applicable requirements, including review of complaints against such agencies and persons in accordance with procedures established by the accrediting entity and approved by the Secretary.

(3) Enforcement

Taking of adverse actions (including requiring corrective action, imposing sanctions, and refusing to renew, suspending, or canceling accreditation or approval) for noncompliance with applicable requirements, and notifying the agency or person against whom adverse actions are taken of the deficiencies necessitating the adverse action.

(4) Data, records, and reports

Collection of data, maintenance of records, and reporting to the Secretary, the United States central authority, State courts, and other entities (including on persons and agencies granted or denied approval or accreditation), to the extent and in the manner that the Secretary requires.

(c) Remedies for adverse action by accrediting entity

(1) Correction of deficiency

An agency or person who is the subject of an adverse action by an accrediting entity may re-apply for accreditation or approval (or petition for termination of the adverse action) on demonstrating to the satisfaction of the accrediting entity that the deficiencies necessitating the adverse action have been corrected.

(2) No other administrative review

An adverse action by an accrediting entity shall not be subject to administrative review.

(3) Judicial review

An agency or person who is the subject of an adverse action by an accrediting entity may petition the United States district court in the judicial district in which the agency is located or the person resides to set aside the adverse action. The court shall review the adverse action in accordance with section 706 of Title 5, and for purposes of such review the accrediting entity shall be considered an agency within the meaning of section 701 of such title.

(d) Fees

The amount of fees assessed by accrediting entities for the costs of accreditation shall be subject to approval by the Secretary. Such fees may not exceed the costs of accreditation. In reviewing the level of such fees, the Secretary shall consider the relative size of, the geographic location of, and the number of Convention adoption cases managed by the agencies or persons subject to accreditation or approval by the accrediting entity.

(Pub.L. 106-279, Title II, s 202, Oct. 6, 2000, 114 Stat. 831.)

Sec. 14923. Standards and procedures for providing accreditation or approval

(a) In general

(1) Promulgation of regulations

The Secretary, shall, by regulation, prescribe the standards and procedures to be used by accrediting entities for the accreditation of agencies and the approval of persons to provide adoption services in the United States in cases subject to the Convention.

(2) Consideration of views

In developing such regulations, the Secretary shall consider any standards or procedures developed or proposed by, and the views of, individuals and entities with interest and expertise in international adoptions and family social services, including public and private entities with experience in licensing and accrediting adoption agencies.

(3) Applicability of notice and comment rules

Subsections (b), (c), and (d) of section 553 of Title 5 shall apply in the development and issuance of regulations under this section.

(b) Minimum requirements

(1) Accreditation

The standards prescribed under subsection (a) shall include the requirement that accreditation of an agency may not be provided or continued under this subchapter unless the agency meets the following requirements:

(A) Specific requirements

(i) The agency provides prospective adoptive parents of a child in a prospective Convention adoption a copy of the medical records of the child (which, to the fullest extent practicable, shall include an English-language translation of such records) on a date which is not later than the earlier of the date that is 2 weeks before: (I) the adoption; or (II) the date on which the prospective parents travel to a foreign country to complete all procedures in such country relating to the adoption.

(ii) The agency ensures that a thorough background report (home study) on the prospective adoptive parent or parents has been completed in accordance with the Convention and with applicable Federal and State requirements and transmitted to the Attorney General with respect to each Convention adoption. Each such report shall include a criminal background check and a full and complete statement of all facts relevant to the eligibility of the prospective adopting parent or parents to adopt a child under any requirements specified by the central authority of the child's country of origin under section 14912(b)(3) of this title, including, in the case of a child emigrating to the United States for the purpose of adoption, the requirements of the child's country of origin applicable to adoptions taking place in such country. For purposes of this clause, the term "background report (home study)" includes any supplemental statement submitted by the agency to the Attorney General for the purpose of providing information relevant to any requirements specified by the child's country of origin.

(iii) The agency provides prospective adoptive parents with a training program that includes counseling and guidance for the purpose of promoting a successful intercountry adoption before such parents travel to adopt the child or the child is placed with such parents for adoption.

(iv) The agency employs personnel providing intercountry adoption services on a fee for service basis rather than on a contingent fee basis.

(v) The agency discloses fully its policies and practices, the disruption rates of its placements for intercountry adoption, and all fees charged by such agency for intercountry adoption.

(B) Capacity to provide adoption services

The agency has, directly or through arrangements with other persons, a sufficient number of appropriately trained and qualified personnel, sufficient financial resources, appropriate organizational structure, and appropriate procedures to enable the agency to provide, in accordance with this chapter, all adoption services in cases subject to the Convention.

(C) Use of social service professionals

The agency has established procedures designed to ensure that social service functions requiring the application of clinical skills and judgment are performed only by professionals with appropriate qualifications and credentials.

(D) Records, reports, and information matters

The agency is capable of—

(i) maintaining such records and making such reports as may be required by the Secretary, the United States central authority, and the accrediting entity that accredits the agency;

(ii) cooperating with reviews, inspections, and audits;

(iii) safeguarding sensitive individual information; and

(iv) complying with other requirements concerning information management necessary to ensure compliance with the Convention, this chapter, and any other applicable law.

(E) Liability insurance

The agency agrees to have in force adequate liability insurance for professional negligence and any other insurance that the Secretary considers appropriate.

(F) Compliance with applicable rules

The agency has established adequate measures to comply (and to ensure compliance of their agents and clients) with the Convention, this chapter, and any other applicable law.

(G) Nonprofit organization with State license to provide adoption services

The agency is a private nonprofit organization licensed to provide adoption services in at least one State.

(2) Approval

The standards prescribed under subsection (a) shall include the requirement that a person shall not be approved under this subchapter unless the person is a private for-profit entity that meets the requirements of subparagraphs (A) through (F) of paragraph (1) of this subsection.

(3) Renewal of accreditation or approval

The standards prescribed under subsection (a) shall provide that the accreditation of an agency or approval of a person under this subchapter shall be for a period of not less than 3 years and not more than 5 years, and may be renewed on a showing that the agency or person meets the requirements applicable to original accreditation or approval under this subchapter.

(c) Temporary registration of community based agencies

(1) One-year registration period for medium community based agencies

For a 1-year period after the entry into force of the Convention and notwithstanding subsection (b), the Secretary may provide, in regulations issued pursuant to subsection (a), that an agency may register with the Secretary and be accredited to provide adoption services in the United States in cases subject to the Convention during such period if the agency has provided adoption services in fewer than 100 intercountry adoptions in the preceding calendar year and meets the criteria described in paragraph (3).

(2) Two-year registration period for small community-based agencies

For a 2-year period after the entry into force of the Convention and notwithstanding subsection (b), the Secretary may provide, in regulations issued pursuant to subsection (a), that an agency may register with the Secretary and be accredited to provide adoption services in the United States in cases subject to the Convention during such period if the agency has provided adoption services in fewer than 50 intercountry adoptions in the preceding calendar year and meets the criteria described in paragraph (3).

(3) Criteria for registration

Agencies registered under this subsection shall meet the following criteria:

(A) The agency is licensed in the State in which it is located and is a nonprofit agency.

(B) The agency has been providing adoption services in connection with intercountry adoptions for at least 3 years.

(C) The agency has demonstrated that it will be able to provide the United States Government with all information related to the elements described in section 14914(b) of this title and provides such information.

(D) The agency has initiated the process of becoming accredited under the provisions of this chapter and is actively taking steps to become an accredited agency.

(E) The agency has not been found to be involved in any improper conduct relating to intercountry adoptions.

(Pub.L. 106-279, Title II, s 203, Oct. 6, 2000, 114 Stat. 832.)

Sec. 14924. Secretarial oversight of accreditation and approval

(a) Oversight of accrediting entities

The Secretary shall—

(1) monitor the performance by each accrediting entity of its duties under section 14922 of this title and its compliance with the requirements of the Convention, this chapter, other applicable laws, and implementing regulations under this chapter; and

(2) suspend or cancel the designation of an accrediting entity found to be substantially out of compliance with the Convention, this chapter, other applicable laws, or implementing regulations under this chapter.

(b) Suspension or cancellation of accreditation or approval

(1) Secretary's authority

The Secretary shall suspend or cancel the accreditation or approval granted by an accrediting entity to an agency or person pursuant to section 14922 of this title when the Secretary finds that—

(A) the agency or person is substantially out of compliance with applicable requirements; and

(B) the accrediting entity has failed or refused, after consultation with the Secretary, to take appropriate enforcement action.

(2) Correction of deficiency

At any time when the Secretary is satisfied that the deficiencies on the basis of which an adverse action is taken under paragraph (1) have been corrected, the Secretary shall—
(A) notify the accrediting entity that the deficiencies have been corrected; and
(B)(i) in the case of a suspension, terminate the suspension; or
(ii) in the case of a cancellation, notify the agency or person that the agency or person may re-apply to the accrediting entity for accreditation or approval.

(c) Debarment
(1) Secretary's authority
On the initiative of the Secretary, or on request of an accrediting entity, the Secretary may temporarily or permanently debar an agency from accreditation or a person from approval under this subchapter, but only if—
(A) there is substantial evidence that the agency or person is out of compliance with applicable requirements; and
(B) there has been a pattern of serious, willful, or grossly negligent failures to comply or other aggravating circumstances indicating that continued accreditation or approval would not be in the best interests of the children and families concerned.
(2) Period of debarment
The Secretary's debarment order shall state whether the debarment is temporary or permanent. If the debarment is temporary, the Secretary shall specify a date, not earlier than 3 years after the date of the order, on or after which the agency or person may apply to the Secretary for withdrawal of the debarment.
(3) Effect of debarment
An accrediting entity may take into account the circumstances of the debarment of an agency or person that has been debarred pursuant to this subsection in considering any subsequent application of the agency or person, or of any other entity in which the agency or person has an ownership or control interest, for accreditation or approval under this subchapter.

(d) Judicial review
A person (other than a prospective adoptive parent), an agency, or an accrediting entity who is the subject of a final action of suspension, cancellation, or debarment by the Secretary under this subchapter may petition the United States District Court for the District of Columbia or the United States district court in the judicial district in which the person resides or the agency or accrediting entity is located to set aside the action. The court shall review the action in accordance with section 706 of Title 5.

(e) Failure to ensure a full and complete home study
(1) In general
Willful, grossly negligent, or repeated failure to ensure the completion and transmission of a background report (home study) that fully complies with the requirements of section 14923(b)(1)(A)(ii) of this title shall constitute substantial noncompliance with applicable requirements.
(2) Regulations
Regulations promulgated under section 14923 of this title shall provide for—
(A) frequent and careful monitoring of compliance by agencies and approved persons with the requirements of section 14923(b)(1)(A)(ii) of this title; and
(B) consultation between the Secretary and the accrediting entity where an agency or person has engaged in substantial noncompliance with the requirements of section

14923(b)(1)(A)(ii) of this title, unless the accrediting entity has taken appropriate corrective action and the noncompliance has not recurred.

(3) Repeated failures to comply

Repeated serious, willful, or grossly negligent failures to comply with the requirements of section 14923(b)(1)(A)(ii) of this title by an agency or person after consultation between Secretary and the accrediting entity with respect to previous noncompliance by such agency or person shall constitute a pattern of serious, willful, or grossly negligent failures to comply under subsection (c)(1)(B).

(4) Failure to comply with certain requirements

A failure to comply with the requirements of section 14923(b)(1)(A)(ii) of this title shall constitute a serious failure to comply under subsection (c)(1)(B) unless it is shown by clear and convincing evidence that such noncompliance had neither the purpose nor the effect of determining the outcome of a decision or proceeding by a court or other competent authority in the United States or the child's country of origin.

(Pub.L. 106-279, Title II, s 204, Oct. 6, 2000, 114 Stat. 835.)

Subsection III—Recognition of Convention Adoptions in the United States

Sec. 14931. Adoptions of children immigrating to the United States

(a) Legal effect of certificates issued by the Secretary of State

(1) Issuance of certificates by the Secretary of State

The Secretary of State shall, with respect to each Convention adoption, issue a certificate to the adoptive citizen parent domiciled in the United States that the adoption has been granted or, in the case of a prospective adoptive citizen parent, that legal custody of the child has been granted to the citizen parent for purposes of emigration and adoption, pursuant to the Convention and this chapter, if the Secretary of State—

(A) receives appropriate notification from the central authority of such child's country of origin; and

(B) has verified that the requirements of the Convention and this chapter have been met with respect to the adoption.

(2) Legal effect of certificates

If appended to an original adoption decree, the certificate described in paragraph (1) shall be treated by Federal and State agencies, courts, and other public and private persons and entities as conclusive evidence of the facts certified therein and shall constitute the certification required by section 1154(d)(2) of Title 8.

(b) Legal effect of Convention adoption finalized in another Convention country

A final adoption in another Convention country, certified by the Secretary of State pursuant to subsection (a) of this section or section 14932(c) of this title, shall be recognized as a final valid adoption for purposes of all Federal, State, and local laws of the United States.

(c) Condition on finalization of Convention adoption by State court

In the case of a child who has entered the United States from another Convention country for the purpose of adoption, an order declaring the adoption final shall not be entered unless the Secretary of State has issued the certificate provided for in subsection (a) with respect to the adoption.

(Pub.L. 106-279, Title III, s 301, Oct. 6, 2000, 114 Stat. 837.)

Sec. 14932. Adoptions of children emigrating from the United States

(a) Duties of accredited agency or approved person

In the case of a Convention adoption involving the emigration of a child residing in the United States to a foreign country, the accredited agency or approved person providing adoption services, or the prospective adoptive parent or parents acting on their own behalf (if permitted by the laws of such other Convention country in which they reside and the laws of the State in which the child resides), shall do the following:

(1) Ensure that, in accordance with the Convention—

(A) a background study on the child is completed;

(B) the accredited agency or approved person—

(i) has made reasonable efforts to actively recruit and make a diligent search for prospective adoptive parents to adopt the child in the United States; and

(ii) despite such efforts, has not been able to place the child for adoption in the United States in a timely manner; and

(C) a determination is made that placement with the prospective adoptive parent or parents is in the best interests of the child.

(2) Furnish to the State court with jurisdiction over the case—

(A) documentation of the matters described in paragraph (1);

(B) a background report (home study) on the prospective adoptive parent or parents (including a criminal background check) prepared in accordance with the laws of the receiving country; and

(C) a declaration by the central authority (or other competent authority) of such other Convention country—

(i) that the child will be permitted to enter and reside permanently, or on the same basis as the adopting parent, in the receiving country; and

(ii) that the central authority (or other competent authority) of such other Convention country consents to the adoption, if such consent is necessary under the laws of such country for the adoption to become final.

(3) Furnish to the United States central authority—

(A) official copies of State court orders certifying the final adoption or grant of custody for the purpose of adoption;

(B) the information and documents described in paragraph (2), to the extent required by the United States central authority; and

(C) any other information concerning the case required by the United States central authority to perform the functions specified in subsection (c) or otherwise to carry out the duties of the United States central authority under the Convention.

(b) Conditions on State court orders

An order declaring an adoption to be final or granting custody for the purpose of adoption in a case described in subsection (a) shall not be entered unless the court—

(1) has received and verified to the extent the court may find necessary—

(A) the material described in subsection (a)(2); and

(B) satisfactory evidence that the requirements of Articles 4 and 15 through 21 of the Convention have been met; and

(2) has determined that the adoptive placement is in the best interests of the child.

(c) Duties of the Secretary of State

In a case described in subsection (a), the Secretary, on receipt and verification as necessary of the material and information described in subsection (a)(3), shall issue, as applicable, an official certification that the child has been adopted or a declaration that custody for purposes of adoption has been granted, in accordance with the Convention and this chapter.

(d) Filing with registry regarding nonconvention adoptions

Accredited agencies, approved persons, and other persons, including governmental authorities, providing adoption services in an intercountry adoption not subject to the Convention that involves the emigration of a child from the United States shall file information required by regulations jointly issued by the Attorney General and the Secretary of State for purposes of implementing section 14912(e) of this title.
(Pub.L. 106-279, Title III, s 303, Oct. 6, 2000, 114 Stat. 839.)

Subchapter IV — Administration and Enforcement

Sec. 14941. Access to Convention records
(a) Preservation of Convention records

(1) In general

Not later than 180 days after October 6, 2000, the Secretary, in consultation with the Attorney General, shall issue regulations that establish procedures and requirements in accordance with the Convention and this section for the preservation of Convention records.

(2) Applicability of notice and comment rules

Subsections (b), (c), and (d) of section 553 of Title 5 shall apply in the development and issuance of regulations under this section.

(b) Access to Convention records

(1) Prohibition

Except as provided in paragraph (2), the Secretary or the Attorney General may disclose a Convention record, and access to such a record may be provided in whole or in part, only if such record is maintained under the authority of the Immigration and Nationality Act and disclosure of, or access to, such record is permitted or required by applicable Federal law.

(2) Exception for administration of the Convention

A Convention record may be disclosed, and access to such a record may be provided, in whole or in part, among the Secretary, the Attorney General, central authorities, accredited agencies, and approved persons, only to the extent necessary to administer the Convention or this chapter.

(3) Penalties for unlawful disclosure

Unlawful disclosure of all or part of a Convention record shall be punishable in accordance with applicable Federal law.

(c) Access to non-Convention records

Disclosure of, access to, and penalties for unlawful disclosure of, adoption records that are not Convention records, including records of adoption proceedings conducted in the United States, shall be governed by applicable State law.
(Pub.L. 106-279, Title IV, s 401, Oct. 6, 2000, 114 Stat. 841.)

Sec. 14942. Documents of other Convention countries

Documents originating in any other Convention country and related to a Convention adoption case shall require no authentication in order to be admissible in any

Federal, State, or local court in the United States, unless a specific and supported claim is made that the documents are false, have been altered, or are otherwise unreliable.
(Pub.L. 106-279, Title IV, s 402, Oct. 6, 2000, 114 Stat. 841.)

Sec. 14943. Authorization of appropriations; collection of fees
(a) Authorization of appropriations
(1) In general
There are authorized to be appropriated such sums as may be necessary to agencies of the Federal Government implementing the Convention and the provisions of this chapter.
(2) Availability of funds
Amounts appropriated pursuant to paragraph (1) are authorized to remain available until expended.

(b) Assessment of fees
(1) The Secretary may charge a fee for new or enhanced services that will be undertaken by the Department of State to meet the requirements of this chapter with respect to intercountry adoptions under the Convention and comparable services with respect to other intercountry adoptions. Such fee shall be prescribed by regulation and shall not exceed the cost of such services.
(2) Fees collected under paragraph (1) shall be retained and deposited as an offsetting collection to any Department of State appropriation to recover the costs of providing such services. Such fees shall remain available for obligation until expended.

(c) Restriction
No funds collected under the authority of this section may be made available to an accrediting entity to carry out the purposes of this chapter.
(Pub.L. 106-279, Title IV, s 403, Oct. 6, 2000, 114 Stat. 841; Pub.L. 107-228, Div. A, Title II, § 211(a), Sept. 30, 2002, 116 Stat. 1365.)

Sec. 14944. Enforcement
(a) Civil penalties
Any person who—
(1) violates section 14921 of this title;
(2) makes a false or fraudulent statement, or misrepresentation, with respect to a material fact, or offers, gives, solicits, or accepts inducement by way of compensation, intended to influence or affect in the United States or a foreign country—
(A) a decision by an accrediting entity with respect to the accreditation of an agency or approval of a person under subchapter II of this chapter;
(B) the relinquishment of parental rights or the giving of parental consent relating to the adoption of a child in a case subject to the Convention; or
(C) a decision or action of any entity performing a central authority function; or
(3) engages another person as an agent, whether in the United States or in a foreign country, who in the course of that agency takes any of the actions described in paragraph (1) or (2), shall be subject, in addition to any other penalty that may be prescribed by law, to a civil money penalty of not more than $50,000 for a first violation, and not more than $100,000 for each succeeding violation.

(b) Civil enforcement
(1) Authority of Attorney General

The Attorney General may bring a civil action to enforce subsection (a) against any person in any United States district court.

(2) Factors to be considered in imposing penalties

In imposing penalties the court shall consider the gravity of the violation, the degree of culpability of the defendant, and any history of prior violations by the defendant.

(c) Criminal penalties

Whoever knowingly and willfully violates paragraph (1) or (2) of subsection (a) shall be subject to a fine of not more than $250,000, imprisonment for not more than 5 years, or both.

(Pub.L. 106-279, Title IV, s 404, Oct. 6, 2000, 114 Stat. 842.)

Subchapter V — General Provisions

Sec. 14951. Recognition of Convention adoptions

Subject to Article 24 of the Convention, adoptions concluded between two other Convention countries that meet the requirements of Article 23 of the Convention and that became final before the date of entry into force of the Convention for the United States shall be recognized thereafter in the United States and given full effect. Such recognition shall include the specific effects described in Article 26 of the Convention.

(Pub.L. 106-279, Title V, s 501, Oct. 6, 2000, 114 Stat. 843.)

Sec. 14952. Special rules for certain cases

(a) Authority to establish alternative procedures for adoption of children by relatives

To the extent consistent with the Convention, the Secretary may establish by regulation alternative procedures for the adoption of children by individuals related to them by blood, marriage, or adoption, in cases subject to the Convention.

(b) Waiver authority

(1) In general

Notwithstanding any other provision of this chapter, to the extent consistent with the Convention, the Secretary may, on a case-by-case basis, waive applicable requirements of this chapter or regulations issued under this chapter, in the interests of justice or to prevent grave physical harm to the child.

(2) Nondelegation

The authority provided by paragraph (1) may not be delegated.

(Pub.L. 106-279, Title V, s 502, Oct. 6, 2000, 114 Stat. 843.)

Sec. 14953. Relationship to other laws

(a) Preemption of inconsistent State law

The Convention and this chapter shall not be construed to preempt any provision of the law of any State or political subdivision thereof, or prevent a State or political subdivision thereof from enacting any provision of law with respect to the subject matter of the Convention or this chapter, except to the extent that such provision of State law is inconsistent with the Convention or this chapter, and then only to the extent of the inconsistency.

(b) Applicability of the Indian Child Welfare Act

The Convention and this chapter shall not be construed to affect the application of the Indian Child Welfare Act of 1978 (25 U.S.C. 1901 et seq.).

(c) Relationship to other laws

Sections 3506(c), 3507, and 3512 of Title 44 shall not apply to information collection for purposes of sections 14914, 14922(b)(4), and 14932(d) of this title or for use as a Convention record as defined in this chapter.
(Pub.L. 106-279, Title V, s 503, Oct. 6, 2000, 114 Stat. 843.)

Sec. 14954. No private right of action

The Convention and this chapter shall not be construed to create a private right of action to seek administrative or judicial relief, except to the extent expressly provided in this chapter.
(Pub.L. 106-279, Title V, s 504, Oct. 6, 2000, 114 Stat. 843.)

B. Code of Federal Regulations

Title 8—Aliens and Nationality

Chapter I—Immigration and Naturalization Service, Department of Justice
Part 204—Immigrant Petitions

Sec. 204.2 Petitions for relatives, widows and widowers, and abused spouses and children.

(a) *Petition for a spouse—*

(1) *Eligibility.* A United States citizen or alien admitted for lawful permanent residence may file a petition on behalf of a spouse.

(i) *Marriage within five years of petitioner's obtaining lawful permanent resident status.*

(A) A visa petition filed on behalf of an alien by a lawful permanent resident spouse may not be approved if the marriage occurred within five years of the petitioner being accorded the status of lawful permanent resident based upon a prior marriage to a United States citizen or alien lawfully admitted for permanent residence, unless:

(1) The petitioner establishes by clear and convincing evidence that the marriage through which the petitioner gained permanent residence was not entered into for the purposes of evading the immigration laws; or

(2) The marriage through which the petitioner obtained permanent residence was terminated through death.

(B) Documentation. The petitioner should submit documents which cover the period of the prior marriage. The types of documents which may establish that the prior marriage was not entered into for the purpose of evading the immigration laws include, but are not limited to:

(1) Documentation showing joint ownership of property;

(2) A lease showing joint tenancy of a common residence;

(3) Documentation showing commingling of financial resources;

(4) Birth certificate(s) of child(ren) born to the petitioner and prior spouse;

(5) Affidavits sworn to or affirmed by third parties having personal knowledge of the bona fides of the prior marital relationship. (Each affidavit must contain the full name

and address, date and place of birth of the person making the affidavit; his or her relationship, if any, to the petitioner, beneficiary or prior spouse; and complete information and details explaining how the person acquired his or her knowledge of the prior marriage. The affiant may be required to testify before an immigration officer about the information contained in the affidavit. Affidavits should be supported, if possible, by one or more types of documentary evidence listed in this paragraph.); or

(6) Any other documentation which is relevant to establish that the prior marriage was not entered into in order to evade the immigration laws of the United States

(C) The petitioner must establish by clear and convincing evidence that the prior marriage was not entered into for the purpose of evading the immigration laws. Failure to meet the "clear and convincing evidence" standard will result in the denial of the petition. Such a denial shall be without prejudice to the filing of a new petition once the petitioner has acquired five years of lawful permanent residence. The director may choose to initiate deportation proceedings based upon information gained through the adjudication of the petition; however, failure to initiate such proceedings shall not establish that the petitioner's prior marriage was not entered into for the purpose of evading the immigration laws. Unless the petition is approved, the beneficiary shall not be accorded a filing date within the meaning of section 203(c) of the Act based upon any spousal second preference petition.

(ii) *Fraudulent marriage prohibition.* Section 204(c) of the Act prohibits the approval of a visa petition filed on behalf of an alien who has attempted or conspired to enter into a marriage for the purpose of evading the immigration laws. The director will deny a petition for immigrant visa classification filed on behalf of any alien for whom there is substantial and probative evidence of such an attempt or conspiracy, regardless of whether that alien received a benefit through the attempt or conspiracy. Although it is not necessary that the alien have been convicted of, or even prosecuted for, the attempt or conspiracy, the evidence of the attempt or conspiracy must be contained in the alien's file.

(iii) *Marriage during proceedings—general prohibition against approval of visa petition.* A visa petition filed on behalf of an alien by a United States citizen or a lawful permanent resident spouse shall not be approved if the marriage creating the relationship occurred on or after November 10, 1986, and while the alien was in exclusion, deportation, or removal proceedings, or judicial proceedings relating thereto. Determination of commencement and termination of proceedings and exemptions shall be in accordance with § 245.1(c)(9) of this chapter, except thatthe burden in visa petition proceedings to establish eligibility for the exemption in § 245.1(c)(9)(iii)(F) of this chapter shall rest with the petitioner.

(A) *Request for exemption.* No application or fee is required to request an exemption. The request must be made in writing and submitted with the Form I-130. The request must state the reason for seeking the exemption and must be supported by documentary evidence establishing eligibility for the exemption.

(B) *Evidence to establish eligibility for the bona fide marriage exemption.* The petitioner should submit documents which establish that the marriage was entered into in good faith and not entered into for the purpose of procuring the alien's entry as an immigrant. The types of documents the petitioner may submit include, but are not limited to:

(1) Documentation showing joint ownership of property;

(2) Lease showing joint tenancy of a common residence;

(3) Documentation showing commingling of financial resources;

(4) Birth certificate(s) of child(ren) born to the petitioner and beneficiary;

(5) Affidavits of third parties having knowledge of the bona fides of the marital relationship (Such persons may be required to testify before an immigration officer as to the information contained in the affidavit. Affidavits must be sworn to or affirmed by people who have personal knowledge of the marital relationship. Each affidavit must contain the full name and address, date and place of birth of the person making the affidavit and his or her relationship to the spouses, if any. The affidavit must contain complete information and details explaining how the person acquired his or her knowledge of the marriage. Affidavits should be supported, if possible, by one or more types of documentary evidence listed in this paragraph); or

(6) Any other documentation which is relevant to establish that the marriage was not entered into in order to evade the immigration laws of the United States.

(C) *Decision.* Any petition filed during the prohibited period shall be denied, unless the petitioner establishes eligibility for an exemption from the general prohibition. The petitioner shall be notified in writing of the decision of the director.

(D) *Denials.* The denial of a petition because the marriage took place during the prohibited period shall be without prejudice to the filing of a new petition after the beneficiary has resided outside the United States for the required period of two years following the marriage. The denial shall also be without prejudice to the consideration of a new petition or a motion to reopen the visa petition proceedings if deportation or exclusion proceedings are terminated after the denial other than by the beneficiary's departure from the United States. Furthermore, the denial shall be without prejudice to the consideration of a new petition or motion to reopen the visa petition proceedings, if the petitioner establishes eligibility for the bona fide marriage exemption contained in this part: Provided, That no motion to reopen visa petition proceedings may be accepted if the approval of the motion would result in the beneficiary being accorded a priority date within the meaning of section 203(c) of the Act earlier than November 29, 1990.

(E) *Appeals.* The decision of the Board of Immigration Appeals concerning the denial of a relative visa petition because the petitioner failed to establish eligibility for the bona fide marriage exemption contained in this part will constitute the single level of appellate review established by statute.

(F) *Priority date.* A preference beneficiary shall not be accorded a priority date within the meaning of section 203(c) of the Act based upon any relative petition filed during the prohibited period, unless an exemption contained in this part has been granted. Furthermore, a preference beneficiary shall not be accorded a priority date prior to November 29, 1990, based upon the approval of a request for consideration for the bona fide marriage exemption contained in this part.

(2) *Evidence for petition for a spouse.* In addition to evidence of United States citizenship or lawful permanent residence, the petitioner must also provide evidence of the claimed relationship. A petition submitted on behalf of a spouse must be accompanied by a recent ADIT-style photograph of the petitioner, a recent ADIT-style photograph of the beneficiary, a certificate of marriage issued by civil authorities, and proof of the legal termination of all previous marriages of both the petitioner and the beneficiary. However, non-ADIT-style photographs may be accepted by the district director when the petitioner or beneficiary reside(s) in a country where such photographs are unavailable or cost prohibitive.

(3) *Decision on and disposition of petition.* The approved petition will be forwarded to the Department of State's Processing Center. If the beneficiary is in the United States and is eligible for adjustment of status under section 245 of the Act, the approved peti-

tion will be retained by the Service. If the petition is denied, the petitioner will be notified of the reasons for the denial and of the right to appeal in accordance with the provisions of 8 CFR 3.3.

(4) *Derivative beneficiaries.* No alien may be classified as an immediate relative as defined in section 201(b) of the Act unless he or she is the direct beneficiary of an approved petition for that classification. Therefore, a child of an alien approved for classification as an immediate relative spouse is not eligible for derivative classification and must have a separate petition filed on his or her behalf. A child accompanying or following to join a principal alien under section 203(a)(2) of the Act may be included in the principal alien's second preference visa petition. The child will be accorded second preference classification and the same priority date as the principal alien. However, if the child reaches the age of twenty-one prior to the issuance of a visa to the principal alien parent, a separate petition will be required. In such a case, the original priority date will be retained if the subsequent petition is filed by the same petitioner. Such retention of priority date will be accorded only to a son or daughter previously eligible as a derivative beneficiary under a second preference spousal petition.

(b) *Petition by widow or widower of a United States citizen*—[Omitted from these materials. Ed.]

(c) *Self-petition by spouse of abusive citizen or lawful permanent resident*—
   (1) *Eligibility*—
   (i) *Basic eligibility requirements.* A spouse may file a self-petition under section 204(a)(1)(A)(iii) or 204(a)(1)(B)(ii) of the Act for his or her classification as an immediate relative or as a preference immigrant if he or she:
   (A) Is the spouse of a citizen or lawful permanent resident of the United States;
   (B) Is eligible for immigrant classification under section 201(b)(2)(A)(i) or 203(a)(2)(A) of the Act based on that relationship;
   (C) Is residing in the United States;
   (D) Has resided in the United States with the citizen or lawful permanent resident spouse;
   (E) Has been battered by, or has been the subject of extreme cruelty perpetrated by, the citizen or lawful permanent resident during the marriage; or is that parent of a child who has been battered by, or has been the subject of extreme cruelty perpetrated by, the citizen or lawful permanent resident during the marriage;
   (F) Is a person of good moral character;
   (G) Is a person whose deportation would result in extreme hardship to himself, herself, or his or her child; and
   (H) Entered into the marriage to the citizen or lawful permanent resident in good faith.
   (ii) *Legal status of the marriage.* The self-petitioning spouse must be legally married to the abuser when the petition is properly filed with the Service. A spousal self-petition must be denied if the marriage to the abuser legally ended through annulment, death, or divorce before that time. After the self-petition has been properly filed, the legal termination of the marriage will have no effect on the decision made on the self-petition. The self-petitioner's remarriage, however, will be a basis for the denial of a pending self-petition.
   (iii) *Citizenship or immigration status of the abuser.* The abusive spouse must be a citizen of the United States or a lawful permanent resident of the United States when the petition is filed and when it is approved. Changes in the abuser's citizenship or lawful permanent resident status after the approval will have no effect on the self-petition. A

self-petition approved on the basis of a relationship to an abusive lawful permanent resident spouse will not be automatically upgraded to immediate relative status. The self-petitioner would not be precluded, however, from filing a new self-petition for immediate relative classification after the abuser's naturalization, provided the self-petitioner continues to meet the self-petitioning requirements.

(iv) *Eligibility for immigrant classification.* A self-petitioner is required to comply with the provisions of section 204(c) of the Act, section 204(g) of the Act, and section 204(a)(2) of the Act.

(v) *Residence.* A self-petition will not be approved if the self-petitioner is not residing in the United States when the self-petition is filed. The self-petitioner is not required to be living with the abuser when the petition is filed, but he or she must have resided with the abuser in the United States in the past.

(vi) *Battery or extreme cruelty.* For the purpose of this chapter, the phrase "was battered by or was the subject of extreme cruelty" includes, but is not limited to, being the victim of any act or threatened act of violence, including any forceful detention, which results or threatens to result in physical or mental injury. Psychological or sexual abuse or exploitation, including rape, molestation, incest (if the victim is a minor), or forced prostitution shall be considered acts of violence. Other abusive actions may also be acts of violence under certain circumstances, including acts that, in and of themselves, may not initially appear violent but that are a part of an overall pattern of violence. The qualifying abuse must have been committed by the citizen or lawful permanent resident spouse, must have been perpetrated against the self-petitioner or the self-petitioner's child, and must have taken place during the self-petitioner's marriage to the abuser.

(vii) *Good moral character.* A self-petitioner will be found to lack good moral character if he or she is a person described in section 101(f) of the Act. Extenuating circumstances may be taken into account if the person has not been convicted of an offense or offenses but admits to the commission of an act or acts that could show a lack of good moral character under section 101(f) of the Act. A person who was subjected to abuse in the form of forced prostitution or who can establish that he or she was forced to engage in other behavior that could render the person excludable under section 212(a) of the Act would not be precluded from being found to be a person of good moral character, provided the person has not been convicted for the commission of the offense or offenses in a court of law. A self-petitioner will also be found to lack good moral character, unless he or she establishes extenuating circumstances, if he or she willfully failed or refused to support dependents; or committed unlawful acts that adversely reflect upon his or her moral character, or was convicted or imprisoned for such acts, although the acts do not require an automatic finding of lack of good moral character. A self-petitioner's claim of good moral character will be evaluated on a case-by-case basis, taking into account the provisions of section 101(f) of the Act and the standards of the average citizen in the community. If the results of record checks conducted prior to the issuance of an immigrant visa or approval of an application for adjustment of status disclose that the self-petitioner is no longer a person of good moral character or that he or she has not been a person of good moral character in the past, a pending self-petition will be denied or the approval of a self-petition will be revoked.

(viii) *Extreme hardship.* The Service will consider all credible evidence of extreme hardship submitted with a self-petition, including evidence of hardship arising from circumstances surrounding the abuse. The extreme hardship claim will be evaluated on a case-by-case basis after a review of the evidence in the case. Self-petitioners are encouraged to cite and document all applicable factors, since there is no guarantee that a particular reason or reasons will result in a finding that deportation would cause extreme hardship. Hardship to persons other than the self-petitioner or the self-petitioner's child cannot be considered in determining whether a self-petitioning spouse's deportation would cause extreme hardship.

(ix) *Good faith marriage.* A spousal self-petition cannot be approved if the self-petitioner entered into the marriage to the abuser for the primary purpose of circumventing the immigration laws. A self-petition will not be denied, however, solely because the spouses are not living together and the marriage is no longer viable.

(2) *Evidence for a spousal self-petition—*

(i) *General.* Self-petitioners are encouraged to submit primary evidence whenever possible. The Service will consider, however, any credible evidence relevant to the petition. The determination of what evidence is credible and the weight to be given that evidence shall be within the sole discretion of the Service.

(ii) *Relationship.* A self-petition filed by a spouse must be accompanied by evidence of citizenship of the United States citizen or proof of the immigration status of the lawful permanent resident abuser. It must also be accompanied by evidence of the relationship. Primary evidence of a marital relationship is a marriage certificate issued by civil authorities, and proof of the termination of all prior marriages, if any, of both the self-petitioner and the abuser. If the self-petition is based on a claim that the self-petitioner's child was battered or subjected to extreme cruelty committed by the citizen or lawful permanent resident spouse, the self-petition should also be accompanied by the child's birth certificate or other evidence showing the relationship between the self-petitioner and the abused child.

(iii) *Residence.* One or more documents may be submitted showing that the self-petitioner and the abuser have resided together in the United States. One or more documents may also be submitted showing that the self-petitioner is residing in the United States when the self-petition is filed. Employment records, utility receipts, school records, hospital or medical records, birth certificates of children born in the United States, deeds, mortgages, rental records, insurance policies, affidavits or any other type of relevant credible evidence of residency may be submitted.

(iv) *Abuse.* Evidence of abuse may include, but is not limited to, reports and affidavits from police, judges and other court officials, medical personnel, school officials, clergy, social workers, and other social service agency personnel. Persons who have obtained an order of protection against the abuser or have taken other legal steps to end the abuse are strongly encouraged to submit copies of the relating legal documents. Evidence that the abuse victim sought safe-haven in a battered women's shelter or similar refuge may be relevant, as may a combination of documents such as a photograph of the visibly injured self-petitioner supported by affidavits. Other forms of credible relevant evidence will also be considered. Documentary proof of non-qualifying abuses may only be used to establish a pattern of abuse and violence and to support a claim that qualifying abuse also occurred.

(v) *Good moral character.* Primary evidence of the self-petitioner's good moral character is the self-petitioner's affidavit. The affidavit should be accompanied by a local police clearance or a state-issued criminal background check from each locality or state in the United States in which the self-petitioner has resided for six or more months during the 3-year period immediately preceding the filing of the self-petition. Self-petitioners who lived outside the United States during this time should submit a police clearance, criminal background check, or similar report issued by the appropriate authority in each foreign country in which he or she resided for six or more months during the 3-year period immediately preceding the filing of the self-petition. If police clearances, criminal background checks, or similar reports are not available for some or all locations, the self-petitioner may include an explanation and submit other evidence with his or her affidavit. The Service will consider other credible evidence of good moral character, such as affidavits from responsible persons who can knowledgeably attest to the self-petitioner's good moral character.

(vi) *Extreme hardship.* Evidence of extreme hardship may include affidavits, birth certificates of children, medical reports, protection orders and other court documents, police reports, and other relevant credible evidence.

(vii) *Good faith marriage.* Evidence of good faith at the time of marriage may include, but is not limited to, proof that one spouse has been listed as the other's spouse on insurance policies, property leases, income tax forms, or bank accounts; and testimony or other evidence regarding courtship, wedding ceremony, shared residence and experiences. Other types of readily available evidence might include the birth certificates of children born to the abuser and the spouse; police, medical, or court documents providing information about the relationship; and affidavits of persons with personal knowledge of the relationship. All credible relevant evidence will be considered.

(3) *Decision on and disposition of the petition—*

(i) *Petition approved.* If the self-petitioning spouse will apply for adjustment of status under section 245 of the Act, the approved petition will be retained by the Service. If the self-petitioner will apply for an immigrant visa abroad, the approved self-petition will be forwarded to the Department of State's National Visa Center.

(ii) *Notice of intent to deny.* If the preliminary decision on a properly filed self-petition is adverse to the self-petitioner, the self-petitioner will be provided with written notice of this fact and offered an opportunity to present additional information or arguments before a final decision is rendered. If the adverse preliminary decision is based on derogatory information of which the self-petitioner is unaware, the self-petitioner will also be offered an opportunity to rebut the derogatory information in accordance with the provisions of 8 CFR 103.2(b)(16).

(iii) *Petition denied.* If the self-petition is denied, the self-petitioner will be notified in writing of the reasons for the denial and of the right to appeal the decision.

(4) *Derivative beneficiaries.* A child accompanying or following-to-join the self-petitioning spouse may be accorded the same preference and priority date as the self-petitioner without the necessity of a separate petition, if the child has not been classified as an immigrant based on his or her own self-petition. A derivative child who had been included in a parent's self-petition may later file a self-petition, provided the child meets the self-petitioning requirements. A child who has been classified as an immigrant based on a petition filed by the abuser or another relative may also be derivatively included in a parent's self-petition. The derivative child must be unmarried, less than 21 years old, and otherwise qualify as the self-petitioner's child under section 101(b)(1)(F) of the Act until he or she becomes a lawful permanent resident based on the derivative classification.

(5) *Name change.* If the self-petitioner's current name is different than the name shown on the documents, evidence of the name change (such as the petitioner's marriage certificate, legal document showing name change, or other similar evidence) must accompany the self-petition.

(6) *Prima facie determination.*

(i) Upon receipt of a self-petition under paragraph (c)(1) of this section, the Service shall make a determination as to whether the petition and the supporting documentation establish a "prima facie case" for purposes of 8 U.S.C. 1641, as amended by section 501 of Public Law 104-208.

(ii) For purposes of paragraph (c)(6)(i) of this section, a prima facie case is established only if the petitioner submits a completed Form I-360 and other evidence supporting all of the elements required of a self-petitioner in paragraph (c)(1) of this section. A finding of prima facie eligibility does not relieve the petitioner of the burden of providing additional evidence in support of the petition and does not establish eligibility for the underlying petition.

(iii) If the Service determines that a petitioner has made a "prima facie case," the Service shall issue a Notice of Prima Facie Case to the petitioner. Such Notice shall be valid until the Service either grants or denies the petition.

(iv) For purposes of adjudicating the petition submitted under paragraph (c)(1) of this section, a prima facie determination—

(A) Shall not be considered evidence in support of the petition;

(B) Shall not be construed to make a determination of the credibility or probative value of any evidence submitted along with that petition; and,

(C) Shall not relieve the self-petitioner of his or her burden of complying with all of the evidentiary requirements of paragraph (c)(2) of this section.

(d) *Petition for a child or son or daughter—*

(1) *Eligibility.* A United States citizen may file a petition on behalf of an unmarried child under twenty-one years of age for immediate relative classification under section 201(b) of the Act. A United States citizen may file a petition on behalf of an unmarried son or daughter over twenty-one years of age under section 203(a)(1) or for a married son or daughter for preference classification under section 203(a)(3) of the Act. An alien lawfully admitted for permanent residence may file a petition on behalf of a child or an unmarried son or daughter for preference classification under section 203(a)(2) of the Act.

(2) *Evidence to support petition for child or son or daughter.* In addition to evidence of United States citizenship or lawful permanent resident, the petitioner must also provide evidence of the claimed relationship.

[Ed. Note: Subsections (i) Primary evidence for a legitimate child or son or daughter; (ii) Primary evidence for a legitimated child or son or daughter; (iii) Primary evidence for an illegitimate child or son or daughter; (iv) Primary evidence for a stepchild; (v) Secondary evidence; and (vi) Blood Tests, are omitted.]

(vii) *Primary evidence for an adopted child or son or daughter.* A petition may be submitted on behalf of an adopted child or son or daughter by a United States citizen or lawful permanent resident if the adoption took place before the beneficiary's sixteenth birthday, and if the child has been in the legal custody of the adopting parent or parents and has resided with the adopting parent or parents for at least two years. A copy of the adoption decree, issued by the civil authorities, must accompany the petition.

(A) *Legal custody* means the assumption of responsibility for a minor by an adult under the laws of the state and under the order or approval of a court of law or other appropriate government entity. This provision requires that a legal process involving the courts or other recognized government entity take place. If the adopting parent was granted legal custody by the court or recognized governmental entity prior to the adoption, that period may be counted toward fulfillment of the two-year legal custody requirement. However, if custody was not granted prior to the adoption, the adoption decree shall be deemed to mark the commencement of legal custody. An informal custodial or guardianship document, such as a sworn affidavit signed before a notary public, is insufficient for this purpose.

(B) Evidence must also be submitted to show that the beneficiary resided with the petitioner for at least two years. Generally, such documentation must establish that the petitioner and the beneficiary resided together in a familial relationship. Evidence of parental control may include, but is not limited to, evidence that the adoptive parent owns or maintains the property where the child resides and provides financial support and day-to-day supervision. The evidence must clearly indicate the physical living arrangements of the adopted child, the adoptive parent(s), and the natural parent(s) for the period of time during which the adoptive parent claims to have met the residence requirement. When the adopted child continued to reside in the same household as a natural parent(s) during the period in which the adoptive parent petitioner seeks to establish his or her compliance with this requirement, the petitioner has the burden of establishing that he or she exercised primary parental control during that period of residence.

(C) Legal custody and residence occurring prior to or after the adoption will satisfy both requirements. Legal custody, like residence, is accounted for in the aggregate. Therefore, a break in legal custody or residence will not affect the time already fulfilled. To meet the definition of child contained in sections 101(b)(1)(E) and 101(b)(2) of the Act, the child must have been under 16 years of age when the adoption is finalized.

(3) *Decision on and disposition of petition.* The approved petition will be forwarded to the Department of State's Processing Center. If the beneficiary is in the United States and is eligible for adjustment of status under section 245 of the Act, the approved petition will be retained by the Service. If the petition is denied, the petitioner will be notified of the reasons for the denial and of the right to appeal in accordance with the provisions of 8 CFR 3.3.

(4) *Derivative beneficiaries.* A spouse or child accompanying or following to join a principal alien as used in this section may be accorded the same preference and priority date as the principal alien without the necessity of a separate petition. However, a child of an alien who is approved for classification as an immediate relative is not eligible for derivative classification and must have a separate petition approved on his or her behalf.

(5) *Name change.* When the petitioner's name does not appear on the child's birth certificate, evidence of the name change (such as the petitioner's marriage certificate, legal document showing name change, or other similar evidence) must accompany the petition. If the beneficiary's name has been legally changed, evidence of the name change must also accompany the petition.

(e) *Self-petition by child of abusive citizen or lawful permanent resident—*
(1) *Eligibility.*
(i) A child may file a self-petition under section 204(a)(1)(A)(iv) or 204(a)(1)(B)(iii) of the Act if he or she:
(A) Is the child of a citizen or lawful permanent resident of the United States;
(B) Is eligible for immigrant classification under section 201(b)(2)(A)(i) or 203(a)(2)(A) of the Act based on that relationship;
(C) Is residing in the United States;
(D) Has resided in the United States with the citizen or lawful permanent resident parent;
(E) Has been battered by, or has been the subject of extreme cruelty perpetrated by, the citizen or lawful permanent resident parent while residing with that parent;

(F) Is a person of good moral character; and

(G) Is a person whose deportation would result in extreme hardship to himself or herself.

(ii) *Parent-child relationship to the abuser.* The self-petitioning child must be unmarried, less than 21 years of age, and otherwise qualify as the abuser's child under the definition of child contained in section 101(b)(1) of the Act when the petition is filed and when it is approved. Termination of the abuser's parental rights or a change in legal custody does not alter the self-petitioning relationship provided the child meets the requirements of section 101(b)(1) of the Act.

(iii) *Citizenship or immigration status of the abuser.* The abusive parent must be a citizen of the United States or a lawful permanent resident of the United States when the petition is filed and when it is approved. Changes in the abuser's citizenship or lawful permanent resident status after the approval will have no effect on the self-petition. A self-petition approved on the basis of a relationship to an abusive lawful permanent resident will not be automatically upgraded to immediate relative status. The self-petitioning child would not be precluded, however, from filing a new self-petition for immediate relative classification after the abuser's naturalization, provided the self-petitioning child continues to meet the self-petitioning requirements.

(iv) *Eligibility for immigrant classification.* A self-petitioner is required to comply with the provisions of section 204(c) of the Act, section 204(g) of the Act, and section 204(a)(2) of the Act.

(v) *Residence.* A self-petition will not be approved if the self-petitioner is not residing in the United States when the self-petition is filed. The self-petitioner is not required to be living with the abuser when the petition is filed, but he or she must have resided with the abuser in the United States in the past.

(vi) *Battery or extreme cruelty.* For the purpose of this chapter, the phrase "was battered by or was the subject of extreme cruelty" includes, but is not limited to, being the victim of any act or threatened act of violence, including any forceful detention, which results or threatens to result in physical or mental injury. Psychological or sexual abuse or exploitation, including rape, molestation, incest (if the victim is a minor), or forced prostitution shall be considered acts of violence. Other abusive actions may also be acts of violence under certain circumstances, including acts that, in and of themselves, may not initially appear violent but are a part of an overall pattern of violence. The qualifying abuse must have been committed by the citizen or lawful permanent resident parent, must have been perpetrated against the self-petitioner, and must have taken place while the self-petitioner was residing with the abuser.

(vii) *Good moral character.* A self-petitioner will be found to lack good moral character if he or she is a person described in section 101(f) of the Act. Extenuating circumstances may be taken into account if the person has not been convicted of an offense or offenses but admits to the commission of an act or acts that could show a lack of good moral character under section 101(f) of the Act. A person who was subjected to abuse in the form of forced prostitution or who can establish that he or she was forced to engage in other behavior that could render the person excludable under section 212(a) of the Act would not be precluded from being found to be a person of good moral character, provided the person has not been convicted for the commission of the offense or offenses in a court of law. A self-petitioner will also be found to lack good moral character, unless he or she establishes extenuating circumstances, if he or she willfully failed or refused to support dependents; or committed unlawful acts that adversely reflect upon his or her moral character, or was convicted or imprisoned for such acts, although the acts do not require an automatic finding of lack of good moral character. A self-petitioner's claim of good moral character will be evaluated on a case-by-case basis, taking into account the provisions of section 101(f) of the Act and the standards of the average citizen in the community. If the results of record checks conducted prior to the issuance of an immigrant visa or approval of an application for adjustment of status disclose that the self-petitioner is no longer a person of good moral character or that he or she has not been a person of good moral character in the past, a pending self-petition will be denied or the approval of a self-petition will be revoked.

(viii) *Extreme hardship.* The Service will consider all credible evidence of extreme hardship submitted with a self-petition, including evidence of hardship arising from circumstances surrounding the abuse. The extreme hardship claim will be evaluated on a case-by-case basis after a review of the evidence in the case. Self-petitioners are encouraged to cite and document all applicable factors, since there is no guarantee that a particular reason or reasons will result in a finding that deportation would cause extreme hardship. Hardship to persons other than the self-petitioner cannot be considered in determining whether a self-petitioning child's deportation would cause extreme hardship.

(2) *Evidence for a child's self-petition—*

(i) *General.* Self-petitioners are encouraged to submit primary evidence whenever possible. The Service will consider, however, any credible evidence relevant to the petition. The determination of what evidence is credible and the weight to be given that evidence shall be within the sole discretion of the Service.

(ii) *Relationship.* A self-petition filed by a child must be accompanied by evidence of citizenship of the United States citizen or proof of the immigration status of the lawful permanent resident abuser. It must also be accompanied by evidence of the relationship. Primary evidence of the relationship between:

(A) The self-petitioning child and an abusive biological mother is the self-petitioner's birth certificate issued by civil authorities;

(B) A self-petitioning child who was born in wedlock and an abusive biological father is the child's birth certificate issued by civil authorities, the marriage certificate of the child's parents, and evidence of legal termination of all prior marriages, if any;

(C) A legitimated self-petitioning child and an abusive biological father is the child's birth certificate issued by civil authorities, and evidence of the child's legitimation;

(D) A self-petitioning child who was born out of wedlock and an abusive biological father is the child's birth certificate issued by civil authorities showing the father's name, and evidence that a bona fide parent-child relationship has been established between the child and the parent;

(E) A self-petitioning stepchild and an abusive stepparent is the child's birth certificate issued by civil authorities, the marriage certificate of the child's parent and the stepparent showing marriage before the stepchild reached 18 years of age, and evidence of legal termination of all prior marriages of either parent, if any; and

(F) An adopted self-petitioning child and an abusive adoptive parent is an adoption decree showing that the adoption took place before the child reached 16 years of age, and evidence that the child has been residing with and in the legal custody of the abusive adoptive parent for at least 2 years.

(iii) *Residence.* One or more documents may be submitted showing that the self-petitioner and the abuser have resided together in the United States. One or more documents may also be submitted showing that the self-petitioner is residing in the United States when the self-petition is filed. Employment records, school records, hospital or medical records, rental records, insurance policies, affidavits or any other type of relevant credible evidence of residency may be submitted.

(iv) *Abuse.* Evidence of abuse may include, but is not limited to, reports and affidavits from police, judges and other court officials, medical personnel, school officials, clergy, social workers, and other social service agency personnel. Persons who have obtained an order of protection against the abuser or taken other legal steps to end the abuse are strongly encouraged to submit copies of the relating legal documents. Evidence that the abuse victim sought safe-haven in a battered women's shelter or similar refuge may be relevant, as may a combination of documents such as a photograph of the visibly injured self-petitioner supported by affidavits. Other types of credible relevant evidence will also be considered. Documentary proof of non-qualifying abuse may only be used to establish a pattern of abuse and violence and to support a claim that qualifying abuse also occurred.

(v) *Good moral character.* Primary evidence of the self-petitioner's good moral character is the self-petitioner's affidavit. The affidavit should be accompanied by a local police clearance or a state-issued criminal background check from each locality or state in the United States in which the self-petitioner has resided for six or more months during the 3-year period immediately preceding the filing of the self-petition. Self-petitioners who lived outside the United States during this time should submit a police clearance, criminal background check, or similar report issued by the appropriate authority in the foreign country in which he or she resided for six or more months during the 3-year period immediately preceding the filing of the self-petition. If police clearances, criminal background checks, or similar reports are not available for some or all locations, the self-petitioner may include an explanation and submit other evidence with his or her affidavit. The Service will consider other credible evidence of good moral character, such as affidavits from responsible persons who can knowledgeably attest to the self-petitioner's good moral character. A child who is less than 14 years of age is presumed to be a person of good moral character and is not required to submit affidavits of good moral character, police clearances, criminal background checks, or other evidence of good moral character.

(vi) *Extreme hardship.* Evidence of extreme hardship may include affidavits, medical reports, protection orders and other court documents, police reports, and other relevant credible evidence.

(3) *Decision on and disposition of the petition—*

(i) *Petition approved.* If the self-petitioning child will apply for adjustment of status under section 245 of the Act, the approved petition will be retained by the Service. If the self-petitioner will apply for an immigrant visa abroad, the approved self-petition will be forwarded to the Department of State's National Visa Center.

(ii) *Notice of intent to deny.* If the preliminary decision on a properly filed self-petition is adverse to the self-petitioner, the self-petitioner will be provided with written notice of this fact and offered an opportunity to present additional information or arguments before a final decision is rendered. If the adverse preliminary decision is based on derogatory information of which the self-petitioner is unaware, the self-petitioner will also be offered an opportunity to rebut the derogatory information in accordance with the provisions of 8 CFR 103.2(b)(16).

(iii) *Petition denied.* If the self-petition is denied, the self-petitioner will be notified in writing of the reasons for the denial and of the right to appeal the decision.

(4) *Derivative beneficiaries.* A child of a self-petitioning child is not eligible for derivative classification and must have a petition filed on his or her behalf if seeking immigrant classification.

(5) *Name change.* If the self-petitioner's current name is different than the name shown on the documents, evidence of the name change (such as the petitioner's marriage certificate, legal document showing the name change, or other similar evidence) must accompany the self-petition.

(6) *Prima facie determination.*

(i) Upon receipt of a self-petition under paragraph (e)(1) of this section, the Service shall make a determination as to whether the petition and the supporting documentation establish a "prima facie case" for purposes of 8 U.S.C. 1641, as amended by section 501 of Public Law 104-208.

(ii) For purposes of paragraph (e)(6)(i) of this section, a prima facie case is established only if the petitioner submits a completed Form I-360 and other evidence supporting all of the elements required of a self-petitioner in paragraph (e)(1) of this section. A finding of prima facie eligibility does not relieve the petitioner of the burden of providing additional evidence in support of the petition and does not establish eligibility for the underlying petition.

(iii) If the Service determines that a petitioner has made a "prima facie case" the Service shall issue a Notice of Prima Facie Case to the petitioner. Such Notice shall be valid until the Service either grants or denies the petition.

(iv) For purposes of adjudicating the petition submitted under paragraph (e)(1) of this section, a prima facie determination:

(A) Shall not be considered evidence in support of the petition;

(B) Shall not be construed to make a determination of the credibility or probative value of any evidence submitted along with that petition; and,

(C) Shall not relieve the self-petitioner of his or her burden of complying with all of the evidentiary requirements of paragraph (e)(2) of this section.

[Ed. Note: Subsections (f), Petition for a parent; (g), Petition for a brother or sister; (h), Validity of approved petition; (i), Automatic conversion of preference classification, are omitted.]

[30 FR 14773, Nov. 30, 1965; 48 FR 4453, Feb. 1, 1983; 48 FR 19155, April 28, 1983; 48 FR 52689, Nov. 22, 1983; 49 FR 8422, March 7, 1984; 50 FR 38969, Sept. 26, 1985; 52 FR 16233, May 4, 1987; 54 FR 11161, March 17, 1989; 54 FR 36754, Sept. 5, 1989; 54 FR 40239, Sept. 29, 1989; 57 FR 41057, Sept. 9, 1992; 60 FR 34090, June 30, 1995; 60 FR 38948, July 31, 1995; 61 FR 7207, Feb. 27, 1996; 61 FR 13073, 13075, 13077, March 26, 1996; 62 FR 10336, March 6, 1997; 62 FR 60771, Nov. 13, 1997]

Sec. 204.3 Orphans.

(a) *General*—

(1) *Background.* This section addresses a number of issues that have arisen in the recent past because of the increased interest by United States citizens in the adoption of foreign-born orphans and is based on applicable provisions of the Act. It should be noted that this section was not drafted in connection with possible United States ratification and implementation of the Hague Convention on Protection of Children and Cooperation in Respect of Inter-country Adoption.

(2) *Overview.* The processing and adjudication of orphan cases is a Service priority. A child who meets the definition of orphan contained in section 101(b)(1)(F) of the Act is eligible for classification as the immediate relative of a United States citizen. Petitioning for an orphan involves two distinct determinations. The first determination concerns the advanced processing application which focuses on the ability of the prospective adoptive

parents to provide a proper home environment and on their suitability as parents. This determination, based primarily on a home study and fingerprint checks, is essential for the protection of the orphan. The second determination concerns the orphan petition which focuses on whether the child is an orphan under section 101(b)(1)(F) of the Act. The prospective adoptive parents may submit the documentation necessary for each of these determinations separately or at one time, depending on when the orphan is identified. An orphan petition cannot be approved unless there is a favorable determination on the advanced processing application. However, a favorable determination on the advanced processing application does not guarantee that the orphan petition will be approved. Prospective adoptive parents may consult with the local Service office on matters relating to an advanced processing application and/or orphan petition.

(b) *Definitions*—

As used in this section, the term:

Abandonment by both parents means that the parents have willfully forsaken all parental rights, obligations, and claims to the child, as well as all control over and possession of the child, without intending to transfer, or without transferring, these rights to any specific person(s). Abandonment must include not only the intention to surrender all parental rights, obligations, and claims to the child, and control over and possession of the child, but also the actual act of surrendering such rights, obligations, claims, control, and possession. A relinquishment or release by the parents to the prospective adoptive parents or for a specific adoption does not constitute abandonment. Similarly, the relinquishment or release of the child by the parents to a third party for custodial care in anticipation of, or preparation for, adoption does not constitute abandonment unless the third party (such as a governmental agency, a court of competent jurisdiction, an adoption agency, or an orphanage) is authorized under the child welfare laws of the foreign-sending country to act in such a capacity. A child who is placed temporarily in an orphanage shall not be considered to be abandoned if the parents express an intention to retrieve the child, are contributing or attempting to contribute to the support of the child, or otherwise exhibit ongoing parental interest in the child. A child who has been given unconditionally to an orphanage shall be considered to be abandoned.

Adult member of the prospective adoptive parents' household means an individual, other than a prospective adoptive parent, over the age of 18 whose principal or only residence is the home of the prospective adoptive parents. This definition excludes any child of the prospective adoptive parents, whose principal or only residence is the home of the prospective adoptive parents, who reaches his or her eighteenth birthday after the prospective adoptive parents have filed the advanced processing application (or the advanced processing application concurrently with the orphan petition) unless the director has an articulable and substantive reason for requiring an evaluation by a home study preparer and/or fingerprint check.

Advanced processing application means Form I-600A (Application for Advanced Processing of Orphan Petition) completed in accordance with the form's instructions and submitted with the required supporting documentation and the fee as required in 8 CFR 103.7(b)(1). The application must be signed in accordance with the form's instructions by the married petitioner and spouse, or by the unmarried petitioner.

Application is synonymous with *advanced processing application*.

Competent authority means a court or governmental agency of a foreign-sending country having jurisdiction and authority to make decisions in matters of child welfare, including adoption.

Desertion by both parents means that the parents have willfully forsaken their child and have refused to carry out their parental rights and obligations and that, as a result, the child has become a ward of a competent authority in accordance with the laws of the foreign-sending country.

Disappearance of both parents means that both parents have unaccountably or inexplicably passed out of the child's life, their whereabouts are unknown, there is no reasonable hope of their reappearance, and there has been a reasonable effort to locate them as determined by a competent authority in accordance with the laws of the foreign-sending country.

Foreign-sending country means the country of the orphan's citizenship, or if he or she is not permanently residing in the country of citizenship, the country of the orphan's habitual residence. This excludes a country to which the orphan travels temporarily, or to which he or she travels either as a prelude to, or in conjunction with, his or her adoption and/or immigration to the United States.

Home study preparer means any party licensed or otherwise authorized under the law of the State of the orphan's proposed residence to conduct the research and preparation for a home study, including the required personal interview(s). This term includes a public agency with authority under that State's law in adoption matters, public or private adoption agencies licensed or otherwise authorized by the laws of that State to place children for adoption, and organizations or individuals licensed or otherwise authorized to conduct the research and preparation for a home study, including the required personal interview(s), under the laws of the State of the orphan's proposed residence. In the case of an orphan whose adoption has been finalized abroad and whose adoptive parents reside abroad, the home study preparer includes any party licensed or otherwise authorized to conduct home studies under the law of any State of the United States, or any party licensed or otherwise authorized by the foreign country's adoption authorities to conduct home studies under the laws of the foreign country.

Incapable of providing proper care means that a sole or surviving parent is unable to provide for the child's basic needs, consistent with the local standards of the *foreign sending country*.

Loss from both parents means the involuntary severance or detachment of the child from the parents in a permanent manner such as that caused by a natural disaster, civil unrest, or other calamitous event beyond the control of the parents, as verified by a competent authority in accordance with the laws of the foreign sending country.

Orphan petition means Form I-600 (Petition to Classify Orphan as an Immediate Relative). The petition must be completed in accordance with the form's instructions and submitted with the required supporting documentation and, if there is not an advanced processing application approved within the previous 18 months or pending, the fee as required in 8 CFR 103.7(b)(1). The petition must be signed in accordance with the form's instructions by the married petitioner and spouse, or the unmarried petitioner.

Overseas site means the Department of State immigrant visa-issuing post having jurisdiction over the orphan's residence, or in foreign countries in which the Services has an office or offices, the Service office having jurisdiction over the orphan's residence.

Petition is synonymous with *orphan petition*.

Petitioner means a married United States citizen of any age, or an unmarried United States citizen who is at least 24 years old at the time he or she files the advanced processing application and at least 25 years old at the time he or she files the orphan petition.

In the case of a married couple, both of whom are United States citizens, either party may be the petitioner.

Prospective adoptive parents means a married United States citizen of any age and his or her spouse of any age, or an unmarried United States citizen who is at least 24 years old at the time he or she files the advanced processing application and at least 25 years old at the time he or she files the orphan petition. The spouse of the United States citizen may be a citizen or an alien. An alien spouse must be in lawful immigration status if residing in the United States.

Separation from both parents means the involuntary severance of the child from his or her parents by action of a competent authority for good cause and in accordance with the laws of the foreign-sending country. The parents must have been properly notified and granted the opportunity to contest such action. The termination of all parental rights and obligations must be permanent and unconditional.

Sole parent means the mother when it is established that the child is illegitimate and has not acquired a parent within the meaning of section 101(b)(2) of the Act. An illegitimate child shall be considered to have a sole parent if his or her father has severed all parental ties, rights, duties, and obligations to the child, or if his or her father has, in writing, irrevocably released the child for emigration and adoption. This definition is not applicable to children born in countries which make no distinction between a child born in or out of wedlock, since all such children are considered to be legitimate. In all cases, a sole parent must be *incapable of providing proper care* as that term is defined in this section.

Surviving parent means the child's living parent when the child's other parent is dead, and the child has not acquired another parent within the meaning of section 101(b)(2) of the Act. In all cases, a surviving parent must be *incapable of providing proper care* as that term is defined in this section.

(c) *Supporting documentation for an advanced processing application*—

The prospective adoptive parents may file an advanced processing application before an orphan is identified in order to secure the necessary clearance to file the orphan petition. Any document not in the English language must be accompanied by a certified English translation.

(1) *Required supporting documentation that must accompany the advanced processing application.* The following supporting documentation must accompany an advanced processing application at the time of filing:

(i) Evidence of the petitioner's United States citizenship as set forth in §204.1(g) and, if the petitioner is married and the married couple is residing in the United States, evidence of the spouse's United States citizenship or lawful immigration status;

(ii) A copy of the petitioner's marriage certificate to his or her spouse, if the petitioner is currently married;

(iii) Evidence of legal termination of all previous marriages for the petitioner and/or spouse, if previously married; and

(iv) Evidence of compliance with preadoption requirements, if any, of the State of the orphan's proposed residence in cases where it is known that there will be no adoption abroad, or that both members of the married prospective adoptive couple or the unmarried prospective adoptive parent will not personally see the child prior to, or during, the adoption abroad, and/or that the adoption abroad will not be full and final. Any preadoption requirements which cannot be met at the time the advanced processing application is filed because of operation of State law must be noted and explained when the application is filed. Preadoption requirements must be met at the time the petition is filed, except for those which cannot be met until the orphan arrives in the United States.

(2) *Home study.* The home study must comply with the requirements contained in paragraph (e) of this section. If the home study is not submitted when the advanced processing application is filed, it must be submitted within one year of the filing date of the advanced processing application, or the application will be denied pursuant to paragraph (h)(5) of this section.

(3) After receipt of a properly filed advanced processing application, the Service will fingerprint each member of the married prospective adoptive couple or the unmarried prospective adoptive parent, as prescribed in § 103.2(e) of this chapter. The Service will also fingerprint each additional adult member of the prospective adoptive parents' household, as prescribed in § 103.2(e) of this chapter. The Service may waive the requirement that each additional adult member of the prospective adoptive parents' household be fingerprinted when it determines that such adult is physically unable to be fingerprinted because of age or medical condition.

(d) *Supporting documentation for a petition for an identified orphan—*

Any document not in the English language must be accompanied by a certified English translation. If an orphan has been identified for adoption and the advanced processing application is pending, the prospective adoptive parents may file the orphan petition at the Service office where the application is pending. The prospective adoptive parents who have an approved advanced processing application must file an orphan petition and all supporting documents within eighteen months of the date of the approval of the advanced processing application. If the prospective adoptive parents fail to file the orphan petition within the eighteen-month period, the advanced processing application shall be deemed abandoned pursuant to paragraph (h)(7) of this section. If the prospective adoptive parents file the orphan petition after the eighteen-month period, the petition shall be denied pursuant to paragraph (h)(13) of this section. Prospective adoptive parents who do not have an advanced processing application approved or pending may file the application and petition concurrently on one Form I-600 if they have identified an orphan for adoption. An orphan petition must be accompanied by full documentation as follows:

(1) *Filing an orphan petition after the advanced processing application has been approved.* The following supporting documentation must accompany an orphan petition filed after approval of the advanced processing application:

(i) Evidence of approval of the advanced processing application;

(ii) The orphan's birth certificate, or if such a certificate is not available, an explanation together with other proof of identity and age;

(iii) Evidence that the child is an orphan as appropriate to the case:

(A) Evidence that the orphan has been abandoned or deserted by, separated or lost from both parents, or that both parents have disappeared as those terms are defined in paragraph (b) of this section; or

(B) The death certificate(s) of the orphan's parent(s), if applicable;

(C) If the orphan has only a sole or surviving parent, as defined in paragraph (b) of this section, evidence of this fact and evidence that the sole or surviving parent is incapable of providing for the orphan's care and has irrevocably released the orphan for emigration and adoption; and

(iv) Evidence of adoption abroad or that the prospective adoptive parents have, or a person or entity working on their behalf has, custody of the orphan for emigration and adoption in accordance with the laws of the foreign-sending country:

(A) A legible, certified copy of the adoption decree, if the orphan has been the subject of a full and final adoption abroad, and evidence that the unmarried petitioner, or married petitioner and spouse, saw the orphan prior to or during the adoption proceeding abroad; or

(B) If the orphan is to be adopted in the United States because there was no adoption abroad, or the unmarried petitioner, or married petitioner and spouse, did not personally see the orphan prior to or during the adoption proceeding abroad, and/or the adoption abroad was not full and final:

(1) Evidence that the prospective adoptive parents have, or a person or entity working on their behalf has, secured custody of the orphan in accordance with the laws of the foreign-sending country;

(2) An irrevocable release of the orphan for emigration and adoption from the person, organization, or competent authority which had the immediately previous legal custody or control over the orphan if the adoption was not full and final under the laws of the foreign-sending country;

(3) Evidence of compliance with all preadoption requirements, if any, of the State of the orphan's proposed residence. (Any such requirements that cannot be complied with prior to the orphan's arrival in the United States because of State law must be noted and explained); and

(4) Evidence that the State of the orphan's proposed residence allows readoption or provides for judicial recognition of the adoption abroad if there was an adoption abroad which does not meet statutory requirements pursuant to section 101(b)(1)(F) of the Act, because the unmarried petitioner, or married petitioner and spouse, did not personally see the orphan prior to or during the adoption proceeding abroad, and/or the adoption abroad was not full and final.

(2) *Filing an orphan petition while the advanced processing application is pending.* An orphan petition filed while an advanced processing application is pending must be filed at the Service office where the application is pending. The following supporting documentation must accompany an orphan petition filed while the advanced processing application is pending:

(i) A photocopy of the fee receipt relating to the advanced processing application, or if not available, other evidence that the advanced processing application has been filed, such as a statement including the date when the application was filed;

(ii) The home study, if not already submitted; and

(iii) The supporting documentation for an orphan petition required in paragraph (d)(1) of this section, except for paragraph (d)(1)(i) of this section.

(3) *Filing an orphan petition concurrently with the advanced processing application.* A petition filed concurrently with the advanced processing application must be submitted on Form I-600, completed and signed in accordance with the form's instructions. (Under this concurrent procedure, Form I-600 serves as both the Forms I-600A and I-600, and the prospective adoptive parents should not file a separate Form I-600A). The following supporting documentation must accompany a petition filed concurrently with the application under this provision:

(i) The supporting documentation for an advanced processing application required in paragraph (c) of this section; and

(ii) The supporting documentation for an orphan petition required in paragraph (d)(1) of this section, except for paragraph (d)(1)(i) of this section.

(e) *Home study requirements—*

For immigration purposes, a home study is a process for screening and preparing prospective adoptive parents who are interested in adopting an orphan from another country. The home study should be tailored to the particular situation of the prospective adoptive parents: for example, a family which previously has adopted children will require different preparation than a family that has no adopted children. If there are any additional adult members of the prospective adoptive parents' household, the home study must address this fact. The home study preparer must interview any additional adult member of the prospective adoptive parents' household and assess him or her in light of the requirements of paragraphs (e)(1), (e)(2)(i), (iii), (iv), and (v) of this section. A home study must be conducted by a home study preparer, as defined in paragraph (b) of this section. The home study, or the most recent update to the home study, must not be more than six months old at the time the home study is submitted to the Service. Only one copy of the home study must be submitted to the Service. Ordinarily, a home study (or a home study and update as discussed above) will not have to be updated after it has been submitted to the Service unless there is a significant change in the household of the prospective adoptive parents such as a change in residence, marital status, criminal history, financial resources, and/or the addition of one or more children or other dependents to the family prior to the orphan's immigration into the United States. In addition to meeting any State, professional, or agency requirements, a home study must include the following:

(1) *Personal interview(s) and home visit(s).* The home study preparer must conduct at least one interview in person, and at least one home visit, with the prospective adoptive couple or the unmarried prospective adoptive parent. Each additional adult member of the prospective adoptive parents' household must also be interviewed in person at least once. The home study report must state the number of such interviews and visits, and must specify any other contacts with the prospective adoptive parents and any adult member of the prospective adoptive parents' household.

(2) *Assessment of the capabilities of the prospective adoptive parents to properly parent the orphan.* The home study must include a discussion of the following areas:

(i) *Assessment of the physical, mental, and emotional capabilities of the prospective adoptive parents to properly parent the orphan.* The home study preparer must make an initial assessment of how the physical, mental, and emotional health of the prospective adoptive parents would affect their ability to properly care for the prospective orphan. If the home study preparer determines that there are areas beyond his or her expertise which need to be addressed, he or she shall refer the prospective adoptive parents to an appropriate licensed professional, such as a physician, psychiatrist, clinical psychologist, or clinical social worker for an evaluation. Some problems may not necessarily disqualify applicants. For example, certain physical limitations may indicate which categories of children may be most appropriately placed with certain prospective adoptive parents. Certain mental and emotional health problems may be successfully treated. The home study must include the home study preparer's assessment of any such potential problem areas, a copy of any outside evaluation(s), and the home study preparer's recommended restrictions, if any, on the characteristics of the child to be placed in the home. Additionally, the home study preparer must apply the requirements of this paragraph to each adult member of the prospective adoptive parents' household.

(ii) *Assessment of the finances of the prospective adoptive parents.* The financial assessment must include a description of the income, financial resources, debts, and expenses of the prospective adoptive parents. A statement concerning the evidence that was considered to verify the source and amount of income and financial resources must be included. Any income designated for the support of one or more children in the care and custody of the prospective adoptive parents, such as funds for foster care, or any income designated for the support of another member of the household must not be counted towards the financial resources available for the support of a prospective orphan. The Service will not routinely require a detailed financial statement or supporting financial documents. However, should the need arise, the Service reserves the right to ask for such detailed documentation.

(iii) *History of abuse and/or violence.*

(A) *Screening for abuse and violence.*

(1) *Checking available child abuse registries.* The home study preparer must ensure that a check of each prospective adoptive parent and each adult member of the prospective adoptive parents' household has been made with available child abuse registries and must include in the home study the results of the checks including, if applicable, a report that no record was found to exist. Depending on the access allowed by the state of proposed residence of the orphan, the home study preparer must take one of the following courses of action:

(i) If the home study preparer is allowed access to information from the child abuse registries, he or she shall make the appropriate checks for each of the prospective adoptive parents and for each adult member of the prospective adoptive parents' household;

(ii) If the State requires the home study preparer to secure permission from each of the prospective adoptive parents and for each adult member of the prospective adoptive parents' household before gaining access to information in such registries, the home study preparer must secure such permission from those individuals, and make the appropriate checks;

(iii) If the State will only release information directly to each of the prospective adoptive parents and directly to the adult member of the prospective adoptive parents' household, those individuals must secure such information and provide it to the home study preparer. The home study preparer must include the results of these checks in the home study;

(iv) If the State will not release information to either the home study preparer or the prospective adoptive parents and the adult members of the prospective adoptive parents' household, this must be noted in the home study; or

(v) If the State does not have a child abuse registry, this must be noted in the home study.

(2) *Inquiring about abuse and violence.* The home study preparer must ask each prospective adoptive parent whether he or she has a history of substance abuse, sexual or child abuse, or domestic violence, even if it did not result in an arrest or conviction. The home study preparer must include each prospective adoptive parent's response to the questions regarding abuse and violence. Additionally, the home study preparer must apply the requirements of this paragraph to each adult member of the prospective adoptive parents' household.

(B) *Information concerning history of abuse and/or violence.* If the petitioner and/or spouse, if married, disclose(s) any history of abuse and/or violence as set forth in paragraph (e)(2)(iii)(A) of this section, or if, in the absence of such disclosure, the home study preparer becomes aware of any of the foregoing, the home study report must contain an evaluation of the suitability of the home for adoptive placement of an orphan in light of this history. This evaluation must include information concerning all arrests or convictions or history of substance abuse, sexual or child abuse, and/or domestic violence and the date of each occurrence. A certified copy of the documentation showing the final disposition of each incident, which resulted in arrest, indictment, conviction, and/or any other judicial or administrative action, must accompany the home study. Additionally, the prospective adoptive parent must submit a signed statement giving details including mitigating circumstances, if any, about each incident. The home study preparer must apply the requirements of this paragraph to each adult member of the prospective adoptive parents' household.

(C) *Evidence of rehabilitation.* If a prospective adoptive parent has a history of substance abuse, sexual or child abuse, and/or domestic violence, the home study preparer may, nevertheless, make a favorable finding if the prospective adoptive parent has demonstrated appropriate rehabilitation. In such a case, a discussion of such rehabilitation which demonstrates that the prospective adoptive parent is and will be able to provide proper care for the orphan must be included in the home study. Evidence of rehabilitation may include an evaluation of the seriousness of the arrest(s), conviction(s), or history of abuse, the number of such incidents, the length of time since the last incident, and any type of counseling or rehabilitation programs which have been successfully completed. Evidence of rehabilitation may also be provided by an appropriate licensed professional, such as a psychiatrist, clinical psychologist, or clinical social worker. The home study report must include all facts and circumstances which the home study preparer has considered, as well as the preparer's reasons for a favorable decision regarding the prospective adoptive parent. Additionally, if any adult member of the prospective adoptive parents' household has a history of substance abuse, sexual or child abuse, and/or domestic violence, the home study preparer must apply the requirements of this paragraph to that adult member of the prospective adoptive parents' household.

(D) *Failure to disclose or cooperate.* Failure to disclose an arrest, conviction, or history of substance abuse, sexual or child abuse, and/or domestic violence by the prospective adoptive parents or an adult member of the prospective adoptive parents' household to the home study preparer and to the Service, may result in the denial of the advanced processing application or, if applicable, the application and orphan petition, pursuant to paragraph (h)(4) of this section. Failure by the prospective adoptive parents or an adult member of the prospective adoptive parents' household to cooperate in having available child abuse registries in accordance with paragraphs (e)(2)(iii)(A)(1) and (e)(2)(iii)(A)(1)(i) through (e)(2)(iii)(A)(1)(iii) of this section will result in the denial of the advanced processing application or, if applicable, the application and orphan petition, pursuant to paragraph (h)(4) of this section.

(iv) *Previous rejection for adoption or prior unfavorable home study.* The home study preparer must ask each prospective adoptive parent whether he or she previously has been rejected as a prospective adoptive parent or has been the subject of an unfavorable home study, and must include each prospective adoptive parent's response to this question in the home study report. If a prospective adoptive parent previously has been rejected or found to be unsuitable, the reasons for such a finding must be set forth as well as the reason(s) why he or she is not being favorably considered as a prospective adoptive parent. A copy of each previous rejection and/or unfavorable home study must be attached to the favorable home study. Additionally, the home study preparer must apply the requirements of this paragraph to each adult member of the prospective adoptive parents' household.

(v) *Criminal history.* The prospective adoptive parents and the adult members of the prospective adoptive parents' household are expected to disclose to the home study preparer and the Service any history of arrest and/or conviction early in the advanced processing procedure. Failure to do so may result in denial pursuant to paragraph (h)(4) of this section or in delays. Early disclosure provides the prospective adoptive parents with the best opportunity to gather and present evidence, and it gives the home study preparer and the Service the opportunity to properly evaluate the criminal record in light of such evidence. When such information is not presented early in the process, it comes to light when the fingerprint checks are received by the Service. By that time, the prospective adoptive parents are usually well into preadoption proceedings of identifying a child and may even have firm travel plans. At times, the travel plans have to be rescheduled while the issues raised by the criminal record are addressed. It is in the best interests of all parties to have any criminal records disclosed and resolved early in the process.

(3) *Living accommodations.* The home study must include a detailed description of the living accommodations where the prospective adoptive parents currently reside. If the prospective adoptive parents are planning to move, the home study must include a description of the living accommodations where the child will reside with the prospective adoptive parents, if known. If the prospective adoptive parents are residing abroad at the time of the home study, the home study must include a description of the living accommodations where the child will reside in the United States with the prospective adoptive parents, if known. Each description must include an assessment of the suitability of accommodations for a child and a determination whether such space meets applicable State requirements, if any.

(4) *Handicapped or special needs orphan.* A home study conducted in conjunction with the proposed adoption of a special needs or handicapped orphan must contain a discussion of the prospective adoptive parents' preparation, willingness, and ability to provide proper care for such an orphan.

(5) *Summary of the counseling given and plans for post-placement counseling.* The home study must include a summary of the counseling given to prepare the prospective adoptive parents for an international adoption and any plans for post-placement counseling. Such preadoption counseling must include a discussion of the processing, expenses, difficulties, and delays associated with international adoptions.

(6) *Specific approval of the prospective adoptive parents for adoption.* If the home study preparer's findings are favorable, the home study must contain his or her specific approval of the prospective adoptive parents for adoption and a discussion of the reasons for such approval. The home study must include the number of orphans which the prospective adoptive parents may adopt. The home study must state whether there are any specific restrictions to the adoption such as nationality, age, or gender of the orphan. If the home study preparer has approved the prospective parents for a handicapped or special needs adoption, this fact must be clearly stated.

(7) *Home study preparer's certification and statement of authority to conduct home studies.* The home study must include a statement in which the home study preparer certifies that he or she is licensed or otherwise authorized by the State of the orphan's proposed residence to research and prepare home studies. In the case of an orphan whose adoption was finalized abroad and whose adoptive parents reside abroad, the home study preparer must certify that he or she is licensed or otherwise authorized to conduct home studies under the law of any State of the United States, or authorized by the adoption authorities of the foreign country to conduct home studies under the laws of the foreign country. In every case, this statement must cite the State or country under whose authority the home study preparer is licensed or authorized, the specific law or regulation authorizing the preparer to conduct home studies, the license number, if any, and the expiration date, if any, of this authorization or license.

(8) *Review of home study.* If the prospective adoptive parents reside in a State which requires the State to review the home study, such a review must occur and be documented before the home study is submitted to the Service. If the prospective adoptive

parents reside abroad, an appropriate public or private adoption agency licensed, or otherwise authorized, by any State of the United States to place children for adoption, must review and favorably recommend the home study before it is submitted to the Service.

(9) *Home study updates and amendments—*

(i) *Updates.* If the home study is more than six months old at the time it would be submitted to the Service, the prospective adoptive parents must ensure that it is updated by a home study preparer before it is submitted to the Service. Each update must include screening in accordance with paragraphs (e)(2)(iii) (A) and (B) of this section.

(ii) *Amendments.* If there have been any significant changes, such as a change in the residence of the prospective adoptive parents, marital status, criminal history, financial resources, and/or the addition of one or more children or other dependents to the family, the prospective adoptive parents must ensure that the home study is amended by a home study preparer to reflect any such changes. If the orphan's proposed State of residence has changed, the home study amendment must contain a recommendation in accordance with paragraph (e)(8) of this section, if required by State law. Any preadoption requirements of the new State must be complied with in the case of an orphan coming to the United States to be adopted.

(10) *"Grandfather" provision for home study.* A home study properly completed in conformance with the regulations in force prior to September 30, 1994, shall be considered acceptable if submitted to the Service within 90 days of September 30, 1994. Any such home study accepted under this "grandfather" provision must include screening in accordance with paragraphs (e)(2)(iii) (A) and (B) of this section. Additionally, any such home study submitted under this "grandfather" provision which is more than six months old at the time of its submission must be amended or updated pursuant to the requirements of paragraph (e)(9) of this section.

(f) *State preadoption requirements—*

(1) *General.* Many States have preadoption requirements which, under the Act, must be complied with in every case in which a child is coming to such a State as an orphan to be adopted in the United States.

(2) *Child coming to be adopted in the United States.* An orphan is coming to be adopted in the United States if he or she will not be or has not been adopted abroad, or if the unmarried petitioner or both the married petitioner and spouse did not or will not personally see the orphan prior to or during the adoption proceeding abroad, and/or if the adoption abroad will not be, or was not, full and final. If the prospective adoptive parents reside in a State with preadoption requirements and they plan to have the child come to the United States for adoption, they must submit evidence of compliance with the State's preadoption requirements to the Service. Any preadoption requirements which by operation of State law cannot be met before filing the advanced processing application must be noted. Such requirements must be met prior to filing the petition, except for those which cannot be met by operation of State law until the orphan is physically in the United States. Those requirements which cannot be met until the orphan is physically present in the United States must be noted

(3) *Special circumstances.* If both members of the prospective adoptive couple or the unmarried prospective adoptive parent intend to travel abroad to see the child prior to or during the adoption, the Act permits the application and/or petition, if otherwise approvable, to be approved without preadoption requirements having been met. However, if plans change and both members of the prospective adoptive couple or the unmarried prospective adoptive parent fail to see the child prior to or during the adoption,

then preadoption requirements must be met before the immigrant visa can be issued, except for those preadoption requirements that cannot be met until the child is physically in the United States because of operation of State law.

(4) *Evidence of compliance.* In every case where compliance with preadoption requirements is required, the evidence of compliance must be in accordance with applicable State law, regulation, and procedure.

(g) *Where to file*—

(1) *Where to file an advanced processing application.* An advanced processing application must be filed with the Service as follows:

(i) *Prospective adoptive parents residing in the United States.* If the prospective adoptive parents reside in the United States, the application must be filed with the Service office having jurisdiction over their place of residence.

(ii) *Prospective adoptive parents residing in Canada.* If the prospective adoptive parents reside in Canada, the application must be filed with the stateside Service office having jurisdiction over the proposed place of residence of the prospective adoptive parents in the United States.

(iii) *Prospective adoptive parents residing in a foreign country other than Canada.* If the prospective adoptive parents reside outside of the United States or Canada, the application may be filed with the overseas Service office having jurisdiction over the current place of residence pursuant to § 100.4(b) of this chapter, or with the stateside Service office having jurisdiction over the proposed place of residence of the prospective adoptive parents in the United States.

(2) *Where to file an orphan petition when the advanced processing application has been approved.* An orphan petition must be filed with the appropriate Service office or immigrant visa-issuing post of the Department of State as follows:

(i) *Prospective adoptive parents residing in the United States who do not travel abroad to locate and/or adopt an orphan.* If the prospective adoptive parents reside in the United States and do not travel abroad to locate and/or adopt an orphan, the petition must be filed with the Service office having jurisdiction over the place of residence of the prospective adoptive parents.

(ii) *Prospective adoptive parents residing in the United States, with one or both members of the prospective adoptive couple, or the unmarried prospective adoptive parent, traveling abroad to locate and/or adopt an orphan.* If the prospective adoptive parents reside in the United States, and one or both members of the prospective adoptive couple, or the unmarried prospective adoptive parent, travel abroad to locate and/or adopt an orphan, the petition may be filed with the stateside Service office having jurisdiction over the place of residence of the prospective adoptive parents in the United States or at the overseas site. The petitioner may file the orphan petition at the overseas site only while he or she is physically present within the jurisdiction of the overseas site. If only one member of a married couple, which includes an alien, travels abroad to file the petition, it must be the United States citizen who travels abroad so that the overseas site will have jurisdiction over the petition.

(iii) *Prospective adoptive parents residing outside the United States.* Prospective adoptive parents residing outside of the United States may file the petition with the overseas site, or with the stateside Service office having jurisdiction over the proposed place of residence of the prospective adoptive parents in the United States.

(3) *Where to file an orphan petition when the advanced processing application is pending.* When the advanced processing application is pending, the petition must be filed at the Service office at which the application is pending.

(4) *Where to file an orphan petition concurrently with the advanced processing applica-tion.* When the petition is filed concurrently with the advanced processing application, it must be filed in accordance with the instruction for filing an advanced processing application in paragraphs (g)(1)(i) through (g)(1)(iii) of this section.

(h) *Adjudication and decision—*

(1) *"Grandfather" provision for advanced processing application and/or orphan peti-tion.* All applications and petitions filed under prior regulations which are filed before and are still pending on September 30, 1994, shall be processed and adjudicated under the prior regulations.

(2) *Director's responsibility to make an independent decision in an advanced processing application.* No advanced processing application shall be approved unless the director is satisfied that proper care will be provided for the orphan. If the director has reason to believe that a favorable home study, or update, or both are based on an inadequate or erroneous evaluation of all the facts, he or she shall attempt to resolve the issue with the home study preparer, the agency making the recommendation pursuant to paragraph (e)(8) of this section, if any, and the prospective adoptive parents. If such consultations are unsatisfactory, the director may request a review and opinion from the appropriate State Government authorities.

(3) *Advanced processing application approved.* If the advanced processing application is approved, the prospective adoptive parents shall be advised in writing. The application and supporting documents shall be forwarded to the overseas site where the orphan resides. Additionally, if the petitioner advises the director that he or she intends to travel abroad to file the petition, telegraphic notification shall be sent overseas as detailed in paragraph (j)(1) of this section. The approved application shall be valid for eighteen months from its approval date. During this time, the prospective adoptive parents may file an orphan petition for one orphan without fee. If approved in the home study for more than one orphan, the prospective adoptive parents may file a petition for each of the additional children, to the maximum number approved. If the orphans are siblings, no additional fee is required. If the orphans are not siblings, an additional fee is required for each orphan beyond the first orphan. Approval of an advanced processing application does not guarantee that the orphan petition will be approved.

(4) *Advanced processing application denied for failure to disclose history of abuse and/or violence, or for failure to disclose a criminal history, or for failure to cooperate in checking child abuse registries.* Failure to disclose an arrest, conviction, or history of substance abuse, sexual or child abuse, and/or domestic violence, or a criminal history to the home study preparer and to the Service in accordance with paragraphs (e)(2)(iii) (A) and (B) and (e)(2)(v) of this section may result in the denial of the advanced processing application, or if applicable, the application and orphan petition filed concurrently. Failure by the prospective adoptive parents or an adult member of the prospective adoptive parents' household to cooperate in having available child abuse registries checked in accordance with paragraphs (e)(2)(iii)(A)(1) and (e)(2)(iii)(A)(1)(i) through (e)(2)(iii)(A)(1)(iii) of this section will result in the denial of the advanced processing application or, if applicable, the application and orphan petition filed concurrently. Any new application and/or petition filed within a year of such denial will also be denied.

(5) *Advanced processing denied for failure to submit home study.* If the home study is not submitted within one year of the filing date of the advanced processing application, the application shall be denied. This action shall be without prejudice to a new filing at any time with fee.

(6) *Advanced processing application otherwise denied.* If the director finds that the prospective adoptive parents have otherwise failed to establish eligibility, the applicable provisions of 8 CFR part 103 regarding a letter of intent to deny, if appropriate, and denial and notification of appeal rights shall govern.

(7) *Advanced processing application deemed abandoned for failure to file orphan petition within eighteen months of application's approval date.* If an orphan petition is not properly filed within eighteen months of the approval date of the advanced processing application, the application shall be deemed abandoned. Supporting documentation shall be returned to the prospective adoptive parents, except for documentation submitted by a third party which shall be returned to the third party, and documentation relating to the fingerprint checks. The director shall dispose of documentation relating to fingerprint checks in accordance with current policy. Such abandonment shall be without prejudice to a new filing at any time with fee.

(8) *Orphan petition approved by a stateside Service office.* If the orphan petition is approved by a stateside Service office, the prospective adoptive parents shall be advised in writing, telegraphic notification shall be sent to the immigrant visa-issuing post pursuant to paragraph (j)(3) of this section, and the petition and supporting documents shall be forwarded to the Department of State.

(9) *Orphan petition approved by an overseas Service office.* If the orphan petition is approved by an overseas Service office located in the country of the orphan's residence, the prospective adoptive parents shall be advised in writing, and the petition and supporting documents shall be forwarded to the immigrant visa-issuing post having jurisdiction for immigrant visa processing.

(10) *Orphan petition approved at an immigrant visa-issuing post.* If the orphan petition is approved at an immigrant visa-issuing post, the post shall initiate immigrant visa processing.

(11) *Orphan petition found to be "not readily approvable" by a consular officer.* If the consular officer adjudicating the orphan petition finds that it is "not readily approvable," he or she shall notify the prospective adoptive parents in his or her consular district and forward the petition, the supporting documents, the findings of the I-604 investigation conducted pursuant to paragraph (k)(1) of this section, and any other relating documentation to the overseas Service office having jurisdiction pursuant to § 100.4(b) of this chapter.

(12) *Orphan petition denied: petitioner fails to establish that the child is an orphan.* If the director finds that the petitioner has failed to establish that the child is an orphan who is eligible for the benefits sought, the applicable provisions of 8 CFR part 103 regarding a letter of intent to deny and notification of appeal rights shall govern.

(13) *Orphan petition denied: petitioner files orphan petition more than eighteen months after the approval of the advanced processing application.* If the petitioner files the orphan petition more than eighteen months after the approval date of the advanced processing application, the petition shall be denied. This action shall be without prejudice to a new filing at any time with fee.

(14) *Revocation.* The approval of an advanced processing application or an orphan petition shall be automatically revoked in accordance with § 205.1 of this chapter, if an applicable reason exists. The approval of an advanced processing application or an orphan petition shall be revoked if the director becomes aware of information that would have resulted in denial had it been known at the time of adjudication. Such a revocation or any other revocation on notice shall be made in accordance with § 205.2 of this chapter.

(i) *Child-buying as a ground for denial.—*

An orphan petition must be denied under ths section if the prospective adoptive parents or adoptive parent(s), or a person or entity working on their behalf, have given or will given money or other consideration either directly or indirectly to the child's parent(s), agent(s), other individual(s), or entity as payment for the child or as an inducement to release the child. Nothing in this paragraph shall be regarded as precluding reasonable payment for necessary activities such as administrative, court, legal, translation, and/or medical services related to the adoption proceedings.

(j) *Telegraphic notifications—*

(1) *Telegraphic notification of approval of advanced processing application.* Unless conditions preclude normal telegraphic transmissions, whenever an advanced processing application is approved in the United States, the director shall send telegraphic notification of the approval to the overseas site if a prospective adoptive parent advises the director that the petitioner intends to travel abroad and file the orphan petition abroad.

(2) *Requesting a change in visa-issuing posts.* If a prospective adoptive parent is in the United States, he or she may request the director to transfer notification of the approved advanced processing application to another visa-issuing post. Such a request shall be made on Form I-824 (Application for Action on an Approved Application or Petition) with the appropriate fee. The director shall send a Visas 37 telegram to both the previously and the newly designated posts. The following shall be inserted after the last numbered standard entry. "To: [insert name of previously designated visa-issuing post or overseas Service office]. Pursuant to the petitioner's request, the Visas 37 cable previously sent to your post/office in this matter is hereby invalidated. The approval is being transferred to the other post/office addressed in this telegram. Please forward the approved advanced processing application to that destination." Prior to sending such a telegram, the director must ensure that the change in posts does not alter any conditions of the approval.

(3) *Telegraphic notification of approval of an orphan petition.* Unless conditions preclude normal telegraphic transmissions, whenever a petition is approved by a stateside Service office, the director shall send telegraphic notification of the approval to the immigrant visa-issuing post.

(k) *Other considerations—*

(1) *I-604 investigations.* An I-604 investigation must be completed in every orphan case. The investigation must be completed by a consular officer except when the petition is properly filed at a Service office overseas, in which case it must be completed by a Service officer. An I-604 investigation shall be completed before a petition is adjudicated abroad. When a petition is adjudicated by a stateside Service office, the I-604 investigation is normally completed after the case has been forwarded to visa-issuing post abroad. However, in a case where the director of a stateside Service office adjudicating the petition has articulable concerns that can only be resolved through the I-604 investigation, he or she shall request the investigation prior to adjudication. In any case in which there are significant differences between the facts presented in the approved advanced processing application and/or orphan petition and the facts uncovered by the I-604 investigation, the overseas site may consult directly with the appropriate Service office. In any instance where an I-604 investigation reveals negative information sufficient to sustain a denial or revocation, the investigation report, supporting documentation, and petition shall be forwarded to the appropriate Service office for action. Depending on the circumstances surrounding the case, the I-604 investigation shall include, but

shall not necessarily be limited to, document checks, telephonic checks, interview(s) with the natural parent(s), and/or a field investigation.

(2) *Authority of consular officers.* An American consular officer is authorized to approve an orphan petition if the Service has made a favorable determination on the related advanced processing application, and the petitioner, who has traveled abroad to a country with no Service office in order to locate or adopt an orphan, has properly filed the petition, and the petition is approvable. A consular officer, however, shall refer any petition which is "not clearly approvable" for a decision by the Service office having jurisdiction pursuant to § 100.4(b) of this chapter. The consular officer's adjudication includes all aspects of eligibility for classification as an orphan under section 101(b)(1)(F) of the Act other than the issue of the ability of the prospective adoptive parents to furnish proper care to the orphan. However, if the consular officer has a well-founded and substantive reason to believe that the advanced processing approval was obtained on the basis of fraud or misrepresentation, or has knowledge of a change in material fact subsequent to the approval of the advanced processing application, he or she shall consult with the Service office having jurisdiction pursuant to § 100.4(b) of this chapter.

(3) *Child in the United States.* A child who is in parole status and who has not been adopted in the United States is eligible for the benefits of an orphan petition when all the requirements of sections 101(b)(1)(F) and 204(d) and (e) of the Act have been met. A child in the United States either illegally or as a nonimmigrant, however, is ineligible for the benefits of an orphan petition.

(4) *Liaison.* Each director shall develop and maintain liaison with State Government adoption authorities having jurisdiction within his or her jurisdiction, including the administrator(s) of the Interstate Compact on the Placement of Children, and with other parties with interest in international adoptions. Such parties include, but are not necessarily limited to, adoption agencies, organizations representing adoption agencies, organizations representing adoptive parents, and adoption attorneys.
[30 FR 14775, Nov. 30, 1965; 57 FR 41063, Sept. 9, 1992; 59 FR 38881, Aug. 1, 1994; 59 FR 42878, Aug. 19, 1994; 63 FR 12986, March 17, 1998]

Title 22 — Foreign Relations

Chapter I — Department of State
Subchapter J — Legal and Related Serices
Part 94 — International Child Abduction

Sec. 94.1 Definitions.

For purposes of this part —

(a) "Convention" means the Hague Convention on the Civil Aspects of International Child Abduction, Appendix B to Department of State notice, 51 FR 10498, March 26, 1986.

(b) "Contracting State" means any country which is a party to the Convention.

(c) "Child" and "children" mean persons under the age of sixteen.
[53 Fed. Reg. 23608 (June 23, 1988); 54 Fed. Reg. 1353 (Jan. 13, 1989)]

Sec. 94.2 Designation of central authority.

The Office of Children's Issues in the Bureau of Consular Affairs is designated as the U.S. Central Authority to discharge the duties which are imposed by the Convention and the International Child Abduction Remedies Act upon such authorities.

[53 Fed. Reg. 23608 (June 23, 1988); 54 Fed. Reg. 1353 (Jan. 13, 1989); 60 Fed. Reg 25843 (May 15, 1995)]

Sec. 94.3 Functions of the Central Authority.

The U.S. Central Authority shall cooperate with the Central Authorities of other countries party to the Convention and promote cooperation by appropriate U.S. state authorities to secure the prompt location and return of children wrongfully removed to or retained in any Contracting State, to ensure that rights of custody and access under the laws of one Contracting State are effectively respected in the other Contracting States, and to achieve the other objects of the Convention. In performing its functions, the U.S. Central Authority may receive from, or transmit to, any department, agency, or instrumentality of the federal government, or of any state or foreign government, information necessary to locate a child or for the purpose of otherwise implementing the Convention with respect to a child.

[53 Fed. Reg. 23608 (June 23, 1988); 54 Fed. Reg. 1353 (Jan. 13, 1989)]

Sec. 94.4 Prohibitions.

(a) The U.S. Central Authority is prohibited from acting as an agent or attorney or in any fiduciary capacity in legal proceedings arising under the Convention. The U.S. Central Authority is not responsible for the costs of any legal representation or legal proceedings nor for any transportation expenses of the child or applicant. However, the U.S. Central Authority may not impose any fee in relation to the administrative processing of applications submitted under the Convention.

(b) The U.S. Central Authority shall not be a repository of foreign or U.S. laws.

[53 Fed. Reg. 23608 (June 23, 1988); 54 Fed. Reg. 1353 (Jan. 13, 1989)]

Sec. 94.5 Application.

Any person, institution, or other body may apply to the U.S. Central Authority for assistance in locating a child, securing access to a child, or obtaining the return of a child that has been removed or retained in breach of custody rights. The application shall be made in the form prescribed by the U.S. Central Authority and shall contain such information as the U.S. Central Authority deems necessary for the purposes of locating the child and otherwise implementing the Convention. The application and any accompanying documents should be submitted in duplicate in English or with English translations. If intended for use in a foreign country, two additional copies should be provided in the language of the foreign country.

[53 Fed. Reg. 23608 (June 23, 1988); 54 Fed. Reg. 1353 (Jan. 13, 1989)]

Sec. 94.6 Procedures for children abducted to the United States.

The National Center for Missing and Exploited Children shall act under the direction of the U.S. Central Authority and shall perform the following operational functions with respect to all Hague Convention applications seeking the return of children wrongfully removed to or retained in the United States or seeking access to children in the United States:

(a) Receive all applications on behalf of the U.S. Central Authority;

(b) Confirm the child's location or, where necessary, seek to ascertain its location;

(c) Seek to ascertain the child's welfare through inquiry to the appropriate state social service agencies and, when necessary, consult with those agencies about the possible need for provisional arrangements to protect the child or to prevent the child's removal from the jurisdiction of the state;

(d) Seek through appropriate authorities (such as state social service agencies or state attorneys general or prosecuting attorneys), where appropriate, to achieve a voluntary agreement for suitable visitation rights by the applicant or for return of the child;

(e) Assist applicants in securing information useful for choosing or obtaining legal representation, for example, by providing a directory of lawyer referral services, or pro bono listing published by legal professional organizations, or the name and address of the state attorney general or prosecuting attorney who has expressed a willingness to represent parents in this type of case and who is employed under state law to intervene on the applicant's behalf;

(f) Upon request, seek from foreign Central Authorities information relating to the social background of the child;

(g) Upon request, seek from foreign Central Authorities information regarding the laws of the country of the child's habitual residence;

(h) Upon request, seek from foreign Central Authorities a statement as to the wrongfulness of the taking of the child under the laws of the country of the child's habitual residence;

(i) Upon request, seek a report on the status of court action when no decision has been reached by the end of six weeks;

(j) Consult with appropriate agencies (such as state social service departments, the U.S. Department of Health and Human Services, state attorneys general) about possible arrangements for temporary foster care and/or return travel for the child from the United States;

(k) Monitor all cases in which assistance has been sought and maintain records on the procedures followed in each case and its disposition;

(l) Perform such additional functions as set out in the "Cooperative Agreement Adjustment Notice" between the Department of State, Department of Justice, and National Center for Missing and Exploited Children.
[53 Fed. Reg. 23608 (June 23, 1988); 54 Fed. Reg. 1353 (Jan. 13, 1989); 60 FR 66073 (Dec. 21, 1995); 61 FR 7069 (Feb. 26, 1996)]

Sec. 94.7 Procedures for children abducted from the United States.

Upon receipt of an application requesting access to a child or return of a child abducted from the United States and taken to another country party to the Convention, the U.S. Central Authority shall—

(a) Review and forward the application to the Central Authority of the country where the child is believed located or provide the applicant with the necessary form, instructions, and the name and address of the appropriate Central Authority for transmittal of the application directly by the applicant;

(b) Upon request, transmit to the foreign Central Authority requests for a report on the status of any court action when no decision has been reached by the end of six weeks;

(c) Upon request, facilitate efforts to obtain from appropriate U.S. state authorities and transmit to the foreign Central Authority information regarding the laws of the child's state of habitual residence;

(d) Upon request, facilitate efforts to obtain from appropriate U.S. state authorities and transmit to the foreign Central Authority a statement as to the wrongfulness of the taking of the child under the laws of the child's state of habitual residence;

(e) Upon request, facilitate efforts to obtain from appropriate U.S. state authorities and transmit to the foreign Central Authority information relating to the social background of the child;

(f) Upon request, be available to facilitate possible arrangements for temporary foster care and/or travel for the child from the foreign country to the United States;

(g) Monitor all cases in which assistance has been sought; and

(h) Perform such additional functions as the Assistant Secretary of State for Consular Affairs may from time to time direct.

[53 Fed. Reg. 23608 (June 23, 1988); 54 Fed. Reg. 1353 (Jan. 13, 1989)]

Sec. 94.8 Interagency Coordinating Group.

The U.S. Central Authority shall nominate federal employees and may, from time to time, nominate private citizens to serve on an interagency coordinating group to monitor the operation of the Convention and to provide advice on its implementation. This group shall meet from time to time at the request of the U.S. Central Authority.

[53 Fed. Reg. 23608 (June 23, 1988); 54 Fed. Reg. 1353 (Jan. 13, 1989)]

Part V

Selected Uniform Acts

Uniform Interstate Family Support Act (1996)
9, Part 1B U.L.A. 235 (1999)

**Reprinted with the permission of the National Conference
of Commissioners on Uniform State Laws**

[Ed. Note: The 1996 version of the Uniform Interstate Family Support Act has been adopted in every U.S. state and the District of Columbia. In 2001, the National Conference of Commissioners on Uniform State Laws approved an amended version of UIFSA. Although the 2001 amendments did not make many substantive changes, they provided clarification in many areas and also addressed the international application of the Act more explicitly.

As of March 2003, however, the 2001 version of the Act had only been enacted in three states, California, Washington, and West Virginia, and introduced in six other states. Therefore, the 1996 version, which is still in effect in the majority of states, is included in this edition. The 2001 UIFSA, 9, Part 1B U.L.A. 41 (West Supp. 2002), is available at http://www.nccusl.org., which also contains current information regarding the states that have adopted it and the states in which legislation to adopt it is pending. The 2001 amendments are also discussed in detail in Chapter 10 of Family Law in the World Community.]

Table of Contents

Article 1. General Provisions

Sec. 101. Definitions.

In this [Act]:

(1) "Child" means an individual, whether over or under the age of majority, who is or is alleged to be owed a duty of support by the individual's parent or who is or is alleged to be the beneficiary of a support order directed to the parent.

(2) "Child-support order" means a support order for a child, including a child who has attained the age of majority under the law of the issuing State.

(3) "Duty of support" means an obligation imposed or imposable by law to provide support for a child, spouse, or former spouse, including an unsatisfied obligation to provide support.

(4) "Home State" means the State in which a child lived with a parent or a person acting as parent for at least six consecutive months immediately preceding the time of filing of a [petition] or comparable pleading for support and, if a child is less than six months old, the State in which the child lived from birth with any of them. A period of temporary absence of any of them is counted as part of the six-month or other period.

(5) "Income" includes earnings or other periodic entitlements to money from any source and any other property subject to withholding for support under the law of this State.

(6) "Income-withholding order" means an order or other legal process directed to an obligor's employer [or other debtor], as defined by [the income-withholding law of this State], to withhold support from the income of the obligor.

(7) "Initiating State" means a State from which a proceeding is forwarded or in which a proceeding is filed for forwarding to a responding State under this [Act] or a law or procedure substantially similar to this [Act], the Uniform Reciprocal Enforcement of Support Act, or the Revised Uniform Reciprocal Enforcement of Support Act.

(8) "Initiating tribunal" means the authorized tribunal in an initiating State.

(9) "Issuing State" means the State in which a tribunal issues a support order or renders a judgment determining parentage.

(10) "Issuing tribunal" means the tribunal that issues a support order or renders a judgment determining parentage.

(11) "Law" includes decisional and statutory law and rules and regulations having the force of law.

(12) "Obligee" means:

(i) an individual to whom a duty of support is or is alleged to be owed or in whose favor a support order has been issued or a judgment determining parentage has been rendered;

(ii) a State or political subdivision to which the rights under a duty of support or support order have been assigned or which has independent claims based on financial assistance provided to an individual obligee; or

(iii) an individual seeking a judgment determining parentage of the individual's child.

(13) "Obligor" means an individual, or the estate of a decedent:

(i) who owes or is alleged to owe a duty of support;

(ii) who is alleged but has not been adjudicated to be a parent of a child; or

(iii) who is liable under a support order.

(14) "Register" means to [record; file] a support order or judgment determining parentage in the [appropriate location for the recording or filing of foreign judgments generally or foreign support orders specifically].

(15) "Registering tribunal" means a tribunal in which a support order is registered.

(16) "Responding State" means a State in which a proceeding is filed or to which a proceeding is forwarded for filing from an initiating State under this [Act] or a law or procedure substantially similar to this [Act], the Uniform Reciprocal Enforcement of Support Act, or the Revised Uniform Reciprocal Enforcement of Support Act.

(17) "Responding tribunal" means the authorized tribunal in a responding State.

(18) "Spousal-support order" means a support order for a spouse or former spouse of the obligor.

(19) "State" means a State of the United States, the District of Columbia, Puerto Rico, the United States Virgin Islands, or any territory or insular possession subject to the jurisdiction of the United States. The term includes:

(i) an Indian tribe; and

(ii) a foreign jurisdiction that has enacted a law or established procedures for issuance and enforcement of support orders which are substantially similar to the procedures under this [Act], the Uniform Reciprocal Enforcement of Support Act, or the Revised Uniform Reciprocal Enforcement of Support Act.

(20) "Support enforcement agency" means a public official or agency authorized to seek:

(i) enforcement of support orders or laws relating to the duty of support;

(ii) establishment or modification of child support;

(iii) determination of parentage; or

(iv) to locate obligors or their assets.

(21) "Support order" means a judgment, decree, or order, whether temporary, final, or subject to modification, for the benefit of a child, a spouse, or a former spouse, which

provides for monetary support, health care, arrearages, or reimbursement, and may include related costs and fees, interest, income withholding, attorney's fees, and other relief.

(22) "Tribunal" means a court, administrative agency, or quasi-judicial entity authorized to establish, enforce, or modify support orders or to determine parentage.

Sec. 102. Tribunal of State.

The [court, administrative agency, quasi-judicial entity, or combination] [is the tribunal] [are the tribunals] of this State.

Sec. 103. Remedies Cumulative.

Remedies provided by this [Act] are cumulative and do not affect the availability of remedies under other law.

Article 2. Jurisdiction
Part 1. Extended Personal Jurisdiction

Sec. 201. Bases for Jurisdiction over Nonresident.

In a proceeding to establish, enforce, or modify a support order or to determine parentage, a tribunal of this State may exercise personal jurisdiction over a nonresident individual [or the individual's guardian or conservator] if:

(1) the individual is personally served with [citation, summons, notice] within this State;

(2) the individual submits to the jurisdiction of this State by consent, by entering a general appearance, or by filing a responsive document having the effect of waiving any contest to personal jurisdiction;

(3) the individual resided with the child in this State;

(4) the individual resided in this State and provided prenatal expenses or support for the child;

(5) the child resides in this State as a result of the acts or directives of the individual;

(6) the individual engaged in sexual intercourse in this State and the child may have been conceived by that act of intercourse;

(7) the individual asserted parentage in the [putative father registry] maintained in this State by the [appropriate agency]; or

(8) there is any other basis consistent with the constitutions of this State and the United States for the exercise of personal jurisdiction.

Sec. 202. Procedure When Exercising Jurisdiction over Nonresident.

A tribunal of this State exercising personal jurisdiction over a nonresident under Section 201 may apply Section 316 (Special Rules of Evidence and Procedure) to receive evidence from another State, and Section 318 (Assistance with Discovery) to obtain discovery through a tribunal of another State. In all other respects, Articles 3 through 7 do not apply and the tribunal shall apply the procedural and substantive law of this State, including the rules on choice of law other than those established by this [Act].

Part 2. Proceedings Involving Two or More States

Sec. 203. Initiating and Responding Tribunal of State.

Under this [Act], a tribunal of this State may serve as an initiating tribunal to forward proceedings to another State and as a responding tribunal for proceedings initiated in another State.

Sec. 204. Simultaneous Proceedings in Another State.

(a) A tribunal of this State may exercise jurisdiction to establish a support order if the [petition] or comparable pleading is filed after a pleading is filed in another State only if:

(1) the [petition] or comparable pleading in this State is filed before the expiration of the time allowed in the other State for filing a responsive pleading challenging the exercise of jurisdiction by the other State;

(2) the contesting party timely challenges the exercise of jurisdiction in the other State; and

(3) if relevant, this State is the home State of the child.

(b) A tribunal of this State may not exercise jurisdiction to establish a support order if the [petition] or comparable pleading is filed before a [petition] or comparable pleading is filed in another State if:

(1) the [petition] or comparable pleading in the other State is filed before the expiration of the time allowed in this State for filing a responsive pleading challenging the exercise of jurisdiction by this State;

(2) the contesting party timely challenges the exercise of jurisdiction in this State; and

(3) if relevant, the other State is the home State of the child.

Sec. 205. Continuing, Exclusive Jurisdiction.

(a) A tribunal of this State issuing a support order consistent with the law of this State has continuing, exclusive jurisdiction over a child-support order:

(1) as long as this State remains the residence of the obligor, the individual obligee, or the child for whose benefit the support order is issued; or

(2) until all of the parties who are individuals have filed written consents with the tribunal of this State for a tribunal of another State to modify the order and assume continuing, exclusive jurisdiction.

(b) A tribunal of this State issuing a child-support order consistent with the law of this State may not exercise its continuing jurisdiction to modify the order if the order has been modified by a tribunal of another State pursuant to this [Act] or a law substantially similar to this [Act].

(c) If a child-support order of this State is modified by a tribunal of another State pursuant to this [Act] or a law substantially similar to this [Act], a tribunal of this State loses its continuing, exclusive jurisdiction with regard to prospective enforcement of the order issued in this State, and may only:

(1) enforce the order that was modified as to amounts accruing before the modification;

(2) enforce nonmodifiable aspects of that order; and

(3) provide other appropriate relief for violations of that order which occurred before the effective date of the modification.

(d) A tribunal of this State shall recognize the continuing, exclusive jurisdiction of a tribunal of another State which has issued a child-support order pursuant to this [Act] or a law substantially similar to this [Act].

(e) A temporary support order issued ex parte or pending resolution of a jurisdictional conflict does not create continuing, exclusive jurisdiction in the issuing tribunal.

(f) A tribunal of this State issuing a support order consistent with the law of this State has continuing, exclusive jurisdiction over a spousal-support order throughout the existence of the support obligation. A tribunal of this State may not modify a spousal-support order issued by a tribunal of another State having continuing, exclusive jurisdiction over that order under the law of that State.

Sec. 206. Enforcement and Modification of Support Order by Tribunal Having Continuing Jurisdiction.

(a) A tribunal of this State may serve as an initiating tribunal to request a tribunal of another State to enforce or modify a support order issued in that State.

(b) A tribunal of this State having continuing, exclusive jurisdiction over a support order may act as a responding tribunal to enforce or modify the order. If a party subject to the continuing, exclusive jurisdiction of the tribunal no longer resides in the issuing State, in subsequent proceedings the tribunal may apply Section 316 (Special Rules of Evidence and Procedure) to receive evidence from another State and Section 318 (Assistance with Discovery) to obtain discovery through a tribunal of another State.

(c) A tribunal of this State which lacks continuing, exclusive jurisdiction over a spousal-support order may not serve as a responding tribunal to modify a spousal-support order of another State.

Part 3. Reconciliation of Multiple Orders

Sec. 207. Recognition of Controlling Child-Support Order.

(a) If a proceeding is brought under this [Act] and only one tribunal has issued a child-support order, the order of that tribunal controls and must be so recognized.

(b) If a proceeding is brought under this [Act], and two or more child-support orders have been issued by tribunals of this State or another State with regard to the same obligor and child, a tribunal of this State shall apply the following rules in determining which order to recognize for purposes of continuing, exclusive jurisdiction:

(1) If only one of the tribunals would have continuing, exclusive jurisdiction under this [Act], the order of that tribunal controls and must be so recognized.

(2) If more than one of the tribunals would have continuing, exclusive jurisdiction under this [Act], an order issued by a tribunal in the current home State of the child controls and must be so recognized, but if an order has not been issued in the current home State of the child, the order most recently issued controls and must be so recognized.

(3) If none of the tribunals would have continuing, exclusive jurisdiction under this [Act], the tribunal of this State having jurisdiction over the parties shall issue a child-support order, which controls and must be so recognized.

(c) If two or more child-support orders have been issued for the same obligor and child and if the obligor or the individual obligee resides in this State, a party may request a tribunal of this State to determine which order controls and must be so recognized under subsection (b). The request must be accompanied by a certified copy of every support order in effect. The requesting party shall give notice of the request to each party whose rights may be affected by the determination.

(d) The tribunal that issued the controlling order under subsection (a), (b), or (c) is the tribunal that has continuing, exclusive jurisdiction under Section 205.

(e) A tribunal of this State which determines by order the identity of the controlling order under subsection (b)(1) or (2) or which issues a new controlling order under subsection (b)(3) shall state in that order the basis upon which the tribunal made its determination.

(f) Within [30] days after issuance of an order determining the identity of the controlling order, the party obtaining the order shall file a certified copy of it with each tribunal that issued or registered an earlier order of child support. A party who obtains the order and fails to file a certified copy is subject to appropriate sanctions by a tribunal in which the issue of failure to file arises. The failure to file does not affect the validity or enforceability of the controlling order.

Sec. 208. Multiple Child-Support Orders for Two or More Obligees.

In responding to multiple registrations or [petitions] for enforcement of two or more child-support orders in effect at the same time with regard to the same obligor and different individual obligees, at least one of which was issued by a tribunal of another State, a tribunal of this State shall enforce those orders in the same manner as if the multiple orders had been issued by a tribunal of this State.

Sec. 209. Credit for Payments.

Amounts collected and credited for a particular period pursuant to a support order issued by a tribunal of another State must be credited against the amounts accruing or accrued for the same period under a support order issued by the tribunal of this State.

Article 3. Civil Provisions of General Application

Sec. 301. Proceedings under [Act].

(a) Except as otherwise provided in this [Act], this article applies to all proceedings under this [Act].

(b) This [Act] provides for the following proceedings:

(1) establishment of an order for spousal support or child support pursuant to Article 4;

(2) enforcement of a support order and income-withholding order of another State without registration pursuant to Article 5;

(3) registration of an order for spousal support or child support of another State for enforcement pursuant to Article 6;

(4) modification of an order for child support or spousal support issued by a tribunal of this State pursuant to Article 2, Part 2;

(5) registration of an order for child support of another State for modification pursuant to Article 6;

(6) determination of parentage pursuant to Article 7; and

(7) assertion of jurisdiction over nonresidents pursuant to Article 2, Part 1.

(c) An individual [petitioner] or a support enforcement agency may commence a proceeding authorized under this [Act] by filing a [petition] in an initiating tribunal for forwarding to a responding tribunal or by filing a [petition] or a comparable pleading directly in a tribunal of another State which has or can obtain personal jurisdiction over the [respondent].

Sec. 302. Action By Minor Parent.

A minor parent, or a guardian or other legal representative of a minor parent, may maintain a proceeding on behalf of or for the benefit of the minor's child.

Sec. 303. Application of Law of State.

Except as otherwise provided by this [Act], a responding tribunal of this State:

(1) shall apply the procedural and substantive law, including the rules on choice of law, generally applicable to similar proceedings originating in this State and may exercise all powers and provide all remedies available in those proceedings; and

(2) shall determine the duty of support and the amount payable in accordance with the law and support guidelines of this State.

Sec. 304. Duties of Initiating Tribunal.

(a) Upon the filing of a [petition] authorized by this [Act], an initiating tribunal of this State shall forward three copies of the [petition] and its accompanying documents:

(1) to the responding tribunal or appropriate support enforcement agency in the responding State; or

(2) if the identity of the responding tribunal is unknown, to the state information agency of the responding State with a request that they be forwarded to the appropriate tribunal and that receipt be acknowledged.

(b) If a responding State has not enacted this [Act] or a law or procedure substantially similar to this [Act], a tribunal of this State may issue a certificate or other document and make findings required by the law of the responding State. If the responding State is a foreign jurisdiction, the tribunal may specify the amount of support sought and provide other documents necessary to satisfy the requirements of the responding State.

Sec. 305. Duties and Powers of Responding Tribunal.

(a) When a responding tribunal of this State receives a [petition] or comparable pleading from an initiating tribunal or directly pursuant to Section 301(c) (Proceedings Under this [Act]), it shall cause the [petition] or pleading to be filed and notify the [petitioner] where and when it was filed.

(b) A responding tribunal of this State, to the extent otherwise authorized by law, may do one or more of the following:

(1) issue or enforce a support order, modify a child-support order, or render a judgment to determine parentage;

(2) order an obligor to comply with a support order, specifying the amount and the manner of compliance;

(3) order income withholding;

(4) determine the amount of any arrearages, and specify a method of payment;

(5) enforce orders by civil or criminal contempt, or both;

(6) set aside property for satisfaction of the support order;

(7) place liens and order execution on the obligor's property;

(8) order an obligor to keep the tribunal informed of the obligor's current residential address, telephone number, employer, address of employment, and telephone number at the place of employment;

(9) issue a [bench warrant; capias] for an obligor who has failed after proper notice to appear at a hearing ordered by the tribunal and enter the [bench warrant; capias] in any local and state computer systems for criminal warrants;

(10) order the obligor to seek appropriate employment by specified methods;

(11) award reasonable attorney's fees and other fees and costs; and

(12) grant any other available remedy.

(c) A responding tribunal of this State shall include in a support order issued under this [Act], or in the documents accompanying the order, the calculations on which the support order is based.

(d) A responding tribunal of this State may not condition the payment of a support order issued under this [Act] upon compliance by a party with provisions for visitation.

(e) If a responding tribunal of this State issues an order under this [Act], the tribunal shall send a copy of the order to the [petitioner] and the [respondent] and to the initiating tribunal, if any.

Sec. 306. Inappropriate Tribunal.

If a [petition] or comparable pleading is received by an inappropriate tribunal of this State, it shall forward the pleading and accompanying documents to an appropriate tribunal in this State or another State and notify the [petitioner] where and when the pleading was sent.

Sec. 307. Duties of Support Enforcement Agency.

(a) A support enforcement agency of this State, upon request, shall provide services to a [petitioner] in a proceeding under this [Act].

(b) A support enforcement agency that is providing services to the [petitioner] as appropriate shall:

(1) take all steps necessary to enable an appropriate tribunal in this State or another State to obtain jurisdiction over the [respondent];

(2) request an appropriate tribunal to set a date, time, and place for a hearing;

(3) make a reasonable effort to obtain all relevant information, including information as to income and property of the parties;

(4) within [two] days, exclusive of Saturdays, Sundays, and legal holidays, after receipt of a written notice from an initiating, responding, or registering tribunal, send a copy of the notice to the [petitioner];

(5) within [two] days, exclusive of Saturdays, Sundays, and legal holidays, after receipt of a written communication from the [respondent] or the [respondent's] attorney, send a copy of the communication to the [petitioner]; and

(6) notify the [petitioner] if jurisdiction over the [respondent] cannot be obtained.

(c) This [Act] does not create or negate a relationship of attorney and client or other fiduciary relationship between a support enforcement agency or the attorney for the agency and the individual being assisted by the agency.

Sec. 308. Duty of [Attorney General].

If the [Attorney General] determines that the support enforcement agency is neglecting or refusing to provide services to an individual, the [Attorney General] may order the agency to perform its duties under this [Act] or may provide those services directly to the individual.

Sec. 309. Private Counsel.

An individual may employ private counsel to represent the individual in proceedings authorized by this [Act].

Sec. 310. Duties of [State Information Agency].

(a) The [Attorney General's Office, State Attorney's Office, State Central Registry or other information agency] is the state information agency under this [Act].

(b) The state information agency shall:

(1) compile and maintain a current list, including addresses, of the tribunals in this State which have jurisdiction under this [Act] and any support enforcement agencies in this State and transmit a copy to the state information agency of every other State;

(2) maintain a register of tribunals and support enforcement agencies received from other States;

(3) forward to the appropriate tribunal in the place in this State in which the individual obligee or the obligor resides, or in which the obligor's property is believed to be located, all documents concerning a proceeding under this [Act] received from an initiating tribunal or the state information agency of the initiating State; and

(4) obtain information concerning the location of the obligor and the obligor's property within this State not exempt from execution, by such means as postal verification and federal or state locator services, examination of telephone directories, requests for the obligor's address from employers, and examination of governmental records, including, to the extent not prohibited by other law, those relating to real property, vital statistics, law enforcement, taxation, motor vehicles, driver's licenses, and social security.

Sec. 311. Pleadings and Accompanying Documents.

(a) A [petitioner] seeking to establish or modify a support order or to determine parentage in a proceeding under this [Act] must verify the [petition]. Unless otherwise ordered under Section 312 (Nondisclosure of Information in Exceptional Circumstances), the [petition] or accompanying documents must provide, so far as known, the name, residential address, and social security numbers of the obligor and the obligee, and the name, sex, residential address, social security number, and date of birth of each child for whom support is sought. The [petition] must be accompanied by a certified copy of any support order in effect. The [petition] may include any other information that may assist in locating or identifying the [respondent].

(b) The [petition] must specify the relief sought. The [petition] and accompanying documents must conform substantially with the requirements imposed by the forms mandated by federal law for use in cases filed by a support enforcement agency.

Sec. 312. Nondisclosure of Information in Exceptional Circumstances.

Upon a finding, which may be made ex parte, that the health, safety, or liberty of a party or child would be unreasonably put at risk by the disclosure of identifying information, or if an existing order so provides, a tribunal shall order that the address of the child or party or other identifying information not be disclosed in a pleading or other document filed in a proceeding under this [Act].

Sec. 313. Costs and Fees.

(a) The [petitioner] may not be required to pay a filing fee or other costs.

(b) If an obligee prevails, a responding tribunal may assess against an obligor filing fees, reasonable attorney's fees, other costs, and necessary travel and other reasonable expenses incurred by the obligee and the obligee's witnesses. The tribunal may not assess fees, costs, or expenses against the obligee or the support enforcement agency of either the initiating or the responding State, except as provided by other law. Attorney's fees may be taxed as costs, and may be ordered paid directly to the attorney, who may enforce the order in the attorney's own name. Payment of support owed to the obligee has priority over fees, costs and expenses.

(c) The tribunal shall order the payment of costs and reasonable attorney's fees if it determines that a hearing was requested primarily for delay. In a proceeding under Article 6 (Enforcement and Modification of Support Order After Registration), a hearing is presumed to have been requested primarily for delay if a registered support order is confirmed or enforced without change.

Sec. 314. Limited Immunity of [Petitioner].

(a) Participation by a [petitioner] in a proceeding before a responding tribunal, whether in person, by private attorney, or through services provided by the support enforcement agency, does not confer personal jurisdiction over the [petitioner] in another proceeding.

(b) A [petitioner] is not amenable to service of civil process while physically present in this State to participate in a proceeding under this [Act].

(c) The immunity granted by this section does not extend to civil litigation based on acts unrelated to a proceeding under this [Act] committed by a party while present in this State to participate in the proceeding.

Sec. 315. Nonparentage as Defense.

A party whose parentage of a child has been previously determined by or pursuant to law may not plead nonparentage as a defense to a proceeding under this [Act].

Sec. 316. Special Rules of Evidence and Procedure.

(a) The physical presence of the [petitioner] in a responding tribunal of this State is not required for the establishment, enforcement, or modification of a support order or the rendition of a judgment determining parentage.

(b) A verified [petition], affidavit, document substantially complying with federally mandated forms, and a document incorporated by reference in any of them, not excluded under the hearsay rule if given in person, is admissible in evidence if given under oath by a party or witness residing in another State.

(c) A copy of the record of child-support payments certified as a true copy of the original by the custodian of the record may be forwarded to a responding tribunal. The copy is evidence of facts asserted in it, and is admissible to show whether payments were made.

(d) Copies of bills for testing for parentage, and for prenatal and postnatal health care of the mother and child, furnished to the adverse party at least [ten] days before trial, are admissible in evidence to prove the amount of the charges billed and that the charges were reasonable, necessary, and customary.

(e) Documentary evidence transmitted from another State to a tribunal of this State by telephone, telecopier, or other means that do not provide an original writing may not be excluded from evidence on an objection based on the means of transmission.

(f) In a proceeding under this [Act], a tribunal of this State may permit a party or witness residing in another State to be deposed or to testify by telephone, audiovisual means, or other electronic means at a designated tribunal or other location in that State. A tribunal of this State shall cooperate with tribunals of other States in designating an appropriate location for the deposition or testimony.

(g) If a party called to testify at a civil hearing refuses to answer on the ground that the testimony may be self-incriminating, the trier of fact may draw an adverse inference from the refusal.

(h) A privilege against disclosure of communications between spouses does not apply in a proceeding under this [Act].

(i) The defense of immunity based on the relationship of husband and wife or parent and child does not apply in a proceeding under this [Act].

Sec. 317. Communications Between Tribunals.

A tribunal of this State may communicate with a tribunal of another State in writing, or by telephone or other means, to obtain information concerning the laws of that State, the legal effect of a judgment, decree, or order of that tribunal, and the status of a proceeding in the other State. A tribunal of this State may furnish similar information by similar means to a tribunal of another State.

Sec. 318. Assistance with Discovery.

A tribunal of this State may:

(1) request a tribunal of another State to assist in obtaining discovery; and

(2) upon request, compel a person over whom it has jurisdiction to respond to a discovery order issued by a tribunal of another State.

Sec. 319. Receipt and Disbursement of Payments.

A support enforcement agency or tribunal of this State shall disburse promptly any amounts received pursuant to a support order, as directed by the order. The agency or tribunal shall furnish to a requesting party or tribunal of another State a certified statement by the custodian of the record of the amounts and dates of all payments received.

Article 4. Establishment of Support Order

Sec. 401. [Petition] to Establish Support Order.

(a) If a support order entitled to recognition under this [Act] has not been issued, a responding tribunal of this State may issue a support order if:

(1) the individual seeking the order resides in another State; or

(2) the support enforcement agency seeking the order is located in another State.

(b) The tribunal may issue a temporary child-support order if:

(1) the [respondent] has signed a verified statement acknowledging parentage;

(2) the [respondent] has been determined by or pursuant to law to be the parent; or

(3) there is other clear and convincing evidence that the [respondent] is the child's parent.

(c) Upon finding, after notice and opportunity to be heard, that an obligor owes a duty of support, the tribunal shall issue a support order directed to the obligor and may issue other orders pursuant to Section 305 (Duties and Powers of Responding Tribunal).

Article 5. Enforcement of Order of Another State Without Registration

Sec. 501. Employer's Receipt of Income-Withholding Order of Another State.

An income-withholding order issued in another State may be sent to the person or entity defined as the obligor's employer under [the income-withholding law of this State] without first filing a [petition] or comparable pleading or registering the order with a tribunal of this State.

Sec. 502. Employer's Compliance with Income-Withholding Order of Another State.

(a) Upon receipt of an income-withholding order, the obligor's employer shall immediately provide a copy of the order to the obligor.

(b) The employer shall treat an income-withholding order issued in another State which appears regular on its face as if it had been issued by a tribunal of this State.

(c) Except as otherwise provided in subsection (d) and Section 503, the employer shall withhold and distribute the funds as directed in the withholding order by complying with terms of the order which specify:

(1) the duration and amount of periodic payments of current child-support, stated as a sum certain;

(2) the person or agency designated to receive payments and the address to which the payments are to be forwarded;

(3) medical support, whether in the form of periodic cash payment, stated as a sum certain, or ordering the obligor to provide health insurance coverage for the child under a policy available through the obligor's employment;

(4) the amount of periodic payments of fees and costs for a support enforcement agency, the issuing tribunal, and the obligee's attorney, stated as sums certain; and

(5) the amount of periodic payments of arrearages and interest on arrearages, stated as sums certain.

(d) An employer shall comply with the law of the State of the obligor's principal place of employment for withholding from income with respect to:

(1) the employer's fee for processing an income-withholding order;

(2) the maximum amount permitted to be withheld from the obligor's income; and

(3) the times within which the employer must implement the withholding order and forward the child support payment.

Sec. 503. Compliance with Multiple Income-Withholding Orders.

If an obligor's employer receives multiple income-withholding orders with respect to the earnings of the same obligor, the employer satisfies the terms of the multiple orders if the employer complies with the law of the State of the obligor's principal place of employment to establish the priorities for withholding and allocating income withheld for multiple child support obligees.

Sec. 504. Immunity from Civil Liability.

An employer who complies with an income-withholding order issued in another State in accordance with this article is not subject to civil liability to an individual or agency with regard to the employer's withholding of child support from the obligor's income.

Sec. 505. Penalties for Noncompliance.

An employer who willfully fails to comply with an income-withholding order issued by another State and received for enforcement is subject to the same penalties that may be imposed for noncompliance with an order issued by a tribunal of this State.

Sec. 506. Contest by Obligor.

(a) An obligor may contest the validity or enforcement of an income-withholding order issued in another State and received directly by an employer in this State in the same manner as if the order had been issued by a tribunal of this State. Section 604 (Choice of Law) applies to the contest.

(b) The obligor shall give notice of the contest to:

(1) a support enforcement agency providing services to the obligee;

(2) each employer that has directly received an income-withholding order; and

(3) the person or agency designated to receive payments in the income-withholding order or if no person or agency is designated, to the obligee.

Sec. 507. Administrative Enforcement of Orders.

(a) A party seeking to enforce a support order or an income-withholding order, or both, issued by a tribunal of another State may send the documents required for registering the order to a support enforcement agency of this State.

(b) Upon receipt of the documents, the support enforcement agency, without initially seeking to register the order, shall consider and, if appropriate, use any administrative procedure authorized by the law of this State to enforce a support order or an income-withholding order, or both. If the obligor does not contest administrative enforcement, the order need not be registered. If the obligor contests the validity or administrative enforcement of the order, the support enforcement agency shall register the order pursuant to this [Act].

Article 6. Enforcement and Modification of Support Order After Registration
Part 1. Registration and Enforcement of Support Order

Sec. 601. Registration of Order for Enforcement.

A support order or an income-withholding order issued by a tribunal of another State may be registered in this State for enforcement.

Sec. 602. Procedure to Register Order for Enforcement.

(a) A support order or income-withholding order of another State may be registered in this State by sending the following documents and information to the [appropriate tribunal] in this State:

(1) a letter of transmittal to the tribunal requesting registration and enforcement;

(2) two copies, including one certified copy, of all orders to be registered, including any modification of an order;

(3) a sworn statement by the party seeking registration or a certified statement by the custodian of the records showing the amount of any arrearage;

(4) the name of the obligor and, if known:

(i) the obligor's address and social security number;

(ii) the name and address of the obligor's employer and any other source of income of the obligor; and

(iii) a description and the location of property of the obligor in this State not exempt from execution; and

(5) the name and address of the obligee and, if applicable, the agency or person to whom support payments are to be remitted.

(b) On receipt of a request for registration, the registering tribunal shall cause the order to be filed as a foreign judgment, together with one copy of the documents and information, regardless of their form.

(c) A [petition] or comparable pleading seeking a remedy that must be affirmatively sought under other law of this State may be filed at the same time as the request for registration or later. The pleading must specify the grounds for the remedy sought.

Sec. 603. Effect of Registration for Enforcement.

(a) A support order or income-withholding order issued in another State is registered when the order is filed in the registering tribunal of this State.

(b) A registered order issued in another State is enforceable in the same manner and is subject to the same procedures as an order issued by a tribunal of this State.

(c) Except as otherwise provided in this article, a tribunal of this State shall recognize and enforce, but may not modify, a registered order if the issuing tribunal had jurisdiction.

Sec. 604. Choice of Law.

(a) The law of the issuing State governs the nature, extent, amount, and duration of current payments and other obligations of support and the payment of arrearages under the order.

(b) In a proceeding for arrearages, the statute of limitation under the laws of this State or of the issuing State, whichever is longer, applies.

Part 2. Contest of Validity or Enforcement

Sec. 605. Notice of Registration of Order.

(a) When a support order or income-withholding order issued in another State is registered, the registering tribunal shall notify the nonregistering party. The notice must be accompanied by a copy of the registered order and the documents and relevant information accompanying the order.

(b) The notice must inform the nonregistering party:

(1) that a registered order is enforceable as of the date of registration in the same manner as an order issued by a tribunal of this State;

(2) that a hearing to contest the validity or enforcement of the registered order must be requested within [20] days after notice;

(3) that failure to contest the validity or enforcement of the registered order in a timely manner will result in confirmation of the order and enforcement of the order and the alleged arrearages and precludes further contest of that order with respect to any matter that could have been asserted; and

(4) of the amount of any alleged arrearages.

(c) Upon registration of an income-withholding order for enforcement, the registering tribunal shall notify the obligor's employer pursuant to [the income-withholding law of this State].

Sec. 606. Procedure to Contest Validity or Enforcement of Registered Order.

(a) A nonregistering party seeking to contest the validity or enforcement of a registered order in this State shall request a hearing within [20] days after notice of the registration. The nonregistering party may seek to vacate the registration, to assert any defense to an allegation of noncompliance with the registered order, or to contest the remedies being sought or the amount of any alleged arrearages pursuant to Section 607 (Contest of Registration or Enforcement).

(b) If the nonregistering party fails to contest the validity or enforcement of the registered order in a timely manner, the order is confirmed by operation of law.

(c) If a nonregistering party requests a hearing to contest the validity or enforcement of the registered order, the registering tribunal shall schedule the matter for hearing and give notice to the parties of the date, time, and place of the hearing.

Sec. 607. Contest of Registration or Enforcement.

(a) A party contesting the validity or enforcement of a registered order or seeking to vacate the registration has the burden of proving one or more of the following defenses:

(1) the issuing tribunal lacked personal jurisdiction over the contesting party;

(2) the order was obtained by fraud;

(3) the order has been vacated, suspended, or modified by a later order;

(4) the issuing tribunal has stayed the order pending appeal;

(5) there is a defense under the law of this State to the remedy sought;

(6) full or partial payment has been made; or

(7) the statute of limitation under Section 604 (Choice of Law) precludes enforcement of some or all of the arrearages.

(b) If a party presents evidence establishing a full or partial defense under subsection (a), a tribunal may stay enforcement of the registered order, continue the proceeding to permit production of additional relevant evidence, and issue other appropriate orders. An uncontested portion of the registered order may be enforced by all remedies available under the law of this State.

(c) If the contesting party does not establish a defense under subsection (a) to the validity or enforcement of the order, the registering tribunal shall issue an order confirming the order.

Sec. 608. Confirmed Order.

Confirmation of a registered order, whether by operation of law or after notice and hearing, precludes further contest of the order with respect to any matter that could have been asserted at the time of registration.

Part 3. Registration and Modification of Child-Support Order

Sec. 609. Procedure to Register Child-Support Order of Another State for Modification.

A party or support enforcement agency seeking to modify, or to modify and enforce, a child-support order issued in another State shall register that order in this State in the same manner provided in Part 1 if the order has not been registered. A [petition] for modification may be filed at the same time as a request for registration, or later. The pleading must specify the grounds for modification.

Sec. 610. Effect of Registration for Modification.

A tribunal of this State may enforce a child-support order of another State registered for purposes of modification, in the same manner as if the order had been issued by a tribunal of this State, but the registered order may be modified only if the requirements of Section 611 (Modification of Child-Support Order of Another State) have been met.

Sec. 611. Modification of Child-Support Order of Another State.

(a) After a child-support order issued in another State has been registered in this State, the responding tribunal of this State may modify that order only if Section 613 does not apply and after notice and hearing it finds that:

(1) the following requirements are met:

(i) the child, the individual obligee, and the obligor do not reside in the issuing State;

(ii) a [petitioner] who is a nonresident of this State seeks modification; and

(iii) the [respondent] is subject to the personal jurisdiction of the tribunal of this State; or

(2) the child, or a party who is an individual, is subject to the personal jurisdiction of the tribunal of this State and all of the parties who are individuals have filed written consents in the issuing tribunal for a tribunal of this State to modify the support order

and assume continuing, exclusive jurisdiction over the order. However, if the issuing State is a foreign jurisdiction that has not enacted a law or established procedures substantially similar to the procedures under this [Act], the consent otherwise required of an individual residing in this State is not required for the tribunal to assume jurisdiction to modify the child-support order.

(b) Modification of a registered child-support order is subject to the same requirements, procedures, and defenses that apply to the modification of an order issued by a tribunal of this State and the order may be enforced and satisfied in the same manner.

(c) A tribunal of this State may not modify any aspect of a child-support order that may not be modified under the law of the issuing State. If two or more tribunals have issued child-support orders for the same obligor and child, the order that controls and must be so recognized under Section 207 establishes the aspects of the support order which are nonmodifiable.

(d) On issuance of an order modifying a child-support order issued in another State, a tribunal of this State becomes the tribunal having continuing, exclusive jurisdiction.

Sec. 612. Recognition of Order Modified in Another State.

A tribunal of this State shall recognize a modification of its earlier child-support order by a tribunal of another State which assumed jurisdiction pursuant to this [Act] or a law substantially similar to this [Act] and, upon request, except as otherwise provided in this [Act], shall:

(1) enforce the order that was modified only as to amounts accruing before the modification;

(2) enforce only nonmodifiable aspects of that order;

(3) provide other appropriate relief only for violations of that order which occurred before the effective date of the modification; and

(4) recognize the modifying order of the other State, upon registration, for the purpose of enforcement.

Sec. 613. Jurisdiction to Modify Child-Support Order of Another State When Individual Parties Reside in This State.

(a) If all of the parties who are individuals reside in this State and the child does not reside in the issuing State, a tribunal of this State has jurisdiction to enforce and to modify the issuing State's child-support order in a proceeding to register that order.

(b) A tribunal of this State exercising jurisdiction under this section shall apply the provisions of Articles 1 and 2, this article, and the procedural and substantive law of this State to the proceeding for enforcement or modification. Articles 3, 4, 5, 7, and 8 do not apply.

Sec. 614. Notice to Issuing Tribunal of Modification.

Within [30] days after issuance of a modified child-support order, the party obtaining the modification shall file a certified copy of the order with the issuing tribunal that had continuing, exclusive jurisdiction over the earlier order, and in each tribunal in which the party knows the earlier order has been registered. A party who obtains the order and fails to file a certified copy is subject to appropriate sanctions by a tribunal in which the issue of failure to file arises. The failure to file does not affect the validity or enforceability of the modified order of the new tribunal having continuing, exclusive jurisdiction.

Article 7. Determination of Parentage

Sec. 701. Proceeding to Determine Parentage.

(a) A tribunal of this State may serve as an initiating or responding tribunal in a proceeding brought under this [Act] or a law or procedure substantially similar to this [Act], the Uniform Reciprocal Enforcement of Support Act, or the Revised Uniform Reciprocal Enforcement of Support Act to determine that the [petitioner] is a parent of a particular child or to determine that a [respondent] is a parent of that child.

(b) In a proceeding to determine parentage, a responding tribunal of this State shall apply the [Uniform Parentage Act; procedural and substantive law of this State,] and the rules of this State on choice of law.

Article 8. Interstate Rendition

Sec. 801. Grounds For Rendition.

(a) For purposes of this article, "governor" includes an individual performing the functions of governor or the executive authority of a State covered by this [Act].

(b) The governor of this State may:

(1) demand that the governor of another State surrender an individual found in the other State who is charged criminally in this State with having failed to provide for the support of an obligee; or

(2) on the demand by the governor of another State, surrender an individual found in this State who is charged criminally in the other State with having failed to provide for the support of an obligee.

(c) A provision for extradition of individuals not inconsistent with this [Act] applies to the demand even if the individual whose surrender is demanded was not in the demanding State when the crime was allegedly committed and has not fled therefrom.

Sec. 802. Conditions of Rendition.

(a) Before making demand that the governor of another State surrender an individual charged criminally in this State with having failed to provide for the support of an obligee, the governor of this State may require a prosecutor of this State to demonstrate that at least [60] days previously the obligee had initiated proceedings for support pursuant to this [Act] or that the proceeding would be of no avail.

(b) If, under this [Act] or a law substantially similar to this [Act], the Uniform Reciprocal Enforcement of Support Act, or the Revised Uniform Reciprocal Enforcement of Support Act, the governor of another State makes a demand that the governor of this State surrender an individual charged criminally in that State with having failed to provide for the support of a child or other individual to whom a duty of support is owed, the governor may require a prosecutor to investigate the demand and report whether a proceeding for support has been initiated or would be effective. If it appears that a proceeding would be effective but has not been initiated, the governor may delay honoring the demand for a reasonable time to permit the initiation of a proceeding.

(c) If a proceeding for support has been initiated and the individual whose rendition is demanded prevails, the governor may decline to honor the demand. If the [petitioner] prevails and the individual whose rendition is demanded is subject to a support order, the governor may decline to honor the demand if the individual is complying with the support order.

Article 9. Miscellaneous Provisions

Sec. 901. Uniformity of Application and Construction.

This [Act] shall be applied and construed to effectuate its general purpose to make uniform the law with respect to the subject of this [Act] among States enacting it.

Sec. 902. Short Title.

This [Act] may be cited as the Uniform Interstate Family Support Act.

Sec. 903. Severability Clause.

If any provision of this [Act] or its application to any person or circumstance is held invalid, the invalidity does not affect other provisions or applications of this [Act] which can be given effect without the invalid provision or application, and to this end the provisions of this [Act] are severable.

Sec. 904. Effective Date.

This [Act] takes effect.....................

Sec. 905. Repeals.

The following acts and parts of acts are hereby repealed:....

Uniform Child Custody Jurisdiction and Enforcement Act (1997)

9, Part 1A U.L.A. 649 (1999)

Reprinted with the permission of the National Conference of Commissioners on Uniform State Laws

[Ed. Note: The Uniform Child Custody Jurisdiction and Enforcement Act (UCCJEA) was drafted under the auspices of the National Conference of Commissioners on Uniform State Laws (NCCUSL), which approved the Act and recommended it for adoption in 1997. The Act was intended to replace the Uniform Child Custody Jurisdiction Act (UCCJA), which was promulgated by NCCUSL in 1968. As of March 2003, the Uniform Child Custody Jurisdiction and Enforcement Act (UCCJEA) was in effect in thirty states and the District of Columbia. In the remaining states, the Uniform Child Custody Jurisdiction Act (UCCJA) was still in effect, although legislation was pending in many of these states to repeal the UCCJA and enact the UCCJEA in its place. Current information regarding state adoption of the UCCJEA can be found on the website of NCCUSL, at http://www.nccusl.org/nccusl/uniformact_factsheets/uniformacts-fs-uccjea.asp.]

TABLE OF CONTENTS

Article 1. General Provisions

Article 1. General Provisions

Sec. 101. Short Title.

This [Act] may be cited as the Uniform Child-Custody Jurisdiction and Enforcement Act.

Sec. 102. Definitions.

In this [Act]:

(1) "Abandoned" means left without provision for reasonable and necessary care or supervision.

(2) "Child" means an individual who has not attained 18 years of age.

(3) "Child-custody determination" means a judgment, decree, or other order of a court providing for the legal custody, physical custody, or visitation with respect to a child. The term includes a permanent, temporary, initial, and modification order. The term does not include an order relating to child support or other monetary obligation of an individual.

(4) "Child-custody proceeding" means a proceeding in which legal custody, physical custody, or visitation with respect to a child is an issue. The term includes a proceeding for divorce, separation, neglect, abuse, dependency, guardianship, paternity, termination of parental rights, and protection from domestic violence, in which the issue may appear. The term does not include a proceeding involving juvenile delinquency, contractual emancipation, or enforcement under [Article] 3.

(5) "Commencement" means the filing of the first pleading in a proceeding.

(6) "Court" means an entity authorized under the law of a State to establish, enforce, or modify a child-custody determination.

→ (7) "Home State" means the State in which a child lived with a parent or a person acting as a parent for at least six consecutive months immediately before the commencement of a child-custody proceeding. In the case of a child less than six months of age, the term means the State in which the child lived from birth with any of the persons mentioned. A period of temporary absence of any of the mentioned persons is part of the period.

(8) "Initial determination" means the first child-custody determination concerning a particular child.

(9) "Issuing court" means the court that makes a child-custody determination for which enforcement is sought under this [Act].

(10) "Issuing State" means the State in which a child-custody determination is made.

(11) "Modification" means a child-custody determination that changes, replaces, supersedes, or is otherwise made after a previous determination concerning the same child, whether or not it is made by the court that made the previous determination.

(12) "Person" means an individual, corporation, business trust, estate, trust, partnership, limited liability company, association, joint venture, government; governmental subdivision, agency, or instrumentality; public corporation; or any other legal or commercial entity.

(13) "Person acting as a parent" means a person, other than a parent, who:

(A) has physical custody of the child or has had physical custody for a period of six consecutive months, including any temporary absence, within one year immediately before the commencement of a child-custody proceeding; and

(B) has been awarded legal custody by a court or claims a right to legal custody under the law of this State.

(14) "Physical custody" means the physical care and supervision of a child.

(15) "State" means a State of the United States, the District of Columbia, Puerto Rico, the United States Virgin Islands, or any territory or insular possession subject to the jurisdiction of the United States.

[(16) "Tribe" means an Indian tribe or band, or Alaskan Native village, which is recognized by federal law or formally acknowledged by a State.]

(17) "Warrant" means an order issued by a court authorizing law enforcement officers to take physical custody of a child.

Sec. 103. Proceedings Governed by Other Law.

This [Act] does not govern an adoption proceeding or a proceeding pertaining to the authorization of emergency medical care for a child.

Sec. 104. Application to Indian Tribes.

(a) A child-custody proceeding that pertains to an Indian child as defined in the Indian Child Welfare Act, 25 U.S.C. § 1901 et seq., is not subject to this [Act] to the extent that it is governed by the Indian Child Welfare Act.

[(b) A court of this State shall treat a tribe as if it were a State of the United States for the purpose of applying [Articles] 1 and 2.]

[(c) A child-custody determination made by a tribe under factual circumstances in substantial conformity with the jurisdictional standards of this [Act] must be recognized and enforced under [Article] 3.]

Sec. 105. International Application of [Act].

(a) A court of this State shall treat a foreign country as if it were a State of the United States for the purpose of applying [Articles] 1 and 2.

(b) Except as otherwise provided in subsection (c), a child-custody determination made in a foreign country under factual circumstances in substantial conformity with the jurisdictional standards of this [Act] must be recognized and enforced under [Article] 3.

(c) A court of this State need not apply this [Act] if the child custody law of a foreign country violates fundamental principles of human rights.

Sec. 106. Effect of Child-Custody Determination.

A child-custody determination made by a court of this State that had jurisdiction under this [Act] binds all persons who have been served in accordance with the laws of this State or notified in accordance with Section 108 or who have submitted to the jurisdiction of the court, and who have been given an opportunity to be heard. As to those persons, the determination is conclusive as to all decided issues of law and fact except to the extent the determination is modified.

Sec. 107. Priority.

If a question of existence or exercise of jurisdiction under this [Act] is raised in a child-custody proceeding, the question, upon request of a party, must be given priority on the calendar and handled expeditiously.

Sec. 108. Notice to Persons Outside State.

(a) Notice required for the exercise of jurisdiction when a person is outside this State may be given in a manner prescribed by the law of this State for service of process or by the law of the State in which the service is made. Notice must be given in a manner reasonably calculated to give actual notice but may be by publication if other means are not effective.

(b) Proof of service may be made in the manner prescribed by the law of this State or by the law of the State in which the service is made.

(c) Notice is not required for the exercise of jurisdiction with respect to a person who submits to the jurisdiction of the court.

Sec. 109. Appearance and Limited Immunity.

(a) A party to a child-custody proceeding, including a modification proceeding, or a petitioner or respondent in a proceeding to enforce or register a child-custody determination, is not subject to personal jurisdiction in this State for another proceeding or purpose solely by reason of having participated, or of having been physically present for the purpose of participating, in the proceeding.

(b) A person who is subject to personal jurisdiction in this State on a basis other than physical presence is not immune from service of process in this State. A party present in this State who is subject to the jurisdiction of another State is not immune from service of process allowable under the laws of that State.

(c) The immunity granted by subsection (a) does not extend to civil litigation based on acts unrelated to the participation in a proceeding under this [Act] committed by an individual while present in this State.

Sec. 110. Communication Between Courts.

(a) A court of this State may communicate with a court in another State concerning a proceeding arising under this [Act].

(b) The court may allow the parties to participate in the communication. If the parties are not able to participate in the communication, they must be given the opportunity to present facts and legal arguments before a decision on jurisdiction is made.

(c) Communication between courts on schedules, calendars, court records, and similar matters may occur without informing the parties. A record need not be made of the communication.

(d) Except as otherwise provided in subsection (c), a record must be made of a communication under this section. The parties must be informed promptly of the communication and granted access to the record.

(e) For the purposes of this section, "record" means information that is inscribed on a tangible medium or that is stored in an electronic or other medium and is retrievable in perceivable form.

Sec. 111. Taking Testimony in Another State.

(a) In addition to other procedures available to a party, a party to a child-custody proceeding may offer testimony of witnesses who are located in another State, including testimony of the parties and the child, by deposition or other means allowable in this State for testimony taken in another State. The court on its own motion may order that the testimony of a person be taken in another State and may prescribe the manner in which and the terms upon which the testimony is taken.

(b) A court of this State may permit an individual residing in another State to be deposed or to testify by telephone, audiovisual means, or other electronic means before a designated court or at another location in that State. A court of this State shall cooperate with courts of other States in designating an appropriate location for the deposition or testimony.

(c) Documentary evidence transmitted from another State to a court of this State by technological means that do not produce an original writing may not be excluded from evidence on an objection based on the means of transmission.

Sec. 112. Cooperation Between Courts; Preservation of Records.

(a) A court of this State may request the appropriate court of another State to:

(1) hold an evidentiary hearing;

(2) order a person to produce or give evidence pursuant to procedures of that State;

(3) order that an evaluation be made with respect to the custody of a child involved in a pending proceeding;

(4) forward to the court of this State a certified copy of the transcript of the record of the hearing, the evidence otherwise presented, and any evaluation prepared in compliance with the request; and

(5) order a party to a child-custody proceeding or any person having physical custody of the child to appear in the proceeding with or without the child.

(b) Upon request of a court of another State, a court of this State may hold a hearing or enter an order described in subsection (a).

(c) Travel and other necessary and reasonable expenses incurred under subsections (a) and (b) may be assessed against the parties according to the law of this State.

(d) A court of this State shall preserve the pleadings, orders, decrees, records of hearings, evaluations, and other pertinent records with respect to a child-custody proceeding until the child attains 18 years of age. Upon appropriate request by a court or law enforcement official of another State, the court shall forward a certified copy of those records.

Article 2. Jurisdiction

Sec. 201. Initial Child-Custody Jurisdiction.

(a) Except as otherwise provided in Section 204, a court of this State has jurisdiction to make an initial child-custody determination only if:

(1) this State is the home State of the child on the date of the commencement of the proceeding, or was the home State of the child within six months before the commencement of the proceeding and the child is absent from this State but a parent or person acting as a parent continues to live in this State;

(2) a court of another State does not have jurisdiction under paragraph (1), or a court of the home State of the child has declined to exercise jurisdiction on the ground that this State is the more appropriate forum under Section 207 or 208, and:

(A) the child and the child's parents, or the child and at least one parent or a person acting as a parent, have a significant connection with this State other than mere physical presence; and

(B) substantial evidence is available in this State concerning the child's care, protection, training, and personal relationships;

(3) all courts having jurisdiction under paragraph (1) or (2) have declined to exercise jurisdiction on the ground that a court of this State is the more appropriate forum to determine the custody of the child under Section 207 or 208; or

(4) no court of any other State would have jurisdiction under the criteria specified in paragraph (1), (2), or (3).

(b) Subsection (a) is the exclusive jurisdictional basis for making a child-custody determination by a court of this State.

(c) Physical presence of, or personal jurisdiction over, a party or a child is not necessary or sufficient to make a child-custody determination.

Sec. 202. Exclusive, Continuing Jurisdiction.

(a) Except as otherwise provided in Section 204, a court of this State which has made a child-custody determination consistent with Section 201 or 203 has exclusive, continuing jurisdiction over the determination until:

(1) a court of this State determines that neither the child, the child's parents, and any person acting as a parent do not have a significant connection with this State and that substantial evidence is no longer available in this State concerning the child's care, protection, training, and personal relationships; or

(2) a court of this State or a court of another State determines that the child, the child's parents, and any person acting as a parent do not presently reside in this State.

(b) A court of this State which has made a child-custody determination and does not have exclusive, continuing jurisdiction under this section may modify that determination only if it has jurisdiction to make an initial determination under Section 201.

Sec. 203. Jurisdiction to Modify Determination.

Except as otherwise provided in Section 204, a court of this State may not modify a child-custody determination made by a court of another State unless a court of this State has jurisdiction to make an initial determination under Section 201(a)(1) or (2) and:

(1) the court of the other State determines it no longer has exclusive, continuing jurisdiction under Section 202 or that a court of this State would be a more convenient forum under Section 207; or

(2) a court of this State or a court of the other State determines that the child, the child's parents, and any person acting as a parent do not presently reside in the other State.

Sec. 204. Temporary Emergency Jurisdiction.

(a) A court of this State has temporary emergency jurisdiction if the child is present in this State and the child has been abandoned or it is necessary in an emergency to protect the child because the child, or a sibling or parent of the child, is subjected to or threatened with mistreatment or abuse.

(b) If there is no previous child-custody determination that is entitled to be enforced under this [Act] and a child-custody proceeding has not been commenced in a court of a State having jurisdiction under Sections 201 through 203, a child-custody determination made under this section remains in effect until an order is obtained from a court of a State having jurisdiction under Sections 201 through 203. If a child-custody proceeding has not been or is not commenced in a court of a State having jurisdiction under Sections 201 through 203, a child-custody determination made under this section becomes a final determination, if it so provides and this State becomes the home State of the child.

(c) If there is a previous child-custody determination that is entitled to be enforced under this [Act], or a child-custody proceeding has been commenced in a court of a State having jurisdiction under Sections 201 through 203, any order issued by a court of this State under this section must specify in the order a period that the court considers adequate to allow the person seeking an order to obtain an order from the State having jurisdiction under Sections 201 through 203. The order issued in this State remains in effect until an order is obtained from the other State within the period specified or the period expires.

(d) A court of this State which has been asked to make a child-custody determination under this section, upon being informed that a child-custody proceeding has been commenced in, or a child-custody determination has been made by, a court of a State having jurisdiction under Sections 201 through 203, shall immediately communicate with the other court. A court of this State which is exercising jurisdiction pursuant to Sections 201 through 203, upon being informed that a child-custody proceeding has been commenced in, or a child-custody determination has been made by, a court of another State under a statute similar to this section shall immediately communicate with the court of that State to resolve the emergency, protect the safety of the parties and the child, and determine a period for the duration of the temporary order.

Sec. 205. Notice; Opportunity to Be Heard; Joinder.

(a) Before a child-custody determination is made under this [Act], notice and an opportunity to be heard in accordance with the standards of Section 108 must be given to all persons entitled to notice under the law of this State as in child-custody proceedings between residents of this State, any parent whose parental rights have not been previously terminated, and any person having physical custody of the child.

(b) This [Act] does not govern the enforceability of a child-custody determination made without notice or an opportunity to be heard.

(c) The obligation to join a party and the right to intervene as a party in a child-custody proceeding under this [Act] are governed by the law of this State as in child-custody proceedings between residents of this State.

Sec. 206. Simultaneous Proceedings.

(a) Except as otherwise provided in Section 204, a court of this State may not exercise its jurisdiction under this [article] if, at the time of the commencement of the proceeding, a proceeding concerning the custody of the child has been commenced in a court of another State having jurisdiction substantially in conformity with this [Act], unless the proceeding has been terminated or is stayed by the court of the other State because a court of this State is a more convenient forum under Section 207.

(b) Except as otherwise provided in Section 204, a court of this State, before hearing a child-custody proceeding, shall examine the court documents and other information supplied by the parties pursuant to Section 209. If the court determines that a child-custody proceeding has been commenced in a court in another State having jurisdiction substantially in accordance with this [Act], the court of this State shall stay its proceeding and communicate with the court of the other State. If the court of the State having jurisdiction substantially in accordance with this [Act] does not determine that the court of this State is a more appropriate forum, the court of this State shall dismiss the proceeding.

(c) In a proceeding to modify a child-custody determination, a court of this State shall determine whether a proceeding to enforce the determination has been commenced in another State. If a proceeding to enforce a child-custody determination has been commenced in another State, the court may:

(1) stay the proceeding for modification pending the entry of an order of a court of the other State enforcing, staying, denying, or dismissing the proceeding for enforcement;

(2) enjoin the parties from continuing with the proceeding for enforcement; or

(3) proceed with the modification under conditions it considers appropriate.

Sec. 207. Inconvenient Forum.

(a) A court of this State which has jurisdiction under this [Act] to make a child-custody determination may decline to exercise its jurisdiction at any time if it determines that it is an inconvenient forum under the circumstances and that a court of another State is a more appropriate forum. The issue of inconvenient forum may be raised upon motion of a party, the court's own motion, or request of another court.

(b) Before determining whether it is an inconvenient forum, a court of this State shall consider whether it is appropriate for a court of another State to exercise jurisdiction. For this purpose, the court shall allow the parties to submit information and shall consider all relevant factors, including:

(1) whether domestic violence has occurred and is likely to continue in the future and which State could best protect the parties and the child;

(2) the length of time the child has resided outside this State;

(3) the distance between the court in this State and the court in the State that would assume jurisdiction;

(4) the relative financial circumstances of the parties;

(5) any agreement of the parties as to which State should assume jurisdiction;

(6) the nature and location of the evidence required to resolve the pending litigation, including testimony of the child;

(7) the ability of the court of each State to decide the issue expeditiously and the procedures necessary to present the evidence; and

(8) the familiarity of the court of each State with the facts and issues in the pending litigation.

(c) If a court of this State determines that it is an inconvenient forum and that a court of another State is a more appropriate forum, it shall stay the proceedings upon condition that a child-custody proceeding be promptly commenced in another designated State and may impose any other condition the court considers just and proper.

(d) A court of this State may decline to exercise its jurisdiction under this [Act] if a child-custody determination is incidental to an action for divorce or another proceeding while still retaining jurisdiction over the divorce or other proceeding.

Sec. 208. Jurisdiction Declined by Reason of Conduct.

(a) Except as otherwise provided in Section 204 [or by other law of this State], if a court of this State has jurisdiction under this [Act] because a person seeking to invoke its jurisdiction has engaged in unjustifiable conduct, the court shall decline to exercise its jurisdiction unless:

(1) the parents and all persons acting as parents have acquiesced in the exercise of jurisdiction;

(2) a court of the State otherwise having jurisdiction under Sections 201 through 203 determines that this State is a more appropriate forum under Section 207; or

(3) no court of any other State would have jurisdiction under the criteria specified in Sections 201 through 203.

(b) If a court of this State declines to exercise its jurisdiction pursuant to subsection (a), it may fashion an appropriate remedy to ensure the safety of the child and prevent a repetition of the unjustifiable conduct, including staying the proceeding until a child-custody proceeding is commenced in a court having jurisdiction under Sections 201 through 203.

(c) If a court dismisses a petition or stays a proceeding because it declines to exercise its jurisdiction pursuant to subsection (a), it shall assess against the party seeking to invoke its jurisdiction necessary and reasonable expenses including costs, communication expenses, attorney's fees, investigative fees, expenses for witnesses, travel expenses, and child care during the course of the proceedings, unless the party from whom fees are sought establishes that the assessment would be clearly inappropriate. The court may not assess fees, costs, or expenses against this State unless authorized by law other than this [Act].

Sec. 209. Information to Be Submitted to Court.

(a) [Subject to [local law providing for the confidentiality of procedures, addresses, and other identifying information], in] [In] a child-custody proceeding, each party, in its first pleading or in an attached affidavit, shall give information, if reasonably ascertainable, under oath as to the child's present address or whereabouts, the places where the child has lived during the last five years, and the names and present addresses of the persons with whom the child has lived during that period. The pleading or affidavit must state whether the party:

(1) has participated, as a party or witness or in any other capacity, in any other proceeding concerning the custody of or visitation with the child and, if so, identify the court, the case number, and the date of the child-custody determination, if any;

(2) knows of any proceeding that could affect the current proceeding, including proceedings for enforcement and proceedings relating to domestic violence, protective orders, termination of parental rights, and adoptions and, if so, identify the court, the case number, and the nature of the proceeding; and

(3) knows the names and addresses of any person not a party to the proceeding who has physical custody of the child or claims rights of legal custody or physical custody of, or visitation with, the child and, if so, the names and addresses of those persons.

(b) If the information required by subsection (a) is not furnished, the court, upon motion of a party or its own motion, may stay the proceeding until the information is furnished.

(c) If the declaration as to any of the items described in subsection (a)(1) through (3) is in the affirmative, the declarant shall give additional information under oath as required by the court. The court may examine the parties under oath as to details of the information furnished and other matters pertinent to the court's jurisdiction and the disposition of the case.

(d) Each party has a continuing duty to inform the court of any proceeding in this or any other State that could affect the current proceeding.

[(e) If a party alleges in an affidavit or a pleading under oath that the health, safety, or liberty of a party or child would be jeopardized by disclosure of identifying information, the information must be sealed and may not be disclosed to the other party or the public unless the court orders the disclosure to be made after a hearing in which the court takes into consideration the health, safety, or liberty of the party or child and determines that the disclosure is in the interest of justice.]

Sec. 210. Appearance of Parties and Child.

(a) In a child-custody proceeding in this State, the court may order a party to the proceeding who is in this State to appear before the court in person with or without the child. The court may order any person who is in this State and who has physical custody or control of the child to appear in person with the child.

(b) If a party to a child-custody proceeding whose presence is desired by the court is outside this State, the court may order that a notice given pursuant to Section 108 include a statement directing the party to appear in person with or without the child and informing the party that failure to appear may result in a decision adverse to the party.

(c) The court may enter any orders necessary to ensure the safety of the child and of any person ordered to appear under this section.

(d) If a party to a child-custody proceeding who is outside this State is directed to appear under subsection (b) or desires to appear personally before the court with or without the child, the court may require another party to pay reasonable and necessary travel and other expenses of the party so appearing and of the child.

Article 3. Enforcement

Sec. 301. Definitions.

In this [article]:

(1) "Petitioner" means a person who seeks enforcement of an order for return of a child under the Hague Convention on the Civil Aspects of International Child Abduction or enforcement of a child-custody determination.

(2) "Respondent" means a person against whom a proceeding has been commenced for enforcement of an order for return of a child under the Hague Convention on the Civil Aspects of International Child Abduction or enforcement of a child-custody determination.

Sec. 302. Enforcement Under Hague Convention.

Under this [article] a court of this State may enforce an order for the return of the child made under the Hague Convention on the Civil Aspects of International Child Abduction as if it were a child-custody determination.

Sec. 303. Duty to Enforce.

(a) A court of this State shall recognize and enforce a child-custody determination of a court of another State if the latter court exercised jurisdiction in substantial conformity with this [Act] or the determination was made under factual circumstances meeting the jurisdictional standards of this [Act] and the determination has not been modified in accordance with this [Act].

(b) A court of this State may utilize any remedy available under other law of this State to enforce a child-custody determination made by a court of another State. The remedies provided in this [article] are cumulative and do not affect the availability of other remedies to enforce a child-custody determination.

Sec. 304. Temporary Visitation.

(a) A court of this State which does not have jurisdiction to modify a child-custody determination, may issue a temporary order enforcing:

(1) a visitation schedule made by a court of another State; or

(2) the visitation provisions of a child-custody determination of another State that does not provide for a specific visitation schedule.

(b) If a court of this State makes an order under subsection (a)(2), it shall specify in the order a period that it considers adequate to allow the petitioner to obtain an order from a court having jurisdiction under the criteria specified in [Article] 2. The order remains in effect until an order is obtained from the other court or the period expires.

Sec. 305. Registration of Child-Custody Determination.

(a) A child-custody determination issued by a court of another State may be registered in this State, with or without a simultaneous request for enforcement, by sending to [the appropriate court] in this State:

(1) a letter or other document requesting registration;

(2) two copies, including one certified copy, of the determination sought to be registered, and a statement under penalty of perjury that to the best of the knowledge and belief of the person seeking registration the order has not been modified; and

(3) except as otherwise provided in Section 209, the name and address of the person seeking registration and any parent or person acting as a parent who has been awarded custody or visitation in the child-custody determination sought to be registered.

(b) On receipt of the documents required by subsection (a), the registering court shall:

(1) cause the determination to be filed as a foreign judgment, together with one copy of any accompanying documents and information, regardless of their form; and

(2) serve notice upon the persons named pursuant to subsection (a)(3) and provide them with an opportunity to contest the registration in accordance with this section.

(c) The notice required by subsection (b)(2) must state that:

(1) a registered determination is enforceable as of the date of the registration in the same manner as a determination issued by a court of this State;

(2) a hearing to contest the validity of the registered determination must be requested within 20 days after service of notice; and

(3) failure to contest the registration will result in confirmation of the child-custody determination and preclude further contest of that determination with respect to any matter that could have been asserted.

(d) A person seeking to contest the validity of a registered order must request a hearing within 20 days after service of the notice. At that hearing, the court shall confirm the registered order unless the person contesting registration establishes that:

(1) the issuing court did not have jurisdiction under [Article] 2;

(2) the child-custody determination sought to be registered has been vacated, stayed, or modified by a court having jurisdiction to do so under [Article] 2; or

(3) the person contesting registration was entitled to notice, but notice was not given in accordance with the standards of Section 108, in the proceedings before the court that issued the order for which registration is sought.

(e) If a timely request for a hearing to contest the validity of the registration is not made, the registration is confirmed as a matter of law and the person requesting registration and all persons served must be notified of the confirmation.

(f) Confirmation of a registered order, whether by operation of law or after notice and hearing, precludes further contest of the order with respect to any matter that could have been asserted at the time of registration.

Sec. 306. Enforcement of Registered Determination.

(a) A court of this State may grant any relief normally available under the law of this State to enforce a registered child-custody determination made by a court of another State.

(b) A court of this State shall recognize and enforce, but may not modify, except in accordance with [Article] 2, a registered child-custody determination of a court of another State.

Sec. 307. Simultaneous Proceedings.

If a proceeding for enforcement under this [article] is commenced in a court of this State and the court determines that a proceeding to modify the determination is pending in a court of another State having jurisdiction to modify the determination under [Article] 2, the enforcing court shall immediately communicate with the modifying court. The proceeding for enforcement continues unless the enforcing court, after consultation with the modifying court, stays or dismisses the proceeding.

Sec. 308. Expedited Enforcement of Child-Custody Determination.

(a) A petition under this [article] must be verified. Certified copies of all orders sought to be enforced and of any order confirming registration must be attached to the petition. A copy of a certified copy of an order may be attached instead of the original.

(b) A petition for enforcement of a child-custody determination must state:

(1) whether the court that issued the determination identified the jurisdictional basis it relied upon in exercising jurisdiction and, if so, what the basis was;

(2) whether the determination for which enforcement is sought has been vacated, stayed, or modified by a court whose decision must be enforced under this [Act] and, if so, identify the court, the case number, and the nature of the proceeding;

(3) whether any proceeding has been commenced that could affect the current proceeding, including proceedings relating to domestic violence, protective orders, termination of parental rights, and adoptions and, if so, identify the court, the case number, and the nature of the proceeding;

(4) the present physical address of the child and the respondent, if known;

(5) whether relief in addition to the immediate physical custody of the child and attorney's fees is sought, including a request for assistance from [law enforcement officials] and, if so, the relief sought; and

(6) if the child-custody determination has been registered and confirmed under Section 305, the date and place of registration.

(c) Upon the filing of a petition, the court shall issue an order directing the respondent to appear in person with or without the child at a hearing and may enter any order necessary to ensure the safety of the parties and the child. The hearing must be held on the next judicial day after service of the order unless that date is impossible. In that event, the court shall hold the hearing on the first judicial day possible. The court may extend the date of hearing at the request of the petitioner.

(d) An order issued under subsection (c) must state the time and place of the hearing and advise the respondent that at the hearing the court will order that the petitioner may take immediate physical custody of the child and the payment of fees, costs, and expenses under Section 312, and may schedule a hearing to determine whether further relief is appropriate, unless the respondent appears and establishes that:

(1) the child-custody determination has not been registered and confirmed under Section 305 and that:

(A) the issuing court did not have jurisdiction under [Article] 2;

(B) the child-custody determination for which enforcement is sought has been vacated, stayed, or modified by a court having jurisdiction to do so under [Article] 2;

(C) the respondent was entitled to notice, but notice was not given in accordance with the standards of Section 108, in the proceedings before the court that issued the order for which enforcement is sought; or

(2) the child-custody determination for which enforcement is sought was registered and confirmed under Section 304, but has been vacated, stayed, or modified by a court of a State having jurisdiction to do so under [Article] 2.

Sec. 309. Service of Petition and Order.

Except as otherwise provided in Section 311, the petition and order must be served, by any method authorized [by the law of this State], upon respondent and any person who has physical custody of the child.

Sec. 310. Hearing and Order.

(a) Unless the court issues a temporary emergency order pursuant to Section 204, upon a finding that a petitioner is entitled to immediate physical custody of the child, the court shall order that the petitioner may take immediate physical custody of the child unless the respondent establishes that:

(1) the child-custody determination has not been registered and confirmed under Section 305 and that:

(A) the issuing court did not have jurisdiction under [Article] 2;

(B) the child-custody determination for which enforcement is sought has been vacated, stayed, or modified by a court of a State having jurisdiction to do so under [Article] 2; or

(C) the respondent was entitled to notice, but notice was not given in accordance with the standards of Section 108, in the proceedings before the court that issued the order for which enforcement is sought; or

(2) the child-custody determination for which enforcement is sought was registered and confirmed under Section 305 but has been vacated, stayed, or modified by a court of a State having jurisdiction to do so under [Article] 2.

(b) The court shall award the fees, costs, and expenses authorized under Section 312 and may grant additional relief, including a request for the assistance of [law enforcement officials], and set a further hearing to determine whether additional relief is appropriate.

(c) If a party called to testify refuses to answer on the ground that the testimony may be self-incriminating, the court may draw an adverse inference from the refusal.

(d) A privilege against disclosure of communications between spouses and a defense of immunity based on the relationship of husband and wife or parent and child may not be invoked in a proceeding under this [article].

Sec. 311. Warrant to Take Physical Custody of Child.

(a) Upon the filing of a petition seeking enforcement of a child-custody determination, the petitioner may file a verified application for the issuance of a warrant to take physical custody of the child if the child is immediately likely to suffer serious physical harm or be removed from this State.

(b) If the court, upon the testimony of the petitioner or other witness, finds that the child is imminently likely to suffer serious physical harm or be removed from this State, it may issue a warrant to take physical custody of the child. The petition must be heard on the next judicial day after the warrant is executed unless that date is impossible. In that event, the court shall hold the hearing on the first judicial day possible. The application for the warrant must include the statements required by Section 308(b).

(c) A warrant to take physical custody of a child must:

(1) recite the facts upon which a conclusion of imminent serious physical harm or removal from the jurisdiction is based;

(2) direct law enforcement officers to take physical custody of the child immediately; and

(3) provide for the placement of the child pending final relief.

(d) The respondent must be served with the petition, warrant, and order immediately after the child is taken into physical custody.

(e) A warrant to take physical custody of a child is enforceable throughout this State. If the court finds on the basis of the testimony of the petitioner or other witness that a less intrusive remedy is not effective, it may authorize law enforcement officers to enter private property to take physical custody of the child. If required by exigent circumstances of the case, the court may authorize law enforcement officers to make a forcible entry at any hour.

(f) The court may impose conditions upon placement of a child to ensure the appearance of the child and the child's custodian.

Sec. 312. Costs, Fees, and Expenses.

(a) The court shall award the prevailing party, including a State, necessary and reasonable expenses incurred by or on behalf of the party, including costs, communication expenses, attorney's fees, investigative fees, expenses for witnesses, travel expenses, and child care during the course of the proceedings, unless the party from whom fees or expenses are sought establishes that the award would be clearly inappropriate.

(b) The court may not assess fees, costs, or expenses against a State unless authorized by law other than this [Act].

Sec. 313. Recognition and Enforcement.

A court of this State shall accord full faith and credit to an order issued by another State and consistent with this [Act] which enforces a child-custody determination by a court of another State unless the order has been vacated, stayed, or modified by a court having jurisdiction to do so under [Article] 2.

Sec. 314. Appeals.

An appeal may be taken from a final order in a proceeding under this [article] in accordance with [expedited appellate procedures in other civil cases]. Unless the court enters a temporary emergency order under Section 204, the enforcing court may not stay an order enforcing a child-custody determination pending appeal.

Sec. 315. Role of [Prosecutor or Public Official].

(a) In a case arising under this [Act] or involving the Hague Convention on the Civil Aspects of International Child Abduction, the [prosecutor or other appropriate public official] may take any lawful action, including resort to a proceeding under this [article] or any other available civil proceeding to locate a child, obtain the return of a child, or enforce a child-custody determination if there is:

(1) an existing child-custody determination;

(2) a request to do so from a court in a pending child-custody proceeding;

(3) a reasonable belief that a criminal statute has been violated; or

(4) a reasonable belief that the child has been wrongfully removed or retained in violation of the Hague Convention on the Civil Aspects of International Child Abduction.

(b) A [prosecutor or appropriate public official] acting under this section acts on behalf of the court and may not represent any party.

Sec. 316. Role of [Law Enforcement].

At the request of a [prosecutor or other appropriate public official] acting under Section 315, a [law enforcement officer] may take any lawful action reasonably necessary to locate a child or a party and assist [a prosecutor or appropriate public official] with responsibilities under Section 315.

Sec. 317. Costs and Expenses.

If the respondent is not the prevailing party, the court may assess against the respondent all direct expenses and costs incurred by the [prosecutor or other appropriate public official] and [law enforcement officers] under Section 315 or 316.

Article 4. Miscellaneous Provisions

Sec. 401. Application and Construction.

In applying and construing this Uniform Act, consideration must be given to the need to promote uniformity of the law with respect to its subject matter among States that enact it.

Sec. 402. Severability Clause.

If any provision of this [Act] or its application to any person or circumstance is held invalid, the invalidity does not affect other provisions or applications of this [Act] which can be given effect without the invalid provision or application, and to this end the provisions of this [Act] are severable.

Sec. 403. Effective Date.

This [Act] takes effect...............

Sec. 404. Repeals.

The following acts and parts of acts are hereby repealed:
(1) The Uniform Child Custody Jurisdiction Act;
(2).......................................
(3).......................................

Sec. 405. Transitional Provision.

A motion or other request for relief made in a child-custody proceeding or to enforce a child-custody determination which was commenced before the effective date of this [Act] is governed by the law in effect at the time the motion or other request was made.